THE MORAL WISDOM OF THE
CATHOLIC CHURCH

Robert J. Spitzer, S.J., Ph.D.

THE MORAL WISDOM
OF THE
CATHOLIC CHURCH

A Defense of Her Controversial
Moral Teachings

Volume Three of the Trilogy:
Called Out of Darkness: Contending with Evil
through the Church, Virtue, and Prayer

IGNATIUS PRESS   SAN FRANCISCO

Cover art:
Detail from "Christ Healing the Sick
(The Hundred Guilder Print)",
etching by Rembrandt van Rijn, c. 1647–1649.
Image in public domain.

Cover design by John Herreid

© 2022 by Ignatius Press, San Francisco
All rights reserved
ISBN 978-1-62164-416-3 (PB)
ISBN 978-1-64229-218-3 (eBook)
Library of Congress Catalogue number 2021941887
Printed in the United States of America ∞

*In loving memory of my mother, who showed me the
goodness of the Church, and my father, who
taught me respect for objective morals and the law.*

*And in sincere gratitude to my colleagues in the pro-life movement,
particularly Camille Pauley and the board of Healing the Culture;
Father Thomas King, S.J.; Father Joseph Koterski, S.J.; and
the founding members of University Faculty for Life; as well as
Dr. Robin Bernhoft, Eileen Geller, and Kenneth Vanderhoef.*

Beware of false prophets, who come to you in sheep's clothing but inwardly are ravenous wolves. You will know them by their fruits. Are grapes gathered from thorns, or figs from thistles? So, every sound tree bears good fruit, but the bad tree bears evil fruit. A sound tree cannot bear evil fruit, nor can a bad tree bear good fruit. Every tree that does not bear good fruit is cut down and thrown into the fire. Thus you will know them by their fruits.

—Matthew 7:15–20

CONTENTS

ACKNOWLEDGMENTS

I am most grateful to Joan Jacoby, whose invaluable work brought mere thoughts into reality through her excellent editing suggestions and research. It is not easy to do research for a blind scholar, transcribe multiple copies of his dictation, clean up the manuscript, and endure his many edits, but she did so with great patience, care, competence, and contribution—a true manifestation of her virtue and dedication.

I am also grateful to Michael Garcia, Matthew Garcia, and Karlo Broussard for their assistance in preparing the manuscript.

I would also like to express my appreciation to the board and benefactors of the Magis Institute who gave me the time and resources to complete this Trilogy.

INTRODUCTION

The Purpose, Perspective, and Method of This Volume

In Volume I of this Trilogy (*Christ versus Satan in Our Daily Lives*), we examined the presence of Christ in our lives, His victory over Satan, the reality of Satan today, the tactics he uses (temptation, deceit, and accusation), and the eight deadly sins (his usual pathways to seduce us into his darkness). In Volume II (*Escape from Evil's Darkness: The Light of Christ in the Church, Spiritual Conversion, and Moral Conversion*), we looked at the invaluable role of the Catholic Church in communicating the sacramental grace, doctrinal and moral teaching, and mystical community of Jesus through the Holy Spirit. Our objective was to give a "best practices" approach to deepening spiritual conversion and moral conversion and catalyze their interaction within our minds and hearts. To this end we discussed essential dimensions of sacramental life (particularly frequent participation at Mass and in confession), starting and deepening a life of contemplative prayer, embracing and cultivating virtue, and resisting temptation. The objective as Saint Paul might have put it is to deepen our communion with the Lord and become "the new man" (Eph 4:24). It now remains to explain specific moral precepts taught by Jesus and interpreted by the Catholic Church.

I. The Purpose of This Volume

If we had but a glimmer of the truly overwhelming love of the Lord for us, and the great peril intended for us by our spiritual enemy (Satan, the Evil One), we would not hesitate to seek, accept, and follow the *whole* moral truth given to us by Jesus Christ and the Catholic

Church. So, why don't we? The Lord has created us with free will, and He cannot give us even an inkling of the love He has for us until we have decided to open ourselves to Him. If He does not do this, He would, in the words of Fyodor Dostoyevsky, "enslave us to a miracle.". In *The Brothers Karamazov*, the Grand Inquisitor tells the prisoner representing Christ:

> Thou wouldst not enslave man by a miracle, and didst crave faith given freely, not based on miracle. Thou didst crave for free love and not the base raptures of the slave before the might that has overawed him for ever.[1]

The Lord, in allowing us to be free, delays the full revelation of His love and the darkness of our enemy (Satan) until we freely choose His way rather than our enemy's. We might ask, why would we choose our enemy's way? Quite simply, we might think that the enemy's way is the path to true happiness—our heart's desire—our treasure.

If we go in that direction, we will resist many of the Church's moral teachings discussed in this volume. Some will find every excuse to call those teachings "anachronistic", "enslaving", "pious pretension", "unfair", and "the work of a domineering church trying to control our lives". However, if we trust in Jesus and open ourselves to the dynamics of love taught by Him in the Beatitudes, we will soon discover that the seemingly unfair impositions of Jesus and the Catholic Church are the path to true freedom and the reality of overwhelmingly sublime loving union with the divine lovers themselves.

So how do we overcome the culture's resistance to the Church's teaching in the minds of our friends, children, students, and ourselves? Even if *we* do not challenge the Church's teaching, many of our friends and children may experience resistance to one or more of these teachings because they might think them to be unreasonable or incomprehensible to the culture around them. Many of us have friends who will find these teachings quite difficult or a significant burden. We ourselves may also find some teachings burdensome or seemingly impossible to live. If we know someone who finds a

---

[1] Fyodor Dostoyevsky, *The Brothers Karamazov*, trans. Constance Garnett (New York: Lowell Press, 2009; Project Gutenberg, 2021), Chapter 5, https://www.gutenberg.org/cache/epub/28054/pg28054-images.html.

particular Church teaching burdensome or unlivable, we naturally want to empathize with them, which might cause us to say, "That teaching is unfair!" or "That group is unfairly burdened or marginalized!" This may cause us to ask why the Lord would lay such a burden on these groups. This puts us in a very precarious position in our spiritual lives, for in our seemingly justifiable compassion and outrage at injustice, we are tempted to go against the teaching of Christ and the Church, and what's worse to abandon the Church herself, thus abandoning the essential sacraments of Reconciliation, the Holy Eucharist, Anointing of the Sick, and even Baptism for our children. The consequences are so profoundly negative and seemingly so justifiable, that we stand on the brink of the abyss.

Given these consequences, we must ask ourselves the following questions *before* we make the judgment that Jesus' and the Church's teachings are unfair and unworthy of belief: Why would Jesus and the Church teach this? Though this teaching seems unfair or insensitive or even prejudicial, might there be a reason why our Lord would ask this of us? Is He trying to help us avoid a path or lifestyle that might lead us into emotional and spiritual darkness? Is He trying to steer us clear of our spiritual enemy who is trying to seduce us into darkness, desolation, and abandonment of God? Is the Lord trying to help us steer clear of false notions of love that seem to be "loving" but really move away from commitment, authentic and humble gift of self, merciful compassion, and self-sacrifice? Even though the culture accepts a particular kind of conduct (or even encourages it), is there a hidden danger that might lead us into a state of profound unhappiness, spiritual emptiness, isolation from true love, and domination by the Evil One? The purpose of this volume is to help the reader answer these questions.

There are twelve moral teachings that have been thrown into question because of seeming insensitivity and outdatedness, putting them at odds with the cultural mainstream:

1. Extramarital sex, premarital sex, and cohabitation (Chapter 1, Sections IV–V)
2. Homosexual lifestyle (Chapter 2, Section I)
3. Sex change and transgender philosophy (Chapter 2, Section III)
4. Pornography (Chapter 2, Section II)

5. Artificial birth control and overpopulation (Chapter 2, Section IV)
6. Abortion and fetal personhood (Chapter 3, Sections I–II)
7. Eugenics and the intrinsic dignity of the mentally disabled (Chapter 3, Section V)
8. Invitro fertilization (Chapter 3, Section VI)
9. Embryonic stem cell research and utilization (Chapter 3, Section VII)
10. Euthanasia and physician-assisted suicide (Chapter 4, Section I)
11. Just war (Chapter 7, Section II.G)

As will be shown, when these teachings are systematically violated, there are several negative consequences for individuals, marriages and families, and society and culture:

- *Individuals* decline significantly in spiritual/religious commitment, ethical/moral commitment, and as a consequence, emotional health. The latter is manifest in steep increases in depression, anxiety, antisocial aggressivity, major psychiatric disorders, substance abuse, familial tensions, and suicides. These consequences are correlated with each of the above twelve moral issues by psychiatric, medical, and sociological studies in Chapters 1–5.
- *Marriages and families* decline significantly in satisfaction, stability, and longevity, which have negative effects on children, communities, and culture.
- *Society and culture*, following the decline of individuals, marriages, and families, decrease significantly in cohesion, shared values, social order, and common purpose, leading to societal angst, dissatisfaction, factioning, unrest, and internal conflict.

These negative consequences are validated by surveys and data, most of which are from peer-reviewed journals and reputable institutes. Though scholarly and scientific surveys are essential, we don't have to look far to see the decline in individual emotional health, marriage and family, and cultural-societal harmony and common cause. Divorce rates and sexual violence have skyrocketed in the last thirty years, our country is increasingly divided and plagued by social unrest, and our young people are filled with a sense of depression and angst. According to a 2019 study by the National Institute of Health, between 2005 and 2017 there have been steep increases in depression and suicides among teens and young adults—52 percent increase in depression/anxiety (among teens), a 63 percent increase in depression among young adults, a 56 percent increase in teen suicides, and a 23 percent increase in teen homicides.[2]

In Chapters 1–5, we will show that these disturbing, disharmonizing, and destructive trends are traceable in many respects to a substantial decline in religious commitment and ethical/moral commitment, a significant rise in ego-comparative identity, and a decline in respect for the intrinsic transcendental dignity of human life and for public exclusive permanent committed love as the true meaning and end of sexuality. These findings are also confirmed by the studies cited in the forthcoming chapters.

So, what is the purpose of this volume? First and foremost, to help educators (particularly in high school and college), catechists (particularly in Confirmation programs), parents, and other Church leaders to give a rational defense of the major controversial moral teachings on the basis of significant deleterious consequences to emotional health, individual identity and stability, marriage and family, and culture and society. In every major study done in the areas of these moral teachings, *secular* institutes confirm again and again that most individuals, our major institutions, and our culture are much worse off than when these moral teachings were believed and observed. This reason alone should give all of us—Catholics, non-Catholics, and unbelievers— significant hesitancy in acceding to the culture's judgment that the Catholic Church's teachings in these areas are insensitive, outdated, and invalid. My hope is that this hesitancy and insight will lead to a

---

[2] Currently, one-third of our young people are expected to have a major incident of depression or anxiety before they reach the age of eighteen. See Jean M. Twenge et al., "Age, Period, and Cohort Trends in Mood Disorder Indicators and Suicide-Related Outcomes in a Nationally Representative Dataset, 2005–2017", *Journal of Abnormal Psychology* 128, no. 3 (2019): 185–99, https://www.apa.org/pubs/journals/releases/abn-abn0000410.pdf. According to the Centers for Disease Control and Prevention, teen suicides have increased by 56 percent over the last decade and teen homicides have increased 23 percent over the same period. See William Wan, "Teen Suicides Are Increasing at an Alarming Pace, Outstripping All Other Age Groups, a New Report Says", *Washington Post*, October 17, 2019, https://www.washingtonpost.com/health/teen-suicides-increasing-at-alarming-pace-outstripping-all-other-age-groups/2019/10/16/e24194c6-f04a-11e9-8693-f487e46784aa_story.html.

secondary reflection on the moral wisdom and truth of Jesus Christ as it has been interpreted by the Church He founded.

My second purpose for writing this volume is to show inductively that objective moral norms are necessary for the emotional and spiritual health of individuals, the stability and strength of marriages and families, and the harmony and high-mindedness of culture and society. Without them, individuals, marriages, and society will unwind and begin a steady process of decline until they become self-destructive. In an age of moral relativism, this claim may seem unrealistic or even preposterous because a large segment of our society has abandoned objective moral norms in favor of consequentialism, situationism, and emotivism, which unfortunately leave us without any solid, identifiable, moral parameters that can act as "absolutes" in the majority of life's situations.

As will be explained in Chapter 1, without these solid identifiable moral parameters (conspicuous lines in the sand), a phenomenon called "social norming" takes hold of our individual and collective consciousness, pulling them toward what we *believe* to be the cultural main stream. Much of the time, we believe that the mainstream is a "safe" place to be, causing us to lower our moral sights until we reach what we perceive to be the mainstream. This has happened almost continuously since the beginning of the sexual revolution, the *Roe v. Wade* decision, and the legalization of euthanasia in Oregon. We have compromised and even numbed our consciences and have allowed our desire for autonomous freedom to eclipse our adherence to objective moral norms that call us to the highest levels of justice, charity, committed love, and the common good. The result, as noted above, has been a steady decline, not only in religious commitment and moral/ethical commitment, but also in emotional health, family stability, and social harmony marked by significantly increased rates of depression, anxiety, substance abuse, familial tensions, homicides, and suicides.

If we grant for a moment that objective moral norms are necessary to prevent moral, emotional, familial, societal, and spiritual decline, and admit further that contemporary society has all but abandoned them, the future of our culture and society seems bleak indeed unless we can restore objective moral norms and revitalize conscience. But how can we do this? In Chapter 5 (Section III.A), we will discuss the three major sources of objective moral norms:

- Religion
- Conscience
- Commonly held beliefs within the culture

We may obtain our moral identity from more than one or all three of these sources. Religion is the most powerful source. Conscience is second to religion and can act independently of it. Nevertheless, religion plays a large role in forming moral norms beyond conscience's six general interior principles:

1. Do not kill an innocent person.
2. Do not unnecessarily harm another person or his reputation, welfare, or family.
3. Do not commit adultery (cheat on one's spouse).
4. Do not steal.
5. Do not lie or bear false witness.
6. Do not defraud or cheat.

Unfortunately, as has been noted above, all three sources of objective moral norms have been compromised in contemporary society—religion is declining, conscience has been "explained away" or numbed, and authoritative social norms have been replaced by the doctrine of "autonomy as fulfillment" and identity politics.

This brings me back to my second purpose for writing this volume: to show people of all age groups that the restoration of all three sources of moral norms—religion, conscience, and authoritative social norms—is necessary, not only for our moral integrity, emotional health, and eternal salvation, but also for marriages, families, culture, and society. If we do not reverse the decline of religion, conscience, and authoritative social norms, our future will be short-lived and bleak. It may be objected that you cannot simply impose religion, objective moral norms, conscience, or authoritative social norms on a population of people. I could not agree more—imposition would be the worst of all possible worlds. What I propose is that we make the rational case for religion, objective moral norms, conscience, and authoritative social norms as clear, accessible, and validated as possible, and as a Church, to make this case integral to our educational and catechetical curricula from middle school through secondary and university education. I have done this in five books and two modular video/PowerPoint programs that give the latest scientific, medical, philosophical, historical, and exegetical evidence for God, the soul, Jesus, and the Catholic Church. (These books are given below in Section II.) The evidence for objective moral norms is given in this present volume, and the explanation of virtue versus the deadly sins is given in Volumes I and II of this Trilogy. In this volume, I have formulated a potential scenario for accomplishing the full range of six steps needed to bring a young person from agnostic (or atheistic) secularism to Christian moral conversion in the Conclusion to the Trilogy (found in this volume).

In sum, my purpose is not only to justify the twelve controversial moral teachings of the Catholic Church (by showing that their systematic violation has led to a significant decline in emotional health and individual stability, marriages and families, and cultural harmony and flourishing) but also to explain that the only way we can restore our culture—let alone our marriages, families, and ourselves—is to recover objective moral norms by the restoration of religion, conscience, and authoritative social norms. There is a tremendous amount of rational evidence for God, Jesus, conscience, and objective moral norms, and so it is incumbent upon all of us to share these resources with as many audiences as possible. Whatever we do will have a positive effect on the people we touch as well as the Church's communities and cultures in which they participate. The task is particularly important for teachers, catechists, priests, religious, and anyone who influences the culture through media, politics, the arts, and social organizations of every kind. It may seem counterintuitive, but the future of our culture and society may well depend on the extent to which we can restore objective moral norms, religion, and conscience. This volume is meant to facilitate that objective along with the other two volumes in this Trilogy as well as the four volumes of the Quartet.

The idea that objective moral norms and religion is vital to the survival of our culture and country is not new. John Adams presciently stated it more than two hundred years ago:

> Because we have no government armed with power capable of contending with human passions unbridled by morality and religion,

Avarice, ambition, revenge and licentiousness would break the strongest cords of our Constitution, as a whale goes through a net. Our Constitution was made only for a moral and religious people. It is wholly inadequate to the government of any other.[3]

The justification for the Church's norms is not limited to longitudinal surveys and natural reason alone. It also extends to spirituality and the heart of God by examining Jesus' revelation of love and the unconditionally loving will of His Father. Though this view of love and God may not be accepted by some non-Catholic audiences, its truth becomes increasingly evident as we examine the studies and surveys showing the deeply negative consequences of violating the objective norms derived from it. Thus, the study and survey results can call non-Catholics and resistant Catholics to a deeper appreciation of Jesus' view of love (given in the Beatitudes and other parts of the Sermon on the Mount).

In view of this, we give extensive treatment to the Christian view of *agapē* (charity and self-sacrificial love), *eros* (Christian sexual love), and *philia* (the modes of deep Christian friendship) in Chapter 1, explaining how the Church's moral teachings support and reinforce this view of love in our lives. This view of love (expressed unconditionally in God) carries through the analysis given in Chapter 2 (on sexual identity, birth control, and population), and Chapters 3–4 (on life issues), as well as Chapter 5 (on charitable deeds) and Chapters 6–7 (the social ethics of the Catholic Church). When readers grasp the centrality of this view of love in the Church's objective moral norms, it becomes increasingly clear that these norms were not given to us as "orders from above" to obey or be punished. They were given to us out of love by an unconditionally loving God to bring us happiness and the purification of our love as well as to help us develop our capacity to care for others, contribute to the common good and culture, and prepare us to enter into the kingdom of unconditional love and joy forever.

When we understand that the Church's objective moral norms are meant solely for our development and happiness in the three loves (*agapē, eros,* and *philia*), they no longer seem unfair or burdensome,

---

[3] Letter from John Adams to Massachusetts Militia, October 11, 1798, National Archives, Founders Online, https://founders.archives.gov/documents/Adams/99-02-02-3102.

but rather gifts that lead us closer to God, one another, and the King-dom of Heaven. This higher, more positive motivation enables us to be insistent gently on the truth and goodness of the Church's (Jesus') moral teachings in the face of an increasingly secularized culture that may see these norms as unfair, repressive, or even oppressive—a needless restriction of human freedom. This positive rationale not only helps Catholics to follow the Church's moral teaching but also gives them a positive entrée to reevangelize the culture (as explained in the Conclusion to the Trilogy, found in this volume).

II. Strengthening the Foundation for Catholic Moral Teaching

Clergy, teachers, catechists, and parents will likely know that the above rationale (showing a direct correlation between the Church's moral teaching and religious commitment, moral commitment, emotional/psychological health, strong marriages and families, and harmonious culture) can be supported and enhanced by intellectual and emotional commitment to God, Jesus, a transcendent soul, and the Catholic Church. The evidence for this intellectual conviction is presented in the four volumes of the Quartet as well as the previous two volumes in this Trilogy. It consists in six major points that may be found in the previous six volumes as follows:

1. *Evidence for a Level Four (transcendent) perspective.* At the end of the second volume of this Trilogy (Appendix I), I gave a brief synopsis of the four levels of happiness and purpose in life.[4] Each level of happiness brings with it a distinct perspective not only on happiness but also on ethics (the good), love, freedom, suffering, personhood, and the common good.[5] The greater one's

---

[4] For those seeking detailed explanations of the four levels beyond the brief synopsis in Volume II of the Trilogy, see Volume I of the Quartet, *Finding True Happiness: Satisfying Our Restless Hearts.* For those seeking an online resource with some detail, see Robert Spitzer, *Credible Catholic Big Book*, vol. 13, *Four Levels of Happiness* (Magis Center, 2017), Credible-Catholic.com, https://www.crediblecatholic.com/pdf/7E-P6/7E-BB13.pdf#P1V13.

[5] These differing perspectives on ethics, love, etc. are explained in detail in two books: Robert Spitzer, *Healing the Culture: A Common-Sense Philosophy of Happiness, Freedom, and the Life Issues* (San Francisco: Ignatius Press, 2000), Chapters 4–7, and also Robert Spitzer, *Ten Universal Principles: A Brief Philosophy of the Life Issues* (San Francisco: Ignatius Press, 2011).

conviction about transcendent meaning in life (Level Four), the greater the motivation to follow religious moral norms. Conviction about transcendent meaning in life depends in great part on intellectual conviction about the existence of God—a personal God who is perfect truth, perfect goodness, perfect love, and perfect beauty—a God who is interested in the transcendent beings He created in His own image. This perspective has been justified through scientific and philosophical evidence in two previous volumes.[6] If this evidence is reasonable and responsible and can be judged true through the eyes and spirit of faith, then it calls us to interpret ethics and morality through its divine transcendental lens.

2. *Evidence for the Christian perspective*. Volume III of the Quartet gave considerable evidence for the life of Jesus Christ about two thousand years ago, showing the likelihood that He performed many miracles within a teaching and evangelizing ministry, was crucified by Pontius Pilate, rose from the dead in glory, and gave us the very Spirit of God—His Holy Spirit. In that volume, we assessed the significance of this full range of evidence and concluded that it points to Jesus' unconditional love as well as His divine Sonship. Inasmuch as this conclusion is reasonable and responsible and can be discerned as true through the eyes and spirit of faith, then Jesus really does have the words of everlasting life (Jn 6:68); He really is "*the way, and the truth, and the life*" (Jn 14:6; italics added)—the summit of divine revelation, and the pathway to eternal salvation and unconditional love. This frees us to turn to Him for the fullness of moral teaching. If Jesus truly is the divine Son, then we are called to obey lovingly His word transmitted through the New Testament and His Church.

3. *Evidence for the Catholic perspective*. In Volume II (Chapter 1) of this Trilogy, we showed that Jesus established the Catholic Church (founded on the supreme teaching office given to Peter) as His definitive interpreter in matters of doctrine and morals. In that volume, it was shown that Jesus intended to

---

[6] Robert Spitzer, *New Proofs for the Existence of God: Contributions of Cotemporary Physics and Philosophy* (Grand Rapids, Mich.: Eerdmans, 2010). See also Volume II of the Quartet, *The Soul's Upward Yearning: Clues to Our Transcendent Nature from Reason and Experience*.

start a church, created an office of supreme teaching and jurid-ical authority ("with the keys to the kingdom of heaven"), appointed Peter as the first holder of that supreme office, and promised that the gates of the netherworld would never prevail against it (Mt 16:18–19). Inasmuch as these affirmations are rea-sonable and responsible and can be affirmed as true through the eyes and spirit of faith, then the Catholic Church is the Church of Jesus Christ, and she has the authority to interpret Jesus' words and intentions definitively through the supreme teaching office held by the successors to Saint Peter. If that is the case, then we are called to listen respectfully and lovingly obey the moral doctrine set out by that Church.

4. *Evidence for the perspective of compassionate self-sacrificial love* (agapē). Jesus intended to establish love as the highest commandment— the highest virtue to which all other virtues are subordinate (see Mt 22:38–39). He defines His unique idea of love through cer-tain teachings and parables, the most important of which are the Beatitudes, the Parable of the Good Samaritan, the Parable of the Prodigal Son, and other teachings from the Sermon on the Mount and other discourses. These teachings reveal that "love" (*agapē*) is humble-hearted, gentle-hearted, forgiving, compas-sionate, chaste, authentic, and self-sacrificial. These affirmations were historically and scripturally justified in two previous vol-umes.[7] Inasmuch as Jesus really is the divine Son and the full-ness of revelation, then we are freed to transform our hearts toward these loving virtues so that we might become like Him and His Father in egoless and compassionate gift of self—to love one another as He has loved us (Jn 15:12).

5. *Evidence for the perspective of a cosmic struggle between Christ and Satan.* One of Jesus' primary mission objectives, along with bringing the Kingdom of God, sharing the good news, and ini-tiating His Church, was to defeat Satan and his minions. Jesus began this mission by defeating Satan in the desert, through His prolific ministry of exorcisms, and absolutely through His

---

[7] This definition of love was scripturally justified in Volume III of the Quartet, *God So Loved the World*, Chapters 1–3. These characteristics of love are explained in detail in Chapter 4 of Volume II of the Trilogy, *Escape from Evil's Darkness*.

self-sacrificial Passion and death. He did not stop there, but also initiated a Church in which He gave His apostles (and their successors) the power to exorcise demons, to forgive sins definitively, and to actualize His body and blood in the Holy Eucharist. These affirmations were scripturally justified (along with examples of exorcism) in Volume I of this Trilogy—*Christ versus Satan in our Daily Lives* (Chapters 2–4). Inasmuch as these affirmations are reasonable and responsible and can be affirmed as true through the eyes and spirit of faith, then we should be cognizant of the presence and power of our spiritual enemy, his objective (to seduce us into Hell), and his tactics (temptation, deceit, and accusation). At the same time, we should be cognizant of the superior power and presence of Jesus Christ, our Lord, and that He will help and protect us from our spiritual enemy. His help and protection cannot be brought to fruition in our lives unless we put our faith in Him, assent to and follow His teachings, and avail ourselves of the sacramental grace He bestows on us through His Church.[8]

6. *Evidence for the perspective of loving obedience.* This is not an intellectual perspective (like the previous five perspectives), but rather a disposition of the will. It does not call us to intellectual assent but suggests an attitude of love and trust of Jesus that opens us to the disposition of discipleship—to follow the word of the One who is at once beloved and master. If we have embraced Jesus Christ as the unconditional personal love of God who came to be with us to reveal His love (see the second perspective), then we are not only called to give *intellectual* assent to His divinity and love but invited to give spiritual assent to Him by entering into relationship with Him through prayer and commitment to His way of life. If we do this, and assent to the third perspective— that Jesus initiated the Church through an office of supreme teaching and juridical authority (the Catholic Church)—and if we believe that He truly does work through the successor of

---

[8] It is important to note that Jesus did not come to be only a teacher of morality. He definitely came to bring moral teaching, but also to protect believers from Satan and to empower and transform them through these teachings within His Church. See the previous two volumes in this Trilogy.

Saint Peter to interpret His word and intention definitively until the end of the age (Mt 28:20), then the commitment to follow Jesus' way is extended to following the teaching of *His* Church. Hence, we are invited by the Lord (through perspectives two and three) to relationship with Christ through prayer as well as commitment to His way of life as interpreted by *His* Church. If we accept His invitation and commit ourselves to Him and His Church, we enter into a whole interior world that I term "trusting discipleship and loving obedience". Obedience out of love is quite different from obedience out of fear and obedience out of coercion. It flows out of our love for the One who has given us everything—even His whole self—to bring us into His unconditional and eternal love and joy. At this juncture, it is not sufficient to look over the evidence and intellectually assent to its probability, reasonableness, or truth. We must make the decision to enter into the interior world of loving commitment—loving discipleship—loving obedience to which He invites us. If we do this, it will change our view on morality, transform our purpose in life, protect us from our spiritual enemy, lead us on the path to salvation, and enable us to be leaders in reevangelizing and restabilizing our declining culture.

III. The Perspective of This Volume: Reason Applied to Revelation

There are some ethical schools of thought that either ignore or suppress the use of reason. The Catholic Church is not one of them. From her very inception, the Catholic Church has used reason to apply the teaching of Jesus to new ethical situations and to defend His teaching. I will use such arguments for these two purposes throughout this volume. As implied above, I will use four rational methods to justify the veracity of Jesus' and the Church's teaching:

1. Showing how ignoring or rejecting the Church's precepts leads to a decline in emotional health (increased depression, substance abuse, anxiety, and suicide)

2. Showing how ignoring the Church's teachings leads to the decline of marriage, family, and the culture
3. Showing how her teaching promotes Jesus' ideal of love (*agapē*), which is our eternal destiny and the hope for a better world
4. Showing how ignoring the Church's teachings leads to a decline in spiritual and moral life

Correlations one and two are quite firmly established by medical, psychological, sociological, and political studies and surveys, most of which are initiated by secular institutes. Correlation three is established through a philosophical, psychological, and theological assessment of the Christian view of love (particularly *agapē*, *philia*, and *eros*—see Chapter 1 of this volume). Correlation four is established by secular and religious studies of the contemporary decline in religion and morality as it manifests itself in the decrease in happiness and collective ethics, as well as the increase in homicides, suicides, sexual assaults, cheating, and bullying, and the decline of family life and internal cultural stability. As implied by these correlations, religion and morality may well be the most important factors in emotional health, family stability, and a stable and fulfilling *secular* society as well as the pathway to eternal salvation.

Before examining the correlation between emotional health and specific moral teachings, it should be noted that there is significant psychological and medical evidence indicating that religious affiliation is integral, and even paramount, to emotional health. The 2004 study of the American Psychiatric Association showed that nonreligious affiliation correlates with significantly higher rates of depression, anxiety, impulsivity, familial tensions, substance abuse, and suicides.[9] These findings have been confirmed by several more recent studies.[10] As we shall see, the negative effects on emotional health caused by

[9] Kanita Dervic et al., "Religious Affiliation and Suicide Attempt", *American Journal of Psychiatry* 161, no. 12 (December 2004): 2303–8, https://ajp.psychiatryonline.org/doi/full /10.1176/appi.ajp.161.12.2303.

[10] See, for example, Harold Koenig, "Research on Religion, Spirituality, and Mental Health: A Review", *Canadian Journal of Psychiatry* 54, no. 5 (2009): 283–91, https://journals. sagepub.com/doi/pdf/10.1177/070674370905400502; Raphael Bonelli et al., "Religious and Spiritual Factors in Depression: Review and Integration of the Research", *Depression and Research Treatment*, August 15, 2012, https://www.hindawi.com/journals/drt/2012/962860/; Stefano Lassi and Daniele Mugnaini, "Role of Religion and Spirituality on Mental Health and

the decline of religion exacerbates the decline in emotional health caused by the rejection of objective moral standards, and vice versa. Hence, decline in emotional health will be more serious in individuals who reject or ignore *both* religion and moral norms. Since religion and moral norms frequently coincide, a decline in one will often lead to a decline in the other, meaning that emotional health will be seriously compromised in our increasingly religiously disaffiliated and morally relativistic culture.

Our contemporary society's cavalier marginalization of religion and objective moral norms—particularly Christian objective moral norms—may well be the undoing of its individual citizens, familial structure, and itself. If we do not want to follow the recipe for insanity—repeating the same unsuccessful behavior and expecting a different result—we may want to reconsider seriously our religious commitment and the twelve controversial moral doctrines of the Catholic Church.

IV. Social Ethics and the Church's Social Teaching

When we turn to social ethics, we encounter a new problem—Jesus did not directly state His position on social ethics. This meant that the Church had to derive that position from four of His teachings:

1. The Golden Rule (versus the Silver Rule)—Do unto others as you have them do to you (see Mt 7:12).
2. "As you did it to one of the least of these my brethren, you did it to me" (Mt 25:40).
3. "The sabbath [the law] was made for man, not man for the sabbath" (Mk 2:27).

Resilience: There Is Enough Evidence", *International Journal of Emergency Mental Health and Human Resilience* 17, no. 3 (2015): 661–63, https://www.omicsonline.org/open-access/role-of-religion-and-spirituality-on-mental-health-and-resilience-there-is-enough-evidence-1522-4821-1000273.pdf; Harold Koenig, "Religion, Spirituality, and Health: A Review and Update", *Advances in Mind-Body Medicine* 29, no. 3 (2015): 19–26, https://pubmed.ncbi.nlm.nih.gov/26026153/; and Corina Ronenberg et al., "The Protective Effects of Religiosity on Depression: A 2-Year Prospective Study", *Gerontologist* 56, no. 3 (2016): 421–31, https://academic.oup.com/gerontologist/article/56/3/421/2605601.

4. "Render therefore to Caesar the things that are Caesar's, and to God the things that are God's" (Mt 22:21).

In Chapter 6, we will show how the Church derived five major principles of social ethics from the above four teachings of Jesus, by examining the work of Christian thinkers throughout the centuries:

1. Every human being has an intrinsically good and transcendent dignity (with which Christ identified).
2. "An unjust law is no law at all" (Saint Augustine).[11]
3. Every being of human origin must be considered equally worthy of protection under the law—personhood (Father Bartolomé de las Casas).
4. Every human being has the inalienable rights of life, self-governance (liberty), the pursuit of happiness, and property (Father Francisco Suarez).
5. The right to life is more fundamental than the right to self-governance, and the right to self-governance is more fundamental than the rights to pursue happiness and own property (because rights that are necessary for other rights are more fundamental).

These five principles developed by Catholic clergy were adopted by non-Catholic political philosophers (such as Hugo Grotius, John Locke, and Thomas Jefferson) and used as the foundation of the charters and constitutions of almost every free country today. But the Church went further—she had to adapt her views on individual dignity, justice, and rights to a complex industrialized society, a need that came to the fore in light of the abuses of the Industrial Revolution. In 1891, Pope Leo XIII wrote the first social encyclical of the Catholic Church that attempted to set out guidelines for political and economic justice and rights within complex economic systems—*Rerum Novarum*. This led to the promulgation of dozens of social encyclicals covering everything from free markets to labor relations, the fundamentality of family, political systems, international relations, just war, and environmental stewardship. In

[11] Saint Augustine, *On Free Choice of the Will* I, 5.

order to do this, the Church developed six additional principles of social ethics:

1. The intrinsic transcendent dignity of every human person
2. The principle of the common good
3. The universal destination of goods
4. The principle of subsidiarity
5. Participation in democracy
6. The principle of solidarity

In Chapter 7, we will give an explanation of these six principles, and an overview on how the Church applies them in several major areas of social ethics—family, economics, politics, international relations, war and peace, and environmental stewardship.

V. Conclusion

As may now be clear, Jesus set out His moral teachings by prescribing charity (*agapē*) and proscribing several actions that undermine the will of His Father and His commandment to love. The Church in her wisdom defended that teaching in different contexts throughout the centuries and applied it to many areas of personal and social ethics that were not even conceived in Jesus' time. Our objective in this volume is to show the intelligibility and rational defensibility of those positions by using the four rational methods mentioned above as well as the social ethical principles the Church derived from Jesus' teaching. Yet this volume—and the Church's teaching—is not the product of reason alone, but rather a blend of reasoning with a heart-felt understanding of His love for us and the love we should show to one another. It also presumes a respect for Jesus' promise to protect the Church until the end of time as well as her teaching office and doctrinal prescription.[12]

---

[12]See the evidence for this in Volume II, Chapter 1 of this Trilogy.

KEY TO ABBREVIATED REFERENCES
TO THE QUARTET AND THE TRILOGY

The Quartet
Happiness, Suffering, and Transcendence

Volume I—*Finding True Happiness: Satisfying Our Restless Hearts* (Ignatius Press, 2015)

Volume II—*The Soul's Upward Yearning: Clues to Our Transcendent Nature from Experience and Reason* (Ignatius Press, 2016)

Volume III—*God So Loved the World: Clues to Our Transcendent Destiny from the Revelation of Jesus* (Ignatius Press, 2016)

Volume IV—*The Light Shines on in the Darkness: Transforming Suffering through Faith* (Ignatius Press, 2017)

The Trilogy
Called Out of Darkness: Contending with Evil
through the Church, Virtue, and Prayer

Volume I—*Christ versus Satan in Our Daily Lives: The Cosmic Struggle between Good and Evil* (Ignatius Press, 2020)

Volume II—*Escape from Evil's Darkness: The Light of Christ in the Church, Spiritual Conversion, and Moral Conversion* (Ignatius Press, 2021)

Volume III—*The Moral Wisdom of the Catholic Church: A Defense of Her Controversial Moral Teachings* (Ignatius Press, forthcoming)

PART ONE

Love and Sexuality:
True and False Promises

Chapter One

True and False Promises of Happiness and Freedom

Introduction

Empirical and rational evidence is sufficient for understanding and assenting to the truth of the Church's moral teaching (see the explanation in the Introduction to this volume). Though a Catholic spiritual life is indispensable for deepening, following, teaching, and defending the Church's moral teaching, it is not necessary for understanding and assenting to it. For this reason, the Church's moral teaching (presented in Chapters 1–7) can be intellectually affirmed by *everyone* capable of understanding empirical and rational evidence. We also noted that this rational evidence consists in medical and psychological studies, sociological surveys and studies, scientific data, philosophical (logical) arguments, and sociopolitical studies of the relationship between ethics, behavior, and culture. These empirical-rational methods and studies give probative evidence for the efficacy of Christ's and the Church's moral teaching in the areas of emotional health, spiritual well-being, marital longevity and stability, and cultural-societal harmony and stability.

In light of this, the rationale and evidence in Chapters 1–7 can be effectively used to justify the Church's teaching to vulnerable populations (such as high school and university students as well as young adults) who are being (or have been) won over to the morally relativistic culture lamented by Joseph Cardinal Ratzinger in his homily for the Mass for the election of the Roman Pontiff (when he was elected and became Pope Benedict XVI) on April 18, 2005:

We are building a dictatorship of relativism that does not recognize anything as definitive and whose ultimate goal consists solely of one's own ego and desires.[1]

He went on to predict the cultural consequences of this relativistic dictatorship which has proved to be remarkably prescient in light of the evidence presented in this volume.

Before proceeding to the Catholic view of love and sexuality, we will first look at the six central precepts of personal morality taught by the Old Testament, Jesus, and the Catholic Church. They are also present in most of the world's religions and tacitly present in the conscience of every human person.[2] For Catholics and most Christians, the Ten Commandments are the foundation of moral teaching and present the minimum standards to be observed by everyone. Jesus formally accepted these commandments as foundational for His moral teaching when He told the rich young man what is needed for eternal life:

> You know the commandments: "Do not kill, Do not commit adultery, Do not steal, Do not bear false witness, Do not defraud, Honor your father and mother." (Mk 10:19; cf. Mt 19:18–19; Lk 18:20)

Jesus identifies six commandments in this passage (five of which are from the latter part of the Decalogue) that He implies are needed for salvation. The texts of the Decalogue in the Old Testament (Ex 20:1–17; Deut 5:6–21) do not include defrauding (cheating). Jesus probably included it in His list of precepts because it is listed elsewhere in the Old Testament,[3] and for Jesus, it is a commandment needed for eternal life. The Greek term used to describe it is *aposterēsēs*, which means to unjustly deprive, to defraud, or to cheat.[4]

---

[1] Mass *Pro Eligendo Romano Pontifice* [for the election of the Roman Pontiff], Homily of His Eminence Joseph Cardinal Ratzinger, Dean of the College of Cardinals (April 18, 2005).

[2] See C.S. Lewis, *The Abolition of Man* (New York: HarperOne, 2001), which makes the case for the natural law in the heart of every person. The Appendix, "Illustrations of the Tao", gives examples of specific precepts known naturally to us. Each of the six precepts mentioned in the chapter is mentioned or implied in many illustrations. See the extensive discussion of this in Chapter 5, Section I.

[3] See Lev 19:13–14; 25:17.

[4] See *Strong's Exhaustive Concordance Online*, s.v. "650: apostereó", where *aposterēsēs* is a transliteration, BibleHub.com, 2021, https://biblehub.com/greek/650.htm.

Jesus goes beyond these six commandments, directing His disciples to pursue a high standard of love defined in the Parable of the Good Samaritan and in the Beatitudes (see below). Notice that the six commandments addressed by Jesus in the above passage are external behaviors while the Beatitudes concern interior attitudes that become the framework for the virtues opposed to the eight deadly sins. As noted in Volume II (Chapter 4) of this Trilogy, the eight deadly sins are also interior attitudes that lead to sinful behaviors. Thus, Jesus was interested not only in external behaviors (the emphasis of the Old Testament law), but also in the interior attitudes that lead to violations of the commandments as well as the attitudes that counter them (the virtues).

Given Jesus' implication that these six commandments are necessary for salvation, we will want to examine each of them. There is another reason for doing this. As noted above, most of these six commandments are mentioned in the ethical codes of most religions. They are also mentioned in philosophical codes and pagan tractates, implying their presence in the conscience of virtually everyone.[5] As such, they are a cross-cultural or, perhaps better, a transcultural language of ethical conduct grounding the objective principles enabling individuals and societies to strive for justice instead of sinking to depths of depravity.

The order of the precepts in the Greek text of Mark 10:19 is as follows:

1. Do not commit adultery (this chapter).
2. Do not kill (Chapters 3–4).
3. Do not steal (Chapter 5, Section I.A).
4. Do not bear false witness (Chapter 5, Section I.B).
5. Do not defraud (Chapter 5, Section I.C).
6. Honor your father and mother (Chapter 5, Section I.D).

We will examine each precept in the order given by Jesus.

Before proceeding to the topic of love and sexuality, it is important to review the three conditions for a mortal sin, because this volume is concerned with only the first condition—grave matter. Since

---

[5] See ibid.

we do not treat the second and third conditions—full knowledge and complete consent of the will[6]—the contents of this volume are incapable of even suggesting that someone has committed a mortal sin (a sin that would jeopardize salvation). Rather, the contents are meant to explain why Jesus and the Church considered particular actions to be grave matter *capable* of jeopardizing salvation. A brief consideration of this teaching in the *Catechism of the Catholic Church* will be sufficient for clarifying this important distinction:

> For a sin to be *mortal*, three conditions must together be met: "Mortal sin is sin whose object is grave matter and which is also committed with full knowledge and deliberate consent" (*Reconciliatio et Paenitentia* 17 §12).... Mortal sin requires *full knowledge* and *complete consent*. It presupposes knowledge of the sinful character of the act, of its opposition to God's law. It also implies a consent sufficiently deliberate to be a personal choice.... *Unintentional ignorance* can diminish or even remove the imputability of a grave offense.... The promptings of feelings and passions can also diminish the voluntary and free character of the offense, as can external pressures or pathological disorders.[7]

In view of this, a person may have committed any of the prohibited actions (mentioned in Chapters 1–5) multiple times, but not be guilty of a mortal sin because they did so without adequate knowledge (unintended ignorance) or impediments to the free use of their will. Such impediments might include strong passions and feelings, extrinsic pressures or constraint, strong habits, serious psychological impediments—such as obsessive compulsive disorder, dissociative identity disorder, schizophrenia, bipolar disorder, psychoses, and strong neuroses—which are explained in Volume II, Chapter 7 of this Trilogy. Therefore, if individuals are involved in the prohibited conduct mentioned in Chapters 1–5, they should examine whether they have full knowledge and complete consent of the will. If there are strong passions, feelings, habits, psychological challenges, or external pressures, they *may* not be guilty of mortal sin. Nevertheless, those individuals should not take chances with their eternal salvation, and so

---

[6] See *Catechism of the Catholic Church*, no. 1857 (hereafter cited as *CCC*).
[7] Ibid., 1857, 1859–60 (italics added).

they should take steps to change their conduct, go to the Sacrament of Reconciliation, and discuss the issues they face with a priest. As we shall see in the forthcoming chapters, the actions prohibited by Jesus and the Church were declared so because they undermine not only our emotional health but also our spiritual well-being and our path to salvation. Regardless of whether one might have committed a mortal sin in the past, it is incumbent on the individual to take at least little steps to change that conduct (within the extrinsic, emotional, habitual, and psychological constraints he faces), and to confess that conduct with sincere contrition. Volume II of this Trilogy (Chapters 3, 5, and 6) gives several techniques to help individuals to resist temptations and make the transition from the old self to the new.

I. The Christian View of Love

There is no more misunderstood commandment than the prohibition of adultery and sexual impropriety. Regrettably, the culture has taken a completely divergent perspective on sexuality from that of Jesus and the Church, leading many Christians to disobey these teachings and to feel considerable resentment and hostility to both the Church and Jesus. A good number of people have cast aside Christ and His path to salvation solely because they felt that Jesus' and the Church's teachings on sexuality are out of date and out of touch with contemporary culture. But are they? Can sexuality be treated as a mere instrument of human passion and fulfillment—a neutral, inconsequential, or collateral dimension to add excitement and adventure to life—or rather is sexuality a deeply mysterious psychic power intertwined with virtually every dimension of our subconscious minds, our biological desires, our conscious interpretation of relationships with others, and our spiritual lives, a mysterious power meant to solidify commitments and build familial loyalties to support the creation of children with transcendental souls destined for eternal life, or something in-between? We will respond to this question in three parts:

1. The Four Levels of Happiness and the Idea of Love and Freedom (Section I.A)

2. Love and Sexuality according to Jesus and the Catholic Church (Section I.B)
3. The Christian View of Eros: Exclusive, Permanent, Family-Oriented, and Christ-Oriented (Section I.C)

A. *The Four Levels of Happiness and the Idea of Love and Freedom*

In our treatment of happiness (See Volume II, Appendix I of the Trilogy), we noted that a Level One or Two view of happiness/ purpose tends to emphasize *personal* gratification and satisfaction of *self* while Levels Three and Four tend to emphasize empathy, contribution, and transcendental purpose. We discuss the problems of Level One-Two views of happiness and purpose in life, giving particular attention to the comparison game, existential emptiness, and lack of fulfillment in contributive and transcendental identity. These are significant problems that can be definitely resolved only by moving to Level Three (contributive-empathetic) happiness and Level Four (transcendent faith-based) happiness-purpose in our lives (see Volume I, Chapters 1–6 of the Quartet). Since our purpose here is to address the Christian view of sexual love, we will not review the comparison game (and the way out of it) here. Interested readers can find a summary in Volume II, Appendix I of this Trilogy.

Before looking at the four levels of freedom and sexual love (*eros*) it will prove helpful to recall C. S. Lewis' distinctions among the four kinds of love:

1. *Storgē*—a *feeling* of affection
2. *Philia*—friendships based on mutual care and commitment
3. *Eros*—in the narrow sense refers to sexual love, but in the broader sense to the exclusive, complete, reciprocal commitment of a man and woman to each other through conjugal union for the sake of mutual support and the generation of children and family
4. *Agapē*—the unselfish and self-sacrificial love oriented solely toward the good of the other that stands at the foundation of forgiveness, compassion for the marginalized, and complete gift of self for the other (describes the essence of Jesus and His Father and is the ideal we are called to by Jesus)

We will defer our treatment of the interrelationship between *eros* and the other three kinds of love to Section I.C. For the moment we will only differentiate the idea of sexual love (*eros*) and freedom from a Level One-Two perspective and from a Level Three-Four perspective. Level One (materialistic and pleasure-based) happiness and Level Two (ego-comparative) happiness tend to run hand in hand because their essential focus is on the *self*—an inward focus. In Level One, *I* obtain pleasure and ownership of things, and in Level Two, *I* have control over others and comparative advantage over others. Conversely, Level Three (contributive and empathetic) happiness and Level Four (transcendent and faith-based) happiness run hand in hand, because their essential focus is on the world beyond the *self*—an outward focus. In Level Three, I invest myself in contribution to *other and the world*, and in Level Four, I invest myself in *God and the good of my church community and the Kingdom of God*. As might be expected, the Level One-Two view of *eros* and freedom will differ significantly from the Level Three-Four view of *eros* and freedom. Evidently, the Christian view of *eros* and freedom is Level Three-Four and is incommensurate with the Level One-Two viewpoint. Therefore, if people wish to understand and follow the Christian viewpoint, they will have to move to Level Three-Four happiness and purpose in life.

Let us now draw the contrast between the Level One-Two view of sexual love and freedom (dominant in popular culture) and the Level Three-Four view of sexual love and freedom (the contributive-transcendent perspective of Christianity). We will begin with the observation that a person who has a Level One or Level Two meaning in life (who is likely to be less personally mature) will have a more superficial view of *eros* than a person in Levels Three and Four (who is more mature and is open to an intimate, generative, and committed relationship). In order to understand this, we will first examine the idea of "freedom" according to both perspectives.

In Volume I (Chapter 4) of the Quartet, we discussed "freedom from" and "freedom for" in which it was shown that individuals on Levels One and Two are likely to have a view of "freedom from" that focuses on immediately attaining strong urges and desires, escaping constraint and commitment, "keeping options open", and resenting unreciprocated sacrifices. Conversely, individuals on Levels Three and Four are likely to view freedom as "freedom for" that focuses on the most pervasive, enduring, and deep purpose in life—one that goes *beyond* self and makes a genuine contribution to family, friends, community, organizations, church, the Kingdom of God, and the culture. In this view, constraint and commitment for the sake of achieving life's higher purpose is seen as worthwhile. Likewise, foreclosing options to pursue truly good directions is deemed essential, and unreciprocated sacrifices are accepted and expected. Once again, these different views of freedom significantly affect individuals' views of a sexual relationship, as well as the feelings coming from it.

We may now give a general profile of the focus and expectations for a sexual relationship in the perspectives of Level One-Two versus Level Three-Four. As might be expected, the Level One-Two perspective of *eros* emphasizes what is more apparent, immediately gratifying, intense, and ego-fulfilling. Hence, its focus is predominantly on the sexual act, beauty, gender complementarity, and romantic excitement and adventure. Furthermore, its expectations are fairly short-term and focused on immediate gratification, keeping options open, increased levels of sexual excitement, and avoiding commitments and unreciprocated sacrifices. As a consequence, it resists movement to Level Three-Four and the intimacy and generativity intrinsic to them (discussed below in this section).

In contrast to this, a Level Three-Four perspective of *eros* focuses on making a difference beyond the self and on making the most pervasive, enduring, and deep contribution possible. It is also open to empathy and care for others (in its quest to make an optimal positive contribution to the world). Though it does not abandon the dimensions of *eros* emphasized in Levels One and Two (sexuality, beauty, gender complementarity, and romantic excitement), it contextualizes these desires within concomitant desires for intimacy, generativity, complementarity, collaboration, common cause, deep friendship, loyalty, commitment, family, and faith. As implied above, a Level Three-Four perspective is not enough to bring about these desires; there must also be psychological stability and personal development and maturation. When these factors are co-present, the expectations of sexual relationships broaden and deepen. As a consequence, there is a willingness to foreclose options, to invest more fully in the relationship, and ultimately to make this relationship exclusive. There is willingness to make the other a "first priority" in the expenditure of physical and emotional resources, which anticipates a lifelong commitment as well as unreciprocated sacrifices. The following chart summarizes the outlooks of both perspectives.

LEVEL	FOCUS	EXPECTATIONS
Eros *(Romantic Love)* Three and Four	Openness to the importance and inclusion of intimacy, generativity, complementarity, collaboration, common cause, deep mutual friendship, long-term commitment, and family (Note: sexuality, beauty, and romantic excitement are still important, but contextualized by the above)	Pervasive, enduring, and deep meaning; foreclosing of options to secure "best option"; mutually supportive communion; constraints for the sake of intimacy, depth, and commitment; unreciprocated sacrifice
Eros *(Romantic Love)* One and Two	The emphasis is on sexual feelings and gratification, beauty of the other, romantic adventure, excitement of the relationship, and control within the relationship.	Immediate and heightened gratification, fulfillment of the desire to be admired and loved, keeping options open, greater levels of excitement, and no unreciprocated sacrifices

When sexual relationships occur in Level Three-Four individuals who are stable and mature, the intimate friendship becomes deeper and deeper. This is well illustrated by the dynamic of friendship (*philia* addressed by C. S. Lewis). When *philia* is reciprocated, it tends to deepen and become more committed. When we commit more of our time, future, and physical and psychic energy to a friend, and that friend reciprocates with a deeper commitment to us, the friendship becomes closer, more supportive, more fulfilling, and more emotionally satisfying. When it is appropriate, this deep friendship can incite intimacy, generativity, and romantic feelings, which in turn can deepen the friendship even more—but now it is not just a deep friendship; it is an *intimate romantic* deep friendship. This distinctive kind of friendship can continue to deepen until both parties are not only ready for, but desirous of, making the other their *number one priority*. As will be explained below, there can be only one number one priority. Hence, the desire to make a deep intimate friend a number one priority is tantamount to wanting an *exclusive* commitment, which cannot be given to anyone else.

Furthermore, this deep friendship anticipates a *lifelong* commitment in which the couple enters into common cause—that is, to do some good through their mutual efforts for the world *beyond* themselves. The most significant dimension of common cause for a couple who are intimately related (anticipating sexuality) is the creation of a *family*. Recall from above that love moves *beyond* itself—we seek to do the good for *the other*, the community, the world, and the Kingdom of God. Just as loving individuals move beyond themselves, so also loving couples move beyond themselves. Though it is very important that the couple have their "alone time" to develop their closeness, affection, generativity, and mutual support, it is likewise important that they do not *stay* within the relationship *alone*. A couple staring into each other's eyes can be as mutually self-obsessive as Narcissus looking at his image in the pool—they can simply fade away doing nothing else. This illustrates the need for intimate friendships to move from *"within* the relationship" to *"beyond* the relationship". The deeply committed sexual relationship cultivates a complementary and collaborative strength—a synergy to move beyond itself to make a positive difference through common cause. Family is the most fundamental aim of such a relationship. But there can be many other objectives as well—for community, church, culture, Kingdom of God, etc. Though the most fundamental objective—family—must come first, the family too must move beyond itself to make a positive difference in ways that will not undermine its depth and cohesiveness.

In sum, the ideal of a Level Three-Four sexual relationship is to bring intimate friendship to its highest level—to make the intimate friend a number one priority through an exclusive and lifelong commitment to enter into mutually supportive and collaborative common cause toward family and other positive objectives that will serve not only friends, but also community, culture, church, and the Kingdom of God.

Let's return to what was said in the above chart about the place of sexuality within Level Three-Four *eros*. Unlike Level One-Two *eros*, which places the priority on need-fulfillment, ego-fulfillment, romance, passion, and sexuality, Level Three-Four *eros* places the priority on friendship based on increasing levels of commitment and the fulfillment of the other. This does not mean that Level Three-Four people do not seek the need-fulfillment and ego-fulfillment. They do, but they subordinate this to the fulfillment of the other through increasing levels of commitment to them. The same thing holds true for romance and sexuality. Unlike Level One-Two individuals who often view romance and sexuality from the vantage point of their need-fulfillment and ego-fulfillment, Level Three-Four individuals tend to view romance and sexuality from the vantage point of the other's needs and fulfillment. This prioritization incites Level Three-Four people to ask the *other* what they would like to do about romance within the framework of their religious and ethical values, comfort level, and purpose in life (normally, Level Three individuals follow an ethical standard, and Level Four individuals follow a religious standard). Level Three-Four individuals then subordinate their needs and preferences to those of their friend (so long as the other's needs and preferences do not violate their ethical religious standards).

B. Love and Sexuality according to Jesus and the Catholic Church

The consideration of religious and ethical values brings us to specifically Christian norms for romance, sexuality, and marriage. A strong belief in Jesus and the Church He initiated (the Catholic Church) will very likely lead to a desire to follow His and His Church's teachings. Before articulating Christian norms for sexuality, we will want to review briefly how to build strong faith in Christ and His Church. Recall from the Introduction to Volume I of this Trilogy that intellectual conversion often precedes spiritual conversion and spiritual conversion often precedes moral conversion. Therefore, if one wants to build a strong foundation for religious and ethical norms that give ultimate purpose to life, eternal significance, and communion with the Creator, one ought to consider seriously the rational evidence for God, the transcendent soul, Jesus, and the Catholic Church (see the list of resources providing evidence for rational assent to these fundamental truths in Section II of the Introduction to this volume). When we complete sufficient studies to meet our needs for intellectual conversion, we can then proceed to spiritual conversion and moral conversion (see Volume II of this Trilogy). This movement begins with commitments to the sacramental life and prayer life (see Volume II, Chapters 2–3 of this Trilogy). When a relationship with the Lord is established (spiritual conversion), we can strongly proceed to moral conversion—appropriating virtue, resisting temptation, and becoming the "new self" (see Volume II, Chapters 5–6 of this Trilogy). The deeper our commitment to spiritual and moral conversion, the deeper our love for Jesus, which in turn deepens our understanding of His (and the Church's) moral teaching and our desire to follow that teaching. We may now proceed to the presentation of Jesus' and the Church's teaching on sexuality.

It may prove helpful to begin with a consideration of the ideal of covenant love described by Pope Saint John Paul II in his important exhortation *Familiaris Consortio*:

> God created man in His own image and likeness (cf. Gen 1:26–27): calling him to existence through love, He called him at the same time for love. God is love (1 Jn 4:8) and in Himself He lives a mystery of personal loving communion. Creating the human race in His own image and continually keeping it in being, God inscribed in the humanity of man and woman the vocation, and thus the capacity and responsibility, of love and communion (cf. Pastoral Constitution on the Church in the Modern World, *Gaudium et Spes*, 12). Love is therefore the fundamental and innate vocation of every human being. As an incarnate spirit, that is a soul which expresses itself in a body and a body informed by an immortal spirit, man is called to love in his unified totality. Love includes the human body, and the body is made a sharer in spiritual love.[8]

Saint John Paul recognized that what we do with our bodies (particularly with respect to sexuality) affects our created souls. If we use our bodies in a nonharmonious way with that intended by the Creator of our souls, we will be divided within ourselves and alienated from others and God. Though the culture teaches that we can use our bodies in a way different from that intended by God, it fails to recognize our higher spiritual nature, and so fails to recognize

---

[8]Pope John Paul II, Apostolic Exhortation on the Role of the Christian Family in the Modern World *Familiaris Consortio* (November 22, 1981), no. 11.

the detrimental effects this behavior has on us and our relationship with others and God. If the culture (and its materialistic view of the human person and sexuality) has it wrong, then we should expect to find the consequences of this alienation from self, others, and God in our individual and relational lives—significantly increased depression, anxiety, substance abuse, sexual assaults, divorce rates, family breakups, suicides, and homicides. As we shall see, this is precisely what has occurred since the beginning of the so-called sexual emancipation and revolution. The revolution has been anything but an emancipation. Indeed, it has been a personal, interpersonal, and societal tragedy.

For Saint John Paul II, covenant love and communion are the meaning of human existence, showing that our *bodies* reveal the meaning and proper end of the specific kind of love that we (following Lewis) have called *eros*—sexual love. For Saint John Paul, this kind of love is deeply good and intended to produce goodness beyond the relationship as well as communion with God. Sexual love was brought into being by the Creator to lead much of the human family to intimacy, complementarity, mutual support, generativity (particularly through children and family life), and relationship with God. This is manifest in Jesus' appeal to Genesis to justify the exclusivity and permanence of marriage:

> Have you not read that he who made them from the beginning made them male and female, and said, "For this reason, a man shall leave his father and mother and be joined to his wife, and the two shall become one"? So they are no longer two but one. What therefore God has joined together, let no man put asunder. (Mt 19:4–6—Jesus appealing to Gen 1:27; 2:24)

If the Creator intended sexual love to bring about a profound exclusive communion between man and woman, leading to generativity and communion with Himself, then separating sexual love from this context is likely to frustrate the ultimate purpose and fulfillment of human persons, leading to significant anxieties, enmity with one another, and separation from God. The statistics given in Sections III through V below give considerable evidence of this. If we really believe that Jesus is the Son of God, then we should take seriously

His words about His Father's intention for sexuality. As we shall see, failure to do so will lead to significant negative consequences for our emotional health, marriages and families, spiritual well-being, and culture.

Saint John Paul goes further, indicating that the physical differences between the bodies of men and women indicate the call to intimate communion with each other and procreation through that union, which points to communion with God (inscribed in our souls[9]). In a series of Wednesday audiences at the Vatican, he presented his Theology of the Body, which has become foundational for discerning the nature and proper end of sexual love. Far from denigrating the body (contended by some critics of the Catholic Church), Saint John Paul indicates the body's significance to call much of the human family to intimate communion and family life, as a primary vehicle for fulfillment in this world and the next. A proper explanation of this theology is beyond our scope, so I will only briefly summarize four important points that show the true end of sexuality, outside of which human persons become alienated from themselves, one another, and God. Following Jesus' interpretation of Genesis to shed light on the Creator's intention for sexual union ("the two shall become one"), Saint John Paul develops what he calls "the nuptial meaning of the human body". I quote a summary of this by Katrina F. Ten Eyck and Michelle K. Borras:

> The first man and woman [also men and women today] bear in their whole being—even in their bodies—call to receive each other and give themselves to one another in a communion that involves every dimension of their persons: physical, emotional and spiritual....
> Adam and Eve's [representing men and women throughout the ages] masculine and feminine bodies are naturally ordered to receiving each other, becoming a gift for one another and participating in a mutual fruitfulness. Adam welcomes Eve and receives her as she is created in her femininity; in doing so, he becomes a gift for her. Likewise, in being welcomed by Adam, Eve "welcomes him in the same

---

[9] Rudolf Otto's assessment of the numinous experience shows the presence of the mysterious, spiritual, wholly Other within every human person, indicating that God is present to our souls from their creation. For a summary and interpretation of Otto's numinous experience, see Chapter 1 in Volume II of the Quartet, *The Souls Upward Yearning*.

way, as he is willed 'for his own sake' by the Creator and constituted by him through his masculinity." They discover that their bodies have a *nuptial* or spousal meaning. That is, their bodies orient them to a complete gift of self that is fruitful and enduringly faithful.[10]

For Saint John Paul, the meaning of sexuality is inscribed in both our bodies and souls (inasmuch as each affects the other), and we are at least intuitively aware that sexuality is a powerful and spiritual force oriented toward procreation, which cannot be used for sexual gratification alone. This is precisely what Jesus teaches about the Creator's intention in creating our first parents and all men and women. If we do not follow the Creator's intention, frustrating His plan for us, Jesus implies that we will be adversely affected by it emotionally and spiritually, as well as in our families and culture (see the statistics below in Sections II through V).

So, what kinds of conduct does Jesus prohibit? What do the Gospels and New Testament letters say about proper sexual conduct? As will be explained below, Jesus (in Mk 7:20–22) prohibits sexual immorality outside of marriage (*porneia*) as well as adultery (*moicheia*—extramarital sex) and licentiousness (*aselgeia*—uncontrolled and unbridled lust). In today's terms, Jesus prohibits extramarital sex, premarital sex, and by implication, a homosexual lifestyle. As will be explained in Chapter 2 (Section I), Jesus does not specifically prohibit a homosexual lifestyle, but rather prohibits *porneia*, sexuality outside of marriage. *Porneia* is the most general term for sexual immorality, and therefore sexual immorality of any kind.[11] If sexual morality is constituted by sex between one man and one woman within marriage (as Jesus interprets the Creator's will), then *porneia* by implication would include the homosexual lifestyle, as well as any other sexual act outside of marriage between one man and one woman.[12] Saint Paul explicitly prohibits the homosexual lifestyle in Romans

---

[10]Katrina F. Ten Eyck and Michelle K. Borras, *Called to Love: John Paul II's Theology of Human Love* (New Haven, Conn.: Catholic Information Service, Knights of Columbus, 2014), pp. 12–13 (italics in original), http://www.kofc.org/en/resources/cis/cis406.pdf.

[11]See *Strong's Concordance*, s.v. "4202: porneia", BibleHub.com, 2021, https://biblehub.com /greek/4202.htm. Also see Thayer's Greek Lexicon: "Strong's G4202—*porneia*", 2021, https:// www.blueletterbible.org/lang/lexicon/lexicon.cfm?t=kjv&strongs=g4202.

[12]See ibid.

1:26–27 and 1 Corinthians 6:9 (see Chapter 2, Section I.A), but seems to reserve the word *porneia* to a general reference for sexual immorality of any kind.

In three subsequent sections, we will examine each of these teachings, not only from the biblical perspective but also from the negative effects they have on emotional health, relationships, and spiritual well-being:

- Extramarital Sex—Section IV of this chapter
- Premarital Sex and Cohabitation—Section V of this chapter
- Homosexual Lifestyle—Chapter 2, Section I

C. The Christian View of Eros: Exclusive, Permanent, Family-Oriented, and Christ-Oriented

The ideal of Christian love may require considerable discipline and patient endurance, but it will ultimately lead to permanence in marriage, satisfaction in marriage, stability and flourishing of children, emotional health and maturity, and above all spiritual well-being (see the statistics below in Section III). It is not an exaggeration to say that the Christian view of sexual love leads to significant fulfillment and dignity for self and others in this world and to eternal life in the next. We began our excursus into the Christian view of sexual love by considering the four levels of happiness. We continue now with some of its objectives.

In Christianity, the goal of sexual love is committed exclusive communion between one man and one woman, which shares itself with children, friends, the culture, and above all, God. Therefore, sexual love (*eros*) is committed to the other, focused on the true good of the other, continually cares for and shares with the other, seeks the freedom of the other, in no way dominates the other, and sacrifices for the other. Jesus asks us to surrender our own preferences, desires, and will to what He has set out before us for the sake of bringing us out of self-deceit, egocentricity, sensual fixation, narcissism, self-idolatry, and domination of others.

Perhaps the best way to sum up Jesus' view of marriage is in a question all potential spouses should ask themselves before proceeding to marriage: Is this the person I wish to *serve* for the rest of my life? Christian marriage is not about both spouses asking what's in it for them personally, but rather what's in it for both of them and their children, as well as the good they can do together for the world and God's Kingdom. This requires faith-filled, generative, intimate, and self-sacrificial love for spouse and children unto the salvation of all. If we enter marriage with the illusion that we will now be set for life—that it will not require disciplined and loving service to the other—our expectations will be dashed sooner rather than later. However, if we enter marriage with the desire to serve the good of the other, we will find deep happiness, meaning, dignity, fulfillment, and salvation through it. As Jesus taught, "Whoever humbles himself will be exalted" (Mt 23:12).

The view of *eros* goes beyond our family and friends, affecting our view of personhood, freedom, and purpose in life. As noted above, if we view sexuality in a superficial way (Level One and Level Two only), then we will be inclined to view love, personhood, freedom, and purpose in life in an equally superficial way. Now we can see the problem. If we learn from the culture to act on our most base sexual desires (self-gratification and the desire to be loved without genuine care, contribution, and commitment), it will significantly influence our view of love, personhood, freedom, purpose in life, etc. Our base actions will turn us into base people, unconcerned for commitment and contribution to others, as well as God's will for our true dignity, destiny, and fulfillment. Alternatively, if we reverse the order of our pursuits, beginning with God's will for us and our commitment and contribution to others, we will arrive at a view of sexuality commensurate with our true purpose, dignity, destiny, and fulfillment.

Hence, when we approach sexuality, our priorities are of paramount importance. If we "seek first [God's] kingdom" (Mt 6:33), then we are likely to arrive at a view of sexuality consistent with our nature and fulfillment (God's will for us). If we seek first mere sexual gratification, we are likely to be alienated from ourselves (pursuing a course of action inconsistent with our ultimate dignity, destiny, and fulfillment), alienated from others (who grow weary of our egocentric motivations), and alienated from God (whom we have chosen to ignore). This is likely to manifest itself in depression, anxiety, aggression, impulsivity, substance abuse, familial tensions, and suicides.[13]

Evidently, there are significant consequences to having a superficial (Level One-Two) view of sexual love—negative effects on individual aspirations, emotional health, spiritual well-being, relationships, marriage, and children's stability, as well as community and cultural interactions. In view of this, we will want seriously to consider Christ's invitation to enter into relationship with Him through participation in the Church He initiated, and with this foundation, to delve into the principles of covenant sexual love.

Let's return to the portrayal of Christian *eros* presented above. Though *storgē* (affection), *philia* (reciprocally committed friendship), and *agapē* (self-sacrificial love for the good of the other) are integral to marriage, marriage has the unique feature of including *eros*, which is not a part of any other vocation within Christianity. For the Christian Church, sexual love goes far beyond romance and sexuality, because they are not ends in themselves. They support and solidify a higher end of love, personhood, and family. Sexual love is at the service of the highest level of "human to human" commitment that brings the highest level of "human to human" love to its earthly fulfillment. When entered into appropriately, it necessarily includes self-sacrificial love aimed at the good of the spouse, the children, and the Kingdom of God.[14]

The ideal of *eros* must be more than *storgē*—feelings of affection—and more than the feelings of romance, even intense romance. It must be built upon the foundation of friendship—that is, upon an ever-deepening reciprocal commitment of two people to each other, which brings trust, care, support, happiness, dignity, and fulfillment that would not otherwise be possible without this commitment. Friendships can

---

[13] Kanita Dervic and others show that *non*religiously affiliated people have significantly higher rates of depression, anxiety, impulsivity, substance abuse, familial tensions, and suicides. See Kanita Dervic et al., "Religious Affiliation and Suicide Attempt", *American Journal of Psychiatry* 161, no. 12 (December 2004): 2303–8, https://ajp.psychiatryonline.org/doi/full/10.1176/appi.ajp.161.12.2303.

[14] Lewis notes that the power of the Greek god Eros is so great that "his" love *appears* to be transcendent—like an end in itself. However, if we treat it this way, it falls apart because it is not a true god, but only a fleeting appearance of a human form of God. See C. S. Lewis, *The Four Loves* (London: Geoffrey Bles, 1960; Project Gutenberg, 2014), Chapter 5, https://gutenberg.ca/ebooks/lewiscs-fourloves/lewiscs-fourloves-00-h.html#chapter05.

grow, but they must do so reciprocally. Thus, if one person commits more of his time, energy, future, and self to another, but the other does not reciprocate, then the friendship will not grow in trust, care, support, happiness, dignity, and fulfillment. However, if the increased commitment is reciprocated, the friendship will grow in these ways.

Eros (in the broader sense of highest, exclusive, reciprocal love) builds on *philia* (friendship). When a man and woman become attracted romantically to each other, the natural course for this romance is not to jump immediately to sexual expression, but to grow in friendship—reciprocal commitment and love—which in the context of romance finds its expression first in deep care, intimacy, tenderness, generativity, and understanding that awakens the desire to support the other in their need (instead of being disappointed or angered by weakness) and to seek out ways of contributing to the other and helping the other toward salvation. Within this high level of commitment and friendship, romance seeks its proper end—the highest level of human commitment, intimacy, and mutual care that will be necessary for raising children and maintaining a high level of familial care and bondedness—that is, a caring home.

So, what is wrong with leaping from romance to sexual expression without developing this commitment and bondedness of friendship? It short-circuits the development of the friendship. It gives the mistaken impression that the libidinal and erotic feelings of union are the true end of romance and marital relationship. Instead of focusing on developing friendship—developing our level of care, support, intimacy, understanding, forgiveness, and common cause through mutual commitment—the premature leap to sexuality focuses us on the continuance of libidinal and erotic passions as ends in themselves. Though this short-circuiting can be more pronounced in some couples than in others, it tends to affect all such relationships to a significant degree (see the statistics on premarital sex, marital satisfaction, and marital longevity below in Sections III through V).

This does not mean that romantic courtships that get off to a false start by premature forays into sexual relationships cannot be redirected toward developing genuine intimacy, care, and commitment needed for a proper expression of *eros*. However, if this is to happen, then sexual expression cannot be the primary focus of the relationship, with care and commitment being relegated to the periphery.

The passion of sexual expression can often impose itself as a priority for the relationship. Nevertheless, love of God and the other can motivate us to discipline our passions and to prioritize the good of the other and the Kingdom of God. This means that courting couples who want to grow in commitment, friendship, intimacy, understanding, and common cause will have to refrain from sexual expression until the other more important dimensions of highest friendship and commitment can be developed. The idea that living together before marriage will be helpful is, in most cases, quite deceptive. The couple should be hyperaware of what is *not* being developed while the focus is on sexual passion (see the statistics on cohabitation and marital satisfaction and longevity below in Section V).

The wisdom of Jesus Christ and the Christian Church, founded on the above ideals of love, teaches us to reserve the passion of sexual expression for the time when the commitment has developed adequately and the couple is willing to declare it publicly. By doing this, the couple makes certain that all of the subtle and exciting work of developing a relationship is not short circuited by the intense passion of sexual expression. When intimacy, common cause, and commitment are first solidified, then passion takes on a new role. Instead of short-circuiting committed relationships, it reinforces them. Though contemporary pop culture can ridicule such traditional wisdom about sexual love, it has no real grounds for doing so, because that traditional wisdom, properly carried out in courtship and marriage, results in high-level, long-lasting, generative families that have interior strength, self-sacrificial contribution, and the salvation of all parties as their objective. This is borne out by several scholarly studies explained below (Sections III through V).

Christian wisdom does not reject premature sexual expression for reasons of prudishness or an imposition of rules on couples who are "in love". It does not do so for motives of repression of sexual desire or a feigned moral high ground ("I am so shocked you could think of that," or "I would never ..."). Christian wisdom is built upon the solid foundation of Christian love, which at its highest level is expressed as *agapē* (self-sacrificial love for the good of the other), and sees in *eros* the needed passionate support to make the highest level of "human to human" commitment come alive for the sake of the couple, their family, and ultimately, their salvation.

Let us now move to the Christian ideal of exclusivity of sexual love. Why must sexual love be within an exclusive relationship—with one person only? Recall the objective of sexual love. As we saw above, if we try to make sexual love an end in itself (without regard for genuine intimacy, care, common cause, and commitment), it alienates us from ourselves, the other, and God. Moreover, sexual expression as an end in itself tends to "objectify" or "thingafy" the other—the other as mere "physical body" or "mere cause of physical arousal" or mere "instrument of physical pleasure". Divorcing sexuality from genuine commitment to the good of others dehumanizes and despiritualizes them. It implicitly says that we care more about the arousal, pleasure, and ego-satisfaction they bring to us than about *them*.

We are remarkably sensitive. We know when we are really cared about and cared for—and know when we are really being used for the pleasure and ego-gratification of others. Some might object that Level One and Level Two people are content with being mere instruments of pleasure and ego-gratification because that brings *them* ego-gratification and pleasure. This is only partially true. Though part of their psychic framework is content with being sought after as an object of arousal, pleasure, and ego-gratification, there are higher levels of the human psyche oriented toward higher levels of purpose, dignity, and fulfillment (arising out of empathy, conscience, and spiritual-numinous awareness) that are not content with this reduction of self to an "it" and reduction of the relationship to "I-it".[15] These higher levels of psyche are actually hurt and demoralized by such degradation.

Even the most popular individuals realize implicitly that it is one thing to be "hot" (sought after as desirable or beautiful) but quite another thing to be a "uniquely good, lovable, and transcendental mystery worthy of the highest levels of care and commitment from human persons and God". Though some may protest that they have no such higher levels of psyche, it may do well for them to look at themselves over the course of time. Are they developing callouses toward real intimacy, a hardness of heart and soul? Do they have increasing feelings of interior emptiness and loneliness both on a

---

[15] Martin Buber distinguishes between three levels of existence—"I-it", "I-thou", "I-Thou". See Martin Buber, *I and Thou* (Eastford, Conn.: Martino Publishing, 2010).

human and cosmic level? Are they beginning to question whether they lived up to their fullest potential, dignity, meaning, and fulfillment—both now and into the future, even an eternal future? These are but a few signs of their emerging—though repressed— higher levels of psyche that are trying to make themselves known before it's too late.

In sum, when sexual love is viewed as an end in itself,[16] it short-circuits the proper development of intimacy, generativity, and committed friendship necessary for long-lasting relationship and family—instead of helping it. Moreover, it dehumanizes and despir-itualizes the person who is reduced from the recipient of committed care and support to a mere object of arousal, pleasure, and ego-gratification. No matter how much one might like being sought after as such an object, it is not enough—not nearly enough to fulfill our higher levels of meaning. Indeed, we receive the hurtful message that we are not worthy of our highest dignity and fulfillment, but only the instrument of another's pleasure.

We now return to the question about why eros must be exclusive— with one person only. If the natural end of eros (sexual love) is to support the highest level of friendship—the highest level of commit-ment of self and future to the care, support, and salvation of another for the purpose of raising children destined for eternal salvation— then eros (sexual expression) is meant to support that highest level of committed love in which children deserve to be raised, the kind of commitment that will give rise to a truly loving home destined for our eternal home. Evidently, sexual expression gives rise to children—and given the above articulation of Christian wisdom, sexual expression is meant to support the highest level of committed human love that leads naturally to a loving home for those children. In this context alone, eros reaches its functional fulfillment (procre-ation) and its ideal fulfillment (a loving home through the *highest* form of committed love), which is, so to speak, a perfect marriage.

---

[16] Lewis indicates that treating sexual love as an end in itself seems almost natural, because it is so powerful and capable of infusing us with a sense of lovability and goodness. However, sexual love cannot bestow absolute meaning, dignity, or destiny on us, because it is limited to the domain of embodiment and infinitude. It may feel ultimate, but it is not; and when we try to make it so, it can only disappoint us and leave us in the emptiness, alienation, and lowliness of dashed expectations. See Lewis, *Four Loves*, Chapter 5.

At this juncture, the answer to our question is mere logic. If *eros* is meant to support the highest level of commitment giving rise to a loving home, then it must be exclusive—with one person only. How many "highest level of commitments" can you have? How many "first priority" commitments can you have? If the marital commitment is the first priority of human commitments, there can be no other priority of equal importance—logically. Every other commitment must be second or third when compared with the first priority.

When *eros* supports this highest level of commitment, and is not separated from it, it attains the true purpose for which the Creator intended it—to support and bond the highest expression of human freedom, leading to the highest manifestation of "human to human" love. When it is separated from this dignity, when it becomes an end in itself, it can become aggressive, demeaning to human personhood, damaging to human intimacy and generativity, and even destructive of our relationship with the Lord. This is born out in the scholarly studies in Sections III–V below, which show that extramarital sex is destructive of marriages, families, and both partners in the marriage. These studies also show that the number of premarital partners is inversely related to marital satisfaction and longevity. Exclusivity before and during marriage goes a long way to securing marriages, families, and the security of each partner within the marriage— precisely as promised by Jesus and the Church.

By now, it will come as no surprise that religiously observant couples who pray and observe moral teachings have significantly greater marital satisfaction and lower rates of divorce. Seven studies carried out by major research universities validate this finding in five areas:

1. Praying with and for your partner correlates with more satisfying and committed relationships (Florida State University and University of Georgia studies).[17]
2. Spiritual intimacy enables couples to resolve conflicts more positively and quickly and to handle the challenges of parenting (Bowling Green State University).[18]

---

[17] David Briggs, "5 Ways Faith Contributes to Strong Marriages, New Studies Suggest", *HuffPost*, February 8, 2015, http://www.huffingtonpost.com/david-briggs/5-ways-faith-con tributes_b_6294716.

[18] Ibid.

3. Belief in the sacredness of marriage leads to an increase in marital satisfaction and compassionate love (Auburn University and East Carolina University).[19]

4. The ability to turn to spiritual and religious resources (giving rise to a sense of forgiveness, peace, hope, and transcendence) increases marital quality and the capacity to deal with struggles and conflicts (University of North Texas).[20]

5. Individuals who are religiously motivated in choosing a spouse and practice their religion after marriage are far less likely to cheat or be unfaithful (University of Calgary).[21]

As will be seen below, the intention toward permanent commitment and children strengthens religious commitment within the marriage (a reciprocal effect).[22] However, cohabitation and long-term premarital relationships weaken religious commitment,[23] which in turn weakens marital satisfaction and commitment after cohabitation (as implied in the above studies of religion and marriage). The reciprocal reinforcement of religion and marriage is exceedingly important, for as religion goes, so goes marriage—and vice versa. As will be seen, this partnership between religion and marriage is one of the most positive factors affecting quality of life and stability of our culture.

We now turn to the question of why the Christian view of *eros* is declining in our culture. One might think initially that this is occurring because of the intensity of sexual passion in the culture versus the need for deferred gratification and disciplined "relationship building" in the Christian view of *eros*. Though this may be part of the explanation for why the Christian view of *eros* is in decline today, there are several other cultural factors involved—such as the social mandate for sexual love of any kind, the increasingly autonomous (versus interpersonal) view of "freedom", and the decline in religion.

[19] Ibid.
[20] Ibid.
[21] Ibid.
[22] See Arland Thornton, William G. Axinn, and Daniel H. Hill, "Reciprocal Effects of Religiosity, Cohabitation, and Marriage", *American Journal of Sociology* 98, no. 3 (1992): 628–51, https://www.journals.uchicago.edu/doi/abs/10.1086/230051?mobileUi=0&.
[23] Ibid.

The combination of these four factors within the culture is truly a recipe for disaster—not only the decline of committed marriages and families, but also the decline in the efficacy of commitment itself. This is leading to a decline in human happiness, dignity, purpose in life, and commitment, as well as steeped increases in depression, anxiety, and homicides, particularly among young people.[24] Given the consequences of falsely prioritizing sexuality over intimacy, care, common cause, commitment, and religion, we must ask the question of how the culture has come to this position, and how we can reverse it.

II. The Instrumentalization of *Eros* in Contemporary Culture

How did our culture lose the bond between sexuality, commitment, and generative familial love? Since the publication of Alfred Kinsey's surveys on sexuality (1948) and, more notably, the extension of it—William Masters' and Virginia Johnson's *Human Sexual Response* in 1966—the interpretation of sexuality has become progressively more empirical, mechanistic, physicalist, and deterministic in orientation.[25] This interpretation of sexuality combined with the introduction of

---

[24] According to a 2019 study by the National Institute of Health, the rate of depression and anxiety has increased by 52 percent among teens and 63 percent among young adults over one decade (between 2005 and 2017). Currently, one-third of our young people are expected to have a major incident of depression or anxiety before they reach the age of eighteen. See Jean M. Twenge et al., "Age, Period, and Cohort Trends in Mood Disorder Indicators and Suicide-Related Outcomes in a Nationally Representative Dataset, 2005–2017", *Journal of Abnormal Psychology* 128, no. 3 (2019): 185–99, https://www.apa.org/pubs/journals /releases/abn-abn0000410.pdf. According to the Centers for Disease Control and Prevention, teen suicides have increased by 56 percent over the last decade and teen homicides have increased 23 percent over the same period. See William Wan, "Teen Suicides Are Increasing at an Alarming Pace, Outstripping All Other Age Groups, a New Report Says", *Washington Post*, October 17, 2019, https://www.washingtonpost.com/health/teen-suicides-increasing -at-alarming-pace-outstripping-all-other-age-groups/2019/10/16/e24194c6-f04a-11e9 -8693-f487e46784aa_story.html.

[25] Sigmund Freud originally developed mechanistic models of the psyche that were applied to sexuality in several works, but Masters' and Johnson's four-step model solidified the physicalist-mechanistic-empirical viewpoint. See David Rowland, "Phases of Human Sexual Response", in *The SAGE Encyclopedia of Abnormal and Clinical Psychology* (Thousand Oaks, Calif.: SAGE Publications, 2017), pp. 1705–6, https://scholar.valpo.edu/cgi/viewcontent .cgi?article=1061&context=psych_fac_pub.

the birth control pill into accessible consumer markets (by Searle) in 1960 had a series of harmful effects on individuals' and the culture's interpretation of sexuality:

1. It undermined Level Three (contributive) and Level Four (spiritual) interpretations of sexuality and placed the focus squarely on Level One (physical/pleasure) and Level Two (ego-comparative) interpretations of sexuality. This separated sexuality from intimacy, generativity, and familial and transcendent purpose—and put the emphasis on achieving enhanced physical pleasure and ego-satisfaction within the sexual act.

2. The Level One-Two interpretation of sexuality as well as the popularization of birth control (allowing for sexuality outside of marriage without fear of pregnancy) led those without contrary religious or philosophical convictions to treat sexuality as an end in itself. This separated sexuality from its original significance of solidifying exclusive commitments in marriage. Commitment was no longer an integral part of the purpose and nature of sexuality.

3. The isolation of sexuality from marital commitment and its transformation into an end in itself weakened the pre-1960s respect and reserve for sexuality. This allowed authors, movie producers, and marketers to become increasingly more explicit about sexual content, which led to increasing superficiality in movies and literature. The creative arts were now less concerned with conveying deeper meaning and values through profound dialogue and more concerned with providing additional libidinal stimulus and audience arousal. This trend also led to an exponential rise in pornography, which was further enhanced by the Internet (see Chapter 2, Section II).

4. The flood of explicit sexually stimulating material in almost every media form led to a need for even more explicit and aggressive portrayals of sexuality in order to maintain and increase libidinal fulfillment. This hypersexualization of media is inciting superficiality within sexual relationships, leading to a loss of intimacy, generativity, and familial love. This has the further consequence of making sexuality more aggressive and callous, allowing the movie *Fifty Shades of Grey* to be an acceptable and even normal form of sexual expression.

In view of the above, it should come as no surprise that the Christian view of sexuality and the culture's view of sexuality are increasingly opposed. What is more troubling is the large percentage of our young people who are unreflectively appropriating the culture's view of sexuality without consulting other points of view. It is easy to see how they can be seduced by a sexual philosophy that is explicit and arousing, and how they can be brought under the spell of literally millions of free pornographic images and movies.[26] In view of this, faith-based parents and teachers will want to reflect on the following questions with young people under their care:

1. How is the culture's view of sexuality affecting my purpose in life—is it moving me away from Level Three-Four purpose toward a dominant Level One-Two purpose?

2. How is the culture's view of sexuality affecting my (or my child's) capacity for intimacy, generativity, exclusive commitment, and self-sacrificial love (all of which are integral to a healthy family)?

3. How is the culture's view of sexuality affecting my (or my child's) practice of ethics, practice of religion, and character?

4. Has the culture's view of sexuality already affected my attitudes and practice of sexuality, leading me to think about it more often, to seek higher levels of libidinal satisfaction, even leading to addiction?[27]

These questions can unmask the consequences of the popular culture's view of sexuality, because, as shown in the studies below, there is a strong likelihood that the longer an individual lives according to the culture's viewpoint, the more entrenched he will become in Level One-Two purpose in life, lose his sense of intimacy, generativity, exclusive commitment, and familial orientation, and become detached from ethical and religious practice. Furthermore,

---

[26] As noted above, sexuality by itself is powerful enough to appear transcendent and ultimate (see Lewis, *Four Loves*, Chapter 5). When this natural power is combined with almost unrestricted availability (on the Internet) and encouragement from the culture toward maximizing sexual pleasure, the result is the suppression of emotional intimacy and generativity, and an addiction (and even obsession) with mere physicality and image manifest in pornography.

[27] "Addiction" here means that cutting back on the amount of sexual stimulation gives rise to classical withdrawal symptoms similar to those associated with alcohol or drugs.

the heightened prioritization of sexuality as an end in itself is negatively undermining religious practice within the culture, because
young people believe that this new view of sexuality is enlightened
and correct, meaning that Christian sexual teaching (which is opposed
to the culture's view) must be unenlightened and incorrect. As this
occurs, one is likely to experience a heightened sense of emptiness,
alienation, loneliness, and guilt, which betrays an inner awareness of
losing one's true self, deeper relationships, higher purpose in life, and
connection to God. Counterintuitive as it may seem, our view of
sexuality can produce all of these negative consequences, alienating
us not only from God but also from others, and from ourselves.

At the beginning of this volume, the reader may have asked why
spend two chapters (Chapters 1–2) on love, adultery, and inappropri-
ate sexuality and two chapters (Chapters 3–4) on life and death, and
only one part of one chapter (Chapter 5) on the other four major
commandments—stealing, cheating, lying, and honoring father and
mother. By now, the answer may be apparent. The consequences of
treating sexuality as an end in itself and reprioritizing sexuality over
the higher dimensions of love (contribution, care, intimacy, common
cause, commitment, and self-sacrifice for the other, the relationship,
and the family) are so grave and so widespread that it threatens the
institution of marriage, the stability of family, and therefore the culture
and society itself. As noted above, the current view of sexuality is inciting significant increases in Level Two (ego-comparative) identity and
fueling the decline in religious morality and religion itself, particularly
among young people. The combination and mutual reinforcement of
these factors is leading to a significant increase in anxiety, depression,
and suicide.[28] It is noteworthy that after decades of stability in teen

---

[28] Millennial unbelief is double that of the Baby Boomer Generation and triple that of
the Silent Generation. About 40 percent of young people are likely to become unbelievers
if they are not helped to see the rational evidence of God, overcome the false dichotomy
between science and faith, and understand the rationale for religious moral teaching (such
as that presented in this volume). See Michael Lipka, "Millennials Increasingly Are Driving Growth of 'Nones'", Pew Research Center, 2015, https://www.pewresearch.org/fact
-tank/2015/05/12/millennials-increasingly-are-driving-growth-of-nones/. The decline in
religion strongly correlates with increased depression, anxiety, substance abuse, familial tension, and suicides. See the six studies given in the Introduction to this volume: Dervic et al.,
"Religious Affiliation and Suicide Attempt"; Harold Koenig, "Research on Religion, Spirituality, and Mental Health: A Review", *Canadian Journal of Psychiatry* 54, no. 5 (2009): 283–91,

depression, anxiety, suicide, and homicide statistics, the last decade (2005 to 2017) has shown steep increases in all of the above negative conditions—a 52 percent increase in depression/anxiety among teens (a 63 percent increase among young adults), a 56 percent increase in teen suicides, and a 23 percent increase in teen homicides.[29]

The further we move away from the teaching of Jesus and the Church, the closer we come to the destruction of self, others, and the culture. My hope is to show in the next two chapters that the Christian (and particularly the Catholic) view of sexuality may be the only way to prevent the culture from undermining the human individual and collective spirit. Additionally, loving obedience of the Lord's teachings will bring "grace upon grace" (Jn 1:16) into the world to support our noble ideals for one another, marriage, family, and the culture itself. This is why I chose to spend two chapters on this issue.

III. Two Pervasive Negative Effects of Social Norming and the Sexual Revolution

Given the consequences of treating sexuality as an end in itself and the reprioritizing of it above the higher ideals of love (intimacy, common cause, commitment, etc.), it would prove helpful to probe more

---

https://journals.sagepub.com/doi/pdf/10.1177/070674370905400502; Raphael Bonelli et al., "Religious and Spiritual Factors in Depression: Review and Integration of the Research", *Depression and Research Treatment*, August 15, 2012, https://www.hindawi.com/journals/drt/2012/962860/; Stefano Lassi and Daniele Mugnaini, "Role of Religion and Spirituality on Mental Health and Resilience: There Is Enough Evidence", *International Journal of Emergency Mental Health and Human Resilience* 17, no. 3 (2015): 661–63, https://www.omicsonline.org/open-access/role-of-religion-and-spirituality-on-mental-health-and-resilience-there-is-enough-evidence-1522-4821-1000273.pdf; Harold Koenig, "Religion, Spirituality, and Health: A Review and Update", *Advances in Mind-Body Medicine* 29, no. 3 (2015): 19–26, https://pubmed.ncbi.nlm.nih.gov/26026153/; and Corina Ronenberg et al., "The Protective Effects of Religiosity on Depression: A 2-Year Prospective Study", *Gerontologist* 56, no. 3 (2016): 421–31, https://academic.oup.com/gerontologist/article/56/3/421/2605601.

As noted above, the sexual revolution and the steep rise in Level Two (ego-comparative) identity is also weakening religious commitment and causing increases in depression and anxiety. When all of these factors are combined, it is leading to the steep increase in depression, anxiety, suicide, and homicide among teens and young adults (see the statistics and references immediately below).

[29]See the references above to Twenge et al., "Age, Period, and Cohort Trends". See also Wan, "Teen Suicides Are Increasing".

deeply into the causes of this cultural decline. Beyond the advent of the birth control pill and studies implying an instrumentalization of sexuality, there is another phenomenon called social norming, which has increased dramatically with the Internet, particularly social media. The power of social norming was advanced by H. Wesley Perkins[30] and Alan D. Berkowitz[31] in the mid-1980s. This theory holds that people form norms for their behavior on the basis of their perceptions about what other people are doing. It seems that in our democratic and pluralistic culture, many people who do not have strong religious or philosophical values, principles, and ideals default to "fitting into the mainstream" as a means of establishing ethical norms for behavior.[32] So, for example, students in a collegiate environment who had the belief that the general population of students was drinking quite heavily would feel comfortable living according to their perception of the mainstream. However, if they subsequently discovered that they had an exaggerated view of how much the mainstream was drinking, they would regulate their behavior to accommodate their new perception.[33] Apparently, students do not want to be in the category of "heavy drinkers" by comparison to their peers.

Though publishing accurate statistics about alcohol use, drug use, cheating, sexual behaviors, etc. can have a healthy effect on students who discover that the reality about these behaviors is lower than their previous perceptions, it can also have a very *unhealthy* effect, if they discover that their perceptions underestimated the reality of those behaviors. In other words, they could well believe that there was more room for them to engage in these negative behaviors while remaining in the mainstream of their peer group.

---

[30] See H. Wesley Perkins, *The Social Norms Approach to Preventing School and College Age Substance Abuse: A Handbook for Educators, Counselors, and Clinicians* (San Francisco: Jossey-Bass, 2003).

[31] See Alan D. Berkowitz, "Applications of Social Norms Theory to Other Health and Social Justice Issues", in ibid., pp. 259–79.

[32] See Hart Blanton, Amber Köblitz, and Kevin D. McCaul, "Misperceptions about Norm Misperceptions: Descriptive, Injunctive, and Affective 'Social Norming' Efforts to Change Health Behaviors", *Social and Personality Psychology Compass* 2, no. 3 (2008), https://online library.wiley.com/doi/abs/10.1111/j.1751-9004.2008.00107.x.

[33] Clayton Neighbors et al., "Are Social Norms the Best Predictor of Outcomes among Heavy-Drinking College Students?", *Journal of Studies on Alcohol and Drugs* 68, no. 4 (2017): 556–65, https://www.jsad.com/doi/abs/10.15288/jsad.2007.68.556.

The expression "What becomes legal eventually becomes normal, and what becomes normal becomes accepted as moral" reflects the same reality. If individuals do not have a strong sense of morality from religion, parents, schooling, or philosophical training, they default to perceptions about mainstream behaviors as the basis for their norms of conduct. Unfortunately, the mainstream may not have a single legitimate ethical criterion on which its perceived norms are based. Furthermore, our perceptions of what the mainstream really believes and does can be quite inaccurate.[34] Additionally, social norming can become a "self-fulfilling prophesy".[35] For example, an exaggerated perception about a certain behavior (e.g., extramarital sex or premarital sex) in the mainstream could mislead people into believing that they can indulge in a heightened level of that behavior. If enough people heighten their level of this behavior to accommodate their misperception about the mainstream, they will ultimately move the reality of mainstream behavior to that heightened perception. Notice that no legitimate ethical criterion—a religious, philosophical, conscience-based,[36] or traditional—need be used to justify the acceptability of this heightened level of negative behavior. Our *perceptions alone* can create an individual and collective decline in morality.

What does this mean? Without a strong sense of morality based on legitimate criteria—religious, philosophical, conscience-based, or tradition—our cultural ethical standards will likely be determined by our perceptions (or misperceptions) of mainstream behavior. We can sink as low as we believe the mainstream to be. Regrettably, Western culture seems to have abandoned the four major criteria of authentic ethics and so has reduced itself to the "perceived ethics of the

---

[34] See Perkins, *Social Norms Approach.*

[35] This now-accepted principle of social influence—and its prediction of how false prophecies become socially accepted truths—was first proposed by Robert K. Merton in 1948. See Robert K. Merton, "The Self-Fulfilling Prophecy", *Antioch Review* 8, no. 2 (Summer 1948): 193–210. This principle has been validated several times in studies of social norming.

[36] Robert George (Princeton University's Chair of Public Law) addresses the breakdown of legitimate ethical criteria—conscious-based, religious, philosophical, and traditional—from both a legal and cultural perspective in his outstanding work *Conscious and Its Enemies: Confronting the Dogmas of Liberal Secularism* (Wilmington, Del.: ISI Books, 2016). Of particular importance is George's summary of the critiques of Richard John Neuhaus (Chapter 27) and GEM Anscombe (Chapter 28).

mainstream" with all its inherent weaknesses and its self-fulfilling downward momentum.

There is one further problem with the "ethical mainstream culture". It puts itself in the manipulative hands of unscrupulous marketers who would encourage low norms, negative behaviors, and cultural decline for the sake of profits and power. One does not have to look far to find examples of how Madison Avenue made cigarette smoking "glamorous" for women, the three-martini lunch acceptable for business executives, and onerous amounts of personal debt acceptable to the middle class. Once marketers had convinced the general public that "everyone in the mainstream is doing this", people began to move toward what they perceived the mainstream to be. If they did not have religious or conscientious objections to the values of the mainstream, they adjusted their perception of right and wrong, softened their conscience, relaxed their ethical hesitations, and eased themselves into the perceived lower ethical level of the mainstream.

What does all this have to do with the sexual mores of Western culture? A lot! We all know the expressions "Sex sells" and "Sex is power"—and so it is for Level One-Two individuals. Needless to say, sexuality has a powerful intrinsic desirability, and so vulnerable human persons are inclined toward it—even if it entails indiscretion, harassment, or even abuse. Now if we add three elements to the powerful intrinsic desirability of sex, we can see how virtually every cultural sexual more was compromised and ultimately abandoned between the 1960s and the current day. Recall the three elements addressed above:

- The clericalization of sexuality by Masters and Johnson (and their successors)
- The birth control pill
- The undermining of authentic ethical criteria by the marketing and media establishment, as well as the Internet and social media

The progressive compromise and abandonment of sexual mores can be seen and even measured by the weakening of censorship standards in television, radio, and print media between 1960 and today. Though this process is nearly complete throughout most countries in Europe, it is still taking place in the United States and Canada. The influence of social norming has played a significant role in this rapid decline of censorship standards regarding sexuality. Marketers and many in the media and film establishment created the perception that the sexual revolution was prevalent not only among young people, but also among the middle aged as well. This led a significant percentage of viewers to believe that the mainstream view of sexuality was more liberal than it actually was. As noted above, those without strong religious, philosophical, conscience-based, or traditional views to the contrary moved toward the mainstream view, dropping previously held mores. What is most interesting in this process is how *unconsciously* this group lost this sense of sexual propriety and appropriate boundaries.

After 1980, nonreligious and nontraditional individuals became progressively more confused about what appropriate standards and boundaries might be, and many young people rejected their parents' views about premarital sex, cohabitation, and pornography. Today, many young people do not believe that there should be any sexual mores beyond the prohibition of adultery (extramarital sex).[37]

A. First Social Effect: Increase in Forcible Rapes and Sexual Assaults

We should not be surprised that the loss of sexual mores and appropriate personal boundaries would result in a dramatic increase in forcible rapes, sexual assaults, and sexual harassment[38]—and so they have. With respect to forcible rapes, the statistics compiled by the FBI UCS (Uniform Crime Statistics) Annual Crime Reports show that forcible rape has increased from 17,190 (in 1960) to 37,990 (in 1970) to 82,990 (in 1980) to 102,560 (in 1990).[39] Beginning in 1994, the rate of forcible

---

[37] See the studies and statistics below.

[38] It is difficult to measure sexual harassment complaints in the workplace because of changing standards and increases in reporting. However, the recent rash of reports of outrageous behavior in the workplace by Harvey Weinstein, Matt Lauer, Charlie Rose, Kevin Spacey, Roy Moore, Al Franken, and Dustin Hoffman—among others—seems to have occurred post-1985. This may indicate that the loss of sexual mores and appropriate boundaries since the mid-1960s has led not only to an increase in numbers of harassment complaints, but also to the egregiousness of offenses.

[39] "United States Population and Number of Crimes 1960–2019", DisasterCenter.com, 1997–2019, http://www.disastercenter.com/crime/uscrime.htm.

rapes began to decrease because of more vigilant police action, special sex crime units, and increased education in the media. As a result, the number of rapes was 90,178 (in 2000) and 85,593 (in 2010). Nevertheless, it increased precipitously again to 132,414 (in 2016). Thus, there was a 557 percent (5.57 times) increase in forcible rapes between 1960 and 2016 (56 years).[40]

The category "sexual assaults" is much larger than "forcible rapes", because it includes assaults that need not have an element of force. They would include forcible rapes, but also unwanted advances, attempts at groping, stalking, and other invasive actions falling short of forcible rape. We might infer from the 557 percent increase in forcible rapes that a parallel increase of sexual assaults without rape has also occurred. Though this trend has not been specifically measured, there are several indicators that point to it—for example, a dramatic increase of 205 percent in campus sexual assaults in fourteen years (2001–2014). Though this statistic includes both forcible rapes and other forms of assault, it is showing the trend among young people who will ultimately constitute the majority of the population in the next twenty years.[41]

The rate of sexual violence in the United States has reached an all-time high and is at a point of "epidemic" according to the National Sexual Violence Resource Center (NSVRC). The NSVRC estimates that one in five women will be raped during their lifetime (including rapes by intimate partners); 12.3 percent of women are victimized before the age of ten, and 30 percent between the ages of eleven and seventeen.[42]

Was the cause of this exceedingly negative social phenomenon attributable to the above cultural trends stemming from the sexual revolution? Though many interpreters have attributed the above significant increase in forcible rapes and sexual assaults to increases in awareness and reporting, this cannot be the sole reason for such a

---

[40] Ibid.

[41] See Lizzie Crocker, "There's Been a Huge Increase in Campus Sex Assaults. Why?", *Daily Beast*, published May 16, 2017, updated May 22, 2017, https://www.thedailybeast.com/theres-been-a-huge-increase-in-campus-sex-assaults-why.

[42] See National Sexual Violence Resource Center, "Statistics about Sexual Violence", 2015, https://www.nsvrc.org/sites/default/files/publications_nsvrc_factsheet_media-packet_statistics-about-sexual-violence_0.pdf.

huge recent increase—a factor of 5.57 times—because the rate of rape reporting has not increased nearly that much. According to the studies of Eric Baumer, the reporting of rapes between 1973 until recently has moved only from 26 percent of women likely to have reported to 31 percent in 1990 and 36 percent in 2000.[43] This 10 percent increase in the reporting of rape does not come close to explaining the recent 557 percent increase in rapes reported. Even if there had been twice the increase in rape reporting calculated by Baumer (20 percent) between 1960 and 2006 without a concomitant increase in rapes themselves, we would have expected the number of reported rapes to be approximately 20,600 in 2016—which is far fewer than the actual number—132,414.

This leads to the conclusion that the decline in sexual ethics has opened the floodgates through social norming to sexual behavior separated from commitment, intimacy, generativity, and mutual support. This had led to the debasing of marriage and strong families, as well as those participating in sexual relationships. As we shall see, forcible rape is but one of the negative outcomes of this decline in sexual morality.

B. Second Social Effect: The Breakdown of Marriage and Family

The sexual revolution, and its concomitant decline in sexual mores, has also fueled another major social problem—the breakdown of the institution of marriage and the family (as seen through increased sexual infidelity and divorce rates, and decreased marriage rates). This has deleterious effects beyond the breakdown of society's primary social bonding unit—namely, the insecurity and destabilization of identity among many divorced children.

According to data from the comprehensive study from the Centers for Disease Control's National Center for Health Statistics, marriage rates have decreased precipitously since the 1950s. In 1950, there were sixteen new marriages for every thousand people; this dropped

---

[43] See Lauren R. Taylor, "Has Rape Reporting Increased Over Time?", *National Institute of Justice Journal*, no. 254 (July 2006): 28–30, https://www.nij.gov/journals/254/Pages/rape_reporting.aspx.

to eleven new marriages per thousand in 1970, then to nine new marriages in 1990, and then to seven new marriages per thousand in 2010.[44] Evidently, the rate of marriage has steadily decreased since the beginning of the sexual revolution—*less than half* the number per thousand people since 1950.

We see a similar trend in the increased rate of divorce since the beginning of the sexual revolution (with a slight amelioration in the last decade). In 1960, there were 2.2 new divorces per year per thousand people; this increased to three new divorces in 1970, then to five new divorces per thousand in 1990 to 3.75 per thousand in 2010 (an improvement from 1990).[45] Despite the improvement in later years, the years of the sexual revolution have seen about a doubling of the annual divorce rate.

When we correlate the decline in the marriage rate with the increase in the divorce rate, we can see the rate at which marriages are likely to end up in divorce per year—in 1950, 16 percent of new marriages ended in divorce (2.5/16), in 1970, this increased to 27 percent (3/11), in 1990, it increased to 56 percent (5/9), and this remained about the same (54 percent) in 2010, where slightly more than 50 percent of new marriages ended in a divorce.[46] This represents a movement from a 16 percent divorce rate in 1950 to a 54 percent divorce rate among new marriages in 2010—more than *triple* the rate of divorce since 1950—during the years of the sexual revolution.

In addition to the decline in new marriages and the increased rate in divorce, the years of the sexual revolution also saw an increased rate in infidelity (cheating among married couples). According to a survey done by YouGov (a polling company), 21 percent of men are unfaithful to their wives and 19 percent of women unfaithful to their husbands (as of 2015).[47] The percentage may well be greater, because 7 percent of those polled said that "they preferred not to answer the

---

[44] Ana Swanson, "144 Years of Marriage and Divorce in the United States, in One Chart", *Washington Post*, June 23, 2015, https://www.washingtonpost.com/news/wonk/wp/2015/06/23/144-years-of-marriage-and-divorce-in-the-united-states-in-one-chart/?utm_term=.54c2dd176ca0.

[45] Ibid.

[46] Ibid.

[47] See Peter Moore, "1 in 5 Americans Say They've Been Unfaithful", YouGov.com, June 2, 2015, https://today.yougov.com/topics/lifestyle/articles-reports/2015/06/02/men-more-likely-think-cheating.

question" and it is likely that a significant percentage did not want to admit even anonymously their indiscretions out of both fear and shame. What is most alarming about this statistic is the rate of increase in infidelity among wives—a 40 percent increase over more than twenty years ago.[48] Additionally, women have now overtaken men in repeated infidelity—with 36 percent of women reporting cheating one to five times (compared with 33 percent of men) and 47 percent of women indicating that they had more than six incidents of infidelity (by comparison with 44 percent of men).[49] Though some commentators "herald" this as a closing of the gender gap, the prospects for marriage and family appear to be quite bleak—since women have been the mainstay of families amid infidelity by their husbands.

These increased rates of infidelity are likely to rise in the future, because young married couples under thirty have significantly higher rates of marital infidelity than their counterparts more than twenty years earlier by a factor of 45 percent (for men) and 20 percent (for women).[50] Furthermore, enrollment in cheating websites such as Ashley Madison is on the rise. Currently, this website supposedly hosts thirty-seven million men and women—though this figure is unofficial and is probably exaggerated.[51] Even if we divide that number by ten, a huge number of people in the United States are apparently intent on cheating. This implies that rising rates of infidelity and divorce are almost inevitable—even within a 50 percent margin of error.

There is a definite correlation between admitted infidelity and divorce. According to surveys compiled by InfidelityFacts.com, only

[48] See the poll by the National Opinion Research Center's General Social Survey cited in Zach Schonfeld, "Wives Are Cheating 40% More Than They Used To, but Still 70% as Much as Men", *Atlantic*, July 2, 2013, https://www.theatlantic.com/national/archive/2013/07/wives-cheating-vs-men/313704/.

[49] See the surveys by the National Opinion Research Center reported by Rebecca Lake, "Infidelity Statistics: 23 Eye-Opening Truths", May 18, 2016, https://www.creditdonkey.com/infidelity-statistics.html.

[50] These statistics were compiled by David Atkins at the University of Washington and were reported by Naomi Schaefer Riley, "The Young and the Restless: Why Infidelity Is Rising among 20-Somethings", *Wall Street Journal*, November 28, 2008, https://www.wsj.com/articles/SB122782458360062499.

[51] Rachel Martin, "Sorting Through the Numbers on Infidelity", National Public Radio (website), July 26, 2015, https://www.npr.org/2015/07/26/426434619/sorting-through-the-numbers-on-infidelity.

31 percent of marriages last after an affair has been admitted or discovered (implying that 69 percent of marriages in which there is infidelity end up in divorce).[52] Furthermore, researchers David Atkins
and Elizabeth Allen strengthen this conclusion in a careful longitudinal study, concluding that an extramarital affair is likely to increase
the rate of divorce by a factor of 2.3 times:

> [O]f those respondents reporting [extramarital affairs], 41% of men
> and 48% of women were either currently divorced or separated, in
> contrast to only 17% of men and 22% of women without a history of
> [extramarital affairs].[53]

The breakdown of marriage is also the breakdown of family—
the primary and essential bonding unit for children, producing
lasting effects to the end of adulthood. Divorce undermines the self-
identity of children, which challenges their emotional stability and
security as well as their sense of lovability. These effects last into
adulthood though they can be hidden from and managed for the
outside world. Elizabeth Marquardt's outstanding study *Between Two
Worlds: The Inner Lives of Children of Divorce*[54] (which includes both
surveys and case studies) demonstrates and illustrates these points in
considerable detail. Marquardt restricts her analysis and case studies to only best-case scenarios in which the divorce was amicable
to the children maintaining contact with both parents into adulthood. Her conclusion is clear: there is no such thing as a "best-case-
scenario divorce". All of them—no matter how well intended—
have significant negative effects upon all the children throughout
their adulthood. Her objective in this study is to stop the process
of social norming that falsely affirms the possibility of a positive and

---

[52]"Infidelity Statistics", InfidelityFacts.com, 2006, https://web.archive.org/web/201602
03140651/http://www.infidelityfacts.com/infidelity-statistics.htmll.
    [53]David Atkins and Elizabeth Allen, "The Association of Divorce and Extramarital Sex
in a Representative U.S. Sample", *Journal of Family Issues*, November 2012, www.research
gate.net/publication/258151224_The_Association_of_Divorce_and_Extramarital_Sex_in_a
_Representative_US_Sample.
    See also Robert Hughes Jr., "Does Extramarital Sex Cause Divorce?", *HuffPost*, August 8,
2012, https://www.huffingtonpost.com/robert-hughes/does-extramarital-sex-cau_b_1567507
.html.
    [54]Elizabeth Marquardt, *Between Two Worlds: The Inner Lives of Children of Divorce* (New
York: Crown Publishers, 2005).

happy divorce for children who find themselves forced into early adulthood and divided identity when caught between two worlds. Inasmuch as the sexual revolution seems to have been a major cause of the doubling of divorce rates (as well as the rate of infidelity), then it must also be held accountable for the undermining of the inner life of its childhood victims throughout their adulthood—a problem that is likely to repeat itself in future generations.[55]

What might we conclude about the breakdown of sexual mores during the sexual revolution? The picture should not be characterized as "progress", for what we see is a systemic breakdown of marriage and family—as well as an undermining of cultural stability (marked by an increase in rapes, sexual assaults, and sexual harassment). Though we cannot definitively conclude that the breakdown of sexual mores in the sexual revolution caused these exceedingly negative familial, social, and cultural conditions solely from their coincidence in time (1966 2010), we can infer such causation from the intrinsic interrelatedness between the weakening of sexual mores and the above-mentioned individual and social behaviors—increased infidelity, decreased marriages, increased divorce, and more aggressive public sexual conduct (rapes, sexual assaults, and sexual harassment). There is significant sociological and social-psychological data showing how strong social mores (in the area of sexuality and other areas of ethics) can prevent these negative behaviors on the part of both individuals and culture.[56]

We have reached a point where we cannot allow the above trends to continue. Further breakdown of the family, increased sexual

[55] See Wayne Parker, "Key Statistics about Kids from Divorced Families", July 15, 2020, https://www.thespruce.com/children-of-divorce-in-america-statistics-1270390.

[56] A seminal article on the influence of social mores on individual and group behavior was written in 1955 by Morton Deutsch and Harold B. Gerard. These principles can be applied to the influence of sexual mores on sexual attitudes and behaviors. See Morton Deutsch and Harold B. Gerard, "A Study of Normative and Informational Social Influences upon Individual Judgment", *Journal of Abnormal and Social Psychology* 51, no. 3 (1955): 629–36, doi:10.1037/h0046408. PMID 13286010.

The original typology of how social mores influence behavior—not only sexually, but in other areas—was set out by Herbert Kelman in 1958. See Herbert Kelman, "Compliance, Identification, and Internalization: Three Processes of Attitude Change", *Journal of Conflict Resolution* 2, no. 1 (1958): 51–60, doi:10.1177/002200275800200106. With respect to how sexual mores influence sexual behavior (based on the above principles), see Donn Byrne, "Social Psychology and the Study of Sexual Behavior", *Personality and Social Psychology Bulletin* 3, no. 1 (December 1976), http://journals.sagepub.com/doi/pdf/10.1177/014616727600300102.

aggressiveness, and the continued deterioration of intimacy, generativity, and committed exclusive love will not only negatively affect future generations of children but also destabilize the internal cultural fabric holding society together through trust, charity, and hope. In the last twenty-plus years, we have tried to bandage symptoms of the above problems by increased counseling, support groups, antidepressants, and diversions (e.g., alcohol and drugs, social media, computer games, and edgy entertainment such aspornography). Though some of these bandages are positive, others are quite negative, furthering the destabilization of individual identity and culture. If we are to restabilize individual and cultural identity, we will have to move beyond treating the symptoms and address the major cause of these problems—namely, the decline of sexual mores. This will mean taking a fresh look at the importance of sexual mores needed for the flourishing of individuals, marriage, and society. But where can we begin this process, for it seems as if we are trying to turn a ship a hundred times bigger than the Titanic? An obvious starting point is the fundamental ground of most societal mores and norms: religion—embodied by the leadership of the major church denominations within our culture.[57] Inasmuch as Christian churches constitute about 75 percent of the U.S. population,[58] there must be a united and concerted effort to make a credible and inspirational case for sexual mores. Though Jesus' and the Church's teaching on these subjects is a clear starting point, it needs to be reinforced by contemporary philosophical teaching and social analysis (similar to what is given above) to reverse the negative social norming process that has undermined the credibility of these teachings in the popular mind. This should include the following:

1. Using "the four levels of happiness" (or another model of purpose in life) to help young people move from dominant Level One-Two purpose to dominant Level Three-Four purpose

---

[57] According to recent data from Gallup, 75.2 percent of the U.S. is Christian (48.9 percent Protestant, 23 percent Catholic, and 1.8 percent Mormon); unaffiliated (none, atheist, and agnostic), 18.2 percent; Jewish, 2.1 percent; Muslim, .8 percent; other non-Christian religions (e.g., Buddhist, Hindu, and Shinto), 2.5 percent. See Frank Newport, "Percentage of Christians in U.S. Drifting Down, but Still High", Gallup, December 24, 2015, https://news .gallup.com/poll/187955/percentage-christians-drifting-down-high.aspx.

[58] See previous note.

2. Presenting a strong justification for the goodness and desirability of family and children (using some of the sources mentioned above), particularly Saint John Paul's Theology of the Body[59]

3. Giving a sobering presentation of the destructiveness of the sexual revolution and its significant negative impact on marriage, sexual fidelity, children, exclusive commitment, and intimacy/ generativity, as well as the increase in sexual assaults—ensuring the use of the statistics given above because they will speak volumes to skeptical listeners

The objective of this heightened teaching is not to make people feel guilty, but rather to portray the consequences truthfully of the above lifestyle choices on individual lives, relationships, families, and culture. Hopefully, the argument and statistics will allow the truth of Jesus' teaching to reemerge so that the truth can set us free—free of the constraints of past social norming and free to reestablish sexual mores within our community of family and friends.

It is important to help young people become countercultural, which is difficult in a society built on social norming and social media. If young people are not yet ready to speak out against the culture, they can still be encouraged to build defenses against the popular culture's false view of sexuality. These defenses are necessary for the protection of themselves and their future spouses, children, and family. Since this truth will be hard to embrace, we might help young people in the following ways:

1. *Expose them to Theology of the Body.* Listen to Christopher West's audio books on Theology of the Body (accessible to young people).[60]

2. *Encourage Level Three-Four peer groups.* Help young people to form peer groups around family members and friends who

---

[59] Parents and teachers may want to begin with Christopher West, *Theology of the Body for Beginners: A Basic Introduction to John Paul II's Sexual Revolution* (West Chester, Penn.: Ascension Press, 2004).

[60] Christopher West, *Our Bodies Tell God's Stories: Discovering the Divine Plan for Love, Sex, and Gender* (Grand Rapids, Mich.: Brazos Press, 2020); Christopher West, *Good News about Sex and Marriage: Answers to Your Honest Questions about Catholic Teaching* (Cincinnati: St. Anthony Messenger Press 2005). Both books are available at the following website: https://www.audible.com/author/Christopher-West/B001K8H50E.

have a strong religious and Catholic affiliation. Peer support is needed until young people are twenty-five but is most necessary from fifteen to twenty years old.

3. *Encourage heroism.* Help young people to risk at least partial social marginalization for the sake of Jesus Christ. We can help them meet the challenges of the culture's skepticism and cynicism by giving them excellent intellectual and scientifically credible justification for God, the soul, and Jesus.[61] The stronger their rational conviction for God and Jesus, the more they will recognize the ultimate significance of religion. This will free them to stand up for Jesus' teaching even at the cost of possible ridicule. If parents and teachers are good role models for nonconformity with objectionable cultural attitudes, children are likely to identify with them (at least in part). When this is combined with families and friends (peer groups) with similar religious and social norms, children have a chance of being countercultural for the sake of God and Jesus (as well as their future families and themselves).

We now proceed to Jesus' and the Church's teaching on particular sexual issues. The first two issues, extramarital sex and premarital sex, will be taken up in this chapter (Sections IV and V, respectively), and four additional topics—the homosexual lifestyle, pornography, gender identity and sex change, and artificial birth control—will be taken up in Chapter 2.

IV. Extramarital Sex

Jesus' teaching on extramarital sex (adultery) is partially based on the Old Testament definition. The books of Deuteronomy and Leviticus understand adultery as a married man having sexual relations with a woman other than his wife, and a married woman having sexual relations with someone other than her husband. The penalty for this was

---

[61] The Magis Center has a prepared a demonstrably effective series to help young people maintain and defend their faith called Credible Catholic. Go to www.crediblecatholic.com and click on 7 Essential Modules and play the videos for each of the seven modules.

death to the offending partners, generally by stoning (see Deut 22:22; Lev 20:10). Though Jesus holds to the seriousness of this sin (because of the injustice to the spouses of adulterers as well as the harm caused to the marriage and family), He is much less interested in exacting the grave penalty. Indeed, He causes the stoning of an adulterous women to be abandoned (see Jn 8:3–11). Though Jesus was not concerned with punishment, He was very concerned with conversion; He concluded his encounter with the woman by saying, "Neither do I condemn you; go, and do not sin again" (8:11).

In the Old Testament, divorce could lead to adultery if a divorced woman remarried because she would then be having sexual relations with someone other than her first husband; however, this did not apply to her husband, who was permitted by Mosaic law to divorce and marry another woman without incurring the sin of adultery (see Deut 24:1–11). Jesus equalized the commandment against adultery for men and women by teaching:

> Whoever divorces his wife and marries another, commits adultery against her; and if she divorces her husband and marries another, she commits adultery. (Mk 10:11–12)

Evidently, Jesus teaches that not only divorced women who remarry commit adultery but also divorced men who remarry. At the same time, He asserts that marriage (by the will of the Creator) is permanent. Recall from Section I.B above that Jesus taught that marriage is permanent and exclusive to one man and one woman. He does this by adding two critical phrases to His citation of Genesis (1:27; 2:24). At the beginning of His citation of Genesis, He adds, "He who made them from the beginning [the Creator] made them male and female"—and at the end of the citation, He adds, "What therefore *God* has joined together, let no man put asunder"[62] (Mt 19:4–6; italics added). Thus, he uses his transformed citation of Genesis to justify the permanence of marriage and declares that

---

[62] With Jesus' two additions the passage reads as follows: "Have you not read that he who made them from the beginning made them male and female, and said, 'For this reason a man shall leave his father and mother and be joined to his wife, and the two shall become one'? So they are no longer two but one. What therefore God has joined together, let no man put asunder" (Mt 19:4–6).

this permanence is the will of the Creator (His Father). From this, it follows that *anyone* who divorces his or her spouse and marries another commits adultery. In doing this, Jesus declared the marriage covenant to be sacrosanct—so holy and good as to be inviolable. This is one of the reasons the Church later declared marriage to be a sacrament.

Jesus taught that adultery is a serious sin not only because it undermines chastity but also because it undermines justice. Inasmuch as fidelity is promised to spouses to obtain their fidelity and loyalty in return, and to form a bond upon which to build a future family, extramarital sex is a sin against justice. It not only breaks a solemn promise but also betrays the spouse who has pledged his or her whole life to the adulterer on the basis of that promise. Thus, adultery "steals" the life of the spouse and undermines the security of the family grounded in the promise now broken.

Jesus extends His teaching on adultery to include the *intention* to commit adultery in His Sermon on the Mount:

> You have heard that it was said, "You shall not commit adultery." But I say to you that every one who looks at a woman lustfully has already committed adultery with her in his heart. (Mt 5:27–28)

The expression "looking lustfully at another" has a very specific meaning—namely, having the intention to commit adultery.[63] It does not so much refer to looking at pornography or looking unchastely at members of the opposite sex, but rather on forming the intention to commit adultery—an intention meant to lead to the act of adultery itself.[64]

Jesus makes this extension of adultery to warn His followers that intending adultery frequently leads to its occurrence, so the sin begins at its conceptualization and is not limited to its completion. If we are to avoid adultery—all sexual relationships outside of marriage—we must avoid intending it and fantasizing about it.

---

[63] See Benedict Viviano, "The Gospel according to Matthew", in *The New Jerome Biblical Commentary*, ed. Raymond E. Brown, Joseph A. Fitzmyer, and Roland E. Murphy (Englewood Cliffs, N.J.: Prentice Hall, 1990), p. 642.

[64] Ibid.

Jesus was deeply interested in the positive reasons for sexuality and chastity. His positive teaching on sexuality may be found within His teaching on love. This is the basis for my explication of the Christian view of *eros* (given above in Section I). This is also the basis for the Christian view of chastity given in Volume II, Chapter 4 of this Trilogy. We may now proceed to an examination of the deleterious effects of adultery and infidelity in contemporary culture.

We have already seen above that infidelity has an exceedingly negative effect on marriage. Recall the research of David Atkins and Elizabeth Allen that extramarital affairs increase divorce by a factor of 2.3 times:

> Of those respondents reporting [extramarital affairs], 41% of men and 48% of women were either currently divorced or separated, in contrast to only 17% of men and 22% of women without a history of [extramarital affairs].[65]

Evidently, extramarital affairs are strongly correlated with divorce but are not necessarily the exclusive cause of divorce. From this we can conclude that adultery is not only a betrayal and injustice to the spouse but also a likely path to divorce and the fallout from it— for both the spouse and children.

Beyond its negative impact on marriage, spouses, and children, sexual infidelity has a particularly insidious nature. There is something quite evil about infidelity, for it manifests a willingness to hurt and undermine both family and children for egotistical motives. Assuming that most people do not enter marriage with the intention to hurt and undermine their spouse and children, we might ask how they allowed themselves to get on the path of egocentric betrayal and destructiveness. Recall from Volume I (Chapter 5), Anna Karenina's progressive self-deceit and rationalization that opened the door to her affair with Count Vronsky, from which she could not extricate herself even when faced with separation from her son, the unjust treatment of her husband (who was willing to forgive her), and the loss of her longtime friends. Recall also from that Volume (Chapter 4) how the Evil One progressively increases temptations and deceits to break

---

[65] Atkins and Allen, "Association of Divorce and Extramarital Sex".

down our will to be good and loving to our spouses, children, and God. Once Anna has stepped over the line, she rationalizes her way progressively to greater infidelity until she has burned almost every bridge back to her family and friends. Her seduction is so complete (and her rationalizations so "perfected"), that when Vronsky loses interest in her, her world falls apart and she sinks into despair, considering herself to be the victim.

Recall that the Evil One moves quickly from tempter and deceiver to "accuser" when he senses despair on his victim's horizon. Given the significantly increased temptation to infidelity in this culture, we should be hypervigilant about letting ourselves go down the path of Anna Karenina. When the temptation comes, we must be prepared to fight every passion within ourselves. As Saint Ignatius of Loyola tells us:

> It is the way of the enemy [Satan] to weaken and lose heart, his temptations taking flight, when the person who is exercising himself in spiritual things opposes a bold front against the temptations of the enemy, doing diametrically the opposite. And on the contrary, if the person who is exercising himself commences to have fear and lose heart in suffering the temptations, there is no beast so wild on the face of the earth as the enemy of human nature in following out his damnable intention with so great malice.[66]

Given the serious darkness and depravity of this offense against one's spouse, children, and God, we must ask ourselves the question of why there has been such a large increase in infidelity over the last twenty-plus years—a 40 percent increase in infidelity among women, and a 45 percent increase among men who are under thirty years of age.[67] The question becomes even more urgent in light of the increasing popularity of cheating websites, such as Ashley Madison. We as Catholics and Christians must ask ourselves how we have arrived at the point where so many people are willing to enter into the dark, destructive, and evil reality of infidelity so readily. Can it

---

[66] Saint Ignatius of Loyola, *Spiritual Exercises*, Twelfth Rule, from "14 Rules for the Discernment of Spirits", *Scepter* (blog), August 3, 2018, https://scepterpublishers.org/blogs/scepter -blog-corner/14-rules-for-the-discernment-of-spirits-by-st-ignatius-of-loyola.

[67] Riley, "Young and Restless".

be that they do not recognize the depravity and destructive power of their actions? Can it be that they do not recognize the evil of their betrayal? We must face up to the reality that many who embark on this dark course do not recognize the interpersonal, moral, and transcendent implications of their actions. Many will likely later discover it when the world around them is falling apart; but at the moment of their betrayal, their sense of love, decency, and connection to God seems to be dulled or even arrested—and they leap into the darkness with reckless abandon.

It is hard to resist the idea that if these individuals had a stronger sense of God and a more acute awareness of the promptings of conscience as well as the help of strong social mores, they would have hesitated before the darkness—recognizing it to be a betrayal not only of the family and God but also of themselves. Unfortunately, these vital interior powers and societal norms have been severely undermined, and popular culture has deliberately filled the vacuum with every kind of rationalization and "new social norms" that shout out, "There is nothing really wrong with it, and besides, everyone is doing it."[68]

One of the best ways of helping our family, church, and culture is to practice Christ's teaching on marriage, fidelity, and sexuality authentically. At the same time, we must reject privately and publicly the promptings of new social norming from the culture—particularly the continued suggestions in the media that sex is merely a physical and morally neutral reality (rather than an intensely generative, moral, and spiritual one). No one is exempt from the pervasive influence of new cultural norming—not even mature married couples or clergy. If we let our guard down, lapse into Level One and Level Two purpose, indulge in the culture's Level One and Level Two suggestions, and marginalize the teachings of Jesus and the Church, we will soon be at the doorstep of darkness—being pulled into a seemingly harmless moment of self-indulgence, which in reality is the height of destructiveness, betrayal, and evil. There is only one way to avoid these temptations—stay close to the Lord in prayer, sacraments, and Church teachings, and vigilantly pursue moral conversion.

---

[68] See the analysis of the foundations and breakdown of objective moral norms in Chapter 5, Section III.

V. Premarital Sex and Cohabitation

What did Jesus say about premarital sex? Though the words "pre-marital sex" are not used per se in the New Testament, this con-duct is included in the meaning of the Greek term *porneia* (Hebrew, *zanah*), which denotes "a *selling off* (surrendering) of sexual purity; *illicit sexual acts* of any type".[69] The Old Testament meaning of *zanah* includes conduct explicitly prohibited by the Deuteronomic and Levitical codes: illicit sexual intercourse—adultery, fornication (see Deut 22:20–28; Lev 18:20), homosexuality (see Lev 18:22; 20:13), and sexual intercourse with close relatives (see Lev 18:6–18).[70] Jesus accepts most of these Deuteronomic and Levitical meanings of *zanah* (translated *porneia* in the New Testament) and adds to it sexual rela-tions with a divorced man or woman (see Mk 10:11–12).

Recall from above that Jesus explicitly prohibits *porneia* in Mark's Gospel in His list of sins that make a person unclean (requiring the forgiveness of God):

> And he said, "What comes out of a man is what defiles a man. For from within, out of the heart of man, come evil thoughts, fornication [*porneia*], theft, murder, adultery, coveting, wickedness, deceit, licen-tiousness, envy, slander, pride, foolishness. All these evil things come from within, and they defile a man." (7:20–23)

So, to what does *porneia* (illicit sexual conduct) refer? As we shall see, it refers to "sexual relations outside of the marital covenant" as he has defined it. We saw above that Jesus considered marriage a permanent covenant between one man and one woman to be the explicit will of the Creator and that the marital covenant is the ap-propriate place for sexual relations. Did Jesus believe that the mar-ital covenant was the *only* appropriate place for sexual relations? If so, then *porneia* refers to all sexual conduct outside of the marital covenant. The answer to this question can be inferred from Jesus' teaching on "adultery of the heart".

In Matthew 5:28, Jesus says, "I say to you that every one who looks at a woman lustfully has already committed adultery with her

---

[69] See *Strong's Concordance*, s.v. "4202: porneia".
[70] See ibid.

in his heart." As noted above (Section IV), "looking lustfully at a woman" has the specific meaning of "intending or planning to have sexual relations with her outside of the marriage covenant". Inasmuch as Jesus called this intention (to have sex outside of marriage) "adultery", He extends the prohibition of adultery to all such intentions, and therefore to any actions resulting from them. Hence, having sexual relations with a woman outside of marriage is seriously sinful ("adultery"). Does this passage apply only to men intending sexual relationships (outside of marriage) with women—or might we infer that it also applies to women intending to have sexual relationships with men outside of marriage? Might it also apply to men intending sexual relationships with men outside of marriage—or women intending sexual relationships with women outside of marriage? Though we cannot say with certainty from the text that Jesus had this in mind, these other relationships apparently fall within the "spirit" of His declaration, and therefore we cannot preclude them from His intention. As such, it is reasonable to infer that Jesus likely viewed all sexual relationships outside of marriage—and even the intention to have such relationships—to be illicit (adultery in the heart). For this reason, Jesus probably intended that *porneia* apply to all sexual activity outside of the marital covenant (permanent, exclusive, covenant relationship between one man and one woman— see the explanation of Mt 19:4–6 in Section IV above). This interpretation of *porneia* is consistent with the meanings of *zanah* in the Deuteronomic and Levitical codes (see above in this section).

With this in mind, let us return to Mark 7:20–23. Recall from that passage that Jesus says that *porneia* (sexual conduct outside of marriage) leads to defilement of the heart. In general, "defilement" refers to "corruption or impairment" and "heart" refers to the "center or origin of emotional, intellectual, moral, and spiritual activity". Hence, for Jesus, *porneia* (sexual activity outside of marriage) leads to corruption or impairment of the "center of our emotional, intellectual, moral, and spiritual activity" and has two major consequences:

1. *Porneia* (like all forms of defilement) causes us to sin against another person. Just as adultery is a sin of injustice against the betrayed spouse, so also sexual relationships outside of marriage (including premarital sex) are sins against the person with

whom one has relations without an exclusive, publicly declared commitment. These sexual acts undermine the dignity of the partner who deserves such a commitment in exchange for sexual and emotional intimacy. Thus, there is a real harm of treating a person as a mere object or thing—using someone for personal gratification—instead of bestowing on the person the commitment he or she deserves for the pledging of one's body, mind, and spirit (as the sexual act connotes).

2. Sexual acts outside of marriage leave us vulnerable to the Evil One. This may be difficult to understand in our culture where premarital sex is seen as a victimless activity practiced by many (see Section III above on the negative effects of social norming). Nevertheless, Jesus sees any form of defilement as opening the door to the Evil One through both disobedience to God and callous disregard for another human person (see 1 Jn 3:10).[71]

Though Jesus does not explain the harmful effects of premarital sex on marriages or future covenant love, we can infer it from His belief that it (like all forms of defilement) weakens our spirit and makes us more vulnerable to the temptations and deceits of the devil. The more we allow ourselves to come under the spell of the Evil One in disobedience to God and disregard for our neighbor, the more we believe his lies and deceits (see Jn 8:44–47), which will ultimately undermine our ability to commit to and live out exclusive permanent commitment to covenant love. We may think that continuous engagement in uncommitted sexual activity is a "harmless tryst", but there is a dark rationalization embedded in this judgment—a rationalization that forces us to devalue the dignity and goodness of the person with whom we are having illicit sexual relations and the goodness of proper marital commitment. This undermines our respect for others, respect for marital commitment, and respect for God, which in turn undermines respect for ourselves.

---

[71] "By this it may be seen who are the children of God, and who are the children of the devil: whoever does not do right is not of God, nor he who does not love his brother" (1 Jn 3:10). The author here implies that anyone who acts unrighteously or acts unlovingly toward his brother or sister makes himself vulnerable to becoming a child of the devil (as opposed to a child of God).

In view of this, it should not be surprising to learn that the more premarital sexual partners we have, the more we will be unhappy in our marriage, and the more likely our marriage will end up in divorce. This is precisely what is revealed in the above-mentioned surveys done by the National Survey of Family Growth (a part of the Centers for Disease Control's National Center for Health Statistics). These surveys correlate the number of women's premarital sexual partners with the divorce rate of their marriages within five years. After the year 2000, those with zero premarital partners had only a 5 percent divorce rate within five years—the lowest rate by far. Women having one premarital partner had a 22 percent divorce rate, those with two to nine partners had an average 30 percent divorce rate, and those with more than ten had a 35 percent-plus divorce rate.[72] Furthermore, according to surveys done by the National Marriage Project, individuals having premarital sexual relationships experienced less marital satisfaction than those who did not. The more premarital partners they had, the less marital satisfaction they experienced.[73]

Additionally, couples who had cohabitated before marriage experienced less marital satisfaction and had a higher divorce rate than those who did not.[74] This correlation between cohabitation and increased risk of divorce is particularly important in light of the huge increase in rates of cohabitation (from 450,000 to more than 7.5 million between 1960 and today).[75] This increase is attributable not only to convenience and economic advantage (see below) but also to a widely held cultural myth that cohabitation before marriage helps the couple to know if they "really get along" and therefore to avoid a

---

[72] See Nicholas H. Wolfinger, "Counterintuitive Trends in the Link between Premarital Sex and Marital Stability", Institute for Family Studies, June 6, 2016, https://ifstudies.org/blog/counterintuitive-trends-in-the-link-between-premarital-sex-and-marital-stability.

[73] See Scott Stanley and Galena Rhoades, "Premarital Cohabitation Is Still Associated with Greater Odds of Divorce", Institute for Family Studies, October 17, 2018, https://ifstudies.org/blog/premarital-cohabitation-is-still-associated-with-greater-odds-of-divorce, and Scott Stanley and Galena Rhoades, "Before 'I Do': What Do Premarital Experiences Have to Do with Marital Quality among Today's Young Adults?", National Marriage Project (University of Virginia), 2014, http://before-i-do.org/.

[74] Ibid.

[75] "In 1960, about 450,000 unmarried couples lived together. Now the number is more than 7.5 million." Meg Jay, "The Downside of Cohabiting Before Marriage", *New York Times*, April 14, 2012.

bad marriage.[76] Current research has revealed that this myth, despite its persuasiveness, is quite wrong. Recent surveys by the Centers for Disease Control as well as by Michael Rosenfeld and Katharina Roesler show precisely the opposite of what the above cultural myth suggests—namely, that the *longer couples* cohabitate, the *more likely* they are to divorce.[77]

Attempts have been made to explain away this correlation by hypothesizing that couples who are likely to cohabitate are also more likely to divorce (so the cause of divorce is supposedly the couple—not the cohabitation experience). Scott Stanley and Galena Rhoades indicate that though the couple's proclivities influence future divorce, the main problem comes from the cohabitation experience itself,[78] pointing to three major factors:[79]

1. The sliding effect and inertia (explained below) weaken the desire and resolve for public, permanent commitment.
2. Cohabitation undermines esteem for marriage.
3. Cohabitation increases acceptance of divorce.

Sheri Stritof[80] (summarizing the *National Health Statistics Reports*[81] and the National Institute of Health study of cohabitation and child well-being[82]) points to several other factors that can contribute to cohabiting couples' increased rate of divorce:

- Living together is considered to be more stressful than being married.

---

[76] See ibid.
[77] See Michael J. Rosenfeld and Katharina Roesler, "Cohabitation Experience and Co-habitation's Association with Marital Dissolution", *Journal of Marriage and Family* 81, no. 1 (September 2018): 42–58, https://doi.org/10.1111/jomf.12530. See Stanley and Rhoades, "Premarital Cohabitation".
[78] See Stanley and Rhoades "Premarital Cohabitation".
[79] Ibid.
[80] Sheri Stritof, "Cohabitation Facts and Statistics You Need to Know", Spruce.com, April 13, 2017, https://web.archive.org/web/20170721011555/https://www.thespruce.com/cohabitation-facts-and-statistics-2302236.
[81] Colleen N. Nugent and Jill Daugherty, "A Demographic, Attitudinal, and Behavioral Profile of Cohabiting Adults in the United States, 2011–2015", *National Health Statistics Reports*, May 31, 2018, https://www.cdc.gov/nchs/data/nhsr/nhsr111.pdf.
[82] Wendy D. Manning, "Cohabitation and Child Wellbeing", *Future Child* 25, no. 2 (2015): 51–66, https://www.ncbi.nlm.nih.gov/pmc/articles/PMC4768758/.

- In the United States and in the UK, couples who live together are at a greater risk for divorce than noncohabiting couples.
- Cohabiting couples had a separation rate five times that of married couples and a reconciliation rate that was one-third that of married couples.
- Cohabiting couples are more likely to experience infidelity.
- Compared to those planning to marry, those cohabiting have an overall poorer relationship quality. They tend to have more fighting and violence and less reported happiness.
- Compared to married individuals, those cohabiting have higher levels of depression and substance abuse.

Cohabitation not only weakens the desire and resolve for permanent marital commitment, but also weakens religious commitment.[83] As noted earlier, religion and prayer significantly heighten marital satisfaction and permanent commitment in five major areas (see the seven major university studies of the positive effects of religion on marriage above in Section I.C[84]). Hence, cohabitation also weakens one of the most important marital and familial bonding factors.

Beyond the above negative factors, is there something intrinsic to the dynamic of cohabitation that leads to increased divorce and marital dissatisfaction? Meg Jay (*New York Times* editorial writer) addresses three causes built into the cohabitation experience itself—the sliding effect, gender asymmetry, and consumer lock-in.[85]

First, cohabitation promotes couples "sliding" into marriage rather than making a deliberate commitment to become engaged and then married for a lifetime (the so-called sliding effect). Couples start with "sleeping over" at each other's places, and then sliding into cohabitating. Thus, they bypass explicit conversations about living together in a committed way, starting a family, and preparing for a future of intimate and generative self-giving love. Since cohabitation offers an easy exit, the couple concentrates on finding a suitable place to live, decorating it, combining their bills, and adjusting to a comfortable level of mutual support. Then, at some point, it seems that marriage is the right thing to do, and so without much discussion about the

---

[83] See Thornton, Axinn, and Hill, "Reciprocal Effects".
[84] See Briggs, "5 Ways Faith Contributes to Strong Marriages".
[85] See Jay, "Downside of Cohabiting before Marriage".

differences between cohabitation and marriage (public permanent commitment, the starting of a family, and the integration of two families of origin), the couple simply slides into it. As it turns out, the lack of deliberation in the sliding effect causes lower levels of commitment, dashed expectations, and a lack of preparation for the challenges that families must almost always face. The result is marital dissatisfaction and increased divorce.[86]

Secondly, there is a problem of "gender asymmetry" in the reasons why men and women cohabitate. Women frequently interpret cohabitation as a step toward marriage (some feel pressured to cohabitate in order to move toward engagement and marriage). Alternatively, men believe that cohabitation is a way to test the relationship and postpone commitment (precisely the opposite of women).[87] This generally results in women pushing men toward engagement and marriage and men trying to postpone it. When the engagement occurs, many men have mental reservations about the permanent public commitment but accede to the pressure and the seeming practicality of continuing the combination of bills and mutual support. Once again, the marriage is grounded less in a deliberate mutual commitment to start a new life and family together, and more in acceding to pressure and practical convenience—evidently less than a solid foundation.

Thirdly, the "consumer lock-in effect" puts additional pressure on couples to enter into marriage as a mere extension of the practical advantages of cohabitation. Meg Jay describes it as follows:

> Sliding into cohabitation wouldn't be a problem if sliding out were as easy. But it isn't. Too often, young adults enter into what they imagine will be low-cost, low-risk living situations only to find themselves unable to get out months, even years, later. It's like signing up for a credit card with 0 percent interest. At the end of 12 months when the interest goes up to 23 percent you feel stuck because your balance is too high to pay off. In fact, cohabitation can be exactly like that. In behavioral economics, it's called consumer lock-in. Lock-in is the decreased likelihood to search for, or change to, another option once an investment in something has been made. The greater the setup

[86] See ibid.
[87] See ibid.

costs, the less likely we are to move to another, even better, situation, especially when faced with switching costs, or the time, money and effort it requires to make a change.[88]

What are the "take-aways" from this new research?

- The cultural myth about cohabitation is false—instead of increasing our freedom to commit in marriage, it deceives us and locks us in; it makes us unfree. Furthermore, it does not increase marital satisfaction and longevity. It decreases it significantly (for the reasons mentioned above).
- If couples are interested in a long-lasting satisfying marriage, they should seriously consider not only the major problems of cohabitation (and its effects on marriage and family) but also the effects of "sleeping over" at each other's places that so easily leads to a slide into cohabitation and then to a nondeliberative and nonpurposeful marriage.
- Women who feel pressured to cohabitate as a condition of moving toward engagement and marriage should present the above data to their partners, and tell them straightforwardly that they are not interested in sliding into a nonpurposeful marriage, but would prefer mutual deliberation toward engagement and marriage without the pressures and consumer lock-in of cohabitation.

We might ask if there are other reasons why marital dissatisfaction and divorce increase so significantly with the increase in premarital sexual relationships beyond the consequences mentioned above (nonpurposeful marriage, disappointed expectations, and consumer lock-in). There are several reasons that are not measured by the above surveys related to the nature of committed sexuality as well as spiritual life. The most fundamental reason is that an extended premarital sexual relationship weakens a couple's association of sexuality with exclusive permanently committed familial love. The longer premarital sexual relationships last, the more sexuality tends to become an end in itself—disconnected from

[88] Ibid.

the permanent familial unifying committed love of marriage. As a result, sexuality within the marriage is less significant as a support of intimate, generative, familial love. This disconnect between sexuality and permanent commitment weakens the commitment, which in turn weakens emotional intimacy and relational stability that are important not only for marital longevity and satisfaction but also for the secure upbringing of children. When permanent commitment is a couple's priority, sexuality is not an end in itself, but *for* the committed marriage. This strengthens the couple's emotional bondedness and intimacy, which in turn strengthens marital satisfaction and longevity. This deeper emotional bondedness and marital security also gives rise to intimate loving joy as relationships continue to grow. Without this strong emotional bond, sexuality can become less significant and even somewhat boring after the luster of romance begins to fade. The opposite is the case when sexuality is embedded within the deeper intimacy and generativity of exclusive permanent commitment toward children, common cause, and religious fulfillment. The marriage's bonding power is not exclusively dependent on sexuality's romantic luster, but also on the power of the couple's committed love, strong family, and religious conviction. If this deeper meaning, agency, and love is significantly weakened by a lengthy premarital sexual relationship, then it will naturally lead to less marital satisfaction and increased rates of divorce.

The negative consequences of premarital sex on marital longevity and satisfaction, as well as Jesus' teaching about the negative consequences of it for spiritual life, present a huge challenge to young people and the future of marriage in our culture, because 95 percent of Americans have unmarried sex before the age of forty-four.[89] What can Catholics and Christians do to mitigate the harm that has been and will be caused by this social reality? First, we cannot afford to be judgmental toward these individuals who obviously are swept up in an immensely successful social norming campaign combined with a

---

[89] See Jennifer Warner, "Premarital Sex the Norm in America: Premarital Sex Research Shows by Age 44, 95% of Americans Have Had Unmarried Sex", WebMD, December 20, 2006, https://www.webmd.com/sex-relationships/news/20061220/premarital-sex-the-norm -in-america.

weakened sense of religion and moral principles. Most of them have followed their peers and educators somewhat unreflectively into this new social reality. In view of this, it is questionable that some or many of them engaged in these activities with sufficient reflection and full consent of the will—the two conditions necessary for mortal sin. Nevertheless, their actions—irrespective of whether they were reflective or free—are harming them spiritually and undermining their capacity for marital satisfaction and longevity.

Since many young people initiate premarital sex in college and move toward cohabitation thereafter, they are in many respects free of parental constraint and guidance, and can ignore the advice given by parents who are frequently marginalized by their "20-something" children. Parents who become aggressive (or even passive-aggressive) rarely succeed in changing their children's attitudes. A better strategy is to inform them about the above data indicating the drawbacks of cohabitation, and to encourage them to reconnect with the Lord in prayer and at Mass. I would recommend the following to the parents of college students who see their children moving into the pattern of increased premarital sex, "sleeping over", and cohabitation:

1. Parents of college students should present the above data on premarital sex, cohabitation, and marital stability and longevity to their children *before* college and encourage them to attend church services at their university Catholic center (sometimes called Newman Centers[90]) where they will find peer support.
2. If possible, encourage your children to participate in a group like FOCUS (Fellowship of Catholic University Students[91]), or in the absence of a campus FOCUS group, participate in the university Catholic center's retreats and education programs. The more students participate, the more they are likely to retain their Christian values. These ministries give peer support for living a Christian life on campus—and if students depart from Christ's teaching, they encourage and provide opportunities for confession.

---

[90] The following website has a directory of Newman Centers and the programs offered at most of them: http://www.newmanconnection.com/locations/.

[91] More information can be obtained at their official website: http://www.focus.org/.

3. If your children have already graduated from college, and are still open to the Church and are not cohabitating, you will want to encourage them to find a parish community that engages them with outstanding adult education and young adult community support. There are several organizations, such as Cursillo, that give encouragement to adults trying to live according to Christian teaching.[92] There are also several men's and women's groups who provide support to live Christian values through weekly reunions or other less formal gatherings.[93]

4. If parents are rebuffed by children who have lost interest or are skeptical about church attendance, it is helpful to enlist the support of some of their peers who are faithful about church commitment. Frequently, young adults will join peers in church participation.

5. If your children have already separated from the Church during or after college, it will be more difficult to help them resist the current trends in premarital sex and cohabitation. It is always worth the effort to help young people find an engaging parish with an active, educated young adult group, and to encourage them to attend that parish. If parents and peers are resistant, and the couple has already moved into cohabitation, then family and friends will have to wait until the prospect of marriage and the anticipated birth of the first child. The desire or prospect for children can move couples from cohabitation to marriage if parents are encouraging, and offer assistance for raising them. Furthermore, the first child can open a couple to renewed interest in the religion of their childhood—so that their child can have everything they had. Remember, the more religious the couple, the more stable and satisfying the marital relationship.

---

[92] Cursillo has a weekly group reunion (after its three-day retreat weekend) that gives encouragement to live Christian values and obtain accelerated spiritual development. For additional information, see the website of the National Cursillo movement (natl-cursillo.org).

[93] The USCCB (United States Conference of Catholic Bishops) has a list of Catholic lay organizations for both men and women having various functions and meeting times. See http://www.usccb.org/about/public-affairs/backgrounders/catholic-lay-organizations.cfm. See also http://www.usccb.org/about/laity-marriage-family-life-and-youth/laity/index.cfm. For international Catholic lay movements and groups (many of whom have large groups in the United States), see http://www.laityfamilylife.va/content/laityfamilylife/en/sezione -laici/repertorio.html.

VI. Further Observations on the Christian View of Love and Sexuality

In Section I above, we explained the Christian philosophy of *eros* (sexual love), which is intended to be the bonding support for the highest level of commitment and "human to human" love oriented toward family and a Christian home. We examined what happens when *eros* is separated from this highest level of commitment, particularly with respect to aggressivity, the depersonalization of sexuality, the "thingification" of the individual, the undermining of intimacy and generativity within relationships, and the emotional and spiritual darkness resulting from this. Recent statistics showing increased infidelity, divorce rates, and sexual aggression (from sexual assault to forcible rape) over the last forty-plus years validate this perspective (see the studies cited in Sections III–V above). The rush to move from feelings of affection and romance to sexual expression has also undermined the development of deep friendships, intimacy, and generativity, which support the highest level of commitment in marriage.

This rush to move from feelings of affection to sexual expression has caused considerable confusion in the minds and hearts of young people with respect to the four loves explained above. Quite often young people view physical attraction and feelings of affection (*storgē*) as an indication of "true love". As a result, they confuse *eros* with mere sexual passion, which falls far short of the ideal of *eros*—sexual passion *for the sake of* expressing and supporting the highest levels of friendship, mutual support, generous self-gift, and commitment over the long-term. This means that *eros* has not only been trivialized but also turned on its head by the popular culture. Sexual passion is no longer a *means* of supporting the highest level of committed friendship and authentic love, but an end in itself—an intense moment of passionate encounter that is frequently self-gratifying and ego-indulgent for both parties.

The sexual revolution has trivialized and undermined not only the ideal of *eros* but also the ideal of *philia* (friendship). Young people frequently believe that strong passionate feelings indicate friendship—not recognizing the mutual support and commitment that genuine friendships require. Genuine friendships entail considerable generosity, hard work, and commitment, while strong feelings of passion can

occur instantaneously without any willingness to be mutually supportive, committed, or self-sacrificial. Furthermore, feelings can die
away in an instant, but friendships by their very nature—the mutual
willingness to commit and make sacrifices for the good of the other—
are enduring. If someone can be a friend by simply being an object of
sexual desire or a stimulus of sexual feelings, then friendship need not
have any mutual self-giving activity. *Philia*, like *eros*, has been trivialized to strong feelings and desires; there is nothing left of the noble
friendship, lauded in the Book of Sirach:

> A faithful friend is a sturdy shelter:
> he that has found one has found a treasure.
> There is nothing so precious as a faithful friend,
> and no scales can measure his excellence.
> A faithful friend is an elixir of life;
> and those who fear the Lord will find him.
> Whoever fears the Lord directs his friendship aright,
> for as he is, so is his neighbor also. (Sir 6.14–17)

If we are to reclaim the profound goodness of deep friendship, intimacy, generativity, exclusive commitment, and the marital-familial
bond supported by them, we will seriously want to reconsider Jesus'
teaching about sexuality being reserved to exclusive, public commitments. This will require self-restraint to allow the development
of deep friendships, intimacy, self-sacrificial generativity, and familial
anticipation *before* moving to sexual expression. This is borne out by
the statistics showing the increased longevity of marriages for those
who reserved sexual expression for a single partner willing to commit
publicly and exclusively.[94]

The rush to move from feelings of affection to sexual expression
has also produced confusion in the psyche of young and middle-aged
individuals who believe that their feelings of attraction and affection for another person (and the reciprocation of those feelings by
that other person) indicate the need for immediate sexual expression
without having developed genuine care and intimacy with the other.

---

[94] As stated previously in Section V, women having no premarital partners had a 5 percent
divorce rate. Women having one premarital partner had a 22 percent divorce rate, those with
two to nine partners had an average 30 percent divorce rate, and those with more than ten had
a 35 percent-plus divorce rate. See Wolfinger, "Counterintuitive Trends".

The truncation of care, generativity, and intimacy within the dating process is causing not only superficiality and depersonalization in dating and courtship, but also a stimulus-response association of feelings of attraction and affection with sexual expression. The idea and ideal of "love" within relationships is progressively becoming reduced to affection, convenient friendship, and sexual expression, leaving out profound intimate generative friendship moving toward exclusive commitment. This explains a host of contemporary challenges— the reticence to have children and to sacrifice personal gains for the sake of spouse and children, as well as delaying marriage.

If this inference is correct, then it would not be surprising to see a trend within society where the absence of sexual expression strongly implies, both intellectually and affectively, the absence of love. This is precisely the opposite of what occurs in Level Three-Four individuals who can be taught to cultivate true friendship, intimacy, and care for one another through the sacrifice of sexual expression before marriage.

If we are to move out of the cultural confusion about love, we will want to begin with restoring the Christian view of *eros*, which goes far beyond mere sexual passion to the objective this passion was meant to support—deep friendship, intimacy, care, common cause, and self-sacrifice directed and committed to a Christian family for a lifetime. If young people recognize that this Christian view of *eros* leads to emotional health and spiritual well-being, as well as the mutually supporting relationship needed for stable family life, and if they make the sacrifices needed to follow the Lord's teaching by delaying the sexual expression until marriage, they will be richly rewarded with deep marital satisfaction, longevity in marriage, and the path to salvation for themselves and their families. They will also find that their view of friendship will be profound and supportive—like Sirach's noble friendship. Though it will be difficult for young people to move away from the popular culture's rush from passionate desire to sexual expression, their sacrifice will be transformed into a "new self" for them and their spouses, and they will be lights of the Lord for the world. No doubt, this will be challenging and countercultural, but it will mean everything in the long run—absolutely everything.

Given the difficulty of being faithful to the Lord's teaching, many well-intended young people are likely to slip and fall, but they must not give up or grow discouraged. Rather, they must trust in the Lord's loving mercy, avail themselves of the Sacrament of Reconciliation, and do everything in their power to follow Him on the road to salvation, which will likely lead them to a lasting, satisfying, and fruitful marriage and family life.

VII. Conclusion

The struggle for virtue makes all the difference to life, identity, purpose, and salvation. Indeed, it is probably the most important dimension of our lives—the supreme dignity. For if we embrace the struggle to move beyond what Saint Paul calls "the flesh" toward "the spirit" in our inmost being, we purify ourselves and gradually take on not only new habits and a new identity, but also a whole new being, which Saint Paul calls "the new man" (Eph 4:24).

Few people willingly seek out the struggles and sacrifices required for a virtuous life, but when we trust in God and accept our crosses, we are gradually interiorly purified toward the image of Christ Himself. As this occurs, we discover that this struggle is worth it, and we see the hand of the Lord guiding us through it. The difference between the old and new self is the difference between a merely sensual-egotistical self and a virtuous-transcendent self, between a base self and a noble self, a shallow self and a deep self, an empty self and one filled with the light of Christ. When we look back on the struggles and sacrifices that transformed us in virtue and faith, we know that they were the most important (albeit painful) times of our lives—not only because they proved our mettle but also because they left an enduring effect on our identity and being. This has certainly been my own experience—not only with progressive blindness but also with some of the most painful and challenging moments of life.

Jesus compares this struggle to the pains of childbirth that give rise to a whole new human person—the prize that makes the pain worthwhile:

> Truly, truly, I say to you, you will weep and lament, but the world will rejoice; you will be sorrowful, but your sorrow will turn into joy. When a woman is in labor, she has pain, because her hour has come; but when she is delivered of the child, she no longer remembers the anguish, for joy that a child is born into the world. (Jn 16:20–21)

Chapter Two

True and False Promises of the Homosexual Lifestyle, Pornography, Gender Change, and Artificial Birth Control

Introduction

We now proceed to four issues in which the Church's teaching stands in opposition to the popular culture—homosexual lifestyle, pornography, gender change, and artificial birth control. It must be stressed from the outset that the Catholic Church did not declare these activities to be immoral for some prudish or controlling motive. Rather, she did so because of a conviction that these teachings were extensions of the teaching of Jesus, and obedience to them would lead to salvation. As we shall see, entering into these lifestyles undermines emotional health and spiritual well-being, opening upon depression, anxiety, and above all, spiritual darkness. As will be shown below, there are many recent studies showing the validity of these contentions, and though some have tried to minimize their findings, I will allow the studies to speak for themselves. If the Church's teachings are faithful to the intention of Jesus, and these lifestyles really do significantly undermine emotional health and spiritual well-being, they should be taken seriously, and steps taken to avoid them.

Popular culture situates the ethical question of these lifestyles within the context of the *right* to free sexual expression. This is not the context in which Jesus and the Church view the ethical question. The Church is primarily interested in whether particular lifestyles are consistent with Jesus' view of love (discussed in the previous chapter), specifically, Jesus' view of *agapē* (seeking the good of the other without expectation, recognition, or reward) and *eros* (sexual love which reinforces committed, mutually supportive, intimate, generative, family-oriented relationships for a lifetime). This ethical context shifts the focus of rights from that of the popular culture to that of Jesus.

A "right" is an entitlement to perform particular activities within a social or societal domain. Rights also obligate individuals to treat others justly. As might be inferred, entitlements are in relationship to the social context in which they occur. So, for example, in a democratic political domain, we may have the right to free sexual expression, but in a religious-spiritual domain (before God), we may not have such a right (entitlement), because God can allow or disallow freedom (entitlement) to which the democratic political domain may be indifferent. This distinction applies to the four topics of this chapter—homosexual lifestyle, birth control, pornography, and gender change.

In the current popular culture, we might think that if we have a right or freedom in the political order, we must also have the same right and freedom in the divine order. However, from an ontological point of view, the opposite is the case. Since God is the highest authority whose domain is the whole of reality, political rights follow from divinely ordained rights—not vice versa.[1] In this sense, the writers of the Declaration of Independence followed this natural law/natural rights ontology:

> We hold these truths to be self-evident, that all men are *created* equal, that they are endowed by their *Creator* with certain unalienable Rights, that among these are Life, Liberty and the pursuit of Happiness.[2]

Evidently, for someone who denies the existence of God (and divine authority), political rights are absolute and not derived from any higher authority. As such, an appeal to divine law or to divinely

---

[1] Saint Thomas Aquinas articulates this position in showing that the eternal/divine law is the ultimate ontological ground of the natural law and that the natural law is the ontological ground of the human law (see *Summa Theologica* I-II, qq. 91–95).

John Finnis, articulating the intrinsic relationship between natural law and natural rights, implies that rights stemming from the eternal/divine law ground natural/human rights. See John Finnis, *Natural Law and Natural Rights*, 2nd ed. (New York: Oxford University Press, 1980), pp. 48–59, 388–403.

[2] From a transcription of the Declaration of Independence on the website of the National Archives, last reviewed on October 7, 2021, https://www.archives.gov/founding-docs/declaration-transcript.

inspired Scripture would have no value. Chapters 1–5 of this volume can still be used by readers who subscribe to a secular ontology, because most of the rationale used in those chapters are based on secular consequences—emotional health, marital longevity and stability, cultural and societal harmony, and an ethic grounded in self-giving love. Thus, secular readers interested in emotional health, self-giving love, marital stability, and cultural harmony can still derive benefit from Chapters 1–5 based on that interest.

Readers who acknowledge a divine authority will likely acknowledge the priority of the divine law over the natural law and the priority of the natural law over human law. In this case, they will not restrict their interest solely to emotional health, self-giving love, marital stability, and cultural harmony, but will also be interested in spiritual well-being and the will of God. Small sections of this chapter as well as Chapters 3–5 are devoted to these two additional considerations. As will become clear, the moral teaching of the Catholic Church is not only good for salvation (though certainly that), but also good for emotional health, generative friendships, marriages, children, culture, and society.

Our feelings (derived perhaps from our sense of fairness within popular culture) may scream out that everyone should have the right to engage in a homosexual lifestyle, to look at pornography, or to have a sex change if they wish, but that's not the *whole* issue. Yes— everyone has a political right within this democracy to do those things, but there are three other issues that Christ and the Church must consider in their moral prescriptions and conveyance of rights:

1. What will a particular lifestyle do to the spiritual well-being of people? Will it lead them into seduction by their spiritual enemy (Satan)? Will it isolate them from God and His call to self-giving love (thereby promoting egocentricity and sensual addiction)? Will it lead to salvation or away from it?
2. What will this lifestyle do to the emotional/psychological health of individuals? Will it increase or decrease depression, anxiety, malaise, or despair?
3. What will this lifestyle do to relationships with others? Will it lead to interpersonal tension, narcissistic tendencies, antisocial behavior, or violence?

Since the Lord cares about these three dimensions of human happiness, purpose, and destiny, so does the Catholic Church. But what about us? If we believe in God (our creator and redeemer), then we too should care about His perspective on the good, evil, salvation, the human condition, and rights—and if we care about His perspective on these subjects, we should give it priority over a purely secular perspective.

So, what does this mean? Believers in God will have to reconfigure their default position from that of popular culture to that of God, and Christians will have to reconfigure it to the perspective and teaching of Jesus, and Catholics will have to further reconfigure it to the teachings of Jesus as interpreted by the Church. So, the next time we feel like defaulting to thinking that everyone has the right to engage in a homosexual lifestyle, to look at pornography, and to have a sex change, we must ask ourselves the questions, what does God think? What does Christ think? Will this lifestyle be good for a person's spiritual well-being and emotional health? Will it be good for their relationships with others? Will it lead to the good life as God understands it?

Yes—everyone has a right to engage in a lifestyle that will be destructive of self, relationships, and salvation, but should we affirm or even encourage such a lifestyle? Would a good parent affirm a child's decision to do something that's self-destructive, alienates him from others, or jeopardizes his salvation? Would Jesus act or think differently from a good parent? Beyond *believing* in Jesus' teaching, what is our responsibility for affirming, encouraging, or teaching contrary positions to others? Can we affirm or encourage a lifestyle that will be deleterious to self, relationships, and salvation even if we would not practice it ourselves? From the vantage point of Jesus Christ, the answer is definitively no! He states his view strongly and graphically:

> Whoever causes one of these little ones who believe in me to sin, it would be better for him to have a great millstone fastened round his neck and to be drowned in the depth of the sea. (Mt 18:6)

This teaching requires us to be countercultural. Christ asks us to risk being unpopular, viewed as "not nice", or even rejected in order to speak the truth that will lead to the good of others, but if we are

to be effective in presenting that truth, we need to go further—to
present an explanation of *why* a specific prohibition is good for our
emotional health, relationships with others, spiritual well-being, and
salvation—*why* it is good for marriages, families, and culture. The
reason for this volume is to help readers understand this rationale
from contemporary psychological, sociological, philosophical, and
cultural studies, in addition to their religious and moral goodness.

We may now return to our initial point—namely, that Jesus and
the Church do not warn us against the above four lifestyles out of a
prudish or controlling motive. Their motive is to reveal God's will
for us, and God's will is always directed toward our good, our perfection in love, and our salvation. So if we follow the teachings of the
Church, we will not only be on the path to optimizing the good for
self and others, our perfection in love, and our and others' salvation
but also avoiding the likely depression, anxiety, disrupted relationships, and spiritual darkness of what is contrary to it. Much of this
chapter will be devoted to showing how the Church's teaching leads
to perfection in love while avoiding emotional and spiritual darkness.

Remember, our feelings can be deceiving and may well be shaped
by social norming from the popular culture of which we are barely
conscious. Even if our feelings are screaming out that anyone should
be able to indulge in the above four lifestyles, place those feelings
in check for a moment and ask yourself if you want to encourage
someone to pursue a lifestyle that is contrary to God's will and that
will likely lead them into emotional and spiritual darkness. If your
answer is no, then it is worth studying the reasons why Jesus and
the Church would warn us against those lifestyles. If those lifestyles
have inherently negative and dark consequences, it would behoove
us to encourage our friends *not* to do them. Be prepared to tell
them *why* you are advising against those lifestyles, for if they are
aware of the potential negative consequences, they may choose the
more challenging path to life rather than the seemingly easier path
to darkness. In this way, you will have encouraged them to move
toward the Lord instead of their spiritual enemy. An *English Book of
Proverbs* (from 1670) expresses it well: "Hell is full of good meanings
and wishes."

Before exploring the Church's teaching in the above four areas, I
repeat an important distinction made at the beginning of the previous

chapter—namely, that the following content is not focused on mortal sin but rather on grave matter leading to sin. Recall that in the *Catechism of the Catholic Church*, the Church teaches that mortal sin requires grave matter as well as full knowledge and complete consent of the will.[3] Since we do not treat the second and third conditions, the contents of this volume are incapable of even suggesting that someone has committed a mortal sin. Nevertheless, it should be emphasized that entering into any of these lifestyles may well be gravely sinful because opening ourselves to the commission of these sins may lead us toward a significant misuse of freedom. If this occurs, make recourse to the Sacrament of Reconciliation and try to return to the teaching of Jesus, who is "the way, and the truth, and the life" (Jn 14:6).

I. Homosexual Lifestyle

Jesus' and the Church's teaching on the homosexual lifestyle is perhaps the most controversial of their doctrinal positions—at least in the United States and Western Europe. At the outset, an important distinction must be made between homosexuality (same-sex attraction) and homosexual lifestyle (the choice to engage actively in homosexual activity).[4] Neither Jesus nor the Church teach that homosexuality (same-sex attraction) is morally problematic—but only engaging in homosexual activity or lifestyle. The *Catechism of the Catholic Church* notes the following:

> [Homosexuals] must be accepted with respect, compassion, and sensitivity. Every sign of unjust discrimination in their regard should be avoided.[5]

---

[3] See *CCC* 1857–60.

[4] There are many terms used to refer to homosexual orientation, such as "gay" or "LGBQTI", but I have chosen to use "homosexuality" throughout this section, because it is the preferred usage in psychological, psychoanalytic, and biological studies, as well as the Christian Scriptures. The Church is not opposed to using these other terms—indeed, Pope Francis has publicly used the term "gay" on various occasions. See, for example, Rachel Donadio, "On Gay Priests, Pope Francis Asks, 'Who Am I to Judge?'", *New York Times*, July 29, 2013, http://www.nytimes.com/2013/07/30/world/europe/pope-francis-gay-priests.html.

[5] *CCC* 2358.

Those with same-sex attraction face a host of challenges from various segments of society. Everyone within the Church should be respectful to them, and also minister to them as they would anyone else—yet it must be remembered that ministry entails fidelity to the truth, goodness, love, rights, and freedom revealed by God through His Son, Jesus Christ. As noted above, ministry that ignores or rejects the truth of God revealed by Jesus could be quite harmful.

Before examining Jesus' teaching, it should be noted that current scientific research indicates that there is no "gay gene", but that genetics may provide some limited contribution to homosexual orientation. According to *Scientific American*:

> The analysis, which examined the genomes of nearly half a million men and women, found that although genetics are certainly involved in who people choose to have sex with, there are no specific genetic predictors.... When the researchers looked at the overall genetic similarity of individuals who had had a same-sex experience, genetics seemed to account for between 8 and 25 percent of the behavior. The rest was presumably a result of environmental or other biological influences.[6]

Evidently, same-sex attraction arises out of a combination of factors including a minority of genetic factors combined with a majority of environmental, psychological, and other cultural factors. It can no longer be said that homosexuals are "born that way", and it should be acknowledged that nurture may be more responsible than nature for same-sex attraction.

Though sexual orientation itself seems strongly engrained and possibly fixed, the American Psychological Association has cited several studies showing that sexual orientation *identity* can be changed in some cases. Sexual orientation concerns feelings of attraction to same-sex or other-sex individuals, while sexual-orientation *identity* refers to one's self-labeling, group association, and chosen marital status. The multiple studies reviewed by the American Psychological Association showed that sexual orientation change efforts

---

[6] Sara Reardon, "Massive Study Finds No Single Genetic Cause of Same-Sex Sexual Behavior", *Scientific American*, August 29, 2019, https://www.scientificamerican.com/article/massive-study-finds-no-single-genetic-cause-of-same-sex-sexual-behavior/.

(SOCE) can be effective in changing sexual orientation identity *in some cases*:

> The available evidence of both early and recent studies suggests that although sexual orientation is unlikely to change, some individuals modified their sexual orientation *identity* (e.g., individual or group membership and affiliation, self-labeling) and other aspects of sexuality (e.g., values and behavior). They did so in a variety of ways and with varied and unpredictable outcomes, some of which were temporary. For instance, in some research, individuals, through participating in SOCE [sexual orientation change efforts], became skilled in ignoring or tolerating their same-sex attractions. Some individuals reported that they went on to lead outwardly heterosexual lives, developing a sexual relationship with an "other sex" partner, and adopting a heterosexual identity.[7]

These studies indicate that some homosexuals who are strongly motivated may be able to choose reconfiguration of their sexual orientation identity, allowing for either heterosexual marriage or a celibate lifestyle. Can such individuals be truly happy and fulfilled? Some can, according to their self-reporting, but they indicate varying degrees of satisfaction and perceptions of success.[8] There are several support groups, such as Courage, to help homosexuals find community and sustain their choice of celibacy or reconfiguration of sexual orientation identity (see below in this section).[9]

There are significant difficulties with the homosexual lifestyle (not homosexuality) that could present personal, relational, and religious challenges. Though these difficulties may not arise in some

---

[7] Judith M. Glassgold et al., *Report of the American Psychological Association Task Force on Appropriate Therapeutic Responses to Sexual Orientation* (Washington, D.C.: American Psychological Association, 2009), pp. 3–4, http://www.apa.org/pi/lgbt/resources/therapeutic-response.pdf.

[8] According to the task force of the American Psychological Association on appropriate therapeutic responses to sexual orientation, "Finally, most individuals in studies of SOCE [sexual orientation change efforts] have tried multiple ways to change their sexual orientation, ranging from individual psychotherapy to religiously oriented groups, over long periods of time and with varying degrees of satisfaction and varying perceptions of success." Ibid., p. 45.

[9] See, for example, the website of Courage, which helps people with same-sex attraction find support, a deep spiritual life, and if desired, a refocusing of their sexual orientation identity: https://couragerc.org/. There are several other Catholic homosexual support groups that can be accessed by a simple Google search of "Catholic Homosexual Support Groups".

homosexual relationships, their prevalence and negative consequences are significant enough to warrant explanation and warning. We will present some survey data on these challenges after a brief explanation of the homosexual lifestyle in the Old and New Testaments.

A. Homosexual Behavior in the Old and New Testaments

The Old Testament is quite clear on this subject and includes homosexual activity in the list of sexual offenses precluded by the Levitical code (see Lev 18:22; 20:13). The New Testament also prohibits the homosexual lifestyle in its general lists of sins endangering salvation (see Rom 1:26–27; 1 Cor 6:9; and 1 Tim 1:10). Jesus did not explicitly prohibit homosexual activity, but as with premarital sex, He implicitly teaches against it in his prohibition of *porneia* in Mark 7:21–22. When this is combined with Jesus' definition of marriage and His view of adultery, it is quite likely that He intended to prohibit all sexual activity outside of the marital covenant (extramarital sex, premarital sex, and homosexual activity).

Let us begin with Jesus' teaching in Mark 7:21–22, in which *porneia* is explicitly prohibited. Recall from Chapter 1 (Section V) that *porneia* very likely refers to sexual activity outside of marriage and includes the offenses prohibited by the Levitical code. Since homosexual behavior is "sexual activity outside of marriage" and is specifically prohibited by the Levitical code (see above), Jesus' use of *porneia* very probably includes it.

It may prove helpful to review the rationale for our inference that *porneia* refers to sexual activity outside of the marital covenant (given in Chapter 1, Section V). Our argument is based on Jesus' teachings on marriage and adultery. Jesus teaches the Creator's will for marriage as follows:

> Have you not read that he who made them from the beginning [the Creator] made them male and female, and said, "For this reason a man shall leave his father and mother and be joined to his wife, and the two shall become one"? So they are no longer two but one. What therefore God has joined together, let no man put asunder. (Mt 19:4–6; Jesus is quoting Gen 1:27; 2:24)

The implication is clear—that marriage is to take place between one man and one woman as an exclusive, permanent commitment. This interpretation is evident from the apostles' subsequent question: "Why then did Moses command one to give a certificate of divorce, and to put her away?" (Mt 19:7). Unless the disciples understood Jesus to mean that marriage was permanent and exclusive, they would never have asked the question.

So how does this definition of marriage help us to interpret Jesus' view of illicit sexual activity (*porneia*)? It does so when seen through the lens of Jesus' view of "adultery in the heart". In Matthew 5:28, Jesus says, "I say to you that every one who looks at a woman lustfully[10] has already committed adultery with her in his heart." In this passage, Jesus extends the notion of "illicit sexual activity" (adultery) to *anyone* (married or unmarried) who intends to engage in sexual activity with a woman outside of marriage. In Chapter 1 (Section V), we showed that this view of "adultery" (illicit sexual conduct) is not limited to men seeking illicit relationships with women. It was probably within Jesus' intention to include women seeking sexual relationships with men, men seeking relationships with men, and women seeking relationships with women. As such, it is reasonable to infer that Jesus likely viewed all sexual relationships outside of marriage—and even the intention of such relationships—to be illicit (adultery in the heart).

Saint Paul is more explicit than Jesus in his prohibition of homosexual activity. He addresses it specifically in Romans 1:18–27, 1 Corinthians 6:9–10, and 1 Timothy 1:9–10. Let's begin with the most explicit passage in Romans 1:18–27, in which he speaks about the unrighteousness of Gentiles who do not heed the law of God within their hearts (consciences):

> For the wrath of God is revealed from heaven against all ungodliness and wickedness of men who by their wickedness suppress the truth. For what can be known about God is plain to them, because God has shown it to them. Ever since the creation of the world his invisible nature, namely, his eternal power and deity, has been clearly perceived in the things that have been made. So they are without excuse;

---

[10] Recall from Chapter 1 that this term, according to Viviano, refers to intending to have a sexual relationship with a woman outside of marriage.

for although they knew God they did not honor him as God or give thanks to him, but they became futile in their thinking and their senseless minds were darkened. Claiming to be wise, they became fools, and exchanged the glory of the immortal God for images resembling mortal man or birds or animals or reptiles. Therefore God gave them up in the lusts of their hearts to impurity, to the dishonoring of their bodies among themselves, because they exchanged the truth about God for a lie and worshiped and served the creature rather than the Creator, who is blessed forever! Amen. For this reason, God gave them up to dishonorable passions. Their women exchanged natural relations for unnatural, and the men likewise gave up natural relations with women and were consumed with passion for one another, men committing shameless acts with men and receiving in their own persons the due penalty for their error.

For Saint Paul, homosexual activity was an offense not only within Judaism and Christianity, but also within the Gentile population, because it goes against God's will for sexuality, which can be known by all people in their conscience. Hence, all people can be held accountable for engaging in homosexual activity. Such activity leaves us vulnerable to other serious sins.[11] As will be explained below, God's will for sexuality can be inferred from nature—specifically through the complementarity of men's and women's bodies for sexual union, procreation, and marital unity. The words "gave them up" in the above passage imply "He let us separate ourselves from Him." He sees this happening through the practice of homosexual activity on two levels:

1. He lets those who reject His will separate themselves from Him (He "gave them up") by their practice of "impurity" (immorality) in "their bodies" (v. 24).

2. He lets those who reject His will separate themselves from Him (He "gave them up") by their practice of dishonorable passions—lesbian activity and male homosexual activity—which is its own penalty, because separation from Him leaves us vulnerable to the sins Paul mentions in verses 29–31.

[11] See Joseph A. Fitzmyer, "The Letter to the Romans", in *The New Jerome Biblical Commentary*, ed. Raymond E. Brown, Joseph A. Fitzmyer, and Roland E. Murphy (Englewood Cliffs, N.J.: Prentice Hall, 1990), p. 836.

So, what is Saint Paul saying? He is saying that homosexual behavior is a manifestation of our rejection of God's intention for creation, just as idolatry is a manifestation of our rejection of the true transcendent God for a worldly image. Just as the true God (the transcendent Creator) should be apparent to anyone who opens themselves to the glories of Heaven and earth, so also God's intention for sexuality should be apparent to anyone open to the complementarity of men's and women's bodies for sexual union, procreation, and marital unity. Thus, both idolatry (the worship of mere images of animals and men) and homosexual behavior (sexuality contrary to the intention of the Creator, manifest in male and female complementarity) are rejections of God's intention that separates us from Him, leaving us vulnerable to darkness and evil.

If Saint Paul believes that homosexual behavior manifests our rejection of God's intention for creation separating us from Him (leaving us vulnerable to evil), it can hardly be imagined that he is not advocating its sinfulness. Indeed, this text implies his belief that homosexual behavior is seriously sinful and dangerous to our salvation. Since Paul believed that the sinfulness of homosexual behavior is applicable to everyone, it includes Jews, Gentiles, and Christians. This conviction was supported by his understanding of homosexual behavior in the Levitical code as well as the moral teachings of Jesus. As such, we as Christians should take seriously Paul's teaching that homosexual behavior is seriously sinful, endangering our salvation.

Some commentators believe that Romans 1:18–27 is not addressing homosexual behavior, but rather, heterosexuals who have abandon their *natural* desires for aberrant ones. For example, John Boswell contends:

> The persons Paul condemns are manifestly not homosexual: what he derogates are homosexual acts committed by apparently heterosexual persons. The whole point of Romans 1, in fact, is to stigmatize persons who have rejected their calling, gotten off the true path they were once on.[12]

---

[12]John Boswell, *Christianity, Social Tolerance and Homosexuality* (Chicago: University of Chicago Press, 1980), p. 335.

Boswell's interpretation of "natural" (*phusikēn/phusikos*) seems at first to be fair, because *phusikos* can refer to the natural propensity or instinct of an animal or man.[13] However, this is not its primary definition in New Testament (mostly Pauline) usage. The primary definition is "according to nature".[14] The meaning of this phrase requires an investigation of Hellenistic philosophical thought that permeated the milieu of Paul's Gentile audience. Saint Paul was quite familiar with Hellenistic thought and used it liberally in his letters.

So, what was the Hellenistic understanding of *phusikos* (natural) derived from *phusis* (nature)? We can here summarize only the major points in this extensive idea. Gerard Naddaf has written a work on the philosophical background of *phusis* that made its way into Hellenistic thought and writing.[15] Central to the idea of *phusis* is *telos* (end), from which we derive "teleology". In Platonic, Neo-Platonic, and Aristotelian thought, "nature" was thought to be oriented toward an end—"what it was meant to be." For both Plato and Aristotle, this end or objective of something's nature occurs by divine intent (Plato and Neo-Platonism) or by the ultimate "final cause"—God (Aristotle).[16] This idea of divine intention/causation in nature made its way into Hellenistic thought, and through it into the mindset of Saint Paul and his Gentile audience.

So, what was Saint Paul's intention in using *phusikanē* (natural) in Romans 1:26–27? Did he have in mind the instinct or the propensity of a person (as Boswell contends) or the divine intent in the nature of sexuality? The context of Paul's usage answers the question quite clearly—it refers to the divine intention inscribed in the nature of sexuality. Consider the following two points:

- "Ever since the creation of the world [God's] invisible nature, namely, his eternal power and deity, has been clearly perceived in the things that have been made" (vs. 20). This passage implies

---

[13] See *Strong's Concordance*, s.v. "5446: phusikos": "governed by (the instincts of) nature: ζῷα γεγεννημένα φυσικά, 2 Peter 2:12 (R. V. born mere animals)", BibleHub.com, 2021, https://biblehub.com/greek/5446.htm.

[14] Ibid.

[15] Gerard Naddaf, *The Greek Concept of Nature* (New York: State University of New York Press, 2005).

[16] See ibid., pp. 17–19, 31–34, 52–54, 65–74.

that nature reveals God's intention, and God's intention reveals Himself.

- "For this reason God gave them up to dishonorable passions. Their women exchanged natural relations for unnatural" (v. 26). The term "relations" is a translation of the Greek *chrésin* from *chrésis*, which means "use or function in a sexual sense".[17] The two words "natural use" suggest the proper use of sexuality according to its nature. Notice that "natural" is not modifying the person practicing homosexual activity but rather the "use or function of sexuality".

These contextual observations show that Paul is not speaking about the propensity or instinct of a particular *person*, but rather about the nature (proper telos—end) of *sexuality itself*. Recall from above that the proper end (nature) of something implies divine intention or causation in designing that nature. And so, the proper interpretation of "natural" in this passage is "the divine intention inscribed in the nature of sexuality". This view of "natural" would have been part of Paul's Hellenistic background, and his argument in the above passage supports this interpretation of it.

Though Saint Paul does not say it, the divine intention in creating sexuality can be known from the design of creation itself (see Rom 1:20 above). In view of this, Paul believes that God's intention in designing sexuality can be recognized in the complementarity of men's and women's bodies not only for sexual union and procreation, but also for the marital covenant itself. So, what does this mean for the interpretation of Romans 1:18–27? Paul is not addressing whether homosexual behavior is "natural" to a particular person, but rather whether it is unnatural in relation to God's intention for sexuality manifest in the complementary design of men's and women's bodies for sexual union, procreation, and the marital covenant. For Paul, it really doesn't matter whether one is naturally homosexual or heterosexual; the pursuit of sexual relationships opposed to the Creator's intention is the problem, because it expresses the willingness to reject God's intention (will)

---

[17] *Strong's Concordance*, s.v. "5540: chrésis", BibleHub.com, 2021, https://biblehub.com/greek/5540.htm.

for creation, which separates us from Him (leaving us vulnerable to spiritual darkness and evil). Inasmuch as Paul has correctly discerned the will of God, we should be quite wary of moving in the direction of homosexual behavior and lifestyle. This is borne out in the studies given below (Section I.B).

It should be noted that Paul's motive for writing the above passage is *not* homophobia. He is not out to "stigmatize" people with same-sex attraction, but rather sincerely seeking to save those who are practicing idolatry and homosexual behavior. For him, acting against God's intention for creation is like acting against God Himself, which is similar to a rejection of God. This (at least implicit) rejection of God separates us from Him, leaving us open to spiritual darkness and our spiritual enemy.

Let's now move to the second passage in which homosexual behavior is prohibited, 1 Corinthians 6:9–10:

> Do you not know that the unrighteous will not inherit the kingdom of God? Do not be deceived: Neither the sexually immoral [*pornoi*], nor idolaters, nor adulterers, nor men who have sex with men [*arsenokoitai* and *malakoi*], nor thieves, nor the greedy, nor drunkards, nor revilers, nor robbers will inherit the kingdom of God. (NIV)

Pornoi comes from the same root as *porneia—porne*. As noted above, it refers to any form of sexual activity outside of marriage as well as sexual activity prohibited by the Deuteronomic and Levitical codes (including homosexual behavior). As he continues his list, he specifically mentions *arsenokoitai*, which means literally male/man (*arsên*) plus "bedding with" (*koitai*) men. This word is used in the Septuagint Greek translation of the Old Testament to refer to sins of homosexual activity prohibited in the Levitical code (see Lev 18:22; 20:13). Thus, it almost certainly refers to homosexual activity. Saint Paul also uses the word *malakoi* in his list of sins, which at the time referred to male prostitutes or "call-boys". However, Paul probably did not mean it in this restricted way, and it likely refers to the passive partner in a homosexual relationship.[18] Paul's prohibition of these sins is serious,

---

[18] See Robin Scroggs, *The New Testament and Homosexuality* (Philadelphia: Fortress Press, 1983), p. 42.

and he warns that practicing them (without attempting to stop) could jeopardize salvation.

The Pauline author[19] of 1 Timothy also shares Saint Paul's view of the danger of a homosexual lifestyle to one's salvation:

> The law is good, if any one uses it lawfully, understanding this, that the law is not laid down for the just but for for the lawless and disobedient, for the ungodly and sinners, for the unholy and profane, for murderers of fathers and murderers of mothers, for manslayers, immoral persons, sodomites, kidnapers, liars, perjurers, and whatever else is contrary to sound doctrine, in accordance with the glorious gospel of the blessed God with which I have been entrusted. (1:9–10)

We have already discussed the meaning of *pornois* and *arsenokoitais* above, and it is clear that the Pauline author of the pastoral letter agrees with his mentor, Saint Paul, about the danger of homosexual activity.

An objective reading of the texts presented above shows considerable unanimity among the Levitical code and the teachings of Jesus, Saint Paul, and the author of 1 Timothy about the danger posed by homosexual activity to our spiritual life.

Is this teaching by Jesus and particularly by Saint Paul anachronistic—that is, outdated and not applicable in today's culture and society in the same way as in the first-century Middle East? Though there may be some anachronistic elements, such as ignorance of the nonchosen, naturally caused dimension of homosexuality (same-sex attraction), the above prohibitions are not focused on sexual attraction or orientation, but on homosexual activity itself. The reason for the prohibition of homosexual *activity* is rooted in Jesus' and Saint Paul's view that this conduct is contrary to the will of the Creator. God does not issue a prohibition arbitrarily—without a good reason. For Jesus, this reason is always linked to justice and *agapē* love—the intention and action to give one's self for the good of another, and in the case of marital love, to give one's self permanently, exclusively, and self-sacrificially for the good of one's spouse

---

[19] According to Robert Wild, S.J., "If Paul were the actual author of the Pastorals, the above chronological reconstruction would then need to be fitted into the full history of the apostle. However, although there is not complete unanimity on the matter, since the early 19th cent. very many exegetes have argued that these letters are the pseudonymous creations of a later follower of Paul." Robert Wild, S.J., "Pastoral Letters," *The New Jerome Biblical Commentary* (Englewood Cliffs, NJ: Prentice Hall, 1990), p. 892.

and children. If this rationale underlies God's (and Jesus') intention for creation and prohibition of homosexual activity, then the prohibition is not merely anachronistic, for it applies in the same way today as it did in the first-century Middle East. Are there any indications that a homosexual lifestyle is inconsistent with the intention to give one's self for the good of one's spouse and children permanently, exclusively, and self-sacrificially? If so, do these inconsistencies pose challenges to spiritual life as well as permanent exclusive commitment and family life? Does a homosexual lifestyle give rise to increased depression, anxiety, and substance abuse? Does it make us vulnerable to other deadly sins and our spiritual enemy? These will be considered in the next section.

B. Studies of the Effects of the Homosexual Lifestyle

Recent studies indicate several challenges of the homosexual lifestyle. We will examine two areas of negative impact substantiated by statistical studies:

1. The impact of the homosexual lifestyle on emotional health (Section I.B.1)
2. Incongruities between the Christian objective of sexuality and the homosexual lifestyle (Section I.B.2)

1. The Impact of the Homosexual Lifestyle on Emotional Health

There is significant scholarly and scientific literature addressing the impact of homosexual behavior on emotional health, but I will limit myself to the studies in the archives of general psychiatry cited by Richard P. Fitzgibbons, M.D., and others in the *National Catholic Bioethics Quarterly*.[20] Fitzgibbons and the others in the study summarized the findings of multiple articles from the archives of general psychiatry that show the negative impact of the homosexual lifestyle

---

[20] See Richard P. Fitzgibbons, Philip M. Sutton, and Dale O'Leary, "The Psychopathology of 'Sex Reassignment' Surgery: Assessing Its Medical, Psychological, and Ethical Appropriateness", *National Catholic Bioethics Quarterly* 9, no. 1 (Spring 2009): 116, http://lc.org/PDFs/Attachments2PRsLAs/2018/061118SexReasssignmentSurgery.pdf.

on emotional health.[21] The following table compares heterosexuals with homosexuals (both men and women) in four dimensions of emotional health: major depression, panic disorder, drug dependency, and at least one psychiatric disorder.

Table 1. Prevalence (%) of Mental Health Disorders
by Gender and Sexual Orientation

	Men		Women	
	Heterosexual	Gay/ Bisexual	Heterosexual	Lesbian/ Bisexual
Major depression	10.2	31.0	16.8	33.5
Panic disorder	3.8	17.9	8.6	17.1
Drug dependence	2.7	9.2	1.5	6.5
At least one disorder	16.7	39.8	24.6	43.7

Source: Cochran, Sullivan, and Mays, "Prevalence of Mental Disorders", p. 56.

[21] Richard Herrell et al., "Sexual Orientation and Suicidality: A Co-Twin Control Study in Adult Men", *Archives of General Psychiatry* 56, no. 10 (October 1999): 867–74; David M. Fergusson, L. John Horwood, and Annette L. Beautrais, "Is Sexual Orientation Related to Mental Health Problems and Suicidality in Young People?", *Archives of General Psychiatry* 56, no. 10 (October 1999): 876–80; Theo Sandfort et al., "Same-Sex Sexual Behavior and Psychiatric Disorders: Findings from the Netherlands Mental Health Survey and Incidence Study (NEMESIS)", *Archives of General Psychiatry* 58, no. 1 (January 2001): 85–91; Stephen E. Gilman et al., "Risk of Psychiatric Disorders among Individuals Reporting Same-Sex Sexual Partners in a National Comorbidity Survey", *American Journal of Public Health* 91, no. 6 (June 2001): 933–39; Susan D. Cochran, J. Greer Sullivan, and Vickie M. Mays, "Prevalence of Mental Disorders, Psychological Distress, and Mental Health Services Use among Lesbian, Gay, and Bisexual Adults in the United States", *Journal of Consulting and Clinical Psychology* 71, no. 1 (February 2003): 53–61; Keren Skegg et al., "Sexual Orientation and Self-Harm in Men and Women", *American Journal of Psychiatry* 160, no. 3 (March 2003): 541–46; Kimberly F. Balsam et al., "Mental Health of Lesbian, Gay, Bisexual and Heterosexual Siblings: Effects of Gender, Sexual Orientation, and Family", *Journal of Abnormal Psychology* 114, no. 3 (August 2005): 471–76; Theo Sandfort et al., "Sexual Orientation and Mental and Physical Health Status", *American Journal of Public Health* 96, no. 6 (June 2006): 1119–25; Susan D. Cochran and Vickie M. Mays, "Physical Health Complaints among Lesbians, Gay Men, and Bisexual and Homosexually Experienced Heterosexual Individuals: Results from the California Quality of Life Survey", *American Journal of Public Health* 97, no. 11 (November 2007): 2048–55; and Michael King, "A Systemic Review of Mental Disorder, Suicide, and Deliberate Self Harm in Lesbian, Gay and Homosexual People", *BMC Psychiatry* 8, no. 70 (2008): 1–17. Cochran and her associates state that lesbians, gays, and bisexuals "use mental health services more and are at a higher risk for suicidal ideation, suicide attempts and self-injurious behavior than heterosexual siblings".

We might explain the statistics in the above table as follows:

- With respect to major *depression*, homosexual men have three times more major depression than heterosexual men, and lesbians have double the rate of major depression as heterosexual women.
- With respect to *panic disorder*, homosexual men have about five times more incidence of panic disorder than heterosexual men, and lesbians have two times the incidence of panic disorder than heterosexual women.
- With respect to *drug dependence*, homosexual men have about three and a half times more drug dependence than heterosexual men, and lesbians have about four times the incidence of drug dependence as heterosexual women.
- With respect to having *at least one psychiatric disorder*, homosexual men have about two and a half times the incidence of psychiatric disorders than heterosexual men, and lesbians have about double the incidence of psychiatric disorders as heterosexual women.

It might be thought that these much higher negative impacts are attributable mostly to social stigmatization of gays and lesbians within the culture. No doubt, social stigmatization plays a role in these increased percentages, but it is not the sole reason for them. As Fitzgibbons and the others in the study point out:

> Some claim that these problems are caused by societal rejection; however, if this were the case, one would expect to see significantly fewer problems among those who live in tolerant countries such as the Netherlands and New Zealand, but psychological maladjustment levels are similarly high in these countries.[22]

The most disturbing statistic is the overall rate of suicidality in homosexual men. Homosexual men experience a five to seven times increased rate of suicidality than the heterosexual population. The breakdown is as follows:

[22] Fitzgibbons, Sutton, and O'Leary, "Psychopathology", p. 116, citing Sandfort et al., "Same-Sex Sexual Behavior", Sandfort et al., "Sexual Orientation", and Fergusson, Horwood, and Beautrais, "Suicidality in Young People".

- *Death wishes*—26.8 percent (homosexual population) vs. 5.8 percent (heterosexual population), almost five times higher
- *Suicide contemplation*—40.2 percent (homosexual population) vs. 7.8 percent (heterosexual population), over five times higher
- *Deliberate self-harm*—14.6 percent (homosexual population) vs. 2.0 percent (heterosexual population), over seven times higher[23]

The fact that *40 percent* (nearly half) of the homosexual population (in a tolerant milieu like the Netherlands) is contemplating suicide should give pause to anyone considering this lifestyle.

As noted above, this study occurred in the Netherlands, where the climate of acceptance is very high, lessening the likelihood that suicidality is caused by social stigmatization. No doubt social stigmatization plays a part in this significantly higher rate of suicidality, but it is most unlikely to be the sole reason. The lifestyle itself—with exponentially larger rates of sexual partners, significantly less duration of relationships, and significantly less monogamy—is likely to be significant, because it points to a lack of fulfillment in love as well as the important qualities coming from committed generative friendships (see below Section I.C.4).

Furthermore, though the acceptance of homosexuality and the homosexual lifestyle has increased considerably over the last three decades, the rates of depression and anxiety among LGBT youth have continued to remain very high (in comparison with heterosexual peers).[24] This provokes the question asked by Stephen Russel and Jessica Fish:

Today's lesbian, gay, bisexual, and transgender (LGBT) youth come out at younger ages, and public support for LGBT issues has dramatically increased, so why do LGBT youth continue to be at high risk for compromised mental health?[25]

[23] See Ron de Graaf, Theo G. M. Sandfort, and Margreet ten Have, "Suicidality and Sexual Orientation: Differences between Men and Women in a General Population-Based Sample from the Netherlands", *Archives of Sexual Behavior* 35 (2006): 253–62, https://link.springer .com/article/10.1007/s10508-006-9020-z.

[24] See Stephen T. Russell and Jessica N. Fish, "Mental Health in Lesbian, Gay, Bisexual, and Transgender (LGBT) Youth", *Annual Review of Clinical Psychology* 12 (2016): 465–87, https://www.ncbi.nlm.nih.gov/pmc/articles/PMC4887282/.

[25] Abstract in ibid.

Though continued social stigmatization plays a part in the high levels of depression, anxiety, and suicidality of LGBT youth (particularly their sense of "minority stress"),[26] there are other reasons for anxiety, perhaps related to "coming out" and the lifestyle itself. In any case, factors related to coming out and lifestyles cannot be ignored, given the increased acceptance of LGBT youth over the years.

When the above statistics showing the significantly higher rates of depression and anxiety among homosexual *adults* (in comparison with heterosexual adults) in the most tolerant countries is combined with the continued high rates of depression among LGBT youth over the years, it seems likely that the homosexual lifestyle itself (described below in section I.B.2) is at least partially responsible for the significantly high rates of depression, anxiety, and psychological disorders among homosexual men and women. If this is the case, young people should be informed of the potential consequences of a homosexual lifestyle before they "come out" and enter into that lifestyle. They should also be informed of alternatives to the lifestyle. Organizations like Courage International provide faith-based community support to live a life commensurate with the teachings of Jesus and the Church (see below Section I.C.5).

2. Incongruities between the Christian Objective of Sexuality and the Homosexual Lifestyle

There are several incongruities between the homosexual lifestyle and the Christian ideal for sexual love. As explained in Chapter 1 (Section I), *eros* (sexual love) is reserved for one man and one woman within a permanent exclusive commitment. Thus, the ideal for Christian sexual love is

- one spouse (one sexual partner),
- permanently committed (lifetime), and
- exclusively committed (monogamous).

Homosexual relationships (in contrast to heterosexual ones) are significantly out of line with these ideals. First, with respect to the

---

[26] See "Mental Health in LGBT Youth", in ibid.

number of sexual partners, the 1997 study by Paul Van de Ven and others of 2,583 older homosexuals (reported in the *Journal of Sex Research*) found the following:

- *Number of sexual partners.* The modal range of sexual partners in homosexual relationships was between 101 and 500. Additionally, 10.2 percent of those studied had between 501 and 1,000 sexual partners. About 13 percent indicated that they had had more than 1,000 lifetime sexual partners.[27] The Van de Ven study showed fewer sexual partners than an earlier Alan Bell and Martin Weinberg (1978) study prior to the Aids epidemic. The earlier study reported the following statistics for white male homosexuals: 43 percent had more than 500 sexual partners and 28 percent had more than 1,000 sexual partners.[28] In contrast to this, the National Center for Health Statistics found in 2007 that the median number of lifetime sexual partners (before and after marriage) for heterosexual men is 7 and the median for women is 4.[29] We might surmise that the reason for this significantly reduced rate of male sex partners is men's concern for their wives and children within marriage relationships, and women's connection of sexual satisfaction with emotional quality and child-bearing needs. Without this feminine, familial, and heterosexual marital component, the number of sexual partners seems to exponentially increase.
- *Duration of relationship.* We must distinguish between unmarried and married committed relationships. With respect to unmarried homosexual relationships, as may be adduced from the large

---

[27] Paul Van de Ven et al., "A Comparative Demographic and Sexual Profile of Older Homosexually Active Men", *Journal of Sex Research* 34, no. 4 (1997): 349–60, https://www .jstor.org/stable/3813477.

[28] Alan P. Bell and Martin S. Weinberg, *Homosexualities: A Study of Diversity among Men and Women* (New York: Simon and Schuster, 1978), pp. 308–9. See also Alan P. Bell, Martin S. Weinberg, and Sue Kiefer Hammersmith, *Sexual Preference* (Bloomington: Indiana University Press, 1981).

[29] Cheryl D. Fryar et al., "Drug Use and Sexual Behaviors Reported by Adults: United States, 1999–2002", *Advance Data from Vital and Health Statistics*, no. 384 (Hyattsville, Md.: National Center for Health Statistics, 2007), pp. 10, 12, https://www.cdc.gov/nchs/data/ad /ad384.pdf.

number of homosexual partners (noted above), a high percentage of homosexual encounters are "transactional" (a one-night stand or slightly longer). Of those which are "relational" (seeking something more intimate or long-term), Michael Pollak (1985), and Marcel Saghir and Eli Robins (1973) found that the average duration of homosexual relationships is two years.[30] With respect to unmarried heterosexual (cohabiting) relationships, those relationships that do not result in marriage last only about two years (about the same as homosexual relationships). However, twice as many heterosexual relationships are likely to result in marriage than homosexual relationships, meaning that heterosexual cohabiting relationships last longer than homosexual ones. With respect to committed relationships that result in marriage, Michael Rosenfeld has developed an index to compare longevity of heterosexual couples with that of same-sex couples. In brief, Rosenfeld shows that a little more than twice as many heterosexual couples marry compared with same-sex couples (74.8% compared to 35%), that heterosexual relationships last 33% longer, and that the heterosexual breakup rate is one-half that of homosexual couples. About 50% of heterosexual marriages will last a lifetime (conservatively 35 years), and 66% will last for ten years or longer.[31]

- *Monogamy of relationships.* A 2003 Canadian study reported that only 25 percent of homosexual relationships lasting more than one year were monogamous—75 percent had multiple partners.[32] With respect to homosexual marriages, a study by Jeffery Parsons and others (*Journal of Family Psychology*) shows that 52% of homosexual marriages are monogamous while 48% are

---

[30] Michael Pollak, "Male Homosexuality", in *Western Sexuality: Practice and Precept in Past and Present Times*, ed. Philippe Ariès and André Béjin, trans. Anthony Forster (New York: B. Blackwell, 1985), pp. 40–61. See Marcel T. Saghir and Eli Robins, *Male and Female Homosexuality* (Baltimore: Williams and Wilkins, 1973), p. 225.

[31] Michael J. Rosenfeld, "Couple Longevity in the Era of Same-Sex Marriage in the U.S.", *Journal of Marriage and Family* 76 (2017): 905–18, http://web.stanford.edu/~mrosenfe/Rosenfeld_Couple_Longevity_Forthcoming_JMF.pdf.

[32] Ryan Lee, "Gay Couples Likely to Try Non-monogamy, Study Shows,", *Washington Blade*, August 22, 2003.

not.[33] In contrast to this, the monogamy rate in "committed heterosexual relationships" is much higher. Recall from Chapter I (Section III) that 21 percent of heterosexual men and 19 percent of heterosexual women are unfaithful to their marital partners[34] (and therefore 79 percent of heterosexual men and 81 percent of heterosexual women are faithful and monogamous within marriage). Though there was a significant increase in heterosexual infidelity over the forty years of the sexual revolution, it is considerably lower than the rate of nonmonogamy reported by homosexuals in committed relationships.

The above statistics indicate that the homosexual lifestyle deviates very significantly from the ideal of marriage (relationships) taught by Jesus—permanent, exclusive, committed relationships for the sake of spouse and children. As such, it points to a lifestyle moving away from covenant love and the heart of Jesus, which may explain the significantly higher rates of depression, anxiety, psychological disorders, and substance abuse detailed above (Section I.B). The negative impact of this lifestyle is not limited to emotional and psychological health but extends to spiritual well-being. Recall from Volume I (Chapter 4) of this Trilogy how the Evil One incites us to separate ourselves from the Lord. First, he tempts us to move away from the Lord's teaching, then presents us with rationalization to support our sinful conduct. These rationalizations are not only part of his temptations but also firmly embedded in the culture. When our consciences have been sufficiently anesthetized, he then presents "opportunities" to increase our sinful conduct along with additional rationalizations to justify further separation. The more we pursue these "opportunities", the more we open ourselves to his influence and close ourselves off to the influence of God.

If the above conjectures are correct, then we would expect to find significantly decreased religious commitment among homosexual men and women than among the heterosexual population. This is

---

[33] Jeffery Parsons, T. Starks, K. Gamaarel, and C. Grov, "Non-monogamy and Sexual Relationship Quality among Same-Sex Male Couples", *Journal of Family Psychology* 26(5) (October 2012): 669-77, https://pubmed.ncbi.nlm.nih.gov/22906124/.

[34] See Peter Moore, "1 in 5 Americans Say They've Been Unfaithful", YouGov.com, June 2, 2015, https://today.yougov.com/topics/lifestyle/articles-reports/2015/06/02/men-more-likely-think-cheating.

precisely what was found by Pew Research Center's 2014 Religious Landscape Study,[35] which delineated its results as follows:

- *Atheism and non-religious affiliation.* In the homosexual population, 41 percent identify as atheist, or nonreligiously affiliated in comparison to 22 percent of the heterosexual population. Therefore, homosexuals are about twice as likely to be nonreligiously affiliated as heterosexuals.
- *Regular religious service attendance.* Approximately 16 percent of homosexuals regularly attend religious services in comparison to 36 percent of the heterosexual population. Therefore, heterosexuals are twice as likely to attend regular church services as homosexuals.
- *Acknowledgement of Scripture as the Word of God.* Approximately 33 percent of homosexuals acknowledge Scripture as the Word of God compared to 61 percent of the heterosexual population. Thus, heterosexuals are about twice as likely as homosexuals to acknowledge Scripture as the Word of God.
- *Religion as important to life.* Approximately 34 percent of homosexuals indicate that religion is important to their lives in comparison with 54 percent of the heterosexual population. Therefore, heterosexuals are about one and a half times more likely than homosexuals to consider religion as important to life.

Though there may be other factors affecting the above differences in religious affiliation and practice (such as homosexuals feeling less welcomed at religious services), the above statistics show that religious disbelief in the homosexual population goes beyond religious affiliation and practice, indicating that homosexuals are much less likely to believe that religion is important in life and that Scripture is the Word of God. At the very least, the statistics indicate that the homosexual lifestyle may be detrimental not only to religious affiliation and practice but also to spiritual well-being.

We conclude from the above that the homosexual lifestyle has a significant negative impact on emotional health and spiritual well-being.

[35] Philip Schwadel and Aleksandra Sandstrom, "Lesbian, Gay and Bisexual Americans Are Less Religious Than Straight Adults by Traditional Measures", Pew Research Center, May 24, 2019, https://www.pewresearch.org/fact-tank/2019/05/24/lesbian-gay-and-bisexual-americans-are-less-religious-than-straight-adults-by-traditional-measures/.

With respect to emotional health, it correlates with substantially higher rates of depression, anxiety, panic disorder, psychological disorders, substance abuse, and suicidality (with 40 percent of the population considering suicide). With respect to spiritual well-being, it is incongruous with the implicit teaching of Jesus, the explicit teaching of Saint Paul, and the ideal of Christian sexual love, giving rise to exponentially higher rates of sexual partners along with substantially shorter duration of relationships and significantly less monogamy. Furthermore, it correlates with a significant reduction in religious affiliation and practice among the homosexual population. In sum, these findings show the likelihood that the homosexual lifestyle will correlate with significant reductions in emotional health, Christian practice, and spiritual well-being, implying that the Christian prohibition of the homosexual lifestyle has significant beneficial consequences for this life and the next.

How can we help and support our brothers and sisters with same-sex attraction? First, we must refrain from judging them, for as noted above, we do not know the impulses and pressures they feel, and we certainly do not know the state of their souls (for example, whether they have full consent of the will—*no* impediments to the free use of their wills). Beyond this, we should be respectful by genuinely according them the full dignity that belongs to them by nature, loving them as Jesus loves all of us.

Secondly, we should do everything we can to help and encourage these "beloveds of Christ" to stay on the path to salvation. This means encouraging them to recognize both their unique goodness and lovability before Christ and the emotional and spiritual dangers inherent in the homosexual lifestyle. This may be difficult for parents relating to children or friends relating to friends, but failure to do this is not loving, because love always seeks the good—particularly the eternal good—of the other. So how can we best point to the truth in love (the eternal good of the other) with loving respect in the heart of Christ? This will be addressed in the next section.

C. Sources of Encouragement on the Path to Christ

In this section, I recommend the following fivefold approach to support friends or family members with same-sex attraction:

1. To read Father Michael Schmitz's book *Made for Love*[36] (Section I.C.1)
2. To present the major dangers of the homosexual lifestyle, particularly regarding emotional health and spiritual well-being (Section I.C.2)
3. To encourage the strengthening of Catholic spiritual life (Section I.C.3)
4. To present material on the profundity of Christian friendship (*philia*) prescinding from sexual love (*eros*) (Section I.C.4)
5. To introduce those with same-sex attraction to supportive Catholic communities, such as Courage International (Section I.C.5)

1. Father Michael Schmitz's Book Made for Love

Father Michael Schmitz's book *Made for Love* is an excellent way to contextualize a discussion with family and friends who have same-sex attraction. He emphasizes throughout the book that all of us are the same in our embodied-ensouled natures, which are oriented toward love. As a Catholic priest, Father Schmitz follows the teachings of the Catholic Church and is fully aware of the Catholic-Christian meaning of *philia* (friendship), *eros* (sexual love), and *agapē* (love without expectation of return for all human persons). He recognizes the cross that those with same-sex attraction must bear and suggests practical spiritual ways of contending with that cross while remaining faithful to the teachings of Jesus and the Catholic Church.

Father Schmitz first helps all readers to recognize our common nature and identity (as body and soul) and then shows the fallacy of identifying ourselves with only one aspect of that nature, such as same-sex attraction. He implies that there is a path to fulfillment in love without a sexual component, emphasizing profound committed friendships of mutual care and support (see below Section I.C.4), contributive love for all human persons without expectation of reward (*agapē*), and love of God manifest in prayer. This ideal of Christian love (in imitation of Jesus) leads to sanctification and holiness through acceptance of the cross, trust in the Lord, and

---

[36]Michael Schmitz, *Made for Love: Same-Sex Attraction and the Catholic Church* (San Francisco: Ignatius Press, 2017).

purification of our interior being. In reminding all readers of the broad Christian meaning of nature, identity, love, and fulfillment, Father Schmitz helps to create a lens of self-understanding for those with same-sex attraction as well as the parents, family members, and friends who love, help, and support them. This self-understanding is grounded in the profound love of Jesus Christ, who is completely dedicated to our salvation so that His joy may be ours and our joy may be complete.

2. Presenting the Dangers to Emotional Health and Spiritual Well-Being

We have all heard the expression "buyer beware", and lifestyle choice is one of the most significant areas to which this expression pertains. As family members and friends of those with same-sex attraction, we should seek to manifest the dangers to emotional health and spiritual well-being that have been documented in Section I.B above. We would probably not hesitate to tell someone about a defect in a car or a computer they were thinking of purchasing or the detrimental side effects of a medication or a procedure they were considering, or warn them about friends who may not have their best interest in mind. Why wouldn't we want to warn people of a lifestyle that has significant emotional and spiritual dangers?

In my view, the answer lies in a misunderstanding of respect, acceptance, love, and compassion. The culture has impressed upon us that the only way to be respectful and loving to those with same-sex attraction is to accept and support them, not only in their orientation but also in the lifestyle associated with it. Though this thinking at first seems right, it is seriously flawed because it implies that respect and love require supporting someone in a lifestyle that endangers not only their emotional health and spiritual well-being in this life but also their salvation in the next. Not even pagan stoic philosophers such as Marcus Aurelias and Epictetus would have suggested this! It is inconceivable that Christ and the saints would recommend this. So why would we as Christians follow this flawed logic—this flawed understanding of love, compassion, respect, and acceptance? As Christians, it is our duty to treat everyone as our own brothers and sisters, which means letting them know about the dangers with which a particular course of action may be fraught. Yes, we must present these dangers with great sensitivity and love, careful to avoid the implication of judgment, moral high ground, or superiority, but doing so should not mitigate our explanation of what undermines and endangers our brothers and sisters. This is what it means to speak the truth in love.

To this end, I would recommend copying Section I.B and presenting it to anyone considering a homosexual lifestyle. You may get a hostile or frustrated response, implying that you are a homophobe or incapable of understanding their needs and desires, but these reactions are perfectly understandable. So, gently reassure your family member or friend that you present these dangers not because you are "holier than thou" but because you really love him. If he says, "I've heard all of these dangers before and I frankly don't care," then I would just ask him respectfully, "If you begin to experience profound emptiness, alienation, loneliness, depression, and anxiety, would you please at least talk to me so that I might be able to help you as a friend?" I would let the subject drop at this point and await the time they might return with reports of increased malaise, emptiness, and anxiety. If they are open to it, I would present the other three resources given below (Sections I.C.3–I.C.5).

3. Encouraging the Strengthening of Catholic Spiritual Life

In Volume II (Chapters 2–3) of this Trilogy, I addressed the necessity of a spiritual life as the ground of Christian love. For Catholics, this essential spiritual life has three interrelated components—sacramental life, prayer life, and moral life (examination of conscience). I noted there that such a spiritual life bestows spiritual freedom and depth. If we are faithful even to a simple spiritual life, we will be able to undertake truly difficult aspects of moral conversion and face the cross with trust and peace. To be sure, resisting temptation and facing the cross will *not* be easy, but with the freedom and grace of the spiritual life, it will be manageable, and more importantly it will lead to eternal life with Jesus Christ (see Volume II, Chapters 5–6 of this Trilogy). If we begin this process now, we will be well prepared when the challenges and crosses of life confront us, and we will gradually find ourselves embracing the life of holiness and love that Jesus promised would make our joy (and the joy of others around us) complete.

4. Profound Love and Friendship Prescinding from Eros

Some people believe that the Lord is being unreasonable in asking those with same-sex attraction to refrain from sexual expression, because it seems that He is asking them to give up the highest expression of "human to human" love. This is not the case, because the highest expression of "human to human" love can occur through *philia*. Recall from Chapter 1 (Section I) that the continuous commitment and mutual support between two parties can actualize the highest expression of committed love without *eros* (sexual expression). *Eros* can support this love (in which case it moves to public, permanent, and exclusive commitment in marriage), but *eros* is not necessary for *philia* to reach this state. A deeper probing of the nature of *philia* will help to explain this.

> *Philia* has been described extensively in pagan, Jewish, and Christian literature. Aristotle distinguishes three kinds of friendships in the *Nicomachean Ethics* (Books 8 and 9)—friendships of utility, pleasure, and "for the good". In the *Rhetoric*, Aristotle speaks specifically about unselfish friendships—friendships that seek the good of the friend without requiring compensatory good for the self.[37] Friendship is praised in the Old Testament and lauded by Ben Sira (see Sir 6:14–17; cited in Chapter 1, Section VI). With respect to the New Testament, *Strong's Concordance* defines *philos* as "a friend; someone *dearly* loved (prized) in a personal, intimate way; a trusted *confidant*, held dear in a close bond of personal affection".[38]

An accompanying note reads that

> the root (*phil-*) conveys *experiential, personal* affection—indicating 5384 (*philos*) expresses *experience-based* love.[39]

This definition captures Jesus' relationship with His disciples, particularly in the Gospel of John. In John 15:15, Jesus extends an unconditional friendship to His apostles:

---

[37] See Aristotle, *Rhetoric* 1380b36–1381a2.
[38] *Strong's Concordance*, s.v. "5384: phílos", BibleHub.com, 2021 (italics in original), https://biblehub.com/greek/5384.htm.
[39] Ibid.

No longer do I call you servants, for the servant does not know what his master is doing; but I have called you friends, for all that I have heard from my Father I have made known to you.

By giving the apostles *everything* that the Father has given Him, Jesus took friendship (a relationship of deep personal intimacy, care, and support) to its perfection.

We can probe the nature of friendship more deeply by examining how and why they develop. Friendships begin with a mutual sense of attraction, affection, and common cause, which stirs empathy and a desire for the good of the other within both parties. Friendships can stay at this level, but they can also deepen considerably if both parties increase their sense of commitment to one another. Normally, this begins with one of the parties extending an increased commitment of time, future fidelity, loyalty, energy, and resources to the other. If the other does not reciprocate, then the friendship stays at its current level. However, if the other party does reciprocate, the friendship grows. As this occurs, the benefits of friendship begin to emerge.

As the bond between both parties strengthens, each party is completed more fully by the other, which provides not only mutual support but also a greater sense of affection, security, care, and peace. As mutual support grows, each party experiences a greater sense of home through the other, which in turn gives them a greater sense of themselves. Each party also experiences actualization through the other as well as self-transcendence (inasmuch as the whole is greater than the sum of its parts). There are feelings that accompany all of these states—feelings of care and being cared for, feelings of loyalty, security, completion, appreciation, and above all, the joy of being in the presence of someone who has committed himself to the other party and to whom the other party has committed. Those who have experienced these high-level friendships without sexual expression will testify that they reach toward the highest levels of love, fulfillment, and interpersonal identity. Some of the greatest self-sacrificial manifestations of love in history and literature are of this nonsexual kind.

Sometimes these high-level friendships move toward sexual expression, but they need not do so. Before moving in this direction, both parties must consider the following:

- Whether such sexual expression is appropriate before the Lord
- Whether it will heighten the true (Level Three-Four) fulfillment and dignity of the other
- Whether it is moved by motives of generosity and permanent, public, and exclusive commitment or moved by more base or selfish motives
- Whether it will find its natural culmination in marriage and family (as defined by Jesus)

If sexual expression does not meet all four conditions, it should not be pursued, because it will not support, but rather undermine, the achieved high-level friendship by separating it from the Lord and true fulfillment while playing to base or selfish motives. However, if it does meet these four conditions, then it will find its natural expression in marriage and family as Jesus has defined it.

In light of the above, those with same-sex attraction can experience the height of human love (and fulfillment through that love) without sexual expression. If they set their sights on this (rather than what they cannot have before Jesus), their lives will have as high an expression of love as can be attained. Nevertheless, resisting the strong pull toward sexual expression within high-level friendships can be quite challenging, and most have described it as a considerable sacrifice and cross. The Lord asks us to follow Him and accept our crosses generously. He promises that through our faith these crosses will lead to our purification and eternal salvation—what Saint Paul calls "the new man" (Eph 4:24).[40] If we keep our eyes focused on the prize, even as we are being purified through our voluntary and involuntary struggles, we will be able to bear them and benefit from them much better; and in the end, we will be led steadily by the Lord not only to the "new man" but also to eternal salvation. As this purification in virtue takes place, it will transform the quality of all our actions, and we will find ourselves leading others by word and example into the Kingdom of God by helping them to benefit from their crosses and struggles.

Saint Paul experienced deeply the interior battle between the pull of the flesh and the pull of the spirit. Though we do not know in

---

[40] See Volume IV of the Quartet, *The Light Shines on in the Darkness: Transforming Suffering through Faith*, which is wholly devoted to this point.

what that interior battle consisted, we know how he dealt with it—through faith in Jesus Christ and his concerted will to follow Him:

> For I know that nothing good dwells within me, that is, in my flesh. I can will what is right, but I cannot do it. For I do not do the good I want, but the evil I do not want is what I do. Now if I do what I do not want, it is no longer I that do it, but sin which dwells within me.... For I delight in the law of God, in my inmost self, but I see in my members another law at war with the law of my mind and making me captive to the law of sin which dwells in my members. Wretched man that I am! Who will deliver me from this body of death? Thanks be to God through Jesus Christ our Lord! (Rom 7:18–20, 22–25)

What about those who are already involved in a homosexual lifestyle? The longer the involvement in the lifestyle, the more difficult it will be to back out of it until levels of depression, anxiety, and spiritual separation become quite acute. But this is a juncture of high risk, for it can move to despair[41] if we do not see the light of Jesus Christ calling us to His unconditional forgiveness, support, and love. In view of this, the best course of action is to back out of the lifestyle as soon as possible by first going to the Sacrament of Reconciliation, planning actualizable steps to back out, and joining a Christian support group such as Courage International (a Catholic group) to help (see below Section I.C.5). This process could be long and challenging, but it will be worth the effort, for as we move toward the light of Christ, He will support us with the grace of the Holy Spirit, not only to be saved but also to find true happiness (Level Three-Four), dignity, and fulfillment in this life as well.

5. Catholic Support Groups—Courage International

Catholic support groups such as Courage International are essential for those with same-sex attraction struggling to live in conformity with the teachings of Jesus. Personal and pastoral support, faith sharing, conferences, and a reliable hand to help during times of struggle can be invaluable for resisting the pull into a homosexual lifestyle and

---

[41] Recall that 40 percent of those engaging in homosexual behavior contemplate suicide—a primary indication of despair. See above Section I.B.I.

for backing out of that lifestyle—particularly within our hypersexu-
alized culture (see Chapter 1, Sections II and III). Courage International states its mission as follows:

> Courage members are men and women who experience same-sex
> attractions and who have made a commitment to strive for chastity.
> They are inspired by the Gospel call to holiness and the Catholic
> Church's beautiful teachings about the goodness and inherent purpose
> of human sexuality. Through our apostolate, people who experience
> same-sex attraction receive pastoral support in the form of spiritual
> guidance, community prayer support, and fellowship.[42]

Courage International has more than a hundred chapters in the
United States (in virtually every major city) as well as many international chapters in Latin America, Europe, and Asia. Courage International also supports EnCourage, which is a support group for
family members and friends trying to support those struggling with
same-sex attraction.[43] Their mission statement is as follows:

> EnCourage is a ministry within Courage dedicated to the spiritual needs
> of parents, siblings, children, and other relatives and friends of persons
> who have same-sex attractions. Standing by the true teachings of the
> Roman Catholic Church, EnCourage members support one another
> and their loved ones through discussion, prayer and fellowship.[44]

There are many testimonies to what Courage has done to provide
a community of rich faith support for those with same-sex attraction.
One of these testimonies is sufficient to show the importance and
efficacy of this Catholic ministry:

> As I looked across the last several years of my life, I kept getting the
> image of me being wrapped in chains. My suffering was silent. How
> could people understand that I had something inside of me that I
> hated? ... The chains of homosexuality kept me miserable. I wanted
> to be listened to, to be hugged, to be understood. I wanted to be the
> man God had made me to be. Five years ago, I felt so alone. I felt no

---

[42] From their website at https://couragerc.org/about/.
[43] From the EnCourage website at https://couragerc.org/encourage/.
[44] Ibid.

one would listen to my heart crying, that no one would really care. I desired to take my own life. In my search for peace, through the help of a close friend, I went to Mass for the first time in my life and felt God's love envelop me. He guided me to Rome, where the Church's teachings on homosexuality gave me great comfort. God, through His Church, cared to love me, to hold me and to listen to me. By way of complicated events, I discovered Courage. Finally, I had arrived at a place where others could relate to me, a place where I could foster chaste friendships with other men who truly cared. We were not afraid to proclaim the truth of Christ, that, in His loving plan for us, we could live a life of holiness and walk down the path, carrying the cross after the One who dies for us. This became a life of chaste holiness—to be the saints that God has called us to be. This is almost impossible without Courage. As we struggle together, the Holy Spirit breaks the chains of homosexuality to free us to be who God calls us to be. Only then are we truly free.[45]

II. Pornography

The Catholic Church views pornography as sinful because of its destructiveness to relationships, its power to addict and undermine viewers of it, and its exploitation of those participating in it. The *Catechism of the Catholic Church* notes the following:

Pornography consists in removing real or simulated sexual acts from the intimacy of the partners, in order to display them deliberately to third parties. It offends against chastity because it perverts the conjugal act, the intimate giving of spouses to each other. It does grave injury to the dignity of its participants (actors, vendors, the public), since each one becomes an object of base pleasure and illicit profit for others. It immerses all who are involved in the illusion of a fantasy world. It is a grave offense.[46]

Despite the astoundingly high rates of pornography use among 98 percent of men and 73 percent of women (over a six-month

---

[45] From the Courage conference testimony by John at https://couragerc.org/resource/conference-testimonies/. Bold font is in original.

[46] *CCC* 2354.

period),[47] and skyrocketing rates of addiction (see below), some Catholics believe that pornography is a victimless and harmless pursuit that should not be viewed as sinful. The following will show the destructive effects of pornography on adult males, marriages, children, adolescence, spiritual life, and the culture.

Since pornography was virtually nonexistent in Old Testament and New Testament times, it is not mentioned by the Deuteronomic and Levitical codes, Jesus, Saint Paul, and the other New Testament writers. Though there were pornographic paintings in Rome, and other ancient cultures, it does not seem to have been used with any frequency prior to the time of photography. We can infer Jesus' likely teaching on it from Matthew 5:28—"But I say to you that every one who looks at a woman lustfully has already committed adultery with her in his heart." Though the person portrayed in a pornographic image is almost always unknown to the viewer, and beyond his capacity to pursue adultery, it reveals the viewer's consent to treat sexuality merely as a matter of self-gratification outside of the domain of spousal relations in marriage. Thus, it would not have been viewed as morally neutral by Jesus, but rather as quite negative. We might also infer the same implicit prohibition of pornography by Saint Paul:

> Do you not know that your bodies are members of Christ? Shall I therefore take the members of Christ and make them members of a prostitute? Never! Do you not know that he who joins himself to a prostitute becomes one body with her? For, as it is written, "The two shall become one." (1 Cor 6:15–16; Paul is quoting Gen 2:24)

Even though pornography facilitates only the imaginary sexual union with a stranger, it shows the wish to engage in sexual relations with someone other than one's spouse. For Saint Paul, this is a sin against our bodies, which are members of Christ—and therefore a sin against Christ.

So, what are the destructive effects of pornography? There are many of them, which negatively impact adult sexual behavior, marriage relationships, and child and adolescent development. The

---

[47] See Marie-Ève Daspe et al., "When Pornography Use Feels Out of Control: The Moderation Effect of Relationship and Sexual Satisfaction", *Journal of Sex and Marital Therapy* 44, no. 4 (May 2018): 343–53, https://pubmed.ncbi.nlm.nih.gov/29281588/.

following combines research from a large array of studies, which can be found in the articles cited below. We will examine the harmful effects of pornography in five areas:

1. Effects on adults (Section II.A)
2. Effects on marriages and marital satisfaction (Section II.B)
3. Effects on developing children and adolescents (Section II.C)
4. Effects on spiritual life (Section II.D)
5. Effects on culture (Section II.E)

A. Negative Effects of Pornography on Adults

In a 2017 survey, 98 percent of men and 73 percent of women reported that they had viewed Internet pornography in the last six months, for a total of 85 percent of respondents.[48] The following summary (from the *Journal of Sex Research*) combines data from thirty-six other studies cited in the article:

> Pornography consumption was associated with having more positive attitudes toward teenage sex, adult premarital sex, and extramarital sex. Pornography consumption was also positively related to actually engaging in extramarital sex. In line with public health researchers' concerns, pornography consumption was associated with having more sexual partners and engaging in paid sex behavior.[49]

The greater the use of pornography, the greater the propensity for extramarital sex, increased sexual partners, and high-risk sexual behavior.[50] Addiction heightens all three negative behaviors over the course of time.[51] Furthermore, these negative behaviors have increased in the general population as accessibility to pornography has increased.[52]

---

[48] Ibid.

[49] Paul J. Wright, "U.S. Males and Pornography, 1973–2010: Consumption, Predictors, Correlates", *Journal of Sex Research* 50, no. 1 (2013), Abstract, https://pubmed.ncbi.nlm.nih.gov/22126160/.

[50] Ibid., pp. 64–68.

[51] Ibid.

[52] Ibid.

Patrick Fagan explains why pornography is so easily addictive, and why it "overrides" normal defensive reactions to high-risk sexual behaviors, negative impacts to spouse and marriage, and moral concerns:

> Pornography changes the habits of the mind, the inner private self. Its use can easily become habitual, which in turn leads to desensitization, boredom, distorted views of reality, and an objectification of women. A greater amount of sexual stimuli becomes necessary to arouse habitual users, leading them to pursue more deviant forms of pornography to fulfill their sexual desires.[53]

Currently, about 10 percent of the adult population is addicted to Internet pornography.[54] Addiction means that the subject has lost control of his impulse to engage in pornographic activity. Though this is a minority of the 98 percent of men and 73 percent of women viewing pornography, it has increased considerably with easier Internet access and can be expected to continue increasing into the future.[55] Pornography addiction has significant negative impacts on individuals and marriages—40 percent of addicts (mostly men) lose their spouses, 58 percent suffer considerable financial losses, and about a third lose their jobs.[56] Evidently, these effects are catastrophic for spouses and marriages, as well as children who experience their fathers (and sometimes mothers) becoming more emotionally distant and uncaring. The increased divorce rate has a particularly significant impact on children and adolescents (see Chapter 1, Section III.B).

Let's put this statistic in context. The addiction rate (10 percent) is very high compared with other addiction and affects a much higher percentage of people with 65 percent of young men visiting pornography sites many times per year.[57] As noted above, frequency

---

[53] Patrick F. Fagan, "The Effects of Pornography on Individuals, Marriage, Family and Community", *Research Synthesis* (Washington, D.C.: Family Research Council, 2009), p. 11, https://downloads.frc.org/EF/EF09K57.pdf. The three aspects of desensitization, habituation, and boredom are documented by separate studies cited in the article.

[54] Megan Hull, ed., *Pornography Facts and Statistics* (Umatilla, Fla.: Recovery Village, updated 2021), under "Online Porn Statistics", https://www.therecoveryvillage.com/process-addiction/porn-addiction/related/pornography-statistics/.

[55] See Fagan, "Effects of Pornography".

[56] See ibid. These three statistics are documented by separate studies cited in the article.

[57] Hull, *Pornography Facts and Statistics*, under "Porn Addiction Trends".

of pornography use tends to increase over time unless individuals deliberately choose to limit consumption and take steps to sensor its availability on their computers (see below Section II.F). Pornography is one of the highest forms of addiction in the U.S. population—nearly twice as high as alcohol addiction (5.3 percent)[58] and drug addiction (6 percent).[59] Though alcohol and drug addiction have more significant impact on physiological degeneration and illness as well as violent and antisocial behavior, the negative effects of pornography on divorce rates, loss of jobs, risky sexual behaviors, and hindrance of development of emotional intimacy, generative care, and self-sacrificial commitment (the capacity for marriage) indicate its seriousness to emotional health, spiritual well-being, marriage, and family stability.

B. Negative Effects of Pornography on Marriages and Marital Satisfaction

A comprehensive study presented at the 2016 American Sociological Association Conference shows significant evidence that pornography probably *doubles* the rate of divorce, even for spouses who begin viewing pornography during marriage.[60] As will be shown, this destructive effect is produced by pornography's negative impact on emotional intimacy, spouses' emotional health, marital trust, and the marital bond. Patrick Fagan reports seven negative impacts from several independent studies:

---

[58] National Institute on Alcohol Abuse and Alcoholism (NIAAA), "Alcohol Facts and Statistics", updated June 2021, under "Alcohol Use Disorder (AUD) in the United States", https://www.niaaa.nih.gov/publications/brochures-and-fact-sheets/alcohol-facts-and-statistics.

[59] American Addiction Centers, "Alcohol and Drug Abuse Statistics", under "Addiction: Treatment Statistics" (video), last updated November 19, 2021, https://americanaddiction centers.org/rehab-guide/addiction-statistics.

[60] The study conducted by authors Samuel Perry and Cyrus Schleifer (at the University of Oklahoma) was a multiyear study based on a 2006–2014 General Social Survey of the United States. It is summarized in David Shultz, "Divorce Rates Double When People Start Watching Porn", *Science*, August 26, 2016, https://www.sciencemag.org/news/2016/08 /divorce-rates-double-when-people-start-watching-porn#:~:text=The%20study%2C%20a %20working%20paper,non–porn%2Dconsuming%20peers.

- Pornography use undermines marital relations and distresses wives.[61]
- Husbands report loving their spouses less after long periods of looking at (and desiring) women depicted in pornography.[62]
- In many cases, wives of pornography users also develop deep psychological wounds, commonly reporting feelings of betrayal, loss, mistrust, devastation, and anger in responses to the discovery or disclosure of a partner's pornographic online sexual activity.[63]
- Wives can begin to feel unattractive or sexually inadequate and may become severely depressed when they realize their husbands view pornography.[64]
- The distress level in wives may be so high as to require clinical treatment for trauma, not mere discomfort.[65]
- Viewers of pornography assign increased importance to sexual relations without emotional involvement,[66] and consequently, wives experience decreased emotional intimacy from their husbands.[67]
- The emotional distance fostered by pornography and "cybersex" (interactive computer contact with another regarding pornographic sexual issues) can often be just as damaging to the

[61] Fagan, "Effects of Pornography", citing Ana J. Bridges, Raymond M. Bergner, and Matthew Hesson-McInnis, "Romantic Partners' Use of Pornography: Its Significance for Women", *Journal of Sex & Marital Therapy* 29, no. 1 (2003): 1–14.

[62] Fagan, "Effects of Pornography", citing Dolf Zillmann and Jennings Bryant, "Pornography's Impact on Sexual Satisfaction", *Journal of Applied Social Psychology* 18, no. 5 (1988): 438–53 (see pp. 439–40), quoting S. E. Gutierres, D. T. Kenrick, and L. Goldberg, "Adverse Effect of Popular Erotica on Judgments of One's Mate" (paper presented at the Annual Meeting of the American Psychological Association, Anaheim, Calif., August 1983).

[63] Fagan, "Effects of Pornography", citing J. P. Schneider, "Effects of Cybersex Addiction on the Family: Results of a Survey", *Sexual Addiction & Compulsivity* 7, nos. 1–2 (2007): 31–58.

[64] Fagan, "Effects of Pornography", citing ibid., p. 38.

[65] Fagan, "Effects of Pornography", citing Barbara A. Steffens and Robyn L. Rennie, "The Traumatic Nature of Disclosure for Wives of Sexual Addicts", *Sexual Addiction & Compulsivity* 13, no. 2–3 (2006): 247–67.

[66] Fagan, "Effects of Pornography", citing Zillmann and Bryant, "Pornography's Impact" p. 448.

[67] Fagan, "Effects of Pornography", citing Raymond M. Bergner and Ana J. Bridges, "The Significance of Heavy Pornography Involvement for Romantic Partners: Research and Clinical Implications," *Journal of Sex & Marital Therapy* 28, no. 3 (2002): 193–206 (see p. 197).

relationship as real-life infidelity,[68] and both men and women tend to put online sexual activity in the same category as having an affair.[69]

How does pornography cause these severely damaging effects within marriage and family? In brief, pornography reorients the marital relationship from emotional intimacy (built on friendship, commitment, generative care, common cause, and love of children) toward sexual intimacy. The longer pornography is viewed, the more sexual intimacy eclipses emotional intimacy, offending and distressing wives while making the relationship superficial. This superficiality puts the emphasis on self-gratification and physical satisfaction while deemphasizing and undermining genuine care and concern, mutual support, and self-sacrifice necessary for maintaining the marital and familial bond. Gary Gilles points to three ways in which pornography causes the above negative consequences to emotional health and marital stability:

1. Breakdown of trust
2. Loss of emotional intimacy
3. Unrealistic expectations of spouses and sexual relations within marriage[70]

With respect to the breakdown of trust, Gilles notes that the emotional intimacy necessary for strong marital bonds entails vulnerability, and this vulnerability requires trust of the partners for each other. As implied above, viewing pornography "feels" like inviting a stranger into the marital bond, causing feelings of violation, broken trust, and even betrayal.[71]

---

[68] Fagan, "Effects of Pornography", citing J. P. Schneider, "Effects of Cybersex Problems on the Spouse and Family", in *Sex and the Internet: A Guidebook for Clinicians*, ed. A. Cooper (New York: Brunner-Routledge, 2002), pp. 169–86 (see p. 180).

[69] Fagan, "Effects of Pornography", citing Bergner and Bridges, "Significance of Heavy Pornography Involvement", p. 197.

[70] See Gary Gilles, "How Pornography Distorts Intimate Relationships", MentalHelp .net, 2020, https://www.mentalhelp.net/blogs/how-pornography-distorts-intimate-relation ships/.

[71] See ibid.

Emotional intimacy is the primary bonding agent of the marital relationship, because as Gilles states, it "makes a person feel valued, cherished, loved, cared for, listened to and appreciated".[72] When emotional intimacy is high, so also is marital satisfaction and sexual satisfaction within the marriage.[73] When one of the spouses views pornography, it shifts the focus from emotional intimacy to sexual intimacy, undermining the primary bonding agent of the marriage as well as the marriage itself.[74]

Pornography has been shown to create unrealistic expectations about a spouse's body as well as sexual behavior, creating dissatisfaction with the spouse's beauty and normal sexual behavior. Pornography shifts the focus from care and love for the spouse to self-gratification that compares the spouse to an unreal sexual ideal. Since the spouse is incapable of satisfying the unrealistic sexual desires of the self-obsessed partner, the latter criticizes and rejects the former, which ultimately undermines the marital bond.[75]

In addition to all the above, pornography causes habitual users to seek additional sexual partners, extramarital relationships, risky sexual behaviors, and paid sex behaviors.[76] This compounds the damage to the spouses' emotional health and the marital bond, thereby *doubling* the rate of divorce.[77]

As can be seen, pornography has a significantly negative impact on marital intimacy, the emotional health of the spouses, the marital bond, and the marital commitment itself. It shifts the focus from care and love for the spouse to self-gratification, which undermines not only the marriage but also the children's sense of love and security. The increased use of pornography has significantly increased the incidence of infidelity[78] and doubled the rate of divorce.[79] Contrary to popular myth, it is anything but victimless.

[72] See ibid.
[73] See ibid.
[74] See ibid.
[75] See ibid.
[76] See Wright, "U.S. Males and Pornography".
[77] Schultz, "Divorce Rates Double".
[78] Wright, "U.S. Males and Pornography".
[79] See Schultz, "Divorce Rates Double".

C. Negative Effects of Pornography on Developing Children and Adolescents

Current research shows that pornography has significant negative effects on the emotional development and sexual proclivities of young people—both preteens and adolescents.[80] The incidence of pornography exposure and use by preteens and adolescents has increased markedly since 2001 primarily because of the Internet; 90 percent of children from the ages of eight to sixteen (in 2013) had viewed pornography on the Internet.[81] "Internationally, between 75% and 90% of teenagers living in developed countries saw pornography on the internet before turning eighteen."[82]

The increasing use of pornography by preteens and adolescents has exacerbated these negative effects,[83] many of which, unless resisted, could last a lifetime. Courtney Bell has listed eight areas in which pornography is undermining the emotional health, development, and relational capacity of young people:[84]

1. Pornography increases young peoples' propensity toward sexual violence.[85]
2. Viewing pornography adversely influences sexual attitudes. Frequent pornographic exposure increases young peoples' acceptance of nonmarital, premarital, extramarital, and recreational sex.[86] Furthermore, teens are likely to imitate more

---

[80] See Courtney Bell, *An Overview of Research on the Impact That Viewing Pornography Has on Children, Pre-Teens and Teenagers* (Arundel BC, Queensland, Australia: Bravehearts Foundation, 2017), https://bravehearts.org.au/wp-content/uploads/2018/01/Research-Report _Overview-of-research-into-the-effects-of-viewing-pornography-on-children....pdf.

[81] "Internet Crime and Abuse Statistics", GuardChild.com, 2013, http://www.guardchild .com/statistics/.

[82] Bell, "Overview of Research", citing the following study: "Teens and Internet Pornography", Christchurch Psychology (website), 2013, http://www.christchurchpsychology .co.nz/news-and-views/teens-internet- pornography.

[83] See ibid.

[84] See ibid.

[85] See P. M. Greenfield, "Inadvertent Exposure to Pornography on the Internet: Implications of Peer-to-Peer File-Sharing Networks for Child Development and Families", *Applied Developmental Psychology* 25, no. 6 (2004): 741–50.

[86] See Michael Flood, "Young Men Using Pornography", in *Everyday Pornography*, ed. K. Boyle (New York: Routledge, 2010), pp. 164–78.

extreme sexual behaviors when they are viewed frequently on pornographic sites.[87]

3. Pornography also depersonalizes sexuality, detaching it from intimate care for the partner, and making it a purely physical act.[88] This depersonalization increases the acceptability of prostitution and other purely physical manifestations of sexuality.[89]

4. Frequent viewing of pornography also leads to the objectification of women by young men, increasing the acceptability of forcing women to have sex.[90]

5. Exposure to pornographic sexual content can be a significant factor in teenage pregnancy. A three-year longitudinal study of teenagers found that frequent exposure to televised sexual content was related to a substantially greater likelihood of teenage pregnancy within the succeeding three years. This same study also found that the likelihood of teenage pregnancy was two times greater when the quantity of that sexual content exposure, within the viewing episodes, was high rather than low.[91]

6. Viewing pornography adversely influences self-image, self-esteem, and self-acceptance. It increases feelings of "shame, guilt, anxiety, confusion, poor social bonds, and addictions".[92] Additionally, pornography increases anxiety, feelings of dissatisfaction with one's body, and sexual adequacy.[93]

7. Pornography is as addictive to young people as it is to adults (see above Section II.A),[94] thereby decreasing the age at which

[87] See ibid.

[88] See ibid. See also T. DeAngelis, "Web Pornography's Effect on Children", *Monitor* 38, no. 10 (2007): 50.

[89] See Flood, "Young Men Using Pornography".

[90] See Michael Flood and Clive Hamilton, "Youth and Pornography in Australia: Evidence on the Extent of Exposure and Likely Effects" (Discussion Paper Number 52, Australia Institute, February 2003).

[91] See Anita Chandra et al., "Does Watching Sex on Television Predict Teen Pregnancy? Findings from a Longitudinal Survey of Youth", *Pediatrics* 122 (2008): 1052. See also Michele L. Ybarra and Kimberly J. Mitchell, "Exposure to Internet Pornography among Children and Adolescents: A National Survey", *CyberPsychology & Behavior* 8, (2005): 479.

[92] See Colleen Bryant, "Adolescence, Pornography and Harm", *Trends and Issues in Crime and Criminal Justice*, no. 368 (February 2009): 3, https://www.aic.gov.au/sites/default/files/2020-05/tandi368.pdf.

[93] See Flood, "Young Men Using Pornography".

[94] See Mary Eberstadt and Mary Anne Layden, *The Social Costs of Pornography: A Statement of Findings and Recommendations* (Princeton, N.J.: Witherspoon Institute, 2010), https://afaofpa.org/wp-content/uploads/Social-Costs-of-Porn-Report.pdf.

pornography addiction occurs and increasing the incidence and percentage of pornography addicts in the United States (currently at 10 percent of the adult population).[95]

8. Pornography viewing in children "short-circuits"[96] the normal personality development process, shifting the focus from caring, loyal, supportive, committed friendships to objectification of desired partners and premature "sexualization" of relationships.[97]

The negative effects of pornography on young people are so significant that it should be considered a public health threat as well as an agent of increasing damage to their personal development, emotional health, and moral proclivities. The increased proclivity toward depersonalizing sex, objectifying women, openness to nonmarital, extramarital, and recreational sex, and hindrance of personality development will have grave consequences, not only for the viewers of pornography but for their future friends, spouses, relationships, and marriages. When this is combined with pornography's influence on teenage pregnancies and violence toward sexual partners, it signals a threat to the future of marriages and families as well as the culture founded upon them.

What can we do to protect our teenagers and reverse this disastrous trend? We cannot remain naïve about the possible impact on our own children, making us guilty bystanders. We have to educate our young people about the negative effects of pornography on their development, their emotional health, morals, and future marriages. Furthermore, we must expect that peer contact and access to Internet pornography *will* affect our children no matter how well we think we are raising them. As noted above, pornography easily becomes habitual and in 10 percent of cases becomes addictive. Therefore, I would recommend purchasing protective software for any teen having free access to the Internet through a smartphone or computer. The following is a sample of programs and apps to help your children:

[95] Hull, "Pornography Facts and Statistics".

[96] Donna Rice Hughes, "How Pornography Harms Children", ProtectKids.com, 2001, http://www.protectkids.com/effects/harms.htm.

[97] Gilles, "How Pornography Distorts".

1. Covenant Eyes (Catholic)[98]
2. Net Nanny[99]
3. Qustodio[100]
4. Ever Accountable[101]
5. Web Safety[102]

D. Spiritual Effects of Pornography

The above negative impacts to adults, children, and marriages reveal a corresponding spiritual impact. As noted above, pornography undermines emotional intimacy; generative, self-sacrificial love; children's security; and the marital bond. As such, it moves us away from the will of Christ for us as individuals and spouses. We can rationalize pornography as victimless and "minor among sins" because so many people are doing it, and social norming suggests that mainstream acceptance is equivalent to moral acceptability (see Chapter 1, Section III). As can be seen from the above studies, this rationalization is completely false. Pornography is contrary to the will of Christ for us and marriage, contrary to the will of the Creator for sexuality, and terribly damaging to emotional health and our ability to live in accordance with the love of Christ (explained in Chapter 1, Section I). Therefore, it is immoral from both a Christian and humanistic point of view.

As noted above, we cannot say that viewing pornography is a mortal sin without assessing the knowledge and freedom of the person viewing it. There may be significant reasons for thinking that pornography viewers do not have full consent of the will (the third condition for a mortal sin), because the high rate of habituation (opening upon addiction) may be a significant impediment to free will. Nevertheless, we are responsible for trying our best to resist and extricate ourselves from pornography because of its damaging effects to our spiritual lives, marriages, children, and emotional health. This may

---

[98] Go to www.covenanteyes.com.
[99] Go to www.netnanny.com.
[100] Go to www.qustodio.com.
[101] Go to www.everaccountable.com.
[102] Go to www.websafety.live.

require assistance from Internet software, accountability partners, and some group therapy (see below Section II.F). Addicts may need ongoing participation in a twelve-step program for sexual addiction. Before discussing these resources, we will briefly examine how pornography negatively affects young people's faith, attendance at church services, prayer life, and relationship with God. In a study published by Oxford Academic, authors Samuel Perry and George Hayward found the following:

> Fixed-effects regression models show that more frequent pornography viewing diminishes religious service attendance, importance of religious faith, prayer frequency, and perceived closeness to God, while increasing religious doubts. These effects hold regardless of gender. The effects of viewing pornography on importance of faith, closeness to God, and religious doubts are stronger for teenagers compared to emerging adults. In light of the rapidly growing availability and acceptance of pornography for young Americans, our findings suggest that scholars must consider how increasingly pervasive pornography consumption may shape both the religious lives of young adults and also the future landscape of American religion more broadly.[103]

The negative effects of the correlation between pornography viewing and the decline in religion, faith, and prayer is so significant that Perry and Hayward believe it could reshape the religious landscape of the United States and the rest of the world. The negative effects of pornography do not stop there. They appear to be influencing the emotional health of the nation and the world—specifically leading to an increase in depression and anxiety.

Recall the six psychological and medical studies correlating religious nonaffiliation and steep increases in depression, anxiety, substance abuse, familial tensions, and suicides. If pornography leads to a decline in religious faith, affiliation, and practice, we might expect that it would also lead to an increase in depression and these other

---

[103] Samuel L. Perry and George M. Hayward, "Seeing Is (Not) Believing: How Viewing Pornography Shapes the Religious Lives of Young Americans", *Social Forces* 95, no. 4 (June 2017), Abstract, https://academic.oup.com/sf/article-abstract/95/4/1757/2877697?redirected From=fulltext.

effects. Furthermore, pornography's negative effect on emotional intimacy,[104] marital and family stability,[105] and job performance[106] would also increase the likelihood and seriousness of depression. Dr. Kevin Skinner obtained a preliminary confirmation of the correlation between frequency of pornography viewing and increased depression determined by a standard depression scale,[107] but these results require further confirmation by additional longitudinal studies. His initial findings are as follows:

- The general population (who may occasionally view pornography) scored about six and a half on the depression scale.
- Those viewing pornography three to five times a week scored eighteen on the depression scale (three times higher), indicating moderate depression.
- Those viewing pornography daily scored over twenty-one on the depression scale, indicating *severe* depression.

These results preliminarily confirm the expected correlation between increased pornography viewing and increased depression. These interrelated negative effects of pornography on faith, religious practice, emotional health, and marital and family stability reveal the presence of our spiritual enemy—Satan.

Recall from Volume I (Chapter 4) how the Evil One works. First, he leads us to an opportunity for sin, then enflames our imagination with the desire for more, then provides rationalizations through interior suggestions and from the culture, hoping that we will freely choose to follow him more deeply into the temptation (pulling us more deeply into his darkness). Pornography is particularly insidious because it enflames desire almost instantly. As noted above, failure to resist it at the outset almost inevitably leads to increased use, and then as boredom sets in, to more and more enhanced and even deviant sexual expression. Throughout this process, habituation takes

---

[104] See Fagan, "Effects of Pornography", and Gilles, "How Pornography Distorts".
[105] See Fagan, "Effects of Pornography".
[106] See ibid.
[107] Kevin Skinner, "Can Pornography Trigger Depression?", *Psychology Today*, November 3, 2011, https://www.psychologytoday.com/us/blog/inside-porn-addiction/201111/can-pornography-trigger-depression.

hold, which makes breaking the spell more and more difficult. As this occurs, we become more forgetful about God and more "casual" about prayer and the sacraments, undermining our path to moral rectitude and relationship with God.[108]

As Saint Ignatius of Loyola notes, the Holy Spirit does not leave us alone in this path toward darkness. He allows us to experience a spiritual emptiness, loneliness, and alienation arising out of our increased separation from God, which imparts a sense of guilt both at night and during the day.[109] He musters his conspiracy of providence to have people make suggestions and warnings while presenting clues to our spiritual danger through books, homilies, and even the media. This oftentimes moves individuals to go to confession and take steps to extricate themselves from their growing habit.

As this happens, the Evil One counters with more rationalizations to minimize our spiritual danger and increase temptations to view more. Rationalizations frequently include resentment toward the Church for teaching her prudish and "out of date" morality. As time passes, victims can even feel resentment toward Jesus and His heavenly Father. When this resentment occurs, victims are in true spiritual danger, because their resentment and indignation may incite voluntary separation from the Church and the Lord, which opens them to direct influence by the Evil One.

As this occurs, victims will feel a significant rise in depression and anxiety (arising out of spiritual emptiness, loneliness, and alienation).[110] This increase in depression and anxiety takes place not because the Holy Spirit incites it but because of their close proximity to the Evil One, who exudes this atmosphere. If this applies to you, do not delay—go to confession as soon as possible, and then take steps to extricate yourself from the pornographic habit. Delays will only increase depression, anxiety, and the pornographic habit's (and the Evil One's) control over you. If the habit is quite strong, you may have to avail yourself of one or more of the four resources mentioned below (Section II.F).

---

[108] See Perry and Hayward, "Seeing Is (Not) Believing".

[109] See Saint Ignatius of Loyola, *Spiritual Exercises*, First Rule, from "14 Rules for the Discernment of Spirits", *Scepter* (blog), August 3, 2018, https://scepterpublishers.org/blogs/scepter-blog-corner/14-rules-for-the-discernment-of-spirits-by-st-ignatius-of-loyola.

[110] See Skinner, "Can Pornography Trigger Depression?"

In sum, the best way to deal with the pervasive problem of pornography is to resist it at the outset. This self-destructive sin is like a snowball moving down a mountain, gathering more snow and momentum as it goes. The longer it rolls, the harder it will be to stop. Do not fall prey to rationalizations about the harmlessness and victimlessness of pornography. As shown above in Sections II.A through this one, pornography is quite harmful, and its path filled with victims. Those who are being increasingly effected need to turn to the Lord in their attempts to resist this temptation and avail themselves of the Sacrament of Reconciliation and frequent reception of the Holy Eucharist, as well as including it in their Examen Prayer (see Volume II, Chapters 2 and 7 of this Trilogy).

If people allow the habit to develop over the course of time, they will have to take more concerted action using not only the grace of the Sacrament of Reconciliation, the Holy Eucharist, and the Examen Prayer, but also one or more of the other four resources given in Section II.F—Catholic videos, courses, written materials, and counseling; accountability software; online accountability groups; and in-person accountability groups (in the case of addiction, a twelve-step program).

E. Cultural Consequences

As shown above, pornography is not a private, harmless predilection deemed immoral by a prudish Church, but a real significant danger to the emotional health, spiritual well-being, and development of adults and children, as well as marriages, families, and the culture dependent on them. This danger is recognized not only by Christian Churches but also by a large number of reputable academic, clinical, therapeutic, and sociological institutes. The undermining of emotional intimacy, the doubling of the divorce rate, and the damage done to personal development, emotional health, and spiritual well-being is so vast that it would be irresponsible to "kick the can down the road" any longer. In view of this, we must take personal responsibility to resist this temptation while exerting social and political influence to limit the almost unmitigated spread of the problem. Before examining the resources to help those habituated (or addicted) to pornography, we will briefly examine its cultural consequences.

A culture is constituted by implicit and explicit general acceptance of certain principles, ideals, and values (as well as the general rejection of certain vices, disvalues, and decadent trends). Thus, a culture can call us to a higher standard, what we have called a Level Three or Level Four purpose in life, or a lower standard, what we have called a Level One or Level Two purpose in life. Level One-Two cultures tend toward disunity (because they emphasize self-gratification and ego-comparative advantage). Their disunity and lack of ideals make them weak, allowing them to be taken over by stronger cultures. Furthermore, Level One-Two cultures have led people toward base lives rather than high-minded ones (which strive for greater contribution, justice, the common good, and spiritual fulfillment). People without ideals have nothing to strive for and no place to go, leaving them purposeless and listless.

The foundation of strong cultures has always been (and always will be) strong, high-minded, socially and religiously responsible *families*, because families are the social unit through which principles, ideals, values, aspirations, and social responsibility are conveyed and developed from one generation to the next. Without strong families, there will not be strong cultures.

Contrary to popular myth, religion is not an impediment to strong principles and ideals, but rather is one of the greatest motivators of them. As noted in Volume II of the Quartet, religion calls us to our highest dignity, destiny, and fulfillment, reminds us of our transcendent status, and moves its adherence to ethical action and social responsibility[111] (this point is developed in Chapter 5 of this volume). When religion and strong families are combined throughout a particular society, its culture will be strong, calling its citizens to contribution, the common good, respect for justice and the law, and even heroic self-sacrifice.[112] These strong cultures can be supported or undermined by other cultural influences, such as the educational system, mass media, and the legal-political system. If these other cultural

[111] See K. Praveen Parboteeah, Martin Hoegl, and John B. Cullen, "Ethics and Religion: An Empirical Test of a Multidimensional Model", *Journal of Business Ethics* 80, no. 2 (2008): 387–98. See also Marie Cornwall et al., "The Dimensions of Religiosity: A Conceptual Model with an Empirical Test", *Review of Religious Research* 2, no. 3 (1986): 266–44.

[112] Note the strong role of family life and religion in the many cases of heroic virtue and self-sacrifice in Tom Brokaw, *The Greatest Generation* (New York: Random House, 2001).

influences are high-minded (Level Three and Level Four), they will reinforce a strong high-minded culture, but if they are Level One and Level Two, they will weaken and undermine that culture.

So how does pornography affect the culture? As noted above, pornography undermines marriages, families, religious commitment, and Level Three-Four principles. Therefore, it cannot help but undermine culture, creating a decadent impetus toward Level One-Two purpose, and even a rejection of conscience and the natural law within our hearts.[113] Given a virtually complete access to pornography on the Internet, it is an increasing threat to our culture and future way of life.

Pornography is by no means alone in influencing cultural decadence. It is accompanied by increasing religious disaffiliation and the steep increase in Level One-Two purpose, inspired in great part by social media. Recall from the Introduction to this volume and Chapter 1 that the decline of religion and the rise of Level One-Two identity has led to a significant increase in depression, anxiety, and suicidality among young people.[114] After decades of stability in teen depression, anxiety, suicide, and homicide statistics, the last decade (2005 to 2017) has shown steep increases in all of the above negative conditions—a 52 percent increase in depression and anxiety among teens (63 percent increase among young adults), a 56 percent increase in teen suicides, and a 23 percent increase in teen homicides.[115]

Inasmuch as pornography incites Level One-Two purpose, and weakens religious affiliation, it contributes to the above negative

---

[113]See Volume I, Chapter 1, Section III of the Quartet. See also C.S. Lewis, *The Abolition of Man* (HarperOne, 2001), Appendix: "Illustrations of the Tao". See also Josephson Institute, "Josephson Institute's Report Card on American Youth: There's a Hole in Our Moral Ozone and It's Getting Bigger", press release, November 30, 2008, http://questgarden .com/85/27/9/091104072905/files/press-release.pdf.

[114]See Jean M. Twenge et al., "Age, Period, and Cohort Trends in Mood Disorder Indicators and Suicide-Related Outcomes in a Nationally Representative Dataset, 2005–2017", *Journal of Abnormal Psychology* 128, no. 3 (2019): 185–99, https://www.apa.org/pubs/journals /releases/abn-abn0000410.pdf. See also William Wan, "Teen Suicides Are Increasing at an Alarming Pace, Outstripping All Other Age Groups, a New Report Says", *Washington Post*, October 17, 2019, https://www.washingtonpost.com/health/teen-suicides-increasing-at -alarming-pace-outstripping-all-other-age-groups/2019/10/16/e24194c6-f04a-11e9-8693 -f487e46784aa_story.html.

[115]See Twenge et al., "Age, Period, and Cohort Trends", and Wan, "Teen Suicides Are Increasing".

impacts (depression, anxiety, and suicidality) in both young people and adults. When this is combined with its negative effects on marriages and families, it should be viewed as a significant undermining agent of a strong high-minded culture.

As noted above, pornography must be resisted by individuals, communities, and society itself. Though doing this seems to impede the full scope of freedom of speech and press, we must prioritize our societal values. What's more important? Unmitigated freedom of speech and press (with its negative individual, familial, and cultural consequences), or mitigation of some freedoms of speech and press (to help resist the damaging effects of pornography)? If we do not choose the latter, our cultural decadence will continue. It seems we may be at a point of no return—smitten by the allure of both pornography and unmitigated freedom. If so, the decision to reverse the decadent trend must rest in the hands of individuals, families, and churches.

F. Resources

In conclusion, we turn our attention to some resources that can help individuals habituated and addicted to pornography. As noted above, habituation (without addiction) can be very strong, but when addiction occurs, 40 percent will lose their spouses, 58 percent will suffer considerable financial loss, and 33 percent will lose their jobs. Without some external help, it will be difficult for both groups to resist pornography and its damaging effects. Four resources are currently available to provide external assistance:

1. *Catholic video resources, courses, written materials, and counseling.* Excellent resources for Catholics are provided by Integrity Restored.com.[116] The website ForYourMarriage.org has a specific page with multiple *Catholic* resources (videos, blogs, online accountability groups, and in-person accountability groups).[117]

---

[116] A blog and events for Catholic men and women working on these challenges, Dr. Peter Kleponis, Matt Fradd, Father Sean Kilcawley, and Ryan Foley provide multiple resources.

[117] For a list of Catholic support groups and recovery programs, see their website at https://www.foryourmarriage.org/help-for-men-and-women-struggling-with-pornography-use-or-addiction/#catholicsgrp.

2. *Accountability software for adults.* There are six major providers that allow screen access to partners (of one's own choosing), which help to form accountability partners—Accountable2You, Covenant Eyes, Ever Accountable, Lion, Router Limits, and X3 Watch. These software options are assessed and compared by Kyle Belden.[118] In order for accountability software to work, users must share their screens with one or more partners who help them remain faithful to their resolutions.

3. *Online and phone conference accountability and support groups.* Online accountability and support groups go beyond monitoring computers to help pornography users maintain their resolutions. They also provide support, counseling expertise, and materials through the Internet and phone. The following websites provide free online and phone conference support groups for addicts and those challenged by pornography habituation: Sex Addicts Anonymous (SAA) electronic meetings,[119] Sex and Love Addicts Anonymous (SLAA) telephone and online meetings,[120] Sexual Compulsives Anonymous phone and online meetings,[121] and Sex/Pornography Addiction Support Forum.[122] Bill Herring.com provides several other widely available free online and phone conference resources for pornography accountability and support groups.[123]

4. *Twelve-step, in-person accountability and support groups.* These support groups are based on principles from Alcoholics Anonymous, making recourse to self-examination and a higher power. They are the best way to attain support and maintain accountability and are essential for addicts. The two most prolific organizations with multiple groups throughout the United States are Sexaholics Anonymous[124] and Sex Addicts Anonymous.[125]

---

[118] See Kyle Belden, "6 Accountability Software Options", CrossPoint Community Church, March 29, 2018, https://cpmodesto.org/2018/03/6-accountability-software-options/.

[119] See saa-recovery.org.

[120] See https://slaafws.org/meetings.

[121] See http://www.sca-recovery.org/find.htm#online.

[122] See https://sca-recovery.org/WP/meetings/#online.

[123] See https://www.billherring.com/sex-addiction-support-forums.

[124] You can find a meeting in almost any locale by clicking on the following URL: https://www.sa.org/meetings/.

[125] Go to the following to find a meeting in your locale: https://saa-recovery.org/meetings/.

III. Gender Identity and Sex Change

In 2019, the Vatican's Congregation for Catholic Education issued a document on sexual identity and gender theory.[126] It clarified the anthropology underlying its principle that sexual identity is genetically and physiologically "given" (intrinsic to one's being), indicating its origin in God for each individual.[127] If educators treat sexual identity as mere cultural influence or personal choice, it denies this biological givenness and rejects its divine origin and goodness.[128] Furthermore, the denial of the objective facticity of sexual identity undermines the objective basis of sexual complementarity in marriage essential for the stability, security, and identity of children. This view of marriage corresponds to the will of the Creator as defined by Jesus:[129]

> Have you not read that he who made them from the beginning [the Creator] made them male and female, and said, "For this reason, a man shall leave his father and mother and be joined to his wife, and the two shall become one"? So they are no longer two but one. What therefore God has joined together, let no man put asunder. (Mt 19: 4–6; Jesus is quoting Gen 1:27; 2:24)

Treating sexual identity as malleable, transient, or merely subjective rejects the Creator's intention for each human person, marriage, and family, which will adversely affect not only the cultural conception of family but also the legislative and juridical decisions impacting it. Evidently, the Vatican is very concerned that these malleable and transient views of sexual identity will destabilize the family within our society, which will further erode our culture, moving it toward what we have called Level One-Two objectives rather than Level Three-Four objectives (see above Section II.E).

A recent comprehensive scientific study of sexual identity done by two professors at Johns Hopkins University[130] vindicates the Vatican

---

[126] Congregation for Catholic Education, *"Male and Female He Created Them": Towards a Path of Dialogue on the Question of Gender Theory in Education* (February 2, 2019).

[127] Ibid., no. 4.

[128] Ibid., no. 2.

[129] See ibid.

[130] Lawrence Mayer and Paul McHugh, "Sexuality and Gender: Findings from the Biological, Psychological, and Social Sciences", special issue, *New Atlantis* 50 (Fall 2016), https://thenewatlantis.com/wp-content/uploads/legacy-pdfs/20160819_TNA50Sexualityand Gender.pdf.

Congregation's view that gender identity cannot be disconnected from biological sex. Drs. Lawrence Mayer and Paul McHugh summarize their findings as follows:

> The hypothesis that gender identity is an innate, fixed property of human beings that is independent of biological sex—that a person might be "a man trapped in a woman's body" or "a woman trapped in a man's body"—is not supported by scientific evidence.... [Brain studies] do not provide any evidence for a neurobiological basis for cross-gender identification.[131]

As noted above, educational theorists and social-political policy makers have used this fictitious anthropology not only to justify malleable and transient sexual identity theories, but also to support partial and total sexual reassignment surgery for both children and adolescents. As Mayer and McHugh show, these efforts are seriously unethical, because they do unnecessary and irreparable damage to the vast majority of preadolescents pursuing this transition. This also can lead postadolescent transgender individuals to a supposed solution to their gender confusion that will in most cases be unsuccessful while leaving their real psychological problems untreated.[132] We will examine each of these points in turn.

First, with respect to the unnecessary irreparable harm to preadolescents, Mayer and McHugh show that

> only a minority of children who experience cross-gender identification will continue to do so into adolescence or adulthood.... No one can determine the gender identity of a two-year-old.[133]

Mayer and McHugh have enhanced previous studies showing that many children will move away from their cross-gender identification back to their biological sex on their own prior to their adolescence.

---

[131] Ibid., p. 8.

[132] See ibid., p. 9. Mayer and McHugh's study confirms a previous study by Drs. Fitzgibbons, Sutton, and O'Leary that provides an invaluable list of excellent medical and psychiatric studies used throughout this section. See Fitzgibbons, Sutton, and O'Leary, "Psychopathology of 'Sex Reassignment' Surgery".

[133] Ibid., pp. 9, 115.

Some children will need assistance in doing this from therapy when there is considerable anxiety in the household[134] or when children have been sexually abused (40 percent to 55 percent of cross-gender identified children have been sexually abused[135]). With respect to anxiety in the household, Kenneth Zucker and Susan Bradley indicate that sensitive boys are vulnerable to cross-gender confusion based mostly on their mothers' anxiety:

> The boy, who is highly sensitive to maternal signals, perceives the mother's feelings of depression and anger. Because of his own insecurity, he is all the more threatened by his mother's anger or hostility, which he perceives as directed at him. His worry about the loss of his mother intensifies his conflict over his own anger, resulting in high levels of arousal or anxiety.[136]

In a separate article, Zucker and Bradley along with others note further that the mothers of eight out of ten boys with gender identity confusion had at least one diagnosed psychological disorder, one had long-term psychotherapy for family issues, and one had continued migraines.[137] The important point here is that most childhood cross-sexual confusion can be resolved if children receive therapeutic counseling before they reach adolescence and their parents participate in that therapy (to lower the anxiety level in the home).[138] This is in agreement with the findings of Mayer and McHugh.[139]

How does this impinge on general and medical ethics? First, sexual reassignment surgery for preadolescents is highly unethical because it is unnecessary, damaging, irreparable, and will not provide an

---

[134] See Kenneth J. Zucker and Susan J. Bradley, *Gender Identity Disorder and Psychosexual Problems in Children and Adolescents* (New York: Guildford Press, 1995), pp. 262–63.

[135] See Darlynne Gehring and Gail Knudson, "Prevalence of Childhood Trauma in a Clinical Population of Transsexual People", *International Journal of Transgenderism* 8, no. 1 (2005): 23–30. See also Holly Devor, "Transsexualism, Dissociation, and Child Abuse: An Initial Discussion Based on Nonclinical Data", *Journal of Psychology and Human Sexuality* 6, no. 3 (1994): 49–72.

[136] See Zucker and Bradley, *Gender Identity Disorder*, pp. 262–63.

[137] See Kenneth J. Zucker et al., "Psychopathology in the Parents of Boys with Gender Identity Disorder", *Journal of the American Academy of Child and Adolescent Psychiatry* 42, no. 1 (January 2003): 2–4, https://pubmed.ncbi.nlm.nih.gov/12500069/.

[138] See Zucker and Bradley, *Gender Identity Disorder*, p. 282.

[139] See Mayer and McHugh, "Sexuality and Gender".

adequate solution to their feelings of anxiety (discussed below). Furthermore, children and adolescents do not have a fully developed frontal lobe (center of judgment and evaluation) until their mid to late twenties and therefore are in no position to make a fully rational judgment about the negative consequences of their actions.[140] Mayer and McHugh validate this finding, implicitly confirming the unethical nature of this unnecessary, irreparable-damaging approach to gender confusion:

> We are disturbed and alarmed by the severity and irreversibility of some interventions being publicly discussed and employed for children.... Therapies, treatments, and surgeries seem disproportionate to the severity of the distress being experienced by these young people, and are ... premature since the majority of children who identify as the gender opposite their biological sex will not continue to do so as adults.[141]

Secondly, it is highly unethical for parents or medical professionals to suggest a surgical option to preadolescents, even if the suggestion pertains to surgery after they have reached adolescence, for the same reasons—it is unnecessary, damaging, irreparable, and does not solve underlying emotional and psychological issues. Instead of suggesting surgical options, parents and medical professionals should be suggesting therapy to help children contend with anxiety in the household, possible sexual abuse, and the emotional issues resulting from these challenges.

Thirdly, parental failure to pursue therapeutic options for children with cross-gender confusion (as well as failure of parents to participate in that therapy) is, at the very least, ethically negligent. Evidently, some parents may not know of the efficacy of therapeutic options and cannot be held responsible for failure to pursue them, but medical professionals should be aware of these options and are therefore ethically negligent for failure to inform parents about them.

---

[140] See Sara Johnson, Robert Blum, and Jay Giedd, "Adolescent Maturity and the Brain: The Promise and Pitfalls of Neuroscience Research in Adolescent Health Policy", *Journal of Adolescent Health* 45, no. 3 (2009): 216–21, https://www.ncbi.nlm.nih.gov/pmc/articles/PMC2892678/.

[141] See Mayer and McHugh, "Sexuality and Gender", pp. 12, 115.

As noted above, most children will transition out of cross-sexual confusion either naturally or through therapeutic assistance before they reach adolescence. Nevertheless, some will be allowed or even encouraged to pursue surgical options after adolescence. This compounds the problems of the adolescent who now becomes convinced that he or she was born with an opposite gender identity than his or her biological sex. Even though scientific investigation does not support the independence of gender identity from biological sex (see above, Mayer and McHugh[142]), most adolescents become convinced of the innateness of their gender identity and want immediate relief from their anxiety without the lengthy efforts of therapeutic options that would be much more helpful to resolving their underlying condition. Many are so convinced of immediate and complete relief from symptoms that they become recalcitrant in refusing any option but surgery. Zucker and Bradley note in this regard:

> Adolescents with gender identity disorder have poor anxiety tolerance. Seeking sex reassignment surgery is a defensive solution and a mechanism for control of anxiety. The thought of not having a "solution" for their distress increases their anxiety, thus making it very difficult to achieve a therapeutic alliance. Despite an understanding (at least at a superficial level) of why they have cross-gender wishes, these adolescents are often unable to relinquish their defense, as they feel too overwhelmed to face their anxiety without it. This leads to demanding behavior and impatience with the therapist as he or she tries to help them explore feelings and behaviors. Many adolescents who seek sex reassignment withdraw from therapy because of their inability to tolerate the anxiety connected with exploration of their wish for surgery.[143]

Though adolescents and adults often express satisfaction with sexual reassignment surgery, they continue to have a significant problem with anxiety, and the sexual reassignment surgery serves only to delay therapy indefinitely for underlying anxiety, anger, depression, and self-hatred. Dr. Charles Socarides notes in this regard:

[142] Mayer and McHugh, "Sexuality and Gender".
[143] Zucker and Bradley, *Gender Identity Disorder*, pp. 315–16.

There is no evidence that gender identity confusion—a gender identity contrary to the anatomical structure—is inborn. Therefore, any
attempt to change this through surgical means forever dooms the individual's chances of overcoming his psychosexual and psychological
difficulties.[144]

In sum, the problem with sexual reassignment surgery is that it
blocks the pathway to help therapeutically relieve anxieties, anger,
narcissism, and other conditions related to gender confusion. Though
patients may be content with the surgery, the preceding anxieties,
anger, and narcissism persist throughout a lifetime.

Mayer and McHugh concur with this analysis, noting:

Compared to the general population, adults who underwent sex-
reassignment surgery continued to have a higher risk of experiencing
poor mental health outcomes.... [They were] *19 times* more likely to
die of suicide.[145]

In a previous article, Paul McHugh summarized the results of
a comprehensive Swedish study that showed the staggering consequences of sex reassignment surgery and untreated anxiety and
self-negation (going back to childhood): "The most thorough
follow-up of sex-reassigned people—extending over 30 years and
conducted in Sweden, where the culture is strongly supportive of
the transgendered—documents their lifelong mental unrest. Ten to
15 years after surgical reassignment, the suicide rate of those who had
undergone sex-reassignment surgery rose to 20 times that of compa-
rable peers."[146] As implied above, the problem with malleable and
subjectivist sexual identity theories is not limited to problems for
marriages, families, education, and spiritual well-being (rejection of
the divine will); it also affects the emotional health and personal well-
being of individuals considering or pursuing partial or total sexual
reassignment surgery.

---

[144]Charles W. Socarides, "The Desire for Sexual Transformation: A Psychiatric Evaluation
of Transsexualism", *American Journal of Psychiatry* 125, no. 10 (1969): 1425.

[145]Mayer and McHugh, "Sexuality and Gender", p. 9 (italics added).

[146]Paul McHugh, "Transgenderism: A Pathogenic Meme", *Public Discourse* (June 10, 2015),
https://www.thepublicdiscourse.com/2015/06/15145/ Discourse.

Dr. Richard Fitzgibbons and others sum up the ethical issues after a comprehensive examination of the medical and psychological literature:

> Failure to protect children from seriously harming themselves or from being harmed by others—let alone enabling this to happen—objectively is abusive. Surgeons and other medical and mental health professionals, however motivated, ethically should not condone, provide, or otherwise cooperate in such disservice to youth.[147]

So, what might we conclude about gender theory and sex change? First, there is no such thing as an innate gender identity opposite of one's biological sex. This throws the entire thesis underlying gender theory into question, disqualifying it as a subject for primary, secondary, and higher education, as well as a candidate for public policy change.

Secondly, "sex change" is a misrepresentation of fact. Sexual reassignment surgery does not make a man into a woman—or a woman into a man. Sexual reassignment surgery can make a man only appear to be like a woman exteriorly, or make a woman appear like a man exteriorly, though these appearances may be inadequate in comparison to the expected result.

Thirdly, sexual reassignment surgery is unnecessary, damaging, irreparable, and incapable of solving the psychopathology, anxiety, anger, and depression underlying preadolescent and postadolescent gender confusion. In view of the fact that the vast majority of gender-confused children will either naturally discontinue their gender confusion or be able to be helped to do so by therapeutic means makes sexual reassignment surgery not only superfluous, but also highly unethical in light of the unnecessary permanent damage it does. Furthermore, sexual reassignment surgery consigns its victims to perpetual underlying psychopathology, anxiety, anger, depression, and self-hatred from which the gender confusion originated. This makes parental cooperation with sexual reassignment surgery for children highly unethical.

[147] Fitzgibbons, Sutton, and O'Leary, "Psychopathology of 'Sex Reassignment' Surgery", p. 115.

Let us return for a moment to the Catholic Church's statement on gender theory, which anticipated the social-medical, public policy, and educational damage that it would do:

> The context in which the *mission of education* is carried out is characterized by challenges emerging from varying forms of an ideology that is given the general name "gender theory" which "denies the difference and reciprocity in nature of a man and a woman and envisages a society without sexual differences, thereby eliminating the anthropological basis of the family. This ideology leads to educational programmes and legislative enactments that promote a personal identity and emotional intimacy radically separated from the biological difference between male and female."[148]

As the Church predicted, the false anthropology of gender theory has done considerable damage not only to children being unnecessarily and harmfully encouraged toward sexual reassignment surgery, but also to the reputation and ethical conduct of the medical, psychiatric, and psychological professions. Furthermore, it continues to damage the ideal of marriage and family and is now co-opting educators and public policy makers into this undermining of the familial foundation of community, culture, and society. As the Vatican's Congregation for Education suggested, this ideology must be stopped for the good of all.

IV. Artificial Birth Control

The promulgation of *Humane Vitae* by Pope Paul VI in 1968 brought with it considerable debate and dissent—perhaps more than any other papal encyclical and moral teaching. The pope rejected the recommendation of his commission on birth control, which had argued in favor of artificial contraception, predicting severe consequences for marriage, family, culture, and societal freedom. Looking back, we might say that Pope Paul VI was not only prudent, but prescient and even prophetic in his reasoning:

[148] Congregation for Catholic Education, *Towards a Path of Dialogue*, no. 2, quoting Pope Francis, Post-Synodal Apostolic Exhortation on Love in the Family *Amoris Laetitia* (March 19, 2016), no. 56.

Responsible men can become more deeply convinced of the truth of the doctrine laid down by the Church on this issue if they reflect on the consequences of methods and plans for artificial birth control. Let them first consider how easily this course of action could open wide the way for marital infidelity and a general lowering of moral standards.... Another effect that gives cause for alarm is that a man who grows accustomed to the use of contraceptive methods may forget the reverence due to a woman, and, disregarding her physical and emotional equilibrium, reduce her to being a mere instrument for the satisfaction of his own desires, no longer considering her as his partner whom he should surround with care and affection. Finally, careful consideration should be given to the danger of this power passing into the hands of those public authorities who care little for the precepts of the moral law.... Who will prevent public authorities from favoring those contraceptive methods which they consider more effective? Should they regard this as necessary, they may even impose their use on everyone.[149]

It is difficult to deny that Pope Paul VI was correct on all of his dire predictions. With respect to increasing marital infidelity and lowering moral standards, there can be little doubt about the rapid increase of marital infidelity, divorce, and every imaginable lowering of sexual standards within the contemporary world (see Chapter 1, Sections II–IV). As noted there, artificial contraception was a primary cause of the sexual revolution that led to this decline of marriage, sexual standards, and sexuality itself within world culture. The objectification of women within marriage is connected to the continuous decline of marital satisfaction since the 1960s. There are other reasons for this decline such as the increase in marital infidelity (see Chapter 1, Section IV) and the increase in the number of premarital partners (see Chapter 1, Section V), but as noted above, these additional factors were also in good part by the sexual revolution incited by artificial contraception. Finally, there is considerable evidence of the imposition of artificial birth control (and abortion) on whole populations of people, such as the "one child policy" of China, the contemporary eugenics movement, and the power politics of the United Nations Population Council (in cooperation with local governments).

---

[149] Pope Paul VI, Encyclical Letter on the Regulation of Birth *Humane Vitae* (July 25, 1968), no. 17.

In view of the destruction done to marriages, families, and women's dignity by the sexual revolution as well as the draconian impositions of artificial birth control and abortion on millions of people, how could anyone suggest that the Catholic Church should be or should have been in favor of artificial birth control? Some may argue that artificial birth control is necessary to control skyrocketing population, but as we shall see, the dire Malthusian consequences of skyrocketing population have never come to pass. Indeed, quite the opposite. Instead of overpopulation, we now face a population implosion that will be quite severe in its economic effects, gender imbalance (toward men), and mass migration (see below Section IV.B).

It may be argued that since artificial birth control is a reality, and many families want to plan the arrival of their children, a church should allow married couples to use artificial contraception for this purpose. Aside from the fact that this is somewhat hypocritical, because it is using a destructive means for a seemingly "good" end, Pope Paul VI and Pope John Paul II argued strongly that the end is in truth not a "good" end, because it undermines the full purpose of sexuality in marriage intended by the Creator. In *Familiaris Cosortio*, Saint John Paul noted the following:

> When couples, by means of recourse to contraception, separate these two [unitive and procreative] meanings [of sexuality] that God the Creator has inscribed in the being of man and woman and in the dynamism of their sexual communion, they act as "arbiters" of the divine plan and they "manipulate" and degrade human sexuality— and with it themselves and their married partner—by altering its value of "total" self-giving. Thus the innate language that expresses the total reciprocal self-giving of husband and wife is overlaid, through contraception, by an objectively contradictory language, namely, that of not giving oneself totally to the other. This leads not only to a positive refusal to be open to life but also to a falsification of the inner truth of conjugal love, which is called upon to give itself in personal totality.[150]

The Catholic Church endorses the use of family planning so long as it is open to both the unitive and procreative objectives of sexuality

---

[150] Pope John Paul II, Apostolic Exhortation on the Role of the Christian Family in the Modern World *Familiaris Consortio* (November 22, 1981), no. 32.

intended by the Creator—called Natural Family Planning (NFP). Currently, there are three major methods of NFP, all of which, if used correctly, are up to 99 percent effective (i.e., only one woman out of a hundred will become pregnant in one year).[151] The third method combines the first two and is the most secure way of predicting fertility and infertility:

1. *The temperature method.* Using a digital thermometer for NFP, a woman records when her temperature rises slightly for at least three days in a row after six days of lower temperature. This indicates when a woman is fertile and when she is not.[152]
2. *The cervical secretion method (the Creighton Model).* Cervical secretions change over the cycle of ovulation, which can be checked manually and recorded to predict accurately when women are fertile and when they are not.[153]
3. *The sympto-thermal method (combination of the above two methods).* The couple crosschecks both the basal body temperature and the cervical fluid to determine with greatest accuracy when a woman is fertile and when she is not.[154]

Inasmuch as Pope John Paul II is correct in his interpretation of the divine will for sexuality in Scripture, we should be able to find ample evidence of its benefits in couples faithfully living the Church's teaching (through openness to fertility and Natural Family Planning) versus those who do not (using artificial birth control). There are three areas in which this should be evident:

1. Lower rate of divorce and greater longevity and satisfaction in marriage among those who faithfully live the Church's teaching
2. Greater emotional intimacy and self-sacrificial love in couples who faithfully live the Church's teaching

---

[151] See United Kingdom National Health Service, "Natural Family Planning (Fertility Awareness)", last reviewed April 13, 2021, https://www.nhs.uk/conditions/contraception/natural-family-planning/.

[152] See ibid.

[153] See ibid.

[154] See Fertility Appreciation Collaborative to Teach the Science (FACTS), "Sympto-Thermal Method", 2014, https://www.factsaboutfertility.org/wp-content/uploads/2014/09/SymptoThermalPEH.pdf.

3. A greater sense of respect and "being honored" by women in couples faithfully living the Church's teaching

We will examine each of these three testable consequences in Section IV.A, after which we will examine the contention that artificial contraception is needed to prevent dire Malthusian consequences of overpopulation (Section IV.B).

A. The Effects of Natural Family Planning on Marriage, Intimacy, Respect, and Religion

We proceed to the first testable consequence of Pope John Paul's explanation of the divine will for sexuality and marriage—decreased rate of divorce and increased marital longevity and satisfaction. In a comprehensive comparative study of 5,530 reproductive-age women in the (2006–2010) National Survey of Family Growth, Dr. Richard Fehring obtained the following results:

> Among the women who ever used NFP [Natural Family Planning] only 9.6 percent were currently divorced compared with the 14.4 percent who were currently divorced among the women who never used NFP ($x^2 = 5.34$, $P < 0.21$). Odds ratio analysis indicated that ever having an abortion, sterilization, and/or methods of contraception increased the likelihood of divorce—up to two times. Frequency of church attendance decreased the risk of divorce.[155]

Fehring did not try to narrow the scope of the study to couples currently using NFP but measured the much broader category of couples "whoever used NFP". This provided for a more accurate comparison to couples using artificial birth control. As noted in the results, couples who made recourse to abortion, sterilization, or artificial birth control had up to *two times* the rate of divorce (after other possible relevant factors had been eliminated).[156]

---

[155] Richard Fehring, "The Influence of Contraception, Abortion, and Natural Family Planning on Divorce Rates as Found in the 2006–2010 National Survey of Family Growth", *Linacre Quarterly* 82, no. 3 (August 2015), Abstract, https://www.ncbi.nlm.nih.gov/pmc/articles/PMC4536625/.

[156] Ibid.

What about marital dynamics, marital satisfaction, and sexual intimacy? In a 2017 U.S. and international comprehensive study of twenty-five hundred couples using the sympto-thermal method of NFP (who had previously used artificial birth control), Matthias Unseld and others obtained the following results:

- Seventy-four percent of men and 65 percent of women indicated that NFP had helped to improve their relationship (by comparison with artificial birth control); 17 percent of men and 26 percent of women said it made little difference. Less than 10 percent of men and women felt that NFP had harmed their relationship. Thus, large majorities of men and women believe that NFP (by comparison to artificial birth control) improved their marital relationship.[157]
- With respect to sexual intimacy, "62% of women and 63% of men said that NFP improved their sex life while 37% of women and 25% of men felt it was unchanged from before they used NFP. Approximately 1% of women and 11% of men felt use of NFP had harmed their sex life."[158] Thus, a majority of men and women believed that NFP helped their sexual intimacy and only a small minority believed that it has harmed them.
- With respect to knowledge and communication about sexuality, 69 percent of women and 72 percent of men felt that NFP helped them to talk about sexuality with their partners while only 8 percent felt it did not. "More than 80% of both men and women felt NFP improved their knowledge and understanding of sexuality."[159]

The Unseld results were further confirmed by a 2018 study of Sergio Barroilhet and others on marital functioning within couples using NFP versus artificial methods of birth control, in structured interviews at health centers in Santiago, Chile:

---

[157] See Matthias Unseld et al., "Use of Natural Family Planning (NFP) and Its Effect on Couple Relationships and Sexual Satisfaction: A Multi-Country Survey of NFP Users from US and Europe", *Frontiers in Public Health* 5, no. 42 (March 13, 2017), under "NFP and Relationship Dynamics", https://www.ncbi.nlm.nih.gov/pmc/articles/PMC5346544/.

[158] Ibid., under "NFP and Sexuality".

[159] See ibid.

On average, the NFP group had a significantly higher DAS score [indicating positive marital functioning] than AMC [artificial methods of birth control]. After controlling for age, socioeconomic status, time in the relationship, and religious commitment in multivariable analysis, the NFP group had a 47 percent (odds ratio = 1.47) greater possibility of having a functional marital score above the cutoff (DAS > 114) when compared with the AMC group. The AMC group reported more frequency of sexual intercourse but similar sexual satisfaction. Most (>60 percent) of the NFP couples mentioned that their methods improved their relationship.[160]

Thus, NFP users have a 47 percent better score in marital functioning than those using artificial birth control, and 60 percent of NFP users believed that NFP had helped them in their relationship.

What about emotional intimacy? In a 2003 study by Leona Vande Vusse and others surveying fourteen hundred randomly selected couples known to use NFP and asking for qualitative responses, 74 percent of the comments made found it "beneficial, often resulting in stronger bonds [emotional intimacy], better communication, and improved knowledge".[161] Approximately one-fourth of the couples found NFP methods challenging.[162] Qualitative comments indicated enhancements in the marital relationship (including closeness and emotional intimacy), spiritual life (both personally and as a couple), knowledge of the partners for one another, and success of the methods used.[163]

In sum, the above four studies show the veracity of Pope Paul VI's and Pope John Paul II's statements about the nature of sexuality within marriage (based on their interpretation of the Creator's will in Matthew 19:4–6[164]). Both popes affirmed that marital longevity,

---

[160] Sergio Barroilhet et al., "Marital Functioning in Couples Practicing Periodic Abstinence for Family Planning", *Linacre Quarterly* 85, no. 2 (May 2018), Abstract, https://www.ncbi.nlm.nih.gov/pmc/articles/PMC6056796/.

[161] Leona Vande Vusse et al., "Couples' Views of the Effects of Natural Family Planning on Marital Dynamics", *National Library of Medicine National Center for Biotechnology Information* 35, no. 2 (2003), Abstract, https://pubmed.ncbi.nlm.nih.gov/12854299/.

[162] See ibid.

[163] See ibid.

[164] "Have you not read that he who made them from the beginning [the Creator] made them male and female, and said, 'For this reason, a man shall leave his father and mother and be joined to his wife, and the two shall become one'? So they are no longer two but one. What therefore God has joined together, let no man put asunder" (Mt 19:4–6; Jesus is quoting Gen 1:27; 2:24).

intimacy, and marital satisfaction would be improved if couples allowed sexual relations to be open to new life indicative of their complete self-gift and permanent commitment to one another. The above four studies confirm a significantly lowered rate of divorce as well as significant improvements in marital relationships, marital bonds (emotional intimacy), marital satisfaction, sexual satisfaction, marital communication, and the couple's knowledge of each other.

We may now answer the question of whether Natural Family Planning is worth the periodic abstinence and the effort to learn the method. As shown in the above studies, significant majorities of the couples using NFP believe that it is, and their belief is borne out by a decreased rate of divorce[165] and objectively measurable enhancements in marital functioning.[166]

One of Pope Paul's and Pope John Paul's predictions was not measured by a quantitative study—namely, a woman's sense of being respected or honored within the relationship. However, this sense of respect and esteem is mentioned often in anecdotal testimonies to the efficacy of Natural Family Planning—for example, the testimony of Dawn Farias:

> What I would learn about God's design for my married life and through the practice of NFP would change my life.... Over time and with some experience, I began to appreciate the gift and beauty of NFP.... When we had used artificial contraception, we ignored this reality [i.e., the possibility of new life].... NFP helped us understand the relationship that God designed between the marital act and procreation.... In using NFP over the years both my husband and I now see that we give ourselves to each other fully in the marital act.... [Artificial contraception] cheapens the marital act. Contraception seems to say: "I love you, honey, but I don't love you THAT much." NFP also guards against the objectification of the woman in the relationship. Contraception often keeps the woman in a defensive position because it allows "intimacy on demand." NFP does not allow this because of the practice of periodic abstinence when not seeking a pregnancy. A deeper equality between husband and wife can be nurtured with NFP.... The sacrifices that NFP entails have only served to make me a better person and more devoted to the Lord. Without

[165] Fehring, "Influence".
[166] Barroilhet et al., "Marital Functioning".

knowing it, using contraception promotes the idea that children are a burden.... NFP has led me to be more open to life, more aware of God's design for intimacy in marriage, more dependent on Him to fulfill these plans. It has strengthened my relationship with my husband, given me personal insight and it has given our children life![167]

Some readers may have found one of the above findings of Matthias Unseld counterintuitive—"couples using NFP (requiring some abstinence) experience higher levels of sexual intimacy."[168] Contemporary culture suggests that unrestricted sexual experience should lead to greater sexual intimacy, but Unseld found precisely the opposite. The reason may be linked to the above testimonial—namely, that NFP elevates the dignity of the couple by calling forth mutual dialogue about how and when to be sexually intimate. This elevates sexual intimacy beyond mere "gratification of the moment" to the means of solidifying the couple's commitments, values, and openness to children and family. Apparently, higher levels of dignity and mutual communication are more important to intimacy than obtaining immediate gratification.

We conclude this section with an observation from Jason Evert:

NFP is the better way, and couples who make the switch are more than pleased with the results. One way to measure a couple's satisfaction with a method of spacing births is to look at how many continue to use it over time. For example, spermicides have a 42 percent annual continuation rate; the condom, 53 percent; the shot, 56 percent; the diaphragm, a 57 percent rate; and the Pill, 68 percent. What about NFP? Research of 1,876 couples using the Creighton Model of NFP showed that it has an annual continuation rate of 89 percent—which is higher than any form of reversible contraception.[169]

---

[167] Dawn Farias, *How Natural Family Planning Changed My Life* (Washington, D.C.: NFPP/United States Conference of Catholic Bishops, 2015), https://www.usccb.org/issues-and-action/marriage-and-family/natural-family-planning/what-is-nfp/couples-stories/upload/Dawn-Farias-English.pdf.

[168] As stated above, with respect to sexual intimacy, "62% of women and 63% of men said that NFP improved their sex life while 37% of women and 25% of men felt it was unchanged from before they used NFP." Unseld et al., "Use of Natural Family Planning", under "NFP and Sexuality".

[169] Jason Evert, *If You Really Loved Me* (Scottsdale, Ariz.: Totus Tuus Press, 2013), p. 66.

B. Overpopulation and a Need for Artificial Contraception?

Artificial birth control, as well as the eugenics movement and forced abortion policies in countries like China, have been not only justified but also foisted upon millions of unwilling individuals throughout the world on the basis of the dire consequences of exponentially growing overpopulation. This belief was initially fostered by Anglican cleric and economist Thomas Malthus in his work *An Essay on the Principle of Population* (1798). In it, he predicts that if overpopulation is not restrained either morally or legally, it will outpace the production of food to maintain minimal standards of living. This will lead to catastrophic consequences—starvation, disease, social strife, among others.[170] Malthus predicted that population would increase at a geometrical rate (doubling every twenty-five years) while resources would grow at an arithmetic rate, thereby giving rise to a world catastrophe without the imposition of legal restraint of population growth.

1. The Negative Impact of Malthusianism

Anthropologist Eric Ross contends that Malthus' work was used to rationalize "the social inequities of the Industrial Revolution, anti-immigration movements, the eugenics movement, and the various international development movements".[171] Malthus' contention was used almost immediately by the British government to reverse laws to help the poor with needed food and medical supplies so that they would die prematurely and reduce superfluous population. According to Michael Shermer:

> The English Poor Law implemented by Queen Elizabeth I in 1601 to provide food to the poor was severely curtailed by the Poor Law Amendment Act of 1834, based on Malthusian reasoning that helping the poor only encourages them to have more children and thereby exacerbate poverty. The British government had a similar Malthusian

---

[170] Thomas Malthus, *An Essay on the Principle of Population* (London: J. Johnson in St. Paul's Church-Yard, 1798).

[171] Eric B. Ross, *The Malthus Factor: Population, Poverty, and Politics in Capitalist Development* (London: Zed Books, 1998).

attitude during the Irish potato famine of the 1840s ... reasoning that famine, in the words of Assistant Secretary to the Treasury Charles Trevelyan, was an "effective mechanism for reducing surplus population."[172]

These draconian ways of controlling population of "inferiors" for the so-called good of humanity have led to terrible, unnecessary hardships and injustices to economically underprivileged individuals for over two hundred years. As noted above, the Malthusian "over population catastrophe" inspired the eugenics movement, which used it to further its more insidious policies to eliminate "racial inferiors", the mentally and physically disabled, and economically underprivileged.[173] Malthus influenced Charles Darwin, and his half-cousin Francis Galton, the founder of the eugenics movement.[174] Throughout the 1920s and 1930s, the eugenics movement experienced considerable growth, not only in Germany, Britain, and other European countries but also in the United States. One of the foremost U.S. advocates of eugenics, Margaret Sanger (founder of Planned Parenthood), declared that birth control was needed not only to control population but to remedy the imbalance in population between "the fit and the unfit". In her essay "The Eugenic Value of Birth Control Propaganda", Sanger asserted:

> As an advocate of Birth Control, I wish to take advantage of the present opportunity to point out that the unbalance between the birth rate of the "unfit" and the "fit", admittedly the greatest present menace to civilization, can never be rectified by the inauguration of a cradle competition between these two classes. In this matter, the example of the inferior classes, the fertility of the feeble-minded, the mentally

---

[172] See Michael Shermer, "Why Malthus Is Still Wrong", *Scientific American*, May 1, 2016, https://www.scientificamerican.com/article/why-malthus-is-still-wrong/. Shermer is citing work from Matt Ridley, *The Evolution of Everything: How New Ideas Emerge* (New York: Harper, 2015).

[173] See Alberto Spektorowski and Liza Ireni-Saban, *Politics of Eugenics: Productionism, Population, and National Welfare* (London: Routledge, 2013).

[174] See Randal Hansen and Desmond Kind, *Sterilized by the State: Eugenics, Race, and the Population Scare in Twentieth-Century North America* (Cambridge: Cambridge University Press, 2013), pp. 107–9, https://www.tandfonline.com/doi/abs/10.1080/14743892.2017.1340068?journalCode=rach20.

defective, the poverty-stricken classes, should not be held up for emulation to the mentally and physically fit though less fertile parents of the educated and well-to-do classes. On the contrary, the most urgent problem today is how to limit and discourage the over-fertility of the mentally and physically defective.[175]

Hitler tried to further eugenics objectives in every sector of what he called "inferiors"—the disabled, Jewish people, gypsies, other racial inferiors, and the economically and educationally underprivileged. The atrocities of Nazism were so grotesque that eugenics lost popularity throughout the world, and so had to slip underground.[176] Nevertheless, it began to reemerge in its Malthusian form in the early 1960s as "population control to avert the population explosion".[177] This worked its way into the policies of Western governments, many Asian countries, and the United Nations Fund for Population Activities (UNFPA).[178]

The population control movement continues to the current day, not only through the official forced abortion policies of China, North Korea, and Peru but also through pressure to use artificial birth control in economically stressed countries by the UNFPA. According to Austin Ruse, the UNFPA directly funded and gave technical assistance to China's forced abortion policy (leading to fifty million coerced abortions in its first six years), the Peruvian forced sterilization/abortion policy, and the coercive distribution of artificial contraceptives in other countries.[179] Most often, forced contraception and sterilization is carried out by local governments in developing countries against their own citizens (sometimes funded by the United Nations or other developed countries).[180] This is often carried out in Asian

---

[175] Margaret Sanger, "The Eugenic Value of Birth Control Propaganda", *Birth Control Review*, October 1921, https://eugenics.us/the-eugenic-value-of-birth-control-propaganda-by-margaret-sanger/128.htm.

[176] See Austin Ruse, "The Myth of Overpopulation and the Folks Who Brought It to You", United States Conference of Catholic Bishops (website), 2022, http://www.usccb.org/about/pro-life-activities/respect-life-program/the-myth-of-overpopulation-and-the-folks-who-brought-it-to-you.cfm.

[177] Ibid.

[178] Ibid.

[179] See ibid.

[180] Ibid.

countries beyond China.[181] Moreover, forced sterilization is also a part of U.S. history beginning officially in 1927, when the Supreme Court voted eight to one to uphold a state's right to force sterilization "on those unfit to procreate".[182] This decision led to the forced sterilization of seventy thousand Americans. It had a resurgence in the 1970s and continues in a more limited way to the present day—sterilization of African Americans in North Carolina and South Carolina, American Indians in Native American Health Centers across the United States, and Latina immigrants in California.[183] It has also been used in Canada to sterilize indigenous women.[184]

Pope Paul VI, in *Humanae Vitae*, presciently foresaw how modern forms of birth control could be used to continue the legacy of injustice, oppression, and eugenic genocide inscribed in the politics of the Malthusian overpopulation catastrophe:

> Careful consideration should be given to the danger of this power passing into the hands of those public authorities who care little for the precepts of the moral law.... Who will prevent public authorities from favoring those contraceptive methods which they consider more effective? Should they regard this as necessary, they may even impose their use on everyone.[185]

2. The Overpopulation Myth

The grave injustices and tragedies arising out of the Malthusian overpopulation catastrophe require an objective assessment of its truth, for if it is false, then it is a most pernicious lie that continues to be used to spawn one unnecessary tragedy after another. It may be argued that since the 1930s, scientists, technology experts, and demographic experts recognized that the Malthusian prediction was simply

---

[181] See Chelsea Follett, "The Cruel Truth about Population Control", commentary, CATO Institute, June 13, 2019 (article originally appeared on the same date in National Interest [online]), https://www.cato.org/publications/commentary/cruel-truth-about-population-control.

[182] Buck v. Bell, 274 U.S. 200 (1927).

[183] See Rachel Benson Gold, "Guarding against Coercion While Ensuring Access: A Delicate Balance", *Guttmacher Policy Review* 17, no. 3 (2014): 8–14, https://www.guttmacher.org/gpr/2014/09/guarding-against-coercion-while-ensuring-access-delicate-balance#.

[184] See Follett, "Cruel Truth about Population Control".

[185] *Humane Vitae*, no. 17.

false and would likely continue to be false, because scientific and technological advances would continue to improve the efficiency and economy of food production, resource availability, communication, and information storage and processing, which would allow per capita income to increase and spread over much larger population segments.[186]

In his book *Unlimited Wealth*, Paul Pilzer argues that Malthusian predictions have never been true because they do not account for the "X factor" of resource multiplication, distribution, and efficient production coming from technology.[187] This is why despite exponentially increasing population rates, per capita income has increased as well as the percentage of people sharing in that wealth. Since 1950, the average person (in both developed and developing countries) has 4.4 times greater wealth than in 1950, moving from an average of $3,300 to $14,574 (adjusted for inflation at 2013 level).[188] It may be thought that this significant increase in wealth does not apply to the poorest of the poor who have neither the education nor the foundational resources to advance their condition. As we shall see, the millennial development goals agreed to by the developing countries at the 1990 United Nations conference on millennial development have made tremendous progress not only in averting starvation, disease, and poverty, but also in closing the educational and technology gap (see Chapter 7, Section III).[189]

Since the time of the Green Revolution, the efforts of Norman Borlaug and others led to a rapid increase of food production, more than doubling grain and rice production (increasing by a factor of 160 percent) by 1985.[190] His basic approach was the development of high-yielding varieties of cereal grains, expansion of irrigation infrastructure, modernization of management techniques, and distribution

---

[186]Paul Zane Pilzer, *Unlimited Wealth: The Theory and Practice of Economic Alchemy* (New York: Crown Publishers, 1990).

[187]Ibid.

[188]See Max Roser, "Economic Growth", Our World in Data (website), 2013, https://ourworldindata.org/economic-growth.

[189]*Millennium Development Goals Report* (New York: United Nations, 2015), http://www.un.org/millenniumgoals/2015_MDG_Report/pdf/MDG%202015%20rev%20%28July%201%29.pdf.

[190]See W. Henery Kindall and David Pimentel, "Constraints on the Expansion of the Global Food Supply", *AMBIO* 23, no. 3 (1994): 198–205.

of hybridized seeds, synthetic fertilizers, and pesticides to farmers.[191] These improvements led to food production for an additional one billion people by 1985. Since then, Green Revolutions have been continuing in India, China, and Southeast Asia. They are starting in Africa and will increase significantly in the next decade.

Will agricultural advances continue as the population rises? Advances in genetics have led to hardier strains of food crops, which are insect resistant[192] and disease resistant.[193] Advances are also being made in irrigation, fertilization, and farm management, which have enabled greater yields and production per acre. Furthermore, as the price of energy decreases (see below), multilevel hydroponic farms will increase food production by a factor of two and a half to five times in the near future.[194]

The world population will reach a maximum of 9.7 billion people in about 2064 (from the current 7.9 billion people),[195] and then decline to 8.8 billion in 2100.[196] Even if the population far exceeds 9.7 billion people in 2064, food production will be able to keep pace with it, because hydroponic farms can be built to enormous sizes with no cessation of production day and night throughout the year (almost completely resistant to diseases and pests). As we shall see, population explosion is not the real problem, but rather population

---

[191]See Graham P. Chapman, "The Green Revolution", in *The Companion to Development Studies* (London: Arnold, 2002), pp. 155–59, https://staff.washington.edu/jhannah/geog 270auto7/readings/GreenGeneRevolutions/Chapman%20-%20GreenRev.pdf.

[192]See A. M. R. Gatehouse et al., "Insect-Resistant Biotech Crops and Their Impacts on Beneficial Arthropods", *Philosophical Transactions of the Royal Society B: Biological Sciences* 366, no. 1569 (2011): 1438–52, https://www.ncbi.nlm.nih.gov/pmc/articles/PMC3081576/#.

[193]See Sophie J. M. Piquerez et al., "Improving Crop Disease Resistance: Lessons from Research on Arabidopsis and Tomato", *Frontiers in Plant Science* 5 (2014): 671, https://www .ncbi.nlm.nih.gov/pmc/articles/PMC4253662/.

[194]Markets and Markets, "Hydroponics Market by Type (Aggregate Systems, Liquid Systems), Crop Type (Vegetables, Fruits, Flowers), Equipment (HVAC, Led Grow Light, Irrigation Systems, Material Handling, Control Systems), Input, and Region—Global Forecast to 2026", January 2021, https://www.marketsandmarkets.com/Market-Reports/hydroponic -market-94055021.html.

[195]See Worldometer, accessed January 10, 2022, https://www.worldometers.info/world -population/.

[196]See Stein Emil Vollset et al., "Fertility, Mortality, Migration, and Population Scenarios for 195 Countries and Territories from 2017 to 2100: A Forecasting Analysis for the Global Burden of Disease Study", *Lancet* 396, no. 10258 (October 17, 2020): 1301, https://www .thelancet.com/journals/lancet/article/PIIS0140-6736(20)30677-2/fulltext.

implosion in which the younger generation in developed countries will be less than 50 percent of the older generation that it will have to sustain.

Given that food production will not run out before the world reaches maximum population (2064), will energy and natural resource production also be able to handle the 24 percent increase in population by 2064? Will the world be out of energy when fossil fuels run out? By no means. Hydrogen is the most plentiful element in the universe (and on the planet). When it is separated from complex molecules (such as water), then combined with oxygen through a fuel cell, it can produce an almost endless amount of energy.[197] This process will be more expensive than fossil fuels, but technological advances and better systems and supply chains will lower that extra expense considerably over the next two decades.[198] Additionally, technologies are being developed to extract CO_2 from the air, which not only cleans up the atmosphere but also can be converted into petroleum resources for decades to come.[199] The cost of this energy supply is higher than the current cost of fossil fuel, but again, as technology and supply chains improve, costs will come down. Furthermore, biofuels (such as ethanol produced by sugar beets and other sugars) are limited only by the amount of farmland and hydroponic capacity available. These new synthetic and bio-options complement significant increases in solar technology,[200] wind technology, geothermal technology, and battery and energy storage (particularly utility scale application of lithium-ion battery technology).[201]

Will we run out of fuel and energy in the next several centuries? If technological improvements of the above synthetic, bio, solar, and

[197] See U.S. Department of Energy, Alternative Fuels Data Center, "Hydrogen Production and Distribution", accessed January 11, 2022, https://afdc.energy.gov/fuels/hydrogen_pro duction.html.

[198] See ibid.

[199] See James Conca, "Extract CO_2 from Our Air, Use It to Create Synthetic Fuels", EnergyPost.eu, October 11, 2019, https://energypost.eu/extract-co2-from-our-air-use-it-to -create-synthetic-fuels/.

[200] See Emily Kerr, "The Future of Solar Is Bright", *Science in the News*, March 21, 2019, http://sitn.hms.harvard.edu/flash/2019/future-solar-bright/.

[201] See Pippa Stevens, "The Battery Decade: How Energy Storage Could Revolutionize Industries in the Next 10 Years", CNBC, December 30, 2019, https://www.cnbc .com/2019/12/30/battery-developments-in-the-last-decade-created-a-seismic-shift-that -will-play-out-in-the-next-10-years.html.

geothermal fuel sources continue apace, we will be able to maintain energy supplies not only for centuries to come but also with continuing population increases. The future of energy, however, does not rest on the above five sources alone. There is another mega source of energy that could lead to an exponential increase in production that would be less than the cost of fossil fuels—fusion.[202] Nuclear fusion would resolve the energy problems of the world indefinitely even with exponential population growth, because there is virtually no limit to its hydrogen fuel source (it can be obtained from modest amounts of sea water), and it has no carbon emissions, no radioactive waste, and no chance of a "meltdown".[203] Recent advances in fusion engineering strongly suggest that fusion reactors will be in operation by about 2050.[204]

There are countless other advances and materials for construction, communication technology, and information storage technology. Moreover, these advances are being used to close the economic gap between developed and developing countries. The inexpensive cost of smartphones[205] (and banking accessibility by smartphones) combined with a huge expansion in microlending access and technology[206] have allowed tens of millions of "new entrepreneurs" to initiate small- and medium-sized ventures in the poorest countries in the world. Furthermore, online education has made trillions of pages of educational content available free of charge to anyone with an inexpensive smartphone anywhere in the world. Though educational gaps will continue between developed and developing countries in graduate and postgraduate education, new online initiatives will lead to the closing of gaps in secondary and basic undergraduate education.

[202] See Slavomir Entler et al., "Approximation of the Economy of Fusion Energy", *Energy* 152, no. 1 (2018): 489–97, https://www.sciencedirect.com/science/article/pii/S0360544218305395.

[203] See Ariel Cohen, "Is Fusion Power within Our Grasp?", *Forbes*, January 14, 2019, https://www.forbes.com/sites/arielcohen/2019/01/14/is-fusion-power-within-our-grasp/#5728af7b9bb4.

[204] See ibid.

[205] In India, an excellent smartphone is the Realme C2, which is available for a little over $200. In the United States, the cheapest smartphone is the Samsung Galaxy A13 for $49.

[206] See Stephanie Wykstra, "Microcredit Was a Hugely Hyped Solution to Global Poverty. What Happened?", *Vox*, January 15, 2019, https://www.vox.com/future-perfect/2019/1/15/18182167/microcredit-microfinance-poverty-grameen-bank-yunus.

We may infer from the above that there will be adequate food, energy, natural resources, and education to supply the world population, even at a more accelerated level of growth than currently predicted into the indefinite future. Yet we must still ask the question whether these resources will be distributed to the neediest, poorest, and most vulnerable populations throughout the world. The problem here is not so much resource availability, because as shown above, resources are available to the world's population. Rather, the problem is whether individuals have the will to share resources with populations who are unable to acquire them competitively within the marketplace. This will entail not only sharing of resources but setting up distribution chains for which compensation will very likely be less than the cost incurred.

3. What about the Poorest of the Poor?

The good news is that most of the governments and people of developed countries *do* have the will to share resources and build distribution chains to help those who are currently unable to help themselves.[207] The Catholic Church, other churches, and hundreds of international NGOs (non-governmental organizations) are dedicated to bringing potable water, food, healthcare, education, and intermediate technologies (smaller scale technology with little installation investment and maintenance cost) to developing countries. The collaboration between public, religious, and private NGOs has increased considerably since 1990, which has enabled these partnerships to make steady progress to meeting the United Nations millennium development goals.[208] The United Nations *Millennium Development Goals Report* (2015) showed considerable progress in several important areas.[209] (The specific areas in improvements are reported in Chapter 7, Section III.) These impressive results confirm the efficacy of concerted commitment to sustainable development goals (SDGs). It should be

---

[207] As explained in Chapter 7 (Section III), international efforts have improved the lives of billions of people in the last few decades, providing them with potable water, food, medicine, and healthcare sufficient to move them out of destitution and poverty. See *Millennium Development Goals Report.*

[208] See ibid.

[209] See ibid.

noted that the above results (and the SDG strategy that incited them) would not have been possible without the productivity, creativity, efficiency, technology, and communication coming directly and indirectly from business enterprises within a free market system.

If the goodwill and collaboration of governments, churches, NGOs, and individual people in developed countries continues apace, we might be able to achieve double the current impressive results before 2045, which will enable developing countries to make significant progress to sustain themselves, grow in technological and transportation infrastructure, and increase the levels of primary, secondary, undergraduate, and graduate education.

Education is the key not only to economic self-sufficiency and growth but also to democratic societal self-determination that respects cultural and individual autonomy. Online education is part of the solution, but significant investments also need to be made by religious, governmental, and non-governmental organizations to build educational institutions with general accessibility and affordability. Given the continued goodwill of the above organizations, there is hope that higher educational infrastructure will grow in developing countries allowing them to become competitive players on the international stage.

So, what does the above mean for the Malthusian overpopulation catastrophe? It shows that the Malthusian prediction is unfounded and untrue. Unfortunately, Malthusianism has been used to justify the most heartless economic and political objectives toward those in developing countries and the poor within developed countries. It has led both indirectly and directly to the eugenics movement, forced abortion and sterilization, and the mistreatment of poor populations throughout the world. In addition to all this, Malthusianism (the overpopulation myth) is leading to yet another catastrophe today—population implosion (discussed immediately below).

4. Impending Population Implosion

In 2019, Elon Musk warned, "The world's population is accelerating towards collapse, but few seem to notice or care."[210] Musk

---

[210] Elon Musk, "The World's Population Is Accelerating toward Collapse and Nobody Cares", CNBC, July 6, 2017, https://www.cnbc.com/2017/07/06/elon-musk-the-worlds-population-is-accelerating-toward-collapse-and-nobody-cares.html.

was reacting to an article in the *New Scientist* that showed that the overpopulation myth is causing the world's nations to hurtle toward population implosion by 2076:

> Half the world's nations have fertility rates below the replacement level of just over two children per woman. Countries across Europe and the Far East are teetering on a demographic cliff, with rates below 1.5. On recent trends, Germany and Italy could see their populations halve within the next 60 years.... Many demographers expect a global crash to be under way by 2076.[211]

According to Abhijit Roy and Mousumi Roy, there are three major kinds of negative consequences coming from population implosion—demographic consequences, economic consequences, and cultural consequences.[212] For the sake of brevity, we will focus on only demographic and economic consequences.

With respect to demographic consequences, the aging of population is the most significant negative consequence because the elderly need more resources than younger people (requiring younger people to support them). As long as there are about four younger people to support one older person (over seventy), the social cost to young families will not be unduly burdensome. However, if the ratio of young people to old people declines significantly, the burden to young people will increase proportionately to the point of being unmanageable. In 1960, the ratio of young to elderly people (the age-dependency ratio) was 6.8 young people for every elderly person. In 1999, there were only 4.5 young people for every elderly person. In 2030 the ratio is expected to be 2.5 young people for every elderly person, which will continue to decline for decades to come.[213] Social security in the United States and international pension systems will not

[211] Fred Pearce, "The World in 2076: The Population Bomb Has Imploded", *New Scientist*, November 16, 2016, https://www.newscientist.com/article/mg23231001-400-the-world-in-2076-the-population-bomb-did-go-off-but-were-ok/.

[212] Abhijit Roy and Mousumi Roy, "Antecedents and Consequences of Impending Population Implosion in the Developed World: Implications for Business Systems", *International Journal of Sustainable Society* 7, no. 2 (2015): 151, https://www.researchgate.net/publication/281422730_Antecedents_and_consequences_of_impending_population_implosion_in_the_developed_world_Implications_for_business_systems.

[213] P. G. Peterson, *Gray Dawn: How the Coming Age Wave Will Transform America and the World* (New York: Random House, 1999).

be able to sustain themselves after 2032 as the age-dependency ratio drops below 2.5 to 1. Furthermore, the cost of healthcare benefits will rise at an accelerated rate (not only because of the rising cost of healthcare but also because of the number and percentage of elderly using Medicare and other healthcare benefits). In order to manage these costs, the percentage of young people's payroll taxes will have to double and then triple within two decades, which is likely to be unduly burdensome even if they make cuts in their standard of living.

As Abhijit and Mousumi Roy note, "Another drawback of aging nations will be the short supply of creativity and innovations. Studies have shown that these qualities flourish at a younger age."[214]

How will the developed nations of the world (eighty-three of them) manage this monumental challenge? There are only two ways: initiate programs to incentivize native populations to have a second, third, and fourth child, and immigration. Japan, Russia, Germany, France, and Singapore have already had to liberalize their strict immigration policies to contend with their population implosion problem.[215] In the future, all developed nations will have to liberalize their immigration policies significantly in order to allow immigrants to take over a rapidly increasing percentage of their workforces.[216] This will present two major challenges: the loss of national identity and considerable social costs to accommodate and educate large immigrant populations.[217] These challenges will become more acute as the need for additional immigrants continues to rise throughout the upcoming decade. Though accommodation and education of large numbers of immigrants will be increasingly needed, it will not be enough. Governments of developed countries will also have to incentivize native people to have a second, third, or fourth child to ease the above social challenges of increasing immigration. As we shall see, a multiple-child incentivization policy will also be crucial to staving off economic problems, such as the rapid decline of household wealth in developed nations.

With respect to economic consequences, growth of the gross domestic product (GDP) is necessary to maintain a high standard of living.

---

[214] Roy and Roy, "Antecedents and Consequences".

[215] See ibid.

[216] See ibid.

[217] See ibid.

According to the National Institute of Aging, GDP growth in Europe is expected to decline to half of what it was in 2007 by 2030.[218] According to the McKinsey Global Institute, the household financial wealth of Germany will decline by 25 percent and Great Britain will decline by 34 percent between the years of 2005 and 2035.[219] All developed European countries will experience similar (though slightly less) declines in household financial wealth.[220] Further economic declines are projected to occur because of a continuing decrease in the availability of high-skilled labor.[221]

These challenges could be quite significant when combined with the rising amount of payroll taxes that will be needed to accommodate the decline in the age-dependency ratio (the number of young people to support older people in the population). Even with generous and farsighted programs to accommodate and educate an increasing number of immigrants, all developed nations must expect a decline in GDP, household financial wealth, and standard of living. This will produce inevitable strain on the majority of people in developed countries, decreasing quality of life and increasing rates of depression, anxiety, and social tension. According to Abhijit Roy and Mousumi Roy, "quality of life" refers not only to the standard of living but also to the social functioning, emotional well-being, and access to goods and services in a society.[222] Declining household financial wealth, increasing payroll taxes, significant cultural changes (by rising numbers of immigrants), and the challenges of dealing with increased age (individually and collectively) will negatively impact quality of life, which will in turn increase rates of depression, anxiety, and social tension.

The severe consequences of population implosion pertain only to *developed* countries. Might it not be argued that artificial contraception will still be needed in Africa and some parts of Asia to help

---

[218] Department of State and the Department of Health and Human Services, *Why Population Aging Matters: A Global Perspective* (Washington, D.C.: National Institute on Aging, National Institutes of Health, 2007), https://2001-2009.state.gov/g/oes/rls/or/81537.htm.

[219] McKinsey Global Institute, "The Demographic Deficit: How Aging Will Reduce Global Wealth", *McKinsey Quarterly*, March 2005, http://www.mickeybutts.com/globalaging Quarterly.pdf.

[220] See ibid.

[221] See Roy and Roy, "Antecedents and Consequences".

[222] See ibid.

alleviate the poverty and economic stress in the most underdeveloped nations? Shouldn't pressure be put on these nations to enforce mandatory artificial contraception among poor populations? There are several problems with limiting populations in developing countries. First, as explained above, developed countries will need an increasing number of immigrants from developing countries to sustain their economies and quality of life. Forced artificial birth control policies in developing countries would effectively cut back on the number of immigrants available to prevent economic implosion.

Secondly, as might be inferred from above (Section IV.B.1), such strategies are unnecessary and abusive. In some cases (such as China, North Korea, and Peru), enforcement is cruel and tyrannical. Why is enforced birth control unnecessary? First, as countries increase the availability of secondary education, populations naturally reduce family size without enforcement. According to the World Bank:

> A negative correlation is most clearly seen between different levels of female education and the total fertility rate (TFR) in a population.... What it shows for all three countries [Ethiopia, Ghana, and Kenya] is that there are striking differences in TFR between women with no schooling and women with a high school education.[223]

High school education for women in the most populous countries of Africa moves the average fertility rate from six per family to about two per family.[224] This occurs without enforcement, and women are free to choose and learn natural family planning or to reject it. In general, the higher the level of education, the lower the fertility rate.

In light of the positive effects of natural family planning on lower divorce rates, marital functioning, marital intimacy, family stability, and respect for women, many high school educated and religiously motivated couples can be expected to choose and learn NFP over artificial contraception as education levels grow. Furthermore, secondary education for both men and women incites families to move

---

[223] Elina Pradhan, "Female Education and Childbearing: A Closer Look at the Data", *World Bank Blogs*, November 24, 2015, https://blogs.worldbank.org/health/female-education -and-childbearing-closer-look-data.
[224] Ibid.

from a rural (agricultural) environment to an urban or suburban environment, which lessens the need for large families.[225] This solidifies the effects of education on lowering average fertility rates. Thus, education is the proper way to lower fertility rates (rather than enforced artificial contraception) because it respects the rights of families to have as many children as they wish, to choose natural family planning, and to be open to fertility in their marital relations. Moreover, higher education rates also increase the standard of living, the growth potential, and the quality of life in developing nations. If we could refocus the efforts and funding mechanisms of international governmental and charitable organizations from fixation on artificial birth control to education of both men and women, developing nations will benefit not only economically and governmentally, but also in freedom, family economy, and family stability.

Let us return now to population implosion in developed nations. Recall that population implosion (partially brought on by the overpopulation myth) will affect future generations of developed countries quite negatively. This should motivate them to cease the current misinformation campaign about overpopulation, and to initiate incentive programs to reward couples to have a second, third, and fourth child. Since immigration alone is unlikely to resolve the problems of population implosion (particularly as increases in education decrease fertility levels in developed countries), the only way to maintain the standard of living for future generations in developing countries is to have more children filling the ranks of those generations. Incentivizing population reduction is tantamount to economic suicide for future generations in the ever-increasing number of developed countries. The only way forward is to increase population in developed countries while increasing education (to naturally and freely moderate population growth) in developing countries. This will allow for significantly increased rates of immigration from developing to developed countries while allowing for higher standards of living in developing countries. As noted above, the world's resources will be able to sustain significantly higher rates of population growth, and in future years, these additional people will be much needed in both developed and developing nations.

[225] See Roy and Roy, "Antecedents and Consequences".

V. Conclusion

Though the Catholic Church has been accused of being "out of step" and behind the times in her moral teaching on the homosexual lifestyle, pornography, gender change, and artificial birth control, deeper analysis of the personal, societal, and spiritual consequences of these four issues reveals a radically different picture. As shown above, a homosexual lifestyle leads to significantly increased rates of depression, anxiety, panic disorder, substance abuse, major psychiatric disorders, and suicidality, which cannot be explained by social stigmatization alone, suggesting that there is something intrinsic to the lifestyle that undermines emotional health. Furthermore, a homosexual lifestyle promotes sexual relationships that are opposite the ideal for committed sexual love taught by Jesus:

- Hundreds of lifetime sexual partners
- Very short duration of relationships (about one and a half years) with an insignificant percentage of permanent relationships
- A virtual absence of monogamy in relationships lasting more than five years

These statistics suggest that this lifestyle has a negative impact not only on emotional health and committed love but also on spiritual well-being. In view of this, the Catholic Church's recommendation of abstinence within support groups like Courage International may well prove to be the best way of achieving emotional health, significantly committed non-sexual friendships, and closeness to the Lord through prayer and walking with Him in carrying the cross.

As explained in Section II above, pornography is not a "victimless sin", but a strong habit (leading toward addiction) that severely impacts the lives of adults, marriages and families, the development of children, and our spiritual lives. Peer-reviewed longitudinal studies show its destructive effects with respect to significantly increased divorce rates, the undermining of emotional intimacy and marital bonds, significant increases in depression, anxiety, sexual partners, infidelity, and dangerous sexual behaviors, as well as a substantial negative impact on the development of children and adolescents and an increase in teen pregnancies and teen sexual violence. Inasmuch as pornography addiction is increasing rapidly (with all these consequences), the Catholic Church's opposition to it can hardly be viewed as a prudish "anti-sex" reaction to social progress. As noted above, pornography is a problem not only for individuals, families, and marriages, but also for the ideal of love and friendship within the culture. If we do not resist it individually and socially, it will severely undermine our culture.

The Catholic Church's teaching on "gender theory" and sex change (Section III) is salutary for emotional health, relational health, spiritual well-being, and culture. Research shows that there is no genetic or anatomical basis for a gender identity opposite one's biological sex. This is borne out by the fact that the vast majority of preadolescents with cross-gender confusion will eventually affirm an identity consistent with their biological sex either naturally or with therapeutic help. Moreover, sexual reassignment surgery is a permanent, unnecessary, damaging procedure that will preempt needed therapy to deal with underlying anxiety, depression, and self-rejection. Therefore, parents and physicians who have knowledge of these facts and encourage preadolescents to affirm a gender identity opposite their biological sex act irresponsibly and unethically. As Jesus and the Catholic Church imply, we should not encourage a person to pursue a destructive course of action in order to be affirming or nice. Rather, our responsibility is to help people pursue directions that are emotionally healthy, relationally healthy, and spiritually healthy—even if it means challenging them in a discomforting way to turn from a destructive path.

The Catholic Church's teaching against artificial birth control (Section IV) has led to a continuous stream of criticism both inside and outside the Catholic Church. Yet her predictions about the destructiveness that artificial contraception would produce (particularly, the sexual revolution) have turned out to be uncannily correct. Indeed, the consequences have been worse than Pope Paul VI predicted—particularly with respect to increased divorce rates, sexual violence, infidelity, marital dissatisfaction, and family instability. Furthermore, as Pope Paul VI feared, artificial birth control and its two partners, abortion and sterilization, have been imposed on citizens of many developing countries and forced on millions of people in China, North Korea, and Peru. Given these harms, why would anyone expect the Catholic Church to change her position?

Pope John Paul II addressed the advantages of Natural Family Planning (up to 99 percent effective) as an alternative to artificial contraception: heightened emotional intimacy, mutual respect, and covenant love that would lead to strong, satisfying, and enduring marriages capable of supporting a stable familial environment for children to learn religion, morality, and respect for others. The above five studies (Section IV.A) prove him correct. Natural Family Planning decreases divorce rates and heightens marital functioning, emotional intimacy, marital communication, sexual intimacy, and marital bondedness. Eighty-nine percent of couples who make the change from artificial contraception to Natural Family Planning stay with it (much higher than any other family planning method). Though NFP entails a commitment to learning the method as well as periodic abstinence, the vast majority of men and women think it is worth it because of the good effects it has on their relationship as well as their openness and devotion to children. Given that these positive consequences will enhance family, children, and culture, we should encourage NFP as a proven means to a happy and fruitful marriage.

The main complaint about the Church's teaching against artificial contraception coming from outside the Church is directed at her so-called irresponsible actions in allowing overpopulation that subjects the world to the Malthusian catastrophe. Yet as we have seen, Malthusianism is simply unfounded and untrue. Population increases will not catastrophically outpace food production, energy, and other needed resources. Furthermore, it has not led to a decrease in world per capita income, which has in fact increased by a factor of 4.4 times (after adjustment for inflation) since 1950. As we saw, Malthus did not account for the "X factor" of human ingenuity, scientific advancement, technological advancement, and social responsibility that would bring huge increases in food production, energy production, communication and transportation technology, and educational dissemination, as well as sustainable development goals that substantially decrease starvation, disease, and poverty. The problem today is not population explosion but population implosion, which is destined to impact developed nations, household financial wealth, quality of life, and social stability severely. Ironically, the only way out of this crisis is for developing nations to open their doors to increase immigration while incentivizing their own citizens to have two, three, or four children. As noted above, continued promotion of the overpopulation myth is tantamount to economic suicide for future generations of all developed countries, which will undermine not only their own stability but that of the entire world.

Is the Catholic Church really out of touch with the needs of contemporary culture, society, and the world? If it is, then the contemporary world is out of touch with its own needs. If the above research is correct, the Catholic Church's countercultural insistence on following the teachings of Christ may be one of the few indispensable lights in our impending cultural darkness.

PART TWO

Matters of Life and Death

Chapter Three

Abortion, Eugenics, Invitro Fertilization, and Embryonic Stem Cells

Introduction

In his encyclical letter *Evangelium Vitae*, Pope John Paul II affirmed the constant infallible teaching of the Catholic Church from the time of Jesus to the present on the inviolability of every innocent human life:

> In effect, the absolute inviolability of innocent human life is a moral truth clearly taught by Sacred Scripture, constantly upheld in the Church's Tradition and consistently proposed by her Magisterium. This consistent teaching is the evident result of that "supernatural sense of the faith" which, inspired and sustained by the Holy Spirit, safeguards the People of God from error when "it shows universal agreement in matters of faith and morals."[1]

The Catholic Church (following Jesus) respects the right to life not only because of the intrinsic dignity of all persons, but also because of their transcendental dignity—for everyone is created in the image and likeness of God Himself (see Gen 1:27; 5:1–5). One of the earliest accounts of sin in Christian Scripture is Cain's murder of his brother, Abel (Gen 4). The Lord says to him:

> "What have you done? The voice of your brother's blood is crying to me from the ground. And now you are cursed from the ground,

---

[1] Pope John Paul II, Encyclical Letter on the Value and Inviolability of Human Life *Evangelium Vitae* (March 25, 1995), no. 57; the pope was quoting Vatican Council II, Dogmatic Constitution on the Church *Lumen Gentium* (November 21, 1964), no. 12.

which has opened its mouth to receive your brother's blood from your hand. When you till the ground, it shall no longer yield to you its strength; you shall be a fugitive and a wanderer on the earth." ... [Cain responds], "You have driven me this day away from the ground; and from your face I shall be hidden." (vv. 10–14)

The Lord metes out an extreme punishment of Cain's injustice toward his brother by driving him from both the land and his presence. This shows the seriousness of his crime as both an injustice to Abel and an act of rebellion against God.

Jesus affirms the prohibition against killing an innocent person (see Mk 10:19) in the Sermon on the Mount (Mt 5:21):

You have heard that it was said to the men of old, "You shall not kill; and whoever kills shall be liable to judgment."

Additionally, He extends the prohibition to any interior attitude that could give rise to the intention to kill:

But I say to you that every one who is angry with his brother shall be liable to judgment; whoever insults his brother shall be liable to the council, and whoever says, "You fool!" shall be liable to the hell of fire. (Mt 5:22)

Jesus goes far beyond the ethical prohibition of killing and requires that Christians refrain from harming others, seek the good of others, and respect the dignity of others.

As will be explained in Chapter 6, Jesus affirms the Silver Rule (avoid unnecessary harm to others), which pertains first and foremost to the killing of an innocent. The Silver Rule is called ethical minimalism and is the most basic requirement of justice that must be accorded to every person. The general form is as follows: "Do not do unto others what you would not have them do unto you"—that is, avoid any unnecessary harm to others, but if a harm is unavoidable, minimize it. This proscription can be found in virtually every religion and every culture because it is so fundamental to basic justice and societal stability.

No doubt, Jesus is aware of this fundamental rule of justice in its two statements in the Old Testament (Tob 4:15; Sir 31:15). He accepts the Silver Rule when He proclaims the Golden Rule, which goes far beyond it. The Golden Rule is called ethical maximalism and is generally stated as follows: "Do unto others as you would have them do unto you"—that is, do the good for others that you would want done to you. When Jesus deliberately removed the "nots" from the Silver Rule, He changed its meaning from merely avoiding unnecessary harms to doing every good for others that we would want done to us—social altruism. Jesus appears to be the first in the history of religions to do this, and as will be explained in Chapter 6 of this volume, it had a huge transformative effect on the ethics, social policy, and legal systems throughout the world.

When Jesus moved His newborn Church from the Silver Rule to the Golden Rule, He extended the notion of love to every person—Jew or Gentile, free person or slave, male or female (Gal 3:28)—proclaiming that every individual is uniquely good, transcendent (made in the image and likeness of God), and therefore worthy of love. He even identified the welfare of every human person with His own welfare:

> The King will answer them, "Truly, I say to you, as you did it to one of the least of these my brethren, you did it to me.... As you did it not to one of the least of these, you did it not to me." (Mt 25:40, 45)

Thanks to the Catholic Church, Jesus' elevation of the personal dignity of every human being eventually led to another socially transformative discovery—inalienable natural rights (see Chapter 6, Section II). This discovery became the cornerstone of the Declaration of Independence, the French and English Revolutions, and the United Nations Charter of Human Rights.

Our contemporary age has attempted to justify abortion as a mother's right, eugenic abortion of the mentally disabled, and physician-assisted suicide for the elderly—and now the young. The Catholic Church contends, *purely on the grounds of natural rights*, that these practices are highly unethical. Furthermore, our society is caught up in a controversy about the legitimacy of capital punishment (on which the Catholic Church's position has developed) and the legitimacy of just war. If we are to form our consciences according to the teaching of Jesus as interpreted by the Catholic Church, we will need to address the rationale behind the Church's position on all four issues. This will be done as follows:

1. The personhood of a unicellular zygote and the injustice of abortion (this chapter, Section I)
2. The immorality of eugenic abortion, invitro fertilization, and embryonic stem cells (this chapter, Sections V–VII)
3. The injustice of physician-assisted suicide and euthanasia (Chapter 4, Section I)
4. The possibility and criteria of just war (Chapter 7, Section II.G)

Chapter 4, Section II will be concerned with three other important issues of the fifth commandment—suicide, self-defense, and torture.

I. The Personhood of Preborn Human Beings and the Injustice of Abortion

Why is the moral question of abortion so important? Each year, approximately 73 million abortions are performed throughout the world.[2] In the United States, the Centers for Disease Control reported 629,898 abortions in 2019.[3] If it can be reasonably and scientifically established that a single-celled zygote is in fact a new unique individual human being, and that legal personhood must be accorded to him or her, then abortion would have to be viewed as the greatest genocide in human history.

Immediately after the death and Resurrection of Jesus, the early Church prohibited abortion. The *Didache* (an early text of Christian instruction, dating to around A.D. 50–120[4]) states this plainly: "You shall not kill the embryo by abortion and shall not cause the newborn

[2] World Health Organization, "Abortion", 2022, https://www.who.int/news-room/fact-sheets/detail/abortion.

[3] Centers for Disease Control and Prevention, "Abortion Surveillance—Findings and Reports", last reviewed November 22, 2021, https://www.cdc.gov/reproductivehealth/data_stats/abortion.htm.

[4] See Peter Kirby, "Didache", *Early Christian Writings*, 2022, http://www.earlychristianwritings.com/didache.html.

to perish."[5] This teaching was reaffirmed in the *Epistle of Barnabas* and Tertullian.[6] The Church has never wavered on this prohibition, asserting that life in the womb be treated identically to any other human life. The huge proliferation of abortions since the *Roe v. Wade* decision in the United States (1973) and similar decisions in Europe and Asia requires a vigorous defense of the rights of unborn children. The Catholic Church has risen to this challenge, which will be summarized throughout this and the next two sections.

Contemporary Western culture has attempted to legitimize abortion by suggesting that preborn human beings are not human persons deserving of protection under the law, because they are not fully developed and dependent on a mother for survival and they are therefore "subhuman" or "subpersons". The Supreme Court of the United States (in *Roe v. Wade*) has explicitly agreed with this justification by noting:

> In areas other than criminal abortion, the law has been reluctant to endorse any theory that life, as we recognize it, begins before live birth or to accord legal rights to the unborn except in narrowly defined situations and except when the rights are contingent upon live birth.... In short, the unborn have never been recognized in the law as persons in the whole sense.[7]

Unfortunately, this interpretation of the majority's view of the unborn is seriously misleading. The life of preborn human beings has been recognized in federal district and state supreme court cases concerned with fetal injury and inheritance.[8] The U.S. Supreme Court

---

[5] *Didache* 2, 2, quoted in *CCC* 2271.

[6] *Ep. Bárnabae* 19, 5: PG 2, 777; Tertullian, *Apol.* 9: PL 1, 319–20.

[7] Roe v. Wade, 410 U.S. 113, 161–62 (1973), https://tile.loc.gov/storage-services/service/ll/usrep/usrep410/usrep410113/usrep410113.pdf.

[8] There are several state supreme court and federal district court decisions acknowledging fetal personhood. For example, the Supreme Court of Nevada decided that a human fetus was a person for purposes of remedying personal fetal injuries, allowing the child to sue after birth (see Weaks v. Mounter, 88 Nev. 118, 493 P.2d 1307, 1309 [1972]). The District Court of the District of Columbia decided in 1971 that "a viable unborn child, which would have been born alive but for the negligence of defendant, is a 'person' within the meaning of the Wrongful Death Statute" (see Simmons v. Howard University, 323 F. Supp. 529 [D.C.D.C. 1971], in *Black's Law Dictionary*, 1979, p. 1029). In 1964, the Supreme Court of New Jersey ordered a pregnant woman who was a Jehovah's Witness to undergo a blood transfusion to save her

also made the fundamental error of framing the issue solely in terms of constitutional rights (rights permitted or secured by the Constitution). However, as we shall see, the right to life has never been viewed exclusively as a constitutional right; rather, it is an inalienable right, which is higher than any right declared by a governmental body, because it belongs to every human being by nature, recognizing that every human being is entitled to these rights as a requirement of fundamental justice itself (see Chapter 6, Section II.D). As we shall see, an inalienable right belongs to all human beings by their very nature—by their very human existence. Since no state declares such rights into existence, no state can abrogate or violate them.[9]

If it can be shown that a unicellular zygote is a new, unique, and individual human being genetically, organically, and metabolically distinct from his or her parents, then he or she should be recognized as a human person with the rights of that unique specifically human being. As such, he or she has the inalienable right to life by nature—by his or her human existence. As our Declaration of Independence declares, this right to life is self-evident, and no governmental body

---

life and that of her fetus (Raleigh Fitkin-Paul Morgan Memorial Hospital v. Anderson [N.J. Sup. Ct. 1964]). The courts of Georgia also held for the personhood of a fetus in 1951, when they allowed an action on behalf of a child who suffered a prenatal, but not fatal, injury at the hands of a negligent party carrying its mother to a hospital (Tucker v. Howard Carmichael & Sons, 208 Ga. 201, 65 S.E.2d 909 [1951]). The courts explicitly declared that the fetus had rights independent of its mother, and made frequent recourse to the well-known *Blackstone Commentaries on the Laws of England*: "The right of personal security consists in a person's legal and uninterrupted enjoyment of his life, his limbs, his body, his health, and his reputation. Life is the immediate gift of God, a right inherent by nature in every individual; and it begins in contemplation of law as soon as an infant is able to stir in the mother's womb.... An infant *in ventre sa mere*, or in the mother's womb, is supposed in law to be born for many purposes. It is capable of having a legacy, or a surrender of a copyhold estate, made to it. It may have a guardian assigned to it; and it is enabled to have an estate limited to its use, and to take afterwards by such limitation, as if it were then actually born." William Blackstone, *Blackstone's Commentaries on the Law: From the Abridged Edition of Wm. Hardcastle Browne* (Washington, D.C.: Washington Law Book Company, 1941), Book I, p. 130.

For additional information, see Robert Spitzer, *Ten Universal Principles: A Brief Philosophy of the Life Issues* (San Francisco: Ignatius Press, 2011), Section IV.A.

[9]Notice that the Constitution and its amendments do not declare life, liberty, and the pursuit of happiness to be rights (though the fourteenth amendment prohibits any state from violating these rights). Rather, the United States has recognized these inalienable rights as self-evident in its Declaration of Independence. By doing this, the Founding Fathers avoided the possibility of inalienable rights being misconstrued as extrinsic rights brought into existence by a governmental body. Since inalienable rights belong to each individual by nature (and are not created by a governmental body), no governmental body can abrogate them.

has the right to abrogate it, for the power to abrogate does not belong to it, but only to God. If governments attempt to abrogate it, the governed have the right to abolish the government:

> We hold these truths to be self-evident, that all men are created equal, that they are endowed by their Creator with certain unalienable Rights, that among these are Life, Liberty and the pursuit of Happiness.—That to secure these rights, Governments are instituted among Men, deriving their just powers from the consent of the governed,—That whenever any Form of Government becomes destructive of these ends, it is the Right of the People to alter or to abolish it.[10]

Therefore, if it can be reasonably established that a unicellular zygote is a new, unique, and individual human being genetically, organically, and metabolically distinct from his or her parents, then the Supreme Court of the United States has made a fundamental error in classifying the preborn human's right to life as merely constitutional (instead of inalienable), in which case its decision must be reversed because it is a gross violation of the principle of fundamental justice.[11]

We will examine the personhood of a unicellular human zygote in three sections:

1. The Biological, Embryological, and Genetic Evidence for the Personhood of a Unicellular Human Zygote (Section I.A)
2. Implications of a Soul in the Unicellular Human Zygote (Section I.B)
3. The Personhood of a Unicellular Zygote (Section I.C)

A. The Biological, Embryological, and Genetic Evidence for the Personhood of a Unicellular Human Zygote

The biological, embryological, and genetic evidence for the existence of human nature and human personhood at the moment of

---

[10] From a transcription of the Declaration of Independence, Preamble, on the website of the National Archives, last reviewed on October 7, 2021, https://www.archives.gov /founding-docs/declaration-transcript.

[11] See Spitzer, *Ten Universal Principles*, pp. 62–70.

conception is significant, so much so that a supermajority of biologists throughout the world confirm that a new, unique, specifically *human* being occurs at fertilization. In an amicus curiae brief submitted by the American Center for Law and Justice to the U.S. Court of Appeals for the Fifth Circuit and the U.S. Supreme Court, seventy-one professors of biology reported data from two surveys and an overview of current scientific literature indicating that a supermajority of biologists affirm that life begins at fertilization (the genetics–based model of assessment).[12] The authors first show that biology is the proper academic discipline to establish the beginning of a unique human being. After which, they present data from three major sources:

1. An international survey of 5,577 biologists, *96 percent* (5,354) of whom affirm that fertilization is the origin of a unique human being

2. A U.S. survey of 2,794 biologists asking for essay responses for four possible criteria for establishing the origin of a unique human being; 68 percent of those biologists selected fertilization as the moment at which a new unique human being comes into existence (explained below)

3. A review of contemporary scientific literature and legislative testimony by scientists showing that the preponderance affirms that a unique human life begins at fertilization.

The U.S. survey of biologists is instructive, because it not only indicates that a supermajority of biologists affirm that a unique human life begins at fertilization, but also examines three alternative criteria and their inadequacy when compared to the genetics–based criterion that affirms fertilization as the point of human origin. Let's begin with a breakdown of the data:

---

[12]Lynn D. Dowd, "Brief of Biologist as Amici Curiae in Support of Neither Party: Thomas E. Dobbs, State Health Officer of The Mississippi Department of Health *et al.*, *petitioners* v. Jackson Women's Health Organization *et al.*, *respondents*", submitted to The United States Court of Appeals for the Fifth Court as well as United States Supreme Court, 2020, https://www.supremecourt.gov/Docket PDF/19/19-1392/185254/20210729125335060_19-1392%20Dobbs%20v.%20 JWHO%20Amicus%20Brief%20of%20American%20Center%20for%20Law%20 and%20Justice%20and%20Bioethics%20Defense%20Fund.pdf.

1. Fertilization (a process that starts with sperm-egg binding and is completed by sperm-egg pronuclear fusion), which was affirmed by a supermajority *68 percent* (1,898) of the responding biologists
2. The initiation of fetal brainwaves (between five and six weeks) or fetal heartbeat (approximately between six and a half and seven weeks)—*10 percent* (268) of the responding biologists
3. Fetal viability outside the womb (approximately twenty-four weeks[13])—*10 percent* (284) of the responding biologists
4. First breath of the fetus outside of the womb (birth)—*12 percent* (343) of the responding biologists.

The reason the supermajority selected fertilization is that it is based on the newest most accurate genetics-based method of establishing a unique human organism. All other methods are older and have intrinsic problems. With respect to the first breath (birth) criterion, the authors respond:

> For this view to gain widespread acceptance, there would need to be a rejection of the human life cycle and the genetics-based method of classifying organisms. The practical consequences could be that it would make obsolete any biological basis for providing independent care to a fetus, as a patient, or performing fetal surgery; it would also remove the biological basis of fetal homicide laws, as a state could not rightfully convict someone for the homicide of a fetus since one would no longer be properly classified as a human.[14]

With respect to the criterion of fetal viability, the authors respond:

> For this theory to take hold, biologists would have to replace the objective genetics-based method of biologically classifying humans with a subjective determination based on the changing state of technology.[15]

---

[13] This is a variable standard that will move downward as technology improves. In 1973 (*Roe v. Wade* decision), viability was at twenty-eight weeks; it is now four weeks less and may go down to immediately after fertilization (a single-celled zygote) if an artificial womb is developed.

[14] Ibid., p. 8.

[15] Ibid., pp. 9–10.

This variable standard would effectively de-objectify when life begins, because in a rural community, viability might be twenty-five weeks, while in a sophisticated urban community, it might be twenty-two weeks. Does the origin of human life really depend on where the fetus is located? Furthermore, the status of a human being would change every time a technological improvement occurs—for example, in 1973, it would have to be said that human life begins at twenty-eight weeks, but today, human life would begin at twenty-two or twenty-three weeks. Does the status and origin of a human being really depend on the date that the fetus is in utero?

With respect to the first fetal brainwave or heartbeat standard, the authors respond:

> For this view to gain prominence, the modern method of genetics-based biological classifications would need to revert to the primitive method of morphology-based biological classifications, whereby organisms are classified based on their physical appearance and abilities rather than their genetics. The practical consequences could be that people can capriciously use arbitrary criteria to classify some biological humans as humans and to deliberately exclude others.[16]

As the authors imply, there are four major reasons why fertilization is the most accurate point at which a unique human being comes into existence:

1. The new complete human genome (distinct from both parents) exists at this stage.
2. The new zygote cell—a special totipotent cell that initiates the self-directing activity from which all cells of a human being will originate and be unified throughout the course of his or her existence (explained below) exists at this stage.
3. At the single-celled zygote stage, the organism is uniquely and specifically human with its complete genome, and will not become any more human throughout the course of its development and aging.

---

[16] Ibid., p. 11.

4. The other three criteria are either subjective and variable (e.g., the viability criterion) or arbitrary, selecting an arbitrary point of development as more indicative of humanity than the complete human genome within a uniquely human zygote (first breath and morphological signs).

In view of the above, it should not be surprising that the preponderance of *contemporary* scientific literature and legislative testimony affirms that a human life (a unique human being) begins at *fertilization*.[17] Inasmuch as biology has the capacity to make an accurate determination about the beginning of a new unique human being, this data indicates that the matter is settled. A supermajority of biologists concur that a unique human being begins to exist at fertilization.

As noted above, the primary reasons for this strong consensus within the community of biologists about the origin of human life comes from the completeness of the human genome within the special totipotent unicellular zygote. This requires explanation for those unfamiliar with this biological criterion.

DNA sequencing[18] shows conclusively that a unique human genome is present at the moment of fertilization. Patricio Ventura-Junca and Manual J. Santos state this as follows:

> The most recent advances in genetics have corroborated with increasingly more precise information that the life of a new individual begins with the union of two highly specialized haploid cells (each with 23 chromosomes), the spermatozoid and the ovum, which give rise to a new cell when they are joined: the zygote. The zygote contains a new genetic code with 46 chromosomes. An individual and unique set of genes arises representing the beginning of the life of a new human organism, or in effect, a new individual or human being. It is thus all the cells of a human being come from an original cell, the zygote.... This new genome, whose fundamental structure will be maintained

---

[17] See ibid, p. 14, as well as explanation and notes on pp. 18–23.

[18] The DNA sequencer was developed and proven capable of establishing a complete unique human genome in 1977 by Frederick Sanger. Since that time, there can be no doubt that a unique human being (which is genetically, organically, and metabolically distinct from his or her mother) exists at the moment of conception.

throughout the development, identifies the unicellular embryo as biologically human.[19]

It is important to note here that this self-moving, self-perfecting, dynamic organism actualizing his or her full unique, specifically *human* genome is the organism through which all cells constituting a fully developed human being throughout a lifetime will be produced. Thus, it is in *potentia* an entire human being throughout his or her lifetime.

Furthermore, mitochondrial DNA in the zygote (which comes from our common ancestor, "mitochondrial Eve", and is present in every human being throughout the world) also indicates that this being is exclusively human.

The unicellular zygote is far more than its unique human genome. It is a unique new organism that must be distinguished from the billions of cells it will produce. An organism is a unified complex which actualizes millions of distinct activities and cellular multiplications directed by the instructions in the genome toward a complete human being. It is a whole that is greater than the sum of its parts. Rev. Nicanor Austriaco explains this by using both philosophical and scientific concepts:

> Philosophically, an organism can be defined as a complete living substance, with its own internal principle of movement and change, that directs it toward its natural perfection; and scientifically, as a discrete unit of living matter that from itself continues a path of robust development, which in turn manifests the specific self-organization of its species.[20]

In view of this, a single-celled zygote is far more than a mere cell. It is a dynamically unified complex with its own principle of

---

[19] Patricio Ventura-Junca and Manual J. Santos, "The Beginning of Life of a New Human Being from the Scientific Biological Perspective and Its Bioethical Implications", *Journal of Biological Research* 44, no. 2 (2011), under "Genetics and Epigenetics", https://scielo.cl/scielo.php?script=sci_arttext&pid=S0716-97602011000200013#:~:text=The%20zygote%20contains%20a%20new,an%20original%20cell%2C%20the%20zygote.

[20] Nicanor Austriaco, "The Moral Case or ANT-Derived Pluripotent Stem Cell Lines", *National Catholic Bioethics Quarterly* 6 (2006): 519, https://www.pdcnet.org/ncbq/content/ncbq_2006_0006_0003_0517_0537.

movement and change actualizing its natural perfection—a fully developed human being. As such, it is the self-moving, self-directing, self-perfecting dynamic unity out of which will develop all cells in their complex interrelationship and interaction that will constitute the full span of its lifetime. This dynamic self-perfecting unity is genetically, organically, and metabolically distinct from its parent gametes and is a completely unique manifestation of the human species. This fulfills all the requirements needed to establish the existence of a unique human being.

On the basis of this evidence, a large number of current embryological textbooks indicate that a unique human being (distinct from his or her mother) begins at fertilization/conception.[21] For example, Keith L. Moore's *Clinically Oriented Embryology* states the following:

> A zygote is the beginning of a new human being. Human development begins at fertilization, the process during which a male gamete ... unites with a female gamete or oocyte ... to form a single cell called a zygote. This highly specialized, totipotent cell marks the beginning of each of us as a unique individual.[22]

The above evidence is sufficient to establish that the unicellular zygote is a unique, self-moving, self-perfecting organism actualizing a full, specifically *human* genome toward its natural perfection that is genetically, organically, and metabolically distinct from his or her parents. As noted above, this organism is that through which all cells constituting a fully developed human being throughout a lifetime will be produced. Thus, it is in *potentia* an entire human being throughout his or her lifetime. This is sufficient to establish that a unicellular human zygote is indisputably a new, unique, individual human being.

[21] See, for example, Keith L. Moore, *The Developing Human: Clinically Oriented Embryology*, 7th ed. (Philadelphia: Saunders, 2003), p. 16. See also Keith L. Moore, *Before We Are Born: Essentials of Embryology*, 7th ed. (Philadelphia: Saunders, 2008), p. 2; Ronan O'Rahilly and Fabiola Miller, *Human Embryology and Teratology*, 3rd ed. (New York: Wiley-Liss, 2001), p. 8; T. W. Sadler, *Langman's Medical Embryology*, 10th ed. (Philadelphia: Lippincott Williams & Wilkins, 2006), p. 11; William J. Larsen, *Essentials of Human Embryology* (New York: Churchill Livingstone, 1998), pp. 1, 14; Bruce Carlson and M. Patten, *Foundations of Embryology*, 6th ed. (New York: McGraw-Hill, 1996), p. 3.

[22] Moore, *Clinically Oriented Embryology*, p. 16.

Inasmuch as the term "person" refers to a unique individual human being, the above embryological and genetic evidence is sufficient to establish that a unicellular zygote is a human person.[23]

B. Implications of a Soul in the Unicellular Human Zygote

Though the existence of human personhood (a unique human being with inalienable rights) can be established on the basis of embryological and genetic evidence alone (see above), a unicellular zygote is far more than the physical-biological reality from which its human identity and personhood is established. It is also a transphysical ("soul-like") reality, which not only is capable of surviving bodily death, but is also the source of transphysical activities such as self-consciousness, conceptual ideas, the five transcendental desires (for perfect truth, perfect love, perfect goodness, perfect beauty, and perfect home), conscience (moral intuition), and communion with God (interiorly manifest as the mysterious, fascinating, numinous "wholly Other").[24] Inasmuch as the evidence for this transphysical dimension of the unicellular zygote is probative, the unicellular zygote would have to be a unity of physical-biological powers and activities as well as transphysical ("soul-like") powers and activities.[25]

There are four kinds of evidence grounding this transphysical dimension of human beings (and by implication, unicellular zygotes—the dynamic source from which developed human beings spring):

[23] For centuries, except in the area of legislation concerned with slavery, the term "person" was indistinguishable from "human being". This view of person was applied to unborn human beings as is reflected in the *Blackstone Commentaries on the Laws of England* (see the extensive quote in note 8, pp. 199–200 above). This view was shared by the courts of the United States until the *Roe v. Wade* decision arbitrarily negated it. This negation of personhood of human beings happened once before—when the courts reduced humans of African descent to property, initiating chattel slavery. See below Section I.C.

[24] Each one of these characteristics is explained in detail in Volume II of the Quartet, *The Soul's Upward Yearning*. See below in this section.

[25] As will be explained below, the Nobel Prize–winning physiologist Sir John Eccles and his colleagues believe this evidence to be probative and set out a philosophy of interactionism between the physical and transphysical dimensions of the human being through quantum meditation. See Sir John Eccles, *Evolution of the Brain: Creation of the Self* (1989; repr., London, UK: Routledge, 1991), pp. 235–51. For a summary explanation of his theory, see Volume II of the Quartet (Chapter 6, Sections IV–V).

1. Medical studies of near-death experiences
2. Medical studies of terminal lucidity
3. Medical studies of cognition in severe hydrocephalic patients
4. Implications of transcendent consciousness from philosophical studies

We will discuss each in turn.

Let us first examine the peer-reviewed medical evidence of near-death experiences. The *Soul's Upward Yearning* (Chapter 5) cites several peer-reviewed medical studies of near-death experiences that give significant probative evidence of consciousness after clinical death (flat EEG, fixed and dilated pupils, and absence of gag reflex).[26] This is confirmed by the fact that 81 percent of blind people (most of whom were blind from birth) see for the first time (and accurately describe visual data both inside and outside the hospital) when they are clinically dead.[27] It is further confirmed by several excellent studies of veridical data, in which patients during the time of their clinical death give completely accurate descriptions of facts occurring outside of the operating room where their bodies lay.[28] The data is summed up by Dr. Pim van Lommel in his peer-reviewed medical study of three hundred patients in the Netherlands (published in Britain's most prestigious medical journal, the *Lancet*):

> How could a clear consciousness outside one's body be experienced at the moment that the brain no longer functions during a period of clinical death with flat EEG? ... Furthermore, blind people have described veridical perception during out-of-body experiences at the time of this experience. [Near-death experience] pushes at the limits of medical ideas about the range of human consciousness and the mind-brain relation. In our prospective study of patients that were clinically dead (flat EEG, showing no electrical activity in the cortex

---

[26] For an online summary of this evidence, see Robert Spitzer, *Credible Catholic Big Book*, vol. 2, *Evidence of Our Transphysical Soul* (Magis Center, 2017), CredibleCatholic.com, https://www.crediblecatholic.com/pdf/7E-P1/7E-BB2.pdf#P1V2.

[27] See Kenneth Ring, Sharon Cooper, and Charles Tart, *Mindsight: Near-Death and Out-of-Body Experiences in the Blind* (Palo Alto, Calif.: William James Center for Consciousness Studies at the Institute of Transpersonal Psychology, 1999).

[28] See Janice Holden, *Handbook of Near-Death Experiences: Thirty Years of Investigation* (Westport, Conn.: Praeger Press, 2009).

and loss of brain stem function evidenced by fixed dilated pupils and absence of the gag reflex) the patients report a clear consciousness, in which cognitive functioning, emotion, sense of identity, or memory from early childhood occurred, as well as perceptions from a position out and above their "dead" body.[29]

These conclusions have been validated by other important studies including those of Dr. Samuel Parnia (University of South Hampton) of over 2,060 patients published in the peer-reviewed journal *Resuscitation*.[30] He summarized his extensive study as follows:

This [study] supports other recent studies [e.g., van Lommel, Greyson, and multiple studies at the University of Virginia Medical School] that have indicated consciousness may be present despite clinically [that is, physically] undetectable consciousness.[31]

The evidence of clear consciousness after death exemplified by the studies of blind people and veridical data is inexplicable by physical processes in the brain, strongly implying a transphysical source of consciousness, such as a soul.[32]

The second kind of evidence for a transphysical source of consciousness (e.g., a soul) comes from medical studies of a phenomenon called "terminal lucidity". Patients with severe neurological disorders having almost no cognitional capacity attributable to brain function (such as advanced Alzheimer's, advanced dementia, and severe neurological damage from strokes) suddenly awaken to consciousness and significant cognitional activity prior to death. There are two types of terminal lucidity:

---

[29] Pim van Lommel et al., "Near-Death Experience in Survivors of Cardiac Arrest: A Prospective Study in the Netherlands", *Lancet* 358, no. 9298 (2001): 2045.

[30] Sam Parnia et al., "AWARE—AWAreness during REsuscitation—A Prospective Study", *Resuscitation* 85, no. 12 (2014):1799–805, http://www.horizonresearch.org/Uploads /Journal_Resuscitation__2_.pdf.

[31] Concluding statement in ibid.

[32] Dr. Mario Beauregard (neuroscientist at University of Arizona) shows that the ten conjectured physical explanations of near-death experiences are completely inadequate for explaining the phenomenon as described in peer-reviewed medical studies. See Mario Beauregard, *Brain Wars: The Scientific Battle over the Existence of the Mind and the Proof That Will Change the Way We Live* (New York: HarperOne, 2012).

1. Gradual terminal lucidity (coming about one week before death)
2. Rapid terminal lucidity (coming hours before death)

In several cases reported by Bruce Greyson, Michael Nahm,[33] Emily Kelly, Erlendur Haraldsson,[34] and Jesse Bering,[35] several individuals with documented atrophying or damage to the brain, rendering them incapable of cognitional activity through brain function alone, regained their capacity for memory, practical and theoretical intellectual functioning, and affective depth prior to death.

Harvard researcher Rudolph Tanzi describes the phenomenon as follows:

> The events of terminal lucidity even in Alzheimer patients who were barely conscious, who were barely responsive, well, we hear them all the time. How suddenly a patient can, just before death, say their goodbyes to their loved ones, remembering their names, maybe recalling an event after a decade or so of not learning, of having lost first their short term memory and then their long term memory. It is a complete mystery.... But it is undeniable that it happens, and it is amazing.[36]

The research on terminal lucidity cannot be explained by brain physiology alone, implying a transphysical source of consciousness such as

[33] See Michael Nahm and Bruce Greyson, "The Death of Anna Katharina Ehmer: A Case Study in Terminal Lucidity", *Omega* 68, no. 1 (2014): 77–87, http://journals.sagepub.com /doi/10.2190/OM.68.1.e; a PDF of the article can be found on the website of the University of Virginia Medical School at https://med.virginia.edu/perceptual-studies/wp-content /uploads/sites/360/2016/12/OTH28.pdf. See also Michael Nahm and Bruce Greyson, "Terminal Lucidity in Patients with Chronic Schizophrenia and Dementia: A Survey of the Literature", *Journal of Nervous and Mental Disease* 197, no. 12 (2009): 942–44; Michael Nahm, "Terminal Lucidity in People with Mental Illness and Other Mental Disability: An Overview and Implications for Possible Explanatory Models", *Journal of Near-Death Studies* 28, no. 2 (2009): 87–106, www.spiritualscientific.com/yahoo_site_admin/assets/docs/Lucidity_at_Death _Nahm_M.9131800.pdf; Michael Nahm, "Reflections on the Context of Near-Death Experiences", *Journal of Scientific Exploration* 25, no. 3 (2011): 453–78.

[34] See the following, where Kelly and Haraldsson are co-authors: Michael Nahm et al., "Terminal Lucidity: A Review and a Case Collection", *Archives of Gerontology and Geriatrics* 55, no. 1 (2012): 138–42, http://www.sciencedirect.com/science/article/pii/S0167494311100 1865?via%3Dihub.

[35] See Jesse Bering, "One Last Goodbye: The Strange Case of Terminal Lucidity", *Scientific American* (blog), November 25, 2014, https://blogs.scientificamerican.com/bering-in-mind /one-last-goodbye-the-strange-case-of-terminal-lucidity/.

[36] Rudolph Tanzi, cited in "Exploring Frontiers of Biology", by Michael Nahm on his website, 2012, http://www.michaelnahm.com/terminal-lucidity.

a soul. These findings corroborate the above findings from medical studies of near-death experiences. A summary of the research on this phenomenon may be found in the *Credible Catholic Big Book*.[37]

The third kind of evidence for transphysical consciousness comes from medical studies of severe hydrocephalic patients. Many of these patients displayed IQ far beyond what their physical brains could sustain. Hydrocephalus is a condition in which spinal fluid replaces brain tissue in the vital parts of the brain needed for cognitional function. Severe cases might have as much as 95 percent of the brain cavity filled with spinal fluid, meaning that the patient effectively has only 5 percent of his brain tissue. By any ordinary understanding of brain physiology and functioning, such individuals should not be able to think and should be effectively reduced to a vegetative state. However, the studies of John Lorber (involving six hundred hydrocephalic patients) found that thirty of these patients (5 percent) actually registered a significant IQ, and some of them registered a genius-level IQ.[38] Michael Nahm's summary of Lorber's findings, as well as those by Roger Lewin, noted the following:

> After performing more than 600 scans on hydrocephalic patients, Lorber put forward the provocative question, "Is your brain really necessary?" (Lewin, 1980; Lorber, 1983). He found that about 30 individuals had a global IQ greater than 100—despite cerebrospinal fluid instead of brain tissue filling 95% or more of their crania. Lorber loved citing the story of a student of mathematics whose global IQ was 126, his verbal IQ even reaching 143. In his case, "instead of the normal 4.5-centimeter thickness of brain tissue between the ventricles and the cortical surface, there was just a thin layer of mantle measuring a millimeter or so.... The boy has virtually no brain" (Lorber in Lewin, 1980, p. 1232).[39]

[37] See Spitzer, "Response to Physicalist Explanations", in *Credible Catholic Big Book*, Chapter 1.

[38] See John Lorber, "Is Your Brain Really Necessary?", in *Hydrocephalus in frühen Kindesalter: Fortschritte der Grundlagenforschung, Diagnostik und Therapie*, ed. D. Voth (Stuttgart, Germany: Enke Verlag, 1983), pp. 2–14. See also Roger Lewin, "Is Your Brain Really Necessary?", *Science* 210, no. 4475 (1980): 1232–34, https://science.sciencemag.org/content/210/4475/1232. For a recent noteworthy hydrocephalus case, see Lionel Feuillet, Henry Dufour, and Jean Pelletier, "Brain of a White-Collar Worker", *Lancet* 370, no. 9583 (2007): 262, https://www.thelancet.com/journals/lancet/article/PIIS0140-6736(07)61127-1/fulltext.

[39] Nahm, "Terminal Lucidity with Mental Illness and Mental Disability", p. 102.

As Lorber, Nahm, Lewin, and others imply, there is no physiological explanation for how these hydrocephalic patients could have any cognitional function, let alone an IQ at a genius level. Michael Nahm examines several hypotheses that have been advanced to enable the 1 percent to 5 percent brain tissue to function like ordinary cerebral and frontal cortices, but such explanations are highly dubious.[40] When we combine the evidence of terminal lucidity with the high-level cognitional functioning of 5 percent of hydrocephalic patients, we are provoked to ask the question posed by Lorber and Lewin—"Is your brain really necessary?" If we treat the evidence seriously, without giving probative value to highly dubious physicalist explanations, we are left with a curious response to their question—it seems that the brain really isn't necessary for consciousness and cognitional functioning, implying that there is a transphysical source of consciousness and cognition (like a soul), a conclusion we previously derived from the evidence of near-death experiences and terminal lucidity.

The fourth kind of evidence for transphysical consciousness comes from philosophy of the mind. Philosophers reflect on scientific data and experiential phenomena that cannot be explained by physical processes and formal structuring or programming of the brain. There are six specific areas that elude such explanation. They will be listed here, but extended explanations of them can be found in Volume II of the Quartet—*The Soul's Upward Yearning* (see the chapter references in the accompanying footnotes below).

1. *Self-consciousness.* David Chalmers refers to this as "the hard problem of consciousness".[41]
2. *Conceptual ideas.* These ideas allow for predicates, objects, and other abstract ideas.[42]
3. *Abstract mathematics.* The mathematician Kurt Gödel implies that human mathematical creativity is not reducible to previous algorithms, programming, or rules.[43]

---

[40] See ibid.

[41] For an extended explanation, see Volume II, Chapter 6 of the Quartet. In his exhaustive work *Conscious Mind*, Oxford philosopher David Chalmers shows the high unlikelihood that human self-consciousness and inner subjectivity can be explained by physical processes alone. David Chalmers, *The Conscious Mind: In Search of a Fundamental Theory (Philosophy of Mind)* (Oxford: Oxford University Press, 1996).

[42] See Volume II, Chapter 3 of the Quartet.

[43] See ibid.

4. *Five transcendental desires.* These desires imply that we have an awareness of what perfect truth, perfect love, perfect goodness/fairness, perfect beauty, and perfect home would be like.[44]

5. *Conscience.* Saint John Henry Newman wrote a proof of theism from the divine inspiration of conscience (briefly summarized in Chapter 5, Section III.A of this volume).[45]

6. *Numinous experience.* Rudolf Otto describes the specifically human interior awareness of the mysterious, fascinating, numinous "wholly Other".[46]

Though the evidence for a transphysical soul with the capacity for consciousness, memory, and even transcendental awareness is quite compelling, we do not need it to establish with reasonable certainty that the single-celled human zygote is the living power (in the present moment) actualizing a unique, specifically *human* being. This conclusion can be established probatively by biological, embryological, and genetic evidence given above in Section I.A. So why spend time elucidating the four kinds of evidence for transphysical consciousness (i.e., a soul) in human beings, and by implication, in a human zygote? For the simple reason that if a unicellular human zygote has a transphysical soul, then that soul would have to be created by a transphysical cause. The most complex organization of all physical powers and processes cannot produce a single transphysical effect.[47] Now if the unicellular human zygote has a transphysical cause, and that cause is a Creator, then this might provoke the question, what would the Creator of a preborn human being's soul think about the deliberate killing of that preborn human being? One need not belong to any specific religion to see the relevance of this question, for it seems

---

[44]See Volume II, Chapter 4 of the Quartet.

[45]See Volume II, Chapter 2 of the Quartet and John Henry Newman's unpublished manuscript entitled "Proof of Theism", in *The Argument from Conscience to the Existence of God according to J. H. Newman*, ed. Adrian Boekraad and Henry Tristram (London: Mill Hill, 1961).

[46]See Volume II, Chapter 1 of the Quartet and Rudolf Otto, *The Idea of the Holy: An Inquiry into the Non-Rational Factor in the Idea of the Divine and Its Relation to the Rational* (Oxford: Oxford University Press, 1923).

[47]As explained in Volume II (Chapters 5–6) of the Quartet, the most complex arrangements of all *physical* powers and processes will not produce a single *transphysical* effect, because the latter entails a higher unity and power (without restrictions intrinsic to spatiotemporal and physical processes). Therefore, the cause of a transphysical effect must itself be transphysical.

likely that the deliberate frustration of the Creator's intention would not be commensurate with His will. The above evidence and question may even be relevant to a sincere agnostic who is searching for the truth. If anyone is open to examining the evidence of a soul from medical studies of near-death experiences, terminal lucidity, and the intelligence of hydrocephalic patients as well as the philosophical evidence for the six nonphysical activities elucidated above, then they may be moved to seek the will of the transphysical cause of the soul of even the smallest human being. This may well be decisive.

The reader may by now be thinking that we have given considerable evidence for a transphysical source of consciousness (a soul) in *postborn* human beings, but really haven't shown that a transphysical Creator infused such a soul in *preborn* human beings. True enough. The reason for this is a lack of evidence. It is virtually impossible to obtain direct testimonies about near-death experiences and terminal lucidity from preborn human beings, let alone obtain evidence of self-consciousness, conceptual ideas, mathematical capacity, and so forth from them. So how will we ever know? It is unlikely that we will ever be able to know this indubitably, so we will have to be content with clues and intuitions, such as speculation about prenatal soul-body unity.

Before examining this clue of prenatal ensoulment, we may glean an insight from clinical reports of near-death experiences of very young children. For example, the journal *Critical Care Medicine* reported several cases of young children having near-death experiences, one as early as six months old.[48] An infant nearly died at a hospital but recounted her vivid memory of it three years later (when she was three and a half years old), at which point she had suitable powers of articulation. Her parents told her that her grandmother was dying, to which she spontaneously responded, "Will Grandma have to go through the tunnel ... to see God?"[49] She

---

[48]See David B. Herzog and John T. Herrin, "Near-Death Experiences in the Very Young", *Critical Care Medicine* 13, no. 12 (December 1985): 1074–75, https://journals.lww.com/ccmjournal/citation/1985/12000/near_death_experiences_in_the_very_young.21.aspx?__cf_chl_jschl_tk__=8797e12212c5dfb336fco9fa8bf733840b007c05-1611342662-0-AbxWfZL68QcZAIH1xunHx7_PrwFWrHNeXcpJa6FlU9it8KKNOYWURTxF9jgAXRBqBy5T4SX2CAd4FJMsbIH_hncfhckmj-.

[49]Ibid., p. 1074.

remembered these classical signs of a near-death experience from earlier in her childhood, which clinicians (and her parents) connected to her clinical death in the ICU for renal failure secondary to hemolytic uremic syndrome. When one considers that 85 percent of children suffering cardiac arrest have a near-death experience,[50] we might infer that this young girl is one among many to have experienced the movement of her soul out of her body toward God.[51] Though we may have evidence of a soul in very young children, it does not mean that a transphysical Creator infused such a soul in preborns.

There is implicit indication of prenatal integration between the transphysical soul (the source of self-consciousness) and the physical brain (the organ through which self-consciousness makes the connection with the senses, the nervous system, and the physical body). In two groundbreaking works, the Nobel Prize–winning physiologist Sir John Eccles and the well-known philosopher of science Sir Karl Popper give a detailed explanation of how the brain might be unified with a transphysical soul/self in a theory called dualistic interactionism.[52] Eccles rejects the "promissory materialism" of Daniel Dennett and other materialistic reductionists as inadequate for explaining human identity and free choice. He concludes his extensive argument as follows:[53]

> I maintain that the human mystery is incredibly demeaned by scientific reductionism, with its claim in promissory materialism to account eventually for all of the spiritual world in terms of patterns of neuronal activity. This belief must be classed as a superstition.... We have to recognize that we are spiritual beings with souls existing in a spiritual world as well as material beings with bodies and brains existing in a material world.[54]

[50] See Pranab Bhattacharya, "Is There Science behind the Near-Death Experience: Does Human Consciousness Survives after Death?", *Annals of Tropical Medicine and Public Health* 6, no. 2 (2013): 151–65, https://go.gale.com/ps/i.do?p=AONE&u=googlescholar&id=GALEA 341721229&v=2.1&it=r&sid=AONE&asid=doab5d7b.

[51] See the other cases in Herzog and Herrin, "Near Death Experiences in Very Young".

[52] See Sir Karl Popper and Sir John Eccles, *The Self and Its Brain: An Argument for Interactionism* (New York: Routledge, 1984). See also Eccles, *Evolution of the Brain*.

[53] David Pratt gives a clear an succinct summary of this extensive argument in "John Eccles on Mind and Brain", *Sunrise Magazine*, June/July 1995, http://systems.neurosci.info/Visual Sub/eccles.htm.

[54] Eccles, *Evolution of the Brain*, p. 241.

If we suppose that Eccles is correct about the need for a transphysical soul to explain human freedom and self-identity, and we further suppose that body-soul integration along the lines of Eccles would have to begin at the moment of conception in order for the soul to be integrated with the physical brain throughout its development, then ensoulment would properly have to occur at conception. Since ensoulment occurs because of an explicitly willed act of a transphysical cause (God), we might conclude that God would want to ensoul a human being at the right moment for full proper integration between the soul and its brain, and so would ensoul the body at the very moment of its conception (as a single-celled zygote).

Beyond this philosophical-physiological implication of integration between soul and body at the inception of a new human being, we enter into the subjective and anecdotal domain of near-death encounters involving preborn (e.g., miscarried) children. One such encounter was described by Colton Burpo in *Heaven Is for Real*.[55] Colton described spontaneously to his mother and father what happened to him when he nearly died of a severe infection from a burst appendix just prior to four years of age. He spoke of sitting on the lap of Jesus, hearing angels sing, meeting his great-grandfather ("Pops"), and a variety of other heavenly phenomena. Most interestingly, he described an encounter with his deceased sister who ran up to him and hugged him while he was in "heaven". She told him that she died in her mother's tummy, and that she had not been named by their parents. When Colton told this to his mother, she was shocked, because neither she nor her husband had ever disclosed to Colton that she had a miscarriage after two months of pregnancy before Colton was conceived. Since she and her husband did not know the biological sex of the child, they had not named her. Though such accounts are evidently subjective and might be manipulated for various agendas, I found this particular account to be believable, because Colton was not yet four years of age (and had no agenda), and it was difficult to believe that he would randomly make up such an account, including details of his sister dying in his mother's tummy. Furthermore, Colton disclosed other facts that indicated he had an authentic near-death experience, such as indicating that when he

[55] See Todd Burpo and Lynn Vincent, *Heaven Is for Real: A Little Boy's Astounding Story of His Trip to Heaven and Back* (Nashville: Thomas Nelson, 2010).

left his body, he saw his father in a small room praying while at the same time his mother was in a different room talking on her cell phone. These two separate rooms were outside the operating room in which Colton's body lay; he was perfectly correct about his facts. If Colton's account accurately reflects what actually occurred, then his sister (a two-month-old embryo) had a soul that survived her bodily death.

As noted above, we do not need to base the case for the personhood of a single-celled human zygote on the evidence for a soul, because the evidence of biology, embryology, and genetics is able to establish this probatively (see above Section I.A). Nevertheless, as noted above, we provide this evidence because it impels us toward a fundamental moral question: If the soul of a unicellular human zygote must have a transphysical cause, and that cause is tantamount to a Creator, then what might that Creator of a preborn human being's soul think about the deliberate killing of that preborn human being? What would the Creator think about our directly frustrating His intention to bring this new transcendental being into the world?

C. The Personhood of a Unicellular Zygote

We may now conclude with a consideration of the idea of personhood. Recall from above that prior to the *Roe v. Wade* decision, personhood was applied to all human beings—and specifically to preborn human beings—without qualification.[56] Besides the *Roe v. Wade* decision, there was only one instance in which personhood was denied to human beings—the attempted justification of slavery. In the law, if a being is not a "person", then it is considered "property". In the 1500s, a distinction was made between "human being" and "person" to justify slavery. It was clear that African natives not only looked like human beings but manifested a rational nature capable of understanding every dimension of European education. Since it was difficult to deny the Africans' humanity, the term "person" was

[56]See the extensive quote in note 8, pp. 199–200 above, from *Blackstone's Commentaries on the Law.*

reconfigured to signify "a legal person" ("a human being deserving of protection under the law") based on that human being's *current* state of education and societal development. This allowed slave traders to classify the slaves as humans who were not persons—humans eligible for slavery because their "inferior" status made them undeserving of protection under the law. Once African natives were classified as nonpersons, they could be transitioned into the legal jurisdiction of property.[57] In the United States, this first occurred in a Virginia statute in 1659–1660.[58] Though there were perceived tensions between the Africans' evident humanity and their legal status as property, their classification as nonpersons facilitated the relegation of them to chattel slavery.[59]

The same specious distinction between "human being" and "person" was made in the *Roe v. Wade* decision to justify the deliberate killing of preborn human beings.[60] The majority indicated that they were uncertain about when life began and so decided that the personhood of the unborn is in question.[61] Hence, they allowed the killing of all unborn life based on their uncertainty about whether human life (and human personhood) began. The denial of personhood led to their denial of inalienable rights to the unborn. In view of the evidence given in Section I.A above, we may adduce three fundamental errors that must be corrected:

1. Since 1977 (four years after the *Roe v. Wade* decision), DNA sequencing and intrauterine photography established with certainty that a unicellular human zygote is a dynamic organism actualizing a unique human genome that is genetically, organically, and metabolically distinct from his or her parents. As noted above, this organism is that through which all cells constituting a fully

---

[57] See Paul Finkelman, "Slavery in the United States: Persons or Property?", in *The Legal Understanding of Slavery: From the Historical to the Contemporary*, ed. Jean Allain (New York: Oxford University Press, 2012), pp. 109–10.

[58] Ibid.

[59] Ibid.

[60] See Spitzer, *Ten Universal Principles*, pp. 26–34.

[61] See ibid., pp. 18–33, for the passages of *Roe v. Wade* about the uncertainty of when life begins, and the majority's use of it to justify the denial of personhood and inalienable rights to the unborn.

developed human being throughout a lifetime will be produced. Thus, it is in *potentia* an entire human being throughout his or her lifetime—indisputably a new, unique, individual human being. For this reason, a super majority of biologists in the United States and throughout the world believe that a single-celled zygote is a new, unique human being. Furthermore, a large number of embryological textbooks classify this unicellular zygote as a "new unique individual human being".[62] This has two consequences. First, it can no longer be said that science is uncertain about the beginning of a new, unique, individual human being. Second, since this is scientifically established, the *Roe v. Wade* decision, which rests on uncertainty about the beginning of life, must be reversed to respect today's scientific facts.

2. The majority should never have used uncertainty about life to justify the killing of an innocent human being. This would never stand as an adequate defense for any other case in a court of law (e.g., I cannot use my uncertainty about someone's personhood to justify killing him). In order to justify killing, there must be certainty—absolute certainty—about whether innocent human life does or does not exist.

3. The majority in *Roe v. Wade* completely ignored the potentiality for *inalienable* rights of the preborn human being following upon their uncertainty about preborn personhood. They therefore turned to the Constitution (and case precedents) to determine the constitutional (extrinsically declared) rights of the preborn. This is precisely what was done to African Americans after 1650 in the United States. They were reclassified as nonpersons, meaning that they were essentially "property" (leading to their reduction to chattel slavery).

As may now be clear, the majority in the *Roe v. Wade* decision acted in a fundamentally unjust way by failing to protect the inalienable rights of preborn human beings (allowing them to be summarily killed). They did this by a series of specious reasoning and sophistries. Using their uncertainty about the beginning of human life, they speciously "justified" the nonpersonhood of the preborn human being,

---

[62] See, for example, Moore, *Developing Human*, p. 16.

which essentially made preborns the property of their mothers. Having done this, they ignored the inalienable rights of these human beings, and sought to find mere constitutional precedents to justify fetal personhood. When they could find no specific precedents justifying fetal personhood, they used the Constitution's and court's *silence* to justify the nonpersonhood of the fetus (when in the law, silence can never be interpreted to mean yes or no[63]). This unfortunate series of specious reasoning and sophistries has led to an unparalleled and ever-increasing genocide.

What is the lesson to be learned from our history of slavery and abortion? In a phrase, we should be incredibly suspicious of any attempt to reclassify a being of human origin as a "nonperson" that effectively makes them property and devoid of inalienable rights. The minute we rob human beings of personhood, we rob them of inalienable rights and leave them open to every form of marginalization and abuse, including slavery and genocide.

Is a unicellular zygote a human person? If we were uncertain, we should await a definitive establishment of the fact (or its negation) before permitting mass killing to occur. However, as it is, biology, embryology, and genetics have in fact established that a unicellular human zygote is a unique and individual human being—a dynamic organism actualizing a unique human genome that is genetically, organically, and metabolically distinct from his or her parents. Inasmuch as fundamental justice requires that personhood belongs to *every* individual human being, and therefore that every human being has inalienable rights, the *Roe v. Wade* decision must be reversed because it is perhaps the most fundamentally unjust legal decision proffered by any court anytime in our history.

We now proceed to a discussion of six issues connected with the injustice of abortion:

1. Response to the First Objection: Incomplete Development of Preborns (Section II)
2. Response to the Second Objection: Preborns' Dependency on Their Mothers (Section III)

[63] See Michael M. Martin, Daniel J. Capra, and Faust F. Rossi, *New York Evidence Handbook: Rules, Theory, and Practice*, 2nd ed. (New York: Aspen Publishers, 2003), p. 181.

3. Post-Abortion Syndrome: Effects of Abortion on Women (Section IV)
4. Eugenic Abortion and the Intrinsic Dignity of the Disabled (Section V)
5. Invitro Fertilization (Section VI)
6. Embryonic Stem Cells (Section VII)

II. Response to the First Objection: Incomplete Development of Preborns

We now examine two major objections that have been raised by some groups within the philosophical and medical community to justify abortion at any time during pregnancy:

1. Since a preborn is not yet fully developed (and is therefore not yet capable of performing the same range of activities as a child after birth), we cannot be sure that it has inalienable rights; therefore, sanctioning its death is without moral culpability.
2. Since a preborn child is dependent upon his or her mother for sustenance and life, the mother has the right to authorize the death of an unwanted child without moral culpability.

We will discuss the first argument below in this section and the second in Section III.

The leap from incomplete development to the nonexistence of human nature and inalienable rights violates two major principles of morality and legal ethics. First, it reverses the common legal presumption of "innocent until proven guilty". If we apply this principle to legal personhood, we would say that every human being (regardless of stage of development) should be presumed to have inalienable rights and therefore legal personhood (deserving of protection by the state) until proven otherwise. Failure to uphold this principle requires that human beings prove they have inalienable rights for the state to grant legal protection. As will be seen below, this requirement for proof of inalienable rights before legal protection was used to justify slavery in the United States, Europe, and Latin America. It was also used to justify the killing of people classified as inferiors or subhuman in countries permitting slavery, as well as in Nazi Germany and Stalinist Russia. This is clearly contrary to the principle of nonmaleficence ("do no unnecessary harm") and this country's fundamental presumption of innocence.

There is a fundamental logical and ontological problem with holding that incomplete stage of development implies the absence of human nature and inalienable rights. It implies that the stage of development is a higher criterion for assessing human nature than the existence of a unique human being (as determined by biological, embryological, and genetic evidence). Restated in Aristotelian language, this is like putting accidents (such as height and weight) above substance (the essential powers that constitute a particular being). Height or weight is literally nonexistent without a substance (such as a living being) in which to inhere. Similarly, the stage of development is literally nothing without a living evolving organism through which it is occurring. Again, our age is literally nothing without a dynamic human substance through which aging is occurring. In view of this, a living being's stage of development cannot be a higher criterion for determining its nature than the living being itself. To suggest that the stage of development is a higher criterion for determining human nature is tantamount to reducing a more fundamental reality to a less fundamental one, which is an absurdity. Therefore, from a logical and ontological point of view, stage of development cannot be used to negate the presence of human nature (and inalienable rights) in a dynamic organism actualizing itself according to a full human genome.

A contemporary computer analogy may prove helpful here. Suppose you spent five years developing the software for a new disc-operating system (an effort that has millions of lines of code and subtle organization), and you proudly show it to your friend who subsequently picks up your memory device (on which the entire system is coded), puts it on a table, and smashes it to pieces with a hammer. You exclaim in alarm, "Hey, what are you doing? It took me five years to develop that system, and you destroyed it." Your friend says in reply, "Don't worry about it—you had not yet loaded the software onto your central processing unit (CPU), and so it was not operational and therefore not a real disc-operating system. In fact, it would not have been a disc-operating system until you *fully* loaded it onto your CPU. I could have destroyed it anytime while you were still loading it, and it would not have been a criminal action." You would probably be screaming, "That's absurd! That was a real disc-operating system because that memory device was the power to actualize a fully operational disc-operating system! You owe me for five years of creative work and genius!"

What are the ethical and public policy implications of making the above logical and ontological error? As might be expected, if our ethical conclusions are based on mistaken logic or a mistaken ontology, they will also be mistaken. So, for example, if we say that height or age can rule out the presence of human nature and inalienable rights, then we can legitimately sanction the killing of individuals who act like human beings, on the absurd basis that they do not have sufficient age or height to have a human nature. The Supreme Court has made precisely the same absurd argument by suggesting that a pre-born's stage of development can rule out the presence of his or her human nature (and inalienable rights). This enabled them to sanction the killing of beings with a human nature legitimately (a unique self-moving, self-perfecting dynamic organism actualizing itself according to a unique human genome).

There are further ethical problems going beyond these logical, ontological, and ethical errors. Once the Court opened the door to the negation of human nature based on stage of development (or any other accident), they effectively removed the power to close it. If the presence of human nature is indicated by stage of development (instead of a unique self-moving, self-perfecting dynamic organism actualizing itself according to a full unique specifically human genome), why not say that the age of a child after birth is similarly determinative of human nature (justifying infanticide)? Why not say that a particular level of IQ is similarly determinative of human nature? Why not say that a certain level of health, athletic capacity, or potential living standard is indicative of human nature? As can be seen, once we have replaced the essential quality of human nature with an accidental quality, there is no end of accidental qualities we can arbitrarily use to define human nature (and sanction the killing of those who do not meet that arbitrary criterion). Inasmuch as accidental qualities are incapable of defining substance, they are also completely arbitrary and open to abuse by anyone allowed to do so by a naive public. The Nazis certainly did this to the fullest extent possible, by using not only IQ genetic defects and physical fitness but also race and ethnicity as substitutes for essential human nature.

We in the current Western world are not so far from this nightmare. As we shall see below, Peter Singer (and many politicians) is already advocating various forms of infanticide, and eugenic abortions are currently being used to eliminate those with Down syndrome and other genetic "defects".

Notice that once we have abandoned an objective substantial criterion for human nature, we are left only with subjective accidental and arbitrary criteria that are not accountable to objective evidence and reason. Therefore, they are open to every form of rhetorical manipulation, and in the end, are determined by the will of those with power, wealth, and influence. Once we allow the power elite to wrest the criterion of human nature from its objective reasonable basis, we allow them to use whatever subjective arbitrary standard they can get away with. They do not have to stop at advocating and sanctioning eugenic abortion and infanticide; they can use almost any arbitrary criterion to sanction the killing of human beings so long as they have enough power and influence to convince the public. This is darkly reminiscent of the words of Lutheran pastor Martin Niemöller, who was released from a Nazi concentration camp by the allies in 1945:

> First they came for the socialists, and I did not speak out—because I was not a socialist.
> Then they came for the trade unionists, and I did not speak out—because I was not a trade unionist.
> Then they came for the Jews, and I did not speak out—because I was not a Jew.
> Then they came for me—and there was no one left to speak for me.[64]

One more observation should be mentioned before leaving this fallacious and dangerous attempt to justify abortion. The very same

---

[64] "Martin Niemöller: 'First They Came for the Socialists ...'", *Holocaust Encyclopedia*, United States Holocaust Memorial Museum, Washington, D.C. (website), last edited March 30, 2012, https://encyclopedia.ushmm.org/content/en/article/martin-niemoeller-first-they-came-for-the-socialists. The quotation is on display in the permanent exhibition of the museum.

"stage of development" criterion has been used to justify slavery since the fifteenth century (the inception of the transatlantic slave trade). This affected Africans throughout the world as well as Indians in Central and South America. With respect to the latter, the Dominican friar Bartolomé de las Casas attempted to defend the rights of the Indians from the Spanish conquistadores who believed that they had the right to enslave all Indian people—and if the Indians resisted, they had the right to kill them. Las Casas found himself in a debate against Juan Gines Sepulveda at the Spanish court in Valladolid in 1550, where Sepulveda made the argument that the Indian people had not yet reached the same level of development in education and intellectual achievement as Europeans, and so it was justified to consider them "subhuman". As subhuman, the Spanish conquistadores had the right to enslave and kill them.[65] Las Casas retorted that the human nature of the Indians could not be determined by their particular level of educational or intellectual achievement at any arbitrary point in their history, because this was merely accidental (not substantial) to their nature. To prove this, he gave examples of the Indian's potential to be as intellectually developed as Europeans within a few years. They were making great strides in mathematics, architecture, agriculture, music, and building design, learning at a very accelerated pace.[66] Las Casas concluded that since these Indians would actualize full intellectual development in a few short years, the Spanish were under a moral obligation to presume that they were fully human, because they had the power (in the present moment) to actualize full educational and intellectual development. The stage of development was subordinate to the nature of the being who is developing.[67]

In conclusion, nature trumps "stage of development"—which is a nonessential characteristic such as weight, height, or color. As discussed above, human nature is identical with a unique human

---

[65] See Ángel Losada, "The Controversy between Sepulveda and las Casas in the Junta of Valladolid", in *Bartolomé de Las Casas in History*, ed. Juan Friede and Benjamin Keen (DeKalb, Ill.: Northern Illinois University, 1971), 279.

[66] See Bartolomé de Las Casas, *In Defense of the Indians: The Defense of the Most Reverend Lord, Don Fray Bartolomé de las Casas, of the Order of Preachers, Late Bishop of Chiapa, against the Persecutors and Slanderers of the Peoples of the New World Discovered across the Seas*, trans. and ed. Stafford Poole (DeKalb, Ill.: Northern Illinois University Press, 1992).

[67] Ibid.

genome, and it is ontologically prior to any stage of development that occurs through it. Notice that the stage of development occurs through the existing nature, making the existing nature ontologically prior to it. It is absurd to think of a stage of development existing without a nature through which it occurs. Therefore, it is a logical and ontological error to suggest that the stage of development can negate the existence of the nature in which it occurs.

The moral errors arising out of this logical and ontological error have been immensely damaging to individual human beings and society, having led to slavery, abortion, and genocide throughout the world. For the sake of humanity, we must insist that all preborn human beings (having a unique human genome) have human nature at every stage of their development. In virtue of this human nature alone, they have the inalienable rights of life, liberty, and the pursuit of happiness, making them legal persons who the state must protect under the law. Furthermore, all beings with a unique human genome must also be considered human beings with a human nature whatever their ethnicity, country of origin, or state of educational or intellectual development. In virtue of this human nature, they too have the inalienable rights of life, liberty, and the pursuit of happiness and are therefore legal persons who must be protected under the law. To say anything else is a logical and ontological error as well as a gross violation of objective morality and fundamental justice.

III. Response to the Second Objection: Preborns' Dependency on Their Mothers

In her 1971 article, "A Defense of Abortion", Judith Jarvis Thomson recontextualized the debate on abortion, moving it from the personhood of the fetus to a mother's right not to involuntarily surrender her body to an unwanted invasion by a stranger who needs it for survival.[68] Thomson concedes for the sake of argument that a

---

[68] Judith Jarvis Thomson, "A Defense of Abortion", *Philosophy and Public Affairs* 1, no. 1 (Fall 1971): 47–66. The article was reprinted in *The Philosophy of Law* (*Oxford Readings in Philosophy*), ed. Ronald Dworkin (Oxford: Oxford University Press, 1977), pp. 112–28. All subsequent citations refer to the reprint.

human fetus is a person—a unique, developing human being similar to human beings having moral rights.[69] She makes her defense of abortion on the basis that "the mother has not given the unborn person a right to the use of her body for food and shelter."[70] She illustrates her case with an analogy in which one wakes up one morning and discovers that he has been attached to a famous violinist who needs the use of the person's kidneys for nine months in order to survive and allow the violinist's kidneys to be repaired.[71] She equates the presence of the fetus with the unwanted invasion of the violinist, suggesting that the mother has the same right to "disconnect" the unwanted invading stranger from her body.[72] This is probably the most well-known defense of abortion since *Roe v. Wade*, and it continues to be used as an adequate defense of abortion even if one concedes to undisputed fetal personhood.

John Finnis responds incisively to the breakdown of the analogy between the violinist and the fetal person.[73] First, he shows that an abortion is a direct act of killing, but unplugging the violinist is an act of "letting die".[74] In Thomson's analogy, the violinist is in the process of dying and trying to stop this process by having himself attached to another person. However, the preborn child is not in a process of dying, but rather is vigorously alive. Yes, the child needs his mother to survive just as the violinist needs the other person. However, the mother must initiate the child's dying process by intentionally killing him, but this need not be done for the violinist who is already in the dying process. We may now get to Finnis' main point. The moral bar for direct killing is much higher than the moral bar for "letting die";[75] it is never morally permissible to kill another innocent human being directly, but there are many circumstances in which it is morally justified to let a person die.[76] On this ground alone, Thomson's analogy fails, invalidating her argument.

---

[69] Ibid., p. 120.
[70] Ibid.
[71] Ibid., p. 113.
[72] Ibid.
[73] John Finnis, "The Rights and Wrongs of Abortion", in *The Philosophy of Law*, ed. Ronald Dworkin (Oxford: Oxford Univ. Press 1977), pp. 129–52.
[74] Ibid., pp. 147–48.
[75] Ibid.
[76] Ibid.

Finnis makes a second morally relevant distinction between the violinist and the preborn child. The violinist could and should have obtained prior consent from the other person before having himself attached to the person during his sleep; therefore, the violinist was in breach of his moral and legal duty to obtain that consent. However, the child has no possibility of obtaining prior consent from his mother to use her body during the pregnancy, and therefore was not in breach of any duty to obtain that consent.[77] This means that the violinist is morally culpable for deceptively and unjustly invading the person's body, but the preborn child is not morally culpable for an unjust action. Therefore, detaching the violinist is an act of rectifying his continued unjust action toward the other. However, since the child has not culpably and unjustly invaded his mother's body, the mother's action is not the rectification of a continuing injustice, but rather the killing of an *innocent*. Again, Thomson's analogy fails, invalidating the supposed moral equivalency between abortion and detaching the violinist.

Finally, since Thomson concedes to the reality of fetal personhood, then she must also concede that this human person has the inalienable right to life, because inalienable rights follow from the existence of human nature. For this reason, Finnis insists that the unborn child has a "prior right claim" to life.[78] Thomson seems to have ignored this important fact by implying that only the mother's rights are being violated. However, this is certainly not the case if fetal personhood exists and inalienable rights are intrinsic to all human persons.

We now confront the problem of resolving the rights conflict between the child and his mother. Who has the higher rights claim? Since the right to life is necessary for the very possibility of the right to liberty (the mother's custody over her own body is a liberty right), then the right to life must take precedence over the right to liberty, making the child's claim to an inalienable right to life higher than the mother's inalienable right to liberty, implying that the conflict be resolved in favor of the child. (This is further explained in Chapter 6, Section II.D.)

So, what might we conclude about Thomson's analogy concerning the moral equivalence between aborting a child and detaching the violinist?

[77] Ibid.
[78] Ibid.

- An abortion is a direct act of killing, which is never morally permissible, but detaching the violinist is an act of "letting die".
- The violinist is in breach of his duty to obtain prior consent to invade the other person's body. His failure to do so constitutes a morally culpable, unjust invasion of another's body. However, the child has no possibility of obtaining prior consent and is not morally culpable for an unjust invasion of his mother's body. Therefore, he is an *innocent*.
- The preborn child's inalienable right to life is a higher right claim than the mother's right to liberty over her body.

Thomson's so-called analogy seriously limps and does not establish moral equivalency between abortion and detaching a culpable violinist.

Dependency can never morally justify the direct killing of an innocent human being—indeed, nothing can. Beyond the principle itself, there is an obvious *reductio ad absurdum*. If society were to allow all people to kill anyone directly who is dependent on them, simply because they were dependent, we might be faced with the intentional killing of all children, teenagers, sick people, disabled people, and elderly people—among others. We may argue about the morality of ignoring the needs of people to whom we are related, but directly killing them is never morally acceptable. Furthermore, abandonment of children who cannot take care of themselves is also considered unjust (and morally unacceptable). If parents are financially destitute, they have the responsibility to find others who might be able to help a child for whom they cannot care. If there are no relatives or friends, there are countless church agencies all over the world, and in developed countries, social agencies and means of adoption. Parents have the highest level of responsibility for their children, both for their survival and well-being. The idea that a child is similar to an unknown violinist forcibly attached to one's body in the middle of the night is an inane characterization of motherhood (and its dignity and responsibilities), regardless of whether her child is a surprise or not.

IV. Post-Abortion Syndrome: Effects of Abortion on Women

In a comprehensive multinational, multiyear (1995–2009) study of 750,000 women for the *British Journal of Psychiatry* (and Cambridge

University), Priscilla K. Coleman details the profound and long-lasting negative effects of abortion on the mental health of women.[79] Overall, she discovered that *81 percent* of women who had an abortion had a significantly higher risk of mental health problems than those who did not.[80] She compared the population of post-abortive women with the populations of women who brought their pregnancies to term as well as those who were not pregnant. With respect to specific mental health problems, she found the following:

- There is a *4.1 times* (311 percent) greater occurrence of suicides in women who had an abortion compared with those who did not.
- There is a *2.5 times* (150 percent) greater occurrence of suicidal contemplation and behaviors in women who had an abortion compared with those who did not.
- There is a *2.1 times* (110 percent) greater occurrence of alcohol abuse in women who had an abortion compared with those who did not.
- There is a *1.4 times* (37 percent) greater occurrence of depression in women who had an abortion compared with those who did not.
- There is a *1.3 times* (34 percent) greater occurrence of anxiety in women who had an abortion compared with those who did not.[81]

Coleman's research shows conclusively that abortion has severe, long-lasting negative effects on many women's mental health. These findings are confirmed by a comprehensive literature review of abortion and women's mental health done by David Reardan in 2018 for the National Center for Biotechnology Information. He discovered that both anti-abortion and pro-abortion advocates found increased symptoms of post-traumatic stress as well as depression, anxiety, and regret experienced by women after an abortion:

[79] Pricilla K. Coleman, "Abortion and Mental Health: Quantitative Synthesis and Analysis of Research Published 1995–2009", *British Journal of Psychiatry* 199, no. 3 (2011): 180–86. Republished online by Cambridge University, January 2, 2018, https://www.cambridge.org/core/journals/the-british-journal-of-psychiatry/article/abortion-and-mental-health-quantitative-synthesis-and-analysis-of-research-published-19952009/E8D556AAE1C1D2F0F8B060B28BEE6C3D.
[80] Ibid., under "Results".
[81] Ibid.

Still, both sides [abortion advocates and opponents] agree that (a) abortion is consistently associated with elevated rates of mental illness compared to women without a history of abortion; (b) the abortion experience directly contributes to mental health problems for at least some women.[82]

Despite the comprehensiveness and academic professionalism of the Coleman study, the Guttmacher Institute (an institute of Planned Parenthood) continues to maintain that there is no substantial link between abortion and women's mental health.[83] The disingenuousness of these claims in the face of comprehensive academic research to the contrary is tragic; it creates the impression that there should be nothing wrong with women who have a four times greater rate of suicide after an abortion. This forces women to blame *themselves* (rather than the abortion) for their feelings of self-destruction. We must redress these harmful fictions of Planned Parenthood to free women to obtain the mental health assistance they need.

The above studies imply that the bond between mother and preborn infant is quite strong even if there is anxiety about the pregnancy. It seems that a significant percentage of women have strong feelings of maternal care, responsibility, and protectiveness even if the pregnancy is surprising or distressing. Women who feel pressured to get an abortion by male partners or friends may also feel anger and hostility toward these individuals as well as themselves for aborting the baby. Evidently, abortions are destructive to preborn babies, but also to the emotional health of a considerable number of women who have them.

---

[82]David Reardon, "The Abortion and Mental Health Controversy: A Comprehensive Literature Review of Common Ground Agreements, Disagreements, Actionable Recommendations, and Research Opportunities", *SAGE Open Medicine* 6 (October 29, 2018), Abstract, https://www.ncbi.nlm.nih.gov/pmc/articles/PMC6207970/.

Another study found the following: "Posttraumatic stress reactions were found to be associated with abortion. Consistent with previous research, the data here suggest abortion can increase stress and decrease coping abilities, particularly for those women who have a history of adverse childhood events and prior traumata. Study limitations preclude drawing definitive conclusions, but the findings do suggest additional cross-cultural research is warranted." Vincent M. Rue et al., "Induced Abortion and Traumatic Stress: A Preliminary Comparison of American and Russian Women", *Medical Science Monitor* 10, no. 10 (2004): SR5, https://www.medscimonit.com/download/index/idArt/11784.

[83]Guttmacher Institute, "Emotional and Mental Health after Abortion", 2022, https://www.guttmacher.org/perspectives50/emotional-and-mental-health-after-abortion.

Since the emotional effects of abortion can be extensive and long term, women who are affected may want to consider a Catholic counseling or retreat program to help them deal with post-traumatic stress, depression, guilt, and anxiety. There are several programs that help with grieving, remorse, and emotional stress:

- Project Rachel, sponsored by the United States Conference of Catholic Bishops,[84] is a network of diocesan ministries (in almost every state) of priests and counselors who provide pastoral and counseling services, retreats, support groups, and referrals to clinical professionals to help women overcome the emotional effects of abortion.

- Rachel's Vineyard is a ministry run by Priests for Life,[85] which offers individual counseling, support groups, and retreat experience to help women overcome the negative emotional effects of abortion.

- Life Perspectives offers education and resources to professionals and care providers to help them offer health and services to women and families suffering from abortion and miscarriage.[86] They offer an extensive list of resources in various geographical areas specifically to help women with emotional problems after abortion.[87] Simply enter your location on the map, and you will be given dozens of resources for counseling and support groups in that location.[88]

There are several other non-Catholic resource centers that also offer services for post-abortion syndrome.

In view of the extensive negative effects of abortion on preborn children, women, and families, the age-old Hippocratic prohibition of abortion and the Catholic Church's teaching against it should be taken seriously, for as Pope John Paul II indicated, it will warp the moral conscience of individuals and societies, leading to a culture of death for those who cannot compete for resources and privilege:

[84] Project Rachel website: https://www.usccb.org/topics/project-rachel-ministry.
[85] Rachel's Vineyard website: https://www.rachelsvineyard.org/.
[86] Life Perspectives website: https://www.lifeperspectives.com/about/.
[87] See the "Find Help" webpage at https://www.abortionchangesyou.com/find-help.
[88] Ibid.

It is at the heart of the moral conscience that the eclipse of the sense of God and of man, with all its various and deadly consequences for life, is taking place. It is a question, above all, of the individual conscience, as it stands before God in its singleness and uniqueness. But it is also a question, in a certain sense, of the "moral conscience" of society: in a way it too is responsible, not only because it tolerates or fosters behaviour contrary to life, but also because it encourages the "culture of death", creating and consolidating actual "structures of sin" which go against life.[89]

This brings us to the next consequence of abortion—eugenics.

V. Eugenic Abortion and the Intrinsic Dignity of the Disabled

"Eugenic abortion" refers to abortion used for eugenic objectives: to limit the reproduction of undesirable groups. In recent history, "undesirable groups" have included various races, sexes, and religions, as well as the mentally disabled, physically disabled, and economically underprivileged. In his 2019 article, "Abortion and Eugenics", Justice Clarence Thomas makes clear that eugenic abortion is currently a reality here in the United States and worldwide:[90]

- In Iceland, eugenic abortion of Down syndrome children is nearly 100 percent. Europe has similarly high rates.
- In the United States, eugenic abortion of Down syndrome children is nearly 66 percent.
- In Asia, 160 million girls were aborted for being undesirable.

Eugenic abortions of those with Down syndrome or other mental disabilities, potential physical disabilities, and other undesirable characteristics have increased considerably with new prenatal-scanning techniques.[91]

---

[89] *Evangelium Vitae*, no. 24.
[90] See Clarence Thomas, "Abortion and Eugenics", *First Things*, May 28, 2019, https://www.firstthings.com/web-exclusives/2019/05/abortion-and-eugenics.
[91] Ibid.

Beyond the fact that eugenic abortion has killed millions of innocent human beings for the sake of a "better world", the increase in its acceptance not only in the medical community but within mainstream culture requires discussion of three ethical issues:

1. Are Fetuses with Genetic Indicators of Intellectual or Physical Limitations Truly Human—or Subhuman? (Section V.A)
2. Does Eugenic Abortion Portend Eugenic Infanticide? (Section V.B)
3. Is a World with Eugenic Purification Truly a Better World? (Section V.C)

A. Are Fetuses with Genetic Indicators of Intellectual or Physical Limitations Truly Human—or Subhuman?

The vast majority of Catholics know how Jesus would have answered the question of whether or not a fetus with intellectual or physical limitations is truly human or subhuman—"As you did it to one of the least of these my brethren, you did it to me" (Mt 25:40). In this passage, Jesus identifies with those who are considered "least" in the human community, imparting His own divine dignity upon them. We will be held accountable for the way we treat Jesus present in the neglected, marginalized, and those considered "inferior".

Though Jesus' teaching is quite clear, we must also make a reasonable (nonrevealed) case for the intrinsic dignity and inalienable rights of everyone in the human community to preserve the future of our culture, society, and world. So, what is the natural ethics rationale against eugenic abortion, and eugenics itself?

First, recall that a unicellular human zygote is a unique, self-moving, self-perfecting, dynamic organism actualizing itself according to a specifically *human* genome. Even if this human being has genetic indicators of physical or intellectual limitations, he is still specifically human not only in parentage, genome, and mitochondrial DNA, but also in various characteristics such as the awareness of God and the spiritual, the sense of authentic self-giving love, the awareness of good and evil, the sense of justice/fairness, and the sense of beauty—even if cognitive abilities are significantly limited. The presence of these abilities points to our five transcendental desires, which in turn point to a transphysical soul.[92] It is not necessary to acknowledge the existence of a transphysical soul to affirm rationally the humanity and inalienable rights of those with genetic indicators of intellectual or physical limitations. Their sense of God and spirit, authentic love, good and evil, justice and injustice, and beauty are sufficient to distinguish them from any other animal species (such as highly trained chimpanzees). Nevertheless, we should investigate the recent compelling evidence for a soul in those with significant cognitive disabilities.

In Section I above, we examined the evidence of terminal lucidity in patients with severe cognitive dysfunction, particularly the studies of Bruce Greyson, Michael Nahm, Emily Kelly, Erlendur Haraldsson, and Jesse Bering, as well as the studies of significant cognitional ability of hydrocephalic patients with less than 5 percent of their brain tissue—particularly, the studies of John Lorber, R. Lewin, and Michal Nahm (see Section I.B). Recall the two findings of these studies:

1. The only way to explain how patients with advanced Alzheimer's and dementia, as well as severe brain trauma and low IQ's (below fifty), can have significant cognitive functioning one hour or so before death (terminal lucidity) is by appealing to a source of self-consciousness and cognition independent of the physical brain, because brain damage is too severe to enable such cognitive functioning.

2. The only way to explain how patients with severe hydrocephalic disorder having less than 5 percent of their brain tissue can have global IQ's over one hundred as well as genius IQ's is to appeal to a source of self-consciousness and cognition independent of the physical brain, because the absence of 95 percent of brain tissue would prevent cognitive functioning on these (and much lower) IQ levels.

The presence of self-consciousness, cognitive functioning, a rich inner life, and spiritual awareness in patients with severe brain injuries caused Dr. Fredrich Happich ethically to prohibit euthanasia in patients with severe cognitive disabilities:

[92] See Volume II, Chapter 4 of the Quartet.

I have lived through various virtually shattering experiences.... Even the most [mentally challenged patient with IQ between twenty and forty-nine] leads a hidden inner life which is just as valuable as my own.... Often in the last hours before death, all pathological obstructions fell away and revealed an inner life of such beauty ... [that] the entire question of legally controlled euthanasia is completely finished.[93]

This view was held by all of Dr. Happich's colleagues.[94] It should be noted that Happich and his colleagues did not comment on the implications of a transphysical origin of their patient's rich inner life (such as a soul). They prohibited controlled euthanasia for these patients on the presence of cognitive functioning and rich inner life *alone*. The evidence of significant cognitive functioning in patients with severe brain trauma has been corroborated in several subsequent studies (listed above), reinforcing Happich's ethical prohibition of euthanasia for these patients.

It might be objected that Happich and his colleagues were addressing the problem of eugenic euthanasia of adults, but the question being considered is eugenic abortion of the preborn. As may be apparent, there is no real distinction between these two actions. Both procedures are eugenic actions meant to eradicate people with intellectual disabilities because they are thought to be subhumans relegated to a subhuman life. Yet there is considerable evidence showing that people with the appearance of severe mental disability have an inner life similar to our own but are unable to manifest it through their physical brains and bodies. The principle of nonmaleficence (ethical minimalism) requires that we not underestimate the powers and intrinsic dignity of any human being, or use such underestimation to justify harming, marginalizing, or killing any of them. Hence if there is significant evidence of a rich inner life in some patients with severe mental disabilities, we should assume that it is present in all patients with similar disabilities—even if it is not fully manifest. As such we should be resolved never to harm or kill such people for eugenic or other motives. Such intentional harm is seriously immoral.

In addition to the studies of terminal lucidity and hydrocephalic patients, there are multiple studies showing that people with severe

---

[93] Fredrich Happich, quoted in Nahm and Greyson, "Death of Anna Katharina Ehmer", p. 82.
[94] See ibid.

cognitive dysfunctions manifest distinctively human qualities and actions, such as a sense of God and spirit, authentic self-giving love, sense of good and evil, sense of justice, and sense of beauty. As noted earlier, these qualities are not found in the most developed non-human primates (such as highly trained chimpanzees) and are singularly human. We will consider each quality in turn.

First, mentally challenged individuals have an awareness of God, the spiritual, and the religious. This awareness is profound and is frequently the ground of personal identity and core value within them.[95] Moreover, religion is quite important to Alzheimer's and dementia patients. As their disease becomes more profound, their ability to connect with hymns and prayers remains quite pronounced until the capacity for verbal production has all but vanished.[96] Furthermore, there may be a correlation between religion-spirituality and the slowing of Alzheimer's and dementia progression.[97] Organizations such as L'Arche International are religiously based communities of disabled and nondisabled individuals that demonstrate the appreciation and importance of religion and spirituality in the lives of the mentally disabled.[98]

Secondly, there is considerable evidence that intellectually challenged individuals have a sense of right and wrong upon which to base a moral life. However, the lower the intellectual ability of these individuals, the less likely they will be to apply their awareness of right and wrong to "cause and effect" and other concepts that allow for a more nuanced personal and social moral life.[99]

[95] See Graeme Watts, "Intellectual Disability and Spiritual Development", *Journal of Intellectual and Developmental Disability* 36, no. 4 (December 2011): 234–41, https://www.ncbi.nlm.nih.gov/pubmed/21992689. See also William C. Gaventa and David Coulter, *Spirituality and Intellectual Disability: International Perspectives on the Effect of Culture and Religion on Healing Body, Mind, and Soul* (Philadelphia, Pa.: Haworth Pastoral Press, 2001).

[96] See Jon C. Stuckey, "Blessed Assurance: The Role of Religion and Spirituality in Alzheimer's Disease Caregiving and Other Significant Life Events", *Journal of Aging Studies* 15, no. 1 (March 2001): 69–84, https://www.sciencedirect.com/science/article/abs/pii/S08904 06500000177.

[97] See Miranda Hitti, "Religion, Spirituality May Slow Alzheimer's", WebMD, April 13, 2005, www.webmd.com/alzheimers/news/20070101/religion-spirituality-slow-alzheimers#1.

[98] See the mission and history of L'Arche at the L'Arche USA website: https://www.larcheusa.org/who-we-are/charter/.

[99] See Glen Thomas, *Teaching Students with Mental Retardation: A Life Goal Curriculum Planning Approach* (New York: Merrill Publishing, 1996), pp.152ff. See also Alfred Baumeister, *Ameliorating Mental Disability: Questioning Retardation* (New York: Routledge, 2009).

Thirdly, intellectually challenged individuals have a profound awareness of not only love, but the authenticity of love. Developmentally disabled individuals are capable of constructive friendships and social interaction. However, friendships among disabled individuals are more frequent and profound than friendships between disabled and nondisabled individuals, because of lack of opportunity and impatience on the part of nondisabled individuals.[100]

Fourthly, developmentally disabled individuals have an awareness of beauty. They are able not only to enjoy nature and art, but also to express themselves emotionally through art and natural symbols.[101]

In sum, though intellectually challenged people may have cognitive dysfunction—even significant cognitive dysfunction—they still manifest specifically human attributes such as an awareness of God and spiritual practice, authentic love and friendship, a sense of good and evil (whose expression may be mitigated by particularly low IQ), and appreciation of beauty. When these capacities are combined with studies of terminal lucidity and significant cognitive functioning among severely hydrocephalic patients (implying a transphysical origin of self-consciousness and cognition independent of the brain, like a soul), it is morally incumbent upon us to presume that the intellectually disabled are fully human even though cerebral dysfunctions may temporarily limit the full manifestation of that humanity. In light of this, we should conclude with Dr. Friedrich Happich "that the entire question of legally controlled euthanasia is completely finished".[102] If it is unethical to euthanize intellectually disabled adults, then it is also unethical to euthanize intellectually disabled preborn children through eugenic abortion. If the preborn are human persons with inalienable rights, then killing them for their disability is morally equivalent to killing adult persons with those disabilities.

Proponents of eugenic abortion contend that the intellectually disabled will force many to make large sacrifices to support functionally unproductive human beings, which justifies killing them through abortion. This radical utilitarian view of life's purpose is highly contestable

---

[100] See Colin Pottie and John Sumarah, "Friendships between Persons with and without Developmental Disabilities", *Mental Retardation: A Journal of Practices, Policy and Perspectives* 42, no. 1 (2004): 55–66.

[101] See Pamela Carter-Birken, "Creative Connections—Art Museums Reach Out to Persons with Disabilities", *Social Work Today* 9, no. 4 (2009): 16.

[102] Happich, quoted in Nahm and Greyson, "Death of Anna Katharina Ehmer", p. 82.

and is contrary to most religious and even humanistic ethical view-points. In addition to religious prohibitions, there is the purely naturalistic prohibition of the principle of nonmaleficence (the Silver Rule)—"do no unnecessary harm." This principle requires that we respect the *intrinsic* value of human life irrespective of any extrinsic valuation. If we abandon the principle of the inviolable intrinsic dignity of every human being (regardless of extrinsic valuation), we open the door to the brutality of genocidal regimes such as the Nazis, Stalinists, and so forth. We discuss this more fully below in Section V.C.

B. Does Eugenic Abortion Portend Eugenic Infanticide?

There is reason to believe that eugenic abortion may open the way to infanticide and ultimately to involuntary euthanasia of adults. We have already seen advocacy of infanticide by the former governor of Virginia Ralph Northam, a medical doctor, as well as several Virginia state legislators for the children of failed abortions as well as those with intellectual disability.[103] This may well foreshadow the reality of what Peter Singer (Princeton) and other theorists have been advocating for years—if abortion for eugenic reasons is permitted until the moment of birth, why stop there? Though "slippery slope" arguments are frequently dismissed because they are not absolutely predictive, they are often relatively predictive and even significantly predictive. Thus, it may be valid to suggest that eugenic abortion could create a momentum toward eugenic infanticide, which may in its turn create a momentum toward eugenic involuntary euthanasia of adults (see Chapter 4, Section I.B). Once society ethically sanctioned eugenic abortions, it has essentially sanctioned involuntary eugenics, which opens the door to infanticide for eugenic reasons. Peter Singer has strongly advocated this position since the early 1980s. The Institute of Social Ecology summarizes Singer's position on eugenic infanticide (from his book *Should the Baby Live?*[104]) as follows:

---

[103] Alexandra Desanctis, "Virginia Governor Defends Letting Infants Die", *National Review*, January 30, 2019, https://www.nationalreview.com/corner/virginia-governor-defends-letting-infants-die/.

[104] Peter Singer, *Should the Baby Live? The Problem of Handicapped Infants (Studies in Bioethics)* (1985; repr., Oxford: Oxford University Press, 1988).

Singer advocates the killing of certain newborn infants at the discretion of their parents. The criteria he proposes for deciding which infants may be killed center on a wide range of hereditary physical conditions which Singer considers "disabilities". He has been forthright and consistent in his advocacy of this position for many years. The second sentence of his 1985 book *Should the Baby Live?* (co-authored with his close colleague Helga Kuhse) reads: "We think that some infants with severe disabilities should be killed." The reason that Singer supports infanticide in such cases is not, as one might expect from a utilitarian, to put an end to the newborn's suffering; as Singer himself repeatedly points out, in many of the cases in which he favors infanticide there is no physical pain or suffering of any kind involved. His stated reason, rather, is that such children have diminished prospects of eventually enjoying an adequate "quality of life", in his words, and to allow them to live would take away resources from what Singer calls "normal" children. He therefore advocates killing "disabled" infants, if the parents so choose, and replacing them with "normal" ones.[105]

Singer considers Down syndrome and hemophilia severe enough handicaps to justify infanticide. In addition to this, he adds the following list:

Spina bifida, a severe physical handicap, chronic urinary infections; kidney disease; paraplegia requiring the use of calipers, crutches, or wheelchairs; severe spinal deformities; precariously controlled hydrocephalus; blindness, fits, and other defects.[106]

As I read Singer's list, I was surprised to discover that I too could have been the victim of infanticide if DNA sequencing had been available in 1952 and Singer's ideas were legalized. I have a congenital retinal disease that would ultimately lead to blindness at the age of sixty-five.

Singer's ethical justification for infanticide of Down syndrome children is simply that they do not have good prospects. Down syndrome children have sufficient cognitional function to do well in certain jobs and are sensitive, loving companions capable of

---

[105] Institute for Social Ecology, "Peter Singer and Eugenics", 2015, http://social-ecology .org/wp/2005/01/peter-singer-and-eugenics/.
[106] Singer, *Should the Baby Live?*, p. 61.

significant awareness of God and religion, right and wrong, and empathy for those in need (as shown below). Singer's philosophy reveals a slippery slope—from severe disabilities and hardship to "not very good prospects".

Is this slippery slope too farfetched for the United States? A clue that it might not be is the continued blocking by Senate Democrats of bills introduced by Republicans in defense of the Born-Alive Abortion Survivors Protection Act.[107] Essentially, the bill guarantees medical assistance for babies who survive a completed abortion—the same assistance that would be offered to infants who are not in the process of being aborted. The blocking of this bill is equivalent to implicit sanctioning of infanticide, because it leaves the decision of whether to help the surviving infant in the hands of the doctor who failed in his attempt to perform a third-trimester abortion. Without legal compulsion, we can expect that many such doctors would let the infants die or "complete the abortion" by killing the infant outside the womb.

The rationale offered by those blocking the Senate bill reveals their virtual indifference to the issue of infanticide:

- Those blocking the bill were concerned about restricting abortion rights, but the abortion had been completed, and no abortion rights had been restricted.[108]
- They advocated *trusting* the doctor who had just attempted the abortion with the decision to help the surviving infant outside the womb.[109]
- Perhaps most disturbing was the testimony by some senators that infanticide might be necessary if a child was disabled—for example, a Down syndrome baby.

[107] For additional information, see Bridget Handy, "Born-Alive Abortion Survivors Protection Act Fails in US Senate", *Live Action News*, February 4, 2021, https://www.liveaction.org/news/born-alive-abortion-survivors-protection-reintroduced-senate/. See also Alexandra Desanctis, "Democrats Block the Born-Alive Abortion Survivors Bill", *National Review*, February 8, 2021, https://www.nationalreview.com/2021/02/democrats-block-the-born-alive-abortion-survivors-bill/.

[108] See Maureen Ferguson, "An Infanticide Question Awaits the Democratic Nominee in 2020", *The Hill*, March 2, 2019, https://thehill.com/opinion/healthcare/432319-an-infanticide-question-awaits-the-democratic-nominee-in-2020.

[109] See ibid.

According to Maureen Ferguson:

Democrats said infanticide is already illegal, yet they seemed to argue that it is sometimes necessary if the baby is severely disabled. Several senators told compelling stories of moms and dads who were devastated at the tragic news of their baby boy or girl's disability. Why did they tell these stories in a debate that by definition only applies to infants already born?[110]

When we look at the advocacy of infanticide by Virginia's ex-governor and the continued blocking of bills in defense of the Born-Alive Abortion Survivors Act in the U.S. Senate, it seems that we are moving dangerously close to the legal sanctioning of infanticide of children with disabilities whether they were born naturally or survived an abortion. If this occurs, where will we draw the line? It may be quite naive to suggest that the momentum against "unfit life" will stop there. Will we allow ourselves to create a eugenic culture where subjective extrinsic evaluations of human worth override the intrinsic dignity and inalienable rights of the human person? If we do, we will compromise not only the inalienable rights of individuals, but also humaneness within the culture.

C. Is a World with Eugenic Purification Truly a Better World?

Up to now we have been examining the immorality of killing innocent human beings based on the false premise that preborn infants and intellectually disabled individuals are not persons, and therefore lack inalienable rights. We now examine the claim of eugenics advocates that much of the world would be better off without the intellectually and physically disabled. Is this really true? Do the sacrifices made for those with intellectual and physical challenges really make the world a worse place in which to live? Certainly, sacrifice and compassion for these individuals require time, effort, and resources, but is the expenditure of these resources for the weak and disabled truly a negative for our world? Would we really be better off without the care, compassion, and empathy bestowed upon our less fortunate

[110] Ibid.

brothers and sisters? We have already seen the answer of Margaret Sanger (founder of Planned Parenthood), which is worth recalling:

> As an advocate of Birth Control, I wish to take advantage of the present opportunity to point out that the unbalance between the birth rate of the "unfit" and the "fit", admittedly the greatest present menace to civilization, can never be rectified by the inauguration of a cradle competition between these two classes. In this matter, the example of the inferior classes, the fertility of the feeble-minded, the mentally defective, the poverty-stricken classes, should not be held up for emulation to the mentally and physically fit though less fertile parents of the educated and well-to-do classes. On the contrary, the most urgent problem today is how to limit and discourage the over-fertility of the mentally and physically defective.[111]

The implicit claim of eugenics advocates is that the lives of "unfit" individuals present excessive burden to the individuals themselves, their caretakers, and the world. Let us examine each of these claims. First, with respect to the *disabled individuals themselves*, we should ask *them* whether they are open to being euthanized for their own good. If we did a comprehensive survey of the reactions of blind people (or any other "defective group" on Peter Singer's list), I strongly suspect the vast majority would not only say no, but also that they would not want this to happen to any other blind person beyond themselves. I suspect that this would be the reply also of Down syndrome children, hemophiliacs, and every other person among the groups that Peter Singer proposes for "justified" involuntary infanticide. More often than not, people who have disabilities and weaknesses, including myself, have a tremendous quality of life, with terrific human relationships, stronger than average faith in God, and interests that promote the common good. Though these individuals struggle more than average and have their sad and hard days, they tend to grow from these struggles, find friends who genuinely value them and their companionship, and provide strength and faith to others who are challenged in life. They also progressively find high (Level Three and

[111] Margaret Sanger, "The Eugenic Value of Birth Control Propaganda", *Birth Control Review*, October 1921, https://eugenics.us/the-eugenic-value-of-birth-control-propaganda-by-margaret-sanger/128.htm.

Level Four[112]) purpose in life. Studies support the contention that disabled people generally have equal or higher quality of life than those considered to be "normal", giving rise to what is called "the disability paradox".[113] This applies not only to the visually impaired, hearing impaired, and intellectually disabled but also to those with severe spinal cord injuries who are paraplegic and quadriplegic (completely dependent on others to provide for their needs).[114] Though quality of life may decrease significantly immediately after a severely disabling accident, the trajectory almost always moves in the opposite direction over the course of one or two years until the disabled person experiences an equivalent or higher quality of life than average (called the "hedonic adaptation").[115] Research indicates that quality of life is determined not by what we can and cannot do, but by what we do with what we have.

We may now proceed to the effects of the disabled on *caretakers*. It may be objected that even if the disabled person does not experience decreased quality of life, the caretakers of the disabled certainly do, particularly if they are not compensated for their effort. This opinion is controverted by studies of uncompensated caretakers. For example, in a comprehensive 2012 study published in the *American Journal of Orthopsychiatry*, the following characteristics were found in uncompensated, nonprofessional caretakers of disabled children and adults:[116]

- Caregivers reported moderate to high levels of social connections (i.e., social support, sense of community, and religious participation).

---

[112] See Volume II, Appendix I of this Trilogy.

[113] See G. L. Albrecht and P. J. Devlieger, "The Disability Paradox: High Quality of Life against All Odds", *Social Science and Medicine* 48, no. 8 (April 1999): 977–88, https://pubmed.ncbi.nlm.nih.gov/10390038/.

[114] Narineh Hartoonian et al., "Evaluating a Spinal Cord Injury—Specific Model of Depression and Quality of Life", *Archives of Physical Rehabilitation* 95, no. 3 (2014): 455–65, https://www.archives-pmr.org/article/S0003-9993(13)01151-9/pdf.

[115] Marcel P. J. M. Dijkers, "Quality of Life of Individuals with Spinal Cord Injury: A Review of Conceptualization, Measurement, and Research Findings", *Journal of Rehabilitation Research and Development* 42, no. 3 (May 2005): 87–110, https://www.rehab.research.va.gov/jour/05/42/3suppl1/dijkers.html.

[116] Eylin Palamaro Munsell et al., "The Effects of Caregiver Social Connections on Caregiver, Child, and Family Well-Being", *American Journal of Orthopsychiatry* 82, no. 1 (2012): 137–45, https://www.ncbi.nlm.nih.gov/pmc/articles/PMC3345204/.

- High levels of subjective well-being were reported.
- Most caretakers (78 percent) did not have above-average depression levels.
- In families with a disabled person, relationships are reported to be cohesive and expressive with about average conflicts.

Several studies indicate that noncaretakers who participate in volunteer service efforts are happier than those who do not, indicating that helping the needy significantly increases quality of life (contrary to eugenic contentions). Consider the following studies:

- People who gave more to charity in 2000 were 43 percent more likely than nongivers to say they were "very happy" about their lives.[117]
- Those who volunteered in 2000 were 42 percent more likely to be "very happy" than nonvolunteers.[118]
- People who gave money away in 2001 were 34 percent less likely than nongivers to say they had felt "so sad that nothing could cheer them up". They were also 68 percent less likely to have felt "hopeless" and 24 percent less likely to have said that "everything was an effort".[119]
- In a 2008 study, giving money to someone else lifted participants' happiness more than spending it on themselves, despite participants' prediction that spending on themselves would make them happier.[120]

To what do we attribute these findings? Caretakers and those who contribute funds and service self-report the following:

- Compassion comes alive when we serve other people. People who take the time to serve others ignite empathy and compassion

[117]Arthur Brooks, "Why Giving Makes You Happy", New York Sun, December 28, 2007, https://www.nysun.com/opinion/why-giving-makes-you-happy/68700/, citing the 2000 Social Capital Community Benchmark Survey (thirty thousand American households surveyed).

[118]See ibid., citing the same 2000 Social Capital Community Benchmark Survey.

[119]See ibid., citing "The University of Michigan's Panel Study of Income Dynamics".

[120]See Jason Marsh and Jill Suttie, "5 Ways Giving Is Good for You", Greater Good Magazine, December 13, 2010, https://greatergood.berkeley.edu/article/item/5_ways_giving_is_good_for_you.

within themselves. It makes their life worth living and fills them with a sense of dignity and spirit and improves their perceived quality of life.

- Volunteer service contributes significantly to the personal, inter-personal, and social development of young people. This effect can also be seen in middle school, high school, and collegiate service-learning programs. Janet Eyler and others from Vander-bilt University assessed multiple dissertations of graduate students studying the effects of service-learning on their development:[121]
  - Service-learning has a positive effect on student personal development such as a sense of personal efficacy, personal identity, spiritual growth, and moral development (compiled from nine-teen dissertations).
  - Service-learning has a positive effect on interpersonal development and the ability to work well with others, as well as leadership and communication skills (compiled from six dissertations).
  - Service-learning has a positive effect on reducing stereotypes and facilitating cultural and racial understanding (compiled from six dissertations).

Almost no negative effects were reported by both volunteer and mandatory service-learning participants. In the vast majority of cases, the person served becomes "beloved" by those who serve, and the person serving becomes beloved by those being served.[122] There is something about "loving and being loved" by those who cannot repay that humanizes and transforms us in our outlook, ideals, and principles.[123]

Speaking personally, when I taught at Georgetown University, I used to participate in retreats where students talked about how they

---

[121] Janet Eyler et al., *At A Glance: What We Know about the Effects of Service-Learning on College Students, Faculty, Institutions and Communities, 1993–2000: Third Edition* (Vanderbilt University, August 31, 2001; funded by the Corporation for National Service Learn and Serve America National Serving Learning Clearinghouse), p. 1. Available on the website of DigitalCommons@UNO, University of Nebraska at Omaha, https://digitalcommons.un omaha.edu/cgi/viewcontent.cgi?referer=https://scholar.google.com/&httpsredir=1&article =1137&context=slcehighered.

[122] This bondedness between those serving and those served is an integral part of personal and interpersonal development coming from service-learning and other service projects. See ibid.

[123] See ibid.

matured in their faith and purpose in life. Over the course of seven years, several students mentioned that this maturity was attributable to their little brother or little sister with Down syndrome. They developed in several areas:

- Changed from an "egotistical adolescent" to being grateful for the gifts they have
- Learned to avoid judging people on the basis of weakness or disability
- Helped them to develop altruistic ideals

No doubt, caretakers experience challenges and make frequent heroic sacrifices, but they are transformed in compassion, ideals, and principles; they are brought alive by the beloved who needs them and wants them, and they are catapulted out of ingratitude and egoism into a heart of genuine love.

We may now proceed to our final consideration. The effects of the disabled on the *community, society, and the world.* Eugenics advocates may object that even if disabilities do not reduce the quality of life of the disabled and their caretakers, they surely put excess burdens on the organizations, communities, and states who must pay at least part of the cost to assist them. Since these funds could be used for other "more productive" purposes, why not "dispense" with the severely disabled? The reader might be thinking that is a heartless question, which is essentially correct. The prioritization of values embedded in this question is clear—matters of the heart have little value compared to investments that will improve our standard of living. From the vantage point of "economic value", they are correct. We can get more velocity and leverage for our money by investing in a technology or business than helping the poor and disabled. However, from the vantage point of humanitarian and transcendent value (Level Three and Level Four), this prioritization of economy over humanity leaves our culture without a "collective heart", because it produces little care, compassion, self-gift, faith, and relationship with God. Without these qualities, we would have a miniscule "collective heart" within our culture and society, similar to the society desired by Ebenezer Scrooge before his discovery of love. When Scrooge is asked for a donation to help the poor, he responds:

"I wish to be left alone," said Scrooge. "Since you ask me what I wish, gentlemen, that is my answer. I don't make merry myself at Christmas and I can't afford to make idle people merry. I help to support the establishments I have mentioned [prisons, treadmills, and union workshops]—they cost enough; and those who are badly off must go there." [The gentleman said,] "Many can't go there; and many would rather die." "If they would rather die," said Scrooge, "they had better do it, and decrease the surplus population."[124]

Every investment we make to ease the deprivation, sufferings, and disabilities of those around us increases the subjective and objective quality of life, not only of the needy but also of their families, caretakers, and those who share in the friendship of the disabled and their families. The disabled bring a humanizing and spiritualizing influence into every environment they enter. Their very presence elicits empathy, natural friendship, and a profound sense of love for the person himself (rather than his esteemable qualities). The encounter with the disabled in the workplace, supermarket, community center, church, or a social setting immediately takes our focus off of practical and utilitarian objectives and places it on the intrinsic goodness and lovability of the person in his transcendent mystery. We may not use these words to describe what is happening to us, but if we reflect on it (and are not jaded), we will find that encounters with the disabled are filled with empathy, delight, peace, and God's presence, which elevate us beyond the merely mundane.

This elevation of our heart and spirit may not be an economic value, but it is an interpersonal and spiritual value. Given that we are more than mere material units of production and consumption (economic valuation) and are relational, interpersonal, affective, caring, moral, transcendent, and spiritual (humanitarian and spiritual valuation), we must make provision not only for goods and services, but also for heart, spirit, family, friendships, community, culture, and society. These qualities truly make life worth living while bringing civility, peace, dignity, respect, care, and self-sacrificial love into our community and society. If all value were economic, we would be a

---

[124]Charles Dickens, *A Christmas Carol* (London: Chapman & Hall, 1843; Project Guttenberg, 2018), Stave One, "Marley's Ghost", https://www.gutenberg.org/files/46/46-h/46-h.htm.

heartless society. We might be wealthier, but there would be little love, appreciation of lovability, and civility in it.

In view of the above, we may now endeavor an answer to the eugenicists' questions. Would we have a better world without people who need our help? Would we be better off without people who are dependent and needy? Let us suppose for a moment that with new gene-mapping techniques, invitro fertilization, germline genetic modification, and other technologies, we could eliminate weakness from the world around us and create a perfect species. Would that be a better world? As noted above, we could say that it would be a more efficient world, a more productive world, and a more progressive world. But is that a better world? I would venture to say unqualifiedly *no*. Can you imagine a world where no one is called out of himself to do an act of compassion, sacrifice, or empathy simply to serve another? Conversely, can you imagine a world without people who have any need? Remember, if you have no needs, you have no vulnerability, and therefore no call to interdependence and humility. Furthermore, you have no need to cooperate with others for any noble endeavor or any common cause, because everyone is self-sufficient and can take care of himself. Can you imagine a world where everyone lives according to the stoic philosophy "I carry my own weight; you carry yours"? Can you imagine a world where there is not some need or weakness that would call or even shock us out of our superficiality and egoism—a world without a call to humility? Can you imagine the level of pride and arrogance there would be? Can you imagine everybody trying to pay his geneticist the highest price for the best gene alterations for himself and his children, because the only thing that makes life worth living is a little marginal advantage over the other near-perfect people? Can you imagine the level of competition that would exist in the "proud and perfect society"? Frankly, I can imagine all these scenarios, and it does not sound like a better or a more perfect society to me. Rather, it sounds like Dante's description of Hell in which everyone is focused on themselves, their marginal comparative advantage, and their ability to use that advantage to dominate (rather than take care of) others. A world without need, vulnerability, humility, compassion, service, self-sacrifice, and empathy for those who are uniquely good and loveable regardless of their extrinsic "qualifications" is to me a world of unadulterated darkness; I think we would bring each other to a speedy end to escape this bleak and painful world of self-sufficiency. It does not take much imagination to see this as the worst possible scenario for a brave new world.

So, what is wrong with eugenics? It assesses human worth not on unique intrinsic goodness and lovability and on the little acts of goodness and love that we can freely muster, but rather on extrinsic characteristics that may boost our esteemability (but not our lovability), our self-sufficiency (but not our goodness), and our contribution to the development of products and services (but not our contribution to the human spirit and the Kingdom of God). The problem with eugenics is its definition of "quality of life" in terms of esteemability, self-sufficiency, and the production of things while ignoring lovability, love, goodness, self-transcendence, the human spirit, and the Lord. If that sounds like a good thing to you, then support the new eugenics, which is resurging throughout the community of "new reproductive technologies". But if this sounds like a nightmare to you, follow the lead of the Catholic Church, who is interpreting the teaching and heart of Jesus for our time. The Church's educational task is challenging because the heart, love, and goodness of Jesus can be reached only by accepting and following objective moral standards that need to be defended if there is going to be any love, goodness, self-transcendence, and spirit and religious fulfillment in our world. Though these objective moral standards may seem like a needless restriction of our freedoms, they are precisely the opposite, for without the prohibition of abortion, embryonic stem cell research, and euthanasia of the preborn and the elderly, we are a much less humane, respectful, caring, and compassionate society. This decline of compassion will ultimately lead to the eclipse of freedom, for where love wanes domination prevails.

VI. Invitro Fertilization

Many married couples who find themselves to be infertile have made recourse to invitro fertilization so they could have a child of their own genetic lineage. When they find out that the Catholic Church has prohibited it, they are baffled and oftentimes indignant because they unknowingly believe that there is nothing wrong with this technology. The Catholic Church does not prohibit actions without substantial moral rationale, so it is incumbent upon us to learn why the Church believes that invitro fertilization is contrary to the teaching and love of Jesus. Aside from the fact that fertilization occurs in a petri dish (instead of in a mother's reproductive system), invitro fertilization almost always entails the extinguishing of multiple human embryos. Recall (from Section I above) that the Church teaches that every human embryo at the moment of fertilization is a human person. This viewpoint is supported by contemporary medical studies in two areas:

- Human embryos at the stage of a unicellular zygote have a full human genome, indicating that they are unique, self-moving, self-perfecting, dynamic organisms actualizing themselves according to a specifically *human* genome.
- There is substantial evidence from peer-reviewed medical studies of near-death experiences and terminal lucidity that all human beings have a soul that is a transphysical source of self-consciousness and intelligence. We may infer that preborn children have such a soul from near-death experiences of babies a few months after birth,[125] as well as the requirements for complete integration of the developing cerebral cortex with a transphysical source of consciousness (see above Section I.B).

Inasmuch as every human embryo is a unique organism actualizing itself according to a full human genome, the extinguishing of multiple human embryos in the process of invitro fertilization is tantamount to killing multiple innocent human beings. The Catholic Church formally set out this position in 1987 in its document *Donum Vitae.*[126]

One of the problems with invitro fertilization is that couples do not *feel* like they are involved in killing multiple innocent human beings (because they do not see the embryos that the doctors are

---

[125] See Herzog and Herrin, "Near Death Experiences in Very Young", pp. 1074–75.

[126] Congregation for the Doctrine of the Faith, Instruction on Respect for Human Life in Its Origin and on the Dignity of Procreation *Donum Vitae* (February 22, 1987), II.

destroying and do not recognize them as human beings). However, these embryos are human beings. Recall from Section I.A above that a unicellular human zygote is a unique, self-moving, self-perfecting, dynamic organism actualizing itself according to a human genome, and that it is the organism through which all cells constituting a fully developed human being throughout a lifetime will be produced. Thus, it is in *potentia* an entire human being throughout his or her lifetime. Recall also the considerable evidence indicating that this unique individual human being has a transphysical soul capable of surviving bodily death that must be created by a transphysical cause (like God).

If couples recognize that invitro fertilization entails the deliberate killing of multiple embryos, and that these embryos are unique individual human beings that may well have a transphysical soul, they would be co-responsible for killing these human beings if they knowingly request a procedure that entails these deaths. We are held responsible for what we knowingly do—not for what we are feeling when we do it. If a couple does not know that invitro fertilization entails multiple killings of innocent human beings, then they are not responsible (culpable) of committing a serious sin. However, if they are aware of these multiple intentional deaths, but proceed with the process to obtain a child of their genetic lineage, then they are co-responsible.

Let us examine the two points at which intentional killing of human embryos occurs during the process of invitro fertilization. The invitro fertilization process has three stages:

1. A woman is given a fertility drug, causing the aspiration of multiple eggs that mature in the ovum simultaneously. These eggs are then removed and combined with semen from a male partner in a petri dish, fertilizing multiple eggs and giving rise to multiple zygotes developing into embryos.[127] Most of these embryos will not be used for implantation, and normally the

---

[127]See John Haas, "Begotten Not Made: A Catholic View of Reproductive Technology", United States Conference of Catholic Bishops, 1998, https://www.usccb.org/issues-and-action/human-life-and-dignity/reproductive-technology/begotten-not-made-a-catholic-view-of-reproductive-technology.

remaining embryos are destroyed. This is the first stage at which intentional destruction of innocent human life occurs.

2. Much of the time several embryos are selected to implant in the woman's uterus in order to obtain implantation of a healthy embryo. All the implanted embryos are allowed to develop for several weeks, after which ultrasound monitoring is used to detect which ones are the healthiest.

3. After forty days, embryos have developed into fetuses with beating hearts. Sometime after this, physicians engage in a second procedure euphemistically called "fetal reduction".[128] Most mothers do not want to have multiple children, and so all of the embryos (except one) have to be "eliminated". A syringe is filled with potassium chloride, then maneuvered through ultrasound monitoring to the fetus' heart. This is injected into the heart, immediately killing it.[129] Fetal reduction is often performed multiple times to ensure that only one fetus is allowed to develop.[130] If fetuses are equally healthy, doctors simply eliminate the ones that are nearest to the needle.[131] These intentional abortions are often erroneously classified as "miscarriages". This is the second stage at which developing human persons (fetuses with beating hearts) are disposed of—this time by intentional abortion.

Given that human embryos and human fetuses are unique individual human beings (see above), which therefore have intrinsic value and dignity, inalienable rights, and transcendent/spiritual dignity before God, invitro fertilization must be considered seriously immoral—it entails the intentional killing of multiple innocent human beings in stages one and three of the commonly used process. Catholics who knowingly engage in this procedure even out of a sincere desire to

---

[128] It is possible to circumscribe this process by taking the risk of implanting only one embryo in the hopes that it will develop normally. Many couples do not take this risk, not only because there is a fair possibility of a nonhealthy embryo but also because each attempt costs at least ten thousand dollars. Furthermore, fetal reduction offers the possibility of selecting the *healthiest* fetus, which brings up the issue of eugenics—the elimination of fetuses with less favorable characteristics. See ibid.

[129] Ibid.

[130] Ibid.

[131] Ibid.

help them bear children of their own lineage are co-responsible for the deaths of the other children they have participated in creating and killing.

In addition to the intentional killing of unwanted living embryos and fetuses, invitro fertilization has also led to a nest of new troubling ethical issues—fetal experimentation, genetic enhancement of embryos, and designer babies through eugenic selection. Advances in gene sequencing and especially gene editing (through CRISPR technologies[132]) have allowed invitro fertilization to be utilized in elitist and eugenic ways. In 2008, the Congregation for the Doctrine of the Faith issued a new document, *Dignitatis Personae*, offering ethical guidance in these new troubling uses of invitro fertilization.[133] In additions to the prohibition of using human embryos and fetuses for experimentation of any kind (also prohibited in *Donum Vitae*), the Congregation addressed two additional areas:

- Gene editing for the sake of curing diseases[134]
- Gene editing for the sake of genetic enhancements of offspring leading to a superior genetic class "that happen[s] to be appreciated by a certain culture or society", for example, possibly among the wealthy[135]

With respect to gene editing of adults for purely therapeutic purposes, the Congregation specified that it is licit so long as it does not entail undue risk and patients give fully informed consent.[136] These procedures would include genetic engineering and CRISPR injections to rectify the conditions brought about by genetically inherited diseases.

There is a new technology called germline genetic editing, which is done through invitro fertilization, that can beneficially affect the

---

[132] CRISPR is an acronym for "clustered regularly interspaced palindromic repeats". See Melody Redman et al., "What Is CRISPR/Cas9?", *Archives of Disease in Childhood—Education and Practice Edition* 101 (2016): 213–15, https://www.ncbi.nlm.nih.gov/pmc/articles/PMC497 5809/.

[133] Congregation for the Doctrine of the Faith, Instruction on Certain Bioethical Questions *Dignitatis Persona* (September 8, 2008).

[134] Ibid., no. 25.

[135] Ibid., no. 27.

[136] Ibid., no. 25.

progeny of those who can afford the procedure. The Congregation declared these technologies to be illicit not only because they use invitro fertilization (entailing the intentional destruction of human embryos and fetuses), but also because they could be used to produce genetic enhancements of the wealthier classes that could afford them. The Congregation considered the future possibility of germline genetic editing not using invitro fertilization, and indicated that so long as this non-IVF technology was used only for therapeutic purposes to prevent genetic disorders, it would be *licit*. However, if germline technology (whether IVF based or non IVF based) were used for enhancement purposes or eugenic attempts to improve the gene pool, it would be *illicit*.[137]

The Congregation's rationale for prohibiting germline genetic editing for enhancement purposes is twofold:

- It could create two classes within the human community—a privileged class that would have the funds to procure intellectual, physical, and longevity enhancements for their progeny versus economically less advantaged classes who would not be able to procure such enhancements. This would give rise to a momentum of elitism among the wealthy with the resultant subordination of the less economically advantaged.
- It would also lead to the unjustified disadvantaging of some groups of people—for example, the disabled (see above) and the female sex (see sex selection in China and Asia in Chapter 2, Section IV.B). Currently, a majority (if not a large majority) of secular ethicists express the same ethical concerns as the Catholic Church—particularly with respect to psychosocial inequality, devaluation of disabilities and the disabled, gene editing for sex selection, and creation of human-animal hybrids and embryoids.[138]

The Congregation summed up its grave concern about germline genetic editing for enhancements (shared by secular ethicists) as follows:

[137] Ibid., nos. 26–27.

[138] Ignacio Macpherson, Maria Victoria Roque, and Ignacia Segarra, "Ethical Challenges of Germline Genetic Enhancement", *Frontiers in Genetics*, September 3, 2019, https://www.frontiersin.org/articles/10.3389/fgene.2019.00767/full. This resource is an excellent, well-referenced summary of the large range of ethical issues raised by germline genetic enhancement.

Some have imagined the possibility of using techniques of genetic engineering to introduce alterations with the presumed aim of improving and strengthening the gene pool. Some of these proposals exhibit a certain dissatisfaction or even rejection of the value of the human being as a finite creature and person. Apart from technical difficulties and the real and potential risks involved, such manipulation would promote a eugenic mentality and would lead to indirect social stigma with regard to people who lack certain qualities, while privileging qualities that happen to be appreciated by a certain culture or society; such qualities do not constitute what is specifically human. This would be in contrast with the fundamental truth of the equality of all human beings which is expressed in the principle of justice, the violation of which, in the long run, would harm peaceful coexistence among individuals.... All of this leads to the conclusion that the prospect of such an intervention would end sooner or later by harming the common good, by favouring the will of some over the freedom of others.[139]

VII. Embryonic Stem Cells

Embryonic stem cells are thought to be a veritable panacea to cure genetic disorders, tissue damage (from almost any cell type), and even organ replacement. Scientists and celebrities promote the use of embryonic stem cells without even questioning the source from which they are derived. Expressing the teaching of the Catholic Church in *Evangelium Vitae*, Pope John Paul II points to an obvious objection that embryonic stem cells have to come from deceased human embryos, and most of these deceased embryos originate from abortions.[140] Inasmuch as abortion is legal, the ethical objection is overlooked. The Church raises another ethical problem showing the extent to which such technologies could be abused. Embryos could be generated through invitro fertilization and allowed to grow to the point where stem cells could be harvested for transplantation and experimentation, resulting not only in the death of the embryo but also in his or her denigration by being reduced from "person" to a mere "thing"—a source of organ cells and tissues.[141]

---

[139] Congregation for the Doctrine of the Faith, instruction *Dignitas Personae* (The Dignity of a Person) (December 8, 2008), no. 27.

[140] See *Evangelium Vitae*, no. 63.

[141] See ibid.

Evangelium Vitae explicitly condemns this killing and utilitarian use of a human embryo:

> This evaluation of the morality of abortion is to be applied also to the recent forms of intervention on human embryos which, although carried out for purposes legitimate in themselves, inevitably involve the killing of those embryos. This is the case with experimentation on embryos, which is becoming increasingly widespread in the field of biomedical research and is legally permitted in some countries.[142]

The Church's ethical rationale for prohibiting embryonic stem cells is twofold:

- The personhood and inalienable rights of every unique embryonic human being must be maintained, to prevent the needless killing of any group of innocent humans based on a merely subjective denial of their personhood.
- Since the end does not justify the means, killing unique embryonic human beings cannot be justified by the ostensibly good end of providing organ tissue (even life-critical organ tissue) to those in need.

It does not matter whether one assigns a greater extrinsic valuation to an adult (who is, for example, in need of an organ transplant) over a developing embryo in a womb or petri dish. The *intrinsic* value of each human being is equal, and it is unethical to kill one human being to improve the health or extend life of another human being on the basis of extrinsic valuation.

The Church also prohibits the production of embryos specifically for the purpose of obtaining stem cells and organ tissue (after which the embryo would be killed). As with experimentation on embryos, this violates an embryo's personhood and right to life, treating it as a mere thing for utilitarian objectives.[143] This utilitarian use and destruction of human embryos has another disturbing consequence. It could incentivize and financially support abortion clinics (such as Planned Parenthood). Increasing the use of fetal stem cells for tissue and transplant therapy could cause an increased demand

---

[142] Ibid.
[143] See ibid.

for those stem cells which in turn would incentivize the marketing and promotion of abortion by abortion clinics for increased profits. Currently it is illegal to sell aborted fetal tissue and organs for profit.[144] Nevertheless, the Center for Medical Progress claimed in May 2020 that Planned Parenthood was in fact selling fetal body parts for profit, which they documented on videos.[145] Though Planned Parenthood denies participation in these activities, videos (including a video of their testimony during their lawsuit) seem to indicate the contrary.[146] At the very least, it looks certain that selling fetal tissue and organs is tempting not only to Planned Parenthood (the largest U.S. provider of abortions), but also to other abortion providers.

What makes this issue particularly troubling is that today embryonic stem cell use is completely superfluous for purposes of tissue and organ repair and replacement. Techniques for obtaining adult stem cells in which an adult can use his or her own stem cells for tissue or organ repair and replacement are safer and more effective than embryonic stem cells. According to an academic article in *Circulation Research*,

> Adult stem cells are the successful standard for stem cells. Although in the past their regenerative/reparative capacity was ignored, misunderstood, or even maligned, a rapidly growing host of clinical applications are being developed, and the clinical utility of adult stem cells is increasingly validated in the literature. Adult stem cells are the true gold standard in regenerative medicine. Adult stem cells are the only stem cell type that has shown evidence of success when it comes to patients, and treating patients is supposedly the ultimate goal for stem cell research.[147]

---

[144] "The sale of tissues and organs of aborted babies for profit is illegal under 42 U.S. Codes 274e and 289g-2." Cheryl Sullenger, "Planned Parenthood Profited from Selling Aborted Baby Parts, One PP [Planned Parenthood] Location Made $25,000 in Three Months", *LifeNews*, April 15, 2020, https://www.lifenews.com/2020/04/15/planned-parenthood -profited-from-selling-aborted-baby-parts-one-clinic-made-25000-in-three-months/.

[145] Center for Medical Progress, "Planned Parenthood Testimony on Selling Baby Parts Unsealed, New Videos Released", May 26, 2020, http://www.centerformedicalprogress.org /2020/05/planned-parenthood-testimony-on-selling-baby-parts-unsealed-new-videos -released/.

[146] See ibid.

[147] David Prentice, "Adult Stem Cells: Successful Standard for Regenerative Medicine", *Circulation Research* 124 (March 2019): 837–39, https://www.ahajournals.org/doi/10.1161 /CIRCRESAHA.118.313664.

In view of the fact that adult stem cells are more effective than embryonic stem cells and require no destruction and "thingification" of human embryos, why is embryonic stem cell research continuing? How can it be ethically justified even from a utilitarian point of view? Embryonic stem cell use constitutes a completely unnecessary destruction and objectification of human beings with inalienable rights, which decreases not increases the efficacy of regenerative and reparative therapies. How can it be viewed as ethical in any way? The Catholic Church encourages Catholics to make use of adult stem cell regenerative protocols for diseases that can be cured by them. There are dozens of diseases currently being treated by regenerative adult stem cell protocols.[148]

VIII. Conclusion

The Catholic Church holds the right to life in the highest regard, insisting that it is higher than all other rights and freedoms—the rights to liberty, property, and the pursuit of happiness, as well as extrinsic rights declared by the state. She uses natural reason and the natural law principle of justice to justify this prioritization—independent of Christian revelation. The right to life belongs to every human being (who can be identified by mitochondrial DNA and a uniquely human genome). The Church also holds that human persons have intrinsic and transcendental dignity, possessing a transphysical soul uniquely created by God with the capabilities of self-consciousness; abstract intelligence; syntactical language; conscience; moral reflection; free choice; the transcendental desires for perfect truth, love, goodness, beauty, and home; spiritual awareness; and survival after bodily death (for which there is considerable evidence from medical, scientific, and philosophical studies[149]). Without making recourse to a transcendental soul, probative arguments can be made for the inalienable right to life of unborn children, disabled individuals, elderly individuals,

---

[148] For a list, see Stem Cell Connect, Charlotte Lozier Institute, "Treatments", 2022, https://stemcellresearchfacts.org/answers/treatments/.

[149] These medical, scientific, and philosophical arguments are summarized in Section I above and fully articulated in Volume II of the Quartet.

and every other human being (see the arguments in Sections I and II). Consideration of evidence for a human soul gives eternal and transcendental significance to human nature and dignity pointing to the prerogative of God in matters of life and death. In view of this, the Church has developed reasonable and responsible natural law arguments to make the moral teaching of Jesus accessible and applicable to a pluralistic secular world.

Based on the above principles, the Church has continuously sought to protect the life and dignity of every human person, particularly the most vulnerable—the preborn and those with disabilities. As we shall see, she extends this protection to the elderly (Chapter 4, Section I) and those who were formerly enslaved (Chapter 6, Section I.B). She pleads not only for the protection and dignity of all people, but also for a culture of life—a culture that seeks to enhance rather than delimit or destroy human persons regardless of how their extrinsic dignity is evaluated. Representing the Lord, who has created and redeemed us, she asks for a vision of all human persons based on their intrinsic and transcendental dignity, who are created for eternal life and joy with the Triune God. If we make this assumption, we will be far better off, striving to foster the intrinsic goodness, lovability, and spirit of every member of the human family, rather than eliminating those who are deemed inconvenient, inferior, and obstacles to materialistic fulfillment.

Chapter Four

Physician-Assisted Suicide, Euthanasia, Self-Defense, and Torture

Introduction

The Catholic Church seeks to protect the life and dignity of several additional vulnerable populations whose extrinsic "worth" may be thrown into question, among whom are the elderly and the disabled. We will again examine the Church's teaching concerning these populations with a view to exposing the callous disregard and injustice to which they are subject by recent legislative activity enacting medical aid in dying and physician-assisted suicide (Section I). We will also examine the Church's teaching on suicide, self-defense, and torture (Section II), as it reflects the teachings of Jesus and a culture of life.

I. Physician-Assisted Suicide and Euthanasia

We now turn to the opposite end of life's spectrum, examining the immorality of physician-assisted suicide and euthanasia. Euthanasia, so-called mercy killing—whether active (an intervention to kill a person) or passive (the removal of ordinary care to kill a person intentionally)—is prohibited by the Catholic Church. The *Catechism of the Catholic Church* states:

> Whatever its motives and means, direct euthanasia consists in putting an end to the lives of handicapped, sick, or dying persons. It is morally unacceptable. Thus an act or omission which, of itself or by intention, causes death in order to eliminate suffering constitutes a murder

gravely contrary to the dignity of the human person and to the respect due to the living God, his Creator.[1]

Though euthanasia was not a major problem in the early Church, the eugenics movement (and the Nazi implementation of it) in the 1930s and 1940s compelled Pope Pius XII to give a general statement prohibiting all forms of direct euthanasia—even in the case of people with terminal illness.[2] This was affirmed by the Sacred Congregation for the Doctrine of the Faith in its 1980 *Declaration on Euthanasia*.[3]

This prohibition is grounded not only in a theological rationale, but also a philosophical one. The Church's prohibition is based on two reasons: First, these practices entail suicide or implicit suicide (a request for lethal injection).[4] Secondly, they lead to the abuse of vulnerable populations and can lead to involuntary euthanasia, as well as undermine the dignity of suffering, lower the cultural view of "quality of life", and encourage a culture of death.[5] This issue and its significant negative consequences is becoming more urgent because of the legal acceptability of physician-assisted suicide in an increasing number of states in the United States (currently ten states and District of Columbia[6]) as well as countries throughout the world (eight countries including parts of the United States[7]). The momentum to increase physician-assisted suicide is increasing not only because of past political successes in the United States and internationally but also because of the efforts and funding of the Hemlock Society (which has

---

[1] *CCC* 2277.

[2] See Pope Pius XII, Address to Participants in the VIII Congress of the World Medical Association (September 30, 1954).

[3] Sacred Congregation for the Doctrine of the Faith, *Declaration on Euthanasia* (May 5, 1980).

[4] See Pope John Paul II, Encyclical Letter on the Value and Inviolability of Human Life *Evangelium Vitae* (March 25, 1995), no. 66.

[5] Ibid., nos. 64–66.

[6] Oregon, Washington, Vermont, Colorado, California, Hawaii, Maine, New Jersey, and New Mexico. Montana also has legal physician-assisted suicide but via court ruling. See "States with Legal Physician-Assisted Suicide", ProCon.org, last updated December 14, 2021, https://euthanasia.procon.org/states-with-legal-physician-assisted-suicide/.

[7] Austria, Canada, Belgium, Finland, Germany, the Netherlands, Luxembourg, New Zealand, Spain, Switzerland, and parts of the United States and Australia (Victoria). See "Euthanasia and Physician-Assisted Suicide (PAS) around the World", ProCon.org, last updated January 10, 2022, https://euthanasia.procon.org/euthanasia-physician-assisted-suicide-pas-around-the-world/#austria.

euphemistically renamed itself Compassion and Choices with its sub-sidiary Caring Friends[8]) and other organizations dedicated to Medical Aid in Dying (MAID) and Physician Assisted Suicide (PAS).[9]

Before examining the negative consequences of MAID and PAS, we must make a distinction between these two illicit means versus refusing extraordinary and burdensome medical treatment. Quoting the Sacred Congregation for the Doctrine of the Faith's *Declaration on Euthanasia*, Pope John Paul II sets out the standard as follows:

> In such situations, when death is clearly imminent and inevitable, one can in conscience "refuse forms of treatment that would only secure a precarious and burdensome prolongation of life, so long as the normal care due to the sick person in similar cases is not interrupted."[10]

Pope John Paul and the Congregation indicate that euthanasia is a deliberate act to end the life of a patient, whether by a direct form of medical intervention (such as a lethal injection) or indirectly by providing a patient with a fatal prescription for self-administration. Such direct or indirect actions to end a person's life intentionally and prematurely are immoral because they constitute either an intentional act of killing or the facilitation of suicide. However, patients have the right to refuse aggressive medical treatments (extraordinary means), such as cardiac resuscitation, ventilators, or amputation, that are incapable of being "objectively proportionate to the prospects for improvement".[11] In other words, if a treatment is burdensome to the patient (or his financial condition) and has a low prospect of improvement and serves mostly to prolong a patient's suffering, the patient has the right to refuse it.[12]

---

[8] Compassion and Choices and Caring Friends are involved in the movement for state-approved physician-assisted suicide and encourage suicide by the helium bag method, promoting suicide by couples if desired. See Patients Rights Council, "Facts about Hemlock and Caring Friends", 2013, http://www.patientsrightscouncil.org/site/hemlock-and-caring-friends/.

[9] See, for example, the contributors to the 2008 Washington Initiative 1000 published by the Patients Rights Council, 2013, http://www.patientsrightscouncil.org/site/funding-watch/.

[10] *Evangelium Vitae*, no. 65.

[11] Ibid.

[12] See Colin B. Donovan, "End of Life Decisions: Ordinary versus Extraordinary Means", EWTN, March 2019, https://www.ewtn.com/catholicism/library/end-of-life-decisions-ordinary-versus-extraordinary-means-12733. See also National Catholic Bioethics Center, *A Catholic Guide to Palliative Care and Hospice*, 2019, https://www.ncbcenter.org/store/catholic-guide-to-palliative-care-and-hospiceenglishpdf-download.

The matter of artificial hydration and nutrition requires further explanation. In brief, if a patient's disease (say, cancer) will cause death before he would die of dehydration or starvation from the removal of artificial hydration and nutrition, then the patient has the right to refuse artificial hydration and nutrition.[13] However, if the removal of artificial hydration and nutrition would cause the death of the patient by dehydration or starvation *before* his underlying disease (say, cancer), then removal of artificial hydration and nutrition would constitute an act of euthanasia (acting to end the life of the patient prematurely), which would be gravely immoral.[14]

There is another important distinction concerned with the administration of pain protocols that must also be considered. In brief, if a dying patient is being given pain medication (intravenously, orally, or by some other method) with the *sole intention* of alleviating pain but the medication unintentionally leads to death (say the cessation of breathing), then the action is not euthanasia but rather an unintentional secondary effect of trying to control pain.[15] This action would not be illicit. However, if medical officials (or others) increased pain medication with the intention of causing death before the patient's underlying disease, then this is an act of euthanasia, which is gravely immoral.[16]

There is other information concerned with end-of-life decisions and palliative care that should be considered by patients and their caretakers. An excellent resource for Catholics is *A Catholic Guide to Palliative Care and Hospice* (written by the National Catholic Bioethics Center).

One final point concerning pain must be considered before proceeding. Many people believe that terminal illness will inevitably be accompanied by unbearable and untreatable pain that incites them to consider assisted suicide without fully examining the protocols

---

[13] See ibid.

[14] See ibid.

[15] According to *Evangelium Vitae*, "Pius XII affirmed that it is licit to relieve pain by narcotics, even when the result is decreased consciousness and a shortening of life, 'if no other means exist, and if, in the given circumstances, this does not prevent the carrying out of other religious and moral duties' (Pius XII, Address to an International Group of Physicians, February 24, 1957)" (no. 65). This is based on the principle of double effect, which is explained below in Section II.

[16] Ibid.

available to control their pain. This assumption is mostly incorrect, and decisions based on it are mostly (and sadly) mistaken.

Martin L. Smith notes that "90% to 99% of terminal cancer pain can be controlled with the use of hospice and palliative care units."[17] This is confirmed by Michael H. Levy and Carol Warfield.[18] Even Derek Humphry (co-founder of the Hemlock Society and author of *Final Exit*, the controversial "self-help" book) admits that "only a small percentage of terminal physical pain cannot be controlled today."[19] Dr. Pieter Admiraal (a Dutch anesthesiologist, clinical pharmacologist, and leading advocate of legalized euthanasia in Holland) has been quoted to the effect that pain control and alertness can be achieved in practically all cases, given sufficient effort and sophistication on the part of all involved, and that euthanasia for pain is therefore unethical.[20] Tremendous progress continues to be made in the development and availability of effective pain protocols, and many national and international organizations are devoted to it, such as the American Pain Society, the International Association for the Study of Pain, the American Society of Hospice Physicians, and the International Psycho-Oncology Society.

Bearing the above considerations in mind, we now proceed to a specific consideration of the negative consequences of medical aid in dying and physician-assisted suicide. Many people complain that the Catholic Church is trying to interfere with the freedoms of non-Catholics by opposing efforts to legalize assisted suicide. It must be stressed here that the Catholic Church is not entering into the public square to impose Catholic morality on non-Catholics, but rather to protect the right of the vulnerable, disabled, those suffering from depression, and people who are disadvantaged in their medical insurance coverage (many of whom have been harmed by the legalization of assisted suicide). Thus, the Church has entered into a large coalition of medical, disabilities, faith-based, and social organizations

---

[17]Martin L. Smith et al., "A Good Death: Is Euthanasia the Answer?" *Cleveland Clinic Journal of Medicine* 59, no. 1 (1992): 107, https://www.ccjm.org/content/ccjom/59/1/99.full.pdf.

[18]Michael H. Levy, "Medical Management of Cancer Pain", in *Principles and Practice of Pain Management*, ed. Carol A. Warfield (New York: McGraw Hill, 1993), p. 235.

[19]Derek Humphry, *Let Me Die before I Wake: Hemlock's Book of Self-Deliverance for the Dying* (New York: Grove Press, 1984), p. 76.

[20]Personal communication of Pieter Admiraal to Carlos Gomez.

to protect the rights of those potentially and actually harmed by the "freedom of assisted suicide". The following six negative consequences of MAID and PAS will make this clear:

1. Creating an Onerous Burden to Die for Vulnerable Populations (Section I.A)
2. Encouragement of Assisted Suicide in Nonterminal Patients and Involuntary Euthanasia (Section I.B)
3. Threats to the Disabled (Section I.C)
4. Lowering the View of "Quality of Life" within the Culture (Section I.D)
5. Undermining the Medical Profession (Section I.E)
6. Normalizing and Morally Sanctioning Suicide within the Culture (Section I.F)

A. Creating an Onerous Burden to Die for Vulnerable Populations

A well-known principle from Natural Law Theory may be expressed as follows: A law permitting freedom to one group cannot impose an excessive or onerous burden on another group.[21] It might at first be difficult to see how permitting assisted suicide for one group of people could impose an onerous burden on another group of people. Nevertheless, many physicians and ethicists have warned against this possibility precisely because "the option to commit assisted suicide" can bring about strong pressures to commit suicide on those who are vulnerable to family or medical coercion as well as those suffering from depression, low self-esteem, or financial constraint. Prior to the legalization of assisted suicide, this pressure did not exist, and it is particularly tragic because it affects the most vulnerable in our society.

Unfortunately, current legislation legalizing assisted suicide allows those deaths to be recorded as caused by the illness from which the

---

[21] John Locke indicates this in his second treatise on government (Book II, Chapter 2, Section VIII), when he notes that the natural freedoms of human beings cannot do unreasonable harm (or lay unreasonable burden) on another human being.

patient was suffering rather than assisted suicide.[22] Hence, we have no idea about the real number of people who have committed assisted suicide let alone the circumstances under which this has occurred. Furthermore, the physician who prescribes the lethal medication is the sole reporter, and he is unlikely to report problems, inadequate diagnosis, or indirect coercion.[23] As a result, we must turn to stories that have leaked to the press or some other public source.

Let us first examine the problem of coercion by family members who may be tired of helping the patient, desirous of inheritance, or resentful for past slights. The case of Kate Cheney shows how these coercive situations are facilitated by family members. The Patients Rights Council sums up Cheney's case (taken from a report of the *Oregonian*, October 17, 1999) as follows:

> Kate Cheney, 85, died of assisted suicide under Oregon's law even though she reportedly was suffering from early dementia. Her own physician declined to provide the lethal prescription. When counseling to determine her capacity was sought, a psychiatrist determined that she was not eligible for assisted suicide since she was not explicitly seeking it, and her daughter seemed to be coaching her to do so. She was then taken to a psychologist who determined that she was competent but possibly under the influence of her daughter who was "somewhat coercive." Finally, a managed care ethicist, who was overseeing her case, determined that she was qualified for assisted suicide, and the drugs were prescribed.[24]

This case illustrates what has come to be known as "physician shopping". As an early dementia patient, Kate was vulnerable to both coercion and suggestion, and her daughter, according to her physicians and psychiatrists, was coercive. For that reason, when Kate's physician refused to write her prescription, her daughter sought another judgment from a psychiatrist, who again indicated that Kate was not

[22] See Ronald Pies and Annette Hanson, "Twelve Myths about Physician Assisted Suicide and Medical Aid in Dying", July 17, 2018, https://www.hcplive.com/view/twelve-myths-concerning-medical-aid-in-dying-or-physicianassisted-suicide.

[23] See ibid.

[24] Patients Rights Council, "Ten Years of Assisted Suicide in Oregon", 2013, http://www.patientsrightscouncil.org/site/oregon-ten-years/. The summary is from Erin Barnett, "A Family Struggle: Is Mom Capable of Choosing to Die?", *Oregonian*, October 17, 1999.

seeking it and that her daughter was coercive. Undaunted, her daughter proceeded to a psychologist, who indicated that she was under the influence of a coercive daughter. Finally, she went to an "ethicist" working for a managed care firm, who determined that she was qualified. Kate soon took the lethal medication without specifically requesting it or having the freedom to resist her daughter's coercion. The fate of Kate Cheney cannot be viewed as unique because there is likely a considerable number of selfishly motivated children who want to rid themselves of a burden, receive inheritance, or repay past slights.

Furthermore, Dr. Leon Kass[25] (professor of medical ethics at the University of Chicago) and Dr. Edmund Pellegrino[26] (former professor of bioethics at the Georgetown University Kennedy Institute of Ethics) write extensively about how seldom the decisions made by dying patients are truly autonomous, and how easily they are influenced or manipulated. In view of the above, it is likely that coercion is present in many cases when vulnerable patients make requests for physician-assisted suicide.

There are many other victims of legalized assisted suicide beyond those vulnerable to coercion. Depressed individuals are also particularly vulnerable because those with a history of depression as well as those suffering from temporary depression (from a terminal diagnosis) can make a tragic decision when they are "least themselves". Of particular concern are those with temporary depression that normally accompanies a diagnosis of terminal illness.[27] In many cases, this depression is resolved naturally,[28] and in most cases, it can be therapeutically resolved with appropriate medication.[29] When depression is treated by available protocols and physicians are caring, the majority of assisted suicide requests are reversed. Dr. Kathleen Foley

[25] See Leon Kass, "Preventing a Brave New World", *New Republic Online*, June 21, 2001, https://web.stanford.edu/~mvr2j/sfsuo9/extra/Kass3.pdf.

[26] See Edmund Pellegrino, "Compassion Is Not Enough", in *The Case against Assisted Suicide: For the Right to End-of-Life Care*, ed. Kathleen Foley and Herbert Hendin (Baltimore: Johns Hopkins University Press, 2002), pp. 41–51.

[27] Elizabeth Kübler-Ross and D. Kessler, On *Grief and Grieving: Finding the Meaning of Grief through the Five Stages of Loss* (New York: Scribner, 2014).

[28] See ibid.

[29] See Herbert Hendin, "Commentary: The Case against Physician-Assisted Suicide: For the Right to End-of-Life Care", *Psychiatric Times* 21, no. 2 (2004), https://dredf.org/wp-content/uploads/2012/10/hendin-psychiatric-times-2004.pdf.

(former director of Palliative Care at Memorial Sloan Kettering Cancer Center) indicates that the great majority of suicide requests are reversed when pain and depression are adequately treated.[30] Since 90–99 percent of pain can be adequately treated (see above, Martin L. Smith, Michael H. Levy, and Carol Warfield), and since much of the depression associated with terminal illness can be reversed naturally or through therapy, love of family and friends, and the understanding of physicians,[31] the vast majority of suicide requests *are* reversed when these conditions are met. Kathleen Foley and Michael Hendin elaborate further on the real meaning behind many patients' requests for suicide:

> Opposition to legalization [of assisted suicide] is strongest among physicians who know most about caring for terminally ill patients (i.e., palliative care specialists, gerontologists, psychiatrists who treat patients who become suicidal in response to medical illness, hospice physicians and oncologist). They know that the patients requesting a physician's assistance in suicide are usually telling us as strongly as they know how that they desperately need relief from their suffering and that without such relief they would rather die. They are making an anguished cry for help and a very ambivalent request to die. When they are treated by a physician who can hear their ambivalence, understand their desperation, and relieve their suffering, *the wish to die usually disappears.*[32]

Unfortunately, many physicians do not meet the above needs of their patients. Instead of helping them to become their true selves once again, they take the easier path of fulfilling patients' ambivalent requests for death rather than honoring their underlying desire to live amid family and friends. Legalized assisted suicide opens the door to this quick and easy path, which short-circuits meaningful and desired life for patients as well as their family and friends.

---

[30] See, for example, Kathleen M. Foley, "The Relationship of Pain and Symptom Management to Patient Requests for Physician-Assisted Suicide", *Journal of Pain and Symptom Management* 6, no. 5 (1991): 289–97. "We frequently see patients referred to our Pain Clinic who have considered suicide as an option, or who request physician-assisted suicide because of uncontrolled pain. We commonly see such ideation and requests dissolve with adequate control of pain and other symptoms, using combinations of pharmacologic, neurosurgical, anesthetic, or psychological approaches", p. 290, https://www.jpsmjournal.com/article/0885-3924(91)90052-6/pdf.

[31] See Foley and Hendin, *Case against Assisted Suicide*, pp. 1–9.

[32] Ibid., p. 4.

The desire to live is present not only in those with temporary depression (from a diagnosis of terminal illness), but also in people with long-term clinical depression. As Dr. Ronald Pies (clinical professor of Psychiatry at Tufts University School of Medicine) and Annette Hanson (assistant clinical professor of psychiatry at Tufts University School of Medicine) state:

> Patients who express suicidal ideation in the context of a condition such as major depression rarely want to die; rather, as numerous suicide prevention websites note: "Most suicidal people do not want to die. They are experiencing severe emotional pain and are desperate for the pain to go away."[33]

When clinical depression is adequately treated by long-term protocols, a patient's depression decreases and the desire to live is rekindled.[34] For this reason, assisted suicide is literally "overkill" as a solution to painful episodes during long-term clinical depression. Though assisted-suicide legislation makes a pretense to protecting patients with temporary or long-term depression (by ostensibly requiring the approval of a clinical professional), it offers little real protection if doctors are not genuinely concerned for the patient or if patients' families are intent on avoiding it (by "physician shopping" as in the case of Kate Cheney). Since there is little government oversight in this area, it is virtually impossible to prevent abuse or sanction violators.[35] As Michael Hendin and Kathleen Foley report in the *Michigan Law Review*:

> Seemingly reasonable safeguards for the care and protection of terminally ill patients written into the Oregon law are being circumvented ... [and that] ... the Oregon Public Health Division (OPHD), which is charged with monitoring the law ... does not collect the information it would need to effectively monitor the law.... OPHD ... acts as the defender of the law rather than as the protector of the welfare of terminally ill patients.[36]

[33] Pies and Hanson, "Twelve Myths".
[34] See ibid.
[35] See ibid.
[36] Herbert Hendin and Kathleen Foley, "Physician-Assisted Suicide in Oregon: A Medical Perspective", *Michigan Law Review* 106, no. 8 (2008): 1613, https://repository.law.umich.edu/mlr/vol106/iss8/7/.

It is irrelevant whether family members, friends, or physicians are well-intentioned or not—if they suggest that a person might be better off dead, then he could take that suggestion seriously if he has no strong religious or philosophical convictions about the immorality of suicide. Is this a real concern? The experiences in the states of Oregon and Washington indicate that it is. The fact is, patients who do not want to commit suicide feel pressured to do so by the simple suggestion that they should consider "the option for it". This pressure never existed prior to assisted-suicide legislation. One person's option has become another person's duty to die.

The new pressure to die by assisted suicide extends beyond the victims of family and physician coercion, the temporarily depressed, and the clinically depressed into the domain of the economically disadvantaged. The advent of assisted suicide allows insurance companies to cover this "service" while tightening up coverage on protocols to extend life in terminal patients. In Oregon, for example, a cancer patient named Barbara Wagner was turned down for a remedial medication and was sent a letter by a company administering one of the state's insurance plans, indicating that they would pay for her assisted suicide and the physician visit for the prescription. She told the *Seattle Times*, "I was absolutely hurt that somebody could think that way. They won't pay for me to live but they will pay for me to die."[37]

Again, shortly after the legalization of assisted suicide in California, Stephanie Packard found her insurance coverage tightened when she asked for chemotherapy treatment for terminal scleroderma. Coverage was denied but assisted suicide was offered as an option for a $1.20 co-pay for the drugs needed to induce her death.[38] Why the bargain rate for assisted suicide? Evidently, replacement of coverage for life-extending treatment with the assisted suicide option will save insurance companies millions of dollars.[39]

But the insurance coverage problem does not stop with patients having a terminal diagnosis. It is now being extended to patients who

[37] Quoted in Hal Bernton, "Washington's Initiative 1000 Is Modeled on Oregon's Death with Dignity Act", *Seattle Times*, October 13, 2008, https://www.seattletimes.com/seattle-news/washingtons-initiative-1000-is-modeled-on-oregons-death-with-dignity-act/.

[38] See Helena Berger, "When Insurance Companies Refuse Treatment 'Assisted Suicide' Is No Choice at All", American Association of People with Disabilities, January 24, 2017, https://www.aapd.com/when-insurance-companies-refuse-treatment-assisted-suicide-is-no-choice-at-all/.

[39] See ibid.

have a greater than 50 percent chance of complete cure. For example, Dr. Brian Callister (associate professor of internal medicine at the University of Nevada) tried to send two patients to Oregon and California for treatments that were not available in his hospital. These treatments would have been covered in Nevada (if available), and in one case would have led to a 50 percent chance of cure and in another case a 70 percent chance of cure. In both cases, the medical insurance director told him, "Brian, we're not going to cover that procedure or the transfer, but would you consider assisted suicide?"[40] In both cases, the patient would have been terminal without treatment.[41] It seems that assisted suicide has given insurance companies an excuse to tighten coverage not only for patients with terminal diagnoses but also for patients who would be terminal without treatment. Given the millions of dollars insurance companies can save by tightening these kinds of coverage, we could be facing a two-tier insurance system within states legalizing assisted suicide—premier insurance coverage for diseases that could be terminal (at a higher rate) and ordinary insurance coverage that replaces curative or life-extending treatment with assisted suicide (at standard rates). If this scenario plays out, assisted suicide will lead to significant disadvantages (and even the duty to die) for the economically less advantaged. Helena Berger (president of the American Association of People with Disabilities) summarizes the problem as follows:

> What voters don't often realize until later is that they are also giving insurance companies and physicians new rights too—the legal means to deny treatment. The romantic notion of assisted suicide as something individuals do at the end of life to make their death more comfortable becomes tainted because without the [economic] means to live, the "right-to-die" becomes the dangerous default.[42]

In sum, physician-assisted suicide cannot be characterized merely as a new freedom or option for those who wish to die, because its

---

[40] Bradford Richardson, "Insurance Companies Denied Treatment to Patients, Offered to Pay for Assisted Suicide, Doctor Claims", *Washington Times*, May 31, 2017, https://www.washingtontimes.com/news/2017/may/31/insurance-companies-denied-treatment-to-patients-o/.

[41] See ibid.

[42] Berger, "When Insurance Companies Refuse Treatment".

legalization has led to the foreclosure of freedom and even the burden to die for a wide range of victims—those who are coerced by family members, the temporarily and clinically depressed, and the economically less advantaged. The fact that states do not require "assisted suicide" to be listed as the cause of death (but rather the illness of the patient) makes it very difficult to investigate the circumstances surrounding assisted suicide.[43] We do not even know how many cases of assisted suicide there are in the United States. It would not be surprising to find that there are far more cases of assisted suicide than currently estimated and that the majority of those cases involve coercion, temporary depression, clinical depression, refusal of insurance coverage, or some combination of these. Evidently, the Church is not trying to take away the freedom to die for those who desire it, but rather protecting the right of life and liberty for the coerced, disabled, depressed, and economically disadvantaged. States and countries currently considering assisted suicide should examine the burdens and injustices they will be imposing upon a large number of their citizens.

B. Encouragement of Assisted Suicide in
Nonterminal Patients and Involuntary Euthanasia

Though "slippery slope" arguments are frequently dismissed out of hand, there appears to be significant evidence that the legalization of assisted suicide expands into the domain of nonterminal patients as well as involuntary euthanasia based solely on the judgment of physicians who consider patients' lives to have insufficient value or quality. Let us begin with the area of assisted suicide for nonterminal patients. In the Netherlands, Belgium, and Luxemburg, many people request and receive assisted suicide for causes completely unrelated to terminal illness. For example, in the Netherlands, two hundred psychiatric patients (between 2008 and 2014) were euthanized by their own request.[44] Among them, 56 percent refused treatment for their psychiatric condition, and 66 percent indicated their primary reason

---

[43] Pies and Hanson, "Twelve Myths".
[44] See ibid.

for requesting euthanasia or suicide was social isolation and loneliness.[45] Since that time, psychiatric euthanasia has increased steadily.
According to Scott Kim (a psychiatrist and philosopher investigating
this phenomenon):

> There has been a steady increase [in psychiatric euthanasia in the
> Netherlands] with 83 cases in 2017; the per-capita equivalent in the
> United States would be about 1,600 cases a year. Unlike euthanasia
> in general, psychiatric euthanasia is predominantly given to women.[46]

One of the problems with psychiatric euthanasia is the absence of
objective criteria to justify it. In the Netherlands, the only requirement to administer a lethal injection is the consent of a patient (sixteen years of age or older) and the physician's subjective judgment
that the patient's emotional suffering is unbearable. This enabled "an
otherwise healthy Dutch woman [to be] euthanized 12 months after
her husband's death for 'prolonged grief disorder' ".[47]

In April 2020, a Dutch member of parliament introduced a bill to
allow any patient over the age of seventy-five to attain assisted suicide
or a lethal injection if he has had a strong wish to do so for at least
two months. "Opponents of the legislation have argued that it preys
on lonely and possibly depressed elderly people, who need support
and resources rather than offers of suicide."[48] Though the legislation
has not been debated and brought to vote, it manifests yet another
decline in the slippery slope. As Dr. Gordon Macdonald (head of the
UK-based alliance Care Not Killing) noted,

> To now consider extending the euthanasia law to people who are
> just tired of life, and may well be depressed, is highly irresponsible,
> immoral and dangerous.[49]

---

[45] See ibid.

[46] Scott Kim, "How Dutch Law Got a Little Too Comfortable with Euthanasia", *Atlantic*,
June 8, 2019, https://www.theatlantic.com/ideas/archive/2019/06/noa-pothoven-and-dutch
-euthanasia-system/591262/.

[47] Ibid.

[48] Catholic News Agency, "Controversial Dutch Bill Would Allow Assisted Suicide
for Healthy People over 75", July 28, 2020, https://www.catholicnewsagency.com/news
/controversial-dutch-bill-would-allow-assisted-suicide-for-healthy-people-over-75-19446.

[49] Ibid.

If this bill passes, it will open the door to a significant increase in physician-assisted suicides, most of which can be prevented by adequately treating depression and administering compassionate physician care.[50]

Could this happen in the United States? It is certainly possible, given the erosion of objective moral norms in the culture. As we shall see (in Chapter 5, Section III), the weakening of objective moral norms undermines resolve to maintain standards essential for emotional health of individuals, stability of marriages and families, and civility within the culture. The foregoing pages show that our culture is experiencing this declining trend in a dangerously accelerating way. Why wouldn't we expect it to occur in the area of euthanasia and physician-assisted suicide?

Let us now turn to the issue of involuntary euthanasia in the Netherlands and other countries that have legalized euthanasia for over a decade. This may give a sense of what is likely to occur in the United States and other countries who have more recently legalized assisted suicide. We begin with the prescient words of Dr. Edmund Pellegrino:

> Assisted suicide is a half-way house, a stop on the way to other forms of direct euthanasia, for example, for incompetent patients by advance directive or suicide in the elderly. So, too, is voluntary euthanasia a half-way house to involuntary and non-voluntary euthanasia. If terminating life is a benefit, the reasoning goes, why should euthanasia be limited only to those who can give consent? Why need we ask for consent?[51]

Since the Dutch courts implicitly allowed voluntary euthanasia in 1997, there has been a steady progression for involuntary euthanasia. John Keown notes that in the Netherlands, official support for nonvoluntary euthanasia is readily found. The State Commission on Euthanasia in 1987 recommended that nonvoluntary euthanasia should not be an offense, if carried out in the context of "careful

---

[50] See Foley and Hendin, *Case against Assisted Suicide*, p. 4.

[51] Edmund Pellegrino, "The False Promise of Beneficent Killing", in *Regulating How We Die: The Ethical, Medical, and Legal Issues Surrounding Physician Assisted Suicide* (Cambridge: Harvard University Press, 1998), p. 89.

medical practice", though that was not defined.[52] In 1988, the Royal Dutch Medical Association working party condoned euthanasia for deformed infants, in some instances thinking it ought to be compulsory.[53] In 1991, the Royal Dutch Medical Association committee condoned the killing of patients in persistent coma.[54] The Remmelink Report on Euthanasia in the Netherlands (1991)[55] noted that involuntary euthanasia is occurring in the Netherlands and is increasing in proportion to the increase in assisted suicide and voluntary euthanasia. This finding is summarized and quantified by the Southern Cross Bioethics Institute as follows:

> By adopting the narrow definition of euthanasia as "active termination of life upon the patient's request", the Dutch reported there were 2,300 instances of euthanasia in the year of the survey, or 1.8% of all deaths. When, however, to these are added instances of killing patients without request and intentionally shortening the lives of both conscious and unconscious patients, the figures are dramatically altered. They now become: 2,300 instances of euthanasia on request; 400 of assisted suicide; 1,000 of life-ending actions without specific request; 8,750 patients in whom life-sustaining treatment was withdrawn or withheld without request, "partly with the purpose" (4,750) or "with the explicit purpose" (4,000) of shortening life; 8,100 cases of morphine overdose "partly with the purpose" (6,750) or "with the explicit purpose" (1,350) of shortening life; 5,800 cases of withdrawing or withholding treatment on explicit request, "partly with the purpose" (4,292) or with the "explicit purpose" (1,508) of shortening life.[56]

---

[52]John Keown, "The Law and Practice of Euthanasia in the Netherlands", *Law Quarterly Review* 108 (1992): 51–78.

[53]See ibid.

[54]See ibid.

[55]Committee to Investigate Medical Practice Concerning Euthanasia, "Medical Decisions about the End of Life (Remmelink Report)" (The Hague, Netherlands: Ministry of Justice and Ministry of Welfare, Public Health, and Culture, 1991).

[56]Southern Cross Bioethics Institute, "Euthanasia Practices in the Netherlands", accessed February 15, 2022, http://www.bioethics.org.au/Resources/Online%20Articles/Other%20Articles/Euthanasia%20practices%20in%20the%20Netherlands%20-%20Brian%20Pollard's%20third%20Document.pdf. The article is citing John Keown, "Further Reflections on Euthanasia in the Netherlands in the Light of the Remmelink Report and the van der Maas Study in Euthanasia", in *Euthanasia, Clinical Practice and the Law*, ed. Luke Gormally (Linacre Centre, 1994), pp. 219–40.

Though ostensibly euthanasia in the Netherlands is voluntary, the Remmelink Report shows demonstrably that a large percentage is involuntary. In the year of the survey (1990–1991), there were 1,000 life-ending actions without request, 1,350 morphine overdoses without request, and 4,000 early withdrawals of treatment explicitly intended to end life without request. Thus, in addition to the 2,300 instances of voluntary euthanasia, there were 2,350 instances of direct (active) involuntary euthanasia and 4,000 involuntary withdrawals of treatment leading to death. Dr. Pellegrino is proven correct in his assertion that voluntary euthanasia leads to involuntary euthanasia almost seamlessly. Since the Remmelink Report, voluntary euthanasia in the Netherlands has tripled (to 6,091 voluntary cases),[57] and lacking additional restraints by the Dutch government, we might infer that involuntary euthanasia has increased proportionately.

More disturbingly, involuntary euthanasia has become more brazen, even in cases where patients actively refused attempts to be euthanized. In 2017, a Dutch doctor determined that one of her patients (an elderly woman with the onset of dementia) was in a state of intolerable suffering and incapable of making a decision in favor of euthanasia. She had requested it in her will, but only when she (the patient) decided that the time was right. Since according to the doctor the patient's dementia prevented her from making such a decision, she took it upon herself to drug the patient's coffee to induce sleep. When the patient awoke and saw the lethal injection coming toward her, she kicked and screamed in an apparent attempt to prevent herself from being killed. When the doctor was unable to control her, she called in family members to hold her down so that she could complete the action of killing her.[58] Though the Regional Review Committee determined that the physician stepped over the line because she had drugged the woman's coffee and did not stop killing her when she actively refused the injection, the committee exonerated her because she "acted in good faith".[59]

---

[57] See Eugene C. Tarne, "Netherlands Forcible Euthanasia Case and the Slippery Slope", Charlotte Lozier Institute Bioethics, July 21, 2017, https://lozierinstitute.org/netherlands-forcible-euthanasia-case-and-the-slippery-slope/.

[58] See ibid.

[59] Ibid.

Once again, we must ask the question of whether this could happen in the United States. It is certainly conceivable, because the United States, like the Netherlands, lacks objective moral norms to the contrary and could seamlessly slip into involuntary euthanasia as predicted by Dr. Pellegrino and demonstrated in the Netherlands. As the Remmelink Report and Eugene Tarni indicate, the slippery slope must be taken seriously because there is no countervening moral will to the contrary within our culture.

C. Threats to the Disabled

Let us begin by examining the professional organizations and institutions adamantly opposed to assisted suicide—World Health Organization, the American Medical Association and many of its state affiliates, the American College of Physicians, the National Hospice and Palliative Care Organization, the American Cancer Society, and many other medical organizations, as well as the League of United Latin American Citizens (LULAC)—and virtually every major national and international disability rights organization.[60] Notice whom these represent: the most weak and vulnerable in our society—those with disabilities, those with physical and psychological illnesses, nonmajority ethnic groups, and those who are terminally ill. Why are these groups so concerned about physician-assisted suicide? They are because these bills can be used to put pressure on the disabled to consider suicide in lieu of their need for assistance. Recall from above that advocates of assisted suicide admit that pain is not an appropriate reason for advocating assisted suicide, because most pain from terminal illness can be adequately controlled by physicians. The real reason for promoting assisted suicide, advocates say, is the indignity of disability and weakness—the indignity of needing help and relying on others.[61] As Marilyn Golden, a former policy analyst for the Disability Rights Education and Defense Fund, retorted:

[60] See Marilyn Golden and Tyler Zoanni, "Killing Us Softly: The Dangers of Legalizing Assisted Suicide", *Disability and Health Journal* 3 (2010): 16–30, https://dredf.org/wp-content/uploads/2012/08/PIIS1.pdf.

[61] See R. Leiby, "Whose Death Is It Anyway? The Kevorkian Debate; It's a Matter of Faith, in the End", *Washington Post*, August 11, 1996.

As many thousands of people with disabilities who rely on personal assistance have learned, needing help is not undignified, and death is not better than reliance on assistance. Have we gotten to the point that we will [advocate] suicides because people need help using the toilet?[62]

Diane Coleman (a disabled attorney) explains the problem in light of data gathered from the state of Oregon several years after legalization of assisted suicide:

What increasingly emerges from the Oregon data is that medical professionals, government officials and assisted suicide proponents see no problem in society assisting suicides of people who feel that they are a "burden on others" (49% in 2013) or feel a "loss of autonomy" (93%) or "loss of dignity" (73%). Did any of the doctors know about consumer controlled attendant services, which could address these concerns? The Oregon law does not require disclosures about any form of home care.[63]

Assisted suicide laws cause many physicians to suggest assisted suicide with people of disabilities before (or instead of) giving them their options to obtain assistance at home, for transportation, and for socialization. Even more concerning is physicians' reticence to give counseling to depressed disabled people about alternatives to suicide before suggesting assisted suicide to them.[64] Indeed, many physicians do not even recognize that suggesting assisted suicide is like telling disabled individuals that their lives are essentially worthless. For Coleman and others upholding disability rights, putting counseling of this nature in the hands of physicians is tantamount to writing off the value and rights of the disabled.[65]

If suicide is to be preferred over needing assistance, what does that say about the worth and dignity of disabled people? What are we saying about the dependent, the vulnerable, and the poor who all need

---

[62] Golden and Zoanni, "Killing Us Softly", p. 18.

[63] Diane Coleman, "Why Do Disability Rights Organizations Oppose Assisted Suicide Laws?" Not Dead Yet, 2022, https://notdeadyet.org/why-do-disability-rights-organizations-oppose-assisted-suicide-laws.

[64] See ibid.

[65] See ibid.

assistance? Are we not saying that death is better than compassion? Are we not reversing the teaching of Jesus Christ, who implied that love conquers death? The influence of culture and cultural trends is amazingly strong, and if this prioritization gains momentum, we will enter into a new level of the culture of death.

D. Lowering the View of "Quality of Life" within the Culture

Dr. Daniel Callahan formerly of the Hastings Center for Bioethics Research states what Catholics and Christians have known for centuries—"noble and heroic life can be achieved by those who have little or no control over the external conditions of their lives but have the wisdom and dignity necessary to fashion a meaningful life without it."[66] Callahan is saying here that we have a fundamental option about how to define "quality of life". Does our quality of life consist in our abilities, strengths, intellectual acuity, and competitiveness—or does it consist in a relationship with the loving God, the compassion we show to others, and the contributions we try to make to the various people and causes around us? If we define "quality of life" in the first way, then suffering has no meaning—and as we lose our mental acuity, physical agility, autonomy, and competitiveness, we will see our quality of life slipping away, leading to a sense of purposelessness, worthlessness, emptiness, and malaise. However, if we put on the mantle of Christ, then we will likely see a remarkable transformation take place during the time of our physical and natural decline—namely, an increased capacity for trust in God, and compassion for and forgiveness of others. As Saint Paul said, "I will all the more gladly boast of my weaknesses, that the power of Christ may rest upon me.... For when I am weak, then I am strong" (2 Cor 12:9–10).

For Christians, weakness and diminishment is a path to salvation with intrinsic dignity, not a scandal, an imposition, or a degradation. We as Christians must stand up for this by word and example, so that the most vulnerable in our society will not only be protected but

---

[66] Quoted in Foley and Hendin, *Case Against Assisted Suicide*, p. 9.

flourish in their true dignity of imparting faith, wisdom, forgiveness, and compassion to their loved ones before they pass to the next life.[67]

We can attain a deeper understanding of the above by recalling the four levels of purpose in life elucidated in Volume I of the Quartet (*Finding True Happiness*). Each level of purpose implies a particular view of "quality of life". Level One views quality of life as material advantage, quality and quantity of material possessions, and abundance of comfort and sensual pleasure. Level Two views quality of life as high autonomy, achievement, comparative advantage, esteem from others, opportunities for advancement, and enhanced control and power.[68] Level Three views quality of life as contribution to others, compassion for others, love and empathy for others, caring for others, listening to others, and forgiving others (Jesus' view of "love").[69] Level Four views quality of life as trusting in God, surrendering to God, being in communion with God, serving God within community, and bringing the saving word of God to others.[70] Frequently, Level One and Level Two views of quality of life go hand and hand; so also do Level Three and Level Four views of quality of life.

As we age, we will ultimately encounter limits to Level One and Level Two quality of life—energy levels, physical stamina, and sometimes even memory and mental acuity begin to diminish. At the same time, Level Three and Level Four quality of life can increase considerably *if we do not impede them*. This is why grandparents, despite diminished physical capacities, can provide deep empathy, affection, care, and religious instruction to children, complementing what is given by their parents. Oftentimes when patients are given a terminal diagnosis, their last year of life can be their best—the time when they show the most compassion, forgiveness, wisdom, religious instruction (evangelization), and peace. If we do not lose heart when Level One and Level Two quality of life decrease, we can focus our energies on Level Three and Level Four quality of life (which may become

[67] I have written an entire book on how the Christian view of suffering can lead to transformation of self, the purification of love, the path to salvation, and an offering of self for the good of the world. See Volume IV of the Quartet—*The Light Shines on in the Darkness: Transforming Suffering through Faith.*

[68] See Volume I, Chapter 3 of the Quartet.

[69] See ibid.

[70] See ibid.

enhanced in the midst of our weakness and limited years). If we do this, we can leave an immense legacy of love, wisdom, and faith for our families and friends. All we need do is refocus from Levels One and Two to Levels Three and Four.

So, what does all this have to do with the passage of assisted-suicide legislation? Recall what was said above that pain is not a good reason to request assisted suicide, because most pain can be controlled adequately by medical protocols. Rather, the primary reason for requesting assisted suicide is diminished autonomy and dignity, as well as the need for assistance. Viewed in terms of the four levels of the quality of life, the primary reason for requesting assisted suicide is a decline in Level One and Level Two quality of life. Thus, assisted suicide presents a serious hindrance to the normal and healthy course of moving from Level One and Level Two quality of life to Level Three and Level Four quality of life during the aging process. When Level One and Level Two are in decline, the mere possibility of assisted suicide incites individuals to consider ending it all in a moment of despair instead of considering how they might best live out the rest of their lives with the gifts they still have—empathy, care, compassion, forgiveness, deepened faith, prayer, and religious instruction. The prospect of assisted suicide focuses them on despair and death rather than love and faith—a corruption of the natural order of life (for those who are open to love and faith). The more we reinforce the normality of assisted suicide, the more we reinforce the indignity of aging, needing assistance, and being a burden, and the more we do this, the more we replace love and faith with despair and death—a recipe for not only individual but cultural suicide. The only way to reverse this propensity toward the culture of death is to teach the four levels of quality of life, emphasizing the dignity and eternal significance of Level Three and Level Four quality of life.[71] If we can do

---

[71] Educating the *elderly* about the four levels of quality of life, and how to transition from Levels One and Two to Levels Three and Four, is particularly important. Oftentimes when the elderly move to an assisted cared or nursing facility, they are asked to fill out forms concerning their wishes for treatment and end of life. If they have no sense of Levels Three and Four quality of life, they are likely to make a disastrous decision for themselves, their families, and friends, undermining the gifts they have, the care and faith they can provide, and the legacy they can leave. See Robert Spitzer, *Healing the Culture: A Common-Sense Philosophy of Happiness, Freedom, and the Life Issues* (San Francisco: Ignatius Press, 2000), Chapter 4.

this in conjunction with reinforcing religious belief and the religious norm of protecting every sacred human life, we may have a chance of staving off an ultimate culture of death.

E. Undermining the Medical Profession

In its Code of Ethics, the American Medical Association declares that physician-assisted suicide is contrary to the physician's role as healer and poses significant societal risks:

> It is understandable, though tragic, that some patients in extreme duress—such as those suffering from a terminal, painful, debilitating illness—may come to decide that death is preferable to life. However, permitting physicians to engage in assisted suicide would ultimately cause more harm than good. Physician-assisted suicide is fundamentally incompatible with the physician's role as healer, would be difficult or impossible to control, and would pose serious societal risks. Instead of engaging in assisted suicide, physicians must aggressively respond to the needs of patients at the end of life.[72]

According to Mark O'Rourke and others, physician-assisted suicide changes the nature of the medical profession, undermines the physician-patient relationship, and co-opts physicians into cooperating with potentially wrongful deaths.[73] The fundamental problem with pressuring physicians to write prescriptions for physician-assisted suicide is the inherent conflict it creates with the Hippocratic oath and their personal identity as healer and life-affirmer. The Hippocratic oath states, "I will use treatment to help the sick according to my ability and judgement, but never with a view to injury or wrongdoing."[74] So long as this identity is fixed in the minds and hearts of

---

[72] American Medical Association, "Code of Medical Ethics Opinion 5.7", 2022, https://www.ama-assn.org/delivering-care/ethics/physician-assisted-suicide.

[73] Mark A. O'Rourke, M. Colleen O'Rourke, and Matthew F. Hudson, "Reasons to Reject Physician Assisted Suicide/Physician Aid in Dying", *Journal of Oncology Practice* 13, no. 10 (2017): 683–86, https://ascopubs.org/doi/full/10.1200/JOP.2017.021840.

[74] Hippocrates, *The Hippocratic Oath*, trans. W. H. S. Jones, in *Oxford Reference*, 2022, https://www.oxfordreference.com/view/10.1093/acref/9780191826719.001.0001/q-oro-ed4-0000 7207.

physicians, they will be determined to heal and save life while they are alleviating suffering. If this is their sole aim, then patients and society will be well served. However, if an inherently contradictory end, such as assisting in suicide, is imposed on physicians and the profession, it will create a dissonant identity, which will undermine the principal aim of healing and saving life.[75] This will likely lead to increasing indifference to patients' welfare progressively, allowing other objectives to become significant and equivalent to the Hippocratic objective. Several alternative objectives are foreseeable, such as lowering the cost of treatment, lowering the time of treatment, dispensing with patient neuralgia, and acquiescing to pressure from insurance companies, hospital officials, and relatives favoring patient suicide.[76] If these alternative objectives become primary, or even replace the Hippocratic one, scenarios such as those in the Netherlands may become commonplace. Recall the case of the doctor who was exonerated for drugging her patient's coffee, and lethally injecting her despite the patient's repeated attempts to stop her (see above Section I.B). Note that the doctor was influenced by the patient's display of fear and anger in the hallway (an inconvenient patient) and was in league with relatives who held the patient down while the physician injected and killed her. As the American Medical Association implies, mixed objectives and bi-furcated identity in physicians entails significant societal risks.[77]

Secondly, as noted above, physician-assisted suicide may ultimately lead to direct active euthanasia by physicians (i.e., dispensing lethal injections),[78] which may in turn lead to involuntary euthanasia (as it has in the Netherlands—see above Section I.B). If this occurs, it will accelerate physician indifference to the life and welfare of the patient. Giving periodic lethal injections to patients cannot but undermine physicians' determination to save the life of the patient. Indeed, it may insight physicians to encourage patients to seek death to ease the cost, time, and efforts of treatment (as has occurred in the Netherlands—see above Section I.B). This course of action further increases societal risks.

[75] See ibid.
[76] See ibid.
[77] See American Medical Association, "Code of Medical Ethics".
[78] See ibid.

Thirdly, physician–assisted suicide may co-opt physicians into causing unnecessary deaths. As O'Rourke and others indicate, many diagnoses of terminal illness in cancer patients have proven to be wrong, and if doctors dispense a lethal prescription believing a wrongly diagnosed terminal illness, they will be co-opted into causing an unnecessary wrongful death. All oncologists know the uncertainty of diagnoses of terminal illness and the risks of acting on them against their patients' welfare. Furthermore, diagnoses of terminal illness cause depression, which is very often naturally or therapeutically reversible, and when reversed leads to a reversal of suicide requests (see above Section I.A). If a physician writes a prescription for assisted suicide, which might well be reversed with proper counseling, he cooperates with an unnecessary and undesired suicide. This is why most oncologists, palliative-care specialists, and hospice physicians are against physician–assisted suicide.[79]

Fourthly, dispensing lethal prescriptions for patients' suicides can be deeply disturbing to physicians, causing depression and withdrawal from the profession. According to doctors Ronald Pies and Annette Hanson,

> Many doctors who have participated in euthanasia and/or PAS are adversely affected—emotionally and psychologically—by their experiences. In a structured, in-depth telephone interview survey of 38 US oncologists who reported participating in euthanasia or PAS, nearly a quarter of the physicians regretted their actions. Another 16% reported that the emotional burden of performing euthanasia or PAS adversely affected their medical practice.[80]

Similarly, European doctors report strong negative emotional reactions to assisted suicide and lethal injection.[81]

[79] "Opposition to legalization [of assisted suicide] is strongest among physicians who know most about caring for terminally ill patients (i.e., palliative care specialists, gerontologists, psychiatrists who treat patients who become suicidal in response to terminal illness, hospice physicians and oncologist)." Foley and Hendin, *Case against Assisted Suicide*, p. 4.

[80] Pies and Hanson, "Twelve Myths", citing K. R. Stevens Jr., "Emotional and Psychological Effects of Physician-Assisted Suicide and Euthanasia on Participating Physicians", *Issues Law and Medicine* 21, no. 3 (2006): 187–200.

[81] See Pies and Hanson, "Twelve Myths", citing American Academy of Hospice and Palliative Medicine, "Statement on Palliative Sedation", December 5, 2014, aahpm.org/positions /palliative-sedation.

In sum, physician-assisted suicide causes negative emotional reactions in physicians, undermines the medical profession, co-opts physicians into premature wrongful deaths and undesired suicides, and compromises physicians' determination to preserve life, entailing significant societal risks. This explains why virtually every major medical organization opposes physician-assisted suicide.

F. Normalizing and Morally Sanctioning Suicide within the Culture

There is an old expression in the philosophy of law: "What becomes legal, soon becomes normalized, and what becomes normalized, soon becomes 'moral'" (because "everyone" is doing it). Recall from Chapter 1 (Section III) the power of social norming. When people lack objective moral norms to the contrary, they tend to adjust their conduct toward what they believe to be the conduct of the "mainstream". If they believe the mainstream to be more principled than themselves, they will move toward those principles—and if they believe that the mainstream is less principled, they will move toward the abandonment of principles.

So, what might we expect to occur especially among young people when we legalize assisted suicide for the elderly (who have comparatively less Level One and Level Two opportunities than the young)? They are likely to infer that suicide is a societally acceptable solution to a decrease in autonomy, capability, status, and opportunity for advancement, inciting them to conclude that it is moral. This belief in suicide as a solution to life's problems and the anxiety coming from comparative disadvantage may help to explain the meteoric rise in suicides among young people over twelve years (2005–2017)—a 56 percent increase in teen suicides.[82]

---

[82] See Jean M. Twenge et al., "Age, Period, and Cohort Trends in Mood Disorder Indicators and Suicide-Related Outcomes in a Nationally Representative Dataset, 2005–2017", *Journal of Abnormal Psychology* 128, no. 3 (2019): 185–99, https://www.apa.org/pubs/journals/releases/abn-abn0000410.pdf. See also William Wan, "Teen Suicides Are Increasing at an Alarming Pace, Outstripping All Other Age Groups, a New Report Says", *Washington Post*, October 17, 2019, https://www.washingtonpost.com/health/teen-suicides-increasing-at-alarming-pace-outstripping-all-other-age-groups/2019/10/16/e24194c6-f04a-11e9-8693-f487e46784aa_story.html.

The culture of death is alive and growing in the United States and throughout the world. The fact that many parents and teachers allowed (and even encouraged) their teens to watch the Netflix series *13 Reasons Why*, advocating suicide as a solution to life's problems, speaks volumes. Dr. Sansea Jacobson (director of the Child and Adolescent Psychiatry Residency Training Program at the University of Pittsburgh School of Medicine) indicates that this program romanticizes suicide, focuses on blaming others (instead of underlying psychiatric problems), suggests that suicide is a result of rational thought (rather than cognitive dissonance arising out of psychiatric problems), and focuses on graphic imagery of self-injury and the suicide itself, all of which encourage imitation and provide rationalization for unsound and unbalanced self-destructive judgment.[83] Would this series have been tolerated (let alone encouraged) thirty years ago? Twenty years ago? What has provoked the obvious change in attitude over the last two decades? I would submit that it is social norming of the culture of death and suicide. Legalizing death and suicide as a solution to the problems of unwanted pregnancy and the problems of aging is becoming socially acceptable and normalized, making it implicitly "moral" within the culture. It should then not be surprising that Hollywood directors would seize upon the eros of death in this tragic self-destructive act to make a profit from teenagers who are vulnerable to its masochistic suggestions. What reveals the presence of the culture of death is the number of parents and teachers who not only allowed their teens to watch it, but believe that its distortions and self-destructive suggestions would somehow be beneficial for their teens to view. Perhaps they felt pressured by their teens who indicated their friends were all watching it. If so, it shows the power of social norming moving our attitudes and behaviors to the perceived cultural mainstream—the culture of death. If we are serious about avoiding this travesty, we would do well to reinvigorate religion and moral norms within the minds and hearts of our young people,[84]

---

[83] See Sansea Jacobson, "Thirteen Reasons to Be Concerned about *13 Reasons Why*", *Brown University Child and Adolescent Behavior Letter* 33, no. 6 (2017): 8, https://onlinelibrary.wiley.com/doi/10.1002/cbl.30220.

[84] Encouragement of religion and objective moral norms requires a rational explanation for both. If the sound evidence from science, social science, and right reasoning can be provided, many teens will move toward both religion and moral norms, because they are predisposed toward them (see Volume II of the Quartet, *The Soul's Upward Yearning*, Chapters 1–2). Parents

reverse the trend toward assisted suicide and euthanasia, and encourage love and faith over death and despair as solutions to life's challenges.

II. Suicide, Self-Defense, and Torture

The Catholic Church has explicitly prohibited *suicide* since the early second century,[85] because our bodies and lives are not our own, but a free gift of the Creator who made us in His own image and likeness (see Gen 1:27). Thus, suicide is a rejection of the Creator's gift of life and transcendental nature. Furthermore, suicide has a terrible adverse effect on family members and friends who can be emotionally injured for a lifetime by such a radical action. They may feel guilty and rejected in their love, and in the case of children, abandoned and rejected. Such consequences constitute very grave matter, but we must remember that many individuals who commit suicide are deeply depressed, emotionally distraught, and overwhelmed by life, meaning that they may have taken their own life without sufficient reflection and complete consent of the will—the two conditions necessary for mortal sin. Therefore, there is reason to believe that Christ will extend mercy to relatives and friends who are in this unreflective and unfree state. As the *Catechism of the Catholic Church* states:

> We should not despair of the eternal salvation of persons who have taken their own lives. By ways known to him alone, God can provide the opportunity for salutary repentance. The Church prays for persons who have taken their own lives.[86]

---

and teachers seeking evidence of this kind designed for middle schools and high schools may want to visit CredibleCatholic.com. The middle school and high school modules provide a basic foundation for belief in God, the soul, Jesus, the Church, and moral teachings. The advanced modules provide an in-depth explanation that can be used by teachers as well as seniors in high school and college students. There is an opportunity to become a master teacher in this material (certification by Catholic Distance University) on the website.

[85] Though Scripture is silent on the prohibition of suicide, there is a very strong negative reaction to the suicide of Judas Iscariot, which is associated with his being influenced by the devil (see Jn 13:27). The first tractate against suicide was written by Justin Martyr in about A.D. 150. See *The Second Apology of Justin Martyr*, Chapter 4, "Why the Christians Do Not Kill Themselves", from *Ante-Nicene Fathers*, vol. 1, ed. Alexander Roberts, James Donaldson, and A. Cleveland Coxe (Buffalo, N.Y.: Christian Literature Publishing, 1885), revised and edited for New Advent by Kevin Knight, https://www.newadvent.org/fathers/0127.htm.

[86] CCC 2283.

With respect to *self-defense*, the Catholic Church has held to the legitimacy of this right since the time of Saint Augustine, who advocated it as the foundation of his just war theory.[87] Saint Thomas Aquinas formalized the principle as part of his moral doctrine:

> If a man, in self-defense, uses more than necessary violence, it will be unlawful: whereas if he repel force with moderation his defense will be lawful.... Nor is it necessary for salvation that a man omit the act of moderate self-defense to avoid killing the other man, since one is bound to take more care of one's own life than of another's.[88]

The justification for self-defense is based on the universal right to protect one's self from an unjust aggressor who intends to cause death or bodily harm—and the duty he may have to help others preserve their lives from an unjust aggressor. As Saint Thomas Aquinas implies above, this is not an unrestricted right to use lethal power in any way to preserve one's own (or others') life. Legitimate self-defense is restricted to the amount of potential harm needed to dissuade an attacker. If lethal power is really needed, then a person is justified in using it. Additionally, the use of lethal force in self-defense is justified by the principle of double effect.

This important ethical principle was developed by Saint Thomas Aquinas in the same article of the *Summa Theologica* in which he justifies the moral legitimacy of self-defense.[89] Saint Thomas states here that one cannot *directly intend* to kill another person. However, if we are primarily intending to defend our lives (or the lives of family members or others dependent on us), and we are constrained to use force (including potentially lethal force) to do so, and it so happens that the use of that force does in fact kill an unjust assailant, then this killing is morally justifiable. The killing of the person is an *unintended*

---

[87] See Saint Augustine, *The City of God* 1, 7, in *Nicene and Post-Nicene Fathers*, series 1, vol. 2, ed. Philip Schaff, trans. Rev. Marchs Dods (Edinburgh: T&T Clark/Grand Rapids, Mich.: Wm. B. Eerdmans Publishing, 1886), https://web.archive.org/web/20130725190746/http://etext.lib.virginia.edu/etcbin/toccer-new2?id=AugCity.xml&images=images%2Fmodeng&data=%2Ftexts%2Fenglish%2Fmodeng%2Fparsed&tag=public&part=all. See Chapter 7 (Section II.G) of this volume for a more complete explanation of just war.

[88] *Summa Theologica* II-II, q. 64, art. 7, from *The Summa Theologiæ of St. Thomas Aquinas*, 2nd and rev. ed., trans. Fathers of the English Dominican Province, 1920, New Advent, online ed. by Kevin Knight, 2017, https://www.newadvent.org/summa/3064.htm.

[89] Ibid.

consequence (a "double effect") of trying to defend one's self (or others); it is not directly intended.[90] In sum, we are permitted only to intend a good end (the preservation of one's own or another's life), but not an evil end (the killing of another person). Thus, in legitimate self-defense, one can kill another person (an evil effect) if it is the unintended consequence of preserving one's own (or another's) life (a good effect).[91]

With respect to *torture*, the Church prohibits *this practice* as an extension of the Silver Rule—"avoid unnecessary harm, but if a harm to others is unavoidable, minimize it." The *Catechism of the Catholic Church* states:

> *Torture* which uses physical or moral violence to extract confessions, punish the guilty, frighten opponents, or satisfy hatred is contrary to respect for the person and for human dignity.[92]

The *Compendium of the Social Doctrine of the Church* teaches that all forms of torture in all cases are prohibited, because they are a violation of the rights and dignity of both the innocent and guilty, and even an affront to the torturer himself:

> In carrying out investigations, the regulation against the use of torture, even in the case of serious crimes, must be strictly observed: "Christ's disciple refuses every recourse to such methods, which nothing could justify and in which the dignity of man is as much debased in his torturer as in the torturer's victim."[93]

Some philosophers, such as Uwe Steinhoff, have made a very narrow case for nonpunitive, nonsadistic torture on the basis of the right to self-defense, sometimes called the "ticking time bomb argument".

[90] Recall from above (Section I) that the principle of double effect is also used to justify the legitimacy of killing someone unintentionally while trying to give adequate medication to control pain during terminal illness. So long as the physician or nurse administering the pain protocol *is not* intending to kill the patient by an overdose but does kill the patient while trying to administer adequate medication to control his pain, the death of the patient is unintentional and morally justified. It is a secondary unintended consequence a—"double effect"—of trying to prevent severe pain.

[91] See *CCC* 2263–67.

[92] Ibid., 2297 (italics in original).

[93] The *Compendium of the Social Doctrine of the Church* quotation is from John Paul II, Address to the International Committee of the Red Cross (Geneva, June 15, 1982), no. 5, in *L'Osservatore Romano*, English edition, July 26, 1982, p. 3.

According to this scenario, a bomb with the potential for mass destruction has been hidden and the perpetrator, who has crucial information to defuse the bomb, has been captured. He will not divulge the needed information without torture. Steinhoff believes that torture can be justified on the basis of self-defense to extract the information needed to defuse the bomb, reasoning that if potentially lethal force can be used in self-defense, than nonlethal "extraordinary methods of interrogation" can be used to protect an innocent person or population from an unjust aggressor.[94] His argument is not *consequentialist*, but a rights-based threshold deontological argument.[95] "Threshold deontology" holds to the absoluteness of a principle (such as the prohibition of torture) until a threshold of unacceptable consequences makes it necessary to override the principle. Steinhoff's "threshold of unacceptable consequence" occurs when the violation of a principle could reasonably prevent the death of an innocent person or population. He justifies this principle on the basis of the innocent person's (or population's) right of self-defense, which is almost universally held (including by the Catholic Church).

The Catholic Church has not commented specifically on Steinhoff's argument, but she may need to do so in light of the actions of terrorists in the post-9/11 era. It would be important to establish whether the right of self-defense (an accepted principle of the Catholic Church) can override the absolute prohibition of torture in certain narrow thresholds of unacceptable consequences. Recall that this is not strictly speaking consequentialism, but a problem of the prioritization of principles. What is the higher principle: The right of self-defense of the innocent or the absolute prohibition of torture? The United States Conference of Catholic Bishops has published a workbook on the ethics of torture that addresses the "ticking time bomb argument", but unfortunately it does not respond to the question of the prioritization of principles (the right to self-defense versus the absolute prohibition of torture) needed to respond definitively to the "ticking time bomb" argument.[96] Instead, it makes recourse to some studies implying that torture generally

---

[94] See Uwe Steinhoff, *On the Ethics of Torture* (Albany, N.Y.: SUNY Press, 2013), pp. 11–60.

[95] See ibid., pp. 53–60.

[96] United States Conference of Catholic Bishops, "Torture Is an Intrinsic Evil", 2012, https://www.usccb.org/issues-and-action/human-life-and-dignity/torture/upload/torture-is-an-intrinsic-evil-study-guide1.pdf.

does not work.[97] Though these studies seem to be generally accurate, Steinhoff gives real-life cases that disprove the contention of the nonworkability of torture—for example, the Mook case in Germany where a child was hidden in a wooden box and would certainly have died had police not used torture (a beating) to extract the information from the criminal who caused the child's peril.[98] In the Daschner case, the kidnapper, who had originally refused to disclose the location of the child he kidnapped, revealed the location when threatened with torture. Unfortunately, the child was already murdered.[99] If there are a few exceptions to the contention of the nonworkability of torture, it opens the door to the possibility of other exceptions that brings to light the right to self-defense of victims like these two innocent children.

No doubt, the Catholic Church is correct that even very narrow exceptions to the prohibition of torture could open a Pandora's box of very negative social consequences; these consequences cannot be ignored because of their gravity. Furthermore, the principle of double effect may be difficult to apply in cases of torture. For example, can a policeman solely intend to save the life of a child while beating a kidnapper to extract the child's location? Though it is not out of the question, it may be more difficult than primarily intending self-defense when fending off a threat from a violent aggressor. Notwithstanding these important considerations, it would be helpful in the post-9/11 era of terrorism (threatening innocent populations) to have a definitive ruling about the prioritization of principles (the right to self-defense of the innocent versus the absolute prohibition of torture); this would allow Catholic ethicists to respond to philosophers like Steinhoff and address the difficult problem of the rights of the innocent in terrorist situations. In particular, it would be helpful to know if the possibility or feasibility of getting information is enough to justify the use of nonpunitive, nonsadistic limited torture to protect an innocent population's right of self-defense. For the moment, we must accept the Church's absolute prohibition of torture prima facie until a response can be given to the above question of the prioritization of moral principles.

[97] See ibid.
[98] See Steinhoff, *On Ethics of Torture*, p. 49.
[99] See ibid.

III. Conclusion

In Chapter 3, we explained the justification for the intrinsic dignity and inalienable right to life of all human persons regardless of their state of development, capacities (or incapacities), productivity, and station in life. This justification was based on natural reason, empirical data, and the principle of justice—the most basic tenet of personal and social ethics affirmed by all cultures and all religions.[100] Based on this justification, we showed the immorality of abortion, eugenics (particularly of the disabled), physician-assisted suicide, euthanasia, invitro fertilization, embryonic stem cell research, suicide, and torture. The Church also uses this justification to show the enduring dignity of criminals for whom we should provide opportunities for repentance (conversion) and rehabilitation.

Though the Church's teaching on the right to life and the immorality of killing pertains to Catholics, it also has validity for non-Catholics in civil society, because, as noted above, she establishes the intrinsic dignity of every human being (beginning with a unique, self-moving, self-perfecting, dynamic organism actualizing itself according to a full human genome) on the basis of reasonable arguments, empirical data, and the universally accepted principle of justice. The protection of all human beings, and the existence of free societies and states, depends not only on recognition of the inalienable right to life of every human being but also on a culture of life that upholds the intrinsic value and dignity of every person. Without a culture of life, human flourishing will be impossible. All that will remain are the powerful, wealthy, and influential, competing with each other for marginal advantage in controlling the lives and liberties of those who are increasingly branded as marginal and inconsequential. This culture of death will not survive for long, for competition among those who lack appreciation of humane and divine principles will ultimately result in mutual destruction.

The way out of the culture of death is the recognition of the intrinsic dignity and inalienable rights of every human being from

---

[100] For an explanation of the fundamentality of justice as an ethical principle, see Chapter 6 (Section II). For an explanation of the universality of justice among different cultures and religions, see Chapter 6 (Section I).

conception to natural death by every individual and state. Whether we do this for reasons of rational arguments, divine authority, cultural persuasion, or all of the above is less important than the conviction that every human being must be protected and allowed to flourish because of his or her intrinsic dignity and unique goodness and lovability. If we accept this, the light of Jesus' revelation will pour into our hearts, revealing our transcendental and eternal nature called to perfect communion with one another through the Lord of life and love. This transformation cannot help but bring about a culture of life, leading toward a humane, just, peaceful, and mutually caring society and state.

PART THREE

Charity and Social Ethics

Chapter Five

Honesty, Charity, and the Need for Objective Moral Norms

Introduction

This chapter may seem to be a hodgepodge of three distinct themes, but I would beg the reader's indulgence to read to the end of the chapter before making that judgment. Honesty and charity free the human heart to see Jesus' preaching of self-sacrificial compassionate love in every moral norm proclaimed by the Catholic Church. As we shall see, the loss of objective moral norms within our culture (and in some respects in our churches) has led to the decline of love, civility, and faith—to a destructive moral and intellectual relativism, which has opened the way to steep increases in depression, anxiety, substance abuse, and suicides, as well as the decline of marriage, family, and culture. As Aleksandr Solzhenitsyn, the great Russian dissident who contributed to the fall of Communism, put it in his commencement speech at Harvard in 1978:

> Destructive and irresponsible freedom has been granted boundless space. Society appears to have little defense against the abyss of human decadence, such as, for example, misuse of liberty for moral violence against young people, such as motion pictures full of pornography, crime, and horror.... Such a tilt of freedom in the direction of evil has come about gradually, but it was evidently born primarily out of a humanistic and benevolent concept according to which there is no evil inherent to human nature.[1]

---

[1] Aleksandr Solzhenitsyn, "A World Split Apart" (commencement address at Harvard University, 1978), https://www.americanrhetoric.com/speeches/alexandersolzhenitsynharvard.htm.

Section III will explore how the Enlightenment ideal led to a progressively more radical view of freedom as an end in itself and the meaning of life in contemporary culture. As it did so, it undermined our awareness of the true meaning of love preached by Jesus, the presence of evil within ourselves, the world, and the spiritual domain, and our need for religion and conscience to bring us out of darkness. If our culture can appropriate this fundamental truth, we can begin to move out of our increasing malaise, meaninglessness, and social unrest. Short of this, we will progressively sink into a darkness that will be our collective undoing. There is a way out of this progressive decline grounded in the truth, love, and goodness of Jesus Christ, brought to contemporary light through the teaching of the Catholic Church (see the Conclusion to the Trilogy, found in this volume). The Lord has always raised up saints even in the most decadent of times to bring his hope and grace into the world. As in those past ages, we the citizens of the world today are called to be those saints who respectfully yet firmly bring the light of Jesus' truth and love to a culture embracing darkness.

This chapter will first consider the themes of honesty (Section I) and charity (Section II) to set the ground of our heart's freedom, and then proceed to the truth that will set not only us free but also our whole culture—our need to embrace objective moral norms, particularly those taught by Jesus Christ and brought to contemporary light through the Catholic Church (Section III).

I. Honesty

The reader may be thinking that this book is quite lopsided; it is spending four long chapters on two commandments (the prohibition of adultery and killing) and a quarter of a chapter on the four other commandments preached by Jesus (the prohibition of stealing, lying, cheating, and dishonoring father and mother [see Mk 10:19]). The only excuse I have is that our culture is almost obsessed with violating the fifth and sixth commandments. No doubt our culture is also inclined toward stealing, lying, cheating, and dishonoring mother and father, but these transgressions have not become idols—the hallmarks of our radical freedom over against God and conscience.

Furthermore, unlike adultery, cohabitation, a homosexual lifestyle, pornography, abortion, assisted suicide, and selective eugenics, our culture still believes that most instances of stealing, lying, cheating, and dishonoring parents are fundamentally wrong. Hence, there is no need to make the case that these transgressions are evil and undermine the good of self, neighbor, culture, and the Kingdom of God. Therefore, though they are very important for our spiritual and moral lives, I have given them comparatively less attention. We will briefly examine the implications of these prohibitions in contemporary culture (in Sections I.A through I.D).

A. Stealing

The Seventh Commandment's most general contemporary context prohibits violations of "commutative justice" and "distributive justice". Commutative justice concerns the equitable exchange of goods, remuneration for services, and honoring of contracts between *individuals*. Distributive justice is concerned with the equitable allocation of goods, services, and monetary remuneration according to work productivity, contribution to the market, and provision of basic necessities within a group, society, or state. We will be concerned with only commutative justice in this chapter on personal ethics and will take up distributive justice in considerable detail in Chapter 7, concerned with social ethics and Catholic social teaching.

Plato provided the background that enabled Justinian to formulate his foundational definition that justice is "giving each person his due",[2] implying that injustice is taking a person's goods (that rightfully belong to him) or depriving him of goods or funds due to him. In the first four centuries, the Church focused more on distributive justice—particularly, meeting the basic needs of the poor and marginalized both inside and outside the church community—and saw violations of commutative justice (stealing) within this larger context. The Church advocated sharing wealth and detaching ourselves from the "love of wealth". Within this worldview, theft would be

---

[2] Plato provides the background on justice and proportional good in *Republic* 4, 433, and Justinian formulates the definition in his *Institutes* 1, 1.

an extreme example of not only love of wealth but lust for it, leading one to commit injustice against others. Accordingly, stealing always requires restitution of the property stolen except in cases where a person steals basic necessities needed for the survival and safety of self and family.[3]

In today's complex business, organizational, and economic arena, stealing encompasses a large number of activities. According to the *Catechism of the Catholic Church*, stealing includes the following:

> Deliberate retention of goods lent or of objects lost; business fraud; paying unjust wages; forcing up prices by taking advantage of the ignorance or hardship of another ... speculation in which one contrives to manipulate the price of goods artificially in order to gain an advantage to the detriment of others; corruption in which one influences the judgment of those who must make decisions according to law; appropriation and use for private purposes of the common goods of an enterprise; work poorly done; tax evasion; forgery of checks and invoices; excessive expenses and waste. Willfully damaging private or public property.[4]

Some of these offenses overlap with the prohibition against defrauding or cheating (see below Section I.C), but all of them concern the intention to take what in justice belongs to another.

Commutative justice also requires the honoring of promises, commitments, and contracts as well as the payment of debts, and so the *Catechism of the Catholic Church* states:

> A significant part of economic and social life depends on the honoring of contracts between physical or moral persons—commercial contracts of purchase or sale, rental or labor contracts. All contracts must be agreed to and executed in good faith.... Commutative justice obliges strictly; it requires safeguarding property rights, paying debts, and fulfilling obligations freely contracted. Without commutative justice, no other form of justice is possible.[5]

The Church affirms the majority of precepts in modern business ethics concerned with theft and commutative justice. Readers interested in

---

[3] See *CCC* 2408, referring to *Gaudium et Spes*, no. 69.
[4] *CCC* 2409.
[5] Ibid., 2410–11.

cases and complex issues in these areas will want to examine some of the many books and articles specializing in Catholic business ethics.[6]

The Christian prohibition of stealing also includes the vast area of intellectual property theft that includes the theft of copyrighted material, trade secrets, and trademarked material. A copyright is "the legal right of an author, publisher, composer, or other person who creates a work to exclusively print, publish, distribute, or perform the work in public".[7] Today, a huge amount of intellectual property theft occurs through what is known as "cybercrime", and includes "computer software, recorded music, movies, and electronic games" as well as traditional materials such as copyrighted articles and books.[8] Christian ethics requires the honoring of these copyrights. Hence, using these materials without permission and referencing the author is unethical.

The American Law and Legal Information library defines trademarks as the following:

> A trademark is the registered name or identifying symbol of a product that can be used only by the product's owner. A trademark violation involves counterfeiting or copying brand name products such as well-known types of shoes, clothing, and electronics equipment and selling them as the genuine or original product.[9]

There are many specialized sources dealing with the theft of intellectual property that give cases and examples of this large and nuanced area of ethics concerned with the Seventh Commandment.[10]

---

[6] See, for example, Brian Engelland, *Force for Good: The Catholic Guide to Business Integrity* (Manchester, N.H.: Sophia Institute Press, 2017); James L. Nolan, *Doing the Right Thing at Work: A Catholic's Guide to Faith, Business and Ethics* (Cincinnati: St. Anthony Messenger Press, 2005); Alejo Jose G. Sison, Ignacio Ferrero, Gregorio Guitian, eds., *Business Ethics: A Virtue Ethics and Common Good Approach* (New York: Routledge, 2018). There is also an excellent volume on Catholic social teaching and social ethics within contemporary business, which puts together quotations from various Catholic documents; see Andrew V. Abela and Joseph E. Capizzi, eds., *A Catechism for Business: Tough Ethical Questions and Insights from Catholic Teaching* (Washington, D.C.: Catholic University of America Press, 2014).

[7] American Law and Legal Information, "Cyber Crime", under "Intellectual Property Theft", 1992, http://law.jrank.org/pages/11992/Cyber-Crime-Intellectual-property-theft.html.

[8] See ibid.

[9] Ibid.

[10] One excellent resource is ibid. For a good introduction to this area of ethics, see the website Philosophia at the University of North Carolina at Greensboro: https://philosophia.uncg.edu/phi361-matteson/module-6-privacy-property-and-technology/property-and-intellectual-property/.

B. Bearing False Witness and Lying

The prohibition of bearing false witness arises out of the long-recognized commandment to live in the truth, because God is truth, and we are made in His image and called to be united with Him forever. The *Catechism of the Catholic Church* states the following:

> The Old Testament attests that *God is the source of all truth*. His Word is truth. His Law is truth. His "faithfulness endures to all generations." Since God is "true," the members of his people are called to live in the truth.[11]

The New Testament, particularly the Gospel of John, reveals that Jesus Christ is God's word and truth, and He came into the world to reveal that truth to us. Jesus *is* "the way, and the truth, and the life" (Jn 14:6)—to know Him is to know the Truth itself. The *Catechism of the Catholic Church* notes:

> In Jesus Christ, the whole of God's truth has been made manifest. "Full of grace and truth," he came as the "light of the world," *he is the Truth.*[12]

Bearing false witness concerns seven subordinate issues: (1) offenses of false testimony; (2) offenses of detraction, calumny, and slander; (3) offenses of lying and deliberate deception; (4) offenses against secrecy and discretion; (5) intentional errors of omission; (6) offenses against appropriate transparency; and (7) the ethical use of media and mass communications. We will discuss each in turn.

Offenses of false testimony are quite serious because their intention is to cause harm to another's reputation *falsely*, which is a grave injustice. If one testifies falsely against another in court, it is called "perjury", which is even more serious because it is a violation of the public trust as well as the name of God, by whom one swears. All acts of false testimony and perjury require reparation, and as best as one can, restoration of the harmed individual's reputation and compensation for the pain caused to that individual and his family.

---

[11] CCC 2465, citing Ps 119:90; cf. Prov 8:7; 2 Sam 7:28; Ps 119:142; Lk 1:50 (italics in original).
[12] CCC 2466, citing Jn 1:14; 8:12; cf. 14:6 (italics in original).

Offenses of detraction, calumny, and slander are violations of the virtues of justice and charity because every individual has the right to be honored in his reputation, and to be protected against the social harms caused by false detraction of his good name. Gossiping and caricaturing of behavior can be quite harmful if they falsely undermine an individual's dignity, reputation, or welfare. They are violations of the virtue of charity even if the gossip or caricaturing is not false. If false detraction and gossip are particularly harmful, they are tantamount to character assassination (calumny), and all such offenses require reparation, restoration of the individual's reputation, and even compensation for pain and damage.

Offenses of lying and deliberate deception are fundamental injustices not only because they can cause harm to others, but also because they breach and injure trust within a relationship. According to the *Catechism of the Catholic Church*, "The *gravity of a lie* is measured against the nature of the truth it deforms, the circumstances, the intentions of the one who lies, and the harm suffered by its victims."[13] Lies of exaggeration for self-enhancement that cause no real harm are less grave, though they do undermine the expectation of truth, to which every individual has a right. Lies that mislead people into harmful courses of action are particularly grave and require reparation for the harm and pain caused by the deception.

Offenses against secrecy and discretion occur when an individual violates a pledge of secrecy or reveals information that prudence dictates would be better kept secret. The *Catechism of the Catholic Church* states, "Even if not confided under the seal of secrecy, private information prejudicial to another is not to be divulged without a grave and proportionate reason."[14] The *Catechism* also states, "The duty to avoid scandal often commands strict discretion. No one is bound to reveal the truth to someone who does not have the right to know it."[15]

Offenses of intentional omission are frequently as unjust and harmful as direct lying. They produce the same harms against individuals and breach of trust as sins of commission. The gravity of these sins is determined by the damage caused to the harmed individual or groups of individuals. Reparation must be made to individuals injured in

---

[13] *CCC* 2484 (italics in original).
[14] Ibid., 2491.
[15] Ibid., 2489.

their reputation or welfare. If the error of omission causes an undermining of someone's religious belief or principles, then every effort must be made to inform him of the *whole* truth.

Offenses against appropriate transparency most frequently occur in business relationships. Though every business, nonprofit, and governmental agency has the right to keep secrets that affect market competitiveness and patented ideas and property, certain information should be disclosed or made available to stakeholders (such as investors, bond holders, and regulators) who have a right to know. Intentionally hiding, disguising, or misrepresenting information to which stakeholders have a reasonable right can cause harm not only to the directly affected stakeholders, but also to indirectly affected ones (e.g., consumers and the community). If harm is caused to individual investors or bondholders, reparation should be made. If the harm is caused to a corporation, agency, community, or other group, reparation should also be made to those bodies and groups. There is a whole area of management and accounting ethics devoted to best practices in appropriate information disclosure to specific stakeholders as well as the public.[16]

There are special rules pertaining to truth in the area of *mass communications and media*. Given the influence of mass media, directors of media news outlets must be particularly careful to balance the common good within individual rights to privacy. The common good requires reporting any truth that bears upon the rights and common good of the public to which it is entitled. However, this does not mean slandering and gossiping about public figures in a way that undermines their reputation falsely or needlessly. False statements require public reparation and restoration of reputation. Furthermore, the media must be particularly careful to avoid lying through culpable omissions of important data influencing the public's perception of the truth. Such omissions are tantamount to direct lies and, therefore, should be avoided. When media outlets give prejudicial reports (through culpable omission), they are responsible for making public clarifications sufficient to correct the misleading or prejudicial

---

[16]Matteo Turilli and Luciano Floridi, "The Ethics of Information Transparency", *Ethics and Information Technology* 11 (June 2009): 105–12, https://link.springer.com/article/10.1007/s10676-009-9187-9.

information reported. The *Catechism of the Catholic Church* sums up the ethics of this important domain as follows:

> By the very nature of their profession, journalists have an obligation to serve the truth and not offend against charity in disseminating information. They should strive to respect, with equal care, the nature of the facts and the limits of critical judgment concerning individuals. They should not stoop to defamation.[17]

There is considerable professional and scholarly writing devoted to this special area of media ethics.[18]

Today, a whole new area of media ethics is burgeoning—social media ethics. There seems to be a consensus among some social media outlets that they are protected by the First Amendment in a way that relieves them of the responsibility to tell the truth, to protect the innocent from detraction, calumny, and slander, and to ensure the common good. From a Christian and natural law perspective, this view is in many respects irresponsible and unethical. No media outlet—whether social or traditional—can be relieved of the responsibility to uphold the common good and the fundamental rights of individuals, particularly with respect to their reputation, safety, and appropriate place within society and culture. The First Amendment of the Constitution cannot be used to excuse the dissemination of harmful, false, irresponsible, and calumnious content—or content that undermines public welfare and peace. The freedoms guaranteed by the U.S. Constitution should not be used to protect unethical and harmful behavior, particularly in the area of public dissemination. Therefore, social media outlets have the responsibility to monitor and exclude content that is clearly contrary to the rights of individuals and the public good. The Ethics Resource Center (concerned with business ethics in general) has begun to assess the effects of social media and their ethical implications.[19]

---

[17] CCC 2497.

[18] See Philip Patterson and Lee Wilkins, *Media Ethics: Issues and Cases*, 8th ed. (New York: McGraw-Hill, 2013). There is also a journal devoted to this—*The Journal of Mass Media Ethics*.

[19] See Sharlyn Lauby, "Ethics and Social Media: Where Should You Draw the Line?", Ethics Resource Center, March 12, 2012, https://www.americanexpress.com/us/small-business/openforum/articles/ethics-and-social-media-where-should-you-draw-the-line/.

C. Defrauding and Cheating

Though the Ten Commandments do not cover cheating per se, Jesus includes it in His list of commandments—"Do not defraud" (Mk 10:19). The *Catechism of the Catholic Church* treats cheating under the categories of "stealing" and "lying", which frequently underlie acts of cheating. In today's complex society, cheating, which is incredibly widespread, requires particular study. In general, cheating has three elements—(1) *misrepresenting* facts about oneself or one's organization, (2) which is contrary to stated or assumed *rules* or *customs*, (3) in order to gain an *unfair* advantage. The unfair advantage causes harm to the disadvantaged parties being cheated, and so involves an act of injustice. Hence, it is contrary to the Christian precept to be just or fair to others.

Today, cheating has become an important ethical topic in many areas of personal organizational, professional, and workplace life. It is discussed under several subsidiary areas, including academia, taxes, insurance, sports, organizational life, professional life, the workplace, and the marketplace. There are other areas of cheating, such as marriage (which is covered in Chapter 1 with respect to adultery) and copyright infringement (covered above in Section I.A with respect to stealing). We will give a brief overview of some of these areas with references to basic ethical literature.

Academic cheating occurs when one misrepresents another's work as one's own. In high schools and universities, it has become quite widespread. According to the Educational Testing Service, only 20 percent of students reported cheating in high school in the 1940s, while 75 percent to 98 percent reported cheating in the 1990s.[20] These statistics apply to test taking, plagiarism (from file sharers and purchasing of term papers), and paying others to do online work or tests. Cheating at the university level has also risen significantly, particularly in university settings where there is no honor code, little monitoring by faculty members, and organized efforts to assist in cheating (e.g., in fraternities or sororities).[21] Apparently,

---

[20] Educational Testing Service, "Academic Cheating Fact Sheet", 1999, http://www.glass-castle.com/clients/www-nocheating-org/adcouncil/research/cheatingfactsheet.html.

[21] See ibid.

social norming (see Chapter 1, Section III) has made cheating more acceptable, not only among students but also among parents and teachers as well.[22] The increased competitiveness to get into the right college fueled by parental expectations has undermined what used to be a strong moral inclination toward academic honesty and integrity. Unfortunately, this increased inclination to resort to cheating to obtain unfair advantage is spilling over into the workplace, business leadership, and professional life.[23] It seems that the decline in the desire and expectation for integrity and honesty in academia is spilling over not only into the business environment, but also into other areas of dishonesty, such as stealing and lying. If we do not reaffirm and reemphasize the importance of academic honesty in middle school and high school, the decline in ethics throughout the culture will continue to grow.

Several actions have been found to be successful in helping students to refrain from cheating and to take personal integrity seriously honor codes, educational programs in ethical integrity, and peer-faculty support.[24] Traditional means of preventing cheating also need to be rekindled—increased faculty monitoring of test taking and papers as well as academic penalties (such as a "zero" on a paper or test). Each institution should have a limit to the number of incidents of cheating allowable by any student with real penalties, such as suspension or dismissal for frequent violators. If the above trends are to be reversed in the culture, it will require efforts not only by Catholic religious and educational leaders, but also by parents, public school teachers, leaders, and student peers who must get involved with new and traditional efforts to decrease cheating and to insist that being honest is more important than having an ill-gained academic or competitive advantage.

Cheating on taxes and insurance claims are really forms of stealing more than misrepresentation of personal or organizational facts to gain an unfair advantage. Therefore, their prohibition is included in the teaching and rationale against stealing discussed above (Section I.A).

---

[22] See ibid.

[23] Josephson Institute, "Josephson Institute's Report Card on American Youth: There's a Hole in Our Moral Ozone and It's Getting Bigger", November 30, 2008, http://questgarden .com/85/27/9/091104072905/files/press-release.pdf.

[24] See Educational Testing Service, "Academic Cheating Fact Sheet".

Cheating in *sports* is sometimes underemphasized, because the misrepresentation by the cheating party does not seem to harm disadvantaged parties or organizations. However, this is far from the truth. Cheating in sports deprives real champions of the awards they deserve for their hard work and training, and when disclosed gives young people (who hang on the words and actions of sports figures) a terrible example of how to conduct their lives in the present and future. Thus, cheating in sports, which has increased significantly over time,[25] almost inevitably leads to other forms of cheating—in academia, professional life, and business. Cheating has almost come to be expected, and like increases in academic cheating, it undermines the sense of integrity and character in young people.

Pope Francis (among other popes) has taught the high importance of using sports to model good character, develop integrity, and learn how to "lose well".[26] Though the teaching of Christ concerning defrauding or cheating (Mk 10:19) does not mention specific areas, we can infer that it applies to all areas of cheating, including sports, because they involve misrepresentation of skills and achievements in order to gain an unfair or unjust advantage.[27] Furthermore, cheating undermines character and models dishonesty. Therefore, efforts must be made—on the part of not only coaches but also parents—to establish soundly the prioritization of honesty over winning. Young people have consciences, and they are very capable of understanding that winning a game is not worth undermining their character both inwardly and publicly. Nevertheless, they are susceptible to the example of leaders and parents, and so they will follow that example almost unquestioningly, even if it encourages dishonesty for an ill-gained reward.

Cheating in *organizations* is treated under the topic of "corporate fraud" in the area of accounting ethics. The objective of its perpetrators is to misrepresent information deliberately about their

[25] See Adam Hartung, "Why Cheating In Sports Is Prevalent—And We Can't Stop It", *Forbes*, January 23, 2016, https://www.forbes.com/sites/adamhartung/2016/01/23/why-cheating-is-prevalent-and-we-cant-stop-it/?sh=788ae944a0e7.

[26] See James Schall, S.J., "Captain Francis: The Pope and Sports", *Catholic World Report*, June 30, 2014, http://www.catholicworldreport.com/2014/06/30/captain-francis-the-pope-and-sports/.

[27] See Pope Francis, "Pope Francis: Cheating to Win in Sport Is 'Ugly and Sterile'", Vatican Radio, August 5, 2015, http://en.radiovaticana.va/news/2015/05/08/pope_francis_cheating_to_win_in_sport_is_ugly_and_sterile/1142609.

organization, which is clearly contrary to generally accepted rules of business ethics and accounting principles, in order to gain an unfair advantage over their competitors in market share, investor funding, brand recognition, loan funding, etc. Generally, these activities are disguised in layers of complex accounting and finance, and are only uncovered with whistleblowing, leaks of information, or the public manifestation of egregious misrepresentation. These acts of fraud create not only unfair advantage, but an unlevel playing field, and are injustices against the investors, consumers, and disadvantaged competitors who are clearly harmed by these misrepresentations.

Cheating in *professional life* occurs on several levels, including misrepresentation of abilities, education, background experience, and leadership on one's resume or *curriculum vitae*, exaggerating one's accomplishments (or underreporting one's failures) in self-evaluations or organizational reports, misrepresenting one's relationships with potential clients or funders, taking or claiming credit for work or leadership accomplished by colleagues or subordinates, and other acts of misrepresentation aimed at gaining unfair advantage over colleagues, subordinates, or competitors in professional life. As noted above, these acts are unjust because they cause harm to the disadvantaged parties. They also create an exaggerated impression of the skill level and leadership qualities of the cheating party upon which a company or division within a company might rely. When the problem is discovered, the company or division may find itself in an unnecessarily disadvantaged position or in financial trouble.

Cheating in the *workplace* pertains to all employees and overlaps many of the areas of cheating in professional life. With respect to being hired and promoted, it includes dishonesty or misrepresentation on one's resume, falsification of reference letters, and exaggeration of skills and experience. With respect to work performance, employees might exaggerate hours worked, results obtained, and the origination or ownership of creative ideas or accomplishments. Cheating also applies to employers who might misrepresent the financial position of the company, work requirements for particular positions, and other information to attract employees unfairly to their company or to maintain employees' loyalty amid unfair or uncompetitive work conditions. These attitudes and behaviors are likewise contrary to Christian ethics and to accepted business ethics generally.

With respect to the *marketplace*, cheating includes the attitudes and behaviors mentioned above with respect to organizations obtaining unfair market share and brand domain by misrepresentation of production, research, and financial facts. It also includes any attempt to create a monopoly—which unfairly runs competitors out of the market—and to raise prices to consumers beyond competitive levels. Governments can also give unfair advantage in the international marketplace by fraudulently manipulating currency valuation to favor domestic products, failing to enforce international patents, and surreptitiously intervening in international competition. These acts of cheating are likewise contrary to Christian and generally accepted business ethics.

D. Dishonoring Parents

Though Jesus mentions the commandment to honor parents at the end of his list (Mk 10:19), it is given as the Fourth Commandment in the Decalogue, immediately after the three commandments concerned with the worship of God Himself. This shows the importance of family and parental authority in God's plan, community, and civil society. The Pauline author affirms this teaching when he says:

> Children, obey your parents in the Lord, for this is right. "Honor your father and mother" (this is the first commandment with a promise), "that it may be well with you and that you may live long on the earth." (Eph 6:1–3)

The author continues by noting the duties of both parents and children while affirming the importance of the family to the Kingdom of God and civil society.

The *Catechism of the Catholic Church* summarizes the nature and importance of the family as follows:

> The relationships within the family bring an affinity of feelings, affections, and interests, arising above all from the members' respect for one another. The family is a *privileged community* called to achieve a "sharing of thought and common deliberation by the spouses as well as their eager cooperation as parents in the children's upbringing" (*Gaudium et Spes*, no. 52).[28]

---

[28] *CCC* 2206 (italics in original).

In order for the family to assume its important role in the raising, evangelization, and education of children—and to become a building block of the Church, the community, and civil society—it is essential that children accept parental authority, respect their parents, and submit to their rightful authority. Furthermore, parents must not abuse their authority, but use it within the context of authentic, affectionate Christian love. This entails using their authority to guide their children, prevent them from harm, and create a setting of security, faith, and wisdom.

The *Catechism of the Catholic Church*, borrowing from the Books of Sirach and Proverbs as well as the Letters to the Colossians and Ephesians, sets out a series of Christian norms to support and solidify healthy families, to enable children to grow in virtue, education, and faith, and to ensure that families will edify the Kingdom of God, the community, and civil society. It treats first children's duties to their parents[29] and then parent's responsibilities to their children.[30]

Parental authority is an extension of God's sovereignty and authority over all of us. This authority is necessary to maintain order and to raise children in faith, wisdom, knowledge, and efficacy. Therefore, children owe their parents obedience to the divine and just authority parents have over them. Furthermore, children owe their parents an inestimable gift of gratitude, not only for the gift of life, sustenance, protection, and education, but also for the love given them and for their moral and religious upbringing. As the Book of Sirach notes:

> With all your heart honor your father, and do not forget the birth pangs of your mother. Remember that through your parents you were born; and what can you give back to them that equals their gift to you? (7:27–28)

The Book of Proverbs reinforces this debt of gratitude and specifies the duties associated with it:

> My son, keep your father's commandment, and forsake not your mother's teaching.... When you walk, they will lead you; when you lie down, they will watch over you; and when you awake, they will talk with you. (6:20, 22)

[29] Ibid., 2214–20.
[30] Ibid., 2221–31.

In view of their parents' divinely ordained and just authority and the immense debt of gratitude they owe to them, children should submit to the duties prescribed by biblical writ and the Church. The first and most important duty is to obey every morally acceptable request asked by parents. Children do not have an obligation to obey a command that is morally unconscionable or harmful to them physically, emotionally, or spiritually. The second duty of children is to obey and respect anyone to whom their parents have entrusted them—teachers, religious authorities, grandparents, and others. Again, they do not have to obey any requests that are morally unconscionable or harmful to them physically, emotionally, or spiritually. When children leave the domicile of their parents, they are free from their obligation to obey requests, but must continue to respect their parents throughout their lives in virtue of God's command and their debt of gratitude.[31]

Jesus teaches His disciples a third duty to parents—to take care of them physically, emotionally, and financially in their elderly years or when they are rendered incapable, indicating that this is the will of His father. In a passage addressed to the Pharisees, Jesus repudiates the interpretation of the Torah that prioritizes gifts to God over the filial duty to take care of one's parents:

> For Moses said, "Honor your father and your mother"; and, "He who speaks evil of father or mother, let him surely die"; but you say, "If a man tells his father or his mother, What you would have gained from me is Corban" (that is, given to God)—then you no longer permit him to do anything for his father or mother, thus making void the word of God through your tradition which you hand on. And many such things you do. (Mk 7:10–13)

Jesus makes our continued obligation to parents throughout their lives so essential that He prohibits using funds needed by parents even as a pledge to God. Though these three duties of children are owed to their parents, children will be rewarded for their obedience, respect, and care in this life and the next. Their filial respect will make for a peaceful and loving household, will extend to brothers, sisters, and grandparents, and will help to integrate the family into the

---

[31] See ibid., 2217.

community, society, and Kingdom of God. For this, God will richly reward them:

> Whoever honors his father atones for sins, ... and whoever glorifies his mother is like one who lays up treasure. Whoever honors his father will be gladdened by his own children, and when he prays, he will be heard. Whoever glorifies his father will have long life, and whoever obeys the Lord will refresh his mother. (Sir 3:3–6)

The Bible also enjoins parents to heed various responsibilities to their children. First, parents have a duty to protect, care for, and love their children, which lays the groundwork for their additional responsibilities to educate them in morals and faith. According to the *Catechism of the Catholic Church*, "[Parents] bear witness to this responsibility [to educate their children] first by *creating a home* where tenderness, forgiveness, respect, fidelity, and disinterested service are the rule."[32] Thus, education in morals and faith are not merely talked about but modeled in parental behavior. Both parents, particularly fathers, must be involved in religious and moral education. If fathers do not go to church, the likelihood of their children following their example is quite high—making them responsible for their weak or nonexistent faith. Robbie Low summarizes the statistics from the 1994 Swiss demographic survey showing fathers' influence on children's religious behavior as follows:

> It is the religious practice of the father of the family that, above all, determines the future attendance at or absence from church of the children. If both father and mother attend regularly, 33 percent of their children will end up as regular churchgoers, and 41 percent will end up attending irregularly. Only a quarter of their children will end up not practicing at all. If the father is irregular and mother regular, only 3 percent of the children will subsequently become regulars themselves, while a further 59 percent will become irregulars. Thirty-eight percent will be lost. If the father is non-practicing and mother regular, only 2 percent of children will become regular worshippers, and 37 percent will attend irregularly. Over 60 percent of their children will be lost completely to the church.[33]

---

[32] Ibid., 2223 (italics in original).
[33] Robbie Low, "The Truth about Men and Church", *Touchstone*, June 2003, https://www.touchstonemag.com/archives/article.php?id=16-05-024-v.

In addition to modeling virtue and faith, parents should create an atmosphere of family prayer as well as moral and catechetical education. Furthermore, parents should teach their children community and social responsibility—particularly for the poor and those in need. According to the *Catechism of the Catholic Church*:

> The family should live in such a way that its members learn to care and take responsibility for the young, the old, the sick, the handicapped, and the poor. There are many families who are at times incapable of providing this help. It devolves then on other persons, other families, and, in a subsidiary way, society to provide for their needs.[34]

Finally, parents must also teach their children how to enter properly into the local community and civil society as good, law-abiding, and productive citizens, respectful of governing authorities, laws, and other regulations needed for good order and civility.

Church teaching also addresses the importance of the family within the community, society, and the state—as well as the community's and state's responsibility to protect, uphold, and foster the family, particularly its freedoms to raise children according to the religious and moral standards that families deem appropriate. In Chapter 7, we discuss the importance of the family in community, society, and the state as articulated in Catholic social teaching. Therefore, we will give only a brief summary from the *Catechism of the Catholic Church* indicating the family's importance to the whole interrelated network of civil society:

> The family is the *original cell of social life*. It is the natural society in which husband and wife are called to give themselves in love and in the gift of life. Authority, stability, and a life of relationships within the family constitute the foundations for freedom, security, and fraternity within society. The family is the community in which, from childhood, one can learn moral values, begin to honor God, and make good use of freedom. Family life is an initiation into life in society.[35]

The principle of honoring father and mother is no less significant than the other principles of Christian personal ethics, because it is

---

[34] *CCC* 2208.
[35] Ibid., 2207 (italics in original).

the foundation for the family, which is the key building block for community, society, the state, and the Church, as well as the Kingdom of God. Without adherence to this central precept, we might expect that children would have little education or models for either morality or religion, in which case, the other principles—necessary as they are—would have little effect within the hearts and minds of society's members. We might look at this commandment, then, as a *sine qua nom*—as a "that without which" other moral principles are compromised and sometimes rendered ineffective.

II. Charity

Up to this point in the book, we have been addressing moral norms that are required by justice and the Silver Rule—"Do not do a harm to others that you do not want done to you." The Silver Rule is ethical minimalism and is so fundamental that failure to comply with it almost certainly entails culpable and unnecessary injustice (evil). Since violation of the fourth through eighth commandments almost always entails a violation of the Silver Rule, which is culpably and unnecessarily unjust, adherence to these commandments is *required* by justice.

Charity is different. Recall from Chapter 2 that *agapē* (oftentimes translated as charity) is unselfish self-sacrificial care for the other that does not seek reciprocity or reward. It comes from the recognition of the intrinsic dignity and unique goodness and lovability of the other, which incites us to do the good for the other for the sole reason of allowing him to flourish—nothing more. Thus, charity goes beyond the Silver Rule (do no unnecessary harm to others) to the Golden Rule—"Do unto others as you would have them do unto you." Of course, what we would want done for us goes far beyond the avoidance of harm. The sky is the limit, for we desire the good in virtually unlimited ways to promote our flourishing. This is ethical maximalism because it goes far beyond the requirements of justice. As will be explained in the next chapter, Jesus moved the world from ethical minimalism (the requirements of justice) to ethical maximalism (charity—doing the good for others without expectation of reciprocity and reward), when He asked His followers to show unselfish compassion to whomever is in need to the extent we can.

Though charity is not a requirement of justice, Jesus made it an obligation for His followers—for those who trust and love Him, because it is not only the divine nature but also the only way to heal a fallen world in need of forgiveness, a suffering world in need of compassion, and a struggling world in need of a helping hand. Jesus taught that He has prepared a kingdom of eternal love and joy for those whose hearts are disposed to it—moving away from ego-centricity and self-interest to genuine care and service for others. If we want to participate in eternal love, then we must be committed and transformed in that love which cares for others unselfishly and serves the needy to the extent possible.

As noted in the Introduction of Chapter 1, the Synoptic Gospels (Mark, Matthew, and Luke) recount Jesus telling a rich young man the six ethical commandments required by justice—that is, needed for salvation (Mk 10:19; cf. Mt 19:18–19; Lk 18:20). Matthew adds a seventh commandment: "Love your neighbor as yourself" (19:19). He did so because he recognized that Jesus taught that charity as well as justice was essential not only for salvation, but for a humane world. Though charity goes beyond the requirements of justice, it is essential for human decency, civility, peace, and fulfillment. If we care about this, says Jesus, we will be welcome in the Kingdom of Heaven, which is defined by that love. However, if we shun charity, then we exclude ourselves from the kingdom of love, by the hardness of our hearts. This is why Matthew includes it in the list of essential commandments.

Jesus illustrates this need for a compassionate heart in several passages of Scripture. In Luke (16:19–31), the rich man who day after day ignored the poor beggar Lazarus is consigned to Hades, and in Matthew, the king (Christ) consigns those who did nothing to serve the needy to the same domain (25:31–46). Clearly, for Jesus, having a heart of compassion is essential for the Kingdom of Heaven. James states the necessity for charity succinctly:

> What does it profit, my brethren, if a man says he has faith but has not [charitable] works? Can his faith save him? If a brother or sister is poorly clothed and in lack of daily food, and one of you says to them, "Go in peace, be warmed and filled," without giving them the things needed for the body, what does it profit? So faith by itself, if it has no [charitable] works, is dead. (2:14–17)

Jesus gives the ideal of charity and the heart of compassion in His Parable of the Good Samaritan, in which the Samaritan, seeing a Jew (a sworn enemy of his people) beaten to the point of death, has compassion on him, treats his wounds, finds an inn where he can recover, and pays for his expenses without asking anything in return (see Lk 10:25–37).

How can we live up to this ideal in a culture like our own? There are three "habits of the heart" that are addressed in several ways throughout the New Testament, discussed below:

1. Developing a Heart of Compassion (Section II.A)
2. Serving Family and Friends (Section II.B)
3. Serving the Needy in Our Community and Beyond (Section II.C)

A. Developing a Heart of Compassion

The first habit (developing a heart of compassion) is not so much a discipline or an action as a cultivation of empathy for others—to feel what another feels. Empathy is natural to most people, but egocentricity, emotional pain, and busyness about life sometimes block it. If empathy is completely suppressed, it leads to sociopathic behavior, but if we cultivate it, it leads to sainthood.[36] Every effort we make to temper egocentricity helps in the cultivation of empathy. Forgiveness, prayer, and therapy help to overcome the emotional pain of a hard childhood or adolescence. Making a concerted effort to carve out time for those in need helps those who are goal-driven to bracket that drive in order to attend to the needy or marginalized (many of whom simply want a few minutes of our counsel or a sympathetic ear).

Speaking personally, I did not have an overly stressed childhood or adolescence, but I did think a lot of myself, which led to self-serving

---

[36] Edith Stein (Saint Teresa Benedicta of the Cross) provides perhaps the most deep and comprehensive phenomenological exposition of this remarkable human and divine dynamic that breaks down the barrier between our self-consciousness and the self-consciousness of others. For the philosophically inclined, it is a profound pathway into charity, prayer, and even mystical communion with the God of Jesus Christ. See Edith Stein, *On the Problem of Empathy*, vol. 3, *The Collected Works of Edith Stein*, trans. Waltraut Stein (Washington, D.C.: Institute of Carmelite Studies Press, 1989).

and egocentric drives for success, wealth, and power. I was not able to sublimate these egocentric drives naturally, which led to a suppression of empathy and compassion for others in my early collegiate years. I applauded those who tutored kids and worked for others but felt no urge to do it myself. One of my close friends befriended a mentally challenged young man and would bring him to some of our social events, which bewildered and irritated me. I also came to appreciate him but only after three graces came to my rescue:

1. Faith and grace that revealed God's love for me (Section II.A.1)
2. Moving from an ego-comparative identity to a contributive identity through suffering interpreted by faith (Section II.A.2)
3. The example of saintly individuals (Section II.A.3)

I will briefly speak of these three blessings in my life, but I believe that they are the blessings that rescue all of us—if we let them.

1. Faith, Grace, and the Recognition of God's Love

As I have related elsewhere, I was challenged to go to daily Mass early in my collegiate career, and it had a tremendous effect. Recognizing God's love for me in the Scriptures, the homilies, the community, and above all, the Holy Eucharist, freed me from the need to pursue status, wealth, and power relentlessly in the world. Going to Mass gave me an interior sense of God's presence, love, and peace, guiding me to eternal salvation. I did not have to establish myself in the world (over against others) to find meaning and dignity in life. The awareness of a higher purpose and dignity from God (coming from the grace of the Holy Eucharist and the goodness of His Word) allowed me to let go of the transitory glory of this world. I did not even know how profoundly that grace was working in my life until people began to tell me that I was changing for the better—less egocentric and less oriented toward power, money, and status.

Faith, knowledge of Christ, and the grace of the Holy Eucharist, as well as my association with friends and the daily Mass community, gave me a sense not only of being loved but of *being* lovable (intrinsically). This awareness gradually moved me from being a "seeker of the esteem of others" to being an "acceptor of the love of others".

In this way, the love of God and others freed me to shift my focus from the esteemable self to the lovable self, which in turn freed me to invest myself not only in personal friendships but also in relationship with God and service to the needy. Grace, friendship, and religious community helped me to develop a heart.

Slowly but surely, I was able to let go of my worldly pretensions in the serenity and love I experienced in the innermost part of my soul. Yes—I constantly searched for rational confirmation of my newly deepened faith, but as this emerged, grace took hold of my heart and freed me to help others within the church community and among my friends. Recognizing God's love for me helped me to love others. I was probably the last person to recognize the interior transformation I was undergoing, but it finally came to my attention when I realized that my friend's intellectually challenged "buddy" (who had formerly irritated me) was becoming my "buddy" too. This uniquely good and lovable being began to affect me—his smile, his voice, and his innocent and unusual mannerisms became a source of pleasure rather than irritation. God's grace had worked a miracle in my stagnant power of empathy to establish a connection of affection, sympathy, and friendship, which ultimately led to compassion and charity.

2. The Move from Ego-Comparative to Contributive Identity through Suffering Interpreted by Faith

Suffering or, perhaps better, challenges were also very helpful. Though I found academics fascinating and satisfying, and had truly wonderful friends and mentors, I began to be tormented by questions of meaning in life, the problem of suffering, and the suggestions of life's insignificance posed by existentialist philosophers I respected. Though my faith helped me tremendously to respond to these challenges, I felt quite alone in dealing with them because unlike other friends I could not shake off the negative existentialist's suggestions and "just have a beer".

As I intimate in my book *The Light Shines on in the Darkness* (Volume IV of the Quartet), I began to see that the resolution to these challenges came not only from faith, but also by helping others. Putting it into the language of the four levels of happiness, my interior torment caused me to move from a Level Two (ego-comparative) purpose in life to a Level Three (contributive) and Level Four (faith-based) purpose in life. I discovered that my feelings of meaningless-ness, insignificance, and valueless suffering came from living beneath myself—living mostly for ego-comparative gratification. I knew I would never be ultimately satisfied by being better than others, smarter than others, more energetic than others, and having more status than others. In the ultimate order of things, they could not bring any lasting significance or purpose. When I started teaching catechism class, helping fellow students to succeed, spending time with those who had greater problems than I, I felt a surge of higher purpose and significance, because I was making a positive difference *beyond* myself.

My life had greater significance because I was making the world beyond myself (not just myself) better by my time and effort. Suf-fering, when combined with faith, frequently gives us the freedom to supersede Level Two purpose in favor of Level Three and Level Four purpose in life—and higher purpose in life gives the freedom to empathize with others, which motivates service and charitable love.

3. The Examples of Saintly Friends

The third path to empathy (away from egocentricity) is the example of the unheralded saints around us. Just as Saint Augustine was moved by the goodness of his mother, his profoundly good friends, and Saint Ambrose, and as Saint Ignatius of Loyola was moved by reading the life of Christ and the saints, and as Malcom Muggeridge was moved by the example of Mother Teresa of Calcutta, I also was called out of myself by the example, goodness, and love of people who had a more perfected faith-filled empathy and compassion than myself. I had many friends in college who were involved in service projects and took it upon themselves to accept and help those who were marginal-ized. The contributive identity coming from my faith and challenges was calling me to serve others, and my "saintly" friends provided me with *concrete* examples of serving the needy. What impressed me most was how this service transformed their hearts. Though they had to commit time to these projects, their efforts instilled in them a natural goodness, love, and joy that I was only beginning to discover and value.

This process came to fruition when I was invited to go on a Search Retreat by a few of my friends. During the retreat, I saw Malcom Muggeridge's movie on Mother Teresa, *Something Beautiful for God.* I resolved at that moment that I would make time in my schedule to serve the needy in some way, and in the future when I would be earning enough income, to share some of my funds with faith-based charities—Mother Teresa in particular. Above all, I wanted to imitate Mother Teresa's empathy for the poor and suffering as well as Malcolm Muggeridge's change of heart inspired by the little sister of Calcutta.

This process of recognizing God's love for me, moving my identity from ego-comparative to contributive and faith-based, using my suffering to detach from my ego, and experiencing the goodness, love, and joy of my "saintly" friends in their service to others opened my heart, increased my empathy for the needy, and helped me recognize my vocation to the Jesuits. When I entered the Jesuit novitiate, and began working and living with the men on skid row, visiting the elderly in nursing homes, and teaching students with learning challenges, I felt right at home—in communion with the Lord, who created me for this love. By then, it was effortless to see the unique goodness and lovability of the "guys on the street" and the elderly whose prime had passed. Recognizing this good news in these "little ones" freed me to empathize with them, love them, and in most cases, like them. The Holy Spirit was guiding my transformation of heart—all I had to do was be open to this guidance and be willing to make the commitment needed to fulfill the Lord's call. If I did not have faith, the sacraments, the readings and homilies of daily Mass, the example of Jesus and His saints, and the Catholic community, I fear that my empathy would not have awakened; without this, I would not have discovered the beauty and goodness of a life of contributing to the good of others by commitment of time and energy. I realize that other people have found their way to charitable service seemingly without faith, but I was far too egocentric and goal-driven to have done that. I suspect that there are many people like me who discovered the dignity and purpose of contribution and service through faith and grace that led to the recognition of God's love and the intrinsic goodness, beauty, and lovability of every human person.

B. Serving Family and Friends

In the First Letter to Timothy, we read:

> Command this, so that they may be without reproach. If any one does not provide for his relatives, and especially for his own family, he has disowned the faith and is worse than an unbeliever. (5:7–8)

The Pauline author here is stressing the primacy of family, relatives, and close friends as divinely ordained. We have all heard the clichés "Charity begins at home" and "Our first responsibility is to our family." No truer words have been spoken. As explained in Chapter 1, sacramental marriage is based on committed love that makes spouse and children our first priority in time, energy, and resources.

Time and presence are the most important gifts we have to offer, because they are the proof not only of *our* love, but also of our family members' belovedness and lovability. When we spend time with spouse and children, we affirm in them their lovability and goodness, but when we do not, we negate them. Obviously, this is a balancing act, because we have very real demands from our workplace and other institutions that must be fulfilled lest our finances and security fall on hard times. Perhaps the best way to fulfill our duty to both family and employer is to make commitment to our family the highest priority so long as necessary work requirements have been reasonably fulfilled. This often entails putting other desires for entertainment, socializing, community involvement, and other commitments on the back burner to make time for our families. These are a few tips that all committed family members know well:

- *Plan* your family time at the beginning of the week and stick to it (unless it would jeopardize your job or a priority commitment to visit a sick relative or assist a friend with high needs).
- *Pledge* the time for family commitments with generosity, avoiding implicit resentments. If you are saying to yourself, "I *have to* do X with my family," you already believe it to be a duty more than a joy or privilege. However, if you are saying, "I am *looking forward* to doing X with my family," it changes the entire experience. Not only will you feel the difference, but your spouse and children will as well.

- *Decide* as a couple where to put the boundaries between family time, entertainment time, socializing time, and other time away from family.
- When you are with your family, *talk and listen* to them, and encourage them to enter the conversation. Do not underestimate the importance of having dinner together even if it means asking sacrifices of your teenage children, because it not only reinforces familial bonds, but elicits communication that might reveal problems and challenges with which you might be able to help or be a consoling presence.
- *Attend* church services together and try to arrange a brunch or family meal around the services. Plan and spend time on sacramental preparation beyond sending your child to religious education classes. Recall from Chapter 1 that religion and prayer bring the family together and make for greater stability in marriage as well as in the hearts of children. According to Father Patrick Peyton, "The family that prays together, stays together," and major university studies have proven this to be the case.[37]
- *Involve* your spouse and children in faith-based and community service. This enables your charitable service to also be service to your family and shares the value of charitable service with them, as well as sets a lifetime pattern for your children. I have seen families bring their children as helpers to food distribution centers, juvenile detention centers, blood drives, Meals on Wheels, home-refurbishment projects for the poor, and even international service projects. This allows family, faith, and service to reinforce each other in the minds and hearts of children and parents.
- *Socializing* at home, and sharing your friends with your children, and vice-versa, is valuable to the children, giving them a sense of extended family and security.

The underlying principle is to give time and emotional intimacy, and focus energy on family members, relatives, and friends who are

---

[37]See the four large studies at seven universities—Florida State University, University of Georgia, Bowling Green State University, Auburn University, East Carolina University, University of North Texas, and University of Calgary—in David Briggs, "5 Ways Faith Contributes to Strong Marriages, New Studies Suggest", *HuffPost*, February 8, 2015, http://www.huffingtonpost.com/david-briggs/5-ways-faith-contributes_b_6294716.

like family, bringing God into family life wherever it is appropriate because this is the proof of your love, your family members' lovability, and God's loving intention for them. Every moment of love invested in your first priority will lead to a lifetime of dividends for your spouse and children, and very likely, for an eternity.

C. Serving the Needy in Our Community and Beyond

As noted above, Jesus taught that having a heart for the needy—a heart of compassion—is integral to our salvation, and as such, is equal in importance to the other Ten Commandments. There are four ways that we can serve the needy:

- By direct service according to our time, talent, and family obligation
- Attending to the needs of those we encounter during the day
- Giving alms to organizations who work with the needy
- Praying for the needy

Jesus did all these things and recommended that we follow His example. I will briefly discuss each in turn.

With respect to direct service of the poor, it is essential to plan specific time to a particular service, organization, or project. One of my truisms runs like this: "If it is on my calendar, it is likely to occur," but if it is only a good intention in my mind, it is not. For me, putting something on the calendar is like making a commitment. Once I have committed the time, I have won half the battle against inertia and my desire to keep my time to myself.

When planning, remember the adage that the perfect or best is frequently the worst enemy of the good. It is simply impossible to do everything because there are literally thousands of individuals in every area of need—religious instruction, evangelization, tutoring students, working with youth, the elderly and disabled, helping the poor, hungry, homeless, and the sick, as well as working in international efforts, environmental efforts, and social justice initiatives. So where can we begin? Take a clue from Saint Paul's First Letter to the Corinthians:

Now there are varieties of gifts, but the same Spirit; and there are varieties of service, but the same Lord; and there are varieties of working, but it is the same God who inspires them all in every one. To each is given the manifestation of the Spirit for the common good. To one is given through the Spirit the utterance of wisdom, and to another the utterance of knowledge according to the same Spirit, to another faith by the same Spirit, to another gifts of healing by the one Spirit.... All these are inspired by one and the same Spirit, who apportions to each one individually as he wills. (12:4–9, 11)

As Saint Paul implies, in order to serve the Lord and the community well, we need to know where we can get the most effect for our efforts, as well as what will engage our interests and passions. If we have the triple combination of capacity, interest, and desire, we are likely to make a well-motivated, quality contribution that engages us personally with those we serve. Take a moment (with your spouse if you are married) to reflect on where your passion and talents are strongest, such as teaching religion,[38] tutoring or mentoring needy kids,[39] working with underprivileged youth,[40] delivering meals to the homebound,[41] working in an organization that serves the poor (e.g., Saint Vincent de Paul, Catholic Charities, and Second Harvest),

[38] The best place to start if you are interested in teaching religion to young people is *your parish*. Call your parish faith formation director, who can direct you to opportunities in catechetics, Confirmation programs, and adult education in the parish.

[39] There are many programs that have opportunities to tutor and mentor the underprivileged. Simply put the following in your search engine: "tutoring and mentoring opportunities for underprivileged" plus the city in which you live. You will be given a fairly extensive list of opportunities. Also, check with your parish justice and service committee for opportunities sponsored by your parish.

[40] There are several programs that work with Catholic youth that are oriented toward teaching and religion. The place to start is your parish youth ministry outreach. If your parish does not have youth ministry, connect with the parish next door. Life Teen is a national organization that works with teens through prayer and catechesis. There are also several youth programs like Catholic Youth Organization (CYO), YMCA, and Boys and Girls Clubs that are athletically oriented, skills oriented, and socially oriented. Simply put in the organization in which you are interested like CYO Los Angeles (or whatever city you are in) and you will see opportunities to volunteer.

[41] Meals on Wheels is the largest organization to deliver meals free of charge or at a very low cost to the underprivileged. It works through Catholic Charities, Salvation Army, and dozens of other charitable organizations. Simply put "Meals on Wheels" plus your city into your search engine and you will see volunteer opportunities and a volunteer agreement to sign up and help right away.

assisting youth in detention or on probation,[42] or volunteering in another organization.[43]

The people you serve are not the sole beneficiaries of your charity. Almost every volunteer will tell you that serving the needy is just as beneficial to the volunteer! Charitable service forms new vital friendships, lifts your spirits, connects you more closely with the heart of Christ, and can help you move beyond your personal challenging situation. This has happened to me so many times in virtually every apostolate in which I have volunteered. In my undergraduate years at Gonzaga University, I was asked to teach catechism class to ninth-grade boys. At first, I was quite reticent to do so because I felt pressured by studies and work, but a nice girl convinced me to "do something for someone beyond yourself!" So, I indicated that I would teach one class as a favor to her. Unsure of what I should teach, I decided to introduce the students to the evidence of Creation from new contemporary studies in physics-cosmology. When the boys came to the class, I could tell that they did not want to be there, but as I continued my presentation, they became progressively more interested. At the end of the class, one young man came up to me and asked, "Are you going to be our catechism teacher for the rest of the year?" I had planned to teach only the one class, but he was looking at me with such longing and hopefulness that I could not resist, and so I responded, "Yes." This resulted in not only a wonderful relationship with those boys, but also the discovery of my teaching vocation, which is one of the best things that ever happened to me.

Several years later when I was teaching at Georgetown University, I was asked by a fellow Jesuit if I would be able to do some

---

[42] These young people have made mistakes, but the love and help of volunteers makes a huge difference to their transformation into productive citizens. They seek everything from companionship to tutoring, skills training, and coaching. Put "youth detention volunteer opportunities" plus your city in a Google search, and you will see several opportunities to provide volunteer services.

[43] To find a list of organizations, ask your parish priest or your parish justice and service committee for a list of organizations with which the parish works. You can also contact Catholic Charities to find opportunities for volunteer service in your area. Many of these organizations are flexible about hours and do much of their volunteer assistance on weekends. The following link to Catholic Charities gives the categories and organizations in which volunteer opportunities are possible: https://www.catholiccharitiessf.org/fundraising/page.html?gclid=EAIaIQobChMIkMz67f3h6wIV3xatBh2EFAAjEAAYAiAAEgJXcfD_BwE.

accounting and filing of government forms for a Jesuit boys' home in Maryland outside of Washington, D.C. I agreed to do so, thinking it would be fairly routine desk work. It was certainly not routine. I had to do all the work at the dining room table that was at the center of the house, with the boys passing by in and out of the kitchen, the backyard, and the rest of the house. After about an hour, the boys came by and asked what I was doing, and so I began to explain a little bit about accounting, government forms, and the like. I soon discovered that they were really not that interested in accounting, but rather in my time, attention, and friendship. Most of them did not have a father in their lives, and if they did, many were insulting and abusive. Of course, they would dream up questions just to be in communication with someone who cared about them.

I truly had no idea how much my presence, attention, and care could mean, but watching these kids' faces come alive when they received just a little attention and care showed me not only the power of love, but also the value of a little time, caring presence, and a smile. I continued working at the boys' home throughout the year, because I found it almost irresistible, and it occurred to me that the good I was doing for these recovering "juvenile delinquents" was as profound as any contribution I could make being a professor at Georgetown. The happiness of those kids filled me to the brim, lifted my spirits, and elevated my relationship with the Lord. I would come back from the boys' home, go to the chapel, and reminisce with the Lord about how rewarding it was to be their father figure and friend. The fact is, anyone could do what I had done—because care, understanding, and positive demeanor are possible for everyone. Care is universal, and giving it to those in need fills our spirit in beautiful and incomprehensible ways.

As noted above, there are other opportunities beyond direct service to those in need. Simply being responsive to the needy we encounter throughout the day can do tremendous good—a kind word to someone who looks like he is having a tough day, a few dollars to someone who is begging or manifestly homeless, paying attention to someone who is ignored or excluded, listening to someone who needs to share a difficult situation, answering the phone call of a person who might demand more time than you have, defending a person who is intimidated or ostracized, offering a positive remark in a negative gossip session, simply respecting a person who seems to get little respect, befriending someone who others seem to avoid. Keeping an eye out for the needy we encounter almost every day and making an effort to help them in little ways can make a big difference to individuals and the community. Once again, our acts of kindness redound back to us and to our relationship with the Lord.

A third way of practicing charitable love is through almsgiving. Regardless of our economic capacity, almsgiving is integral to Christian life. Jesus, who was not wealthy, kept a money box for provisions and contributions to the poor (see Jn 13:29), and He taught the importance of almsgiving (see Mt 6:1–4); Saint Paul made considerable efforts to raise money from the Gentile churches to help poor Christians in Jerusalem (see 2 Cor 8; Acts 21:1–5). Virtually every saint preached the importance of almsgiving and made provisions for the poor. Having been a fundraiser myself for many years while president of Gonzaga University, I can attest that I was able to see people at their best when they made a sacrifice to respond to the needs of the Church, as well as the economically challenged, the sick, and the marginalized.

The fourth way of responding to the needs of the community is prayer. Sometimes we unintentionally relegate prayer to the most ineffective rung of charitable service after attending to the needs of people around us and almsgiving, but prayer is complementary to all of these areas of charity. Sometimes, prayer is all we can do—for we may not have the opportunity or means to serve more directly.

Though double-blind studies on the correlation between intercessory prayer and healing are inconclusive, there is considerable anecdotal evidence of intercessory prayer causing remarkable healing and reversal of illness in people who have faith.[44] Patients who have faith and pray for themselves have significantly higher rates of health and healing than those who do not. Dr. Harold Koenig of Duke University, in a comprehensive study of research on religion and health, states that there is a strong correlation between religion and lower mortality

---

[44] Some Duke Medical School studies indicate that intercessory prayer not known by subjects may help with healing and recovery. See Jeanie Lerche Davis, "Can Prayer Heal?", WebMD, 2001, https://www.webmd.com/balance/features/can-prayer-heal#1. There are many books detailing stories of healing through prayer, such as Laura Jamison Wright, *Chosen to Heal: Gifted Catholics Share Stories of God's Miraculous Healing Power* (Immaculate Heart Press, 2013).

and longer survival in 75% of the very best studies.[45] Dr. Koenig also notes that there is a strong correlation between religion and better immune functioning in 71% of the very best studies.[46] He also shows significant correlations between church attendance and lower blood pressure, endocrine functioning, cardiovascular functions, coronary heart disease, survival after open heart surgery, cancer, and all-cause mortality.[47] Perhaps this is why 72 percent of physicians in the United States believe in the reality of miracles both past and present.[48] If religion and prayer can have beneficial effects on the sick, why would God deny His grace to those with other needs—for example, those needing housing, a job, and help with family members?

When I offer Mass, I pray the following intercessory prayer every day: "for the sick and dying, the poor and the homeless, the oppressed and the depressed, those without faith or hope, the vulnerable, the unborn, and the elderly". Scripture tells us, "When the righteous cry for help, the LORD hears" (Ps 34:17), and, "They caused the cry of the poor to come to him, and he heard the cry of the afflicted" (Job 34:28). Why would God not hear the cry of those who intercede on behalf of the righteous and poor? The obvious answer is, He would and He does. I can testify to this.

The common thread throughout this entire section is that charitable service liberates our hearts. Whether we are doing direct service for the needy in our community, serving our families' needs, giving alms, or praying, something happens to us when we take the time and make the effort to extend charitable love to our neighbor—we grow in empathy, experience the unique goodness and lovability of others, and enter into deeper communion with the Lord of love whom we imitate. In loving our neighbor, our hearts are opened to love the Lord more deeply, and even to love ourselves. All of this leads not only to eternal salvation with the loving Lord, but also to the

---

[45] Dr. Harold Koenig, "Religion, Spirituality & Health: Research and Clinical Implications" *International Scholarly Research Notices* (2012), https://www.hindawi.com/journals/isrn /2012/278730/.

[46] Ibid.

[47] Ibid.

[48] See Bill Freeman, "Science or Miracle? Holiday Season Survey Reveals Physicians' Views of Faith, Prayer and Miracles", WorldHealth.net, December 22, 2004, reporting survey by HCD Research and Louis Finkelstein Institute, https://www.worldhealth.net/news /science_or_miracle_holiday_season_survey/.

freedom for deeper spiritual and moral conversion. As Jesus implied, those who love much are also forgiven much (Lk 7:47). We might infer from this that when we are so greatly loved and forgiven, we are incited to love Him even more and incited to greater spiritual and moral conversion. This is the spiritual freedom upon which assent to the moral teaching of Jesus and the Catholic Church is built.

III. The Need for Objective Moral Norms

In the Introduction to this volume, we showed the need for objective moral norms to prevent individuals from declining in emotional and spiritual well-being, and to maintain the stability and efficacy of marriage and family as well as society itself. The studies presented in Chapters 1–4 will have brought at least partial confirmation to this contention. It now remains to explain it more fully. The multiple studies and statistical analyses presented in defense of the Church's teaching on extramarital sex, premarital sex (and cohabitation), a homosexual lifestyle, pornography, sex change, artificial birth control, abortion, overpopulation, eugenics, invitro fertilization, embryonic stem cells, and physician-assisted suicide (euthanasia) provide significant evidence to make a strong *inductive* argument for the necessity of objective moral norms—specifically those taught by Jesus and the Catholic Church.

An inductive argument moves from the bottom up, while deductive arguments move from the top down. We frequently use deductive arguments in mathematics and formal logic, such as, "If all A is B and all B is C, then all A must be C." If the first premise is true and the second premise is true, then the conclusion must be true. In contrast to this, inductive arguments work from the bottom (observable data) to general laws by inferring causation from repeated quantifiable correlations. For example, in the natural sciences, the observation of correlations in rigorously designed experiments verifying predicted outcomes of hypothetical laws has led to encyclopedias of new knowledge about the natural world not accessible to purely deductive proof. Inductive arguments do not have the same universal certitude as deductive arguments, but they offer a sound way of making highly probable predictions about the natural world through this new hypothetical-experimental-quantitative method. The social sciences are similarly inductive, making use of statistical methods to predict outcomes of human behavior and opinion on the basis of rigorous sampling of human populations. This method was used in the studies in Chapters 1–4 to show the correlation between objective moral norms and emotional health and spiritual well-being of individuals, marital and family stability, and cultural cohesion and stability.

The broad question we have been examining is whether individuals, marriages, families, society, and culture would be in better condition if the majority of individuals had a strong sense of objective moral norms (particularly Christian-Catholic moral norms)—or whether they are in better condition with the current moral relativism and adherence to autonomous freedom. "Better condition" means the following:

- *Individuals* having high incidence of emotional health (marked by low rates of depression, anxiety, substance abuse, familial tensions, antisocial aggressivity, and suicide) and spiritual well-being (marked by high rates of hope, significant purpose in life, respect for the dignity of self and care for others' welfare, as well as low rates of narcissism, cheating, lying, and stealing)
- *Marriages and families* having high incidence of internal satisfaction, stability, longevity, security for children, and ethical influence on culture
- *Society and culture* having high incidence of unity, mutual respect among different groups, and social stability as well as low rates of division and social unrest

Needless to say, multiple causes can be found to explain each of these indicators of a good condition of individuals, marriages, families, and society. Yet our question persists: Do objective Christian-Catholic moral norms have a pervasive positive influence on all the factors defining the "good condition" of individuals, marriages, families, and societies within Western culture? Could this one cause make a huge difference to the malaise, familial decline, division, and unrest in our society today? Though other causes can be found to explain the very challenged state of individuals, marriages, families, and society today, the comparative data given in the studies and statistical analyses in the previous four chapters implies strongly that objective moral norms (particularly Christian-Catholic objective moral norms) would help significantly in reversing the declining—and often steeply declining—trends in individuals' emotional health, spiritual well-being, marital and familial satisfaction and stability, and societal unity, stability, and peace. My objective here is not to review the data given in those studies, but to draw the evident inductive conclusion that if our society had a stronger sense of objective moral norms (particularly Christian-Catholic norms), we would be in a much higher state of emotional health, spiritual well-being, marital and familial stability, and societal unity and peace. Readers may want to review the data presented in Chapters 1–4 to validate this inductive conclusion for themselves. If you find the data to be probative, let it strengthen your resolve to embrace the moral norms taught by Jesus and the Church He instituted.

Some people may object that our society seems to be happier, more purposeful, and hopeful than before. Unfortunately, this objection is *not* supported by the data. We are far less happy, purposeful, and hopeful than previous generations (as the data indicates, particularly the 56 percent rise in suicides, 63 percent increase in depression and anxiety, and 23 percent rise in homicides among young people in twelve years, from 2005 to 2017[49]). No one can dispute that our society has more material wealth, technological assistance, and economic security than previous generations, but at the same time we cannot lose sight of the fact that all of this material and technological advantage has not helped to allay the accelerating decline of emotional health and spiritual well-being, marriage and family satisfaction, and stability and societal unity, as well as peace. Indeed, as our material and technological advantage has increased,

---

[49] See Jean M. Twenge et al., "Age, Period, and Cohort Trends in Mood Disorder Indicators and Suicide-Related Outcomes in a Nationally Representative Dataset, 2005–2017", *Journal of Abnormal Psychology* 128, no. 3 (2019): 185–99, https://www.apa.org/pubs/journals/releases/abn-abn0000410.pdf. See also William Wan, "Teen Suicides Are Increasing at an Alarming Pace, Outstripping All Other Age Groups, a New Report Says", *Washington Post*, October 17, 2019, https://www.washingtonpost.com/health/teen-suicides-increasing-at-alarming-pace-outstripping-all-other-age-groups/2019/10/16/e24194c6-f04a-11e9-8693-f487e46784aa_story.html.

our happiness, unity, and peace have decreased. The conclusion is evident—amid all our societal advantages, we are missing something, and as the data of the previous four chapters indicate, this "something" is religion[50] and objective moral norms, particularly Christian-Catholic norms.

Before we can address a solution, we need to examine what caused the decline in objective moral norms. To do this we need to further examine the sources of moral norms so that we can determine what factors undermine those sources. There are three major sources of objective moral norms—religion, conscience, and cultural traditions. We will examine each in turn.

A. The Sources of Objective Moral Norms

For about four millennia before the Enlightenment, religion and moral norms were closely interrelated—religion imparted moral norms, and moral norms bound the consciences of individuals.[51]

Though both religion and conscience had an impact on individual and collective moral norms, religion was the primary source. As will be explained below, religion is grounded in our strong interior sense of the numinous, mysterious, and sacred "wholly Other", which virtually all cultures identify as "God" or "the Divine". This sense of a sacred, divine, creative presence is also associated with the moral obligations of conscience and several specific norms to which we feel obligated. These two contentions are borne out by many comprehensive studies as well as philosophical analyses of conscience. A brief explanation of five of these studies will give the general contours of the evidence not only for the connection between religion and moral

---

[50] Recall from the Introduction to this volume (Section III) the six studies indicating that religious affiliation correlates with significantly lower rates of depression, anxiety, substance abuse, aggressivity, and suicides. See Kanita Dervic et al.; Harold Koenig (two studies); Raphael Bonelli et al.; Stefano Lassi and Daniele Mugnaini; and Corina Ronenberg et al. Complete references are given below in note 56.

[51] For a very well-referenced survey of the historical connection between religion and morality and its close connection to cultural identity and social cohesion in the West and Middle East, see John Hare, "Religion and Morality", *Stanford Encyclopedia of Philosophy*, Fall 2019 ed., ed. Edward N. Zalta, https://plato.stanford.edu/archives/fall2019/entries/religion-morality.

norms throughout history, but also for the divine source of this inter-related awareness of divinity and morality:

- Rudolf Otto's study of the numinous experience
- Mircea Eliade's study of the intuition of the sacred
- Friedrich Heiler's seven common characteristics of major religions
- Saint John Henry Newman's analysis of conscience
- C. S. Lewis' study of the common moral norms of religion and conscience

I have discussed these studies in much greater detail in other works (see Volume II, Chapters 1–2 of the Quartet). For the moment we will briefly summarize these studies and examine their implications for the interrelated origin of our interior awareness of the divine presence and objective moral norms. As we shall see, the first two of the above sources of objective moral norms (religion and conscience), though distinct, are inextricably interrelated.

Let us begin with Rudolf Otto, whose seminal comprehensive study of religious experience, *The Idea of the Holy*,[52] has provided the basis for many systematic analyses of religious awakening and awareness to this day. Based on the studies of William James[53] and others, Otto articulates the fundamental interior precognitive sense of the "numen" (divine presence and power) manifesting itself as a mysterious, spiritual, fascinating, inviting "wholly Other" that elicits from us a sense of awe, reverence, creatureliness, sacredness, and mystery. This presence as "wholly Other" is overwhelmingly superior to us, yet fascinating and inviting. It is also connected to our sense of moral obligation. Otto indicates that the more we reflect on our awareness of God (the "numen") and our sense of moral obligation, the more we recognize their interrelationship.[54] Our sense of moral obligation is imbued with divine authority, and we hear the same divine "voice" in our religious experience as well as in our conscience (see the explanation of Saint John Henry Newman below).

---

[52] See Rudolf Otto, *The Idea of the Holy: An Inquiry into the Non-Rational Factor in the Idea of the Divine and Its Relation to the Rational* (Oxford: Oxford University Press, 1923).

[53] See William James, *The Varieties of Religious Experience: A Study in Human Nature* (New York: Longmans, Green, 1902).

[54] See Otto, *Idea of the Holy*, pp. 40–47, 97–101.

Throughout his study, Otto implies that the numinous experience is common to every human person,[55] which as we shall see is borne out by the other four studies mentioned below, as well as studies showing the correlation of religion with human happiness, emotional health (significantly lower rates of depression and anxiety),[56] and marriage and family stability.[57] Otto's contention gives rise to the question of the source of the numinous in every human consciousness. Is it given to us by the world's religions (an exterior source)? Is it innate to the human psyche? If so, what caused this prerational awareness of the mysterious, sacred "wholly Other" whose "otherness" seems to be more powerful than our own subjectivity? As we shall see at the end of Section III.A, the most likely explanation is a transcendent personal source.

[55] For Otto, the numinous is an a priori element in human experience and an a priori dimension of human understanding (in the Kantian sense), implying that it is universal—that is, common to every human person. See ibid., Chapters 14 and 17.

[56] A longitudinal study published by the American Psychiatric Association correlated religious affiliation not only with decreased depression and suicides, but decreased substance abuse, aggression, and familial tensions. See Kanita Dervic et al., "Religious Affiliation and Suicide Attempt", *American Journal of Psychiatry* 161, no. 12 (2004): 2303–8, http://ajp.psy chiatryonline.org/article.aspx?articleid=177228. Recall the other studies confirming Kanita Dervic et al. given in the Introduction to this volume (Section III): Harold Koenig, "Research on Religion, Spirituality and Mental Health: A Review", *Canadian Journal of Psychiatry* 54, no. 5 (2009): 283–91, https://journals.sagepub.com/doi/pdf/10.1177/070674370905400502; Raphael Bonelli et al., "Religious and Spiritual Factors in Depression: Review and Integration of the Research", *Depression and Research Treatment* August 15, 2012, https://www.hindawi .com/journals/drt/2012/962860/; Stefano Lassi and Daniele Mugnaini, "Role of Religion and Spirituality on Mental Health and Resilience: There Is Enough Evidence", *International Journal of Emergency Mental Health and Human Resilience* 17, no. 3 (2015): 661–63, https:// www.omicsonline.org/open-access/role-of-religion-and-spirituality-on-mental-health-and -resilience-there-is-enough-evidence-1522-4821-1000273.pdf; Harold Koenig, "Religion, Spirituality, and Health: A Review and Update", *Advances in Mind-Body Medicine* 29, no. 3 (2015): 19–26, https://pubmed.ncbi.nlm.nih.gov/26026153/; Corina Ronenberg et al., "The Protective Effects of Religiosity on Depression: A 2-Year Prospective Study", *Gerontologist* 56, no. 3 (2016): 421–31, https://academic.oup.com/gerontologist/article/56/3/421/2605601.

[57] Married couples who take their sacramental life and prayer life seriously will palpably sense the Lord's presence, reassurance, peace, inspiration, and guidance individually and collectively. They will also have an increased sense of satisfaction in their marriage, hope in salvation, resilience in times of challenge, and determination to be faithful to their spouses throughout their lifetime. These findings are confirmed by five recent large studies at seven universities—Florida State University, University of Georgia, Bowling Green State University, Auburn University, East Carolina University, University of North Texas, and University of Calgary. See Briggs, "5 Ways Faith Contributes to Strong Marriages".

The second study of the interior source of religion and moral norms was carried out by the Romanian historian and philosopher of religion Mircea Eliade, who examined and systematized religious experience throughout four millennia and edited the *Macmillan Encyclopedia of Religion*.[58] He showed through his study of world religions throughout history that human beings have a profound interior and collective sense of the sacred, which has influenced the drive of all peoples and cultures toward religion. His studies showed that for more than four millennia, human beings from virtually every culture around the world yearned for and sought the sacred. In virtually every culture, the expression and the fulfillment of that yearning is similar in four general areas:[59]

1. There is a belief in the sacred (transcendent reality) in which there is absolute truth and goodness.

2. The sacred (transcendent reality) desires to connect with human beings and so enters into the profane world at a particular place and time. Its entrance into the world is the originative or creative moment. The physical world may have existed before the sacred's entrance into it, but the world was not significant or real prior to its entrance. Thus, for traditional man, true reality and meaning began when the sacred reality broke through.

3. When the sacred reality broke through, it sacralized (made holy) the place and time it entered. When human beings draw close to the place of entrance, it makes them holy. Similarly, when human beings celebrate the ritual of origin and recount the myth of origin,[60] time collapses, and they reenter the sacred time of origin again, connecting them with the sacred, which strengthens them.

4. The celebration of rituals and recounting of myths not only strengthens the participants but also imparts what Eliade terms

---

[58] Mircea Eliade, *Macmillan Encyclopedia of Religion*, 15 vols. (New York: Macmillan Publisher, 1966).

[59] See Mircea Eliade, *The Sacred and the Profane: The Nature of Religion*, trans. Willard R. Trask (New York: Harcourt, 1987).

[60] The myth of origin is not only the precise moment at which the sacred enters the world; it includes unfolding of the originative moment through the actions and virtues of heroes, the overcoming of evil, and the teaching and development of human beings.

"paradigmatic models"—that is, lessons about *purpose in life, the goods to be pursued, evils to be avoided, the virtues and laws that will help to achieve the good, and the vices that will undermine it.* Thus, traditional man receives purpose, direction, and virtue from reentering the sacred time through ritual and myth.

Eliade has added to Otto's studies that the human awareness of the numinous led to public religious expression (in religious ceremonies, recounting of sacred myths, and public worship and symbols). It is quite remarkable that virtually every religion in the world shares the above four characteristics, even though many of them developed independently of one another.[61] Once again, we are led to the question of what the source of this commonality among independent developing religions could be. What is it within individual consciousness that causes a belief in the need for sacralization, and the sacred divine presence breaking into profane reality, allowing us to draw closer to it through public expression of religion? It seems that this common source of collective human awareness is at once universal, interior, and as sacred and transcendent as the feelings and consciousness it evokes. If so, then Eliade is correct in implying that the sacred (the Divine) is not only real, but also efficaciously present within each individual consciousness and collective (cultural) milieu. How is this sacred divine reality efficaciously present? As Eliade indicates, it shows us the path to sacralization (being purified or made holy), gives us the virtues to be pursued and the vices to be avoided, and shows us a path to life beyond this world. Once again, we see that our sense of the sacred, numinous, divine presence includes moral obligation and precepts. We will discuss this more fully at the end of this section.

The third study of the interior sources of religion and moral norms comes from the German historian of religion and ecumenical theologian Friedrich Heiler, who elucidated seven common characteristics among the world's major religions:[62]

---

[61] See John L. McKenzie, *Dictionary of the Bible* (New York: Macmillan, 1965), p. 754.

[62] Friedrich Heiler, "The History of Religions as a Preparation for the Cooperation of Religions", in *The History of Religions*, ed. Mircea Eliade and J. Kitagawa (Chicago, Ill.: University of Chicago Press, 1959), pp. 142–53.

1. The transcendent Being, the Holy One, the Divine, the Other is real.
2. The transcendent reality is immanent in human awareness.
3. This transcendent reality is the highest truth, highest good, and highest beauty.
4. This transcendent reality is loving and compassionate—and seeks to reveal its love to all of us.
5. The way to God requires prayer, *ethical self-discipline, purgation of self-centeredness, asceticism, and redressing of offenses.*
6. The way to God also includes service and responsibility to people.
7. The highest way to eternal bliss in the transcendent reality is through love.

Though the interpretation of specific moral norms and the definition of "love" differs significantly among the world's religions,[63] Heiler's "seven common characteristics" give rise to the same question raised by the studies of Otto and Eliade—namely, since many of the world's religions developed independently of one another,[64] what could be the source of these seven common characteristics among those religions? Once again, we are led to a common interior awareness of the divine sacred presence, which when it is combined with our sense of moral obligation arising out of conscience, leads almost inexorably to the seven common characteristics of Heiler. Can this universal, transcendent, sacred, and moral phenomenon be explained by anything other than the divine, sacred, moral reality? If not, then God is not only real but efficaciously present in the individual consciousness and the cultural ethos of humanity. This will be discussed at the end of this section.

The fourth study of the interior source of religion and moral norms is Saint John Henry Newman's phenomenological assessment of conscience. John Henry Newman was an influential theologian and philosopher of religion who wrote extensively about epistemology,

---

[63] I have discussed this in much greater detail relative to Christianity's most profound and distinctive definition of love affecting the interpretation of the general moral norms of conscience and the specific moral norms of Jesus. See Volume II (Chapter 1) and Volume III (Chapter 1) of the Quartet.

[64] See McKenzie, *Dictionary of the Bible*, p. 754.

philosophy of religion, philosophy of education, and the development of Christian doctrine. One of his seminal contributions was a phenomenological assessment of conscience articulated in several short works, as well as an unpublished manuscript entitled "Proof of Theism".[65] His proof can be synthesized in four major steps:

1. *The presence of moral obligation.* Newman begins by observing that the feelings of conscience are quite different from other kinds of feelings, such as those associated with experiencing beauty, joy, or sadness. He describes this difference as follows: "The feeling of beauty or ugliness is attended by no sanction; no hope or fear, no misgiving of the future, no feeling of being hurt, no tender sorrow, no sunny self-satisfaction, no lightness of heart."[66] What differentiates the feelings of conscience from other kinds of feelings is that it *does* have a sense of sanction (moral obligation) and a sense of hope or dread (which has a spiritual dimension going beyond ordinary optimism or fear) as well as a dimension of misgiving about the future.

2. *The presence of a personal authority figure.* These feelings also include a dimension of being praised for good deeds and being faulted for evil ones. This sense of being praised or faulted reveals an authority figure who is higher than we are—who has the right to bestow praise or fault on our conduct. This authority figure is instructing and charging us to do or avoid certain actions. Thus, our conscience—our sense of moral obligation—has a *personal* component who is not only guiding us but obliging us to do right and avoid wrong.

3. *The presence of a loving fatherly authority figure.* Newman then shows that the feelings of conscience are not simple moral obligation, praise, fault, and spiritual hope and dread. At their deepest level they are filled with love, revealing that the authority source is not just a lawgiver or a moral commander, but rather like a loving parent. Newman expresses it as follows: "The

---

[65]John Henry Newman, unpublished manuscript entitled "Proof of Theism", in *The Argument from Conscience to the Existence of God according to J. H. Newman*, ed. Adrian Boekraad and Henry Tristram (London: Mill Hill, 1961).

[66]Ibid., pp. 117–18.

feeling is one analogous or similar to that which we feel in human matters towards a *person* whom we have offended; there is a tenderness almost tearful when we go wrong, and a grateful cheerfulness when we go right which is just what we feel in pleasing or displeasing a father."[67] This is why conscience does not plunge us into sheer dread of spiritual punishment or abject despair when we do wrong, but rather to feelings of regret, disappointment, and alienation for having displeased the authority who *loves* us. The reason we do not plummet into sheer dread, despair, and hopelessness is because we know the authority figure still loves us, yet we regret having disappointed the one who does love us like a parent. This is also why conscience fills us with a sense of spiritual restoration and hope going far beyond sentimental happiness when we are forgiven. It fills us with a sense of spiritual restoration, like being invited back to our true home after separating ourselves from it. That is why confession can elevate our spirits and sense of "being at home" when we have had a long period of straying from doing right.

4. *The presence of a divine, loving fatherly authority figure.* There is one final dimension to conscience that resembles the numinous experience—it shows the higher authority figure to be divine. Newman puts it this way: "[When we are] contemplating and revolving on this feeling the mind will reasonably conclude that it is an unseen father who is the object of the feeling. And this father has necessarily some of those special attributes which belong to the notion of God. He is invisible— He is the searcher of hearts—He is omniscient as far as man is concerned—He is (to our notions) omnipotent."[68] This recognition of the *Divine* within conscience draws us out of ourselves to seek out the divine, loving fatherly authority figure standing behind our feelings of disappointment, regret, guilt, and disgust for doing wrong as well as feelings of spiritual nobility, elevation, and "being at home" when we do right. Newman describes it as follows: "Its very existence throws us out of ourselves and beyond ourselves, to go and seek for Him in the

[67] Ibid.
[68] Ibid., pp. 118–19.

height and depth, whose voice it is." Just as the fascinating and inviting dimension of the numinous experience enkindles in us a desire to seek the numen, so also the divine, loving fatherly authority figure enkindles in us the desire to please Him and come closer to Him by reforming our lives and following His guiding light.

Newman's assessment of conscience cannot be explained without making recourse to a *real* divine, loving fatherly authoritative presence, which is intrinsic to the human experience of moral obligation. He follows Immanuel Kant in asserting that our sense of moral duty cannot be explained without the presence of a divine binding moral authority,[69] but goes beyond Kant by showing that conscience is more than binding moral authority; it is fatherly, loving, and filled with a divine subjectivity seeking our good and ultimate fulfillment. In both cases, divine authority is needed to explain the phenomenon, but each philosopher's conception of the divine consciousness giving rise to that authority is quite different—with Newman's view being more complete, affectively nuanced, and in my view, truer to experience.

Newman's assessment of conscience affirms from the opposite direction what Otto, Eliade, and Heiler affirm from their studies of religious experience and religion. Newman recognizes the presence of divine authority and presence in the moral obligations of conscience, while Otto, Eliade, and Heiler recognize moral obligation in our interior awareness of the sacred divine presence. We may infer from this that the two sources of moral obligation—religion and conscience—are inextricably interrelated, and our awareness of the Divine is imbued with moral obligation and our experience of moral obligation (and conscience) is imbued with divine authority. We will discuss this more specifically at the end of this section.

Our fifth and final study of the interior source of religion and moral norms comes from C. S. Lewis' perceptive and wide-ranging assessment of the precepts of conscience in various religions and

---

[69] See Immanuel Kant, *Kant's Critique of Practical Reason and Other Works on the Theory of Ethics*, trans. T. K. Abbott (New York: Barnes and Noble, 2004), p. 233. See also Immanuel Kant, *Opus Postumum*, vol. 21, Berlin Critical Edition (Berlin: Georg Reimer, 1960), p. 12.

philosophies in his work *The Abolition of Man*.[70] In the Appendix, "Illustrations of the Tao", Lewis elucidates eight common laws that pervade most religions and many moral philosophies. Though Lewis makes no pretense about being a historian of religion or showing comprehensive or critical analysis, he suggests that the commonality of the eight laws (that may well resonate with the reader's own moral sensibility) points to a universal moral authority that binds us, as well as some general "laws" or precepts by which most people (and most religions) believe themselves to be bound:

1. The law of general beneficence
2. The law of special beneficence
3. Duties to parents, elders, ancestors
4. Duties to children and posterity
5. The law of justice
6. The law of good faith and veracity
7. The law of mercy
8. The law of magnanimity

Within these eight general laws, we find the Ten Commandments, as well as an incipient manifestation of the Golden Rule and the commandment to love one's neighbor as oneself. When we combine Lewis' eight moral laws with Newman's phenomenological assessment of "the divine voice" in conscience, we may infer that each of these precepts has the power to bind us precisely because its source is divine. Though there are many different specific interpretations of these eight general laws, the general laws themselves are common to most people and religions throughout the world and they find these laws to have an obligating or binding force. What gives these laws a virtually universal binding force? Is it simply that we can see a good consequence for ourselves and others in practicing them? Kant, Newman, and Lewis would submit that it is more than that. We sense the goodness and sacredness of the laws (as well as the evil and ignobility of their violation), which arises out of our sense of their divine author. Each general moral law carries a trace of the divine presence within

---

[70] See C. S. Lewis, *The Abolition of Man* (New York: HarperOne, 2001), Appendix, "Illustrations of the Tao".

it—a divine presence known to us through our conscience (as Newman describes it). When we consider these general laws, we sense at once their intrinsic goodness as well as the consummate goodness of their source.

Once again, we are led to the same question raised throughout this section: Can the source of our universal awareness of the binding force of these eight laws be anything other than a divine consciousness that can permeate and authoritatively bind every human being? Given the diversity and privacy of each human being, the answer would seem to require a sacred divine authoritative presence who is consummate goodness, truth, and beauty. A closer inspection of all five studies (given immediately below) will confirm this conjecture.

We may infer three conclusions from the interrelated results of the above five studies:

1. In the three studies concerned with the interior origin of the awareness of the sacred, divine reality (Otto, Eliade, and Heiler), the sense of the Divine is imbued with a sense of moral obligation—obligations pertaining to sacred worship as well as conduct with others.
2. In the two studies concerned with the interior awareness of moral obligation and precepts (Newman and Lewis), the awareness of moral obligation to specific norms is imbued with the presence of divine authority.
3. In all five studies (Otto, Eliade, Heiler, Newman, and Lewis), the sense of divine sacred presence as well as the general moral obligations (imbued with divine authority) are quite similar throughout most religions and cultures.

This coincidence is quite remarkable, because many religions in the ancient world developed independently of one another,[71] raising the question of how they could all have common characteristics concerned with the Divine, the relationship between the sacred and profane, and the general precepts of moral obligation. If these multiple commonalities did not come from some common cultural origin (such as one religion borrowing from another), where did

[71] McKenzie, *Dictionary of the Bible*, p. 754.

they come from? Given that cultures have significant differences, we might hypothesize that the commonalities originate from some common feature innate to the human psyche. It is virtually impossible to explain the multiple commonalities concerned with religious experience and moral obligation among most human beings—such as the interior sense of the mysterious, sacred, divine presence (Otto), the four characteristics of the sacred's entry into the profane world (Eliade), the seven common characteristics of religion (Heiler), and the eight common general precepts of morality (Lewis)—*unless* there is a single common source of these commonalities. Since the divine presence is intrinsic to all these commonalities, and it would require nothing short of divine power to communicate interiorly with billions of human beings throughout the world, we might infer that the common source of *both* our interior awareness of the sacred divine presence and the general precepts of morality is the divinity itself—what monotheistic religions would call "God" or "the Creator"—what Otto calls "the sacred, mysterious, overwhelmingly powerful 'wholly Other'". In brief, what these five studies imply is that a sacred, divine "wholly Other" is interiorly present to every human being communicating a sense of itself, its holiness, the way to connect with it, and the general moral precepts it asks us to observe.

If the above conjecture is correct, then the decline in religion (as we are experiencing today) will lead to a decline in objective moral norms (with the negative consequences noted above). Furthermore, inasmuch as the general moral precepts are connected with divine authority and obligation, the failure to abide by them—and the denial of them—will result in alienation from the Divine, as well as self-alienation. This alienation is experienced as profound emptiness, loneliness, and guilt. Could this lie at the foundation of the steep increase in depression, anxiety, substance abuse, suicides, and homicides among young people between 2005 and 2017?[72] Recall the six psychological studies above (particularly the study of the American Psychiatric Association) correlating *non*religious affiliation

---

[72] There was a 52 percent increase in depression/anxiety among teens (63 percent increase among young adults), a 56 percent increase in teen suicides, and a 23 percent increase in teen homicides between 2005 and 2017. See Twenge et al., "Age, Period, and Cohort Trends", pp. 185–99. Also, see Wan, "Teen Suicides Are Increasing".

with increased rates of depression, anxiety, substance abuse, familial tensions, and suicides.[73]

In addition to the above, several contemporary studies have correlated religion with increased motivation to act ethically in particular situations. The empirical study of K. Praveen Parboteeah[74] used the religious typology of Marie Cornwall[75] to confirm the findings of previous studies,[76] showing that "belief in church authority, religiosity's affective component, and the behavioral component are negatively related to individuals' willingness to justify unethical behaviors."[77] Thus, religion influences—and frequently strongly influences—people's unwillingness to be unethical. In view of these findings, the decline of religion is likely to lead to the continued decline of ethics in our culture.

If the decline in religion and objective moral norms is having such a significant negative effect on individuals and society, should we not collectively address this problem before it becomes insurmountable? If God really is the source of our interior awareness of Him, and the general moral norms imbued with His authority, then why would we let our obsession with autonomy and free expression alienate us from Him anymore than it already has? Even if we have no fear of the final judgment, wouldn't it behoove us to investigate a way out of our increasing sense of depression, anxiety, and self-alienation? If we find

[73] See the six studies correlating religious nonaffiliation and decline in emotional health given above in this section: Dervic et al., "Religious Affiliation and Suicide Attempt"; Koenig, "Research on Religion"; Bonelli et al., "Religious and Spiritual Factors"; Lassi and Mugnaini, "Role of Religion and Spirituality"; Koenig, "Religion, Spirituality, and Health"; Ronenberg et al., "Protective Effects of Religiosity".

[74] See K. Praveen Parboteeah, Martin Hoegl, and John B. Cullen, "Ethics and Religion: An Empirical Test of a Multidimensional Model", *Journal of Business Ethics* 80, no. 2 (June 1, 2008): 387–98.

[75] See Marie Cornwall et al., "The Dimensions of Religiosity: A Conceptual Model with an Empirical Test", *Review of Religious Research* 27, no. 3 (March 1986): 226–44.

[76] See Charles R. Tittle and Michael R. Welch, "Religiosity and Deviance: Toward a Contingency Theory of Constraining Effects", *Social Forces* 61, no. 3 (March 1983): 653–82; Gary R. Weaver and Bradley R. Agle, "Religiosity and Ethical Behavior in Organizations: A Symbolic Interactionist Perspective", *Academy of Management Review* 27, no. 1 (January 2002): 77–97; Jonathan H. Turner, *The Institutional Order* (New York: Addison-Wesley Educational Publishers, 1997); and Thomas J. Fararo and John Skvoretz, "Action and Institution, Network and Function: The Cybernetic Concept of Social Structure", *Sociological Forum* 1, no. 2 (March 1, 1986): 219–50.

[77] Parboteeah, Hoegl, and Cullen, "Ethics and Religion", p. 393.

that God and His moral precepts are the only way to mitigate what Mircea Eliade calls "the anxiety of modern nonreligious man",[78] would we be willing to subordinate our ego—our autonomy—to the call of that divine sacred consciousness? If Newman, Otto, and Heiler are correct, then this divine sacred consciousness is not a tyrannical ego competing with ours, but rather a good and loving father who uses his overwhelming creative power not to subjugate us, but to invite us to the fullness of goodness, love, truth, and beauty for which we yearn.[79] Are social norming, cultural conformity, and social and traditional media so strong that we will not break out of our desire for autonomy and ego-satisfaction even for the sake of our own happiness, fulfillment, preservation, and eternal salvation? If so, then an increasing number of individuals and the culture itself will find themselves caught in a downward implosive momentum, which today's social unrest incipiently betokens. However, if we can recognize the implications of the above studies and can further recognize their fulfillment in the call of Jesus Christ through His Church, then we may have a chance of collectively reversing this implosive momentum. Throughout the Church's history, the Lord has raised up generations of canonized and unheralded saints right at the moment the culture and the Church needed them most. We will further explain this call in the Conclusion to the Trilogy (found at the end of this volume).

B. The Power and Norms of Conscience and Practical Reason

In the previous section, we explored the interrelationship between religious experience and conscience giving rise to our interior conviction of the morality/goodness of God and divine authority in the general norms of conscience. This intersection of religion and morality has existed for four millennia and remains strong among more than 80 percent of the world's population.[80] Does conscience exert

---

[78] Eliade, *Sacred and Profane*, p. 211.

[79] For further explanation of this, see Volume II, Chapter 4 of the Quartet.

[80] See Conrad Hackett and David McClendon, "Christians Remain World's Largest Religious Group, but They Are Declining in Europe", Pew Research Center, April 5, 2017, https://www.pewresearch.org/fact-tank/2017/04/05/christians-remain-worlds-largest-religious-group-but-they-are-declining-in-europe/.

a strong normative influence on those who are nonreligious in the contemporary world? As we shall see, it does, and in many cases, it is imbued with a powerful spiritual and cosmic significance. We will first examine this influence in modern literature's portrayal of nonreligious characters—specifically, in Edgar Allen Poe, Theodore Dostoyevsky, and Franz Kafka. If these diverse portrayals of conscience are correct, we may infer that there is a universal natural law that is a common ground of moral norms within pluralistic societies.

These norms exert themselves so powerfully within the human psyche that their violation alienates us from ourselves and the whole cosmic order. If Aquinas, Kant, and Newman are correct, then the origin of this powerful sense of duty within the cosmic order is God. Conversely, if secularists such as Nietzsche and Freud are correct, then conscience is the result of training by parents or society to associate self-punishment with particular norms. This diversity of explanations prompts us to ask whether the portrayals of conscience in Poe, Dostoyevsky, and Kafka are best explained by theists or secularists. As we ask this question, we will want to focus on the spiritual, ultimate, and urgent dimensions of the exertions of conscience. Do these really result from mere training and associative self-punishment—or do they have a truly spiritual, ultimate, and urgent cause, such as God? In either case, the power and ultimacy of conscience is in the minds of almost everyone, which is sufficient to show that conscience and its general moral norms should be taken seriously in every area of human life, particularly when those norms are almost universally acknowledged and affirmed.

Let us proceed to three portrayals of conscience as experienced by nonreligious characters in the stories of Poe, Dostoyevsky, and Kafka. Edgar Allan Poe's short story *The Tell-Tale Heart* exemplifies the power and ultimate significance of conscience. The story's narrator decides to kill an old man who is residing in a house with him because the old man's "vulture eye" disturbs him. After killing the old man, during which he hears the old man's heart stricken with terror, the narrator dismembers his body, cleans the room, and places the body under the floorboards. When the police arrive, he is so confident about his handiwork that he invites them into the old man's room, placing their chairs on top of the floorboards under which the old man is buried. Though the police suspect nothing, the narrator begins to hear the old man's heart beating louder and louder in his mind. It becomes so horrific that he confesses his crime to the police to make it stop.

Another classic example is Fyodor Dostoyevsky's portrayal of the power of guilt—*Crime and Punishment*. The novel tells the story of Rodion Raskolnikov, who decides to kill an unprincipled pawn-broker in order to procure resources for supposedly good purposes. Like the narrator of the *Tell-Tale Heart*, he is wracked with guilt, emptiness, shame, and disgust for what he has done, which ulti-mately causes him to confess his crime to the authorities in order to be punished—the only way to overcome his more severe feelings of guilt. This theme is one of the most common in great literature, because the power and ultimacy of conscience and guilt are so great.[81]

This feeling of guilt and shame in the face of wrongdoing is fre-quently so powerful that we cannot control it. It is filled with a sense of our inauthenticity and injustice calling us "to make it right". Though we try to suppress it, it frequently persists like the *Tell-Tale Heart*. Most of the time, conscience manifests itself in much gentler ways than in the case of killers, but it nevertheless reveals that we seem to be obligated and guided by a moral force that is beyond our control.

Franz Kafka's *The Trial* illustrates the above sense of spiritual guilt within a character who is neither religiously nor morally formed. The central character, Josef K, is besieged by feelings of guilt as if he were on trial in an endless series of appeals without the possibility of ulti-mate resolution. After every conviction, he is given the opportunity to appeal, but his appeals all result in further convictions.

Joshua Still notes that K's endless appeals and retrials are the product not of an absurd legal system, but rather of his refusal to acknowledge and repent of his life of sexual license, family neglect, and preoccupation with status, which is destroying not only his family, friends, and colleagues but also himself. Though K does not consciously acknowledge either God or his sin, his interior subcon-scious awareness of both convicts him at every turn. When a priest admonishes him to stop protesting his innocence and to seek the

---

[81] See David Crossen, "Guilt Is a Recurring Theme in Literature and Drama", *New York Times Archives*, July 24, 1979, https://www.nytimes.com/1979/07/24/archives/guilt-is-a-recurring-theme-in-literature-and-drama-crediting-the.html.

source of his guilt, he does not heed the warning and finds himself being ultimately judged and executed,[82] dying "like a dog" at the end of the book.[83]

Let us return to the question asked above. Are the vignettes of Poe, Dostoyevsky, and Kafka best explained by the theistic explanation of conscience (e.g., Aquinas, Kant, and Newman), or by the secularist interpretation (e.g., Nietzsche and Freud)? Can the spiritual, ultimate, and urgent dimensions of conscience be fully explained by parental and societal training associated with self-punishment? If so, how does parental training incite spiritual and ultimate foreboding and judgment? Can parental training really fill us with a sense of dread beyond fear? Rudolf Otto indicates that dread is distinct from fear. Fear gives an adrenaline rush, increases heartrate, and boosts energy (e.g., when we see a car rushing toward us), but dread (coming from, say, a ghost story) has an uncanny, spiritual, and horrifying element that slows the heart down, turns us pale, and causes our skin to crawl.[84] Though parental training has been shown to incite fear, disappointment, and shame, it does not seem to bring these qualities to the spiritual level of dread—to the uncanny emptiness and horror of evil turned in on ourselves. Thus, it seems to fall short of the experience of Poe's narrator, Dostoyevsky's Raskolnikov, and Kafka's Josef K, as well as Oedipus, Macbeth, Lady Macbeth, and so many others.

Readers must make up their own minds, but if guilt has a spiritual quality (such as the empty and horrifying sense of spiritual evil turned in on ourselves—a dimension unexplained by merely temporal fear, disappointment, and shame), then we should take seriously the explanation of Aquinas, Kant, and Newman—that a loving divine source with whom we yearn to be in communion lies at the source not only of our guilt and shame, but also of the dread and evil we feel when we are separated from Him. If we are to avoid the ultimate futility, insanity, and tragedy of the above literary characters, it will be worthwhile to investigate the cause of this sense of spiritual or ultimate guilt, for if it truly arises out of a divine agency speaking through our

---

[82] See Joshua Stills, "How Franz Kafka's 'The Trial' Hides a Religious Narrative", *The Social Matter*, 2017.

[83] Franz Kafka, *The Trial* (Gloucestershire, Eng.: Simon and Brown, 2016), p. 231.

[84] See Otto, *Idea of the Holy*, pp. 12, 14, 19.

conscience, then acknowledging that divine agency would lead to an acknowledgment of our sinfulness, which in turn would lead to our repentance, forgiveness, and the reform of our lives.

Let us pause for a moment and shift the focus from the spiritual and ultimate significance of guilt to the question of natural law. Can the moral awareness and feelings of conscience be the ground of a natural law that applies to all human persons independent of the time, culture, and individual circumstances in which they are raised? Whether or not we acknowledge the presence of God within our conscience, the many guilt-stricken characters of literature show us that conscience is a powerful and ultimate interior convicting force, which is universal in its mandate for us to be just to our fellowman, avoid unnecessary harms, and be true to our commitments. Regardless of the culture, religion, or circumstances of our lives, we all appear to be *obligated* to live by these general moral norms. The interpretation of these general norms can vary from epic to epic and culture to culture, but the three general norms themselves appear to be invariant, universal, and infused with spiritual and ultimate significance.

The above implies that every human person is interiorly obligated to (1) avoid unnecessary harm, (2) act justly toward others, and (3) honor commitments. The application of these principles to particular situations occurs through reason (what most philosophers would call practical reason as distinct from speculative reason). Inasmuch as conscience binds every human person to act justly, avoid unnecessary harms, and be true to their commitments, and inasmuch as most individuals are capable of using reason to apply these norms to particular situations, then there is a natural law that binds every person in every culture and epic. What would happen if we ignored the interior mandate of conscience and reject religion and its moral mandates? As the above stories indicate (as well as Oedipus, Macbeth, Richard III, and Anna Karenina, among many others), there are two consequences:

1. Interior self-alienation moving toward despair (unless appeal is made to divine forgiveness)
2. An increasing detachment from morality leading to harm of others and even criminality

What might we infer from this? If any society attempts as a whole to ignore or reject both religion and conscience, we might expect a huge increase in self-destructive, harmful, and even cruel behavior—the loss of our collective human heart. It would also lead to a loss of self-motivated moral norms, opening upon a movement toward absolute autonomy of will and action. If this scenario played out to its logical conclusion, it would mean the ultimate demise of civilized society. A society without religion stands on the brink of despair and self-destruction; a society without religion *and* conscience is destined for both.

As we shall see in Section III.C, conscience (and its three natural norms) does not exhaust the range of moral principles. Indeed, they are only foundational principles (needed for ethical minimalism), but not the highest principles (giving rise to ethical maximalism). Jesus Christ uniquely addressed the idea of a "greatest commandment"—the commandment that all other commandments must serve—the commandment to love (as Jesus defined it in the Beatitudes). Conscience does not obligate us to love in this way (but only to be just, nonmaleficent, and to keep our word), and so we need the revelation of Jesus to show us the highest level of morality, dignity, and destiny. We can know the truth of Jesus' ethical maximalism by assessing where it leads—to the highest levels of respect and care for others, contribution, reconciliation, peaceful coexistence, and the common good. Notice that Jesus indicates that this self-giving love is the nature of God (His Father) as well as Himself (demonstrated in His ministry and ultimately in His complete gift of self on the Cross). As such, Christianity reveals a path to move us to the highest levels of ethical propriety—the path of true dignity, fulfillment, destiny, and purpose in life, the path of the unconditionally loving God. If readers believe that these effects of Jesus' moral teaching are worth the sacrifice, and indeed, point the way to the true meaning of life and the fulfillment of our nature, then we should take seriously Jesus' claim to be the only begotten Son of God (His Father). This brings us to our next topic.

C. The Formation of Conscience:
Religion, Christianity, and the Catholic Church

Up to this point, we have given evidence from five studies showing the likelihood that a divine sacred reality (God) is present to our consciousness (the numinous experience) and is acting through our conscience enjoining us to do good and avoid evil by adhering to certain general principles (such as the eight laws compiled by C. S. Lewis). As might be inferred from Lewis' eight laws, conscience gives us only *general* guidance—a *general* direction for doing good and avoiding evil. If we are to get additional guidance to specify these eight laws, we will have to turn to another source beyond that of conscience. What source? Inasmuch as the divine sacred reality (God) is the source of the general principles of conscience (as shown by Newman and implied by Lewis), we will want to discover how that divine reality gives specificity to those general norms. The obvious candidate is indicated by Eliade and Heiler—*revealed religion.*

Throughout the last four millennia, religion has been involved in specifying norms within each of the general principles of conscience.[85] As Eliade and Heiler imply, religion teaches specific moral norms that help believers move toward God and avoid separation from Him. Most of the time, religious norms are commensurate with the general principles of conscience, particularly the honoring of parents and prohibition of killing the innocent, adultery, stealing, defrauding, and lying. There are a few exceptions to this, the most glaring of which is human sacrifice for the purpose of pleasing divinities. Over the course of human history, human sacrifice and other exceptions to the norms of conscience were corrected by the major religions and their missionary efforts.[86] Christianity was notably active in curtailing and ending the practice of human sacrifice in Central and South America, Africa, and other places under European colonial government.[87] In most contexts, the major religions have supported the general principles of conscience and enhanced them in ways that promoted a more just and humane society.

Evidently, there are significant differences between major religions' teachings on specific moral norms. How might we decide which religion (or religions) best reflects the will of God? We may

---

[85] See Hare, "Religion and Morality".

[86] Judaism moved away from human sacrifice after the period of the Judges (1230 B.C. to 1020 B.C.), and ultimately condemned it as antithetical to divine law. Christianity condemned human sacrifice from its inception. See J. Pohle, "Sacrifice", *The Catholic Encyclopedia*, vol. 13 (New York: Robert Appleton, 1912), https://www.newadvent.org/cathen/13309a.htm.

[87] See ibid.

find a clue in Heiler's seven common characteristics of world religions. Inasmuch as these characteristics represent general *agreement* among world religions, we might infer that they point to God's universal will for humanity. The seventh common characteristic (the *highest* way to eternal bliss in the transcendent reality is through *love*) implies that love is the highest moral and salvific principle in all major religions. As such, it would seem to represent God's universal moral will for humanity. This enables us to prioritize the moral teaching of various religions. The question is, which religion has the deepest, most comprehensive, and broadly applicable doctrine of love—that is, which religion has grounded its moral teaching almost entirely in its doctrine of love?

As explained in Volume III (Chapters 1–3) of the Quartet, Christianity is unparalleled among world religions in its articulation of moral norms and methods based on the principle of charitable love taught by Jesus. The Sermon on the Mount (Mt 5–7, particularly the Beatitudes [5:1–12]), the Parable of the Good Samaritan (Lk 10:25–37), and Jesus' establishment of charitable love as the highest commandment define the heart of universal unconditional charitable love. Jesus defines the attitudes needed for love in the Beatitudes and demonstrates this love in His ministry to sinners, the sick, the spiritually deprived, and even His enemies (see Volume II, Chapter 4 of this Trilogy). He brings this demonstration of love to perfection and completion in His freely offered self-sacrificial Passion and death, which He intended as an unconditional act of love whose healing power would redeem everyone who tries to follow God according to the dictates of his conscience.[88]

This view of love transformed the world. As will be shown in Chapter 6 of this volume, Jesus taught His unique view of charitable love (*agapē*) to move human society from the Silver Rule (do no unnecessary harm) to the Golden Rule (do optimal good for your neighbor). He taught His followers to show this love to all human beings (including slaves, enemies, and criminals), asking them to go beyond justice—to mercy, compassion, and the forgiveness of others without limit. These developments gave rise in later centuries to the

---

[88] See Second Vatican Council, Dogmatic Constitution on the Church *Lumen Gentium* (November 21, 1964), no. 16. See also Volume III (Chapter 3) of the Quartet.

recognition of personhood in every human being, to the four inalienable rights of life, liberty, property, and the pursuit of happiness, and to the principles of humane social ethics manifest in the Church's social teaching (see Chapters 6–7 of this volume). These principles have transformed the world, giving rise to social equality and global systems of education, social welfare, and public health. Jesus' teaching and example inspired the Catholic Church to become the largest international healthcare, educational, and social welfare system in the world (see Chapter 6, Section I of this volume).

What might we conclude from this? First, Jesus' teaching on love not only enhanced the principle of justice and inspired the principles of inalienable rights, social welfare, and the common good, but also inspired a movement that transformed the world from the cruelties of Rome to the 1948 United Nations Universal Declaration of Human Rights.[89] Secondly, the fact that Jesus' teaching on love and its moral precepts had such a transformative effect on individual human beings, communities, society, and the world, shows that His revelation of God's will for humanity is true—indeed, truth itself. This is the proof of the pudding. Jesus' moral teaching (based on His unique articulation of charitable love) is not only the deepest and most comprehensive moral teaching in the history of religions, it also has a transformative humanitarian effect unparalleled by any other. More importantly, beyond its humanitarian effect, His teaching has the power of spiritual transformation that can lift its practitioners to the highest levels of hope and trust in God based on the unconditional love of Jesus and His Father—the unconditional love that moves not only the saints but ordinary people of faith to heroic acts of compassion and sacrifice. What deeper and more comprehensive morality could there be?

Now let us return to the subject of this section. Inasmuch as conscience reveals only general principles of morality (such as Lewis' eight laws), we need an additional source of morality to help us articulate the *specific* norms for applying these general principles in a clear and proper way. As noted above, we want to find a divine source of these moral norms commensurate with the divine sacred reality speaking through our conscience. Given what was said above about

---

[89] The UN document can be found on the website of the United Nations at https://www.un.org/en/universal-declaration-human-rights/.

the depth, comprehensiveness, individual efficacy, and societal efficacy of Jesus' moral teaching, we might infer that it comes from a divine source. This inference is confirmed by the fact that Jesus lived what He preached, indicated that He and His Father are at the heart of this unconditional love, and promised that He would give us His Spirit (so manifest in the interior and exterior charisms[90]) to help us live according to this love. Furthermore, as indicated in Volume III of the Quartet, there is considerable historical and scientifically accessible evidence for Jesus' Resurrection, miraculous power, and gift of the Holy Spirit (which enabled His disciples to work miracles in His name to this day[91]). When all of this is combined with the contemporary scientifically validated miracles connected with Jesus, the Blessed Mother, the saints, and the Holy Eucharist (see the Appendix of Volume I of this Trilogy), it becomes reasonable and responsible to believe that the moral teaching of Jesus is the fullest and most accurate manifestation of the revelation of the heart and will of the unconditionally loving God. When we combine this evidence with our interior conviction about the truth of Jesus' preaching on love, and the interior presence of His Holy Spirit within our hearts, we are transformed in the attitude of Saint Peter, who when asked by Jesus, "Will you also go away?" responded, "Lord, to whom shall we go? You have the words of eternal life; and we have believed, and have come to know, that you are the Holy One of God" (Jn 6:67–69).

[90] Paul describes the exterior charisms of the Spirit as follows: "To each is given the manifestation of the Spirit for the common good. To one is given through the Spirit the utterance of wisdom, and to another the utterance of knowledge according to the same Spirit, to another faith by the same Spirit, to another gifts of healing by the one Spirit, to another the working of miracles, to another prophecy, to another the ability to distinguish between spirits, to another various kinds of tongues, to another the interpretation of tongues. All these are inspired by one and the same Spirit, who apportions to each one individually as he wills" (1 Cor 12:7–11). The interior charisms of the Holy Spirit are *graced* love/compassion, hope, trust/faith, joy, and peace. Though all of these dispositions have a natural component, the Holy Spirit infuses them with a power and efficacy beyond our natural powers. See Volume III (Chapter 5) of the Quartet.

[91] For an extensive treatment of miracles from Jesus to today, see Craig Keener, *Miracles: The Credibility of the New Testament* (Grand Rapids, Mich.: Baker Academic Publishing, 2011). For an excellent scholarly study of the historicity of Jesus' miracles, see John P. Meier, *A Marginal Jew: Rethinking the Historical Jesus*, vol. 2, *Mentor, Message, and Miracles* (New York: Doubleday, 1994). As previously mentioned, there was a study concerned with 72 percent of physicians affirming their belief in past and present miracles; see Freeman, "Science or Miracle?"

Though Jesus' revelation is manifestly true in its humanitarian and spiritual effects, its meaning is not perfectly transparent to imperfect believers living in situations of increasing complexity. As noted in Volume II (Chapter 1) of this Trilogy, there are literally thousands of different interpretations and specifications of Jesus' moral teaching by Christian churches throughout the world. Indeed, these differences of interpretation have led to thousands of Protestant denominations in five hundred years.[92] Evidently, the meaning and applicability of Jesus' teaching (including His moral teaching) has not been perfectly clear. Moreover, the application of His moral teaching within contemporary (previously unknown) ethical situations in more highly complex societies has often been unclear.

Did Jesus anticipate that this would happen? Absolutely. As noted in Volume II, Chapter 1 of this Trilogy, Jesus foresaw possible factions and divisions; because of this, He established a highest teaching and juridical *office* (marked by the keys to the Kingdom of Heaven) that would be able to resolve disputes concerning His teaching and its application until the end of the world:

> Blessed are you, Simon Bar-Jona! For flesh and blood has not revealed this to you, but my Father who is in heaven. And I tell you, you are Peter, and on this rock I will build my church, and the gates of Hades shall not prevail against it. I will give you the keys of the kingdom of heaven, and whatever you bind on earth shall be bound in heaven, and whatever you loose on earth shall be loosed in heaven. (Mt 16:17–19)

Recall from Volume II (Chapter 1) that the above passage has several indications validating its origin in Jesus Himself:

- There are five Semitisms indicating an early Palestinian origin (uttered in the spoken language of Jesus).

---

[92] The number of Protestant denominations given by the Center for the Study of Global Christianity, Gordon-Conwell Theological Seminary (Evangelical), identifies the number as forty-seven thousand denominations, but these include denominational differences throughout various countries, implying that the number should be lower—perhaps in the low thousands. See Todd M. Johnson et al., "Christianity 2017: Five Hundred Years of Protestant Christianity", Center for the Study of Global Christianity, Gordon-Conwell Theological Seminary, 2017, https://www.gordonconwell.edu/wp-content/uploads/sites/13/2019/04/IBMR2017.pdf.

- There are four parallels between Matthew 16:17–19 and the commissioning narrative in Galatians 1 and 2 indicating Saint Paul's awareness of a narrative similar to Matthew's narrative of the commissioning of Peter. This shows the likelihood of another source of the commissioning of Peter earlier than Matthew's narrative. This means that Matthew did not author his commissioning passage. It was a tradition known to both him and Saint Paul.

- There are four unique expressions of Jesus (indicating authorship of the commissioning passage by Him) in Matthew 16:17–19:
  - The use of Abba ("my Father") as an address to God.[93] This address is typical of Jesus, but there are very few instances of this use of Abba in the whole of Jewish literature, meaning that the expression in verse 17 very likely originated with Him.
  - The emphatic *ego*.[94] This method of solemnizing a pronouncement is typical of Jesus and very rare in other Jewish biblical literature. Hence, the expression in verse 18 likely originated with Jesus.
  - Peter's change in name (from Simon to Cephas/Peter). Changing a name requires a greater authority than that possessed by parents. Jesus is the only one in Peter's company that could have formally proclaimed this in verse 18.[95]
  - The conveyance of divine authority to Peter in verse 19. The only one in Peter's company who would or could have done this is Jesus.

Recall also from Volume II (Chapter 1) of this Trilogy that the phrase "keys of the kingdom of heaven" signifies the power and authority particular to the *office* of prime minister—the highest office with the power to act on behalf of the king himself—as shown in the

---

[93] See Joachim Jeremias, *New Testament Theology* (New York: Charles Scribner's Sons, 1971), p. 65.

[94] That is, adding the pronoun "I" (*ego*) before a verb such as *lego*. In Semitic languages and Greek, the pronoun is unnecessary because it is contained in the conjugation of the verb, but as Jeremias indicates, when Jesus is making a declaration tantamount to a law or a doctrine, He adds the pronoun, i.e., "ego lego—*I* say." See ibid., pp. 252–54.

[95] See W.D. Davies and Dale C. Allison, *International Critical Commentary*, vol. 2, *Matthew 8–18* (New York: T&T Clark, 1991), pp. 626–29.

parallel passage of Isaiah 22:20–23. In this passage, the prophet Isaiah takes the keys of the office of prime minister from Shebna, and gives them to Eliakim with words of commissioning similar in form and content to Jesus' commission of Peter: "He shall open, and none shall shut; and he shall shut, and none shall open" (Is 22:22, paralleling Mt 16:19: "Whatever you bind on earth shall be bound in heaven, and whatever you loose on earth shall be loosed in heaven"). This passage is explained in greater detail in the Conclusion to the Trilogy (found in Section V of this volume). In view of this, it is likely that Jesus created an *office* of prime minister on earth to bind on behalf of Him (the King) in Heaven. Was this office meant only for Peter, or also for Peter's successors? A clue may be found in Jesus' proclamation that the "gates of Hades shall not prevail against [the Church]" (v. 18).

"Hadés" refers to "the abode of the departed spirits";[96] "the gates of hades" is an expression in the Old Testament (Job 38:17; Is 38:10; Wis 16:13) referring to "the power of death that will prevail over everything in the transitory world".[97] When Jesus used the phrase "the gates of Hades shall not prevail against it", His listeners understood Him to say that the Church (built on the foundation of Peter, the rock) was not subject to death and corruption—that is, the Church has an enduring, indeed, eternal, quality. When this promise is combined with the fact that Jesus said He did not know the time of the end of the world (Mk 13:32), indicating that He was open to the *possibility* that the Church could last for many generations after Peter, the question arises, why would He not intend that the supreme office (necessary to prevent factions in the Church) be held by Peter's successors? It is unfathomable that He would have either implicitly or explicitly restricted this office to only one holder when the problem of disputes and factions would evidently persist until the end of the world.

Inasmuch as Jesus did initiate such a supreme office of teaching and juridical authority applicable to Peter and his successors, we may properly infer that Jesus intended the Catholic Church (acting under

---

[96] *Strong's Concordance*, s.v. "86: hades", BibleHub.com, 2021, https://biblehub.com/greek/86.htm.

[97] See Charles John Ellicott, "Matthew 16:18: Ellicott's Commentary for English Readers", 2021, https://biblehub.com/commentaries/matthew/16-18.htm.

the authority of the holder of that supreme office) to be the definitive interpreter of Jesus' doctrine and moral teaching as well as the definitive authority to apply that moral teaching to new ethical contexts and situations. This was the view of first- and second-century popes and bishops (as explained in Section V of the Conclusion to the Trilogy, found in this volume). In light of the above, it is reasonable and responsible to believe that the objective moral norms taught by Jesus and interpreted by the Catholic Church are the highest revelation of God Himself to form our conscience—that is, to specify the general norms given by Him within our conscience.

If the moral norms of the Catholic Church really do represent the highest revelation of God through Jesus, then we should expect that the violation of those norms in the last six decades would produce the multifold negative effects on individuals, marriages, and culture shown in the studies and statistics presented in Chapters 1–4. As shown in those chapters, the abandonment of those norms has led to significant increases in depression, anxiety, substance abuse, homicides, and suicides, as well as instability and dissatisfaction with marriage and family and concomitant increases in sexual crime, social unrest, and cultural division. This implies that we need—desperately need—to return to those moral norms before we undermine Western culture and significantly increase internal strife. Too dire a prediction? In his historical classic *Religion and the Rise of Western Culture*, Christopher Dawson shows how Christianity and Catholicism are embedded in the historical-cultural fabric of the West, and "can never be entirely undone except by the total negation and destruction of Western man himself."[98]

D. The Separation of Religion and Morality in the Post-Enlightenment Era

The reader may by now be wondering about the third source of moral norms—cultural traditions. As noted above, for about four millennia, religion and morality were inextricably interrelated and

---

[98] Christopher Dawson, *Religion and the Rise of Western Culture: The Classic Study of Medieval Civilization* (New York: Double Day/Image, 1991), p. 224.

associated with cultural tradition.[99] Religion revealed the divine will for good moral conduct, which infused morality with objectivity and divine authority. These two powerful interrelated influences form the foundation of culture—the communal sense of virtue, vice, sacredness, dignity, destiny, purpose in life, and fulfillment. There are many influences on culture, but religion and conscience are by far the most basic and influential—the superstructure upon which hang rational reflection, migratory and social customs, the opinions of influential people, and other influences. In sum, we might say that for nearly four millennia, the moral traditions of culture were almost indistinguishable from norms of religion and conscience.

This unity of normative sources changed drastically in the Enlightenment era when religion was questioned (and undermined) and conscience was reduced to social conditioning. The Enlightenment era may be generally defined from the time of René Descartes (1636 to the conclusion of the French Revolution, 1789). Though some Enlightenment thinkers were religious, most were deists who believed that God and morality could be known through reason without making recourse to revealed religion. Most deists hold that God does not providentially interact with human beings and deny the possibility of miracles and special divine revelation. As a consequence, deistic Enlightenment thinkers separated ethics from religion and its formation of conscience. For this reason, philosophers in the post-Enlightenment era searched for ways to ground ethics in either rational reflection on harms-benefits analysis (utilitarianism and other forms of consequentialism), or intuitions and feelings of right and wrong (situational emotivism). Though the history of philosophical ethics is much more complex than this, we might say the effect of Enlightenment thinking was to detach morality from religion, while reducing conscience to psychological or social conditioning. This trend found its apex in the nineteenth century in Freud's *Future of an Illusion*, Friedrich Nietzsche's *Beyond Good and Evil*, and Karl Marx's *Communist Manifesto*.

Since the eighteenth century, political philosophy, psychology, natural anthropology, and natural science became increasingly secularized (though many scientists, psychologists, political theorists,

---

[99] See Hare, "Religion and Morality".

and anthropologists maintained faith, which continues to this day[100]). These secularized disciplines began to have a progressively greater influence on culture—first in the West and gradually throughout the non-Western world. These new cultural nonreligious moral norms were often grounded in political ideologies that turned to a secular interpretation of science, psychology, and anthropology for justification. As these political secular ideologies became more materialistic, so did the implicit and explicit norms they professed. This materialistic, sociopolitical trend spawned extreme movements, such as secular nationalism, Fascism, Marxism-Communism, and Maoism, which not only abandoned the idea of objective moral norms, but ran contrary to the two most fundamental principles of the natural law: nonmaleficence and justice. The crises of World War I and World War II brought a temporary return to objective moral norms and religion, but secular cultural norms had become a reality in competition with religion, and frequently with conscience and the natural law.

In the 1960s, the West went through yet another metamorphosis— inspired by educators professing autonomous freedom, sexual liberation, and rejection of tradition. These three new interrelated foundations of progressive culture had considerable influence on public morality and opened the door to the phenomenon of social norming. In Chapter 1 of this volume, we discussed the effects of social norming on sexual ethics, marriage and family, and social cohesion. Recall that when religion-based and conscience-based moral norms are weak, social norming grows in influence. In the absence of other sources of moral norms, people orient themselves toward what they *perceive* the mainstream to be. So long as they *believe* they are in the "mainstream", they alleviate tension within their conscience, believing themselves

[100]The Pew Research Center survey of the American Association for the Advancement of Science (one of the largest scientific organizations in the world) found that 51 percent of scientists profess belief in God or a spiritual reality, while 41 percent are agnostics or atheists. See Pew Research Center, "Religion and Science in the United States: Scientists and Belief", November 5, 2009, https://www.pewforum.org/2009/11/05/scientists-and-belief/. Physicians have an even higher rate of religious belief. In a National Institute of Health random survey of 1,144 physicians, 88 percent indicated they were affiliated with a religion, while only 10 percent had no religious affiliation. See National Center for Biotechnology Information (National Institute for Health), "Physicians' Observations and Interpretations of the Influence of Religion and Spirituality on Health", 2010, https://www.ncbi.nlm.nih.gov/pmc/articles/PMC2867458/. Sixty-seven percent of those religiously affiliated physicians reported having moderate to high religiosity. See ibid.

morally upright. As noted earlier, in the absence of religion and conscience, what becomes socially normative eventually becomes moral. The effects of this phenomenon in the United States and Western Europe are detailed throughout Chapters 1–4—a significant increase in rape, sexual harassment, premarital and extramarital sex, the homosexual lifestyle, abortion, substance abuse, depression, anxiety, antisocial aggressivity, incidents of major psychiatric disorders, homicides, suicides, destabilization of marriage and family, and social unrest. From any perspective, this is not a good result. The decline of religion and objective moral norms in Western society lies at the root of this self-destructive scenario so presciently foreseen by Aleksandr Solzhenitsyn (the Nobel Prize–winning Soviet dissident who challenged the Marxist state and exposed the Soviet Gulag) in his commencement speech at Harvard University in 1978:

Destructive and irresponsible freedom has been granted boundless space. Society appears to have little defense against the abyss of human decadence, such as, for example, misuse of liberty for moral violence against young people, such as motion pictures full of pornography, crime, and horror.... Such a tilt of freedom in the direction of evil has come about gradually, but it was evidently born primarily out of a humanistic and benevolent concept according to which there is no evil inherent to human nature. The world belongs to mankind and all the defects of life are caused by wrong social systems, which must be corrected.... But the fight for our planet, physical and spiritual, a fight of cosmic proportions, is not a vague matter of the future; it has already started. The forces of Evil have begun their offensive; you can feel their pressure, and yet your screens and publications are full of prescribed smiles and raised glasses. What is the joy about? ... [The mistaken logic of today's Western thinking comes from a view that] was first born during the Renaissance and found its political expression from the period of the Enlightenment. It became the basis for government and social science and could be defined as rationalistic humanism or humanistic autonomy: the proclaimed and enforced autonomy of man from any higher force above him. It could also be called anthropocentricity, with man seen as the center of everything that exists.... This new [autonomous materialistic] way of thinking, which had imposed on us its guidance, did not admit the existence of intrinsic evil in man nor did it see any higher task than the attainment of happiness on earth.... Is it true that man is above everything?

Is there no Superior Spirit above him? Is it right that man's life and society's activities have to be determined by material expansion in the first place? Is it permissible to promote such expansion to the detriment of our spiritual integrity? If the world has not come to its end, it has approached a major turn in history, equal in importance to the turn from the Middle Ages to the Renaissance.... This ascension will be similar to climbing onto the next anthropologic stage. No one on earth has any other way left but—upward.

After reviewing the studies and statistics cited in Chapters 1–4, can anyone doubt that Solzhenitsyn's appraisal of the future of culture without religion and moral norms is coming to an unmitigated fruition? If we are to escape the clutches of what he rightfully acknowledges as the "forces of evil", we will have to "ascend upward", which means rediscovering the religious and moral components of human nature, and bringing them to the forefront of our culture and society.

IV. Conclusion

This chapter may at first have seemed a mixture or even a hodgepodge of three topics—honesty (the prohibition of stealing, lying, cheating, and dishonoring parents), charity (in action as well as belief), and following the objective moral norms taught by the Catholic Church. Yet, as now may be clear, these three themes are wholly interrelated in the human heart. The intention toward honesty and the practice of charitable love free us to surrender to the Lord of unconditional, unselfish, self-sacrificial compassionate love. God's truth is not simply a matter of probative rational and empirical evidence, but above all, a matter of the truth of the heart—a truth that is captured through prayer, the formation of conscience, the practice of charity, and participation in the Church founded by Christ. We might exclaim, "All of this is too much to remember—I can't keep it all in my head!" The Lord does not ask us to keep it all in our heads, but rather to be open to the inspiration of the Holy Spirit, who will remind us of everything we need to know in our hearts. Judging from my life, the Holy Spirit will do this precisely as Jesus proclaimed.

Chapter Six

How Christ and the Catholic Church Transformed the World: Institutions of Charity and Principles of Social Ethics

Introduction

Up to this point, we have been discussing mostly personal morality, and now we will move into another area of ethics in which the Catholic Church has been involved since its inception: sociopolitical ethics, which is concerned with justice, rights, and the common good. As we shall see, Jesus and the Catholic Church are in many respects responsible for the gigantic developmental leaps in this area which led from the elitism of Greece and Rome and the barbarity of the coliseum to the sociopolitical and socioeconomic principles and structures most cultures enjoy today. To be sure, brilliant seminal contributions to justice theory were made by Plato,[1] Aristotle,[2] and

---

[1] In the *Republic* (Books 1–6), Plato lays the groundwork for viewing justice as a virtue (a guiding habit) that implicitly links justice to keeping one's word and avoiding excess. He does not yet reach the Justinian universal standard of "giving each person his due" (*Institutes* 1,1), but lays the foundation for it. He moves between justice as a personal virtue and justice as a guiding principle of the polity (city-state). He concludes by paralleling justice in the soul and justice in the polity. Just as there are three parts of the soul (reason, "spirited", and appetitive) so also there are three corresponding parts of the state (the guardians, the enforcers, and the merchants). If each part of the soul does what it is supposed to do (without being slothful or interfering with the other parts) and each part of the state does what it's supposed to do, justice will eventually occur in both the individual and the polity. Though this is an improvement upon the position of the materialists and sophists, it is incomplete in many respects and awaits developments from Aristotle, Cicero, and Christianity.

[2] Like Plato, Aristotle is concerned with justice in both the individual and polity, but limits his concept of it to a character virtue in both areas. In Book 5 of the *Nicomachean Ethics*,

Cicero,[3] but they were mitigated in many respects by social classism (man versus woman and free versus slave), an absence of universal standards (conditioned by merit), and subservience to the positive law and social structures. These undeveloped areas of justice theory allowed Plato's "guardian state" to take children away from their parents (to be raised by the state),[4] and the justification of gender exclusion and slavery, as well as the cruelties visited upon conquered foreigners, unproductive slaves, and religious dissidents (such as Christians). Shortly after Cicero, a light came into the world, and along with it, a persecuted Church that gradually transformed world

---

he associates character virtue with achieving the mean between vices of excess and vices of defect. He distinguishes between the general and the particular application of justice, in which the former seeks to avoid the vices of lying (deceiving) and refusing to honor one's agreements and obligations, and the latter seeks to avoid the excesses of giving too much or too little than a person deserves for his work. He determines this mean by appealing to comparative proportionality, indicating that those who are more talented and work hardest deserve more than those with proportionately less talent or effort. Though Aristotle makes many contributions to the development of justice theory, his idea of justice does not move to a universal standard for all human persons, and rests upon merit and social class (e.g., man versus woman, free versus slave) awaiting developments from Christianity to provide the basis for a universal standard (natural law) and inalienable rights.

[3] Markus Tullius Cicero (106–43 B.C.) came closer than any other pre-Christian philosopher to formulating a natural law universal standard in his works *The Republic* and *On the Laws*. As a stoic, Cicero believed that all manifestations of particular natures arose out of a divine-like totality, and he surmised that this "divine spark" would be most evidently present in the highest reason of mankind. In Book 3 of *The Republic*, he asserts that there is a "true law" (a universal law that applies to all people and things) that can be known by "right reason" (prudence), the acknowledgment of which differentiates good from wicked people. In Book 1 of *On the Laws*, he implies that the origin of this "right reason" lies in a divine presence pervading the whole cosmos. This sense of universal standard present to "right reason" is a foreshadowing of Saint Paul's view of conscience in Romans 2:14–15 (see below Section II.A), with the notable exception that Paul's view is grounded in a personal God who is both just and loving, while Cicero's view is based on the intrinsic rightness within the cosmic order. Cicero influenced Saint Ambrose and Saint Augustine, and the latter rewrote Cicero's insights within a Christian framework that became the foundation of a fully developed natural law theory (particularly in Saint Thomas Aquinas) and natural rights theory (particularly in Father Francisco Suarez). Through these philosopher-theologians, Christianity's influence transformed Cicero's insight into the universal standard that became the ground of John Locke's and our Founding Fathers' view of inalienable rights (see below Section II.D).

[4] In Book 5 (449a–472a), Plato proposes that all spouses live in common and that sexual intercourse take place only in festivals, at which point they are spouses only during the time of intercourse. All the children are taken away from their mothers and are raised by a group of guardians who will provide the best education for the good of the state.

culture through the teaching and example of Jesus and the blood of the martyrs.

Christian social ethics had from its inception one overarching objective: to make a better world for every person. The originator of Christian social ethics is none other than Jesus, and without Him the world would be a very different place—not for the better. Since His remarkable contribution to personal and social ethics, the world has been transformed in public healthcare, welfare, education, and social equality (see below Section I). In addition to this, Christian philosophers and theologians devoted themselves to showing how Jesus' teaching could be applied to society and the common good. They knew that applying Christian teaching to these social contexts would influence populations beyond the Christian world. In order to provide broader justification of social ethics (for non-Christians), they grounded their theory of justice and the common good on principles of natural law accessible to reason (without recourse to revelation). As we shall see, this effort began with Saint Paul and was brought to a new level of sociopolitical applicability by Saint Augustine, and then expanded by Saint Thomas Aquinas, Father Bartolomé de las Casas, Father Francisco Suarez, Hugo Grotius, and John Locke. This gave rise to five fundamental principles of justice that hold the key to resolving problems in the area of justice and rights (see below Section III). Later, these political principles were complemented with socioeconomic principles by Pope Leo XIII after the terrible abuses of the Industrial Revolution. His encyclical *Rerum Novarum* (1891) gave rise to what is now called Catholic social teaching (see Chapter 7 of this volume).

We will examine and explain this rich tradition of social ethics and its sociopolitical and socioeconomic application in three parts:

1. The Effect of Jesus on World Culture and Social Institutions (Section I)
2. The Sources of Christian Social Ethics: Jesus, Saint Paul, Saint Augustine, Saint Thomas Aquinas, and Father Francisco Suarez (Section II)
3. A Summary of the Five Fundamental Principles of Justice (Section III)

I. The Effect of Jesus on World Culture and Social Institutions

Jesus' teaching on love changed the course of world history. Its socio-political benefits were so vast in the West that they spread to the farthest parts of the globe—not only through the missionaries but through international political organizations, international courts, and non-governmental organizations.

Jesus' distinctive teaching on the love of God and neighbor had five profound sociopolitical effects that will be taken up in the following four subsections:

1. Jesus' distinctive teaching on love (Section I.A)
2. The ideal of social equality and the diminution of slavery in the ancient world (Section I.B).
3. The rise of public healthcare, hospitals, and welfare (Section I.C)
4. The rise of public education (Section I.D)

If these developments had not taken root and proliferated throughout Western and global culture, we would live in a world with vastly more social inequalities, and vastly less healthcare, social welfare, education, justice, and civil rights. There were of course other causes of this positive social momentum besides Christ's teaching on love, and its main proponent—the Catholic Church—but without these two mainstays, the other influences would have had considerably less foundation on which to build. The source of this momentum is captured in Saint Paul's prayer for the Christian Church:

> That you, being rooted and grounded in love, may have power to comprehend with all the saints what is the breadth and length and height and depth, and to know the love of Christ which surpasses knowledge, that you may be filled with all the fullness of God. (Eph 3:17–19)

There is of course a danger in writing about this positive social momentum—namely, that there have been (and are) many Christians (including clergy) who have not lived up to, and even undermined,

Jesus' teaching on love, because of cowardice, lack of resolve, self-ishness, narcissism, and every other form of the eight deadly sins. I certainly view myself as an imperfect Christian, but Christ's call to love and the grace given by the Holy Spirit through the Church have helped in my transition from the "old self" to the "new self" (see Col 3:9–10).

Though there are failures among some leaders and members in the Church, it is best to judge the Church by her thousands of saints rather than her serious sinners, so that we will not underestimate or under-mine the transformative power Jesus bestows on us and the world through that Church. The light of Jesus working through Scripture, Church teaching, the sacraments, moral conversion, and charitable service is the hope of a better future in this world as well as eternal salvation in the next. Jesus tells us, "I am the light of the world" (Jn 8:12; 9:5; cf. 12:35), and if we look for this Light, find inspiration in it, and try to put it into practice—however imperfectly—we too can join the Church's saints in bringing light into our cultural darkness.

A. The Sociopolitical Implications of Jesus' Teaching on Love

Three aspects of Jesus' teaching on love are quite distinct if not unique in the history of religions:

1. God is not only loving; He is *unconditionally* loving (like the father of the prodigal son whom Jesus addresses as "Abba").
2. Love is the highest commandment, which summarizes all com-mandments and virtues.
3. Love of God and love of neighbor are inseparable and complementary.

Jesus places this distinctive teaching on love at the heart of His gospel message, and further teaches that it must begin with an interior transformation that allows us spontaneously to feel compassion for those in need—and indeed for everyone (like the good Samaritan) This interior transformation will naturally manifest itself in exterior actions that Jesus describes throughout His preaching.

Jesus then shows how these interior attitudes should manifest themselves in exterior actions: love of enemies; prayer for those who hate us; turning the other cheek; forgiving one another seventy times seven times (an innumerable number of times); having mercy on the marginalized, ignored, and displaced; and loving sinners and even criminals. Jesus says that these actions represent the heart and perfection of His Father.

Jesus extends His teaching on love into the domain of ethics in three other distinctive ways:

1. The Golden Rule and ethical maximalism (Section I.A.1)
2. The intrinsic *transcendent* dignity of *every* human person (Section I.A.2)
3. The valuation of each individual person over the law itself (Section I.A.3)

These social ethical dimensions of Jesus' teaching on love enabled the Christian Church to be the agent of considerable social reform, which ultimately resulted in such social and legal doctrines as the intrinsic dignity of all human persons, universal inalienable rights, social altruism, and the prioritization of justice and human dignity over the positive law and the power of the state (see below Section II).

1. The Golden Rule and Ethical Maximalism

Though many contemporary thinkers use the phrase of the Golden Rule to refer to any doctrine of ethical reciprocity, I am using it here in the restricted sense proposed by Jesus—namely, "Do the good for others that you would want done for you." This view must be sharply distinguished from the Silver Rule, which emphasizes only the avoidance of harm ("Do not do unto others what you would not have them do unto you"—that is, "Avoid harms to others that you do not want done to you"). The Golden Rule should also be distinguished from reciprocity doctrines that are essentially reprisal, such as the *lex talionis* ("an eye for an eye and a tooth for a tooth"), and from reciprocity doctrines that are essentially ethical pragmatism—"Do the good for others, so that others will do good back to you."

As far as I can determine, non-Christian religions do not have an explicit and central teaching of the Golden Rule in the maximalistic sense mentioned above. They emphasize the negative or pragmatic reciprocity doctrines—namely, the Silver Rule, the *lex talionis*, and ethical pragmatism.[5] Most religions emphasize the Silver Rule (*lex talionis* and pragmatic reciprocity continue to be influential in some modern religions). The Silver Rule is mentioned explicitly in the Old Testament two times (Tob 4:15; Sir 31:15). It can be roughly translated as, "Do not do a harm to others that you do not want done to you." This is generally termed "ethical minimalism" because it places the emphasis on avoiding harm rather than on doing good.

When Jesus removed the "nots" from the Silver Rule, He converted it from "ethical minimalism" to "ethical maximalism". The emphasis is no longer on merely avoiding harm, but also on doing good (beyond the avoidance of harm)—indeed, doing every good to another that you would want done to you. There is really no limit to these goods, and so the Golden Rule might be viewed as "open-ended altruism".

Jesus not only emphasized the Golden Rule, but also made it *central* to His ethical doctrine. He superseded the Silver Rule and rejected the *lex talionis*:

> You have heard that it was said, "An eye for an eye and a tooth for a tooth." But I tell you, Do not resist one who is evil. But if any one strikes you on the right cheek, turn to him the other also. (Mt 5:38–39; Jesus was quoting Ex 21:24)

Jesus' positive ethical maximalism has its origins in His doctrine on love. He asks us to imitate the Father's love of enemies (Mt 5:44–48), to forgive everyone from the heart (6:12), not to judge others negatively (7:1–5), to consider *everyone* our neighbor—worthy of compassionate love (like the Good Samaritan [Lk 10:25–37]). When we look at these teachings collectively, we can see Jesus' underlying viewpoint that love, mercy, and compassion are higher than justice (which is derived from the Silver Rule). Love and mercy (from which the

---

[5] See W. A. Spooner, "The Golden Rule", in *Encyclopedia of Religion and Ethics*, ed. James Hastings (New York: Bloomsbury T&T Clark, 2000), 6:310–12. There is one possible exception to this: in the Indian epic *Mahābhārata Shānti-Parva* 167:9, which says, "Hence (keeping these in mind), by self-control and by making dharma (right conduct) your main focus, treat others as you treat yourself." This positive phrasing is not central to either the epic or the ethical doctrines of ancient India that emphasize the Silver Rule and ethical pragmatism.

Golden Rule is derived) go beyond justice (the Silver Rule), and encourage a positive, altruistic, and compassionate social order. This emphasis had a profound effect on the development of sociopolitical theory in the West, particularly with respect to the development of universal public healthcare and welfare (Section I.C) and universal public education (Section I.D), and on the development of inalienable rights and social responsibility (Sections II through III). The influence of these doctrines spread to the rest of the world in the fifteenth century as exploration and migration expanded.

2. The Intrinsic Transcendent Dignity of All Human Persons

Another distinctive extension of Jesus' teaching on love is the intrinsic *transcendent* dignity of *every* human person—particularly the lowliest and most challenged. Jesus establishes this principle by identifying every human person with Himself—indicating that He not only is present to every human person, but imparts His own divine dignity upon each person:

> Truly, I say to you, as you did it to one of the least of these my brethren, you did it to me.... Truly, I say to you, as you did it not to one of the least of these, you did it not to me. (Mt 25:40, 45)

Though there is precedent for the idea of divine dignity in human beings in the Hebrew Scriptures (particularly Genesis 1:26—"Let us make man in our image, after our likeness"), this is truly an extraordinary teaching, because Jesus elevates the *ontological* teaching in Genesis to a *moral and ethical imperative*. He accomplishes this by combining the ethical dimension of "treating others justly and compassionately" with the ontological dimension of our sharing in His divine status. Thus, He is not only saying that human beings have a quasi-divine status (created in the image and likeness of God), but also that to mistreat a human being is the same as mistreating Him (the divine Son).

Three aspects of this ethical doctrine had a profound effect on social-political theory. First, *every* human being has a divine-like status in virtue of being created in God's image and being adopted by Jesus. This lies at the foundation of the doctrine of social equality

(Section I.B) and the doctrine of universal inalienable natural rights (Sections II.D and III). Secondly, since human beings have this divine-like dignity from God, they are not given it by any human authority. Thus, our dignity is *intrinsic*—that is, it belongs to us in virtue of our creation by God and adoption by Jesus. We can see the effects of this principle in the Declaration of Independence: "[All people] are endowed by their *Creator* with certain unalienable Rights, that among these are Life, Liberty and the pursuit of Happiness."[6] Thirdly, no human authority (such as a state or court) can remove, negate, or abuse that intrinsic divine-like dignity without having a just cause for doing so (such as self-defense). Negating anyone's intrinsic dignity is tantamount to human authority suppressing divine authority.

As will be seen below, this doctrine of universal intrinsic transcendent dignity will have several major effects: the end of the coliseum's atrocities, the end of slavery in the Roman world, the end of slavery of Indians and Blacks in the New World (see below Section I.B), and the development of the doctrines of social equality and inalienable rights (Sections II through III).

3. Individual Dignity and the Law

One of the more radical passages in Jesus' teaching occurs in Mark 2:23–28, which tells of Jesus' disciples plucking grain on the Sabbath, inciting the Pharisees to ask Jesus, "Why are they doing what is not lawful on the sabbath?" (v. 24). The Pharisees believe they have caught Jesus in the violation of *God's* law, because they assume that the Sabbath law is virtually absolute, and that it cannot be compromised for any reason.

Jesus contradicts their interpretation of the law by implying that God wants compassion to be exercised along with obedience to the law, and if need be, to supersede strict observance of the law to prevent serious harm. He tells them about King David's violation of the law (eating the bread reserved for the priests) to assuage the extreme hunger of his men. He then comes out with a statement that will

---

[6] From a transcription of the Declaration of Independence on the website of the National Archives, last reviewed on October 7, 2021 (italics added), https://www.archives.gov /founding-docs/declaration-transcript.

shake the foundations of state authority for centuries: "The sabbath was made for man, not man for the sabbath" (Mk 2:27).

The Sabbath here represents the law (Torah) itself. This implies that the law was created not as a higher reality independent of human persons, but rather as a subordinate reality for the good of human persons. The law has no purpose apart from the people it is intended to serve. This means that the law cannot be an absolute above the humane treatment of human persons, and that the needs of individuals can create legitimate exceptions to the practice of the law. This is precisely why David had the right to feed his men bread reserved for the priests (a violation of the law).

This idea of valuing individuals above the law is so disturbing to the Pharisees that Jesus needs to justify it beyond making an appeal to David's actions. He makes the extraordinary claim that "the Son of man [Jesus] is lord even of the sabbath [the law]" (2:28). The Pharisees may not have been clear on what Jesus meant by this, but many of them were familiar with Daniel 7:13–14, in which the eschatological Son of Man would descend from Heaven on the clouds with His angels and be given divine authority and judgment for all time:

> I saw in the night visions, and behold, with the clouds of heaven there came one like a son of man, and he came to the Ancient of Days and was presented before him. And to him was given dominion and glory and kingdom, that all peoples, nations, and languages should serve him; his dominion is an everlasting dominion, which shall not pass away, and his kingdom one that shall not be destroyed.

The Pharisees may have recognized Jesus' reference to the "son of man" in Daniel but may not have been certain that He was using this title to refer to Himself. Nevertheless, His disciples believed (after His Resurrection) that He had made this utterance with divine authority (like that given to the Son of Man). As a consequence, they initiated the Christian doctrine that the law was not absolute, was not higher than human persons, was made for human persons, and could have legitimate exceptions when humane necessity required it.

This doctrine had a significant impact on the course of history, especially with respect to the elimination of slavery in the Ancient and New Worlds, the development of the doctrine of social equality

(Section I.B), and the development of the doctrine of inalienable rights (Sections II.D and III).

Jesus' ethical imperative that equates the treatment of each individual with the treatment of Himself, and the social-political imperative that individual dignity can supersede the law when humane treatment requires it, is quite distinctive in the history of religions. Once again, it emanates from Jesus' teaching about the unconditional love of God; for if God loves us unconditionally, then each of us must be *unconditionally lovable*, implying a supreme dignity and value. Immanuel Kant later described this supreme value in his categorical imperative that each human being must be treated as an end in himself.[7]

Jesus' teaching on the unconditional love of God changed the social fabric of the world with an incredible momentum. Prior to Constantine's Edict of Toleration toward Christianity (313), the rapidly growing Christian community had already begun a vigorous process of humanizing the harsh, unequal, stoic culture of the Roman Empire. This process began in the Christian community itself, but soon spread into the wider culture. This occurred in three major areas:

1. The equality of all people and concomitant diminishment of slavery (Section I.B)
2. The initiation of social welfare programs from hospitals and healthcare to care for widows and the poor (Section I.C)
3. Education of community members and the public (Section I.D)

When Constantine legalized Christianity, he incorporated many of its institutions into the Roman civil and social structure. Though these humanizing factors waxed and waned during the barbarian conflicts with Rome and their subsequent conquest of it, Christian social institutions made their way back into the social and cultural fabric through the monasteries. We may now turn to each of the three Christian social transformations of Rome and the new culture of the Early Middle Ages.

---

[7] Immanuel Kant, *Grounding for the Metaphysics of Morals*, 3rd ed., trans. James W. Ellington (Indianapolis, Ind.: Hackett Publishing, 1993), p. 36.

B. The Christian Impact on Social Equality and Slavery

The Roman Empire exemplified social values that in many ways opposed those of Christianity. Rome embraced the hierarchical social view that accorded peerage to the top rungs of society and almost nothing to the bottom ones. The very bottom rung, of course, were slaves, which constituted about 40 percent[8] of the Roman population and were oppressed in many ways—including abuses in the Roman colosseum.[9]

Almost immediately after the arrival of Saints Peter and Paul in Rome, the Christian resocialization of the empire began. Jesus' teaching about the unconditional love of God (e.g., the father of the prodigal son), His teaching to imitate Him and the Father in compassion (e.g., the Good Samaritan), and His identification of Himself with every person, most especially the poor, forms the basis for Saint Paul's proclamation of social equality within the Christian community:

> For in Christ Jesus you are all sons of God, through faith. For as many of you as were baptized into Christ have put on Christ. There is neither Jew nor Gentile, there is neither slave nor free, there is neither male nor female; for you are all one in Christ Jesus. (Gal 3:26–28)

For Paul, being baptized into Christ is to receive the highest attainable status—"sons of God" who "put on Christ". This means that all Christians have equal status, which Paul makes explicit, by saying that there are no class distinctions (such as slave or free person), ethnic distinctions (such as Jew or Greek), or gender distinctions (male or female). This radical notion of equality is made customary within Christian communities by the leaders of the Christian Church. This teaching moved into the larger culture, which initiated

---

[8] See Walter Scheidel, "Human Mobility in Roman Italy, II: The Slave Population", *Journal of Roman Studies* 95 (2005): 64–79. Scheidel estimated that there were between 1 and 1.5 million slaves in the first century B.C. (p. 170).

[9] It is estimated that four hundred thousand-plus people died in the coliseum, most of whom were slaves, gladiators, and enemies of the state, such as Christians. It was one of the most bloody and barbaric displays of cultural decadence in the West. See Kate Zusmann, "How Many People and Animals Died in the Colosseum?", Rome.Us, 2022, https://rome.us/ask-us/how-many-people-and-animals-died-in-the-colosseum.html.

a transformation of the Roman social hierarchy by giving the lowest rungs social status, education, and the essentials of life and health. According to Koester:

> This is a sociological formula that defines a new community. Here is a community that invites you, which makes you an equal with all other members of that community which does not give you any disadvantages. On the contrary, it gives even the lowliest slave personal dignity and status. Moreover, the commandment of love is decisive. That is, the care for each other becomes very important. People are taken out of isolation. If they are hungry, they know where to go. If they are sick, there is an elder who will lay hands on them to heal them.[10]

Some historians have questioned Christianity's commitment to the elimination of slavery because of Paul's Letter to Philemon, in which Paul sends Philemon's slave, Onesimus, back to Philemon. This has apparently provoked the question of why Paul would do this if he were against slavery. In brief, Paul very probably was not in favor of slavery. Indeed, the Letter to Philemon reveals that he held precisely the opposite view. However, he was not in a position to take on the institution of slavery while sitting in a Roman prison.

Instead, Paul takes an indirect approach by showing Philemon that Onesimus has the same dignity as both Paul and Philemon before Jesus (they are both children of God and brothers in the Lord). On this basis, Paul calls Onesimus his "child" and asks Philemon to treat Onesimus accordingly (v. 10). He heightens the sense of Onesimus' dignity by referring to him as his "heart" (v. 12), indicating not only the love of a son, but the love of a peer. Paul continues building his case by shifting the focus from him (Paul) to Philemon, indicating that he is sending Onesimus back as a *brother* (equal) to Philemon— "[You have him back] *no longer as a slave* but more than a slave, as a beloved brother" (v. 16; italics added). Finally, Paul tells Philemon to treat Onesimus as if he were Paul himself: "So if you consider me your partner, receive him as you would receive me" (v. 17).

---

[10]Helmut Koester, "The Great Appeal: What Did Christianity Offer Its Believers That Made It Worth Social Estrangement, Hostility from Neighbors, and Possible Persecution?", Frontline, WGBH Educational Foundation, April 1998, pbs.org/wgbh/pages/frontline/shows /religion/why/appeal.html. See also Helmut Koester with James M. Robinson, *Trajectories through Early Christianity* (Philadelphia: Fortress, 1971; repr., Eugene, Ore.: Wipf & Stock, 2006).

Paul's argument to Philemon can scarcely be considered an endorsement of slavery. Rather, it is a strong testimony to the intrinsic transcendent dignity of Onesimus—stated precisely as Jesus taught it. As Christians taught this doctrine (that every slave has the dignity of sons, brothers, and even Saint Paul and Jesus Himself) within their communities, it gave every slave a sense of immense dignity that would inevitably be communicated not only to other slaves, but also to their masters.

As Christianity spread throughout the empire, its view of social equality and mutual care began to seep outside of the Christian community into the larger culture. This had several long-term effects: the significant diminishment of slavery, the end of massacres in the colosseum,[11] social equality within the family, and the initiation of a public welfare system (see below).

The Middle Ages were initiated by the invasion and conquest of the barbarians, which had the effect of bringing non-Roman and non-Christian social and cultural views to Europe. This meant that the Church and the Christian community had to restart its program of social equality and social welfare. The fall of the Roman Empire left Europe without a fundamental unifying power and bureaucracy, which placed power into the hands of feudal lords (landowners who could provide military protection). Feudalism brought with it a class of serfs who were not slaves (property to be owned and disposed of by their masters), but rather peasants who belonged to the land. If a feudal manor changed hands, the serfs would continue to work the land on which they had been situated. Though serfdom was a difficult existence, it certainly was not slavery. Serfs could not be treated as property and had the rights to protection from the lord, just treatment, and subsistence from the land on which they worked. The monasteries and churches in various locales would provide healthcare, assistance, and education to serfs (see below).

The Black Plague and the subsequent rise of the guilds and merchant class brought an end to Feudalism, after which the proclamation of inalienable rights became more influential. This put an end to serfdom, but soon thereafter, slavery of Africans and Indians in the

---

[11] Christian influence after the time of Constantine gradually led to the end of gladiatorial combat in the colosseum in the sixth century. See "Colosseum", History.com, June 6, 2019, https://www.history.com/topics/ancient-history/colosseum.

New World presented a new challenge to the Catholic Church and society.

Colonial slavery (sometimes called "racial slavery") in the New World was condemned on multiple occasions by the Magisterium of the Catholic Church from 1435 to 1890.[12] The first papal condemnation of slavery occurred shortly after its initiation in 1435 (sixty years before the discovery of the New World) when Black natives of the Canary Islands were forced into slavery by Portuguese colonists. Pope Eugene IV not only condemned the practice but ordered all slave owners to return full liberty to their captives under pain of immediate excommunication:

> [Slave holders] have deprived the natives of the property, or turned it to their own use, and have subjected some of the inhabitants of said islands to perpetual slavery, sold them to other persons, and committed other various illicit and evil deeds against them.... Therefore, We ... exhort, through the sprinkling of the Blood of Jesus Christ shed for their sins, one and all, temporal princes, lords, captains, armed men, barons, soldiers, nobles, communities, and all others of every kind among the Christian faithful of whatever state, grade, or condition, that they themselves desist from the aforementioned deeds, cause those subject to them to desist from them, and restrain them rigorously. And no less do We order and command all and each of the faithful of each sex, within the space of fifteen days of the publication of these letters in the place where they live, that they restore to their earlier liberty all and each person of either sex who were once residents of said Canary Islands ... who have been made subject to slavery. These people are to be totally and perpetually free, and are to be let go without the exaction or reception of money.[13]

In the 1537 bull *Sublimes Dei* (Sublime God), Pope Paul III condemned under pain of sin and excommunication the practice of

---

[12] Joel S. Panzer, "The Popes and Slavery: Setting the Record Straight", *Catholic Answers*, January/February 1996, from the website of EWTN, https://www.ewtn.com/catholicism /library/popes-and-slavery-setting-the-record-straight-11119.

[13] Pope Eugene IV, Against the Enslaving of Black Natives from the Canary Islands *Sicut Dudum* (January 13, 1435), nos. 2–4, from Joel S. Panzer, *The Popes and Slavery* (Society of St. Paul, 1996), Appendix B, on p. 75 in Baronius, *Annales Ecclesiastici*, ed. O. Raynaldus (Luca, 1752), 28:226–27, PapalEncyclicals.Net, last updated February 20, 2020, https://www .papalencyclicals.net/eugene04/eugene04sicut.htm.

enslaving any and all people anywhere in the world.[14] He also ordered the immediate restoration of any enslaved people to full liberty and the immediate restitution of all confiscated property under the same pain of sin.[15] Though this bull was focused on the apparently new practice of enslaving the Indian peoples in the New World, Pope Paul made certain to give it universal applicability and reinforced these points in two subsequent papal bulls.[16] One of his important contributions was a justification that would be later used by Father Bartolomé de las Casas to defend the Indians against Portuguese and Spanish enslavement—that any person capable of receiving and understanding the faith and sacraments must have a full and true human nature, and therefore cannot be considered subhuman.[17]

The above two encyclicals were followed by multiple encyclicals and letters issued by six popes that further reenforced the condemnation of slavery and the necessary restoration of liberty and restitution of property for communion with Christ and the Church:

- Gregory XIV (1591), *Bulla Cum Sicuti*
- Urban VIII (1639), *Commissum Nobis*
- The Holy Office under Innocent XI (1686), *Response of the Congregation of the Holy Office*
- Benedict XIV (1741), *Immensa Pastorum*
- Pius VII (1814–1815), Letters to the kings of Spain and Portugal as well as the Congress of Vienna on the abolition of slavery
- Gregory XVI (1839), *In Supremo Apostolatus*

Pope Pius VII's contribution is important, because he attempts to convince the kings of Spain and Portugal to abolish slavery regardless of economic consequences. In a separate letter, he tried to convince the Congress of Vienna that the victors over Napoleon should use their worldwide influence to enforce the suppression of the slave trade.

---

[14] Pope Paul III, Papal Bull on the Enslavement and Evangelization of Indians *Sublimus Dei* (May 29, 1537), PapalEncyclicals.Net, last updated February 20, 2020, https://www .papalencyclicals.net/paulo3/p3subli.htm.

[15] Ibid.

[16] "Two other bulls would be published to implement the teaching of Sublimis, one to impose penalties on those who fail to abide by the teaching against slavery, and a second to specify the sacramental consequences of the teaching that the Indians are true men." Panzer, "Popes and Slavery".

[17] See *Sublimus Dei*.

The 1839 encyclical letter of Gregory the XVI, *In Supremo Apostolatus*, is particularly important because Pope Gregory moves beyond the Catholic Church to exhort strongly all the Christian faithful "of every condition" to abandon slavery as a complete injustice to Blacks, Indians, and any other human being victimized by the practice of slavery:

> We, by apostolic authority, warn and strongly exhort in the Lord faithful Christians of every condition that no one in the future dare to bother unjustly, despoil of their possessions, or reduce to slavery Indians, Blacks or other such peoples. Nor are they to lend aid and favor to those who give themselves up to these practices, or exercise that inhuman traffic by which the Blacks, as if they were not humans but rather mere animals, having been brought into slavery in no matter what way, are, without any distinction and contrary to the rights of justice and humanity, bought, sold and sometimes given over to the hardest labor.[18]

In his wording, Pope Gregory moved beyond all faithful Christians to all people throughout the world by appealing to a natural law argument grounded in the universal necessity of justice, rights, and the humane treatment of all peoples. This argument is borne out of principles from the Salamanca school,[19] brought to fruition by Francisco Suarez (*De Legibus on the Laws*, 1612), who formulated the doctrine of the inalienable rights of life, liberty, property, and the pursuit of happiness as a universal standard for all human beings[20] (see below Section II.D).

---

[18] Gregory XVI, Apostolic Letter Condemning the Slave Trade *In Supremo Apostolatus* (December 3, 1839), PapalEncyclicals.Net, last updated February 20, 2020, https://www.papalencyclicals.net/greg16/g16sup.htm.

[19] The esteemed Salamanca School, one of the oldest universities in the world, in the sixteenth century attempted to fuse Thomism with humanistic philosophy and some early principles of free market economics to articulate a standard of universal international law. See Goncalo L. Fonseca, "The School of Salamanca", History of Economic Thought (website), accessed February 20, 2022, https://www.hetwebsite.net/het/schools/salamanca.htm.

[20] As the editors of *Encyclopedia Britannica* indicate, "Arguing for the natural rights of the human individual to life, liberty, and property, [Suarez] rejected the Aristotelian notion of slavery as the natural condition of certain men. He criticized most of the practices of Spanish colonization in the Indies in his *De Bello et de Indis* ('On War and the Indies')." *Encyclopedia Britannica*, s.v. "Francisco Suárez", last updated January 1, 2020, https://www.britannica.com/biography/Francisco-Suarez.

The Catholic Church's clergy and religious orders were also very active in combating slavery in the New World, particularly Father Bartolomé de las Casas (who wrote extensively on the defense of the Indians and famously debated Juan Gines de Sepulveda in the Spanish courts to stop the "blood thirsty" acts of the conquistadores in the New World); Saint Peter Claver (who devoted himself to assisting and defending the slaves in Cartagena Colombia); and the Jesuit reductions throughout Paraguay and Brazil. Las Casas' legacy was explained (in Chapter 3, Section II), but the contributions of Claver and the Jesuit reductions merit brief discussions here.

Saint Peter Claver felt called to give much-needed assistance to the Negro slaves in the New World. Shortly after his entrance into the Society of Jesus, he was moved in 1610 to Cartagena, Colombia, which was the center of the slave trade in the New World. He was so disturbed by the conditions of the slaves, and inspired by his mentor Father Alonso de Sandoval (who preceded him in this ministry), that he resolved not only to provide humane treatment to every slave arriving in the New World, but also to share their plight by living in their quarters and initially riding with them in the atrocious conditions of the lower decks of a slave ship. He attended to the needs of hundreds of thousands of slaves, baptized three hundred thousand, defended their rights against abusive treatment by property owners, and made frequent appeals to government officials for their humane treatment.[21]

The Jesuit reductions were large Jesuit missions in the south of Brazil as well as Paraguay, Argentina, and parts of Uruguay, which were portrayed in Robert Bolt's film *The Mission*. At their peak, there were thirty reductions inhabited by about two hundred thousand Guarini Indians.[22] Each reduction had a large irrigated communal farm with each family also having their own private garden and perhaps a cow or horse.[23] The Jesuits educated every member of the reductions, and they were the first societies in the world to have completely literate populations.[24]

---

[21] *Encyclopedia Britannica*, s.v. "St. Peter Claver", last updated January 1, 2020, https://www.britannica.com/biography/Saint-Peter-Claver.

[22] *New Catholic Encyclopedia*, s.v. "Reductions of Paraguay", Encyclopedia.com, 2019, https://www.encyclopedia.com/religion/encyclopedias-almanacs-transcripts-and-maps/reductions-paraguay.

[23] Ibid.

[24] Ibid.

In the early 1600s, the Jesuits received permission from the Spanish government to use the vast domain occupied by the Guarani Indians for autonomous socioeconomic missions that would not be disturbed by colonialists.[25] The Indians were quite gifted in music, art, architecture, handcrafts, construction, and farming techniques. They built cathedrals, aqueducts, educational facilities and offices, and fashioned art, statuary, and literary manuscripts rivaling anything in Europe.[26] The Indians worked for six hours per day on the communal farms, leaving the rest of their time to be free for education, raising families, and recreation.[27] The reductions broke down when the Society of Jesus was suppressed in Europe and the Spanish ceded reduction territory to the Portuguese, who were much less inclined to forego materialistic gain for the sake of the Indians.[28] When the reductions broke up, many of the Indians went back to the jungles (without immunities) and a substantial part of the population died of disease and were subjugated to slavery—a tragic end to what many called the paradise of the New World.[29]

The Catholic Church did not distinguish itself in the southern United States. Prior to the Civil War, seven U.S. Southern bishops—Baltimore, Bardstown, Charleston, Saint Louis, Mobile, New Orleans, and Nashville—at the Council of Baltimore misinterpreted Pope Gregory the XVI's condemnation of slavery in *In Supremo*.[30] These bishops falsely contended that Pope Gregory XVI had condemned only the slave trade but not the institution of slavery itself.[31] Given the clarity of Pope Gregory XVI's statement about the injustice of slavery in *In Supremo* (see the quotation above), it must be concluded that these bishops intentionally misrepresented the pope's words as well as the clear consensus of papal teaching since 1435. This act of disobedience to the Magisterium provided support for Bishop John England (of Charleston) to misinterpret the

---

[25] Ibid.
[26] See C.J McNaspy, *Lost Cities of Paraguay: Art and Architecture of the Jesuit Reductions, 1607–1767* (Chicago: Loyola University Press, 1982).
[27] See *New Catholic Encyclopedia*, "Reductions of Paraguay".
[28] Ibid.
[29] Ibid.
[30] See Panzer, "Popes and Slavery".
[31] Ibid.

papal encyclical in his response to Secretary of State John Forsyth (during the administration of Martin Van Buren), which gave the impression not only to the presidential administration and Congress but also to the Catholic public that the Catholic Church was not against domestic slavery. This had the effect of dampening potential Catholic opposition to slavery for twenty years prior to the Civil War. No excuse can be made for this deliberate act of disobedience, but the Magisterium of the Catholic Church should not be blamed for it.

As can be seen from the above, the Catholic Church was on the forefront of opposition to slavery since its inception. The Church was essential in securing the abolition of slavery in the African Colonies, Latin American Colonies, the Philippines, and throughout the world (with the notable exception of the United States twenty years prior to the Civil War).[32] Moreover, when colonists and government officials ignored the Church's prohibitions, clergy, religious, and lay people were able to restrict and limit abuses, provide humanitarian assistance, and seek legal remedies for the abused.[33] Notwithstanding the inexcusable abrogation of ecclesial duty on the part of some U.S. bishops, the Church played a vital role in putting an end to one of the greatest injustices imposed upon many of the world's most helpless people for over four hundred years.

C. The Christian Impact on Social Welfare and Healthcare

Care of the sick and needy was of great importance to Jesus, who engaged in a prolific ministry of healing the sick—particularly outcasts such as lepers and the possessed. He taught His disciples to care for the sick and the poor, indicating that helping them was equivalent to helping Him (see Mt 25:36–41). He used the Parable of the Good Samaritan (Lk 10:25–37) to exemplify the ideal of service to the needy. Jesus' words and actions were put into rigorous practice by the early church community. As Luke notes in the Acts of the Apostles:

[32] Ibid.
[33] Ibid.

> All who believed were together and had all things in common; and they sold their possessions and goods and distributed them to all, as any had need. (2:44)

The ministry to the poor was so important that when Paul separated from Peter, James, and John (working with Jewish converts in Jerusalem) to work with the Gentiles, the one request the three founders made of Paul was to "remember the poor" (Gal 2:10).

Paul also created a network of Jewish and Gentile churches to provide for the needs of the Jerusalem Church, which experienced considerable deprivation. He speaks often of this collection in several of his letters (e.g., 1 Cor 16:1–4; 2 Cor 8:1—9:15; Rom 15:14–32). In 1 Corinthians, he revealed that he had also asked the Galatian Church for this offering, and he specified the process by which he intended to collect and distribute the gifts of the Gentiles:

> Now concerning the contribution for the saints: as I directed the churches of Galatia, so you also are to do. On the first day of every week, each of you is to put something aside and store it up, as he may prosper, so that contributions need not be made when I come. And when I arrive, I will send those whom you accredit by letter to carry your gift to Jerusalem. If it seems advisable that I should go also, they will accompany me. (16:1–4)

There were, of course, many poor within the Gentile Church, and Paul expects that they will be taken care of through the ordinary methods explained in the Acts of the Apostles. The reason for asking an additional sacrifice of the Gentiles for the Jerusalem Church seems to have been their greater need. Many of the Jerusalem converts had lost their social and financial status as the early Church separated from the synagogue, and Paul felt the call of Christ to help and serve them.

James believes so strongly in the mandate of Jesus to help the poor that he claims faith without works is dead:

> If a brother or sister is poorly clothed and in lack of daily food, and one of you says to them, "Go in peace, be warmed and filled," without giving them the things needed for the body, what *does it* profit? So faith by itself, if it has no works, is dead. (2:15–17; italics added)

Prior to the arrival of Christianity in Rome, social welfare was not widespread—and it certainly did not affect the lowest rungs of the social order. Some wealthy Romans, who mostly embraced the stoic philosophy of Seneca and others, built centers of public good works, but they did this only out of a sense of duty and the desire for recognition by peers. The idea of loving persons in the lower classes (or recognizing a unique intrinsic dignity in them) was quite foreign. Furthermore, love and compassion were considered weaknesses within the largely held stoic philosophy that advocated that compassion *not* be felt by the wise and strong man. Seneca phrases it this way:

> The sage will console those who weep, but without weeping with them. He will succor the shipwrecked, give hospitality to the proscribed, and alms to the poor, ... but in all his mind and his countenance will be alike untroubled. He will feel no pity.... His countenance and his soul will betray no emotion as he looks upon the withered legs, the tattered rags, the bent and emaciated frame of the beggar. But he will help those who are worthy, and, like the gods, his leaning will be towards the wretched.... It is only diseased eyes that grow moist in beholding tears in other eyes.[34]

Christianity turned stoic philosophy on its head by appealing to Jesus' teaching that compassion is the highest of all the virtues (exemplifying God's perfection [e.g., see Lk 6:36]) and His identification of the poor with Himself (see Mt 25:31–46). As a result, serving the sick and the poor with empathy, love, affection, and joy became characteristic of and central to the Christian way of life. For Christianity, this beneficent view of others was more than a philosophy; it was a pervasive ethos within the community. This spirit of love had the effect of changing the stoic *philosophy* of "charity with a cold heart" into a *spirit* of compassion for uniquely good and lovable others that shows itself in good works done joyfully and lovingly. Christians and Christian communities took upon themselves the mission to serve not only community members, but also the sick and needy on every rung of the social ladder. This led to a proliferation of healthcare

---

[34] Seneca, *De Clementia* 2, 6–7, in *History of European Morals from Augustus to Charlemagne*, by William Edward Hartpole Lecky (New York: D. Appleton, 1870), 1:199–200.

services, small hospitals, orphanages, and social welfare networks for widows and the poor.

As the Catholic Church grew in influence throughout the Roman Empire (during the fourth and fifth centuries), these charitable works became formalized and institutionalized, and extended far beyond the church community. According to Koester:

> [There was] increasingly in the Christian churches, in the time up to Constantine, the establishment of hospitals and some kind of health service. We have a clear establishment of social service— everything from soup kitchens to money for the poor if they need it. We have the very important establishment of the institution of widows, because a widow in the Roman society who had lost her husband and did not have money of her own was at the very bottom of the social ladder. One of the first welfare institutions we find in the church was all the widows who were recognized as virgins of the church. Considered particularly precious possessions of the church, they were paid by the church and therefore were rescued from utter poverty in most instances.[35]

The historian Geoffrey Blainey noted that this early healthcare network was the beginning of the social welfare system.[36] This dedication to public healthcare and welfare was progressively integrated into the Roman Empire after Constantine's Edict of Toleration in 313. In addition to local Church communities, the monasteries took up the charge to take care of the needs of non-Christian people and prioritized their resources for this effort. *The Rule of St. Benedict* (written at the beginning of the sixth century), which became a model for all other monasteries, requires that "before all things and above all things, care must be taken of the sick, so that they will be served as if they were Christ in person."[37] This apostolic emphasis led to the profusion of Christian hospitals and healthcare (for everyone in need) throughout the Middle Ages.

---

[35] Koester, "Great Appeal".

[36] See Geoffrey Blainey, *A Short History of Christianity* (Lanham, Md.: Rowan, Littlefield, 2014), pp. 67, 148, 214.

[37] Saint Benedict, *St. Benedict's Rule for Monasteries*, trans. Leonard J. Doyle (Collegeville, Minn.: Liturgical Press, 1948; Project Gutenburg, 2015), Chapter 36, http://www.gutenberg .org/files/50040/50040-h/50040-h.html.

In 1204, Saint Francis of Assisi brought Christian service to the poor and sick to an even higher level. He started what was to become the first of many religious orders dedicated to compassionate and joyful service of the needy. His intention was to tend not merely to their exterior needs, but also to their interior needs, so that even the most marginalized and neglected would know that they are loved by God and neighbor. He hoped to be God's instrument for bringing a peace beyond all understanding (Phil 4:7). His prayer (which he left as a model not only for the Franciscan order, but for all Christians) sums up the Christian mission to every human being of every station of life:

> Lord, make me an instrument of your peace:
> where there is hatred, let me sow love;
> where there is injury, pardon;
> where there is doubt, faith;
> where there is despair, hope;
> where there is darkness, light;
> where there is sadness, joy.
> O divine Master, grant that I may not so much seek
> to be consoled as to console,
> to be understood as to understand,
> to be loved as to love.
> For it is in giving that we receive,
> it is in pardoning that we are pardoned,
> and it is in dying that we are born to eternal life.[38]

The example of the Franciscan mission led to an even greater proliferation of Catholic charities and healthcare institutions, going far beyond the monasteries. Imitating Saint Francis' itinerant style, dozens of holy men and women started new hospitals, relief works, soup kitchens, and religious orders devoted to service of the poor and needy. Dozens of religious orders of sisters were founded specifically for this purpose. The nineteenth and twentieth centuries saw a huge expansion in these efforts, and today, the Catholic Church has

---

[38] Saint Francis, "Peace Prayer of Saint Francis", Loyola Press (website), 2022, https://www.loyolapress.com/catholic-resources/prayer/traditional-catholic-prayers/saints-prayers/peace-prayer-of-saint-francis/.

become the largest public healthcare and welfare system in the world. With respect to healthcare, the Church oversees more than a quarter of all worldwide healthcare facilities and hospitals.[39] With respect to public welfare, the Church provides services in 15,423 homes for the elderly, chronically ill, and disabled; 9,295 orphanages; and 12,515 marriage counseling centers.[40] Furthermore, the Catholic Church runs some of the largest international relief agencies in the world, such as Caritas International, Catholic Charities USA, and Catholic Relief Services. The mission is still the same—the humble, loving, joyful service of every human person's bodily, psychological, and spiritual needs in the imitation of Jesus.

D. The Christian Impact on Education

We might think it unusual that Jesus' teaching on love would provide the impetus to build the largest educational structure in the world, but this is precisely what happened. The Christian dedication to loving service lies at the heart of its interest in education. Jesus' teaching on the intrinsic, transcendent dignity of every human being manifests the worthiness of every person to be educated. The ancient Romans' disdain for people in the lower strata dissuaded them from investing in their education. However, Christians' respect for all people moved them to provide education to everyone as the most effective way to overcome poverty and social marginalization. Education has the power to lift the lowly to the status that is their true dignity; it led to the breakdown of the hierarchical social structure of Rome, initiating the Christian vision of social equality.

There were many educated Jewish scribes and Gentile converts in the early Church who understood the benefits of both religious and secular education. Saint Paul possessed a unique combination of Jewish (religious) and Greek (secular) learning, which he synthesized and contributed to the early Church's initial formulations of theology.

---

[39] Catholic News Agency, "Catholic Hospitals Comprise One Quarter of World's Healthcare, Council Reports", February 10, 2010, https://www.catholicnewsagency.com/news/catholic_hospitals_represent_26_percent_of_worlds_health_facilities_reports_pontifical_council.

[40] See *Agenzia Fides* (Fides News Agency), "Vatican—Catholic Church Statistics 2020", October 16, 2020, http://www.fides.org/en/news/68840-VATICAN_CATHOLIC_CHURCH_STATISTICS_2020.

As a young man, Paul was sent to Jerusalem for his education and attended the school of one of Israel's most respected rabbis, Gamaliel, the son of Rabbi Hillel. The Hillel School of Learning was balanced, allowing Paul to synthesize the best of Jewish education with other philosophies of the day, most notably stoicism, wisdom speculation, and other forms of Hellenistic thought. Paul recognized the complementarity of Jewish and Greek thought and used both his sacred and secular learning to create the seminal theological and philosophical synthesis lying at the heart of the Christian approach to education. It is likely that Paul and other educated Christians (both Jewish scribes and Gentile converts, such as Luke) encouraged and inspired the education of Christian community members.

Within a few decades after the arrival of Christianity in Rome, the Church's educational efforts began to spread and attracted additional converts. As Christian schools began to develop in the third century, the Roman bureaucracy hired Christians into its ranks, because they were among the few people capable of reading, writing, and rhetoric. Koester notes in this regard:

> We find that in the administration of the last pagan emperors, before Constantine, at the very end of the third century, a large number of the people in the imperial administration were Christians, because they could read and write ... which constituted a big problem with the persecution of the Christians because they were thrown out of their office first when the persecution began, and suddenly the government didn't work anymore.[41]

After Constantine's Edict of Toleration in 313, Christian schools began to proliferate, giving rise to a great synthesis of Christian religious and Greek philosophical thought. Though the seeds of this synthesis are found in the letters of Paul and the writings of John, it found a remarkable new depth in the Church Fathers from Ignatius of Antioch (A.D. 107) through Augustine of Hippo (A.D. 430). Augustine created one of the most elaborate theological and philosophical syntheses in Western history. He was familiar with Plato's (and Platonic) philosophy as well as Old and New Testament Scripture, and he influenced the Christian philosophy of education by elaborating the complementarity of faith and reason. In one of his sermons, he

---

[41] Koester, "Great Appeal".

states, "I believe, in order to understand; and I understand, the better to believe."[42]

Augustine created a master synthesis of philosophy and theology—including systematic explanations of epistemology, ontology, metaphysics, ethics, Christian Scripture, Christian doctrine (e.g., the Trinity and Incarnation), and a variety of other subjects. He also developed the initial Christian philosophy of education beginning with his work *The Teacher* and concluding with his later work *Reconsiderations*. This philosophy of education encouraged dialogue and dialectic within the classroom and differentiated the many styles of students and learning. It became a model for Christian education prior to the barbarian conquests.

The barbarian conquests interrupted both Christian and secular education throughout Europe. Schools were destroyed, libraries were burned, and a general disdain for education took over the continent for nearly one hundred years. However, the Irish monastic movement, as Thomas Cahill put it, "saved civilization".[43] The Irish monks copied hundreds of Latin and classical manuscripts, and later translated Neo-Platonic works from Greek into Latin,[44] preserving them from extinction. Through the efforts of Saints Columban and Columba, they began a concerted missionary movement, using their monasteries as a place to educate and minister to the spiritual and temporal needs of local residents. Schools began to spring up around the monasteries that enabled a significant number of people to learn classical and Christian education for the first time. Between 575 and 725, the Irish started over 150 monasteries—many of them quite large. They first educated new European (non-Irish) members of their community, and then used their well-qualified monks to be teachers of the general population.[45]

About one hundred years after the arrival of the monastery schools, many bishops instituted cathedral schools (associated with a specific diocese). These were established mostly to teach the sons of nobility who had an interest in serving the Church, but eventually the

---

[42] Saint Augustine, *Sermon* 43, 7, 9: PL 38, 257–58, quoted in *CCC* 158.

[43] Thomas Cahill, *How the Irish Saved Civilization* (New York: Anchor, 1996).

[44] John Eriugena and Nicholas of Cusa translated the works of Pseudo-Dionysius the Areopagite from Greek into Latin, which brought Neo-Platonic thought into postbarbarian Europe. These kinds of texts lay at the foundation of higher education in the Irish monasteries.

[45] Paul Gallagher, "The Irish Monastery Movement", *Federalist*, March 1995, http://american_almanac.tripod.com/monks.htm.

curriculum expanded to meet the needs and desires of people who wanted to serve in the bureaucracies and governmental agencies initiated in the pre-Carolingian era. In 789, Charlemagne issued a general admonition requiring schools to be established in every monastery and bishopric in which children could learn to read so that "psalms, notation, chant, computation, and grammar be taught".[46] This led to a proliferation of monastery and cathedral schools and to the standardization of the seven liberal arts: grammar, astronomy, rhetoric, music, logic, arithmetic, and geometry. This primary and secondary education was later complemented by courses in literature, philosophy, and theology, as well as courses in medicine and law (for those seeking employment by the expanding governmental system).

As European unity and bureaucracy developed, so did the need for higher education in Europe. Eventually, some of the larger and more prestigious cathedral schools developed into universities where the faculties of philosophy (progenitor of natural science and humanistic studies), theology, medicine, and law were combined in a single locale.

The rise of medieval universities occurred under the auspices of the Catholic Church, because as historian Lowrie Daly states, "The Church was the only institution in Europe that showed consistent interest in the preservation and cultivation of knowledge."[47] Some newly formed secular universities arose out of the need for additional faculties of government, law, and medicine, but the Catholic Church was committed to the pursuit of knowledge for its own sake. Though she was careful to ensure orthodoxy in faith, she gave significant latitude to creativity in reason and natural knowledge. The philosopher Edward Grant put it this way:

What made it possible for Western civilization to develop science and the social sciences in a way that no other civilization had ever done before? The answer, I am convinced, lies in a pervasive and deep-seated spirit of inquiry that was a natural consequence of the emphasis on reason that began in the Middle Ages. With the exception of revealed truths, reason was enthroned in medieval universities as the ultimate arbiter for most intellectual arguments and controversies....

[46] Pierre Riché, *Daily Life in the World of Charlemagne* (Philadelphia: University of Pennsylvania Press, 1988), p. 191.

[47] Lowrie J. Daly, *The Medieval University: 1200–1400* (New York: Sheed and Ward, 1961), p. 47.

The creation of the university, the commitment to reason and rational argument, and the overall spirit of inquiry that characterized medieval intellectual life amounted to a gift from the Latin Middle Ages to the modern world ... though it is a gift that may never be acknowledged. Perhaps it will always retain the status it has had for the past four centuries as the best-kept secret of Western civilization.[48]

Medieval universities were anything but "dark" and "constrained by Church laws"; they were fertile fields of creativity and questioning that arose out of a firm conviction that reason did not threaten faith, but complemented it (since they arose from the same source—the intelligent and loving God).

The great medieval universities of Oxford, Paris, Bologna, and Salamanca flourished, but they became overcrowded, and so various religious orders within the Church started additional universities in smaller cities. This trend continued through the Protestant Reformation, particularly with the Jesuits who were opening new universities throughout Europe and the New World. Protestants also started universities in Europe and the New World, and the combined effect of Christian education was brought to new heights. Though many of these universities became secularized within a century, many remained faithful to the mission of exploring faith and reason as envisioned by Augustine,[49] Aquinas,[50] and John Henry Newman.[51]

---

[48] Edward Grant, *God and Reason in the Middle Ages* (Cambridge: Cambridge University Press, 2001), p. 152.

[49] As previously mentioned above, in his works *The Teacher* and *Reconsiderations*, Augustine sets out the complementarity of faith and reason, and uses it as the ideal for Christian education. As he noted, "I believe, in order to understand; and I understand, the better to believe." This ideal became a model for education in Europe for nearly eight hundred years. See Augustine, *Sermon* 43, 9.

[50] Much of Saint Thomas' work exemplified a synthesis of philosophy and theology (e.g., the *Summa Contra Gentiles* and *Summa Theologica*), which Etienne Gilson termed "the Christian philosophy of St. Thomas Aquinas". Though Aquinas believed that philosophy had its own proper methodology and objectives (apart from theology), he believed that the two methodologies could complement each other, and move intellectual pursuit beyond the domain of natural reason alone. In the *Summa Contra Gentiles*, he states: "Although the truth of the Christian faith which we have discussed surpasses the capacity of the reason, nevertheless the truth that the human reason is naturally endowed to know cannot be opposed to the truth of the Christian faith." *Summa Contra Gentiles* 1, 7, 1, trans. Anton C. Pegis, ed. Joseph Kenny, O.P. (New York: Hanover House, 1955–57), https://isidore.co/aquinas /ContraGentiles1.htm.

[51] In his work *The Idea of a University*, John Henry Newman (who founded University College Dublin) espoused five major principles of Catholic higher education: (1) the

Some have contended that the Catholic Church stood in the way of the development of natural sciences (and that the medieval university was antithetical to its spirit). As we have seen, Edward Grant holds the contrary position, believing that the medieval university embraced the essential commitment to free inquiry, creativity, and the whole range of reason needed for the development of science—"the best kept secret in Western civilization". Grant's view is supported by the contributions of 244 clergy-scientists in the development of all branches of the natural sciences.[52] For example, Nicolaus Copernicus (1473–1543), the originator of the heliocentric universe and its mathematical justification (1540), was a Catholic cleric.[53] Nicolas Steno (1638–1686), a Catholic Danish bishop, was one of the founders of modern stratigraphy and geology.[54] The Augustinian monk and abbot Gregor Mendel (1822–1884) was the founder of modern quantitative genetics.[55] Monsignor Georges Lemaître (a Belgian priest and colleague of Albert Einstein) is acknowledged to be the founder of contemporary cosmology (the Big Bang Theory in 1927).[56]

---

cultivation of the love of knowledge for its own sake; (2) the teaching of natural theology (metaphysics and the philosophy of God) as the highest science—in which the human mind soared to ultimate principles, causes, unities, and the necessary highest being; (3) commitment to the complementarity of faith and reason; (4) commitment to the moral life (and the belief in the objectivity of virtues and moral norms); and (5) the commitment to the common good as complementary to the service of faith. See John Henry Newman, *The Idea of a University* (South Bend, Ind.: Notre Dame Press, 1982).

[52] See Angelo Stagnaro, "A List of 244 Priest-Scientists (from Acosta to Zupi)", *National Catholic Register*, November 29, 2016, https://www.ncregister.com/blog/a-list-of-244-priest -scientists-from-acosta-to-zupi.

[53] See John Macke, "Religious Scientists: Canon Nicolaus Copernicus", *Religious Scientists of the Catholic Church* (blog), 2020, https://www.vofoundation.org/blog/religious-scientists -canon-nicolaus-copernicus-1473-1543-heliocentricism/.

[54] Jens Morten Hansen indicates that Steno was not only a great scientist but also a philosopher of science, a master of theology and spirituality, and a bishop. See Jens Morten Hansen, "On the Origin of Natural History: Steno's Modern but Forgotten Philosophy of Science", in *The Revolution in Geology from the Renaissance to the Enlightenment*, by Gary D. Rosenberg (Boulder, Colo.: Geological Society of America, 2009), pp. 159–80.

[55] Robin Marantz Henig, *The Monk in the Garden: The Lost and Found Genius of Gregor Mendel, the Father of Genetics* (Boston: Houghton Mifflin, 2000).

[56] Though Father Lemaître was too humble to assert the primacy of his discovery over that of Edwin Hubble (two years later), Lemaître is widely acknowledged today to be the true founder of the Big Bang Theory—one of the most rigorously established theories in contemporary physics. The theory has undergone many modifications since the time of Father Lemaître (1927), but the general theory of the expanding universe remains the same. See Mauricio Livio, "Comments", *Nature*, November 10, 2011. See also Tammy Plotner, "The Expanding Universe—Credit to Hubble or Lemaitre?", *Universe Today*, November 10, 2011.

Several Jesuit priests were responsible for important discoveries in the natural sciences. Giovanni Battista Riccioli was the first person to discover the rate of acceleration of a freely falling body. Father Roger Boscovich, one of the great geniuses of Yugoslavia, is acknowledged to be one of the founders of modern atomic theory. Father J.B. Macelwane wrote the first seismology textbook in America in 1936 and was head of the American Geophysical Union.[57]

Jonathan Wright describes the extent of the Jesuit contribution to natural science as follows:

[By the eighteenth century], the Jesuits had contributed to the development of pendulum clocks, pantographs, barometers, reflecting telescopes and microscopes, to scientific fields as various as magnetism, optics and electricity. They observed, in some cases before anyone else, the colored bands on Jupiter's surface, the Andromeda nebula and Saturn's rings. They theorized about the circulation of the blood (independently of Harvey), the theoretical possibility of flight, the way the moon affected the tides, and the wave-like nature of light. Star maps of the southern hemisphere, symbolic logic, flood-control measures on the Po and Adige rivers, introducing plus and minus signs into Italian mathematics—all were typical Jesuit achievements, and scientists as influential as Fermat, Huygens, Leibniz and Newton were not alone in counting Jesuits among their most prized correspondents.[58]

Some historians have suggested that the Catholic Church manifested an "antiscientific attitude" during the controversy with Galileo, but the controversy was not about the veracity of scientific method or its seeming heliocentric conclusion. The Jesuits of the Roman College helped Galileo to confirm mathematically his version of the heliocentric theory and considered him to be an esteemed colleague and friend. The relationship broke down only when Galileo broke his promise to the pope and claimed heliocentrism as *fact* (before adequate astronomical observations could be made to confirm the theory through a technique

---

[57] See Thomas Woods, *How the Catholic Church Built Western Civilization* (New York: Regnery History, 2012), pp. 67–114.

[58] Jonathan Wright, *The Jesuits: Missions, Myths and Histories* (New York: Harper Perennial, 2005), p. 189.

called "stellar parallax").[59] He exacerbated the strained relationship when he called the pope and the Jesuits "fools" because of their reservation. In brief, the Catholic Church was not against the scientific method (which she had helped to develop) or heliocentrism (whose initial proponent, Nicolaus Copernicus, was a Catholic cleric). The strained relationship between the Church and Galileo stemmed from his broken promise to the pope to refrain from publishing heliocentrism as fact prior to its empirical verification. As noted above, Galileo never did have empirical verification. Indeed, stellar parallax could not be accurately measured until two hundred years later.

The Catholic Church's dialogue with the natural sciences is embedded in its structures. It is the only church to have an academy of sciences with Nobel Prize winners from every area of science. Its lineage goes back to 1601 and is very active today. The Pontifical Academy of Sciences has 73 Nobel Prize winners as well as about 175 highly esteemed scientists who are elected by their fellow colleagues.[60] Additionally, the Church supports scientific research institutes (independent of and attached to universities), such as the pontifical observatories and Jesuit observatories in Rome, Tucson (Arizona), and Santiago (Chile).

The contention that the Catholic Church stood in the way of the development of natural science is clearly false. Natural science grew out of the creative, free, and methodical use of reason within the medieval university, and was aided in its development by priests who saw the natural order (as described by natural scientific method) as an extension of God's intelligence, glory, and love. Discovering the mathematical intricacies, symmetries, and beauty of nature through

---

[59] The stellar parallax technique is essential to confirming the earth's movement around the sun, but astronomical observations of distant stars were not accurate enough to confirm the earth's movement relative to the sun until over two hundred years after Galileo—in 1839 by Friedrich Bessel. The pope and the Jesuits were justified in asking Galileo not to claim his theory as fact until this critical astronomical observation had been made. Unfortunately, he chose not to do so, and the controversy (and breakdown of a longstanding collegial relationship) began. See William Wallace, *Galileo and His Sources: Heritage of the Collegio Romano in Galileo's Science* (Princeton, N.J.: Princeton University Press, 2014). See also Donald DeMarco, "The Dispute between Galileo and the Catholic Church (Part I and Part II)", *Homiletic and Pastoral Review* 86, no. 8 (1986): 23–32, 50–51, and vol. 86, no. 9 (1986): 23–51, 53–59.

[60] See the list of member and Nobel Prize winners in the Pontifical Academy of Science's website, http://www.pas.va/content/accademia/en/academicians/nobel.html.

the rigorous use of empirical-mathematical method was akin to a mystical experience of the grandeur of God. The Jesuit priest, scientist, and anthropologist Pierre Teilhard de Chardin described progress in science and technology as follows:

> The greater man becomes, the more humanity becomes united, with consciousness of, and mastery of, its potentialities, the more beautiful creation will be, the more perfect adoration will become, and the more Christ will find, for mystical extensions, a body worthy of resurrection.[61]

We conclude this brief summary on Catholic education by reflecting on the maxim with which we started—ancient cultures were not inclined to educate those they believed were unworthy of this honor. If we do not see the unique dignity and goodness of people, we will not attempt to elevate them to a status beyond lowliness. The teaching of Jesus about the uniquely good transcendent dignity of every human being—especially the least of his brothers and sisters—inspired the Catholic Church to see this dignity, and to elevate it to its full status through education in every discipline. Education is the "mind's road to God", and belief in this vision enabled the Catholic Church to educate the lowest rungs of Roman society, reeducate Europe after the barbarian invasions, establish a foundational curriculum for primary and secondary education, initiate the university system, contribute to both the natural and social sciences, and become the largest international educational organization in the world. Throughout the world today, there are 95,200 Catholic primary schools and 43,800 Catholic secondary schools,[62] educating 62.2 million students (K–12).[63] There are also 1,358 Catholic universities around the world[64] of which 244 are in the United

---

[61] Pierre Teilhard de Chardin, *The Divine Milieu*, trans. Sion Cowell (Sussex: Sussex Academic Press, 2004), p. 117.

[62] See "Preparing for the Year of Creation", *Vermont Catholic*, Winter 2016–2017, http://www.onlinedigeditions.com/publication/index.php?i=365491&m=&l=&p=1&pre=&ver=html5#{%22page%22:74,%22issue_id%22:365491}.

[63] See International Office of Catholic Education, "Global Catholic Education Report 2020", June 2020, http://oiecinternational.com/wp-content/uploads/2020/06/GCE-Report-2020.pdf.

[64] See Congregation for Catholic Education, *Index: Universitates et IM Instituta Studiorum Superiorum Ecclesiae Catholicae* (Vatican City: Vatican Press, 2005), p. 464.

States.[65] Without the teaching of Jesus Christ and the work of the Catholic Church, Western and even international culture would arguably be vastly different than it is today. Contrary to those who claim that the Middle Ages were dark, it seems to have been a period in which the light of reason was enkindled by a Church convinced of the need for universal education and her belief that reason springs from the mind and heart of God.

II. The Sources of Christian Social Ethics: Jesus, Saint Paul, Saint Augustine, Saint Thomas Aquinas, and Father Francisco Suarez

As we have seen, Jesus' teaching on love, particularly the Golden Rule, the intrinsic transcendent dignity of *every* person, and the subordination of the law to the good of individuals, transformed human history in many important *concrete* ways—for example, social equality, diminishment of slavery, and the proliferation of healthcare, welfare, and education. Additionally, it influenced the course of theoretical and philosophical reflection on social ethics, politics, law, and natural rights that were to influence the organization and culture of Europe, the United States, and the international community beyond them.

Throughout seventeen centuries, Christian thinkers developed a body of political principles and doctrines that would hold the power of government to a standard of justice that could be recognized as self-evident by everyone (without having to make recourse to divine revelation) and to conjoin it with a complementary doctrine of natural rights. This eventually led to three fundamental and inviolable principles: (1) the prioritization of justice over the positive law, (2) the universality of rights, and (3) the inalienability of natural rights. In my view, it is unlikely that these three principles would have emerged within the West or anywhere else in world culture without the teaching of Jesus and the Catholic Church. As we examine the work of Saint Paul (Section II.A), Saint Augustine (Section II.B), Saint Thomas Aquinas (Section II.C), and Father Francisco

---

[65] Ibid.

Suarez (Section II.D), we will see the inherent connection between Jesus' teaching and the three fundamental principles safeguarding the justice of democracy.

A. Saint Paul and Conscience

Jesus' teaching on the intrinsic transcendent dignity of *every* human being meant that each person, regardless of his religious background, had a loving connection to God. This raises a question of how God connects with the uncatechized and unbaptized (namely, the Gentiles). Inasmuch as He loves them, He cannot leave them without a sense of His presence, teaching, and principles, and He must also allow them to have a place in eternal salvation. To do anything less would contradict Jesus' teaching on the love of God, for an unconditionally loving God would not condemn anyone because of an accident of birth (e.g., being born before Jesus or into a culture that has barely heard of Him). Condemnation for an accident of birth simply cannot be reconciled with Jesus' teaching on the Good Samaritan, the father of the prodigal son, the love of enemies, and Jesus' words after encountering a centurion—"I tell you, not even in Israel have I found such great faith" (Lk 7:9).

This teaching is clearly stated by the Second Vatican Council's Dogmatic Constitution on the Church, *Lumen Gentium*:

> Those also can attain to salvation who through no fault of their own do not know the Gospel of Christ or His Church, yet sincerely seek God and moved by grace strive by their deeds to do His will as it is known to them through the dictates of conscience. Nor does Divine Providence deny the helps necessary for salvation to those who, without blame on their part, have not yet arrived at an explicit knowledge of God and with His grace strive to live a good life.[66]

From her inception, the Catholic Church, following Jesus, believed that every human being has an interior awareness of God's

---

[66] Second Vatican Council, Dogmatic Constitution on the Church *Lumen Gentium* (November 21, 1964), no. 16.

law through the dictates of conscience (see Chapter 5, Section III.B). Saint Paul explicitly addresses God's presence and conscience in Romans 2:14–15, which becomes a cornerstone for the theory of natural law:

> When Gentiles who have not the law do by nature what the law requires, they are a law to themselves, even though they do not have the law. They show that what the law requires is written on their hearts, while their conscience [suneidēseōs] also bears witness and their conflicting thoughts accuse or perhaps excuse them.

Paul's response to the question of God's love and salvation for the Gentiles is that God has *written the law on their hearts*—that is, He has given them an interior awareness of the general precepts of the law (without the specific precepts of Torah and Christian morality). These general precepts are enough for the Gentiles to accuse themselves or defend themselves before their understanding of the law (and hence, before God). For Paul, the God of Jesus Christ does not expect the Gentiles to be judged by the same specific standards as Jews and Christians—how could they be? They would be doomed from the outset. They can be judged only on what they understand— namely, the general precepts that God has made known to them in their consciences—the interior thoughts that inform, accuse, and defend (see Chapter 5, Section III.B).

Paul gives evidence of this interior awareness of God's law in two ways:

1. The Gentiles doing what is required by the law without knowing the Jewish or Christian law
2. The fact that the Gentiles have a sense of conscience (an interior sense of good and evil), which accuses or defends them in their thoughts

If the Gentiles did not have an interior sense of the general precepts of the law, why would so many of them consistently do what is required by the law without explicitly knowing it? Similarly, if they did not have a conscience—an interior awareness of good and evil— why would they feel accused or defended by it in their thoughts?

Paul believed that our conscience could be corrupted by the culture around us but could be redeemed by the teaching and love of Christ, and the power of the Holy Spirit. This view did not mitigate his belief that "God's law in our hearts" was sufficient for the Gentiles to be judged and made worthy of salvation. Thus, for Paul, conscience not only informs us but binds us. It binds the Gentiles in a virtually unqualified way, and it is one of the significant factors, along with the teaching of Christ and the power of the Spirit, binding all Christians.

Paul's teaching on conscience would evolve into the rationale for the natural law in Saint Thomas Aquinas and Francisco Suarez.

B. Saint Augustine and Unjust Laws

Though Augustine did not influence the notion of natural law or natural rights, he made contributions to political theory that enabled Aquinas and later philosophers to apply the natural law to the political order. In his work *On Free Choice of the Will*, Augustine states, "An unjust law is no law at all."[67] In so doing, he makes a crucial distinction between justice and law, implying that justice is higher than the positive law (laws enacted by human beings—through legislatures, plebiscites, and courts). He further implies that since an unjust law is not true to its nature (to promote justice), it need not be obeyed.

Augustine's view of justice (in the political sense) was influenced by the Platonists and Justinian. He recognized that justice is equivalent to "giving each person his due" (what belongs to him and what is owed to him), and with Plato and Cicero, he believed that we have an interior sense of what justice is (albeit imperfect prior to the enlightenment of grace).[68] This imperfect sense of justice, though not ideal, is capable of guiding even Gentile (pagan) lawmakers and city-states to a proper end. In this sense, justice can guide the positive law to its proper end. Thus, justice is higher than the positive law,

---

[67] *On Free Choice of the Will* 1, 5. It is now one of the most frequently quoted adages in political theory. See Robert Spitzer, *Ten Universal Principles: A Brief Philosophy of the Life Issues* (San Francisco: Ignatius Press, 2011), pp. 125–27.

[68] See Saint Augustine, *The City of God* 19.

and it is the end to which all positive laws must aim. Any positive law that does not aim at justice (an unjust law) runs contrary to its purpose and end, and so is "no law at all".

Saint Thomas Aquinas developed the doctrine by articulating the ways in which unjust laws can occur:

> Laws may be unjust in two ways: first, by being contrary to human good, through being opposed to the things mentioned above—either in respect of the end, as when an authority imposes on his subjects burdensome laws, conducive, not to the common good, but rather to his own cupidity or vainglory—or in respect of the author, as when a man makes a law that goes beyond the power committed to him—or in respect of the form, as when burdens are imposed unequally on the community, although with a view to the common good. The like are acts of violence rather than laws; because, as Augustine says (*De Lib. Arb.* i, 5), "a law that is not just, seems to be no law at all."[69]

Augustine's insight became one of the key ways to correct the injustices of government—not only in Rome, but in the Early Middle Ages, High Middle Ages, the Renaissance, and in the Modern Age. It was used by virtually every political theorist from the time of Aquinas onward to manifest the nonbinding nature of unjust laws, and it became the key principle of civil disobedience. A few such advocates have been Francisco Suarez,[70] John Locke,[71] Edmund Burke,[72]

---

[69] *Summa Theologica* I-II, q. 96, art. 4, from *The Summa Theologiæ of St. Thomas Aquinas*, 2nd and rev. ed., trans. Fathers of the English Dominican Province, 1920, New Advent, online ed. by Kevin Knight, 2017, https://www.newadvent.org/summa/2096.htm. Hereafter, all translations of the *Summa Theologica* are from this reference and are cited as *ST*.

[70] For an explanation, see below Section II.D.

[71] "As usurpation is the exercise of power, which another hath a right to; so tyranny is the exercise of power beyond right, which nobody can have a right to. And this is making use of the power anyone has in his hands, not for the good of those who are under it, but for his own private separate advantage. When the governor, however intitled, makes not the law, but his will, the rule; and his commands and actions are not directed to the preservation of the properties of his people, but the satisfaction of his own ambition, revenge, covetousness, or any other irregular passion." John Locke, *Second Treatise on Government* 18, 199, ed. C.B. Macpherson (Indianapolis: Hackett Publishing, 1980).

[72] "It is not what a lawyer tells me I may do; but what humanity, reason, and justice tell me I ought to do." Edmund Burke, *Second Speech on Conciliation*, 1775.

Mahatma Gandhi,[73] and Martin Luther King Jr.[74] Perhaps the most nuanced expositor of this doctrine was Henry David Thoreau—the father of American civil disobedience.[75]

This doctrine did not arise *directly* out of Jesus' teaching, though one can detect the teaching of Jesus in it. Jesus' teaching that the law was made for man, not man for the law (see Mk 2:27), subordinates the law to the good of individuals. According to Jesus, the purpose of law is the good of the individual; so, inasmuch as injustice is contrary to the good of the individual, an unjust law has lost its purpose and legitimacy.

C. Saint Thomas Aquinas and the Natural Law

In his *Summa Theologica*, Saint Thomas Aquinas wrote the most comprehensive synthetic treatise on philosophy and theology in history. In addition to his groundbreaking work in metaphysics, philosophical theology, and systematic theology, Aquinas made two major breakthroughs in the area of natural law, which were foundational for the later development of natural rights by Francisco Suarez, Hugo Grotius, and John Locke (see below Sections II.D and III).

First, Aquinas returns to the doctrine of "the law written on the Gentile's hearts" in Paul's Letter to the Romans (see 2:15). Aquinas asserts that conscience (*synderesis*), though not a power, is a natural habit (intrinsic to human intellection) that "incites us to good and

---

[73] "Civil Disobedience ... becomes a sacred duty when the state has become lawless or, which is the same thing, corrupt. And a citizen who barters with such a state shares its corruption or lawlessness." Mahatma Gandhi, *Young India*, January 5, 1922.

[74] "One may well ask: 'How can you advocate breaking some laws and obeying others?' The answer lies in the fact that there are two types of laws: just and unjust. I would be the first to advocate obeying just laws. One has not only a legal but a moral responsibility to obey just laws. Conversely, one has a moral responsibility to disobey unjust laws. I would agree with St. Augustine that 'an unjust law is no law at all.'" Martin Luther King Jr., *Letter from a Birmingham Jail*, April 16, 1963.

[75] "If the injustice is part of the necessary friction of the machine of government, let it go, let it go: perchance it will wear smooth—certainly the machine will wear out. If the injustice has a spring, or a pulley, or a rope, or a crank, exclusively for itself, then perhaps you may consider whether the remedy will not be worse than the evil; but if it is of such a nature that it requires you to be the agent of injustice to another, then, I say, break the law. Let your life be a counter friction to stop the machine. What I have to do is to see, at any rate, that I do not lend myself to the wrong which I condemn." Henry David Thoreau, *On the Duty of Civil Disobedience* (London: Simple Life Press, 1903), p. 39.

causes us to murmur [feel discontent and lack of peace] at evil".[76] This "attraction to the good and revulsion at evil" works through practical principles of the intellect to inform us about what we should or should not do. The practical reason is oriented toward *doing* the *good* (action), while the theoretical (speculative) reason is oriented toward knowing the true or the real. For Aquinas then, our interior awareness and drive toward the good has two dimensions—conscience (which inclines us toward good and repels us from evil) and practical reason (which informs us about *what* is good for us). When we combine these two dimensions, we (any human being—including non-Christians) can *naturally* know "God's law" in a general way. Aquinas phrases it as follows:

> Now as "being" is the first thing that falls under the apprehension simply, so "good" is the first thing that falls under the apprehension of the practical reason, which is directed to action: since every agent acts for an end under the aspect of good. Consequently, the first principle of practical reason is one founded on the notion of good, viz. that "good is that which all things seek after." Hence this is the first precept of law, that "good is to be done and pursued, and evil is to be avoided." All other precepts of the natural law are based upon this: so that whatever the practical reason naturally apprehends as man's good (or evil) belongs to the precepts of the natural law as something to be done or avoided.[77]

For Aquinas, then, God gave human persons, through the combined effects of conscience and practical reason, the capacity to know the general precepts of *His* law by natural means. This means not only that the non-Christians can have knowledge of God's eternal law (and can therefore be judged and saved), but also that all can have an awareness of and attraction to what is good for *us*.

Aquinas believed that the natural law was part of God's eternal law:

> Since all things subject to Divine providence are ruled and measured by the eternal law ... it is evident that all things partake somewhat of the eternal law, in so far as, namely, from its being imprinted on

---

[76] *ST* I, q. 79, art. 12.
[77] *ST* I-II, q. 94, art 2.

them, they derive their respective inclinations to their proper acts and ends. Now among all others, the rational creature is subject to Divine providence in the most excellent way, in so far as it partakes of a share of providence, by being provident both for itself and for others. Wherefore it has a share of the Eternal Reason, whereby it has a natural inclination to its proper act and end: *and this participation of the eternal law in the rational creature is called the natural law.*[78]

For Aquinas, God shares his own eternal reason with us by "imprinting" it on our natural reason so that we might have a *natural* inclination toward God's eternal goodness and law. This means that the natural law can bind our conscience even though it is known through natural reason alone (without divine or Christian revelation).

Though Aquinas did not have a theory of natural rights, he laid the foundation for it in his theory of natural law. The natural law is concerned with the naturally known goods we should pursue and the naturally known evils we should avoid. Thus, the natural law tells us our most fundamental *obligations* or *duties*. For Aquinas, the three most evident naturally known goods are the self, the family, and the community/society. Correspondingly, the three most evident evils are what opposes or undermines these three natural goods.[79]

The theory of natural rights is not concerned with *our* duties and obligations *to others* (like the natural law) but rather with the duties or obligations that are *owed to us by others*. Father Francisco Suarez would make this clear three hundred years after Aquinas in 1612. Nevertheless, one rationale for deriving natural rights from the natural law is implicit in Aquinas' theory.

If we take Aquinas' three natural goods—self, family, and community/society—we might ask what is required to avoid doing evil to them (opposing them or undermining them). The answer is given in Aquinas' Treatise on Justice,[80] in which he explains that *injustice* is a fundamental undermining of the good of any person— and that injustice can be naturally known. For Aquinas, injustice deprives persons of their proper due (what belongs to them and

---

[78] *ST* I-II, q. 91, art. 2 (italics added).

[79] See John Finnis, "Aquinas' Moral, Political, and Legal Philosophy", *Stanford Encyclopedia of Philosophy*, last updated March 16, 2021, https://plato.stanford.edu/entries/aquinas-moral-political/.

[80] *ST* II-II, qq. 57–61.

what is owed to them). According to the natural law, we owe to *all* people (in virtue of their being human) at least the minimal capacity to pursue the three natural goods. If we deprive them of this minimal capacity, we prevent them from being human, which Aquinas sees as being the antithesis of justice and the natural law (the good of self, family, and community/society). Stating it in reverse, we violate the natural law by undermining the good of self, family, and community/society, which is the most fundamental kind of injustice. Therefore, we owe everybody *the right* to the minimal pursuit of the three natural goods, and if we prevent them from so doing, we violate not only the natural law but also their natural rights. As will be seen below (Section II.D), Suarez recognized this relationship between natural law and natural rights in Aquinas' theory. For the moment, suffice it to say that Aquinas builds a philosophical foundation (based on natural reasoning) that enables Suarez, and later, Grotius, Locke, and Jefferson, to formulate the doctrine of natural rights that will become the basis for redressing the weaknesses of democracy and rectifying the abuses of governmental power.

D. Francisco Suarez and Inalienable Rights

Father Francisco Suarez, S.J., was a Spanish Jesuit priest who is acknowledged to be one of the most important scholastic philosophers after Saint Thomas Aquinas. He was an early member of the School of Salamanca—an influential post-Reformation Catholic intellectual movement initiated by Francisco de Vitoria, O.P., and named after the University of Salamanca in which it resided. The Jesuits took control of the school after the Dominicans, and their combined efforts moved the Catholic Church from the medieval era into the modern era in legal and economic theory and practice.[81] The works of Suarez as well as Luis de Molina and Giovanni Botero formalized the modern doctrine of inalienable rights, just war, international law,[82] and economic theory and justice.[83] With respect to

---

[81] See Fonseca, "School of Salamanca".
[82] See ibid.
[83] See Joseph Schumpeter, *History of Economic Analysis* (New York: Routledge, 1954), pp. 91–118, 155–61.

economic theory, the Salamanca school formulated the justification of charging interest for loans formerly considered to be usury and an initial formulation of market laws such as supply and demand.[84]

In Suarez's work *De Legibus* (*On the Laws*) published in 1612, he, according to John Finnis, "crossed a watershed into the idea of objective natural rights".[85] This transition was to change the landscape of political theory throughout the West and subsequently throughout the rest of the world.

Suarez used Aquinas' natural law theory as a basis for natural rights. As explained above, natural law theory is concerned with what *we owe* to others (the good we should do for them and the evils we should avoid), but natural rights are concerned with what everybody *owes to us* in order to avoid the most fundamental injustice or evil (that would prevent us from being human). Suarez identifies this minimal standard of justice with what is necessary to preserve, govern, and perfect ourselves.[86] If we do not have the minimum capacity for self-preservation, self-governance, and self-perfection, we will not be able to pursue the three natural goods of self, family, and community/society—meaning that we will not be able to be human.

For Suarez, the ability to preserve oneself is the foundation for all natural rights, but this alone does not make us human. What makes us truly human is the ability to govern and perfect ourselves.[87] Self-governance is more fundamental than the ability to perfect ourselves, because we cannot have the latter without the former (since self-governance is the condition necessary for perfection of self). Therefore, to deny a person the power of self-governance is to take away his humanity.

It is not enough to grant self-governance to people; we must also give them the ability to perfect themselves through their power of self-governance. Suarez views this ability to perfect ourselves (as well as our families and communities/societies) in the classical way of Aquinas—namely, "the pursuit of happiness". Aristotle and Aquinas understood happiness to be coincident with the achievement of a good and viewed a "true good" as fulfillment (perfection) of human nature.

---

[84] Ibid.

[85] See John Finnis, *Natural Law and Natural Rights*, 2nd ed. (New York: Oxford University Press, 1980), pp. 207–9.

[86] *De Legibus* II, ch. 14, no.18.

[87] Ibid.

For Suarez, then, the minimal standard of justice (i.e., what is required to be human) entails self-preservation, the capacity for self-governance, and the ability to perfect ourselves,[88] which roughly corresponds to life, liberty,[89] and the pursuit of happiness, respectively. Since everyone owes everyone the minimal standard of justice (required to be human), everyone owes everyone the *rights* of life, self-governance (liberty), and the ability to perfect ourselves (the pursuit of happiness).

Suarez includes a fourth right alongside the other three—namely, the right to *property* (i.e., to own property privately[90]). He specifies that this right extends not only to property that belongs to us, but also to that which is owed to us.[91] Why does Suarez include property in his description of minimal justice? He very likely harkened back to Justinian's definition of "justice"—namely, "giving each person his due".[92] What is "our due"? For Suarez, it is what "belongs to us and what is owed to us". To deprive a person of his just due is to violate the principle of justice.

Is property really necessary to be human? Does it meet the standard of minimal justice? It does, because depriving a person of property reduces him to indentured servitude. It makes him beholding to a master for all the necessities of life. For example, though serfs had rights, they were dependent on their feudal masters for their homes, farmlands, and access to goods, which effectively placed them under their master's control.

We now come to yet another development of Suarez's theory of natural rights. He designates natural rights as a *"moral power"*:

---

[88] Ibid.

[89] Though self-governance describes liberty in a general sense, it does not describe liberty in the Enlightenment sense used by Locke and Jefferson, which carries with it aspects of autonomy, the preeminence of reason, nonreliance on tradition, etc.

[90] Suarez includes the right to private property in his list following Saint Thomas Aquinas' justification of the lawfulness and *natural good* of property ownership: "Two things are competent to man in respect of exterior things. One is the power to procure and dispense them, and in this regard, it is lawful for man to possess property. Moreover, this is necessary to human life for three reasons. First because every man is more careful to procure what is for himself alone than that which is common to many or to all.... Secondly, because human affairs are conducted in more orderly fashion if each man is charged with taking care of some particular thing himself.... Thirdly, because a more peaceful state is ensured to man if each one is contented with his own." *ST* II-II, q. 66, art 2.

[91] See *De Legibus* 1, 2, 5.

[92] See Justinian, *Institutes* 1, 1.

the true, strict and proper meaning [of right—*jus*] ... is a kind of moral power which every man has, either over his own property or with respect to that which is due to him.[93]

How is it that a right (a universal obligation of everybody to everybody) is also a "moral power"? It seems that Suarez considered this universal obligation to be an expectation of the societal privileges needed to be human, and that this "expectation of privileges" was a possession that could *do* something in the world (e.g., a possession that *enables* us to live, govern ourselves, and perfect ourselves). Inasmuch as rights *do* or *enable* something, they are a "power", and inasmuch as they are owed to us, they are "moral". We are now in a position to give a definition of natural rights for Suarez—natural rights exist in all human beings as a moral power bestowing the societal privileges needed to be human as required by fundamental justice.

This view of natural rights as "moral power" enabled Hugo Grotius (the father of international law who wrote shortly after Suarez) to commoditize rights—turning them into possessions that can be held or transferred to others. This development, in turn, allowed John Locke to form a social contract theory based on natural rights.

Notice what Suarez has done. In the three hundred years between Aquinas and him, he has taken the developments in theory of autonomy and governance, which give higher importance to the individual, and invested the minimum standard of justice in *each* human being. Therefore, he held that "a right was something that a man had as his own, that he could exercise in his own name, and that could not be taken away from him without injustice."[94]

The preceding reflection not only gives Suarez's *definition* of natural rights, but also his *justification* of them from reason and nature. Notice that he does not make an appeal to theology, God, or creation in the above justification, but only an appeal to the standard of minimum justice that can be known by "what is required to be human"— self-preservation (life), self-governance (liberty), and self-perfection (the pursuit of happiness). Suarez believed that this "argument from

---

[93] *De Legibus*, bk. 1, ch. 2, sec. 5.

[94] See Brian Tierney, *The Idea of Natural Rights: Studies on Natural Rights, Natural Law, and Church Law 1150–1625* (Grand Rapids, Mich.: Eerdmans Publishing, 1997), p. 308, citing Suarez in *De statu perfectionis, Opera* 15:8.5.29, 571.

natural reason" could bind our consciences because it reflects the natural law, and the natural law is a part of God's *eternal* law.[95]

Suarez goes even further, implying that natural rights are higher than the positive law.[96] This follows naturally from Augustine's principle that justice is higher than the positive law. If we grant Augustine's principle and we grant Suarez's contention that the most fundamental justice is the ability to be human (requiring self-preservation, self-governance, the ability to perfect self, family, community/society, and the protection of property—the four natural rights), then it must follow that natural rights are higher than the positive law.

Suarez extends this thought to the purpose of the state (government). If the state must by its nature uphold and promote justice, and the most fundamental justice is reflected in the four natural rights, then the state *must* uphold and promote natural rights. This means that an integral part of the state's purpose is to preserve and protect the natural rights of the people within its domain. Hence, the positive law and the power of the state can interfere with the four natural rights only if someone has forfeited his rights by violating the rights of others.[97] This forfeiture allows the state, in its function to protect justice and the common good, to incarcerate or punish the violator.[98]

Suarez used his theory of natural rights to criticize slavery and Spanish colonization. The editors of the *Encyclopedia Britannica* summarizes this view as follows:

> Having refuted the divine-right theory of kingly rule, [Suarez] declared that the *people* themselves are the *original* holders of political

[95] Suarez borrows this from *ST* I-II, q. 93, art. 2.

[96] "For a law to be genuine law, it must ... be just and reasonable, because an unjust law is not law" (*De Legibus*, bk. 3, ch. 22, sec. 1 [vol. 6, 84]). He explicates this principle as follows: "The human lawmaker ... does not have the power to bind through unjust laws, and, therefore, were he to command unjust things, such prescriptions would not be law, because they have neither the force nor the validity necessary to bind" (*De Legibus*, bk. 1, ch. 9, sec. 4, [vol. 2, 6]).

[97] Heinrich Rommen notes the following: "In Book 2, Chapter 14 of *De Legibus*, Suarez asserts that Liberty, i.e. the *dominium suae libertatis* of positive natural law. Nature makes men free, *positive (Ut sic dicum)* with the intrinsic Right of liberty; and only the Body Politic may take away a man's liberty *ex justa causa* [for a just cause]—as, for instance, in punishment for crimes, just as it may, in capital punishment, take away a man's life." Heinrich Rommen, "*De Legibus* of Francisco Suarez", *Notre Dame Law Review* 24, no. 1 (1948): 71–81.

[98] Ibid.

authority; the state is the result of a social contract to which the people consent. Arguing for the natural rights of the human individual to life, liberty, and property, he rejected the Aristotelian notion of slavery as the natural condition of certain men. He criticized most of the practices of Spanish colonization in the Indies in his De Bello et de Indis ("On War and the Indies").[99]

There is another consideration of Suarez's doctrine of natural rights arising out of his belief (along with Aquinas) that natural law binds our conscience. In *De Legibus* he states:

> To break the natural law without sinning [violating God's eternal law] involves an inconsistency ... and therefore the existence of an obligation which is imposed by the natural law but which is not a matter of conscience also involves an inconsistency.[100]

For Suarez and Aquinas, the natural law can be known by reason alone, but this does not mean that it pertains only to nature. It pertains also to the eternal law (God's law) because God has allowed human reason (through *synderesis* and practical reason) to naturally discover His eternal law. Just because the natural law is discovered by reason, and pertains to nature, does not mean that it is not part of God's eternal law. Did Aquinas and Suarez arbitrarily assert that the natural law was part of God's eternal law? They did not, for they both believed that justice was the "middle term" (the demonstrable common ground) between the natural law and the eternal law.

For Aquinas and Suarez, justice can be known to be morally good by *both* natural reason (as discovered, for example, by Socrates, Plato, and Aristotle) and divine revelation (as it is taught in both the Old and New Testaments). Justice is a common ground between the natural law and the divinely revealed law, which are *both* part of God's eternal law. Since the four natural rights follow from fundamental *justice*, and justice is part of God's eternal law, the four natural rights must also be part of God's eternal law (and therefore, bind human conscience).

---

[99] *Encyclopedia Britannica*, s.v. "Francisco Suárez" (italics mine).
[100] *De Legibus* bk. 2, ch. 9, sec. 6.

Hugo Grotius understood Suarez's view of the power of both the natural law and natural rights to bind human conscience,[101] and in his turn, conveyed it to John Locke. John Locke apparently believed that the natural rights were moral goods (even moral necessities) that bind human conscience. This may be what gave him the moral authority to declare that people have a right to revolt against any government who violates the natural rights of citizens.[102] Such governments violate not only the universal moral authority of justice, but also God's law, and so they violate the purpose intended for them by both universal moral authority and divine authority.[103]

We may infer from the above that the seventeenth-century Jesuit Francisco Suarez was the father of natural rights theory, and that he derived this theory from natural reasoning about human nature. Now the question arises: Did Suarez have to be a Christian to discover and formulate the natural rights doctrine? Perhaps these ideas could have developed in another religious tradition or in a purely secular context. In point of fact, they did not develop in another context throughout the course of world history. Was there something about Christianity that allowed the notion of natural rights to develop that was not clearly articulated by other religious traditions or a purely secular context? I believe that two of Jesus' teachings led Christian thinkers to the discovery of natural rights. Other religions may have had an awareness of these ideas, but in Christianity, they were so clear and central that they inevitably found their way from the domain of revelation into the domain of natural reason:

1. The intrinsic transcendent dignity of human beings (which is so substantial that the law was created to serve human beings, and not human beings to serve the law)
2. The *universality* of that intrinsic transcendent dignity (i.e., it belongs to *every* human being), including slaves and the lowest strata of society (see Mt 25:31–46)

---

[101] See Jon Miller, "Hugo Grotius", *Stanford Encyclopedia of Philosophy*, last updated January 8, 2021, http://plato.stanford.edu/entries/grotius.

[102] See Locke, *Second Treatise on Government* 222 and 225. See below Section II.D.

[103] Locke makes an appeal to both kinds of authority—universal moral authority and divine authority—throughout the *Second Treatise on Government*. This may be what allowed Jefferson the freedom to appeal directly to divine authority in the Declaration of Independence—"That all men are *created* equal and endowed by their *Creator* with certain unalienable rights."

In Christianity, the universality of intrinsic transcendent dignity demands that minimal justice extend to *every* human being in every social class that Saint Paul explicitly describes:

> There is neither Jew nor Gentile, there is neither slave nor free, there is neither male nor female; for you are all one in Christ Jesus. (Gal 3:28)

One need not be a Christian to recognize the obligation, benefits, and authority of natural rights, because they can be known by natural reasoning (without Christian revelation). However, it did fall to Christianity to recognize the *universality and inalienability* of this obligation of minimal justice (following from Jesus' teaching on the intrinsic transcendent dignity of every human being) and to place this obligation *above* the positive law (following from Jesus' subordination of the law to the good of human beings). When Christian thinkers explained the universality and inalienability of the obligation to accord minimum justice (life, self-governance, the pursuit of happiness, and protection of property) through *natural* reason, it became progressively accepted not only by intellectuals and philosophers, but by governments and courts in the West, and then throughout the rest of the world. This logic can also be found in the United Nations Declaration on Human Rights (see below).

Recall that the order in which Suarez lists inalienable rights is self-preservation, self-governance, and self-perfection,[104] which roughly corresponds to life, liberty, and the pursuit of happiness. Though Suarez does not explicitly show why he ordered these three rights in this way (and why he considered property rights separately), we may infer his implicit rationale from his work on metaphysics[105]—that whatever is necessary for something else must be prior to it (in an ontological sense).[106] Such a priority implies an ontological *hierarchy*. In view of this, the right of self-preservation has to be prior to (higher than) the right to self-governance, because a dead person cannot have rights of self-governance (liberty). Since the right to life is necessary for the very possibility of the right to liberty, it must be higher than

---

[104] See *De Legibus*, bk. 3, ch. 2, sec. 7 (vol. 7, 118).

[105] Francisco Suarez, *On Creation Conservation and Concurrence: Disputationes Metaphysicae 20–22*, trans. A.J. Freddoso (South Bend, Ind.: St. Augustine Press, 2002).

[106] This principle of necessary ontological priority grounds all of Suarez's proofs for the existence of God (in *Disputationes Metaphysicae* 17–22). See ibid.

the right to liberty. Similarly, self-governance rights are necessary for the right of self-perfection (the pursuit of happiness), because when we are enslaved, our capacity for self-perfection is virtually nonexistent. Hence, the right of self-governance (liberty) must be ontologically prior to (higher than) the right to perfect oneself (pursue happiness). This ontological hierarchy of rights (based on necessity) grounds an *objective* criterion on which to adjudicate rights conflicts. For example, if there is a dispute between a person's right to life and another person's right to liberty, the dispute should be resolved in favor of the person who has a right to life, because it is an objectively higher rights claim. The same holds true for the priority of the right to liberty over the right to perfect oneself, and the rights of life, liberty, and the pursuit of happiness over the right to property. Hugo Grotius, John Locke, and Thomas Jefferson implicitly assented to this hierarchy of rights, because they followed it assiduously.

One final dimension of Suarez's rights theory should be explicitized. Recall that Suarez based his criticism of slavery and colonization on his proven claim that natural rights belong to human beings by nature—in virtue of being a human, because natural rights represent the minimal standard of justice (what is *necessary* to be human). Justice demands that every human being have the possibility of acting according to human nature. To deprive humans of acting according to their nature unnecessarily is a most fundamental injustice. This means that no state (constitution, government, judicial body, or plebiscite) gives natural rights to anyone (because he possesses those rights in virtue of his human nature). If no state gives natural rights to human beings, then no state has the right to take them away without justification (e.g., a criminal act depriving someone else of his rights). Most importantly, no state has the right to declare that natural rights do not exist for certain individuals or groups, because they belong to *every* human being by nature. Finally, no state has the right to declare that natural rights are within their jurisdiction to grant or rescind (for the same reason).

Lest it be thought that there are other natural rights beyond life, liberty, the pursuit of happiness, and property—such as the right to an abortion or the right to enslave someone—bear in mind that a natural right is one that is *necessary* to be human, necessary to act according to human nature. This presents us with a reasonable test to determine whether something is in fact a natural right—or not. If we want to know whether something is a natural right, we must begin by asking, is this supposed "right" necessary for somebody to be human—to act according to human nature? For example, is abortion a natural right? Though the Supreme Court has declared that abortion is a "right", it cannot be considered a *natural* right, because having an abortion is not necessary for acting according to human nature. Similarly, slavery was implicitly declared by the Supreme Court to be a right of white property owners, but again it cannot be considered a *natural* right because enslaving people is not necessary in order to act according to human nature. If someday the Supreme Court were to declare that having a smartphone is a natural right, we would have to respond that it is not a *natural* right for the same reason. Indeed, if any of these things were natural rights, then we could arguably say that everyone who has not had an abortion, did not have a slave, or did not have a smartphone was not able to act according to human nature, and therefore was unable to be truly human.

The principles of inalienable rights and the necessary prioritization of rights figure prominently in the issues of slavery and abortion. If the Supreme Court of the United States had paid attention to the logical and ontological rationale for the inalienability and prioritization of natural rights in Suarez (and subsequently in Grotius, Locke, and Jefferson), we might have been able to avoid the egregious injustices perpetrated on millions of human beings because of *Dred Scott v. Sanford*[107] and *Roe v. Wade*.[108] As is clear from both decisions, the Court

[107] In *Dred Scott v. Sanford*, the Supreme Court unanimously declared that Black people had no rights to liberty, and therefore that the "dominant race's" property rights had the higher constitutional priority. In the Court's words: "The question is simply this: Can a negro, whose ancestors were imported into this country, and sold as slaves, become a member of the political community formed and brought into existence by the *Constitution* of the United States, and as such *become entitled* to all the rights, and privileges, and immunities, guaranteed *by that instrument* to the citizen? ... We think they are not, and that they are not included, and were not intended to be included, under the word 'citizens' in the *Constitution*, and can therefore claim none of the rights and privileges which that instrument provides for and secures to *citizens of the United States*. On the contrary, they were at that time considered as a *subordinate and inferior class of beings*, who had been *subjugated by the dominant race*, and, whether emancipated or not, yet remained subject to their authority, and *had no rights or privileges but such as those who held the power and the Government might choose to grant them*." Dred Scott v. Sanford, [1] 60 U.S. (How. 19) 393 (1857) (italics added).

[108] In *Ten Universal Principles*, I explain the six fundamental errors made by the Supreme Court in the *Roe v. Wade* decision—errors concerned with inalienable rights, constitutional rights, the prioritization of rights, the rules of legal evidence, embryology, and logic. See pp. 62–70.

completely ignored and neglected the inalienable *natural* rights of two classes of human beings (African Americans in *Dred Scot v. Sanford* and preborn children in *Roe v. Wade*). As a result, they reduced the rights of both classes of human beings to constitutional rights only and, interpreting the Constitution according to their preference, decided that both classes of individuals had no rights or political standing whatsoever in the United States. These egregious injustices could have been used to overthrow the government according to John Locke (in the *Second Treatise on Government*) and Thomas Jefferson (in the Declaration of Independence). The injustice of slavery has been redressed, but the injustice of preborn genocide remains a dark and bloody stain on our country, its courts, and our Constitution. For the sake of justice, rights, and basic decency, this decision must be reversed and recognition of the *natural* rights of preborn human beings as well as the prioritization of life rights over liberty rights must be restored. Failure to do this undermines not only the ethics but the soul of our country.

The legacy of Francisco Suarez and the School of Salamanca is deep, penetrating, and necessary for civility and civilization. As noted above, this legacy was immediately recognized by Hugo Grotius, who incorporated it into his work on international law.[109] Grotius' work was used by John Locke to ground his *Second Treatise on Government*, which in turn influenced Thomas Jefferson[110] (the writer of the Declaration of Independence). Subsequent generations of political theorists and statesmen eventually applied it to the United Nations Universal Declaration on Human Rights.[111]

---

[109] See Terence Irwin, *The Development of Ethics: A Historical and Critical Study* (New York: Oxford University Press, 2008), 2: 98ff.

[110] Locke was an important intellectual influence on Jefferson, who read both the essay *Concerning Human Understanding* and *The Second Treatise on Government* quite carefully. See Luigi Marco Bassani, "The Real Jefferson", Mises Institute, May 23, 2002, https://mises.org/library/real-jefferson.

[111] The Preamble of the 1948 United Nations Declaration of Human Rights states: "Whereas recognition of the inherent dignity and of the equal and inalienable rights of all members of the human family is the foundation of freedom, justice and peace in the world. Whereas disregard and contempt for human rights have resulted in barbarous acts which have outraged the conscience of mankind, and the advent of a world in which human beings shall enjoy freedom of speech and belief and freedom from fear and want has been proclaimed as the highest aspiration of the common people. Whereas it is essential, if man is not to be compelled to have recourse, as a last resort, to rebellion against tyranny and oppression, that human rights should be protected by the rule of law" (from their website at https://www.un.org/en/universal-declaration-human-rights/).

III. A Summary of the Five Fundamental Principles of Justice

As may now be apparent, four fundamental principles of social ethics were developed in the Catholic Church over the fifteen hundred years from the life of Jesus to Father Francisco Suarez. The first principle, the principle of nonmaleficence (the Silver Rule), was not developed by the Catholic Church, but within the various religious and cultural traditions that independently formulated this most fundamental principle of justice and ethics. The other four principles were developed within the Catholic Church through the philosophers and theologians mentioned above (Section II). The following brief summary of those principles represents the theoretical underpinnings of every just political regime as well as the United Nations Declaration of Human Rights. If we do not enshrine these principles in our individual hearts and collective will, we will allow ourselves to be gradually overwhelmed by suppression and oppression. As we reflect on them, consider their origin in Jesus and their gradual unfolding through the Holy Spirit working within the Catholic Church.

1. *The principle of nonmaleficence (the Silver Rule).* "Avoid unnecessary harm to others, and if a harm is unavoidable, minimize it." This principle is the foundation of all ethics and is intrinsic to fundamental justice. It was developed independently in most cultures and religions throughout the world.

2. *The principle of unjust laws.* "An unjust law is no law at all" (Saint Augustine). This principle may be restated as follows: Every positive law (declared into existence by a ruling authority) must be just in order to be considered legitimate (binding on the populace). "Justice" includes three elements:

   a. A positive law cannot deprive a person of what is required to act according to human nature—self-preservation, self-governance, and self-perfection.

   b. A positive law cannot cause unnecessary harms to an individual or group.

   c. A positive law must be equitable and must accord all people "their due"—what is owed to them and properly belongs to them.

Since an unjust law is illegitimate and therefore nonbinding, it can be peacefully resisted or disobeyed.[112]

3. *The principle of full and equal personhood.* "Every being of human origin should be considered a 'person' deserving of full and equal protection under the law" (Father Bartolomé de las Casas). A human being must be considered a "person" regardless of any secondary or accidental characteristic such as race, economic condition, age, or stage of development. In Chapter 3 (Section II), it was shown that human nature (a unique being of human origin) has ontological priority over any secondary or accidental characteristic—such as height, age, stage of development, economic condition, race, etc. Therefore, the presence (or absence) of such secondary or accidental characteristics cannot negate the existence of human nature and personhood in any identifiable human being. In Chapter 3 (Section I), we showed that a human being can be identified definitively through the following scientifically validatable criterion: a unique, self-moving, self-perfecting, dynamic organism actualizing itself according to a full *human* genome. We also noted in Chapter 3 (Section I.C) that any attempt to differentiate human nature from personhood was tantamount to fundamental injustice, because such dissociation could lead to the unjust deprivation of his or her inalienable rights to self-preservation, self-governance, and self-perfection (as in slavery and abortion).

4. *The principle of inalienable rights.* "Every human being (person) by nature possesses the inalienable rights of life, liberty, and the pursuit of happiness" (Father Francisco Suarez). In Section II.D above, we explained Father Francisco Suarez's principle that every human being (person) must be able to act in accordance with his or her nature—to preserve his life, govern himself, and perfect himself. To deprive a person of these three capacities deprives him of his humanity, which causes him fundamental harm and injustice (see number 2 above). Suarez coined the phrase "right" to express this principle of fundamental justice

---

[112] Civil disobedience has been acknowledged as a proper response to unjust laws by many political thinkers and activists. See, for example, David Thoreau, Edmund Burke, Mahatma Gandhi, and Martin Luther King Jr. in the citations above (Section II.B).

as a property belonging to every human being. Thus, every human being has the right (the entitlement from every other human being) to preserve and protect his capacity for self-preservation (life), self-governance (liberty), and self-perfection (the pursuit of happiness).

5. *The principle of the natural hierarchy of rights.* "If one right is necessary for the possibility of another right, it must be higher than that other right, and accorded preference in any rights conflict" (Father Francisco Suarez). In Section II.D above, we explained that certain rights can be shown to be higher than other rights according to their necessity for the others. This reveals a natural ranking among rights. Since the right to life is necessary for the very possibility of the right to liberty (dead people have no liberty rights), then the right to life must be a higher right than the right to liberty. Similarly, the right to liberty (self-governance) must be higher than the right to pursue happiness (self-perfection) because a slave has no capacity to seek his own happiness through self-perfection. Therefore, in rights conflicts, where one person's life right is in conflict with another person's liberty right, preference must be given to the person with the life right over the person with the liberty right. Similarly, in rights conflicts where one person's liberty rights are in conflict with another person's right to pursue happiness, preference should be given to the person with the liberty right.

In the past, these five principles were neglected by governments promoting slavery, and today are neglected by governments promoting abortion. The unnecessary harm and fundamental injustice caused by forsaking these fundamental principles is so grave that they engender continuously growing opposition to redress and reverse them. If we are to maintain humaneness, civility, and justice within our society, we will not only have to correct the gross violations of these principles (such as the legal decisions *Dred Scott v. Sanford* and *Roe v. Wade*),[113] but also keep them close to our hearts and collective will. We cannot be guilty bystanders; we must profess this heritage of

[113] These inherent problems in these legal decisions are explained in detail in Spitzer, *Ten Universal Principles.*

our Christian-Catholic tradition publicly and courageously, lest "the very stones would cry out" (Lk 19:40).

IV. Conclusion

Throughout the last two millennia, Jesus and the Catholic Church have transformed the world—not only religiously and metaphysically but communally, socially, and culturally. Thanks to the Catholic Church's faithfulness to Jesus' mandate in Matthew 25:31–46 (especially verse 40, "As you did it to one of the least of these my brethren, you did it to me"), the world is a much better place to live than the pre-Christian era of slavery, destitution of the lower classes, and cruel public sports. As noted above, the Church, even in her infancy, transformed Roman society by administering public healthcare, welfare, and education for every one of every class. Christian education not only allowed slaves and the lower classes to advance in society but undermined the institution of slavery itself. The Catholic Church, in combination with other Christians, eventually put an end to colonial slavery in the New World, and today the Catholic Church is the largest international education, public health, and public welfare system in the world.

The Church's transformational effects can also be found in the evolution of social ethics within the positive law and political systems. The progressive development of the doctrines of individual intrinsic dignity, equality, the natural law, natural rights, and the prioritization of rights ensures that the polity will not overshadow or cancel out the intrinsic dignity and rights of every human being. Though the Church contributed hugely to the development of the common good and just laws, she emphasized, along with Jesus, that the polity and social order existed for the good of the individual and the family—not vice versa. This inspired the development of inalienable rights as a necessary complement not only to Western monarchies, but eventually to Europe's emerging democracies. As we shall see, the Church also influenced the development of economic rights and sociopolitical doctrines (see Chapter 7).

Jesus was and continues to be the inspiration of all these transformative efforts; the Catholic Church, despite her weaknesses and occasional failures, has been consistently a faithful servant in carrying out the mandate of her Master through the grace of the Holy Spirit working in her saints, educators, and statesmen. Could the Church have done a better job in the past? No doubt—as could we all. Yet in the midst of great internal and external pressures, plagues and famines, rapid social transformations, changing demographics of conquests and migration, and the discovery of new worlds, she persistently moves toward an ideal of faith, goodness, and love that will leave its imprint not only on politics and legal systems, but also on family, community, society, and culture—that is, on humane civilization.

Chapter Seven

The Social Teaching of the Catholic Church

Introduction

In Chapters 3 and 6, we addressed the two most fundamental principles of social ethics, both Catholic and secular:

- The principle of justice (including the principle of nonmaleficence as well as fair and equitable treatment for all)
- The principle of the intrinsic dignity of every human being

The Catholic Church fleshed out the meaning and application of these two founding principles in the five fundamental principles of justice animating most secular governments today and the United Nations Universal Declaration of Human Rights: the principle of nonmaleficence, the principle of unjust laws, the principle of full and equal personhood, the principle of inalienable rights, and the principle of the natural hierarchy of rights (see Chapter 6, Section III).

Catholic social ethics is not restricted to the intrinsic dignity of individuals and their equitable relationship with one another. Though these principles are foundational, social ethics must also include the relationship of intrinsically dignified persons to complex international social, political, and economic systems. As most readers recognize, these complex systems take on a life of their own. They contribute to us, make demands of us, and require ethical responsibilities from individuals as well as themselves. As history has demonstrated, these collective systems can be just or unjust, freedom enhancing or freedom restricting, and contributive or cruel. Arguing from natural law reasoning (giving rise to a universal standard on which most religions and consciences agree), the Church developed a set of principles to optimize justice, freedom, and the common good as well as collective creativity, economic productivity, environmental stewardship, and international cooperation and peace. These principles and their application in seven collective contexts (called "Catholic social teaching") form the most comprehensive natural law standards of social ethics today.

In 1891, Pope Leo XIII issued the encyclical letter *Rerum Novarum* to rectify the abuses of the working class created by unjust practices throughout the Industrial Revolution. It endeavored to set out the responsibilities of labor, capital producers, government, and citizens to achieve justice and free market creativity and production. This entailed the condemnation of Marxist socialism as well as unrestrained capitalism while protecting the rights of individuals and private property. It is the founding document of Catholic social teaching.

Since that time, every pope has expanded the body of Catholic social teaching to apply not only to labor and the economy but also to family, political community, international community, war and peace, and the environment. The history of Catholic social teaching (CST) is rich and interesting, but beyond the scope of this volume. Our purpose in this brief treatment is to give a basic description of its major principles and areas of application so that the reader may delve into it more deeply according to his interests. CST is expressed through twenty papal documents, three documents by the Roman Curia,[1] and two conciliar documents[2] spanning from Pope Leo XIII's *Rerum Novarum*

---

[1] Pope Leo XIII, Encyclical Letter on Capital and Labor *Rerum Novarum* (May 15, 1891).

Pope Pius XI, Encyclical Letter on Reconstruction of the Social Order *Quadragesimo Anno* (After Forty Years) (May 15, 1931).

Pope John XXIII, Encyclical Letter on Christianity and Social Progress *Mater et Magistra* (May 15, 1961).

Pope John XXIII, Encyclical Letter on Establishing Universal Peace in Truth, Justice, Charity, and Liberty *Pacem in Terris* (Peace on Earth) (April 11, 1963).

Pope Paul VI, Encyclical Letter on the Development of Peoples *Populorum Progressio* (March 26, 1967).

Pope Paul VI, Apostolic Letter on a Call to Action on the Eightieth Anniversary of Rerum Novarum *Octogesima Adveniens* (May 14, 1971).

Pope Paul VI, apostolic exhortation *Evangelii Nuntiandi* (Evangelization in the Modern World) (December 8, 1975).

Pope John Paul II, Encyclical on Human Work *Laborem Exercens* (September 14, 1981).

Pope John Paul II, Encyclical Letter for the Twentieth Anniversary for Populorum Progressio *Sollicitudo Rei Socialis* (On Social Concern) (December 30, 1987).

to Pope Francis' *Fratelli Tutti*. The Pontifical Council of Justice and Peace wrote a comprehensive document entitled *Compendium of the Social Doctrine of the Church*, which organizes the content of the above encyclicals according to the six principles and seven major areas of application. (It is very well indexed and free on the Vatican's website.)[3]
The following will briefly explain three dimensions of CST and its articulation in the compendium:

1. The six principles of CST (Section I)
2. Seven major areas of CST application (Section II)

Pontifical Council for Justice and Peace, *Contribution to World Conference against Racism, Racial Discrimination, Xenophobia and Related Intolerance* (August 31–September 7, 2001).

Pope John Paul II, Encyclical Letter on the Hundredth Anniversary of Rerum Novarum *Centesimus Annus* (May 1, 1991).

Pope John Paul II, encyclical *Veritatis Splendor* (The Splendor of Truth) (August 6, 1993).

Pope John Paul II, Encyclical Letter on the Value and Inviolability of Human Life *Evangelium Vitae* (The Gospel of Life) (March 25, 1995).

Congregation for the Doctrine of the Faith, instruction *Dignitas Personae* (The Dignity of a Person) (December 8, 2008).

Pope John Paul II, Post-Synodal Apostolic Exhortation on the Encounter with the Living Jesus Christ *Ecclesia in America* (The Church in America) (January 22, 1999).

Pope John Paul II, Encyclical Letter on the Relationship between Faith and Reason *Fides et Ratio* (September 14, 1998).

Congregation for the Doctrine of the Faith, *Doctrinal Note on Some Questions regarding the Participation of Catholics in Political Life* (November 21, 2002).

Pope Benedict XVI, Encyclical Letter on Christian Love *Deus Caritas Est* (God Is Love) (December 25, 2005).

Pope Benedict XVI, Post-Synodal Apostolic Exhortation on the Eucharist as the Source and Summit of the Church's Life and Mission *Sacramentum Caritatis* (February 22, 2007), especially nos. 47, 49, 82–84, 88–92.

Pope Benedict XVI, Encyclical Letter on Integral Human Development in Charity and Truth *Caritas in Veritate* (June 29, 2009).

Pope Francis, Apostolic Exhortation on the Proclamation of the Gospel in Today's World *Evangelii Gaudium* (The Joy of the Gospel) (November 24, 2013).

Pope Francis, Encyclical Letter on Care for Our Common Home *Laudato Si'* (May 24, 2015).

Pope Francis, Encyclical Letter on Fraternity and Social Friendship *Fratelli Tutti* (October 3, 2020).

[2] Second Vatican Council, Pastoral Constitution on the Church in the Modern World *Gaudium et Spes* (December 7, 1965).

Second Vatican Council, Declaration on Religious Freedom *Dignitatis Humanae* (December 7, 1965).

[3] Pontifical Council for Justice and Peace, *Compendium of the Social Doctrine of the Church* (2004; repr., April 2005). Hereafter, *Compendium*.

3. Sustainable development goals and the alleviation of worldwide famine, disease, and poverty (Section III)

We will conclude this chapter with a discussion of the degree of magisterial authority with which Catholic social doctrine is taught—Extraordinary Magisterium, Ordinary Magisterium, or prudential judgment (Section IV).

I. Six Principles of Catholic Social Teaching

There are six major principles of Catholic social teaching:

1. The Intrinsic Transcendent Dignity of Every Human Person (Section I.A)
2. The Principle of the Common Good (Section I.B)
3. The Universal Destination of Goods (Section I.C)
4. The Principle of Subsidiarity (Section I.D)
5. Participation in Democracy (Section I.E)
6. The Principle of Solidarity (Section I.F)

We will discuss each in turn.

A. The Intrinsic Transcendent Dignity of Every Human Person

As we saw in the previous chapter, the teaching of Jesus in this regard is unequivocal:

> Truly, I say to you, as you did it to one of the least of these my brethren, you did it to me.... As you did it not to one of the least of these, you did it not to me. (Mt 25:40, 45)

When Jesus equates Himself with the least of his brothers and sisters, He elevates everyone—including slaves, prisoners, and the poorest of the poor—to His own divine dignity. Since that time, the Christian Church has recognized the equal intrinsic and transcendent dignity of every human person, bringing it into the realm of natural reason, natural law, and natural rights through the idea and reality of the inalienable rights of life, liberty, the pursuit of happiness, and property. The Church embraces this as her central social teaching in *Rerum Novarum*, and it has remained so to this day. This principle is a part of the Church's Extraordinary Magisterium and is therefore infallible and needed for salvation (explained below, Section IV).[4] The Church has based virtually all of her other social doctrines on this foundation—the equal intrinsic transcendent dignity of all human life from conception to its natural end as well as the justification for the other five principles of CST. Further explanation of this principle can be found in Chapter 3 (Sections I–II) and Chapter 6 (Section II).[5]

B. The Principle of the Common Good

This principle extends the first principle to the domain of groups, communities, cultures, societies, and states as the *Compendium* notes:

> *The principle of the common good, to which every aspect of social life must be related if it is to attain its fullest meaning, stems from the dignity, unity and equality of all people.* According to its primary and broadly accepted sense, *the common good* indicates "the sum total of social conditions which allow people, either as groups or as individuals, to reach their fulfilment more fully and more easily" (*Gaudium et Spes*, no. 26).[6]

The *Compendium* goes on to state that the common good is "the social and community dimension of the moral good".[7]

To fulfill the principle of the common good, every individual, societal group, and governmental body must commit themselves to certain ends and objectives described by the *Compendium* as follows:

> These demands concern above all the commitment to peace, the organization of the State's powers, a sound juridical system, the protection of

---

[4] See *Gaudium et Spes*, nos. 12, 25–27, 41, and *Dignitatis Humanae*, no. 1.

[5] This doctrine is elucidated in the *Compendium*, Chapter 3.

[6] *Compendium*, no. 164 (unless otherwise indicated, all italics in *Compendium* quotes are in the original).

[7] Ibid.

the environment, and the provision of essential services to all, some of which are at the same time human rights: food, housing, work, education and access to culture, transportation, basic health care, the freedom of communication and expression, and the protection of religious freedom.[8]

Gaudium et Spes and several CST encyclicals exhort every Catholic to do their utmost individually, in community, and through participation in government to meet the demands of the common good in the best way possible. This is explained in detail below with regard to the seven major areas of CST applications (Section II).

C. The Universal Destination of Goods

The expression "universal destination of goods" refers to the fact that God wills that His creation of the earth (and its fruitfulness) sustain *all* people. This means that *all* people have a right to share in the earth's goods in order to meet their needs (and their families' needs). These "needs" include the requirements not only for sustenance, shelter, and safety, but also for personal fulfillment—including work, community, education, and culture. The *Compendium* describes it as follows:

> The universal right to use the goods of the earth is based on the principle of the universal destination of goods. Each person must have access to the level of well-being necessary for his full development.[9]

At first glance, one might think that this principle advocates collectivism or socialism, but the Church has been very careful to advocate just the opposite—namely, the advocacy of the universal right to share in the earth's goods as well as the right to private property and the right to participate in the free market. Though these three economic rights could be conflictual when taken to extremes, the Church advocates that they be kept in a perpetual balance so that the intrinsic dignity of every human being and the principle of the

---

[8] Ibid., no. 166. See also *Gaudium et Spes*, no. 26.
[9] *Compendium*, no. 172.

common good can be fulfilled. The right to private property and to participate in a free market merit closer inspection.

Since the time of Saint Thomas Aquinas, and later Francisco Suarez, the Church has recognized the need for a legitimacy of private property as an extension of the right to autonomy and self-governance (liberty). It is also recognized how private property increases responsibility, incentivizes labor and creativity, and helps to provide autonomy for the family. *Gaudium et Spes* states in this regard:

> Private property or some ownership of external goods confers on everyone a sphere wholly necessary for the autonomy of the person and the family, and it should be regarded as an extension of human freedom.... Since it adds incentives for carrying on one's function and charge, it constitutes one of the conditions for civil liberty.[10]

Saint Thomas Aquinas[11] and Francisco Suarez[12] (among many others) recognized that private property was a condition necessary for privacy and self-governance long before the abuses of collectivism and Marxism. When these abuses were recognized after the Russian Revolution, the Church saw private property as a fundamental need to avoid indentured servitude and "promiscuous dominion" of the state.[13]

Nevertheless, the Church has never recognized "private property" as an *absolute* right, but rather as a relative one—subordinated to every person's right to share in the earth's goods.[14] This means that the right to private property must be regulated so that the accumulation of wealth by some individuals will not lead to depravation of the earth's goods from other individuals or groups of individuals. Hopefully, individual citizens will responsibly regulate themselves to prevent exploitation or severe depravation of the world's goods from others. If they do not, they force government to take on this role—a role that the Church believes is integral to the common good.[15]

[10] *Gaudium et Spes*, no. 71.

[11] In his *Summa Theologica*, Aquinas wondered "whether it is natural for man to possess external things" (*ST* II-II, q. 66, art. 1). Also, "Is it lawful for a man to possess something as his own?" *ST* II-II, q. 66, art. 2.

[12] See *De Legibus*, 1, 2, 5.

[13] *Compendium*, no. 176.

[14] Ibid.

[15] Ibid.

The relative right to private property also extends to the right to participate in the free market. Since the writing of *Rerum Novarum*, the Church has recognized not only the right to participate in free markets, but also the effectiveness of those markets for the creative, efficient, and optimized production of goods and services. The *Compendium*, borrowing from Pope John Paul II's encyclical *Centesimus Annus*, states it this way:

> *The free market is an institution of social importance because of its capacity to guarantee effective results in the production of goods and services.* Historically, it has shown itself able to initiate and sustain economic development over long periods. There are good reasons to hold that, in many circumstances, "*the free market* is the most efficient instrument for utilizing resources and effectively responding to needs." The Church's social doctrine appreciates the secure advantages that the mechanisms of the free market offer, making it possible as they do to utilize resources better and facilitating the exchange of products.[16]

Though a free market is essential to the efficient and creative production of goods and services, it cannot be left completely unregulated lest ethical problems (such as greed and pride) undermine workers and the economy itself. The eighty-year history of Industrial Revolution abuses make this proclivity a virtual truism when markets are completely unregulated.[17] For this reason, the state must regulate the free market to protect weaker parties from being exploited by stronger and wealthier ones. Though the state should not interfere with the ordinary means of production or the market itself, it must perform certain functions to protect laborers, consumers, and the competitiveness of the marketplace. This means safeguarding workers from exploitation, consumers from price gauging of inelastic goods (necessities such as bread), and the marketplace from monopolies and monopolizing tendencies.

CST uses two of its principles (discussed below) to provide guidance and balance in setting guidelines for state actions within the marketplace—the principle of subsidiarity and the principle of

---

[16] Ibid., no. 347, quoting *Centesimus Annus*, no. 34; see also nos. 30, 40–41.

[17] In the introductory chapters of *Rerum Novarum*, Pope Leo XIII is quite explicit about the abuses of the Industrial Revolution that require rectification through just governmental systems.

solidarity. The *Compendium* summarizes this "mean" by appealing to Pope John Paul II's *Centesimus Annus*:

> The action of the State and of other public authorities must be consistent with the principle of subsidiarity and create situations favourable to the free exercise of economic activity. It must also be inspired by the principle of solidarity and establish limits for the autonomy of the parties in order to defend those who are weaker. Solidarity without subsidiarity, in fact, can easily degenerate into a "Welfare State", while subsidiarity without solidarity runs the risk of encouraging forms of self-centred localism.[18]

Let us now return to the third principle of CST—universal destination of goods. We may now summarize the principle with the above two important qualifications. Every person, in light of his transcendent soul made in the image and likeness of God, has a right to share in the goods of this earth and cannot be deprived of the goods needed to sustain himself and his family humanely. This principle does not mean that everyone must share equally in the goods of this world. The requirements of private property and free markets as well as differences in productivity, initiative, creativity, and education will give rise to inequalities of wealth, property, status, and privileges. However, such inequalities cannot lead to exploitative, oppressive, and unjust working conditions, wages, and distribution of inelastic goods (i.e., necessities for life and family). Thus, the universal destination of goods should not preclude private property or free markets, but private property and free markets cannot lead to exploitative, oppressive, or unjust conditions for any party.

The universal destination of goods further entails the preferential option for the poor. In Pope John Paul II's address to the bishops of Latin America in Puebla, Mexico, this phrase was used to denote the obligation of all Christians to use the means at their disposal to help alleviate the oppressive conditions of the poor—particularly through meeting their needs of food, shelter, and healthcare as well as education, communication, and technological advancement.[19] It

---

[18] *Compendium*, no. 351. See also *Centesimus Annus*, no. 15.
[19] See Pope John Paul II, Address to the Third General Conference of Latin American Bishops, Puebla, Mexico (January 28, 1979).

also includes encouragement of the Church and influential citizens to rectify unjust and oppressive social and political structures (a mandate intrinsic to the principle of solidarity—see below I.F). Whatever our status, we must be cognizant of the gospel mandates to make a place in our heart, time, and action for the poor—whether it be through contributing funds, service to the less fortunate, exerting influence in the marketplace or politics, developing social entrepreneurial solutions, or other contributions befitting our talents, responsibilities, and abilities (see Chapter 5, Section II).

D. The Principle of Subsidiarity

The principle of subsidiarity is a foundation of Catholic social teaching that *Quadragesimo Anno* elevated to utmost importance in social philosophy.[20] It means that no higher (larger) social unit should undermine and absorb any lower (smaller) social unit—or stated the other way around, that preference for action within society should always be given to the lowest (the smallest) social unit that can accomplish it. For example, if an individual or a family can accomplish a social action or duty, then they should be allowed to do it without interference from (or absorption into) a higher social unit (such as a community organization). Similarly, if a local charity or a community organization can accomplish a particular social action or duty, then it should be allowed to do it without interference from (or absorption into) a higher social unit (such as a city or state bureaucracy). Again, if a local business can accomplish a social action for which it is designed, it should be allowed to do so without interference from a higher social unit (such as a state government).

The Church is interested in this principle for three reasons. First, she is interested in the autonomy of individuals as essential to the intrinsic dignity of transcendent beings made in the image of God. Without subsidiarity, higher social units would absorb the autonomy and the proper duties (and dignity) of individuals. Secondly, the Church is interested in the family—as the original unit through which love, religion, and morals are lived, practiced, and taught.

[20] See *Quadragesimo Anno*, no. 23. See also *Centesimus Annus*, no. 48.

Higher social units are perforce much less intimate than families, and they do not have the same care and specificity about religious and moral practice. To relegate family duties to community, city, or state organizations undermines this essential intimacy, care, and religious and moral practice, which is deleterious to both individuals and society. Thirdly, the Church is interested in protecting community autonomy because local communities are much better suited to solve local problems than larger social units who care and understand far less than local communities.

Harkening back to *Rerum Novarum* and *Quadragesimo Anno*, the *Compendium* urges all authorities in higher governmental and societal positions to observe the principle of subsidiarity to fulfill their ethical duty to protect the autonomy, dignity, and proper functions of lower social units:

> *On the basis of this principle, all societies of a superior order must adopt attitudes of help ("subsidium")—therefore of support, promotion, development—with respect to lower-order societies.* In this way, intermediate social entities can properly perform the functions that fall to them without being required to hand them over unjustly to other social entities of a higher level, by which they would end up being absorbed and substituted, in the end seeing themselves denied their dignity and essential place.[21]

There is a tendency in complex societies to allow larger social units—and even the state—to absorb the functions and duties of lower social units (an extreme example of this is totalitarianism manifest in Communism). This has the effect of undermining individuality, more intimate associations among people, and more effective local associations by replacing them with more bureaucratic, less intimate, and less effective higher ones. If we allow larger social units to absorb the actions and responsibilities of smaller ones, we can expect to see a decrease in individual self-worth, individual initiative, familial intimacy, religious and moral practice, and local effectiveness. It is not enough for the Church to urge leaders within higher social, societal, and governmental units to observe their ethical duty toward subsidiarity. *All* citizens must be vigilant about maintaining subsidiarity

[21] *Compendium*, no. 186.

by insisting on individual freedoms, family autonomy and rights, and the proper duties of community organizations, individual businesses, and local governments.

In the previous subsection, we noted that there seems to be an inherent tension between the principle of subsidiarity and the principle of solidarity, for the former seeks to vest authority and power in the lowest possible social units, while the latter *seems* to vest authority and power in higher social units. As we shall see below (Section I.F), solidarity is not interested in vesting power and authority anywhere, but rather in seeking the common good and mutual care for as many as possible.

E. Participation in Democracy

Since *Rerum Novarum* (1891), the Church has been a champion of democracy and participation in democracy as not only a right, but a duty of every citizen. Democracy, as a *right* of citizens, is derived from two more fundamental principles—the intrinsic transcendent dignity of every human being and the principle of subsidiarity. Participation in democracy is also a *duty* of every citizen and is derived from two other principles—the principle of the common good and the universal destination of goods.

In order for the Church to maintain all four of its more fundamental principles, she must at once urge every state and societal structure to observe every individual's right to self-governance and individual participation in the larger community. At the same time, she must also urge every citizen to participate in the democratic process not only by voting but by using every other means of participation (e.g., participation in local hearings, public discussions, and even protests) to urge civil authorities to take care of those who have less influence and social status.[22] She must also urge citizens to be vigilant about preventing people of influence to receive unfair and unearned privileges within the civil society that undermine justice and the common good.

---

[22] See *Compendium*, nos. 190–91. See also *Sollicitudo Rei Socialis*, nos. 44–45, and *Pacem in Terris*.

F. The Principle of Solidarity

Like the principle of subsidiarity, the principle of solidarity is considered a most fundamental social principle affecting every citizen's participation in social and civil structures as well as those social and civil structures themselves. Though solidarity is an ideal for all social and civil structures, it is first and foremost a moral virtue in every individual. We might define this virtue as a concern and determination to orient social and civil structures toward justice and the common good—and to find ways to change unjust social structures that are contrary to the common good. Summarizing *Sollicitudo Rei Socialis*, the *Compendium* describes it as follows:

> *Solidarity must be seen above all in its value as a moral virtue that determines the order of institutions.* On the basis of this principle the "*structures of sin*" that dominate relationships between individuals and peoples must be overcome. They must be purified and transformed into *structures of solidarity* through the creation or appropriate modification of laws, market regulations, and juridical systems.[23]

The Catholic Church has supported many international solidarity initiatives throughout the last century, such as the United Nation's Millennial Developmental Goals. Pope John Paul II, Pope Benedict XVI, and Pope Francis have encouraged governments, citizens, Catholic charitable organizations, and secular NGOs (non-governmental organizations) to support this effort to alleviate international poverty, famine, disease, and other oppressive conditions to the greatest possible extent. As will be explained below (Section III), these efforts have helped hundreds of millions of people to move out of extreme famine, disease, and poverty.

The principle of solidarity applies not only to social structures of particular communities, states, and nations, but also to social and market structures among nations throughout the world. This means that citizens must be vigilant about ensuring that international market forces and global political structures are oriented toward justice and the common good—that is, that they do not exploit or oppress less

---

[23] *Compendium*, no. 193.

wealthy and less influential peoples and nations. If they do, citizens should do what they can to rectify these unjust and oppressive relationships so that those nations have the opportunity to forge a way out of their economically and politically challenged conditions. Two particularly important vehicles for doing this are education and the introduction of inexpensive new technologies that will advance communication, agriculture, energy production, and banking/financing. Social entrepreneurship has been quite successful in accomplishing these objectives without making recourse to governmental solutions. There are dozens of examples of this new generation of social entrepreneurs, two of whom, for example, have affected the lives of hundreds of thousands of people in developing countries.[24] If citizens find it difficult to move the wills of governmental and international authorities, they might want to investigate this new generation of social entrepreneurs and find ways to support them.

II. Seven Major Areas of Catholic
Social Teaching Application

There are seven major social contexts that Christian citizens should safeguard, maintain, and develop through the application of the six principles of CST:

1. The Family (discussed in Chapter 5 of the *Compendium*)—Section II.A
2. The Working Environment (discussed in Chapter 6 of the *Compendium*)—Section II.B

---

[24] See, for example, the work of Iqbal Quadir (current professor at MIT), who started Grameenphone and Gonofone in his native Bangladesh, making cell phone communication so inexpensive that it is available to almost everyone. See also the work of James Tooley, who is currently organizing networks of inexpensive private schools throughout the world using a remarkable model of integrated private initiatives. Currently his and others' work is positively affecting the education of tens of thousands of students in developing countries. The model is described in his book *A Beautiful Tree*, which won the Sir Anthony Fisher prize in the UK. See Iqbal Quadir, "How Mobile Phones Can Fight Poverty", *TED Talk*, 2006, https://www.ted.com/speakers/iqbal_quadir. See James Tooley, *A Beautiful Tree: A Personal Journey into How the World's Poorest People Are Educating Themselves* (Washington, D.C.: Cato Institute, 2013).

3. The Economic/Business Community (discussed in Chapter 7 of the *Compendium*)—Section II.C
4. The Political Community (discussed in Chapter 8 of the *Compendium*)—Section II.D
5. The International Community (discussed in Chapter 9 of the *Compendium*)—Section II.E
6. The Environment (discussed in Chapter 10 of the *Compendium*)—Section II.F
7. The Pursuit of Peace and the Situation of War (discussed in Chapter 11 of the *Compendium*)—Section II.G

We will discuss each in turn.

A. The Family

Family is foundational, and so also the Sacrament of Matrimony, on which it is based, because it is the original and most influential context into which human life is born and formed, and the most fundamental constituent of local communities, societies, and the state.[25] Thus, it is the culture of every person's origin and the building block and conduit of all other forms of culture and community. As noted above (with respect to the principle of subsidiarity), the family is the most intimate and caring social unit, imparting not only psychological and social stability, but also moral and religious teaching and practice. Therefore, it is incumbent on all Christians to care not only for their own families, but also for the structure, stability, and welfare of all families within society.

In view of this, the Church recognizes the family to be the most foundational social structure and sees the proper rearing of children— the bringing of new transcendent eternal life into the world—as its most important purpose. Thus, the family (and the proper rearing of children) provides the basis on which the Church defines marriage and sexual mores. Yes—the Church derives her definition of marriage and sexuality from Jesus, but these teachings are seen within the

---

[25] See Pope John Paul II, Apostolic Exhortation on the Role of the Christian Family in the Modern World *Familiaris Consortio* (November 22, 1981). See also *Compendium*, Chapter 5.

context of the stability and proper functioning of the family. Hence, it should come as no surprise that the Church sees Jesus' teaching about the indissolubility of marriage within the context of providing a stable, loving, moral, and religious family in which to raise children. The centrality of family (and the raising of children) goes beyond the ideal of indissolubility to issues such as having one male father and one female mother, the exclusivity of marital partners, and even the openness to children within marriage.

Furthermore, it should come as no surprise that the Church sees Jesus' teaching on sexuality within the more foundational context of her view of marriage and family (see Chapter 1, Section I of this volume). For Christ and the Church, sexuality is not an end in itself—it is a support for the exclusive, covenant love of marriage whose purpose is to provide a stable, loving, moral, and religious context for the raising of children. We might say, then, that the family (the generation and raising of transcendent eternal beings) is the foundation on which the Church builds her view of marriage—and that this view of marriage is the foundation on which she builds her view of sexuality. Viewed the other way around, the Church's view of sexuality is derived from her view of marriage, which is derived from her view of family—and is inseparable from them.

Interpreting Jesus' teaching about the intention of His Father to make sexual union the exclusive domain of covenant love in marriage, the Church views sexual relationships outside of marriage to be contrary to God's will. Inasmuch as God's will is oriented solely toward the good of human beings both in this world and toward the life to come, she holds that sexuality outside the marriage covenant (exclusive commitment) will undermine the maturity, capacity for love, generativity, and commitment to God of those engaging in it. In short, engaging in any sexual relationship outside of the covenant love of marriage is destructive of the self, the capacity to relate to others, and our commitment to God (see Chapter 1, Section I). The idea that the Church should adapt to the contemporary view that sexuality can be an end in itself is tantamount to saying that the Church should ignore the teachings of Jesus and allow people to undermine their potential for covenant love, family, and commitment to God. Thus, she will always teach the indissolubility of marriage and the sole place of sexuality within marriage.

What must Christians do to uphold and promote the family within society?

1. Enter into marital relationships with the intention of exclusive and indissoluble commitment to one's spouse and be open to bearing and raising children.
2. Provide an example to friends and community of good marriage and the raising of children.
3. Practice and uphold Jesus' and the Church's view of exclusive indissoluble marriage and the proper place of sexuality within it.
4. Use the principle of subsidiarity to protect the autonomy and dignity of the family within the larger social context.
5. Help other families with advice, friendship, prayer, and other forms of support.

There is one more dimension of upholding the family to which Pope John Paul II calls us—namely, to do everything within our power to create a culture of life.[26] Inasmuch as bearing and raising of children is the most important purpose of family, it is incumbent on Christians to build a culture in which the sacredness and preciousness of life is recognized, appreciated, and supported. Without this culture of life (i.e., a culture of death), we can expect that the intrinsic transcendental dignity of every child will not be recognized, let alone appreciated and supported. Quite the opposite—children will be "under attack", and as we can see, the killing of innocent preborn children will not only be permitted but hailed as a great social triumph.

Furthermore, we can expect that families with large numbers of children will also come under scrutiny—and may also be marginalized socially and civilly. This will allow society to promote "more noble" objectives than bringing eternal transcendental life into the world—such as increased wealth, social status, disposable goods, and creature comforts. This trend will lead inevitably to an increased concern for Level One (materialistic and sensual) objectives and Level Two (ego-comparative) objectives—and a concomitant decline in Level Three (contributive and generative) objectives and Level Four

---

[26] See *Evangelium Vitae*.

(transcendent and religious) objectives. As the culture becomes more materialistic, egocentric, and even narcissistic, the society that it animates will grow weaker and less unified.[27] This trend is already having significant consequences throughout Europe and is beginning to manifest itself in the United States and Canada (see Chapter 1, Sections II–V of this volume). Even as these negative cultural and societal consequences are becoming increasingly apparent, the myth of overpopulation continues to be promulgated by some cultural leaders who simply ignore the data of increased per capita wealth amid rising population due to significant advances in the technology of agriculture, energy production, communication, education, and structural engineering. (This was thoroughly discussed in Chapter 2, Section IV.B.)

If we are to uphold the family, the significance and value of children, and the lives of the unborn, we will have to put Catholic social teaching into action in three other ways within the culture:

1. Uphold the principles of justice and inalienable rights discussed in Chapter 6 (Section II) to defend the life, personhood, and inalienable rights of the unborn—and to reverse the legal decisions upholding abortion.
2. Uphold the inalienable rights and intrinsic transcendent dignity of children within the culture and the state by challenging the myth of overpopulation and other sophistical arguments against children.
3. Promote the transcendental dignity (and transphysical soul) of human beings, and help others to make the transition from Level One-Two purpose to Level Three-Four purpose.

In light of the above, we cannot afford naively to hold that we are promoting social justice and upholding Catholic social teaching without being strong advocates of the Church's teaching on family, children, and the unborn, for if the fundamental value and

---

[27]Interestingly, the former neo-Marxist Christopher Lasch recognized this trend in Western culture, which led him to a rigorous defense of the family. See Christopher Lasch, *The Culture of Narcissism: American Life in an Age of Diminishing Expectations* (Danvers, Mass.: W. W. Norton, 1991).

dignity of family and children are culturally and societally undermined, the society will soon move to a dominant Level One-Two culture. Moreover, its most fundamental social unit will be destabilized, and the value of its most precious constituent—its children— undervalued and implicitly (and sometimes explicitly) marginalized. This will serve only to weaken the moral and social fabric of the culture and society, which will endanger its social cohesiveness, civility, and stability. Let us resolve then to uphold the dignity and value of children, the family, and the unborn as if it were the very foundation of the other six social contexts of Catholic social teaching—the working environment, the economic/business community, the political community, the international community, the environment, and international peace.

B. The Working Environment

The Old Testament, Jesus, Saint Paul, and the Church—all attest to the importance and dignity of work in our temporal and spiritual lives. Using one's gifts, time, and talents to create and produce goods and services to help sustain the lives of others in the community is intrinsically good and an integral part of life's purpose.[28]

The abuses of the Industrial Revolution moved Pope Leo XIII to write the first social encyclical, *Rerum Novarum*, to protect the dignity of workers, prevent their exploitation, uphold their right to organize, and to ensure humane working conditions and just wages. The pope's intention was not only to rectify the abuses of unregulated capitalism, but also to present a Christian alternative to Marxism and Fascism, which were becoming more popular in their attempts to correct the abuses of unregulated capitalism. To do this, the pope crafted a middle course substituting government regulations and labor unions for Marxism's state ownership of the means of production.[29] The *Compendium* summarizes the contribution of *Rerum Novarum* as follows:

[28] See *Compendium*, nos. 261–66.
[29] See *Rerum Novarum*, nos. 10–11. See also *Laborem Exercens*, nos. 1–6, which sums up the prophetic nature and accomplishments of *Rerum Novarum*.

Rerum Novarum is above all a heartfelt defence of the inalienable dignity of workers, connected with the importance of the right to property, the principle of cooperation among the social classes, the rights of the weak and the poor, the obligations of workers and employers and the right to form associations.[30]

Building on this foundation, Pope Pius XI (*Quadragesimo Anno*), and Pope John Paul II (*Centesimus Annus* and *Laborem Exercens*) elaborated what might be called a constitution of the rights and duties of labor and laborers. They address the following four major issues:

1. The dignity of work (including the proper relationship between labor and capital and the proper relationship between labor and private property)[31]
2. The right to work (including the role of the state in promoting it, the proper relationship between family and work, and the rights of special groups—children, women, immigrants, and agricultural workers)[32]
3. The rights of workers (including just remuneration, humane working conditions, and the right to organize and the right to strike)[33]
4. Solidarity among workers (including the importance of unions and other labor associations)[34]

Next to its prolific work on the intrinsic transcendental dignity of every human being and the dignity and rights of the family, Catholic social teaching has distinguished itself in its defense of the dignity and rights of workers. It was the initial point from which Pope Leo XIII entered the world of Catholic social teaching, and it remains one of its major pillars to the present day because of the centrality of work—along with the family—in human dignity, rights, and fulfillment.

[30] *Compendium*, no. 268.

[31] See *Laborem Exercens*, nos. 4, 6, 11–12, 14, 19; also, *Quadragesimo Anno*, no. 23; *Centesimus Annus*, nos. 31–32, 41, 43. See also the summary of these in *Compendium*, nos. 270–86.

[32] See *Compendium*, nos. 287–300. See also *Gaudium et Spes*, no. 26; *Rerum Novarum*, no. 11; *Laborem Exercens*, nos. 9–10, 12, 14, 16–18.

[33] See *Compendium*, nos. 301–4; *Laborem Exercens*, nos. 18–19; *Gaudium et Spes*, nos. 67–68.

[34] See *Compendium*, nos. 305–9; *Laborem Exercens*, 8, 10, 20; *Gaudium et Spes*, no. 68.

C. The Economic/Business Community

Some economists have proffered the myth that the "science of economics" is morally neutral, because it simply assesses the results of its dispassionate laws (the laws of supply and demand, microeconomic analysis, and macroeconomic analysis). The objective of microeconomic analysis is to find the ideal price, quantity, and means to produce various products, while the objective of macroeconomic analysis is to determine the money supply, lending rates, and other aggregate features of the economy necessary to avoid recession and unacceptable rates of inflation. Though these enterprises at first seem more quantitative than ethical, the devil lies in the details. There are countless dimensions of economic analysis that must be subject to the scrutiny of ethical principles, particularly those that effect competitiveness among firms, humane wages, prices of inelastic goods (necessities), accessibility of credit, and several other areas. Economic laws are designed to find the most efficient ways of doing things—ideal prices, ideal quantities, ideal levels of credit, etc. But these efficiencies can, as the Industrial Revolution showed us, be incredibly exploitative—toward workers, the poor, and those without political influence. These gray areas require considerable ethical examination, which has incited the Church to provide some basic guidelines. The *Compendium* summarizes the intent of these guidelines as follows:

> Just as in the area of morality one must take the reasons and requirements of the economy into account, so too in the area of the economy one must be open to the demands of morality: "In the economic and social realms, too, the dignity and complete vocation of the human person and the welfare of society as a whole are to be respected and promoted. For man is the source, the centre, and the purpose of all economic and social life" (*Gaudium et Spes*, no. 63).[35]

The Church has no wish to modify the laws of economics or the methods for financing and initiating business enterprises. However, she is exceedingly interested in ensuring that economists, financiers, and business owners do not narrow the focus of business enterprises

---

[35] *Compendium*, no. 331.

exclusively to the most efficient means and ends of production—or exclusively to the maximization of shareholder wealth. In this sense, the Church separates herself from a vision of economics like that of Milton Friedman, who declared that "the business of business is to maximize shareholder wealth."[36] Instead, the Church proposed, long before it became popular, a "stakeholder" view of business, which holds that the objective of business is to maximize shareholder wealth while respecting and contributing to its stakeholders—that is, its customers, employees, vendors, and community (including its surrounding environment). According to Richard DeGeorge, "A stakeholder analysis of an issue consists of weighing and balancing all of the competing demands on a firm by each of those who have a claim on it, in order to arrive at the firm's obligation in a particular case."[37]

Pius XI long ago recognized that customers, employees, and community have a *claim* on business enterprises because of their contributions to it. Every business executive has the responsibility of assessing these claims and responding to them within the scope of establishing efficient means of production and competitive profits for its investors. It should be mentioned that this way of doing business has been found to be a far better model for guaranteeing the long-term viability of a business—and therefore for guaranteeing *long-term shareholder wealth*. Why? Because customers who believe they have been treated fairly will return to purchase more. Employees who believe they have been treated fairly will not only have high morale and loyalty, but also contribute creativity, personal initiative, and higher effort to company objectives. Community members who believe that they have been treated fairly attempt to accommodate those businesses and provide incentives for them to grow. Thus, stakeholder analysis is not only good ethics; it is also good business.[38]

Though the Church uses different language to speak about stakeholder analysis, she covers all of its major points:

---

[36] This is called the "Friedman Doctrine", which says that the only social responsibility of any company is to maximize profits and to ensure that some of those profits are distributed to the shareholders—nothing more. See Milton Friedman, "The Social Responsibility of Business Is to Increase Its Profits", *New York Times Magazine*, September 13, 1970.

[37] Richard DeGeorge, *Business Ethics*, 7th ed. (London: Pearson, 2009), p. 192.

[38] See Robert Spitzer, *Spirit of Leadership: Optimizing Creativity and Change of Organizations* (Seattle: Pacific Institute Press, 2000), pp. 295–308.

1. Business owners have an obligation to serve the interests not only of the shareholders, but also of those who contribute to and are affected by it. The *Compendium* states it this way:

> In this personalistic and community vision, "a business cannot be considered only as a 'society of capital goods'; it is also a 'society of persons' in which people participate in different ways and with specific responsibilities, whether they supply the necessary capital for the company's activities or take part in such activities through their labour" (*Centesimus Annus*, no. 43).[39]

2. Business owners are responsible not only for establishing the most efficient means of production and the increase of profits, but also for guaranteeing the personal dignity and rights of all those who work for it or relate to it. Summarizing paragraph 2432 of the *Catechism of the Catholic Church*, the *Compendium* states the following:

> *Business owners and management must not limit themselves to taking into account only the economic objectives of the company, the criteria for economic efficiency and the proper care of "capital" as the sum of the means of production. It is also their precise duty to respect concretely the human dignity of those who work within the company.*[40]

3. Civil authorities have a right to tax and impose regulation on private enterprises in order to prevent exploitation, provide social goods, protect competition, and ensure fair practices to customers, employees, and other stakeholders. The *Compendium* phrases it as follows:

> *With a view to the common good, it is necessary to pursue always and with untiring determination the goal of a proper equilibrium between private freedom and public action, understood both as direct intervention in economic matters and as activity supportive of economic development.* In any case, public intervention must be carried out with equity, rationality and effectiveness, and without replacing the action of individuals, which would be contrary to their right to the free exercise of economic initiative.[41]

---

[39] *Compendium*, no. 338.
[40] Ibid., no. 344.
[41] Ibid., no. 354. See also *Centesimus Annus*, no. 48.

4. Private nonprofit organizations (NGOs) are essential to sup-
plying social goods to the needy as well as education and spiritual goods for citizens. The state should observe the principle
of subsidiarity and allow private nonprofits the space to raise
funds and to provide social, educational, and religious goods as
they see fit to enhance the lives and spirits of citizens. There
is good reason to believe that the intrinsic motivation of the
leaders of these nonprofits is much higher than state officials.
Moreover, the state should not deliver religious or spiritual
benefits or try to take over all educational endeavors.[42]

As can be seen, CST's approach to business and the economy is one
of ethics and balance—that is, introducing ethical objectives into the
marketplace alongside of stakeholder analysis and a balance between
private enterprise, civil authorities, and private nonprofit organizations.

D. The Political Community

Since the time of Saint Augustine, the Church has explicitly recognized that the political community is not a higher reality than the
individuals that constitute it.[43] Furthermore, human persons cannot
be reduced to mere social units, political units, or economic units
within the political community. The political community arises out
of the individual persons who assent to it, and it is for those individuals as well as those who are affected by it both inside and outside its
boundaries. We might say that the perennial Catholic social teaching is similar to the declaration of Abraham Lincoln in his Gettysburg Address that government is "of the people, by the people, for
the people".[44] The origin of the declaration may by now be clear—

---

[42] See *Compendium*, no. 357.

[43] See Saint Augustine, *The City of God* 19, in *Nicene and Post-Nicene Fathers*, series 1, vol.
2, ed. Philip Schaff, trans. Rev. Marchs Dods (Edinburgh: T&T Clark/Grand Rapids, Mich.:
Wm. B. Eerdmans Publishing, 1886), https://web.archive.org/web/20130725190746/http://
etext.lib.virginia.edu/etcbin/toccer-new2?id=AugCity.xml&images=images%2Fmodeng
&data=%2Ftexts%2Fenglish%2Fmodeng%2Fparsed&tag=public&part=all.

[44] Abraham Lincoln, Gettysburg Address (Gettysburg, Pa., November 19, 1863), http://
www.abrahamlincolnonline.org/lincoln/speeches/gettysburg.htm.

the principle of the intrinsic transcendent dignity of every human person combined with the principle of subsidiarity.

In view of this prioritization, the Church rejects any form of totalitarianism, Marxism, and extreme socialism. These forms of political community not only eclipse the freedom and dignity of the individual and violate the principle of subsidiarity (absorbing family, community, nonprofit, and local government prerogatives into its influence), but also detract from creativity, personal initiative, and efficient production within the marketplace. To avoid these extremes, CST advocates a democratic form of government that is complemented by a strong sense of individual rights that are adjudicated by a court system responsible for upholding those rights.

Catholic social teaching begins with the cornerstone of political community—the individual, social, transcendent human being. The *Compendium* states it as follows:

> *The human person is the foundation and purpose of political life.* Endowed with a rational nature, the human person is responsible for his own choices and able to pursue projects that give meaning to life at the individual and social level.[45]

In a democracy, the will of the political community is determined by a plebiscite or by representational government (whose officials are elected). This has the good effect of allowing the will of the people to determine the common good for the nation. Remarkable as democracy is, it has one major drawback: it is based on the will of not necessarily *all* the people, but rather the *majority* of the people. This leaves those in the minority in a vulnerable position, because even in the best democracy, the majority could abuse, marginalize, or ostracize people who are in a minority position. These minorities could be ethnic minorities, religious minorities, socioeconomic minorities, and political minorities. So how can they be protected?

Recall from Chapter 6 (Section II.D) that Father Francisco Suarez discovered the solution to this problem of potentially extreme injustice—namely, the inalienable rights to life, liberty, the pursuit of happiness, and property, which belong by nature to every human

---

[45] *Compendium*, no. 384. See also *Gaudium et Spes*, no. 25.

being in order to guarantee his just desserts and claim to minimal justice. The state does not give these rights to anyone—they belong to everyone by one's very human existence. If the state does not give them, then the state cannot take them away, unless they have been used to harm the rights of others. Moreover, these rights are based on every human being's claim to minimum justice, and as we have seen from Saint Augustine, justice is higher than the positive law. If the positive law contradicts justice, then the positive law is "no law at all", and should not be enforced or obeyed. Why is this important? Since individual rights are higher than the positive law, then the power of the state must uphold them for everyone— even if the will of the majority is to ignore or reject those rights. Thus, inalienable rights are the ultimate safeguard for protecting all minorities—and adjudicating minorities' claims against the state, its laws, or the manifest will of a majority that may be contrary to those rights.[46]

The political community's responsibilities do not stop at protecting and promoting the inalienable rights of its citizens. It is also responsible for promoting the *common good*. This means providing social goods (such as roads, water, police protection, and defense) for all individuals within its boundaries, taking special care to protect the rights of everyone *equally*. Thus, the political community must guarantee an atmosphere where every individual has access to the necessities of life, education, dignified work, and entrance to the free market so that he can exercise his creativity, personal initiative, and practical efforts to sustain and enhance himself, his family, his community, and his religion.[47]

Since the Catholic Church holds that the sovereignty of a social group or nation rests in the people as a whole, and that the people can vest this sovereignty in elected representatives and that these representatives must be sworn to uphold the inalienable rights of all people while seeking to represent the majority, she advocates for a constitutional democracy sworn to uphold both the inalienable rights of all individuals and defined constitutional rights.[48]

---

[46] This is summarized in the *Compendium*, no. 387–98.
[47] See ibid., no. 389.
[48] See ibid., nos. 394–95.

Beyond this, the Church insists that the people as well as their elected representatives are bound by the moral order—that is, to adhere to the basic, universally recognized prescripts of justice, so that no political official should violate the Silver Rule (do no unnecessary harm), deprive a person without cause of life, liberty, and property, deprive a person of what is justly owed to him or belongs to him, or act in a way that is clearly contrary to the accomplishment of the common good. As explained in Chapter 6 (Sections II.B–II.D), these prescriptions of justice do not have to be explicitly assigned to political authorities by the positive law, because they belong to the natural law written in the hearts of every human being—what legal authorities would call *bonum per se* (good in itself) and *malum in se* (evil in itself).[49]

The Church holds that the prescripts of the natural law are sufficiently evident that reflective citizens should be able to recognize when the positive law violates these evident prescriptions of natural justice. If citizens recognize such a violation of the natural law by the positive law, they have the right to conscientious objection—to refrain from doing what they believe in conscience is fundamentally unjust or immoral.[50] Furthermore, Christians also have the right to resist positive laws that violate the prescripts of natural justice through civil disobedience.[51]

Catholics who aspire to political office should do so only with the intention to maintain the precepts of natural justice, to defend the inalienable rights of everyone, and to pursue the common good. Political

---

[49] In U.S. law and common law, ignorance is no excuse for violating a precept considered to be *malum in se*. It should be recognized as wrong by any person of conscience. This principle goes back to the Roman law, specifically as elucidated by Cicero in *De Republica* 3, 33: "Law in the proper sense is right reason in harmony with nature. It is spread through the whole human community, unchanging and eternal, calling people to their duty by its commands and deterring them from wrong-doing by its prohibitions. When it addresses a good man, its commands and prohibitions are never in vain; but those same commands and prohibitions have no effect on the wicked. This law cannot be countermanded, nor can it be in any way amended, nor can it be totally rescinded. We cannot be exempted from this law by any decree of the Senate or the people; nor do we need anyone else to expound or explain it. There will not be one such law in Rome and another in Athens, one now and another in the future, but all peoples at all times will be embraced by a single and eternal and unchangeable law; and there will be, as it were, one lord and master of us all—the god who is the author, proposer, and interpreter of that law." Marcus Tullius Cicero, *The Republic and the Laws*, trans. Niall Rudd (New York: Oxford University Press, 2009), pp. 68–69.

[50] See *Compendium*, no. 399.

[51] See ibid., no. 400.

office should never be used to aggrandize oneself, bring undue privileges, or give some constituents unfair advantage over others, because engaging in bribery or any form of corruption is immoral.[52]

The media can be an indispensable help for informing the constituents of a democracy about issues and candidates, but it could also be a manipulative propaganda machine if it is motivated by ideology or profits. Therefore, it is incumbent upon the leaders of the media establishment to present the truth about issues and candidates, trying to avoid deception by either omission or commission. Leaders of the media establishment should be concerned to promote the common good, be fair, and to avoid undermining various points of view to promote personal preferences or ideology.[53]

"Society" refers to the conglomerate of free associations of people within a political community. Hence, a society is constituted by religious associations, ethnic associations, sociopolitical associations, business and economic associations, and cultural associations. These associations have the right to exist within a political community so long as they do not violate the inalienable rights or precepts of natural justice of its citizens. A "state" is a political community (within a particular geographical boundary) with a governing body having political authority to legislate, administer, and render legal judgments. A state in which the political community has *freely vested* its sovereignty in government and political authorities is a "democratic state", but a state in which political authority is imposed on the political community by external force is a "totalitarian state". The Church is opposed to the repression of freedom and the imposition of authority on a political community—and so she is opposed to totalitarian states.

The Church teaches that society (and the free associations that constitute it) is of more fundamental importance than the state. It gives the state its purpose, and not vice versa. Therefore, the society can never be viewed as a mere extension of the state, and the state cannot suppress it or the many groups constituting it unless one or more of those groups violates the precepts of natural justice or inalienable rights of its citizens.

As noted above, every state must be open to all free associations that respect the inalienable rights and the precepts of natural justice of

---

[52] See ibid., nos. 412–13.
[53] See ibid., no. 416.

its citizens. Therefore, every *religious* association has the right to exist in any legitimate state. The principle of the intrinsic transcendent dignity of every human being requires freedom of religion within any legitimate state. This means that any person within the state should be allowed to practice his religion so long as that practice does not violate the inalienable rights or precepts of natural justice of other people. Furthermore, the state should not encourage or give undue influence to any religion or to secularism (nonreligiosity).[54] This corresponds quite closely to the first amendment of the U.S. Constitution: "Congress shall make no law respecting an establishment of religion or prohibiting the free exercise thereof."[55]

Within the scope of the freedom of religion, the Catholic Church reserves the right to be independent and self-governing, free of influence or coercion from the state. Similarly, the Church must respect the autonomy and self-governance within a democratic state that upholds inalienable rights. The Church should not ask the state to give her preference in particular rulings, laws, or judgments. However, the Church has the right to point to moral failings within the states (that violate the inalienable rights or the precepts of natural justice of the people within its boundaries). This closely resembles the so-called doctrine of the separation of church and state, which most of the U.S. Founding Fathers did not intend in an absolute sense. Though Jefferson had a more extreme view of separation,[56] most Founding Fathers did not want religion, religious symbols, or the formation of political conscience by religion to be banished from the public square.[57]

---

[54] See ibid., nos. 421–23. See also *Dignitatis Humanae*, nos. 1–7.

[55] From the website of Constitute, last revised 1992, https://www.constituteproject.org/constitution/United_States_of_America_1992.

[56] This phrase was first used by Thomas Jefferson to interpret the first amendment of the Constitution (in a letter in 1801 to the Danbury Baptist Association); since that time, it has been cited frequently by the Supreme Court (see *Reynolds v. US*).

[57] In an interview with Mark Levin, Professor Michael McConnell (Stanford University) indicated, "[The 'separation of Church and state'] did not mean that the framers believed that the American people should be any less religious than they choose to be.... It didn't mean ... that there was anything wrong with having religious elements in the culture. What it meant is that we would not have a system in which the government was able to tell us what to believe, was able to control churches, decide their doctrines, decide who their personnel would be, and so forth." See Charles Creitz, "Constitutional Expert on 'Separation of Church and State': Framers Said Nothing Wrong with Religion in Culture", Fox News, June 23, 2019, https://www.foxnews.com/politics/separation-of-church-state-levin-michael-mcconnell.

This view of separation between church and state does not entail noncooperation. Indeed, it expects the church and the state to cooperate with each other to best serve the needs of the common good. In sum, the church and the state should cooperate with each other for the individual and common good so long as this cooperation does not lead to favoritism of one religion over another or to the restriction of particular religions or religious liberty.[58]

E. The International Community

The *Compendium* defines the international community as follows:

> The international community is a juridical community founded on the sovereignty of each member State, without bonds of subordination that deny or limit its independence. Understanding the international community in this way does *not in any way mean relativizing or destroying the different and distinctive characteristics of each people but, encourages their expression.*[59]

In order to promote international cooperation to avoid war and unnecessary disputes, and to avoid prejudice (and marginalization based on prejudice), it is necessary to have a body of international law and some international legal structures to facilitate cooperation among states without interfering with their sovereignty. These international laws and legal structures should support the natural law on international cooperation, which is of higher significance than the internal laws of any particular state. The *Compendium* describes this as follows:

> Universal respect of the principles underlying "a legal structure in conformity with the moral order" (Pacem in Terris: AAS 55 [1963], 277) is a necessary condition for the stability of international life.... Juridical and theological reflection, firmly based on natural law, has formulated "universal principles which are prior to and superior to the internal law of States" (John Paul II, Message for 2004 World Day of

---

[58] See *Compendium*, nos. 424–25.

[59] *Compendium*, no. 434. See Pope John Paul II, Address to the Fiftieth General Assembly of the United Nations (October 5, 1995), nos. 9–10.

Peace, 5: *AAS* 96 [2004], 116), such as the unity of the human race, the equal dignity of every people, the rejection of war as a means for resolving disputes, the obligation to cooperate for attaining the common good and the need to be faithful to agreements undertaken (*pacta sunt servanda*).[60]

CST affirms the need for intergovernmental structures, such as the United Nations and international courts, to ensure that the fundamental natural laws noted above will be effective within and among different nations. However, these intergovernmental structures/organizations cannot become de facto a "global super-state"[61] and therefore must respect the sovereignty of every nation. The only way to guarantee this is through *mutual agreement* among nations—both weak and strong.[62] The ideal would be if every nation throughout the world would agree to a set of natural laws (based on fundamental natural principles) for the common good to be administered without prejudice by an international organization or organizations.

The principle of intrinsic transcendent dignity of every individual and the principle of solidarity requires that all nations—as well as citizens having influence and means—cooperate and contribute to the overcoming of worldwide poverty and to development within substantially undeveloped nations (see below Section III). The degree of cooperation among nations depends on the resources, expertise, and capital available for these efforts—beyond the reasonable needs of the nation itself as determined by its citizens. It is incumbent on governmental agencies, non-governmental organizations, and social entrepreneurs (within the free market system) to set aside time, expertise, and resources to make these contributions to global development where and when they have access. At the very least, special provision should be made to help developing nations gain access to free markets and to subsidize loans for infrastructure and business incubation. Furthermore, provision should be made to deliver essential needs for the impoverished and to provide the highest degree of education attainable. Creative efforts should be made to share education through distance technologies, share the infrastructure for new

---

[60] *Compendium*, no. 437.
[61] Ibid., no. 44.
[62] Ibid.

technologies, and to share administrative expertise with developing countries. Without this solid educational, technological, and administrative foundation—along with the promotion of a solid legislative and juridical framework—access to free markets and low-cost loans will be at best fictitious and at worst a road to further indentured servitude to wealthier nations.

F. The Environment

The abuses of the environment caused by the industrial revolution at the turn of the century alerted the Church to the need to protect the environment from long-term abusive, polluting, and depleting activities of industries and governments. The threat to a sound environment in the future became critical at the time of the Second Vatican Council, at which point the Council declared that the Church must make the protection of the environment one of her special charges.[63] Pope John Paul II gave special attention to this dimension of Catholic social teaching in Centesimus Annus[64] and Sollicitudo Rei Socialis,[65] and Pope Francis brought this issue into full light by dedicating an entire encyclical letter to it—Laudato Si'. Church teaching emphasizes a balance between the "environment as resource" and "the environment as home". The environment provides necessary resources for human beings to maintain a healthy and productive life—food, drink, shelter, energy, and the elements for necessary technological growth. The Church encourages nations to share resources and support developing nations in the acquisition of resources needed to sustain their populations, and to ensure that certain nations do not consume (and permanently deplete) the majority of the world's resources. Furthermore, the Church teaches that the proper use of these resources should not lead to their exploitation in such a way that the environment (as common home) is undermined now or in the future.[66] Pope Francis extended this principle by making concrete

---

[63] See Gaudium et Spes, no. 35.
[64] See Centesimus Annus, nos. 37–40.
[65] See Sollicitudo Rei Socialis, no. 28.
[66] See Compendium, no. 461.

recommendations in four specific areas—pollution, climate change, clean water, and biodiversity.[67]

Some of Pope Francis' recommendations make specific judgments about the use of fossil fuels and other resources. Though they have the endorsement of many in the scientific community, they do not enjoy unanimity among scientists, and they should be viewed as prudential judgments—and not as doctrinal teaching (see below Section IV). The key principle for Catholics forming their consciences is to use their best judgment as well as the recommendations of the Holy Father to find ways of balancing the use of resources in the following areas:

1. The balance between wealthier and poorer nations in accessing resources
2. The balance between resources needed to sustain life and the use of resources injurious to the environment
3. The balance between the resources needed to sustain life and the permanent depletion of those resources

Since scientific opinion is not unanimous on where these balances occur, it is difficult to determine the uses of resources that are socially irresponsible—that is, uses of resources that unnecessarily cause poverty or injury, cause irreparable harm to the environment and world climate, and cause a permanently injurious depletion of resources. Nevertheless, the multiple "gray areas" in these critical balances do not excuse individuals from seriously considering the above questions, or determining specific ways in which they or their organizations can help the environment (or at least avoid injuring it).

There is another "gray area" that presents hope for the environment, but further ambiguity about moral responsibility—*new technological advances*. As noted in Chapter 2 (Section IV.B), the bleak Malthusian prediction that scarce resources and unlimited wants will cause poverty, war, and other social disruption has been proven false time and time again by the creation of new technological means to multiply and use resources as well as to clean the environment.[68]

---

[67] See *Laudato Si'*, "Pollution and Climate Change" (Chapter 1, Section I), "The Issue of Water" (Chapter 1, Section II), and "Loss of Biodiversity" (Chapter 1, Section III).

[68] See Paul Pilzer, *Unlimited Wealth: The Theory and Practice of Economic Alchemy* (New York: Crown Publishers, 1990).

Though we must be very conscious to do what we can to prevent the artificial causes of global warming, pollution, and the decline of biodiversity, there may well be several new technological solutions to these problems beyond the abandonment of fossil fuels and economically destructive environmental restrictions.[69] Furthermore, there are several new technological solutions to the food crisis on the horizon, which will not only multiply food but make food available locally in the poorest and harshest environments irrespective of climate conditions.[70] Availability of clean water will continue to increase because of new "low-tech" and "hi-tech" solutions.[71] These new technologies will be available almost everywhere in the world and will transcend environmental and climate conditions. The extreme reduction in cost for energy, water, food, and material resources has great promise for solving the world's resource crises and sustaining the environment. All that is required to implement these new technologies is *the charitable resolve* of influential individuals, industries, and wealthier nations to share these advances irrespective of lower rates of profitability. As each of these technologies emerge, it will be incumbent upon the developers of these technologies, as well as the nations in which they are developed, to sacrifice some of their entitled profits to

[69] There are several new cost-efficient ways to scrub fossil fuels and to recover the residues of fossil fuels from the atmosphere. Furthermore, the probable success of fusion power will make fossil fuels *per force* obsolete. See the multiple technologies discussed in Chapter 2, Section IV.B of this volume.

[70] The most notable advance is the high level of research being done into huge multilevel hydroponic vertical farms. Since these vertical farms are completely enclosed, they are impervious to insects, diseases, and climate conditions. Furthermore, the regulatable frequencies of the light used to grow the products in these farms and the precise regulation of temperatures (with no soil requirements and recyclable water) will allow ten harvests per year instead of 1.5 harvests. Therefore, a five-square-mile, twenty-five-story vertical farm could yield a hundred times the crop yield per acre as conventional farming techniques. There is currently only one obstacle to building these farms—the high cost of energy. If fusion power becomes a reality, the price of energy per megawatt hour will drop to a mere fraction of current power production techniques. See the references to new agricultural technologies in Chapter 2, Section IV.B of this volume.

[71] New low-tech filtration systems can be made by making containers out of straw and local soil that can eliminate a significant amount of the impurities in local water. Additionally, new high-tech solutions are becoming cost efficient, such as devices using only salt and energy to purify large quantities of water continuously at the source. This will allow water purification to occur in every small village. The availability of salt and affordable power will make this possible. These low-tech solutions are in part responsible for the considerable increase in potable water throughout the world. See the achievements in the United Nations Millennial Sustainability Goals below in Section III.

help alleviate the world's resource and environmental problems. At present, governments, businesses, and wealthy individuals and foundations have contributed significantly to the alleviation of famine, disease, and poverty (see below Section III). If this continues, many of the world's most acute poverty and environmental problems will be in good part alleviated, but this will require continued effort and sacrifice from leaders in the international economic community.

The Church also encourages responsible juridical regulation of the environment by both individual nations and the international community.[72] Evidently, these regulations are subject to the balances and ambiguities mentioned above. These balances and ambiguities require that legislators within nations find the most prudential course of action to protect the environment while allowing the proper use and development of resources by responsible industries. This is best worked out by a dialogue between scientists, industrial developers, citizens of local communities, and government officials who are charged with finding a proper balance to protect the environment and international economies both now and in the future. International treaties among nations will be more challenging because environmental protections in developing countries could inadvertently retard the development of industry and social infrastructure in those countries. Furthermore, it is difficult to know how to balance fairly the needs of different countries with vastly different resources and economic potential. The Church encourages all nations to enter into voluntary international protocols to increase environmental protection continually even at the cost of reasonable (non-onerous) sacrifices to the industrial base of wealthier countries. Without such reasonable sacrifices, these needed protocols would be undermined. Such reasonable sacrifices are morally incumbent upon the economic and political leaders of wealthier nations.[73]

G. The Pursuit of Peace and the Situation of War

The pursuit of peace on every level is a mandate of Jesus Christ and is integral to the Beatitude "Blessed are the peacemakers, for they shall

---

[72] See *Compendium*, nos. 468–69.
[73] See ibid.

be called sons of God" (Mt 5:9). The idea of peace (*shalom*) is integral
to every aspect of the Old Testament—from the nature of God to
the purpose of the Israelite nation. It is even the greeting extended
from one person to another. The duty to pursue peace applies to
family members, neighbors, and for Jesus, to enemies. It is the duty of
individuals and communities as well as societies and states and is the
principal outgrowth of justice and charity. The *Compendium* phrases
it as follows:

> *Peace is a value and a universal duty founded on a rational and moral order*
> *of society that has its roots in God himself,* "the first source of being, the
> essential truth and the supreme good" (John Paul II, Message for the
> 1982 World Day of Peace, 4: *AAS* 74 [1982], 328). *Peace is not merely*
> *the absence of war, nor can it be reduced solely to the maintenance of a balance*
> *of power between enemies. Rather it is founded on a correct understanding of*
> *the human person and requires the establishment of an order based on justice*
> *and charity.*[74]

Injustice threatens peace, because unfair treatment, deprivation of
justly acquired property, and deprivation of the necessities of life lead
to resentment and desperation, both of which can incite agitation and
violence. Unrest and violence are almost certainly the outcomes of
the absence of a just societal and governmental order.[75]

Yet justice alone is not sufficient for an ongoing pursuit of peace—
this requires charity (*agapē*, love—see Chapter 5, Section II).[76] Individuals and groups will no doubt make mistakes and act unjustly,
making forgiveness (an integral part of charity) a necessary part of a
peaceful social order. Furthermore, compassion (also a part of charity) is needed to overcome deeply embedded inequities within social
structures that prevent people from rising above a state of social deprivation. A deep sense of contributive altruism that seeks equal
opportunities for everyone (irrespective of economic, social, and ethnic background) is needed to guarantee peace within the social order
over the long term.

[74] Ibid., no. 494.
[75] See ibid.
[76] See *Gaudium et Spes*, no. 78, and *Populorum Progressio*, no. 76.

Even in the midst of radical injustice, violence cannot be considered a proper response. Though one may be compelled to defend oneself by the use of force (see Chapter 4, Section II, and below in this section), the Church (putting its faith in the mandate of Jesus) admonishes us to avoid in every way possible the use of violence, not only because "violence begets violence" but because it corrupts our souls, making us turn from love to anger, resentment, and destruction. The *Compendium*, following Pope Paul VI, phrases it as follows:

> *Violence is never a proper response.* With the conviction of her faith in Christ and with the awareness of her mission, the Church proclaims "that violence is evil, that violence is unacceptable as a solution to problems, that violence is unworthy of man. Violence is a lie, for it goes against the truth of our faith, the truth of our humanity. Violence destroys what it claims to defend: the dignity, the life, the freedom of human beings" (John Paul II, Address at Drogheda, Ireland [September 29, 1979], 9: *AAS* 71 [1979], 1081; cf. *Evangelii Nuntiandi*, 37).[77]

In view of this, war is considered unacceptable as a solution to the problems of national boundaries and injustice—and a war of aggression is in every way immoral. Such wars cause unbelievable harm to countless innocent victims[78] whose rights are violated by aggression, which is almost certainly avoidable. All wars of aggression should therefore be avoided, and every means should be brought to bear by powerful nations and international organizations to negotiate and to mediate potential conflicts that entail such aggression.[79]

Nevertheless, the Church acknowledges a legitimate right to self-defense and national defense in the event of a war of aggression.[80] This right arises out of an aggressor unjustly attacking a country, compelling that country to defend its citizens by force of arms. There

---

[77] *Compendium*, no. 496.

[78] For example, the Second World War cost forty-five million *civilian* deaths, as well as fifteen million military deaths. See the website of the National WWII Museum, "Research Starters: Worldwide Deaths in World War II", accessed February 22, 2022, https://www.nationalww2museum.org/students-teachers/student-resources/research-starters/research-starters-worldwide-deaths-world-war.

[79] See *Compendium*, no. 499.

[80] See ibid., no. 500.

are four major conditions governing the use of force set out by the Catholic Church (called "The Just War Doctrine"[81]):

1. The damage caused by the aggressor must be lasting, grave, and certain.
2. All other means to put an end to the aggression must be shown to be impractical or ineffective.
3. The damage inflicted on the enemy to prevent the aggression cannot be greater than those of the aggressor itself.
4. There must be a reasonable prospect of success.[82]

The application of these four principles is quite complex, but there have been several ethical treatments that attempt to articulate them systematically.[83]

Every nation has a right to raise a military force for its legitimate defense and the defense of peace. Those who serve in the military are in no way unethical or immoral, and are considered to be agents of truth, justice, and peace.[84] Nevertheless, military personnel are bound by the natural law, which must be held above the positive law and military orders that contradict the natural law. Thus, military personnel must resist complying with orders that are criminal or in other ways violations of the natural rights of every human being.[85]

Every state legitimately using military force to resist unjust aggression must take every possible step to minimize harm to innocent civilians—not only harm to their lives and bodies but also harm to their liberty and property. Perpetrating avoidable "collateral damage"

---

[81] This doctrine had a long development within the Catholic Church, beginning with Saint Augustine (in *Contra Faustum Manichaeum* 22, 69–76, and *City of God* 19) and further developed by Saint Thomas Aquinas (in *ST* II-II, q. 40). The doctrine was expanded and formalized by the School of Salamanca (see Chapter 6, Section II.D on Francisco Suarez).

[82] See *Compendium*, no. 500, and *CCC* 2309.

[83] See, for example, Paul Ramsey, *The Just War: Force and Political Responsibility* (Rowman & Littlefield Publishers, 2002).

[84] See *Compendium*, no. 502.

[85] See ibid., no. 503. For example, Lieutenant William Calley was court-martialed for the massacre of twenty-two civilians in My Lai during the Vietnam War. Though controversy surrounded the conviction, Calley's actions clearly violated the inalienable right to life and liberty (through torture) of civilians, though they may have been hiding weapons for North Vietnamese regulars.

to innocent victims is immoral, and international courts have the right to redress these crimes legitimately.[86] The international community also has the right to resist, redress, and punish any attempt to engage in ethnic cleansing or the eradication of a particular ethnic or religious group (genocide). Perpetrators of such crimes against humanity are punishable by the rules of international law.[87] If the innocent are attacked (and their human rights significantly violated) in a nation that cannot defend itself against a more powerful aggressor, then it is incumbent upon the international community to defend the rights of the innocent even if it must use the force of arms to do so.[88] Such defense must adhere to the guidelines and four conditions of the just war doctrine elucidated above. CST elaborates several other precepts concerned with war and the pursuit of peace:

- The legitimate use of economic and political sanctions as disincentives to those who are threatening peace[89]
- The common, multilateral agreement to reduce weapons of mass destruction[90]
- The prohibition of a Cold War–style arms race[91]
- The prohibition of the conscription of children into the military or into fighting situations[92]
- The prohibition of terrorism in any form—and the profanation of God's name and nature by proclaiming terrorist actions to be His will—or to proclaim terrorists as martyrs in the eyes of God[93]

As can be seen, the Church's articulation of the precepts of war and peace are very well nuanced and follow the six principles of her social teaching applied to individuals, societies, political entities, and the international community (see above Section I). It serves as a model not only for Catholics, but also every secular society, for it is based

---

[86] See ibid., no. 505.
[87] See ibid., no. 506.
[88] Ibid.
[89] See ibid., no. 507.
[90] See ibid., nos. 508–9.
[91] See ibid., no. 509.
[92] See ibid., no. 512.
[93] See ibid., nos. 513–15.

primarily on the natural law and natural rights that have become the cornerstone of every free nation. Indeed, Pope John XXIII addressed his famous encyclical on peace and war (*Pacem in Terris*) to *all* men, as expressed in the *Compendium*:

> To "all men of good will" (*Pacem in Terris*, no. 1) who are called to a great task "to establish with truth, justice, love and freedom new methods of relationships in human society" (*Pacem in Terris: AAS* 55 [1963], 301).[94]

III. Sustainable Development Goals and the Alleviation of Worldwide Famine, Disease, and Poverty

In Sections II.E (international community) and II.F (environment), we discussed the ethical responsibility to seek solutions to oppressive and inhumane conditions caused by economic inequities and environmental destruction. Pope John Paul II indicated in his address at the Puebla Conference of Latin American Bishops that the principles of the common good, solidarity, and the universal destination of goods require that governments, world economic leaders, and concerned citizens of economically privileged nations commit themselves to international goals for the alleviation of famine, disease, and poverty. In the face of significant inequities arising out of globalization, climate challenges, migration, and lack of socioeconomic opportunity, he advocated a "preferential option for the poor". He later used this rationale to commit the Church to the sustainable development goals of the United Nations 1990 World Summit.

The term "sustainability" arose out of the Brundtland Report in 1987 and quickly evolved into a socioeconomic-ecological movement adopted by the United Nations and almost immediately subscribed to by Pope John Paul II. The intention behind sustainable development is to create a systemic approach to socioeconomic-ecological development through the integration of economic policy, ecological policy, technological development, and sociopolitical

---

[94] Ibid., no. 95.

cooperation in a fashion that meets the needs of the present as well as those of future generations.

CST has deeply considered the needs of not only sociopolitical and socioeconomic equitable development (see *Compendium*, Chapters 6–9), but also environmental stewardship and development (*Compendium*, Chapter 10). John Paul II recognized almost immediately the importance of integrating these two components through the above scheme of sustainable development, and publicly supported the United Nations' formulation of Millennium Development Goals (oriented toward reducing poverty and social exclusion in developing countries) in 1990 through 2004. Pope Benedict XVI enhanced this effort in several addresses that he brought to fruition in his encyclical *Caritas in Veritate*. Building on these efforts, Pope Francis has formally raised sustainable development goals to a level of a virtual ethical mandate in *Laudato Si'* (May 2015). In addition to reinforcing the socioeconomic Millennium Development Goals (supported by Pope John Paul II and Pope Benedict XVI), Pope Francis advocates the much broader 2015 sustainable development goals of the United Nations that include ecological sustainability goals in both developing and developed countries. These include commitments to avoid ecological crises with respect to climate change, ocean acidification, deforestation, and depletion of water resources, as well as pollution from extensive use of fertilizers and from the massive burning of fossil fuels, and the undermining of ecosystems and the loss of biodiversity. Pope Francis provides a thorough explanation and rationale for integrating these new dimensions into the Catholic commitment to sustainable development goals in *Laudato Si'*.

It should be noted that worldwide commitment to sustainable development goals really works to bring billions of people out of conditions of starvation, disease, and poverty. In 1990, at the United Nations conference on Millennium Development Goals (MDGs), most developed nations committed themselves through specific actions to seven major goals:

1. Providing for livable wages (humane standard)
2. Providing healthcare (humane standard)
3. Providing education (by means of both private and public programs)

4. Providing clean water and accessible energy
5. Shifting to a "sustainable" resource-use model
6. Protection of ecosystems
7. Build more inclusive societies in light of global migration

Between 1990 and 2015, enormous progress (affecting billions of people throughout the world) was made in all seven MDGs with reasonable sacrifices, affordable contributions, reasonable (but concerted) technology sharing, and commitment by a host of new NGOs (nongovernmental organizations). The following points represent some of the amazing results listed in the United Nations *Millennium Development Goals Report* (2015):[95]

- Extreme poverty rate decreased by more than 50 percent from 1.9 billion affected people to 836 million.
- Percentage of malnourished in developing countries down by nearly half from 23 percent to 13 percent of population.
- Deaths of children down by more than half, from 12.7 million to 6 million.
- Maternal mortality rate down by 45 percent.
- Infectious disease rates decreased substantially with respect to HIV, malaria, and tuberculosis.
- Access to proper sanitation increased by 2 billion people.

These results confirm the efficacy of concerted commitment to MDGs.

We may conclude from the above results that the collaboration of governments, private businesses, churches, and religious and nonreligious NGOs toward sustainable development goals is exceedingly worthwhile. If progress continues apace, the levels of famine, disease, poverty, and ecological destruction will again be cut in half (from the 2015 levels) by 2027. This would fulfill the objectives, indeed the dreams, of Saint John Paul II, Pope Benedict XVI, and Pope Francis, as well as thousands of diocese, churches, and charities throughout the world.

[95] *The Millennium Development Goals Report* (New York: United Nations, 2015), http://www.un.org/millenniumgoals/2015_MDG_Report/pdf/MDG%202015%20rev%20%28July%201%29.pdf.

IV. The Doctrinal Authority of Catholic Social Teaching—Magisterium or Prudential Judgment?

The Church has been very clear about the distinction between Ordinary and Extraordinary Magisterium throughout the last century but less clear about the distinction between Ordinary Magisterium and prudential judgment with respect to her social teaching. This ambiguity in combination with the proliferation of CST and the regularity of episcopal conferences led to a series of clarifying pronouncements by the Holy Father, the Pontifical Council for Justice and Peace, and the USCCB. I will give a brief summary of the pronouncements of Vatican I and Vatican II on Ordinary and Extraordinary Magisterium followed by a more in-depth analysis of the Church's recent documents on prudential judgment.

We may begin with *Extraordinary Magisterium*, which concerns defined doctrines of the Church. These are irrevocable decisions, by which the supreme teaching authority in the Church decides a question pertaining to faith or morals, and which bind the whole Church. Four conditions are required for a defined doctrine:

1. It must be a decision by the supreme teaching authority in the Church.
2. The decision must concern a doctrine of faith or morals.
3. The decision must bind the Universal Church.
4. The decision must be irrevocable (definitive).

With respect to the first condition, there are two sources of supreme authority in the Church: (a) the Holy Father, who declares himself to be speaking as supreme teacher of all Christians (*Ex Cathedra*), and (b) the bishops of the Church united in ecumenical council in concert with the pope.

With respect to the second condition (faith and morals), "faith" concerns what must be *believed* by Christians while "morals" concerns what must be *done* by Christians. The third condition requires a decree (from one of the two supreme authoritative sources of the Church) that binds all the faithful (not merely some part of the faithful). Finally, the fourth condition requires that one of the two sources declare that the decision is final and will never be changed (irrevocable).

We may now proceed to *Ordinary Magisterium*, which can be infallible, but is most often noninfallible. It is infallible *only* when the dispersed bishops throughout the world are in union with the pope over a long period of time and a particular teaching is to be held by the faithful for the sake of salvation. The reason that "ordinary" is used in conjunction with "infallible" here is that a particular teaching may begin as noninfallible Ordinary Magisterium, but when the pope and the bishops throughout the world have taught the same doctrine of faith and morals, to be held by the faithful, over the course of some length of time, it takes on an infallible character, and is no longer noninfallible Ordinary Magisterium. This is also referred to as Ordinary Universal Magisterium.[96]

The more common *noninfallible* Magisterium occurs in three ways:

1. When the pope teaches authoritatively but not definitively and infallibly (e.g., an encyclical letter such as the social encyclicals)
2. When an ecumenical council teaches authoritatively but not definitively and infallibly
3. When individual bishops exercise their teaching authority in matters of faith and morals; this may also occur through regional episcopal conferences

Individual bishops do not have infallible teaching authority. If a bishop is not speaking about theological truths or moral principles leading to salvation, then his pronouncement is not Ordinary Magisterium. It is a theological opinion or a prudential judgment (see below). Furthermore, if a bishop is not in communion with other bishops or makes a pronouncement that contradicts the Extraordinary

[96] Many Church teachings have come to their doctrinal (universal, infallible) status in this way. Since there is no definitive declaration about this kind of Magisterium, there is ambiguity surrounding which doctrines qualify. For example, how long must a particular teaching be taught in this manner? Two generations? Five generations? Furthermore, does "universal" mean "all the bishops with the pope (no dissenters)" or "most of the bishops (only a few dissenters)"? Despite these ambiguities, the faithful may be sure that this kind of infallibility exists, and that when there is ambiguity, it is best to assume the infallible character of the teaching in question.

or Ordinary Universal Magisterium of the Church, then his pronouncement is evidently not Ordinary Magisterium. If a regional council of bishops (e.g., the USCCB) is not speaking about theological truths or moral principles leading to salvation, their pronouncements are not Ordinary Magisterium, but only theological opinions or prudential judgments.

We now proceed to the third category of Church teaching—namely, *prudential judgments*. This category is important with respect to *applying* the Church's social teaching to particular times and places and to pronouncements of regional councils of bishops. As will be shown, prudential judgments do *not* bind but only guide the faithful. Thus, Catholics can respectfully disagree with the recommendations of social encyclicals that are prudential judgments. Judgments that are not necessary for salvation may change over the course of time, or have a diversity of expert opinion with respect to application.

Let us begin with papal pronouncements on Catholic social teaching. Papal encyclicals on social teaching contain both *principles* and *applications of principles*. Should both CST principles and their applications be considered Ordinary Magisterium? The answer may be inferred from the above general criteria for Ordinary Magisterium:

1. Since the *principles* of CST lead the faithful to salvation and are not likely to change over time, they qualify for Ordinary Magisterium.
2. Conversely, specific *applications* of these principles may *not* be directly concerned with salvation and may change in different places and times. Therefore, they should be considered prudential judgments.

The Pontifical Council for Justice and Peace (requested by Pope John Paul II in 2004) declared in the *Compendium* that there are five major principles of CST, which are binding on all the faithful:

1. The pursuit of the common good in a spirit of service
2. The development of justice with particular attention to situations of poverty and suffering
3. Respect for the autonomy of earthly realities

4. The principle of subsidiarity (matters ought to be handled by the smallest, lowest, or least centralized competent authority)
5. The promotion of dialogue and peace in the context of solidarity[97]

The Pontifical Council for Justice and Peace further declared that these five principles of CST are Ordinary Magisterium that obligates the Catholic faithful:

> These are the criteria that *must* inspire the Christian laity in their political activity. *All* believers, insofar as they possess rights and duties as citizens, are *obligated* to respect these guiding principles.[98]

There is also a sixth principle of CST that is implicit in the above list of five that forms the foundation of virtually every papal social encyclical—namely, the principle of the intrinsic dignity of every human being (see above Section I.A).

We may now return to the distinction between the principles of CST and the *application* of the *principles* of CST. From the above, it is clear that the six general principles of CST are Ordinary Magisterium, but as the Pontifical Council for Justice and Peace and the U.S. Catholic bishops declare, the applications of these principles are prudential judgments. The *Compendium* states:

> When reality is the subject of careful attention and proper interpretation, concrete and effective choices can be made. However, an *absolute value* must *never* be attributed to these choices because no problem can be solved once and for all. "Christian faith has never presumed to impose a rigid framework on social and political questions, conscious that the historical dimension requires men and women to live in imperfect situations, which are also susceptible to rapid change" (Congregation for the Doctrine of the Faith, *Doctrinal Note on Some Questions regarding the Participation of Catholics in Political Life*, no. 7).[99]

How does this distinction work out in our daily lives? Let's take an example. The principle of the intrinsic dignity of every human being is evidently important for our salvation and will not change over the

---

[97] *Compendium*, no. 565.
[98] Ibid. (italics added).
[99] Ibid., no. 568.

course of time (i.e., it qualifies for Ordinary Magisterium). However, certain applications of this principle—say, membership in a particular Union, which might help workers to obtain their appropriate dignity—does not necessarily lead to salvation and could very well change over the course of time. Such an application of the principle of intrinsic dignity would not qualify for Ordinary Magisterium and would then be a prudential judgment.

This distinction becomes more challenging when we are considering very *general* applications of the six major principles of CST (e.g., the right of labor to organize). Is this application only prudential judgment? Doesn't the right to organize prevent all kinds of exploitation of labor? Wouldn't this qualify as Ordinary Magisterium? It is easy to see how *specific* applications of CST (such as belonging to a particular Union) would not qualify for Ordinary Magisterium, but what about very general applications?

One can see how the right of labor to organize could be considered a natural corollary to the principle of intrinsic human dignity of all people, and how this would lead to salvation. However, a closer examination of this idea reveals that there are many ways in which the organization of labor might not lead to salvation—and indeed, could lead away from it (e.g., many forms of Marxism, totalitarian Communism, etc.). The ambiguity of the word "organize" makes it impossible to say that such an application of the principle of intrinsic human dignity would lead to salvation (and never away from it). Furthermore, the notion of organization of labor could change over the course of time and may be interpreted differently in various cultures. For these reasons, it seems that even *general* applications of CST principles should not qualify for Ordinary Magisterium.

As noted above, this is precisely the conclusion reached by the Pontifical Council for Justice and Peace. It was also anticipated by the National Conference of Catholic Bishops in 1986 in its pastoral letter *Economic Justice for All.* In that letter, the bishops explicitly used and defined "prudential judgment" in the area of applying the principles of Catholic social teaching to concrete situations.[100]

---

[100] For example, "We do not claim to make these prudential judgments with the same kind of authority that marks our declarations of principle." National Conference of Catholic Bishops, *Economic Justice for All: Pastoral Letter on Catholic Social Teaching and the U.S. Economy* (Washington, D.C.: National Conference of Catholic Bishops, 1986), p. xii.

This was reaffirmed and explained in 2007 (after the publication of the *Compendium* in 2005) in another pastoral letter called *Forming Consciences for Faithful Citizenship: A Call to Political Responsibility from the Catholic Bishops of the United States*.[101] Once again, the bishops make a careful distinction between principles and application of principles, and they clearly indicate that the application of principles belongs to the domain of prudential judgment. Their recommendation may be summarized in the following two points:

1. The above six principles of CST apply to all political issues, but in many cases do not lead prudentially to one acceptable Catholic position.

2. While the six major principles of CST (and other teachings of the pope and the bishops on faith and morals that qualify as Ordinary Magisterium) are binding, their prudential judgments on policy, legislation, and other situational applications of principles *guide us but do not bind us*. The only exceptions to this are policies and practices concerned with infallible moral teaching—namely, abortion, euthanasia, and marriage.

V. Conclusion

As can be seen, the Catholic social teaching is incredibly extensive, giving guidance to our individual and collective minds on just about every topic of ethical relevance to the modern world. It is built on five fundamental principles of justice (four of which came from the Catholic Church) that have now been accepted and appropriated by most secular societies and governments, including the United Nations Declaration on Human Rights (see Chapter 6, Section III):

1. The principle of nonmaleficence
2. The principle of unjust laws
3. The principle of full and equal personhood

---

[101] United States Conference of Catholic Bishops, *Forming Consciences for Faithful Citizenship: A Call to Political Responsibility from the Catholic Bishops of the United States—with New Introductory Letter* (Washington, D.C.: United States Conference of Catholic Bishops, 2007).

4. The principle of inalienable rights
5. The principle of the natural hierarchy of rights

Using these fundamental principles of *justice and individual dignity* as a foundation, the Church extended her teaching into the *social* and *societal* domain through six additional CST principles discussed above (Section I), which she applies to seven areas of community, society, commerce, and international relations (see Section II above). There is a remarkable logical and ethical consistency in matching principles with areas of application. Notice the incredible balance achieved by the Second Vatican Council and the popes who issued social encyclicals—a balance between the rights of labor and the common good versus free markets, between abhorrence of war and provision for a just war, between national sovereignty and the need for legitimate international courts, and between the environment as resource and the environment as home. Though the principle of subsidiarity gives primacy to smaller more intimate groups—family before community, community before society, society before state, and state before international governing bodies—the Church also gives great latitude to larger social and governmental units so long as they do not undermine the smaller ones. The balance, judiciousness, and logical application of Christ's teaching to the complex array of contemporary societies, states, and the international community seems to manifest more than just rationality. It manifests the height of compassion (seen in the heart of Jesus) articulated through the best that the natural sciences, social sciences, political theory, and philosophy have to offer. It is not only a guide to social ethics, but a light to the world.

CONCLUSION TO THE TRILOGY

Reevangelizing the Culture

Introduction

In Chapter 5, we concluded that the future of democratic society lies in the hands of religion and conscience insofar as they affect objective moral norms. Inasmuch as this is true, our future will depend on the religious commitment of our citizens, the extent to which we form and obey our consciences, and the moral consensus we bring to the culture. As such, the future of our society depends on the extent to which our citizens believe and listen to God—precisely as John Adams predicted:

> Because we have no government armed with power capable of contending with human passions unbridled by morality and religion— avarice, ambition, revenge and licentiousness would break the strongest cords of our Constitution, as a whale goes through a net. Our Constitution was made only for a moral and religious people. It is wholly inadequate to the government of any other.[1]

How do we restore religion and its moral norms to an increasingly secularized society? How do we even begin this process? Throughout the Quartet and this Trilogy, I have implicitly set out a program that I have tested extensively in high schools, religious education classes, and Catholic campus ministries at Catholic and public universities. It has amazing results because the evidence for God, a transcendent soul, and Jesus from science, philosophy, and history is so probative and mutually corroborative. This rational evidence can form a reasonable

[1] Letter from John Adams to Massachusetts Militia, October 11, 1798, National Archives, Founders Online, https://founders.archives.gov/documents/Adams/99-02-02-3102.

473

and convincing response to contemporary secularization upon which we can critique the absolutizing of freedom and the undermining of objective morality while justifying the reality of Jesus and the truth of His teaching grounded in unselfish, self-sacrificial love. Can reason offer us a way out of past exaggerations of itself manifest in the Enlightenment, scientism, logical positivism, and other movements that attempt to restrict the horizons of human knowledge to particular methodologies? Perhaps it can, if people of faith are willing to reevangelize the culture by using reason's newest revelations.

The age of the Enlightenment, which proclaimed reason and science as its new "bible", initiated the religious, moral, emotional, familial, and cultural decline we are now experiencing (see Chapter 5, Section III.D). It did this by exaggerating the capabilities of reason and science to the exclusion of religion, ethics, and the humanities. In its attempt to capture the fullness of truth, love, goodness, beauty, and being through science and reason alone, it succeeded only in narrowing these five transcendentals to a mere shadow of their former selves.

Fortunately, much of the scientific and intellectual community, particularly the founders of contemporary physics, mitigated this trend by their own spiritual beliefs—Galileo Galilei (the father of observational astronomy and initial laws of dynamics and gravity),[2] Sir Isaac Newton (the father of calculus, classical mechanics, and quantitative optics),[3] James Clerk Maxwell (the father of the classical theory of electromagnetic radiation),[4] Max Planck (the father of quantum theory and co-founder of modern physics),[5] Albert Einstein (the father of the

---

[2] Despite acclaims to the contrary, well-known nuclear physicist Antonino Zichichi has documented Galileo's continuous religious belief from his personal diaries. See Antonino Zichichi, *Galilei, Divine Uomo* (Italy: Casa editrice Il Saggiatore, 2001).

[3] Newton was intensely religious and studied the Bible throughout his life. He had a radical view of Christianity, which some believed to be unorthodox, but was filled with devotion for the God of Jesus Christ. See William H. Austin, "Isaac Newton on Science and Religion", *Journal of the History of Ideas* 31, no 4 (1970): 521–42.

[4] Maxwell was a devoted Christian who defended his biblical faith and gave a religious interpretation of the uniformity of different physical phenomena. See Paul Theerman, "James Clerk Maxwell and Religion", *American Journal of Physics* 54, no. 4 (1986), https://aapt.scitation.org/doi/abs/10.1119/1.14636.

[5] Planck was convinced about not only the existence of God and the human soul, but also the veracity and importance of religion: "Religion is the link that binds man to God—resulting from the respectful humility before a supernatural power, to which all human life is subject and which controls our weal and woe." See Raymond J. Seeger, "Planck, Physicist", *Journal of the American Scientific Affiliation*, 37 (December 1985): 232–33.

theory of relativity and co-founder of modern physics),[6] Kurt Gödel (one of the greatest modern mathematicians and logicians and originator of the incompleteness theorems),[7] Sir Arthur Eddington (the father of the nuclear fusion explanation of stellar radiation),[8] Werner Heisenberg (the father of the matrix theory of quantum mechanics and the uncertainty principle),[9] Freeman Dyson (the originator of multiple theories in contemporary quantum electrodynamics),[10] and many other Nobel Prize winners.[11] Furthermore, the Pew Research Center Survey of the American Association for the Advancement of Science (one of the largest scientific organizations in the world) found that

[6] Einstein viewed God as a principle of intelligibility and rationality—a superior mind— stating it this way: "Certain it is that a conviction, akin to religious feeling, of the rationality and intelligibility of the world lies behind all scientific work of a higher order.... This firm belief, a belief bound up with a deep feeling, *in a superior mind* that reveals itself in the world of experience, represents my conception of God." See Albert Einstein, *Ideas & Opinions*, trans. Sonja Bargmann (New York: Crown Publishers, 1954), p. 262.

[7] Gödel believed in a personal God and believed that such a God could be logically proven. He expressed his thoughts as follows: "I am convinced of this [the afterlife], independently of any theology. It is possible today to perceive, by *pure reasoning* that it is entirely consistent with known facts. If the world is rationally constructed and has meaning, then there must be such a thing [as an afterlife]." See Hao Wang, *A Logical Journey: From Gödel to Philosophy*, (Cambridge: MIT Press, 1996), pp. 104–5.

[8] Eddington was a professed Christian who spoke openly about his faith and wrote a book about his belief in a personal God. See Sir Arthur Eddington, *Why I Believe in God: Science and Religion, as a Scientist Sees It* (London: Hadelman-Julius Publications, 1930). He famously noted, "The idea of a universal Mind, or Logos, would be, I think, a fairly plausible inference from the present state of [physical] theory. Mind, however, perceives two realms, the physical and the spiritual [the mystical]." See Raymond J. Seeger, "Eddington, Mystic Seeker", *Journal of the American Scientific Affiliation* 36, no. 1 (March 1984): 36.

[9] Heisenberg was a devoted Lutheran who believed in God and a transphysical soul. He defended his belief in a personal God to his colleague Wolfgang Pauli. Heisenberg publicly declared that faith goes beyond having a conviction *about* the existence of God and a soul, noting that faith entails trust that moves us to action. See Raymond J. Seeger, "Heisenberg: Thoughtful Christian", *Journal of the American Scientific Affiliation* 37 (December 1985): 231–32.

[10] Dyson is a professed Christian who has written extensively on the interplay between science and religion. One of his well-known quotations is, "Science and religion are two windows that people look through, trying to understand the big universe outside, trying to understand why we are here. The two windows give different views, but they look out at the same universe. Both views are one-sided, neither is complete. Both leave out essential features of the real world. And both are worthy of respect." See Freeman Dyson, "Progress in Religion", Edge.org, May 15, 2000, https://www.edge.org/conversation/freeman_dyson-progress-in-religion.

[11] See Robert Kurland, "23 Famous Scientists Who Are Not Atheists", Magis Center, June 5, 2021, https://www.magiscenter.com/23-famous-scientists-who-are-not-atheists/.

51 percent of scientists profess belief in God or a spiritual reality, while 41 percent are agnostic or atheist.[12] Physicians have an even higher rate of religious belief. In a National Institute of Health random survey of 1,144 physicians, 88 percent indicated they were affiliated with a religion while only 10 percent had no religious affiliation.[13] Sixty-seven percent of those religiously affiliated physicians reported having moderate to high religiosity.[14] Furthermore, HCD Research and the Louis Finkelstein Institute for Religious and Social Studies surveyed 1,100 physicians nationally and found that 73 percent believe that miracles have occurred in the past and can occur today.[15] If all these scientists and physicians profess belief in God and religion (and we suppose that they would not act contrary to reason), then contemporary culture's rejection of religion cannot be attributed mostly to science and reason. What most of these scientists recognize is that the presence of God and the fullness of truth, love, goodness, beauty, and being cannot be narrowed to the methodological confines of science and logic alone. They implicitly proclaim that there is a transcendent soul that yearns upward toward a supreme being, who is the origin of these five transcendentals. In the immortal words of the mathematical physicist Sir Arthur Eddington:

> We all know that there are regions of the human spirit untrammeled by the world of physics. In the mystic sense of the creation around us, in the expression of art, in a yearning towards God, the soul grows upward and finds the fulfilment of something implanted in its nature. The sanction for this development is within us, a striving born with our consciousness or an Inner Light proceeding from a greater power than ours. Science can scarcely question this sanction, for the pursuit of science springs from a striving which the mind is impelled to follow,

[12] See Pew Research Foundation, "Religion and Science in the United States: Scientists and Belief", November 5, 2009, https://www.pewforum.org/2009/11/05/scientists-and-belief/.

[13] National Center for Biotechnology Information (National Institute for Health), "Physicians' Observations and Interpretations of the Influence of Religion and Spirituality on Health", 2010, https://www.ncbi.nlm.nih.gov/pmc/articles/PMC2867458/.

[14] Ibid.

[15] Bill Freeman, "Science or Miracle? Holiday Season Survey Reveals Physicians' Views of Faith, Prayer and Miracles", WorldHealth.net, reporting survey by HCD Research and Louis Finkelstein Institute, December 22, 2004, https://www.worldhealth.net/news/science_or _miracle_holiday_season_survey/.

a questioning that will not be suppressed. Whether in the intellectual pursuits of science or in the mystical pursuits of the spirit, the light beckons ahead and the purpose surging in our nature responds.[16]

It seems that the scientific community is offering us a way out of scientism and the past exaggerations of reason that it admits to be beyond its methodology. This I believe is the way to reestablish and reinvigorate in contemporary culture the existence of God and the soul as well as faith in Jesus Christ. Yet, as powerful as reason can be in mitigating supposedly rational secularism,[17] we cannot content ourselves with the mere rational apprehension of God's existence.[18] It is not enough to be a deist. We need to proceed toward faith, for it is faith that opens us to God's interior presence, and faith that moves us to know, relate to, communicate with, and follow this transcendent, sacred, and ultimately significant divine presence.

If we follow the lead of the God within, we will encounter what most every world religion has discovered—"The highest way to eternal bliss in the Transcendent Reality is through love" (Fredrich Heiler's seventh major common characteristic of world religions).[19] If we accept this universal truth about God, then we may move naturally to the proclamation of Jesus that love is the highest commandment, and that God's nature is unconditional and unrestricted love. As noted in Volume III of the Quartet, the evidence for Jesus' historicity, miracles, and Resurrection is considerable; when this is combined with truth of His proclamation of self-sacrificial love as the nature of God and the meaning of life (which we implicitly know in our hearts), we can reasonably and responsibly pursue the life and salvation that He

[16] Sir Arthur Eddington, *The Nature of the Physical World* (Cambridge: Cambridge University Press, 1928), pp. 327–28.

[17] See the considerable contemporary evidence from science, medicine, and philosophy in Volumes II–III of the Quartet, and Robert Spitzer, *New Proofs for the Existence of God: Contributions to Contemporary Physics and Philosophy* (Grand Rapids, Mich.: Eerdmans, 2010).

[18] I have presented the scientific evidence for God as well as three contemporary philosophical proofs for God in Spitzer, *New Proofs for Existence of God*. For scientific and philosophical evidence for a transphysical soul capable of surviving bodily death, see Volume II of the Quartet.

[19] Friedrich Heiler, "The History of Religions as a Preparation for the Cooperation of Religions", in *The History of Religions*, ed. Mircea Eliade and J. Kitagawa (Chicago, Ill.: University of Chicago Press, 1959), pp. 142–53.

taught. In sum, if we are to reevangelize the culture by means of reason, we will also have to show our secular confreres what Blaise Pascal called "the heart's reasons"—the interior presence of God within us,[20] our sense of the unlimited potential of self-sacrificial love, and the highest of all truths of the heart—"God is love, and he who abides in love abides in God, and God abides in him" (1 Jn 4:16). With this in mind, I will give a brief presentation of six steps that can help the contemporary skeptic to break the inertia of doubt and move to the ultimate reality and significance of divine love—to cross what Pope Saint John Paul called "the threshold of hope".[21] As we shall see, remaining in the hope of Jesus Christ entails membership in a Christian church community (Step 4), which provokes the question, which one? We will give special consideration to the Church initiated by Jesus Himself—the Catholic Church (Step 5)—and then consider what it means to be a practicing Catholic (Step 6).

I. Step 1: The Rational Assent to God and the Soul

In *New Proofs for the Existence of God*, I present the considerable scientific evidence for an intelligent Creator of physical reality (whether this be a multiverse, a string universe, a bouncing universe, or merely our universe),[22] and three contemporary philosophical proofs of God.[23] In *The Soul's Upward Yearning* (Volume II of the Quartet), I present the rational evidence for a transphysical soul capable of surviving bodily death.[24] This brings together seven distinct kinds of

---

[20] In *Pensées* 277, Pascal says the following: "The heart has its reasons, which reason does not know. We feel it in a thousand things. I say that the heart naturally loves the Universal Being, and also itself naturally, according as it gives itself to them." Blaise Pascal, *Pensées* (New York: E. P. Dutton, 1958; Project Gutenberg, 2006), http://www.gutenberg.org/files/18269/18269-h/18269-h.htm.

[21] Pope John Paul II, *Crossing the Threshold of Hope*, ed. Vittorio Messori (New York: Knopf, 1994).

[22] I complement this evidence from physics with additional, more technical arguments and responses to objectors in Robert Spitzer and James Sinclair, "Fine-Tuning and Indications of Transcendent Intelligence", in *Theism and Atheism: Opposing Arguments in Philosophy*, ed. Joseph Koterski and Graham Oppy (New York: Macmillan Reference Library, 2016), pp. 331–58.

[23] See Spitzer, *New Proofs for Existence of God*, Chapters 1–5.

[24] See Chapters 3–6. I update the peer-reviewed medical studies of near-death experiences and complement this research with medical studies of terminal lucidity in the *Credible Catholic Big Book*, vol. 2, *Evidence of Our Transphysical Soul* (Magis Center, 2017), CredibleCatholic.com, Chapter 1, https://www.crediblecatholic.com/pdf/7E-P1/7E-BB2.pdf#P1V2.

scientific evidence and philosophical proofs for God, and six kinds of evidence for a transcendent soul from medical studies and philosophical arguments, which can help those beset by doubt to open themselves to God's presence within them.

As noted above, rational evidence alone will not convince an ardent skeptic who refuses to believe in God for personal motives rather than rational ones, such as a rejection of moral authority beyond himself, resentments toward God (perhaps from a hateful view of God learned in childhood or an inability to explain suffering), or as Aleksandr Solzhenitsyn suggests, "the proclaimed and enforced autonomy of man from any higher force above him".[25] If we are to open ourselves to the interior presence of God, we must be willing to acknowledge and listen to Him. This is the minimum threshold of faith.

II. Step 2: Opening Ourselves to the Numinous, Sacred, and Moral Presence of God within Us

In *The Soul's Upward Yearning* (Chapters 1–2), I present a thorough account of Rudolf Otto's numinous experience, Mircea Eliade's "intuition of the sacred", and John Henry Newman's awareness of the divine fatherly morally authoritative presence to human conscience. Many people will recognize various dimensions of these three acutely perceptive accounts of our interior experience and can focus on them to cross the threshold from "the rational assent to God" to the interior experience of God's presence. This movement is critical, because it entails the essential recognition that God is present to *me*, wants to enter into relationship with *me*, and show *me* the way from darkness and evil into the light of goodness and love. In other words, God does not stand aloof at a distance (deism) but is personally involved with me and my transformation toward the fullness of His love. These signs of God's interior presence can be complemented with other personal experiences of God's mystical presence, which should not be underestimated. As the 2009 Pew Forum survey

---

[25] See Aleksandr Solzhenitsyn, "A World Split Apart" (commencement address at Harvard University, 1978), https://www.americanrhetoric.com/speeches/alexandersolzhenitsynharvard.htm.

shows, 49 percent of Americans indicate that they have had a personal mystical experience defined as a "moment of sudden religious insight or awakening".[26]

Readers attempting to evangelize a person locked in doubt may want to present some of the insights of Otto, Eliade, and Newman while sharing their own interior experiences. Sharing the data from the Pew survey might also help to incite doubters toward a recognition of God's personal presence. Some doubters may say that they have never had any of these experiences of God, suggesting that God may care about others, but not them.

It is difficult to believe that someone has not had any interior experience of the sacred, spiritual, or transcendent, because it is so universal within human history and world religion. It is much more likely that such people have forgotten their experiences of the sacred and mystical because they were unable to understand them at the time of the experience (as happened to C. S. Lewis when he marginalized his childhood experiences of divine "stabs of joy"[27]). Whatever the case, it is best not to push people beyond their recollection or comfort zone and allow them to discover their interior experiences of the sacred in their own time.

Evangelizers may also want to share the experience of conscience, which is truly universal. It may be objected that the guilt or shame of conscience does not originate from God, but merely from social or parental conditioning (as asserted by Freud and other secular psychotherapists). Though it may be difficult to move a skeptic from Freud's interpretation of conscience to Newman's, it is worth presenting Newman's argument (described in Chapter 5, Section III.A) or C. S. Lewis' argument in *Mere Christianity*,[28] because they resonate so deeply with skeptics wrestling with the perturbations of conscience.

If a person cannot relate to any of the above experiences, it may be helpful to point him to what psychiatrists and the American Psychiatric Association predict is likely to result from his implicit separation from God and religion—significant levels of depression, anxiety,

---

[26] Russell Heimlich, "Mystical Experiences", Pew Research Center, December 29, 2009, https://www.pewresearch.org/fact-tank/2009/12/29/mystical-experiences/.

[27] C. S. Lewis, *Surprised by Joy: The Shape of My Early Life* (New York: Harcourt, Brace & World, 1955), pp. 16–22.

[28] See C. S. Lewis, *Mere Christianity* (New York: Macmillan, 1952), Book 1.

antisocial aggressivity, and suicidal ideation.[29] I (along with Christian and atheistic existentialists) refer to this interior disposition as spiritual/cosmic emptiness, alienation, and loneliness. The skeptic may well admit to some or all of these interior states, and if so, the believer may want to indicate that they can be appreciably alleviated when one begins to practice religion—particularly Christianity. If we sincerely open ourselves to God in our religious practice, there is a strong likelihood that the above negative states will begin to subside. This may provide some initial evidence for God's interior presence and companionship.

A skeptic may object that this alleviation comes solely from wishful thinking, but a believer may respond, "Well if it's merely a matter of your subjective disposition, why not alleviate your depression and anxiety right now? Just start the process of wishful thinking right now, and make the anxiety go away." Why make the additional effort to pray, study theology, or become religiously affiliated? I can almost guarantee that he will be unable to do this. When we try to wish ourselves out of anxiety, we subconsciously know that it is merely a wish, which cancels the inauthentic beneficial effect. Furthermore, if we think that we are *mere* wishful thinkers, we prevent ourselves from connecting with God, at which point His grace will be held at bay. However, if we allow for the possibility that God is present and that He can deliver us from our current darkness, and take the risk of

---

[29] See the six studies correlating nonreligious affiliation with decline in emotional health given in the Introduction to this volume: Kanita Dervic et al., "Religious Affiliation and Suicide Attempt", *American Journal of Psychiatry* 161, no. 12 (December 2004): 2303–8, https://ajp.psychiatryonline.org/doi/full/10.1176/appi.ajp.161.12.2303; Harold Koenig, "Research on Religion, Spirituality, and Mental Health: A Review", *Canadian Journal of Psychiatry* 54, no. 5 (2009): 283–91, https://journals.sagepub.com/doi/pdf/10.1177/070674370905400502; Raphael Bonelli et al., "Religious and Spiritual Factors in Depression: Review and Integration of the Research", *Depression and Research Treatment* August 15, 2012, https://www.hindawi.com/journals/drt/2012/962860/; Stefano Lassi and Daniele Mugnaini, "Role of Religion and Spirituality on Mental Health and Resilience: There Is Enough Evidence", *International Journal of Emergency Mental Health and Human Resilience* 17, no. 3 (2015): 661–63, https://www.omicsonline.org/open-access/role-of-religion-and-spirituality-on-mental-health-and-resilience-there-is-enough-evidence-1522-4821-1000273.pdf; Harold Koenig, "Religion, Spirituality, and Health: A Review and Update", *Advances in Mind-Body Medicine* 29, no. 3 (2015): 19–26, https://pubmed.ncbi.nlm.nih.gov/26026153/; and Corina Ronenberg et al., "The Protective Effects of Religiosity on Depression: A 2-Year Prospective Study", *Gerontologist* 56, no. 3 (2016): 421–31, https://academic.oup.com/gerontologist/article/56/3/421/2605601.

praying to Him—if we freely open ourselves to Him—then He has the latitude within the confines of our freedom to make His presence felt, and this He will do. It may not occur in the way or time we think, but if we maintain our openness to Him and continue to pray, He will assuredly surprise us with a lift in spirit, a horizon of hope, and a sense of peace to fill the emptiness, loneliness, and alienation.

The skeptic may ask how the believer can be so sure of this. The answer lies in the statistics. The majority of believers (who are not beset by temporary circumstantial anxieties) tend to have a sense of security, serenity, and joy. Nonbelievers are more likely to have a sense of deep emptiness, alienation, and loneliness—a sense of being "not at home" and "lacking something fundamental and significant". This is confirmed by nonbelievers' significantly higher rates of depression, anxiety, aggressivity, substance abuse, familial tensions, and suicides.[30] On the surface, they may seem to be happy and adjusted, but on a deeper level, they experience Antoine Roquentin's nausea (from Sartre's novel of the same name), Mersault's complete indifference and alienation from the whole of reality (in Albert Camus' The Stranger), Josef K's experience of being unspecifiably judged and convicted (in Franz Kafka's The Trial—see above), or the despair of Kierkegaard's godless individual (in The Sickness unto Death). The common characteristic among these superficially well-adjusted yet deeply disturbed characters is the absence of God in their lives. As Christian existentialists—such as Søren Kierkegaard, Karl Jaspers, Gabrielle Marcel, and Max Scheler—strongly rejoin, the way out of nausea, alienation, despair, meaninglessness, and unspecified guilt is God—not merely belief in the existence of God but openness to God's presence in our lives. These Christian existentialists attribute their security, serenity, and joy to the grace of God.

Ironically, both atheists and Christians validate this conclusion, but from opposite points of view. Atheistic existentialists point to their nausea, alienation, and despair from which they see "no exit",[31] while Christian existentialists in their religious practice point to their security, serenity, and joy. If Christian existentialists are not hopelessly deluded wishful thinkers, then their decidedly positive frame of

[30] See ibid.
[31] See Jean-Paul Sartre, No Exit (New York: Samuel French, 1958).

mind may well be a result of their experience of God—the real God who is present and active in their interior lives.

Skeptics may wonder why God is so subtle—why He doesn't make Himself more evident or even urgently felt. Dostoyevsky succinctly answers this question in the story of the Grand Inquisitor in *The Brothers Karamazov* where the Inquisitor asks the Christ figure, "Why did you not come down from that cross?" The Inquisitor answers his own question, by saying, "[Because] you would not enslave us to a miracle."[32] God must be subtle, for if He made His presence as obvious as our hands and feet, He would eliminate our freedom to accept Him—enslaving us to the evidence. Instead, God prefers to make His presence *just* evident enough to allow us the option to deny Him—a way out if we really *want* it. If we really do not *want* a way out, then God's presence will become more and more evident, as we allow Him to engage us in the deepest recesses of our hearts and minds. Yes—God is quite subtle, but He is also quite evident if we are willing to give Him even a small place in our lives.

Helping the skeptic to see God's interior presence is truly worth the effort, because if successful, it will free him to pray—to open himself to God. It is paramount to encourage the skeptic-turned-"new believer" to persevere in prayer, regardless of whether he feels anything in prayer or not. Tell him with assurance that God will make Himself manifest within the confines of his freedom when it is good for him (the believer). Sometimes this presents itself as a providential turn of events, sometimes as a new manifestation of freedom, sometimes as protection from darkness and evil, sometimes as a greater inclination toward self-sacrificial love, sometimes as alleviation of spiritual emptiness, alienation, and loneliness, sometimes as consolation in prayer, and sometimes in a completely surprising and unmistakable way.

III. Step 3: The Move to Jesus Christ

When the skeptic steps over the line to open himself to God, he will begin to notice what every world religion has acknowledged—that

---

[32] See Fyodor Dostoyevsky, *The Brothers Karamazov* (Edison, NJ: Global Classics), p. 225.

the divine sacred reality is loving.[33] If he practices his religion authentically, he will also likely notice a greater inclination toward unselfish love as the meaning of life. At this point, if the novice believer is unfamiliar with Jesus, it is incumbent upon the experienced believer to help him solidify and develop his inclination toward unselfish love, showing its potential to be our most significant purpose in life. If the novice believer is willing to make unselfish love central to his life, the experienced believer should share with him the good news of Jesus Christ, who proclaimed that unselfish love is the highest commandment and the nature of God.

The novice may have a host of objections to faith in Jesus arising out of popular culture, traditional and social media, and the academic milieu. The majority of these cultural criticisms are formulated without recourse to or familiarity with contemporary historical and scriptural evidence of Jesus, and some of them culpably ignore this evidence. For this reason, I wrote Volume III of the Quartet—*God So Loved the World: Clues to Our Transcendent Destiny from the Revelation of Jesus*. The historical study of Jesus' Resurrection (Chapter 4), His miracles (Chapter 5), and His self-revelation (Chapter 6), as well as the scientific examination of the Shroud of Turin (showing the likelihood of a several billion-watt emanation of light from the corpse inside the Shroud needed to produce the image [Appendix I]), is considerable and probative. When this evidence is combined with that of contemporary scientifically validated miracles,[34] it can redress many of the objections to Jesus' historicity, divine power, and Resurrection to provide a basis for reasonable and responsible belief in Jesus' definition of charitable love, His proclamation of love as the highest commandment, His revelation of His Father's unconditional love, and His actualization of unselfish love in His self-sacrificial Passion and death. The combination of this evidence and Jesus' revelation of the unconditional love of God can rationally support a movement of faith in the novice's heart toward "Jesus as Emmanuel—'God with us'."

At this point, the novice may ask why Jesus had to die. Why couldn't Jesus reveal God's way, truth, life, and love without enduring His

---

[33] See Heiler's seventh major characteristic of world religions in Chapter 5, Section III.C.

[34] See Volume I (Appendix) of this Trilogy for contemporary scientifically validated miracles concerned with the Virgin Mary, the Holy Eucharist, and saints.

painful and ignominious Passion and death? The answer is important for recognizing the unconditional love of God and Jesus as the Son of God. Recall (from Volume I of this Trilogy) that Satan is quite real, and that Jesus' mission was concerned with Satan's ultimate defeat.[35] The Gospels of John and Luke make clear that Jesus intended to do this by His Passion and death. How so?

Jesus was well aware that everyone of us has racked up a huge debt to Satan by deliberately committing sins through which we accept Satan's "gifts" of false happiness—egocentricity, dominion over others, sensual excess, and the many manifestations of the eight deadly sins.[36] Jesus' intention was to cancel our debt to Satan by paying the penalty for our sins by His complete self-sacrificial act (giving everything He, the Son of God, has to give). Of course, Satan could not have demanded this kind of payment from God, because Satan can make no *just* claim against anyone because he is injustice itself. Furthermore, God has complete power over Satan because Satan must be sustained in existence by God. Therefore, Jesus could have simply negated all of Satan's claims with one act of the will instead of voluntarily enduring a painful death. So why didn't He take the easier, "more sensible" way out?

Jesus did not want our liberation from Satan to be based on an act of power, but rather on an act of love. For Him, the true way to liberate us from Satan's dominating power was not another act of dominating power—the conquest of power by power. Rather, Jesus wanted to pay off every claim that Satan had over every person by an act of unconditional self-sacrifice. In this way, He would pay off Satan's claims against *us* in "the right way", for according to His logic of love, self-gift for the sake of every human being is far more righteous than conquest of an adversary. By doing this, Jesus used self-sacrificial love to conquer power and domination that inscribed into created reality and human history the victory of compassionate forgiving self-sacrificial love over force, domination, and supremacy. The way of Heaven conquered the way of Hell.

Jesus' loving way of discharging our indebtedness due to sin had several additional positive effects:

---

[35] See Volume I (Chapter 2) of this Trilogy.
[36] See Volume I (Chapters 5–6) of this Trilogy.

- It revealed His unconditionally loving nature commensurate with His revelation of His Father (the father of the prodigal son). This shows that He shares the same unconditionally loving nature with His Father—"I and the Father are one" (Jn 10:30).
- It means that He *completely* discharged *everyone's* debt to Satan and others due to sin, for He held back nothing in His act of loving forgiveness and redemption through compassionate self-sacrifice; therefore, everyone who freely accepts His forgiveness and redemption through belief and surrender to Him is freed from bondage to all debtors (Satan and others).
- Through His loving way, He created an infinite act of love that could outshine the finite sin of all repentant believers throughout all time.
- His loving way shows us the ideal way to resolve our conflicts due to our and others' sinfulness that forms the foundation for His movement from the Silver Rule to the Golden Rule, His teaching to forgive others without limit, and His promise to extend His merciful salvific love to every repentant believer—even those who come to Him at the last minute (see Mt 20:8–16).

If the novice believer accepts Jesus' redemptive act as Emmanuel (God with us), then it is essential to show him that the best way to actualize unselfish love for the good of all (including himself) is to follow the moral teaching of Jesus. Christianity does not preach a life of convenience and conformity to popular culture. It makes a demand along with its promise of eternal salvation by enjoining us to detach from materialistic and ego-comparative purpose in life, to surrender to the loving God, to follow His teaching, and to take up our crosses and follow Him (see Volume II of this Trilogy).

At this point, Christian faith becomes challenging—particularly for young people, who are drawn by social media into the most powerful cultural and moral conformity ever experienced in the history of mankind. We have to do everything we can to help them move through the separation anxiety from peers and school, community life, and social media. In my view, the best way to help them is to give good scientific, historical, and spiritual evidence for God and Jesus, and introduce them to Christian communities of their peers. The latter may occur through individual parishes or churches (if they have an active youth ministry), through campus ministries in Catholic high schools and universities, or through local or nationwide Christian communities, such as Life Teen (for high school students) and FOCUS (Fellowship of Catholic University Students). There are also several excellent organizations for young adults, such as Young Catholic Professionals.

As by now may be evident, surrendering to Jesus and His moral teaching cannot be merely an individualistic pursuit. It is very much enhanced, guided, supported, and graced through a church community, which leads us to our next step.

IV. Step 4: The Move to a Church Community

Though popular culture embraces the idea that we can have our own private spirituality independent of a church community, nothing could be further from the truth. Of course, we can pray to God privately and He will hear us and respond as best He can, but we cannot orient ourselves toward God (and away from evil) by making a few guesses. As four millennia of human history show, interior spiritual experience unguided by religious doctrine leads to everything from superstition to dream interpretation and even to spirit worship and the occult. Without religious doctrine, we are blind in our pursuit of God, the sacred, and salvation. This may explain why the vast majority of the world (currently 84 percent) subscribes to one of the major religions.

Without a church community, we lack understanding, direction, mutual support, and fulfillment in our faith on four levels:

1. Without divine revelation manifest through authoritative religious figures, we are lost within a myriad of untested ideas about God and salvation and are therefore left clueless about how to understand and practice our faith.
2. Without a faith community to support us, we consign ourselves to our own interior religious consciousness devoid of interpersonal relationships, communal support, and accountability to an authority beyond ourselves. This deprives our faith of the care, insight, and help of others.

3. Without a rite of worship (e.g., the Mass), we relegate our prayer to merely private, subjective expressions devoid of the prayers, rituals, and common beliefs given to us by divine revelation. This is particularly evident in the Catholic Church, which has a specified ritual to receive the very essence and heart (body and blood) of Jesus to transform and help us (see Mt 26:26–28; Mk 14:22–24; Lk 22:17–19) as well as a ritual for definitive absolution from sin originating from Jesus Himself (see Jn 20:21).

4. Without a church's moral teaching, we are left to our own unformed consciences for moral guidance in a complex world with literally thousands of divergent moral prescriptions, making us vulnerable to misleading teachings, evil people, and evil spirits.

This absence of church affiliation leads to the above-mentioned religious emptiness, loneliness, and alienation, because our individual spirituality leaves us unfulfilled, unsupported, and unguided with a profound sense that we are alone in the cosmos and "not at home" with the Divine.[37] Belief in God and individual spirituality are not enough—all major studies correlating religion with human happiness and fulfillment imply that we also need *religious* affiliation—a church community—to avoid depression, anxiety, and meaninglessness.[38] What these studies imply is that without religious teaching *within* a church community, we are likely to be unfulfilled and unhappy, as well as depressed and anxious.

The above observations give an insight into how God created us and the reason He created us: to be ultimately fulfilled by His perfect truth, love, goodness, beauty, and home through a personal relationship with Him arising out of His self-revelation to us—a self-revelation coming through a church community. We can be sure that

[37] See Mircea Eliade's description of what happens to human beings who are naturally religious (*homo religiosus*) when they do not affiliate with a church community bringing an authoritative revelation about the sacred and the divine. See Mircea Eliade, *The Sacred and the Profane: The Nature of Religion* (New York: Harcourt, 1959), pp. 162–215.

[38] See the six studies by the following, cited above in note 29: Kanita Dervic et al.; Harold Koenig (two studies); Raphael Bonelli et al.; Stefano Lassi and Daniele Mugnaini; and Corina Ronenberg et al.

this is what God wants for us and from us, because without a church community we have so little knowledge of His heart and inner being, so little sense of His will for us in our personal, spiritual, and moral lives, so little accountability to an authority beyond ourselves, so little opportunity for interpersonal support for our faith, and so little certainty about divine forgiveness and expiation—all of which restrict our awareness and receptivity to our ultimate fulfillment by Him. We can infer from the above that God truly desires us to be committed to a faith community, adhere to its revealed teachings, and worship Him with others in it so that the community may preserve the truth, support our faith, call us to moral responsibility, mediate grace, provide the means for us to serve others, and through all this, help us toward eternal salvation. Why else would God have created us with these needs that can be fulfilled only by a divinely inspired church? Why else would He have revealed Himself to specific religious communities and churches through prophets, priests, and saints? If God did not intend us to be part of a church community, why would He have created us to be spiritually unfulfilled, unsupported, unguided, and bereft without a church?

The objective of this step is to help religious believers, particularly Christian believers, to move beyond the myth of the adequacy of private spiritualty—including *Christian* private spirituality. As noted above, private spirituality—and even private Christianity—has little guidance, support, accountability, and efficacy without a church community. Individual subjective spirituality loses its conviction, direction, and motivation toward salvation after a relatively short time, allowing the sense of spiritual emptiness, alienation, loneliness, and guilt to reappear amid the absence of conviction about ultimate purpose, dignity, destiny, and home. The best thing we can do for friends, colleagues, and acquaintances who content themselves with private spirituality is to offer them a way out of this malaise. Simply ask them that if they feel an acute sense of spiritual or cosmic emptiness, alienation, loneliness, and guilt, as well as an absence of ultimate purpose and destiny, that they might consider entering a church community; and if they are inclined toward Jesus' teaching of self-sacrificial love, to choose the church community that He initiated: the Catholic Church.

V. Step 5: The Move to the Church Initiated by Jesus—the Catholic Church

This may be the most difficult step in the process of reevangelizing the culture because there are many misconceptions about the Catholic Church among former Catholics, Protestants, and non-Christians. If such misconceptions are blocking the path to a consideration of the Catholic Church, there are a variety of resources developed to respond to hundreds of them.[39] If you know a person who is open to Jesus Christ and a church community, but still searching, it is important to simply ask if he has considered the Catholic Church. If he is open to the Catholic Church as a community, it would be very helpful to invite that person to Mass with your family and introduce him to your friends from church. If he asks why the *Catholic* Church, it is essential to establish three major points:

1. The Catholic Church was initiated by Jesus Christ, who established her on the foundation of Saint Peter and his successors.
2. There are four major benefits of the Catholic Church vital for salvation that no other church provides (with the exception of the Orthodox churches, which offer all seven sacraments):
   - The Holy Eucharist as the real body, blood, soul, and divinity of Jesus Himself
   - The Sacrament of Reconciliation (Confession)
   - The other four unique sacraments of the Catholic Church—Confirmation, Anointing of the Sick, Matrimony, and Holy Orders (Baptism is offered by all Christian churches)
   - The definitive teaching authority of the Church (under the Chair of Peter), which offers both unity of community and doctrine as well as a secure interpretation of the words of Jesus (according to the promise He made to Peter)

---

[39] Catholic Answers has an excellent, accurate searchable website responding to a large number of common questions raised by Protestants and non-Christians. See https://www.catholic.com/. The St. Paul Center teaches Catholics (and inquirers) how to read the Scriptures within the tradition of the Catholic Church, providing excellent resources. See their website at https://stpaulcenter.com/about/. Apologists such as Tim Staples, Patrick Madrid, and Scott Hahn have written a variety of books responding to objections raised about the Catholic Church from scriptural, theological, and philosophical perspectives.

3. Two remarkable dimensions of the Church:
   - Her accomplishments in charitable works and social ethics
   - Her deeply developed spiritual, moral, and intellectual traditions

We will discuss each of these points in turn to give a brief summary of the much more developed points given throughout this Trilogy. References to the Trilogy are provided with each summary explanation.

It is best to begin your conversation with the centrality of Jesus Christ as the source, center, and summit of the Catholic Church, because some people have the misconception that Catholics are different from Christians. Start with a summary of Step 3 above, which shows Jesus Christ to be the highest self-revelation of God by declaring unselfish, self-sacrificial love to be the highest commandment, the meaning of life, the nature of God, and our eternal destiny. When this is complemented by the probative evidence of Jesus' miracles, Resurrection, and gift of the Holy Spirit (still manifest today in the thousands of scientifically validated miracles done in the name of Jesus[40]), we can reasonably and responsibly assent to His doctrinal and moral teaching as our definitive guide to His promised eternal salvation.

The problem is that Jesus' revelation is not perfectly clear in today's complex evolved society. As noted above, there are thousands of Protestant denominations that have been initiated over the last five hundred years, mostly as a result of different interpretations of Jesus' teaching.[41] In view of this, it is difficult to avoid the conclusion that

---

[40] Pope John Paul II canonized 482 saints and Pope Francis canonized 899. It is necessary to have one scientifically validated miracle to canonize a martyr and two scientifically validated miracles to canonize a nonmartyr. Each miracle must be certified by a panel of objective scientists agreeing that there is no natural (scientific) explanation for a particular phenomenon (such as an instantaneous healing of an irreparable injury or disease that continues throughout a lifetime). Evidently, the number of contemporary scientifically validated miracles is considerable. See Michael Lipka and Tim Townsend, "Papal Saints: Once a Given, Now Extremely Rare", Pew Research Center, April 24, 2014, https://www.pewresearch.org/fact-tank/2014/04/24/papal-saints-once-a-given-now-extremely-rare/#:~:text=Recent%20popes%20are%20known%20for,refusing%20to%20convert%20to%20Islam. See also Melissa Butz, "Pope Francis Has Named the Most Saints in History", Rome Reports, August 8, 2020, https://www.romereports.com/en/2020/08/08/pope-francis-has-named-the-most-saints-in-history/.

[41] The number of Protestant denominations given by the Center for the Study of Global Christianity, Gordon-Conwell Theological Seminary (Evangelical), identifies the number as forty-seven thousand denominations, but these include denominational differences throughout

Christian church unity and consistency of doctrine *requires* a single definitive authority to interpret Jesus' teaching. This requirement was not lost on Jesus, who lived at a time when religious factions (such as the Pharisees, Sadducees, and Essenes) were proliferating in Judaism.

There is considerable evidence that Jesus designated Saint Peter as His definitive teaching authority. Volume II (Chapter 1 of this Trilogy) gives a thorough exegesis of Matthew 16:17–19 and John 21:15–17 as well as multiple indications of Peter's supreme teaching authority in the Acts of the Apostles (15:1–21).

Additionally, Matthew 16:19 shows that Jesus created a definitive teaching *office* in the Church, referring to it as "the keys of the kingdom of heaven". As noted in Chapter 5 (Section III.C) of this volume, Isaiah 22:22, "the keys" refers to the *office* of prime minister. In this passage, the prophet Isaiah took the office of prime minister (with the authority to be father over all Israel—Is 22:21) from Shebna and gave it to Eliakim with a proclamation closely paralleling Matthew 16:19. Isaiah 22:22 ("He shall open, and none shall shut; and he shall shut, and none shall open") is so similar in structure to Matthew 16:19 ("Whatever you bind on earth shall be bound in heaven, and whatever you loose on earth shall be loosed in heaven") that it is likely Jesus had it in mind when He gave this *office* ("the keys of the kingdom") to Peter (see Volume II, Chapter 1 of this Trilogy). Thus, it is highly likely that Jesus created an office of supreme teaching authority (to bind and loose in Heaven) and gave it to Peter as its first holder.

There is also considerable evidence that Jesus believed that the Church would last beyond the life of Saint Peter. As noted in Chapter 1 of Volume II of this Trilogy (Section III.B), Jesus believed that there would be an interval of time between the first tribulation (the destruction of Jerusalem) and the second tribulation (the second coming of the Son of Man), admitting that even He did not know when the second tribulation would occur (Mt 24:36). His admission of this shows that He was aware of at least the possibility of the Church lasting beyond the life of Peter. If Jesus created an office of supreme teaching and juridical authority to resolve inevitable disputes about the

various countries, implying that the number should be lower—perhaps in the low thousands. See Todd M. Johnson et al., "Christianity 2017: Five Hundred Years of Protestant Christianity", Center for the Study of Global Christianity, Gordon-Conwell Theological Seminary, 2017, https://www.gordonconwell.edu/wp-content/uploads/sites/13/2019/04/IBMR2017.pdf.

meaning of His teaching, and if He believed that the Church could endure beyond Peter, why would He not intend that this supreme office (necessary to prevent fractioning of the Church) be held by Peter's successors? It would be unfathomable to have restricted this office to only one holder when the problem of disputes and fractioning would evidently persist till the end of the world.

In addition to the scriptural evidence, there is considerable evidence that the early popes and Church Fathers believed that the successors to Peter (occupying his Chair in Rome) had supreme teaching and juridical authority over the whole Church. Pope Clement (fourth holder of the supreme office—from A.D. 88 to 99) believed that he had the power to order rebellious members of the Corinthian Church to restore their bishop and clergy to their offices and to be "obedient to the things which we have written through the Holy Spirit" *under pain of sin.*[42] If he did not have supreme juridical power, how could he have made such a declaration expecting to be obeyed? Furthermore, Saint Ignatius of Antioch, bishop of Antioch, in about A.D. 102, wrote a letter to the Church of Rome acknowledging that it was superior to—and presided over—all other Christian churches.[43] Saint Irenaeus (writing around A.D. 189) declared that the Church of Rome (whose presiding bishop is the pope) is owed obedience in matters of teaching by all other Christian churches.[44] Saint Cyprian of Carthage, one of the greatest Latin apostolic fathers and bishop of Carthage, wrote an important treatise on the unity of the Catholic Church in A.D. 251, where he declared that

> a primacy is given to Peter, whereby it is made clear that there is but one Church and one chair.... If someone does not hold fast to this unity of Peter, can he imagine that he still holds the faith?[45]

These testimonies indicate that Saint Peter and the other apostles communicated clearly to the second generation of disciples that the successors to the office of Peter (located at his See in the heart of the

---

[42] See Clement of Rome, *Letter to the Corinthians* 1, 58–59, 63, CatholicAnswers.com, 2022, http://www.catholic.com/tracts/the-authority-of-the-pope-part-i.

[43] Ignatius of Antioch, *Letter to the Romans* 1, 1.

[44] St. Irenaeus, *Against Heresies* 3, 3, 2.

[45] Cyprian of Carthage, *The Unity of the Catholic Church* 4, 1st ed., Philvaz.com, accessed March 3, 2022, http://philvaz.com/apologetics/num44.htm.

Roman Empire) shared his supreme teaching and juridical authority. In light of all the above, it is highly likely that Jesus intended to give the supreme power of the office of the keys of the Kingdom of Heaven to Peter's successors.

In addition to all this, Jesus has apparently been true to His promise to protect the Catholic Church from the "gates of Hades" (Mt 16:18) throughout history. The great historian of culture and civilization Arnold Toynbee testified to the unique nature of the Catholic Church to endure beyond any other institution throughout history—a conviction that brought him from agnosticism to the light of Christ:

> The Church in its traditional form thus stands forth armed with the spear of the Mass, the shield of the Hierarchy, and the helmet of the Papacy ... and the divine intention ... of this heavy panoply of institutions in which the Church has clad herself is the very practical one of outlasting the toughest of the secular institutions of this world, including all the civilizations. If we survey all the institutions of which we have knowledge in the present and in the past, I think that the institutions created, or adopted and adapted, by Christianity are the toughest and the most enduring of any that we know and are therefore the most likely to last—and outlast all the rest.[46]

In view of the scriptural evidence, the testimony of the early Church Fathers, and the unique longevity of the Church among all other institutions in the world, it is not unreasonable to conclude that Jesus really did initiate the Catholic Church on the rock of the office of Saint Peter (with supreme teaching and juridical authority), and promised to protect that Church until the end of time.

We may now proceed to the second essential point that all prospective Catholics need to know—the four major unique benefits of the Catholic Church that help believers toward eternal salvation in Jesus Christ:

1. The Holy Eucharist, which Jesus intended to be His real crucified and risen body and blood to forgive sins and lead us to eternal life (see Jn 6:35–69)[47]

---

[46] Arnold Toynbee, "Christianity and Civilization", in *Civilization on Trial* (New York: Oxford University Press, 1948), http://www.myriobiblos.gr/texts/english/toynbee.html.

[47] These graces of the Holy Eucharist are explained in detail in Volume II, Chapter 2, Section I of this Trilogy.

2. The Sacrament of Reconciliation, whose power was given by Jesus to the apostles and their successors (see Jn 20:23)
3. The other five sacraments of the Church, four of which (with the exception of Baptism) are unique to the Catholic (and Orthodox) Church—Confirmation, Sacrament of the Sick, Matrimony, and Holy Orders[48]
4. The definitive doctrinal and moral teaching authority vested in the office of Saint Peter and his successors

The first benefit, the Holy Eucharist, was thoroughly discussed in Volume II, Chapter 2, Section I.A of this Trilogy. In that section, we gave detailed historical and exegetical justification for Jesus' intention to give us His *real* crucified and risen body and blood in the Holy Eucharist. Four points are salient:

1. An exegesis of John 6:35–69 shows Jesus' intention to give us his *real* body and blood, particularly the central passage—"I am the living bread which came down from heaven; if anyone eats of this bread, he will live for ever; and the bread which I shall give for the life of the world is my flesh" (6:51). When this is combined with the Jews' question, "How can this man give us his flesh to eat?" (6:52) and the fact that His words produced so much scandal that everyone left Him (6:66–69), it is difficult to believe that this reaction was provoked by Jesus referring to a mere symbol of His body.
2. The Aramaic background of Jesus' Eucharistic words indicates an *identification* of the bread in His hand with his body, and the wine in the cup with His blood.[49]
3. The phrase "Do this in remembrance of me" (Lk 22:19; 1 Cor 11:24) does not mean "call this event to mind". It is an exhortation to relive the event in a prophetic way that collapses the past Eucharistic species into the present bread and wine in the hands of the priest (see the double collapse of time in Volume II, Chapter 2, Section I.A of this Trilogy).

---

[48] A detailed explanation of these sacraments is given in Volume II, Chapter 2, Section III of this Trilogy.

[49] Joachim Jeremias, *The Eucharistic Words of Jesus* (London: SCM Press, 1966), pp. 223–24.

4. The unanimous belief of the early Church Fathers[50]—particularly first-century witnesses, such as the *Didache* (9, 10, and IV) and Saint Ignatius of Antioch (*Letter to the Smyrnaeans* 7)—about the *Real* Presence of Jesus in the Eucharist indicates that the apostles must have unanimously taught this to their disciples.

There are five major graces of the Holy Eucharist that facilitate the believer's entrance into the Kingdom of Heaven (and enabling him to help others to do so):

1. Forgiveness of venial sins and healing from the effects of evil
2. Transformation in the Heart of Jesus
3. Companionship within the Mystical Body
4. Spiritual peace
5. Everlasting life

These graces are explained in detail in Volume II, Chapter 2, Section I.C of this Trilogy. The font of grace arising out of Jesus' crucified risen body and blood in the Eucharist is so powerful that it became the central activity for the spiritual life of the Catholic Church from the first century to the present. It is so spiritually fruitful that Jesus virtually guarantees its worthy reception will lead to eternal life—"If any one eats of this bread, he will live for ever; and the bread which I shall give for the life of the world is my flesh.... He who eats my flesh and drinks my blood has eternal life, and I will raise him up at the last day" (Jn 6:51, 54). With such a gift and assurance, why would anyone willingly ignore or refuse it?

The well-known epic writer J.R.R. Tolkien grasped the significance of Jesus' great gift of self in the Eucharist, which he placed at the center of his life. Writing to his son, Michael, he testified:

In the Blessed Sacrament ... you will find romance, glory, honour, fidelity, and the true way of all your *loves* upon earth, and more than that.[51]

---

[50] See the list of references to virtually all early Church Fathers in J. Pohle, "Eucharist", in *The Catholic Encyclopedia*, vol. 5 (New York: Robert Appleton, 1909), https://www.new advent.org/cathen/05572c.htm.

[51] J.R.R. Tolkien, *The Letters of J.R.R. Tolkien*, ed. Christopher Tolkien and Humphrey Carpenter (Boston: Mariner Books, 2000), p. 53 (italics mine).

In another letter to Michael, he wrote: "The only cure for sagging or fainting faith is Communion."[52] He believed the Catholic Church to be true even in the midst of moments of scandal and imprudence because denying her would be tantamount to denying the Blessed Sacrament, which he viewed as calling Jesus a fraud to His face.[53] Rather than arguing that the Eucharist was true because the Church was true, he believed that the Church was true because the reality of Jesus' body and blood in the Eucharist is evident in the words of Jesus, and the grace of the Eucharist evident in its support of our faith.[54]

In addition to all this, there are several scientifically corroborated Eucharistic miracles that have occurred in the late twentieth and early twenty-first centuries:

- Buenos Aires, Argentina (1996), overseen by Archbishop Bergoglio (Pope Francis)
- Tixtla, Mexico (2006)
- Sokolka, Poland (2008)

These miracles are not merely blood on a host, but the substance of the host transmuted into flesh from the left ventricle of the heart with a proliferation of white blood cells embedded in the ventricle wall (indicating that the tissue was removed from the heart while the body was still alive—a body that was severely beaten before the tissue was removed). The blood type on all three tissue samples is AB+ (the same blood type as the Shroud of Turin and the Eucharistic host of Lanciano). The tissue samples have been examined in top pathology laboratories, and the sample from Sokolka, Poland, has been thoroughly examined by electron microscope. (The scientific studies and photographs are given on the Magis Center website.[55])

The second major benefit, the Sacrament of Reconciliation, was given by Jesus to the apostles and their successors with the proclamation "If you forgive the sins of any, they are forgiven; if you retain the sins of any, they are retained" (Jn 20:23). This sacrament provides

[52] Ibid., p. 338.
[53] See ibid., p. 338.
[54] See ibid.
[55] Go to www.magiscenter.com and click on "Articles", then click on "Contemporary Eucharistic Miracles".

definitive absolution for even the most serious of sins, breaks the grip of the Evil One, and reunites us with the Lord and His Mystical Body (the Church). In Volume II, Chapter 7 of this Trilogy, there is a detailed explanation of its five major graces:

1. Definitive absolution for mortal and venial sins
2. Spiritual solidification of a turning point in life
3. Healing of the damage of sin and release from the grip of the Evil One
4. Graced resolve for continued conversion
5. The peace of Christ

If we can receive definitive absolution for even the most serious sins (and be certain of that absolution and restoration to grace), and this sacrament can break the grip of the Evil One, help break sinful habits, purify our intentions, and lead us to salvation, why would we willingly ignore or refuse it?

The third benefit of the Catholic Church—the other four unique sacraments (Confirmation, Sacrament of the Sick, Matrimony, and Holy Orders)—is explained in Volume II, Chapter 2 (Section II) of this Trilogy, and the fourth benefit—the supreme teaching and juridical authority vested in Saint Peter and his successors—is explained above and in greater detail in Volume II, Chapter 1 of this Trilogy.

These sacraments and the supreme teaching authority of the Church are proclaimed by virtually all the thousands of canonized saints to be the source and summit of their lives of heroic virtue and self-sacrificial love. If these graces of Jesus given to the Catholic Church produced such remarkable benefits for both the saints' salvation and that of the millions of people they served, why wouldn't they do the same for all of us if we receive them as Jesus intended? If the objective of our lives is heroic self-sacrificial love and virtue leading to our and others' salvation, why wouldn't we seek these gifts of Jesus and the Church as the most important dimensions of our lives?

We now proceed to two remarkable dimensions of the Catholic Church—her charitable works and her spiritual, moral, and intellectual tradition. Let us begin with the Catholic Church's accomplishments in charity and social doctrine. As noted in Chapter 6 (Section I), the Catholic Church created such large missions to help the needy, cure the sick, and educate all classes of people that she ultimately undermined the barbarity, social stratification, and slavery of Rome.[56] Throughout her history, the Catholic Church has been the largest public educational system, healthcare system, and public welfare system in the world. It remains so today:

- With respect to public education, the Church provides services in 43,800 secondary schools, 95,200 primary schools,[57] and 1,861 colleges and universities.[58]
- With respect to healthcare, the Church oversees more than one-fourth of all worldwide healthcare facilities and hospitals.[59]
- With respect to public welfare, the Church provides services in 15,423 homes for the elderly, chronically ill, and disabled; 9,295 orphanages; and 12,515 marriage counseling centers.[60]

Additionally, the Catholic Church has published and promulgated the most comprehensive and systematic doctrine on sociopolitical, economic-environmental, international ethics in existence. As previously mentioned, a systematic summary of this vast work is given in the *Compendium of the Social Doctrine of the Catholic Church*.[61] Chapter 7 of this volume gives a detailed summary of the six major principles

[56] See Helmut Koester, "The Great Appeal: What Did Christianity Offer Its Believers That Made It Worth Social Estrangement, Hostility from Neighbors, and Possible Persecution?", Frontline, WGBH Educational Foundation, April 1998, pbs.org/wgbh/pages/frontline /shows/religion/why/appeal.html. See also Christopher Dawson, "The Formation of Christendom" (New York: Sheed & Ward, 1965), pp. 111–37.

[57] See "Preparing for the Year of Creation", *Vermont Catholic*, Winter 2016–2017, http:// www.onlinedigeditions.com/publication/index.php?i=365491&m=&l=&p=1&pre=&ver =html5#{%22page%22:74,%22issue_id%22:365491}

[58] United States Conference of Catholic Bishops, "Catholic Education", under "Catholic Colleges and Universities", 2022, https://www.usccb.org/offices/public-affairs/catholic -education.

[59] Catholic News Agency, "Catholic Hospitals Comprise One Quarter of World's Healthcare, Council Reports", February 10, 2010, https://www.catholicnewsagency.com/news /catholic_hospitals_represent_26_percent_of_worlds_health_facilities_reports_pontifical _council.

[60] See *Agenzia Fides* (Fides News Agency), "Vatican—Catholic Church Statistics 2020", October 16, 2020, http://www.fides.org/en/news/68840-VATICAN_CATHOLIC_CHURCH _STATISTICS_2020.

[61] Pontifical Council for Justice and Peace, *Compendium of the Social Doctrine of the Catholic Church* (2004; repr., April 2005).

of Catholic social teaching as well as the seven major areas to which it is applied—the family, labor/work, business-economics, governmental systems and policy, international relations, environmental stewardship, and war/peace.

We now proceed to the second remarkable dimension of the Catholic Church—her deeply articulated spiritual, moral, and intellectual traditions. There are literally encyclopedic volumes devoted to Catholic spiritual life,[62] moral life,[63] and intellectual life,[64] but this vast content cannot be treated adequately in this chapter. A brief summary of some major contributions is outlined here to give a semblance of the rich tapestry of sacred culture that has been influenced by the Catholic Church—her priests, religious, and lay faithful.

1. *Spiritual life.* The many developments of spirituality (through religious orders and lay associations), the development of Christian mysticism from the Desert Fathers through the current day, and the development of multiple modes of prayer—from *lectio divina* to the discernment of spirits—show the presence of the Holy Spirit animating the Church's awareness and practice of deep, authentic, spiritual life. No other Christian church manifests anything close to this richness of spiritual depth and tradition. When we combine the spiritual traditions arising out of the Church Fathers, the Benedictines, the Franciscans, the Dominicans, the Jesuits, the Carmelites, and the many other religious and spiritual traditions in the Catholic Church, we must ask ourselves, what is the source from which all of these rich spiritual traditions sprang?

---

[62] See, for example, Michael Downey, *The New Dictionary of Catholic Spirituality* (Collegeville, Minn.: Liturgical Press, 1993). See also the Classics of Western Spirituality series (New York; Mahwah, N.J.: Paulist Press, 1978–2013), which consists of 123 volumes, the vast majority of which are Catholic authors and mystics.

[63] Catholic moral theology is divided into four major areas: (1) introductory works (e.g., William E. May, *An Introduction to Moral Theology*, 2nd ed. [Huntington, Ind.: Our Sunday Visitor Publishing, 2007]), (2) Catholic bioethics and medical ethics (e.g., William E. May, *Catholic Bioethics and Gift of Human Life*, 2nd ed. [Huntington, Ind.: Our Sunday Visitor Publishing, 2008]), (3) Catholic social ethics and social teaching (e.g., the *Compendium*), and (4) Catholic business ethics (e.g., Andrew Abela and Joseph E. Capizzi, eds., *A Catechism for Business: Tough Ethical Questions and Insights from Catholic Teaching* [Washington, D.C.: Catholic University of America Press, 2014]).

[64] See, for example, Thomas Carson, *The New Catholic Encyclopedia*, 2nd ed., 15 vols. (Detroit: Gale Research, 2002).

We are led back to what Saint Irenaeus called "the *greatest* and most ancient church known to all.... It is in her that the faithful everywhere have maintained the apostolic tradition."[65]

2. *Moral life.* The Catholic Church applied the teachings of Jesus to almost every aspect of moral, social, cultural, and political life, including the development of the notion of conscience (Saint Paul), the notion of free will (Saint Augustine), the development of systematic moral theology (Saint Thomas Aquinas and others), justice theory (Saint Augustine, Saint Thomas Aquinas, and others), natural law theory (Saint Thomas Aquinas), the systematization of canon laws and its integration with civil law (Italian scholar Gratian), the universality of personhood (Father Bartolomé de las Casas), the first articulation of inalienable rights (Father Francisco Suarez), and as noted above, the social teaching of the Catholic Church, from Pope Leo XIII to today. (The history of these developments is summarized in Chapter 6, Section II of this volume.) The Church also developed specializations in both Catholic medical ethics and Catholic business ethics.[66] There is nothing like this development, systemization, and sociopolitical application of moral thought in any other religion in world history. This again shows the action of the Holy Spirit in the life of the Church.

3. *Intellectual life.* The Catholic Church applied Christian religious and theological thought to virtually every area of science and the humanities.

- With respect to *science*, Catholic clergy made invaluable contributions to the discovery and articulation of
  - Hastronomy (Nicholas Copernicus—a Catholic cleric and the father of heliocentrism[67]),
  - biology-genetics (Abbott Gregor Mendel—the father of quantitative genetics[68]),

---

[65] Saint Irenaeus, *Against Heresies* 3, 3, 2, trans. Robert Schihl and Paul Flanagan, from "Post-Apostolic Fathers of the Church", Catholic Biblical Apologetics (website), last updated 2004, http://www.freerepublic.com/focus/religion/2476599/posts?page=1.

[66] For a summary of Catholic medical ethics, see May, *Catholic Bioethics*. For a summary of Catholic business ethics, see Abela and Capizzi, *Catechism for Business*.

[67] For an explanation and references, see Chapter 6 (Section I.D).

[68] For an explanation and references, see ibid.

- ○ geology (Bishop Nicolas Steno—the father of contemporary geology and stratigraphy[69]), and
- ○ astrophysics-cosmology (Monsignor Georges Lemaître—the father of the Big Bang Theory[70])—to mention but a few (244 clergy-scientists have made major contributions to all fields of science[71]). The Catholic Church hosts the Pontifical Academy of Sciences, which has had eighty Nobel Prize winners in its membership.[72] The Church sponsors multiple astronomical observatories from Rome to the United States to Chile, as well as scientific institutes such as the Society of Catholic Scientists.[73] No other church or religious institution has contributed a fraction of what has been done for science by Catholic clergy and lay Catholic scientists.

- The Catholic Church has also made very significant contributions to philosophy, the social sciences, music, architecture, art, and literature. (These accomplishments are described in detail in Volume II, Chapter 3, Section VIII of this Trilogy.)

The above benefits and wisdom of the Catholic Church build a strong foundation of grace for our pathway to eternal life with Christ. As noted above, no other church or religious tradition provides these benefits, which clearly manifest the grace and love of Christ as well as the power, inspiration, and guidance of the Holy Spirit. They are worth serious consideration, not only for our personal edification and development, but also to provide the best path and access to our eternal salvation with the Triune God—the Catholic Church.

There is a good possibility that prospective reverts and converts to Catholicism who are searching for a church community will be moved toward the Catholic Church by these benefits and edifying

---

[69] For an explanation and references, see ibid.

[70] For an explanation and references, see ibid.

[71] See Angelo Stagnaro, "A List of 244 Priest-Scientists (from Acosta to Zupi)", *National Catholic Register*, November 29, 2016, https://www.ncregister.com/blog/a-list-of-244-Priest-Scientists-from-acosta-to-zupi.

[72] See the Pontifical Academy of Scientists website: https://www.pas.va/en/academicians/nobel.html.

[73] See the Society of Catholic Scientists website: https://www.catholicscientists.org/.

dimensions of her past and present. If you know such people, encourage them to accompany you to Mass or even a parish event where they can experience your faith and friendship from others.

Bringing a revert or convert to the Catholic Church is a great leap forward, but it is not the end of the process. The first five steps in reevangelizing the culture are focused on intellectual conversion and the beginning of spiritual conversion, but they don't make much leeway into moral conversion. As noted in the Introduction to Volume I of this Trilogy, intellectual conversion aims at the rational assent of the mind to God, Jesus, and the Church. Spiritual conversion aims at deep relationship with the Lord, and moral conversion aims at the appropriation of virtue, resistance to temptation, and transformation into what Saint Paul calls "the new man" (Eph 4:24). If we are to help new believers to achieve this, we must direct them to Step 6.

VI. Step 6: Spiritual and Moral Conversion in the Catholic Church

Let us return for a moment to the commencement speech of Aleksandr Solzhenitsyn at Harvard University. In it, he lays out two dimensions of the challenge to restore spiritual integrity and objective morality to the Western world, which if unfaced would leave the West open to interior decay and implosion similar to that of the totalitarian East from which he came:

> Destructive and irresponsible freedom has been granted boundless space. Society appears to have little defense against the abyss of human decadence.... Such a tilt of freedom in the direction of evil has come about gradually, but it was evidently born primarily out of a humanistic and benevolent concept according to which there is no evil inherent to human nature.[74]

The problem, as Solzhenitsyn sees it, is the primacy and unlimited extent of freedom (radical autonomy) as well as the unconscious and

---

[74]Solzhenitsyn, "World Split Apart".

conscious denial of objective and subjective evil. These two problems have been enormously magnified since 1978 by the Internet and social media combined with the efforts of various politicians and jurists. Some cultural critics believe that the situation of Western culture is at the brink of collapse;[75] but I am personally not convinced of the inevitability of this negative scenario, because I have seen the Lord's providential grace reverse historical trends even worse than that of contemporary Western culture. However, if that is to occur, we will have to make recourse to Jesus Christ and the Catholic Church, as well as a multitude of people willing to endure unpopularity and courageously address Christian moral norms in a society that has become increasingly ego-comparative, irreligious, and "intolerant" of Christian doctrine.

How might we approach this challenge with friends, acquaintances, and especially children who practice their faith by at least occasional participation at Mass? We need a strategy for helping them move from "Sunday morning Catholics" toward spiritual and moral conversion—the objective of all three volumes of this Trilogy. Evidently, the three large volumes of this Trilogy will not be able to reach the majority of Christians and Catholics in this culture. Though these volumes can be very effective in educating educators, leaders, and catechists, a more simple and incisive approach is needed to help the ordinary citizen cross the threshold from church participation to moral conversion. I would recommend the following simple "how to" strategy to first incite deeper spiritual conversion and then incite deeper moral conversion:

1. *Spiritual conversion.* Create a "Starting a Life of Prayer" booklet (see Volume II, Chapter 3 of this Trilogy). Photocopy it and go through it with your friends as if it were a home book club selection. If they do not have some of the religious items needed by beginners, offer to buy these resources for them if you can afford it—a crucifix, a rosary, a study Bible, and a blessed religious icon, picture, or statue, as well as *Day by Day:*

---

[75] See George Weigel, "Is Europe Dying? Notes on a Crisis of Civilizational Morale", Columbian College of Arts and Sciences, George Washington University, History News Network, accessed March 8, 2022, http://historynewsnetwork.org/article/12295.

The Notre Dame Prayer Book for Students.[76] If you are able to get your friends to commit to two or more of them, it will be major progress for their happiness and salvation.

2. *Moral conversion.* In a culture of radical autonomy and moral relativism, moral conversion will be more challenging than spiritual conversion. Nevertheless, if a person is trying to live up to some of the commitments of spiritual conversion, there will be a good chance of introducing at least basic points of moral conversion that will be important to their progress. The remainder of this section will be devoted to deepening this more challenging endeavor.

So how can we assist a person endeavoring spiritual conversion to take the challenging step of deepening moral conversion? I would tell him plainly, "I (we) believe in the moral teaching of Jesus as interpreted by the Catholic Church." I am certain that much of the time you will get either a curious or negative reaction. People may write you off as ignorant or an extremist, but at least you have told them the truth and did not leave them in the darkness—the decline in emotional and spiritual health described in Chapters 1–4. Some may ask why or how we could possibly believe the Church's teaching on XYZ. Or wondering if we are saying that the majority of people in our culture are in a state of spiritual decline and endangering their salvation. Any (or all) of these reactions is truly desirable, because it starts a conversation that may open the minds of family or friends beyond the usual cultural intransigence. If you do only that, it would be a partial victory for them and the Lord.

If someone sincerely asks why or how could you, you have an opening that can be filled by one or more of the following three strategies (depending on the person you are talking to):

1. A brief presentation of the four levels of happiness, the objective of which would be to move a person from dominant materialistic/ego-comparative identity (Levels One and Two) to dominant contributive/faith-based identity (Levels Three and Four). There are several helpful resources to do this:

[76] Thomas McNally, C.S.C., and William G. Storey, D.M.S., eds., *Day by Day: The Notre Dame Prayer Book for Students* (Notre Dame, Ind.: Ave Maria Press, 2004).

- Module 6 on the four levels of happiness from Credible Catholic's 7 Essential Modules[77]
- Several written texts on the four levels of happiness on the websites of both the Magis Center and Credible Catholic[78]

2. A presentation on the reality and tactics of the Evil One, the objective of which is to show people that there really is an evil spirit who is trying to undermine them, their family, and their friends, and to seduce them to an eternity of spiritual alienation and darkness. There are several resources that can be helpful:

- Free video interviewing Father Gary Thomas, exorcist[79]
- The movie and book *The Rite*[80]
- Free extended written explanation of modern exorcisms and the tactics of the Evil One on the Credible Catholic website[81]
- Chapters on the reality and tactics of spiritual evil (Volume I, Chapters 3 and 4 of the Trilogy)

3. A presentation on the statistics and studies showing how violating the Church's moral teaching on abortion, euthanasia, and sexuality lead to significant increases in depression, anxiety, substance abuse, familial tensions and instability, and suicides (see Chapters 1–4 of this volume)

We will examine each of these strategies in turn.

[77] There are four short videos (totaling about thirty-eight minutes) on the Credible Catholic website that explain why Levels Three and Four are much more pervasive, enduring, and deep than Levels One and Two. On the website, see the following link for the first video, and you will be led to subsequent links for the other three: https://www.crediblecatholic .com/15vid/7E-P6/u01.mp4.

[78] For the Magis Center scholarly article, go to this link: https://f.hubspotusercontent40 .net/hubfs/7693347/Four_Levels_of_Happiness.pdf. For an extended explanation of all four levels on the website of the Credible Catholic, go to the following link: https://www .crediblecatholic.com/pdf/7E-P6/7E-BB13.pdf#P1V13.

[79] "Interview with Father Gary Thomas, Part 1", Magis Center, April 3, 2017, YouTube, 1:47, https://www.bing.com/videos/search?q=video+interviewing+Father+Gary+Thomas %2c+exorcist&&view=detail&mid=6F8C4BA33B0EB00A10956F8C4BA33B0E B00A1095&&FORM=VDRVRV. "Interview with Father Gary Thomas, Part 2", Magis Center, May 5, 2017, YouTube, 1:52, https://www.bing.com/videos/search?q=video+in terviewing+Father+Gary+Thomas%2c+exorcist&docid=608034461605706274&mid=338011 C07B9E6034D6CA338011C07B9E6034D6CA&view=detail&FORM=VIRE.

[80] Matt Baglio, *The Rite: Making of a Modern Exorcist* (New York: Image/Doubleday, 2010). The movie is available online through most streaming services (Amazon Prime, Netflix, etc.).

[81] Go to https://www.crediblecatholic.com/pdf/P14/BB14.pdf#P1V14.

With respect to the first strategy, the four levels of happiness is a nonthreatening way to show a person that he may be caught up in extreme ego-comparative (narcissistic) identity and purpose in life. The above videos are designed to show the negative emotional, mental, and relational states that come from this ego-comparative orientation, and several techniques to help people move positively to Levels Three and Four. If your family and friends find this helpful (and most people do), then you might want to broach the topic of the eight deadly sins, because every deadly sin is nothing more than a focused manifestation of ego-comparative purpose in life—gluttony/sensuality, greed, lust, sloth, vanity, anger, envy, and pride.

In Volume I (Chapters 5–6) of this Trilogy, I presented a non-threatening literary approach to the deadly sins that will hopefully incite people to fear the deadly sins' destructive consequences to themselves, their families, friends, and salvation. Well-known characters from the Bible and history, as well as from works by Shakespeare, Dickens, Forster, Tolstoy, and Milton, and contemporary movies illustrate the downward spiral initiated by these rationalized destructive attitudes. As suggested above, these chapters could be discussed as a home book club selection.

The hope is to incite the question of how to overcome dominant ego-comparative happiness and the deadly sins (which can become powerful intransigent habits). If asked this question, give the immediate response without hesitation that the best way to overcome these attitudes is to make a weekly examination of conscience using one of the following resources:

- The USCCB youth examination of conscience[82]
- *Day by Day: The Notre Dame Prayer Book for Students* (Chapter 6).
- The USCCB has seven distinct examinations of conscience for different audiences. They can be accessed on the USCCB website.[83]

---

[82] United States Conference of Catholic Bishops, "What Must I Do?: The Sacrament of Reconciliation and Young Adults", 2022, https://www.usccb.org/prayer-and-worship /sacraments-and-sacramentals/penance/sacrament-reconciliation-young-adults-examination -of-conscience.

[83] United States Conference of Catholic Bishops, "Examinations of Conscience", 2022, https://www.usccb.org/prayer-and-worship/sacraments-and-sacramentals/penance/exami nations-of-conscience.

You will also benefit greatly by going to confession (and receiving sacramental absolution) *at least* four times per year or when one is in a state of mortal sin. The Sacrament of Reconciliation is the key to initiating deep moral conversion. As noted in Volume II, Chapter 7 of this Trilogy, the five graces of the sacrament can make a huge difference to transform our lives. The more frequently we go to confession, the more life-transforming fruit we will receive. If people are open, encourage them to go once per month or even more frequently. If they want to do more, suggest going to some weekday Masses. As noted above, the Holy Eucharist is extremely powerful in the process of transformation.

With respect to the second strategy, the presentation of the reality and tactics of the Evil One is definitely more daunting than the four levels of happiness. Nevertheless, large numbers of adults and *young people* willingly listen to these accounts, because they know in their hearts that evil is real. Moreover, many of their friends are experimenting with the occult (causing a negative change in their personalities and relationships). Strange as it may seem, William Peter Blatty's movie *The Exorcist*, based on the diary of several Jesuits who performed the Robbie Mannheim exorcism in Saint Louis (summarized in Volume I, Chapter 3 of this Trilogy), set Hollywood records.[84] *The Rite* explains both the horror of evil and God's power over it, particularly through the name of Jesus. If you have challenging teenagers or young adults who see no need for Jesus, the Church, or the Mass, you may want to watch the movie together.

If your children are willing to watch, emphasize that this is a true story (and that *The Exorcist* was based on the diary of a real exorcism). There are four major points to push home:

1. The Evil One is all around you and intends to seduce you into eternal darkness.
2. The Lord, working through the name of Jesus, has complete power over the Evil One, but He will respect your freedom to enter into the Evil One's seductions.

---

[84] As recently as 2021, it was in the top-ten list of top-grossing movies. See Josie Green, "100 Top-Grossing Movies of All Time", 24/7 Wall St. (website), September 3, 2021, https://247wallst.com/special-report/2021/09/03/100-top-grossing-movies-of-all-time-4/11/#:~:text=Snow%20White%20and%20the%20Seven%20Dwarfs%20%281937%29%20%3E,%241%20billion%20%3E%20Estimated%20ticket%20sales%3A%20%10.6%20million.

3. Your best protections are the sacraments given to the Catholic Church by Jesus Himself, the sacraments of Reconciliation and the Holy Eucharist, as well as the moral teaching that Jesus entrusted to the Catholic Church for her interpretation. The name of Jesus and the Catholic Church are your protection and stronghold. If you neglect them, you leave yourself vulnerable not only to spiritual emptiness, alienation, and loneliness, but also to the bondage of eternal evil and darkness.

4. Therefore, set your sights on regular confession and frequent reception of the Holy Eucharist and resolve to follow the teachings of Jesus, examining your conscience at least once per week using one of the above resources. Start today—and keep going until the end of your life. You will not regret it.

The third strategy—presenting the rationale for the Church's controversial moral teachings—is not meant to be a substitute for the first two strategies but an addition to them. The first and second strategies give a self-motivational incentive for young and old to take seriously the threat of evil, ego-comparative identity, and the deadly sins, inciting them to avail themselves of confession and the Holy Eucharist and to follow the teachings of Jesus Christ as interpreted by the Catholic Church. Failure to do so has both immediate and eternal consequences, all of which lead to profound unhappiness and the undermining of emotional health, relationships, and eternal salvation.

Many people may believe that if they follow the Church's moral teaching in a general way, they can gloss over some of the more challenging teachings that seem to run contrary to popular culture. This is a very real concern, particularly for young people who believe that the Church's teaching on abortion, euthanasia, and sexuality are mean-spirited to vulnerable groups within society. I certainly cannot blame them for believing this, because the propaganda effort to convince them of this false impression is gargantuan. Quite frankly, a cultural ethos has been created around the justification and even the goodness of abortion, euthanasia, cohabitation, a homosexual lifestyle, and gender change, among other issues. However, we must point out the major logical fallacy mentioned time and again throughout this volume: there are far more errors of omission—that is, culpable omission—than commission.

The fact is that most young people have not been told or taught even one of the statistics or studies mentioned in Chapters 1–4. They have literally and figuratively been kept in the dark about abortion as the killing of an innocent that violates the most minimum standards of justice, personhood, and inalienable rights. They have not been exposed to a single study indicating the tragic downside and abuses of physician-assisted suicide, and they certainly have not been told the statistics of the hugely increasing levels of depression, anxiety, substance abuse, sexual crimes, divorce rates, marital infidelity, marital dissatisfaction, and family instability associated with violating the Church's teachings on sexuality. Above all, they have not been told how the Evil One uses these lifestyles to pull them into ever greater separation from God, causing increased emptiness, alienation, loneliness, and guilt, as well as leaving them vulnerable to choose eternal darkness.

To bring our work of evangelization to completion, we must again risk unpopularity and ridicule, taking up the Lord's call for us to be light in the darkness. If our children, students, and friends have at least listened to the first or second strategy concerned with happiness and the Evil One, respectively, we may as well take the opportunity to present to them at least some of the studies and statistics in Chapters 1–4 that justify the Church's controversial moral teachings in ways that are both immediately and eternally comprehensible. Everyone can understand that significantly increased rates of depression, anxiety, antisocial aggressivity, substance abuse, familial tensions, and suicides are conditions best avoided, and most young people have at least an incipient desire to have a long-lasting, stable, satisfying marital relationship. Even if we make only a small impression on them, it might prove very helpful to them if they happen to move into a challenging moral situation, which is producing progressively more profound depression, anxiety, and spiritual alienation. It may occur to them when they reach a point of desperation that they need to turn to Jesus and the Church. If we but plant the seed to do this, we will have helped the Lord immensely.

VII. Conclusion

The above six steps are designed to be a nonthreatening but effective way to help people who have been thoroughly "catechized" in secularism to move beyond the intrinsically narrow limits of this perspective into the merciful and mysterious loving plan of God through evidence of both the mind and heart. The approach to God is both rational (scientific and philosophical) and interiorly intuitive (pointing to the numinous, the sacred, the spiritual, and transcendent). The approach to Jesus is the same—examining the historical evidence as well as the scientific investigation of the Shroud of Turin and miracles. Yet, the foundation for the argument for Jesus does not rest solely on the evidence for His glorious Resurrection, and His miraculous presence through the Holy Spirit yesterday and today, but also the quality and unconditional nature of the love He preached and exemplified in His own life and death. If people know in their hearts that this unconditional love is the meaning of their lives, dignity, and destiny, then the evidence of the Resurrection and miraculous presence of Jesus will be quite probative; but absent this, the evidence will always leave room for doubt. As noted many times in the previous volumes, this is precisely God's plan. He does not want to enslave us to a miracle, to coercion of an undeniable proof or the overwhelming evidence of peer-reviewed medical studies of near-death experiences—or anything else. He wants us to acknowledge and respond to the truth of Jesus' teaching about God's unconditional, unselfish, self-sacrificial compassionate love, and to affirm for ourselves that this unselfish, self-sacrificial compassionate love is the meaning of life for us. If we freely believe and choose this love in our hearts, He will provide us with more than enough probative evidence, not just from history, science, and philosophy, but also from our lives' experience.

Ultimately the truth of the Catholic Church will come through her authentic preaching of the unselfish, self-sacrificial compassionate love of Jesus expressed in her doctrines and lived by her saints. This love speaks so strongly that it cuts through even the worst scandals perpetrated from the time of Judas Iscariot to the present. The blood of the martyrs and the compassion of the saints brilliantly outshine the darkness of our sinfulness. If our young people can apprehend a glimmer of that unselfish, self-sacrificial compassionate love in the Church's controversial moral teachings (addressed in Chapters 1–4), it will be enough to see the Lord's providential hand working through the Church and her saints—through the Holy Eucharist and Reconciliation and through her doctrines and the writings of her mystics and cherished theologians. If that affirmation occurs, spiritual freedom ensues, and eternal salvation becomes a matter of faithfully following its course out of darkness into the unconditional light and love of God.

POSTSCRIPT

Four Scripture Passages on Truth

If we do not have at least a tacit sense of ultimate truth, we cannot orient ourselves toward ultimate significance or destiny, and so we are all confronted with the question that Pontius Pilate insincerely asked Jesus, "Quid est veritas?" ("What is truth?" [Jn 18:38]). The following four Scripture passages have provided me with inspiration and light for many years. I might say that the Quartet and this Trilogy are my attempt to unravel the depth and significance of these passages in contemporary philosophical, scientific, psychological, literary, and theological terms. For me, the passages represent God Himself speaking to the world through His Son and inspired writers telling us how to understand the reality into which we have been born, and the ultimate reality awaiting us.

The first passage is Psalm 19, which initially speaks of the inspiration behind intellectual conversion (vv. 1–6), then the inspiration behind moral conversion (vv. 7–13), and concludes with the inspired prayer of spiritual conversion (v. 14).

> [On intellectual conversion:] The heavens declare the
> glory of God;
> the skies proclaim the work of his hands.
> Day after day they pour forth speech;
> night after night they reveal knowledge.
> They have no speech, they use no words;
> no sound is heard from them.
> Yet their voice goes out into all the earth,
> their words to the ends of the world.
> In the heavens God has pitched a tent for the sun.
> It is like a bridegroom coming out of his chamber,
> like a champion rejoicing to run his course.

It rises at one end of the heavens
and makes its circuit to the other;
nothing is deprived of its warmth.
[On moral conversion:] The law of the LORD is perfect,
refreshing the soul.
The statutes of the LORD are trustworthy,
making wise the simple.
The precepts of the LORD are right,
giving joy to the heart.
The commands of the LORD are radiant,
giving light to the eyes.
The fear of the LORD is pure,
enduring forever.
The decrees of the LORD are firm,
and all of them are righteous.
They are more precious than gold,
than much pure gold;
they are sweeter than honey,
than honey from the honeycomb.
By them your servant is warned;
in keeping them there is great reward.
But who can discern their own errors?
Forgive my hidden faults.
Keep your servant also from willful sins;
may they not rule over me.
Then I will be blameless,
innocent of great transgression.
May these words of my mouth and this meditation
of my heart
be pleasing in your sight,
LORD, my Rock and my Redeemer. (New International
Version)

Though scientific and philosophical evidence can open the path to seeing God's creative power, goodness, and love in creation, the deep mystical dimension of verses 1 through 6 comes from a heart liberated by prayer and grace. Similarly, studies of the psychological, sociological, and political effects of religious practice (or the lack of it) can help us see how the Lord's moral teaching can lead to emotional, marital, familial, and cultural health; but it takes prayer and grace to recognize that His commandments are perfect, refreshing, trustworthy, wisdom-inspiring, right, joy-filled, radiant, light-giving, pure, everlasting, firm, and righteous. Once we recognize these characteristics of the Lord's moral teachings in our hearts, resistance to them from our lower nature breaks down, and we find ourselves content to trust and follow Him.

The attitude and inspiration of spiritual conversion is summed up in the beautiful humble prayer asking that the Lord be pleased with "the prayers of my mouth and the meditations of my heart" (see v. 14), for it represents the objective of the spiritual life—to please the Lord who has given us everything in this life and ultimate meaning and love in the next.

The second of my favorite passages concerns a truth that the Psalmist did not and could not yet know—that God's truth Himself came into the world to give us not only the fullness of revelation, but the fullness of Himself—fullness of light, love, and glory:

> In the beginning was the Word, and the Word was with God, and the Word was God. He was in the beginning with God; all things were made through him, and without him was not anything made that was made. In him was life, and the life was the light of men. The light shines in the darkness, and the darkness has not overcome it.... And the Word became flesh and dwelt among us, full of grace and truth; we have beheld his glory, glory as of the only-begotten Son from the Father. (Jn 1:1–5, 14)

The idea that God Himself would come to be with us face-to-face is so profound that it can be understood only through the "logic" of unconditional, humble-hearted, gentle-hearted, compassionate, self-sacrificial love that reveals His and His Father's nature. In light of this, we would expect that His ultimate commandment—His ultimate revelation of the meaning of life—would be centered on the love He came to reveal. This leads us to the third of my favorite Scripture passages—also from the Gospel of John:

As the Father has loved me, so have I loved you; abide in my love. If
you keep my commandments, you will abide in my love, just as I have
kept my Father's commandments and abide in his love. These things
I have spoken to you, that my joy may be in you, and that your joy
may be full. This is my commandment, that you love one another as
I have loved you. Greater love has no man than this, that a man lay
down his life for his friends. (15:9–13)

There are four revelations in this passage that are mystically profound, requiring a knowledge of Jesus in our hearts—a knowledge
that comes from prayer and devotion:

1. *"As the Father has loved me, so I have loved you."* It is almost
   unimaginable that the Son of God could love us in the same
   way that His Father loves Him. Who can wrap their minds
   around this mystery? Speaking personally, I cannot, and it will
   take an eternity to penetrate the beauty and goodness of it. All
   I can do is try to remain faithful to Him and His love, which
   opens the way to enjoying His loving presence—to stand in
   awe before Him.

2. *"If you keep my commandments, you will abide in my love."* Jesus
   indicates here that there are many commandments, but in
   the next verse implies that all of them are related to the central commandment to love one another as He has loved us.
   Throughout this volume, we have articulated many of those
   commandments, showing how each of them is related to covenant love—the humble-hearted, gentle-hearted, compassionate, self-sacrificial love exemplified by Jesus. Though the quality
   of covenant love may not at first be evident in some of these
   commandments (particularly in this culture), their observance
   produces genuinely deep, long-lasting, relational effects that
   reveal their life-giving character—their capacity to conquer evil
   and death. Jesus says that if we want to "abide" ("bask, enjoy,
   and live") in His love, all we need do is keep His commandments. The hundreds of studies mentioned in this volume point
   to that truth—that obedience to Jesus' commandments leads to
   emotional, marital, familial, cultural, and spiritual health, calling
   us out of darkness into His eternally loving light.

3. *"These things I have spoken to you, that my joy may be in you, and that your joy may be full."* Jesus' promise points to the eternal life He wishes to give us, but it also refers to *this* life. Even though this life can have manifold challenges and sufferings, remaining faithful to prayer in His commandments keeps us in His joy—what Saint Paul called "a peace beyond all understanding" (Phil 4:7).

4. *"This is my commandment, that you love one another as I have loved you. Greater love has no man than this, that a man lay down his life for his friends."* As noted above, all of Jesus' commandments serve one purpose: to help us abide in genuine covenant love—humble-hearted, gentle-hearted, compassionate, self-sacrificial love. If we try to live according to His commandments (albeit imperfectly), we can be sure that we will experience His joy and peace even in the midst of suffering in this life, and fully in the life to come. The many studies in this volume testify to the *truth* of Jesus' promise, and I will add my own. When I am faithful to His commandments, He holds me in joy and peace, and when I veer off the road, the sense of spiritual emptiness, alienation, and loneliness soon ensues. Though there are sacrifices involved in living according to His commandments, the reward is being at home with Him in this life and the next.

Jesus knew that His words would not be perfectly transparent to us not only because of our lack of knowledge, but also because of our egocentricity and bias. He was well aware of religious factioning in His own time and knew that such factioning would also occur among Christians in future generations. He was also aware that our spiritual enemy, Satan, though defeated, would continue to tempt and deceive us in his "mission" to lead us into darkness. In view of this, Jesus would not leave us like sheep without a shepherd, and so He provided an authoritative, spirit-filled voice to interpret His words and administer His sacramental grace. Realizing that the only way to prevent factioning was to make His authoritative voice supreme and definitive, He created an office ("the keys of the kingdom of heaven" [Mt 16:19]) built on the foundation rock of Peter that He would protect until the end of time.

This leads us to our fourth and final Scripture passage:

Blessed are you, Simon Bar-Jona! For flesh and blood has not revealed this to you, but my Father who is in heaven. And I tell you, you are Peter, and on this rock I will build my Church, and the gates of Hades shall not prevail against it. I will give you the keys of the kingdom of heaven, and whatever you bind on earth shall be bound in heaven, and whatever you loose on earth shall be loosed in heaven. (Mt 16:17–19)

As I have indicated multiple times throughout this Trilogy, there is ample evidence to indicate that Jesus has kept His promise to protect His Church from the gates of Hades even in the most decadent and challenging times. Yes—there have been scandals, but amid it all, there have been millions more heralded and unheralded saints who have proved through their lives that living covenant love according to Jesus' commandments interpreted by the Catholic Church is the way to peace and joy in the midst of depravity and suffering. Jesus has been true to His word—true to His identity—He is "the way, and the truth, and the life" (Jn 14:6). If we follow Him through the moral wisdom of His Church, His truth will set us free (see Jn 8:32)—free to follow His light out of darkness into the kingdom of eternal love and joy.

BIBLIOGRAPHY

Abela, Andrew V., and Joseph E. Capizzi, eds. *A Catechism for Business: Tough Ethical Questions and Insights from Catholic Teaching.* Washington, D.C.: Catholic University of America Press, 2014.

Adams, John. Letter from John Adams to Massachusetts Militia, October 11, 1798. National Archives, Founders Online. https://founders.archives.gov/documents/Adams/99-02-02-3102.

Agenzia Fides (Fides News Agency). "Vatican—Catholic Church Statistics 2020". October 16, 2020. http://www.fides.org/en/news/68840-vatican_catholic_church_statistics_2020.

Albrecht, G. L., and P. J. Devlieger. "The Disability Paradox: High Quality of Life against All Odds". *Social Science and Medicine* 48, no. 8 (April 1999): 977–88. https://pubmed.ncbi.nlm.nih.gov/10390038/.

American Academy of Hospice and Palliative Medicine. "Statement on Palliative Sedation". December 5, 2014. http://aahpm.org/positions/palliative-sedation.

American Addiction Centers. "Alcohol and Drug Abuse Statistics". Last updated November 19, 2021. https://americanaddictioncenters.org/rehab-guide/addiction-statistics.

American Law and Legal Information. "Cyber Crime". 1992. http://law.jrank.org/pages/11992/Cyber-Crime-Intellectual-property-theft.html.

American Medical Association. "Code of Medical Ethics Opinion 5.7". 2022. https://www.ama-assn.org/delivering-care/ethics/physician-assisted-suicide.

Aquinas, Thomas. *Summa Contra Gentiles.* Translated by Anton C. Pegis. Edited by Joseph Kenny, O.P. New York: Hanover House, 1955–57. https://isidore.co/aquinas/ContraGentiles1.htm.

———. *Summa Theologica.* Translated by the Fathers of the English Dominican Province. New York: Benziger Brothers, 1947.

————. *Summa Theologica*. Translated by the Fathers of the English Dominican Province. Westminster, Md.: Christian Classics, 1981.

————. *The Summa Theologiæ of St. Thomas Aquinas*. 2nd and rev. ed. Translated by the Fathers of the English Dominican Province, 1920. New Advent, online ed. by Kevin Knight, 2017.

Aristotle. *Nicomachean Ethics*. Translated by W. D. Ross. Internet Classics Archive by Daniel C. Stevenson. 1994–2000. http://classics.mit.edu/Aristotle/nicomachaen.html.

Atkins, David, and Elizabeth Allen. "The Association of Divorce and Extramarital Sex in a Representative U.S. Sample". *Journal of Family Issues*, November 2012. www.researchgate.net/public ation/258151224_The_Association_of_Divorce_and_Extramarital Sex_in_a_Representative_US_Sample.

Augustine. *The City of God*. In *Nicene and Post-Nicene Fathers*. Series 1, vol. 2. Edited by Philip Schaff. Translated by Rev. Marchs Dods. Edinburgh: T&T Clark/Grand Rapids, Mich.: Wm. B. Eerdmans Publishing, 1886. https://web.archive.org/web/20130725190746 /http://etext.lib.virginia.edu/etcbin/toccer-ncw2?id=AugCity .xml&images=images%2Fmodeng&data=%2Ftexts%2Fenglish %2Fmodeng%2Fparsed&tag=public&part=all.

————. *On Free Choice of the Will*. Edited and Translated by Peter King. New York: Cambridge University Press, 2010. https://philo new.files.wordpress.com/2016/08/augustine-augustine-on-the -free-choice-of-the-will-on-grace-and-free-choice-and-other -writings-2010.pdf.

Austin, William H. "Isaac Newton on Science and Religion". *Journal of the History of Ideas* 31, no. 4 (1970): 521–42.

Austriaco, Nicanor. "The Moral Case or ANT-Derived Pluripotent Stem Cell Lines". *National Catholic Bioethics Quarterly* 6 (2006): 517–37. https://www.pdcnet.org/ncbq/content/ncbq_2006_0006_0003 _0517_0537.

Baglio, Matt. *The Rite: Making of a Modern Exorcist*. New York: Image/Doubleday, 2010.

Balsam, Kimberly F., Theodore P. Beauchaine, Ruth M. Mickey, and Esther D. Rothblum. "Mental Health of Lesbian, Gay, Bisexual, and Heterosexual Siblings: Effects of Gender, Sexual Orientation, and Family". *Journal of Abnormal Psychology* 114, no. 3 (August 2005): 471–76.

Barroilhet, Sergio, Camila Señoret, Ximena Mallea, Rosemarie Fritsch, Paul Vöhringer, and José-Antonio Arraztoa. "Marital Functioning in Couples Practicing Periodic Abstinence for Family Planning". *Linacre Quarterly* 85, no. 2 (May 2018): 155–66. https://www.ncbi.nlm.nih.gov/pmc/articles/PMC6056796/.

Bassani, Luigi Marco. "The Real Jefferson". Mises Institute, May 23, 2002. https://mises.org/library/real-jefferson.

Baumeister, Alfred. *Ameliorating Mental Disability: Questioning Retardation*. New York: Routledge, 2009.

Beauregard, Mario. *Brain Wars: The Scientific Battle over the Existence of the Mind and the Proof That Will Change the Way We Live*. New York: HarperOne, 2012.

Belden, Kyle. "6 Accountability Software Options". CrossPoint Community Church, March 29, 2018. https://cpmodesto.org/2018/03/6-accountability-software-options/.

Bell, Allen P., and Martin S. Weinberg. *Homosexualities: A Study of Diversity among Men and Women*. New York: Simon and Schuster, 1978.

Bell, Allen P., Martin S. Weinberg, and Sue Kiefer Hammersmith. *Sexual Preference*. Bloomington: Indiana University Press, 1981.

Bell, Courtney. *An Overview of Research on the Impact That Viewing Pornography Has on Children, Pre-Teens and Teenagers*. Arundel BC, Queensland, Australia: Bravehearts Foundation, 2017. https://bravehearts.org.au/wp-content/uploads/2018/01/Research-Report_Overview-of-research-into-the-effects-of-viewing-pornography-on-children....pdf.

Benedict. *St. Benedict's Rule for Monasteries*. Translated by Leonard J. Doyle. Collegeville, Minn.: Liturgical Press, 1948; Project Gutenburg, 2015. http://www.gutenberg.org/files/50040/50040-h/50040-h.html.

Benedict XVI, Pope. Encyclical Letter on Christian Love *Deus Caritas Est* (God Is Love). December 25, 2005.

———. Encyclical Letter on Integral Human Development in Charity and Truth *Caritas in Veritate*. June 29, 2009.

———. Post-Synodal Apostolic Exhortation on the Eucharist as the Source and Summit of the Church's Life and Mission *Sacramentum Caritatis*. February 22, 2007.

Berger, Helena. "When Insurance Companies Refuse Treatment 'Assisted Suicide' Is No Choice at All". American Association of People with Disabilities, January 24, 2017. https://www.aapd .com/when-insurance-companies-refuse-treatment-assisted-suicide -is-no-choice-at-all/.

Bergner, Raymond M., and Ana J. Bridges. "The Significance of Heavy Pornography Involvement for Romantic Partners: Research and Clinical Implications". Journal of Sex & Marital Therapy 28, no. 3 (2002): 193–206.

Bering, Jesse. "One Last Goodbye: The Strange Case of Terminal Lucidity". Scientific American (blog), November 25, 2014. https:// blogs.scientificamerican.com/bering-in-mind/one-last-goodbye -the-strange-case-of-terminal-lucidity/.

Bernton, Hal. "Washington's Initiative 1000 Is Modeled on Oregon's Death with Dignity Act". Seattle Times, October 13, 2008. https:// www.seattletimes.com/seattle-news/washingtons-initiative-1000 -is-modeled-on-oregons-death-with-dignity-act/.

Bhattacharya, Pramab Kumar. "Is There Science behind the Near-Death Experience: Does Human Consciousness Survives after Death?" Annals of Tropical Medicine and Public Health 6 no. 2 (2013): 151–65.

Blackstone, William. Blackstone's Commentaries on the Law: From the Abridged Edition of Wm. Hardcastle Browne. Washington, D.C.: Washington Law Book Company, 1941.

Blainey, Geoffrey. A Short History of Christianity. Lanham, Md.: Rowan, Littlefield, 2014.

Blanton, Hart, Amber Köblitz, and Kevin D. McCaul. "Misperceptions about Norm Misperceptions: Descriptive, Injunctive, and Affective 'Social Norming' Efforts to Change Health Behaviors". Social and Personality Psychology Compass 2, no. 3 (2008). https://online library.wiley.com/doi/abs/10.1111/j.1751-9004.2008.00107.x.

Bonelli, Raphael, Rachel E. Dew, Harold G. Koenig, David H. Rosmarin, and Sasan Vasegh. "Religious and Spiritual Factors in Depression: Review and Integration of the Research". Depression and Research Treatment, August 15, 2012. https://www.hindawi .com/journals/drt/2012/962860/.

Boswell, John. Christianity, Social Tolerance and Homosexuality. Chicago: University of Chicago Press, 1980.

BP. "Statistical Review of World Energy". 2016. https://www.bp.com/en/global/corporate/energy-economics/statistical-review-of-world-energy/downloads.html.

Bramlett, Matthew D., and William D. Mosher. "First Marriage Dissolution, Divorce and Remarriage: United States". *Advance Data*, no. 323. Hyattsville, Md.: National Center for Health Statistics, 2001.

Bridges, Ana J., Raymond M. Bergner, and Matthew Hesson-McInnis. "Romantic Partners' Use of Pornography: Its Significance for Women". *Journal of Sex & Marital Therapy* 29, no. 1 (2003): 1–14.

Briggs, David. "5 Ways Faith Contributes to Strong Marriages, New Studies Suggest". *HuffPost*, February 8, 2015. http://www.huffingtonpost.com/david-briggs/5-ways-faith-contributes_b_6294716.

Brokaw, Tom. *The Greatest Generation*. New York: Random House, 2001.

Brooks, Arthur. "Why Giving Makes You Happy". *New York Sun*, December 28, 2007. https://www.nysun.com/opinion/why-giving-makes-you-happy/68700/.

Bryant, Colleen. "Adolescence, Pornography, and Harm". *Trends and Issues in Crime and Criminal Justice*, no. 368 (February 2009): 1–6. https://www.aic.gov.au/sites/default/files/2020-05/tandi368.pdf.

Buber, Martin. *I and Thou*. Eastford, Conn.: Martino Publishing, 2010.

Burke, Edmund. *Second Speech on Conciliation*. 1775.

Burpo, Todd, and Lynn Vincent. *Heaven Is for Real: A Little Boy's Astounding Story of His Trip to Heaven and Back*. Nashville: Thomas Nelson, 2010.

Butz, Melissa. "Pope Francis Has Named the Most Saints in History". *Rome Reports*, August 8, 2020. https://www.romereports.com/en/2020/08/08/pope-francis-has-named-the-most-saints-in-history/.

Byrne, Donn. "Social Psychology and the Study of Sexual Behavior". *Personality and Social Psychology Bulletin* 3, no. 1 (December 1976). http://journals.sagepub.com/doi/pdf/10.1177/014616727600300102.

Cahill, Thomas. *How the Irish Saved Civilization*. New York: Anchor, 1996.

Carlson, Bruce, and M. Patten. *Foundations of Embryology*. 6th ed. New York: McGraw-Hill, 1996.

Carson, Thomas. *New Catholic Encyclopedia*. 2nd ed. 15 vols. Detroit: Gale Research, 2002.

Carter-Birken, Pamela. "Creative Connections—Art Museums Reach Out to Persons with Disabilities". *Social Work Today* 9, no. 4 (2009): 16.

Catholic News Agency. "Catholic Hospitals Comprise One Quarter of World's Healthcare, Council Reports". February 10, 2010. https://www.catholicnewsagency.com/news/catholic_hospitals _represent_26_percent_of_worlds_health_facilities_reports_ponti fical_council.

————. "Controversial Dutch Bill Would Allow Assisted Suicide for Healthy People over 75". July 28, 2020. https://www.catholic newsagency.com/news/controversial-dutch-bill-would-allow -assisted-suicide-for-healthy-people-over-75-19446.

Center for Medical Progress. "Planned Parenthood Testimony on Selling Baby Parts Unsealed, New Videos Released". May 26, 2020. http://www.centerformedicalprogress.org/2020/05/planned -parenthood-testimony-on-selling-baby-parts-unsealed-new-videos -released/.

Centers for Disease Control and Prevention. "Abortion Surveillance— Findings and Reports". Last reviewed November 22, 2021. https:// www.cdc.gov/reproductivehealth/data_stats/abortion.htm.

Chalmers, David. *The Conscious Mind: In Search of a Fundamental Theory (Philosophy of Mind)*. Oxford: Oxford University Press, 1996.

Chandra, Anita, Steven C. Martino, Rebecca L. Collins, Marc N. Elliott, Sandra H. Berry, David E. Kanouse, and Angela Miu. "Does Watching Sex on Television Predict Teen Pregnancy? Findings from a Longitudinal Survey of Youth". *Pediatrics* 122 (2008): 1047–54.

Chapman, Graham P. "The Green Revolution". In *The Companion to Development Studies*, pp. 155–59. London: Arnold, 2002. https:// staff.washington.edu/jhannah/geog270aut07/readings/Green GeneRevolutions/Chapman%20-%20GreenRev.pdf.

Cicero, Marcus Tullius. *The Republic and the Laws*. Translated by Niall Rudd. New York: Oxford University Press, 2009.

Classics of Western Spirituality Series. New York; Mahwah, N.J.: Paulist Press, 1978–2013.

Clement of Rome. *Letter to the Corinthians*. CatholicAnswers.com, 2022. http://www.catholic.com/tracts/the-authority-of-the-pope -part-i.

Cochran, Susan D., J. Greer Sullivan, and Vickie M. Mays. "Prevalence of Mental Disorders, Psychological Distress, and Mental Health Services Use among Lesbian, Gay, and Bisexual Adults in the United States". *Journal of Consulting and Clinical Psychology* 71, no. 1 (February 2003): 53–61.

Cochran, Susan D., and Vickie M. Mays. "Physical Health Complaints among Lesbians, Gay Men, and Bisexual and Homosexually Experienced Heterosexual Individuals: Results from the California Quality of Life Survey". *American Journal of Public Health* 97, no. 11 (November 2007): 2048–55.

Cohen, Ariel. "Is Fusion Power within Our Grasp?" *Forbes*, January 14, 2019. https://www.forbes.com/sites/arielcohen/2019/01/14 /is-fusion-power-within-our-grasp/#5728af7b9bb4.

Coleman, Diane. "Why Do Disability Rights Organizations Oppose Assisted Suicide Laws?" Not Dead Yet, 2022. https://notdeadyet .org/why-do-disability-rights-organizations-oppose-assisted -suicide-laws.

Coleman, Priscilla K. "Abortion and Mental Health: Quantitative Synthesis and Analysis of Research Published 1995–2009". *British Journal of Psychiatry* 199, no. 3 (2011): 180–86. Republished online by Cambridge University, January 2, 2018. https://www .cambridge.org/core/journals/the-british-journal-of-psychiatry /article/abortion-and-mental-health-quantitative-synthesis-and -analysis-of-research-published-19952009/E8D556AAE1C1D2F0 F8B060B28BEE6C3D.

"Colosseum". History.com, June 6, 2019. https://www.history .com/topics/ancient-history/colosseum.

Committee to Investigate Medical Practice Concerning Euthanasia. "Medical Decisions about the End of Life (Remmelink Report)". The Hague, Netherlands: Ministry of Justice and Ministry of Welfare, Public Health, and Culture, 1991.

Conca, James. "Extract CO_2 from Our Air, Use It to Create Synthetic Fuels". EnergyPost.eu, October 11, 2019. https://energypost.eu /extract-co2-from-our-air-use-it-to-create-synthetic-fuels/.

Congregation for Catholic Education. *Index: Universitates et IM Instituta Studiorum Superiorum Ecclesiae Catholicae.* Vatican City: Vatican Press, 2005.

———. *"Male and Female He Created Them": Towards a Path of Dialogue on the Question of Gender Theory in Education.* February 2, 2019.

————. *The Religious Dimension of Education in a Catholic School: Guidelines for Reflection and Renewal.* April 7, 1988.

Congregation for the Doctrine of the Faith. *Doctrinal Note on Some Questions regarding the Participation of Catholics in Political Life.* November 24, 2002.

————. Instruction on Certain Bioethical Questions *Dignitatis Personae.* September 8, 2008.

————. Instruction on Respect for Human Life in Its Origin and on the Dignity of Procreation *Donum Vitae.* February 22, 1987.

Constitution of the United States of America. First Amendment. From Constitute (website). Last revised 1992. https://www.constitute project.org/constitution/United_States_of_America_1992.

Cornwall, Marie., Stan L. Albrecht, Perry H. Cunningham, and Brian L. Pitcher. "The Dimensions of Religiosity: A Conceptual Model with an Empirical Test". *Review of Religious Research* 27, no. 3 (1986): 226–44.

Credible Catholic. Magis Center, 2021. https://www.credible catholic.com/.

Creitz, Charles. "Constitutional Expert on 'Separation of Church and State': Framers Said Nothing Wrong with Religion in Culture". Fox News, June 23, 2019. https://www.foxnews.com/politics /separation-of-church-state-levin-michael-mcconnell.

Crocker, Lizzie. "There's Been a Huge Increase in Campus Sex Assaults. Why?" *Daily Beast*, published May 16, 2017, updated May 22, 2017. https://www.thedailybeast.com/theres-been-a-huge -increase-in-campus-sex-assaults-why.

Crossen, David. "Guilt Is a Recurring Theme in Literature and Drama". *New York Times Archives*, July 24, 1979. https://www .nytimes.com/1979/07/24/archives/guilt-is-a-recurring-theme-in -literature-and-drama-crediting-the.html.

Cyprian of Carthage. *The Unity of the Catholic Church.* 1st ed. From Philvaz.com. Accessed March 3, 2022. http://philvaz.com/apolo getics/num44.htm.

Daly, Lowrie J. *The Medieval University: 1200–1400.* New York: Sheed and Ward, 1961.

Daspe, Marie-Ève, Marie-Pier Vaillancourt-Morel, Yvan Lussier, StéphaneSabourin, and Anik Ferron. "When Pornography Use Feels Out of Control: The Moderation Effect of Relationship and

Sexual Satisfaction". *Journal of Sex and Marital Therapy* 44, no. 4 (May 2018): 343–53. https://pubmed.ncbi.nlm.nih.gov/29281588/.

Davies, W. D., and Dale C. Allison. *International Critical Commentary*. Vol. 2, *Matthew 8–18*. New York: T&T Clark, 1991.

Davis, Jeanie Lerche. "Can Prayer Heal?" WebMD, 2001. https://www.webmd.com/balance/features/can-prayer-heal#1.

Dawson, Christopher. *Religion and the Rise of Western Culture: The Classic Study of Medieval Civilization*. New York: Double Day/Image, 1991.

DeAngelis, T. "Web Pornography's Effect on Children". *Monitor* 38, no. 10 (2007): 50.

De Chardin, Pierre Teilhard. *The Divine Milieu*. Translated by Sion Cowell. Sussex: Sussex Academic Press, 2004.

Declaration of Independence. From a transcription on the website of the National Archives. Last reviewed on October 7, 2021. https://www.archives.gov/founding-docs/declaration-transcript.

De Graaf, Ron, Theo G. M. Sandfort, and Margreet ten Have. "Suicidality and Sexual Orientation: Differences between Men and Women in a General Population-Based Sample From the Netherlands". *Archives of Sexual Behavior* 35 (2006): 253–62. https://link.springer.com/article/10.1007/s10508-006-9020-z.

DeGeorge, Richard. *Business Ethics*. 7th ed. London: Pearson, 2009.

DeMarco, Donald. "The Dispute between Galileo and the Catholic Church (Part I and Part II)". *Homiletic and Pastoral Review* 86, no. 8 (1986): 23–32, 50–51; no. 9 (1986): 23–51, 53–59.

Department of State and the Department of Health and Human Services. *Why Population Aging Matters: A Global Perspective*. Washington, D.C.: National Institute on Aging, National Institutes of Health, March 13, 2007. https://2001-2009.state.gov/g/oes/rls/or/81537.htm.

Dervic, Kanita, Maria A. Oquendo, Michael F. Grunebaum, Steve Ellis, Ainsley Burke, and J. John Mann. "Religious Affiliation and Suicide Attempt". *American Journal of Psychiatry* 161, no. 12 (December 2004): 2303–8. https://ajp.psychiatryonline.org/doi/full/10.1176/appi.ajp.161.12.2303.

Desanctis, Alexandra. "Democrats Block the Born-Alive Abortion Survivors Bill". *National Review*, February 8, 2021. https://www

.nationalreview.com/2021/02/democrats-block-the-born-alive
-abortion-survivors-bill/.

—————."Virginia Governor Defends Letting Infants Die". *National Review*, January 30, 2019. https://www.nationalreview.com/corner/virginia-governor-defends-letting-infants-die/.

Deutsch, Morton, and Harold B. Gerard. "A Study of Normative and Informational Social Influences upon Individual Judgment". *Journal of Abnormal and Social Psychology* 51, no. 3 (1955): 629–36. doi:10.1037/h0046408. PMID 13286010.

Devor, Holly. "Transsexualism, Dissociation, and Child Abuse: An Initial Discussion Based on Nonclinical Data". *Journal of Psychology and Human Sexuality* 6, no. 3 (1994): 49–72.

Dickens, Charles. *A Christmas Carol*. London: Chapman & Hall, 1843; Project Guttenberg, 2018. http://www.gutenberg.org/ebooks/19337.

Dijkers, Marcel P.J.M. "Quality of Life of Individuals with Spinal Cord Injury: A Review of Conceptualization, Measurement, and Research Findings". *Journal of Rehabilitation Research and Development* 42, no. 3 (May 2005): 87–110. https://www.rehab.research.va.gov/jour/05/42/3suppl1/dijkers.html.

Donadio, Rachel. "On Gay Priests, Pope Francis Asks, 'Who Am I to Judge?'" *New York Times*, July 29, 2013. http://www.nytimes.com/2013/07/30/world/europe/pope-francis-gay-priests.html.

Donovan, Colin B. "End of Life Decisions: Ordinary versus Extraordinary Means." EWTN, March 2019. https://www.ewtn.com/catholicism/library/end-of-life-decisions-ordinary-versus-extraordinary means-12733.

Dostoyevsky, Fyodor. *The Brothers Karamazov*. Translated by Constance Garnett. New York: Lowell Press, 2009; Project Gutenberg, 2021. https://www.gutenberg.org/cache/epub/28054/pg28054-images.html.

Dowd, Lynn D. "Brief of Biologist as Amici Curiae in Support of Neither Party: Thomas E. Dobbs, State Health Officer of The Mississippi Department of Health *et al*, *petitioners* v. Jackson Women's Health Organization *et al*, *respondents*". Submitted to The United States Court of Appeals for the Fifth Court as well as United States Supreme Court, 2020. https://www.supremecourt.gov/DocketPDF/19/19-1392/185254/20210729125335060_19-1392%20Dobbs%20v.%20JWHO%20Amicus%20Brief%20of%20American%20

Center%20for%20Law%20and%20Justice%20and%20Bioethics%20
Defense%20Fund.pdf.

Downey, Michael. *The New Dictionary of Catholic Spirituality*. Collegeville, Minn.: Liturgical Press, 1993.

Dyson, Freeman. "Progress in Religion". Edge.org, May 15, 2000.
https://www.edge.org/conversation/freeman_dyson-progress-in
-religion.

Eberstadt, Mary, and Mary Anne Layden. *The Social Costs of Pornography: A Statement of Findings and Recommendations*. Princeton, N.J.:
Witherspoon Institute, 2010. https://afaofpa.org/wp-content/up
loads/Social-Costs-of-Porn-Report.pdf.

Eccles, Sir John. *Evolution of the Brain: Creation of the Self*. 1989.
Reprint, London, UK: Routledge, 1991.

Eddington, Sir Arthur. *The Nature of the Physical World*. Cambridge:
Cambridge University Press, 1928.

――. *Why I Believe in God: Science and Religion, as a Scientist Sees It*.
London: Hadelman-Julius Publications, 1930.

Educational Testing Service. "Academic Cheating Fact Sheet".
1999. http://www.glass-castle.com/clients/www-nocheating-org
/adcouncil/research/cheatingfactsheet.html.

Einstein, Albert. *Ideas & Opinions*. Translated by Sonja Bargmann.
New York: Crown Publishers, 1954.

Eliade, Mircea. *Macmillan Encyclopedia of Religion*. 15 vols. New York:
Macmillan Publisher, 1966.

――. *The Sacred and the Profane: The Nature of Religion*. Translated
by Willard R. Trask. New York, Harcourt, 1987.

Ellicott, Charles John. "Matthew 16:18: Ellicott's Commentary for English Readers". 2021. https://biblehub.com/commentaries/matthew
/16-18.htm.

Engelland, Brian. *Force for Good: The Catholic Guide to Business Integrity*. Manchester, N.H.: Sophia Institute Press, 2017.

Entler, Slavomir, Jan Horacek, Tomas Dlouhy, and Vacla Dostal.
"Approximation of the Economy of Fusion Energy". *Energy* 152,
no. 1 (2018): 489–97. https://www.sciencedirect.com/science
/article/pii/S0360544218305395.

Eugene IV, Pope. Against the Enslaving of Black Natives from
the Canary Islands *Sicut Dudum*. January 13, 1435. From Joel S.
Panzer, *The Popes and Slavery*, Appendix B. Society of St. Paul,
1996. In Baronius, *Annales Ecclesiastici*, edited by O. Raynaldus, p.

75. Luca, 1752. PapalEncyclicals.Net. Last updated February 20, 2020. https://www.papalencyclicals.net/eugene04/eugene04sicut .htm.

Evert, Jason. *If You Really Loved Me*. Scottsdale, Ariz.: Totus Tuus Press, 2013.

Eyler, Janet, Dwight E. Giles Jr., Christine M. Stenson, and Charlene J. Gray. *At A Glance: What We Know about the Effects of Service-Learning on College Students, Faculty, Institutions and Communities, 1993–2000: Third Edition*. Vanderbilt University, August 31, 2001. Funded by the Corporation for National Service Learn and Serve America National Serving Learning Clearinghouse. Available on the website of DigitalCommons@UNO, University of Nebraska at Omaha. https://digitalcommons.unomaha.edu/cgi /viewcontent.cgi?referer=https://scholar.google.com/&httpsredir =1&article=1137&context=slcehighered.

Fagan, Patrick F. "The Effects of Pornography on Individuals, Marriage, Family, and Community". *Research Synthesis*. Washington, D.C.: Family Research Council, 2009. https://downloads.frc.org /EF/EF09K57.pdf.

Fararo, Thomas J., and John Skvoretz. "Action and Institution, Network and Function: The Cybernetic Concept of Social Structure". *Sociological Forum* 1, no. 2 (1986): 219–50.

Farias, Dawn. *How Natural Family Planning Changed My Life*. Washington, D.C.: NFPP/United States Conference of Catholic Bishops, 2015. https://www.usccb.org/issues-and-action/marriage -and-family/natural-family-planning/what-is-nfp/couples-stories /upload/Dawn-Farias-English.pdf.

Fehring, Richard. "The Influence of Contraception, Abortion, and Natural Family Planning on Divorce Rates as Found in the 2006–2010 National Survey of Family Growth". *Linacre Quarterly* 82, no. 3 (August 2015): 273–82. https://www.ncbi.nlm.nih.gov/pmc /articles/PMC4536625/.

Ferguson, Maureen. "An Infanticide Question Awaits the Democratic Nominee in 2020". *The Hill*, March 2, 2019. https://thehill .com/opinion/healthcare/432319-an-infanticide-question-awaits -the-democratic-nominee-in-2020.

Fergusson, David M., L. John Horwood, and Annette L. Beautrais. "Is Sexual Orientation Related to Mental Health Problems and

Suicidality in Young People?" *Archives of General Psychiatry* 56, no. 10 (October 1999): 876–80.

Fertility Appreciation Collaborative to Teach the Science (FACTS). "Sympto-Thermal Method". 2014. https://www.factsaboutfertility.org/wp-content/uploads/2014/09/SymptoThermalPEH.pdf.

Feuillet, Lionel, Henry Dufour, and Jean Pelletier. "Brain of a White-Collar Worker". *Lancet* 370, no. 9583 (2007): 262. https://www.thelancet.com/journals/lancet/article/PIIS0140-6736(07)61127-1/fulltext.

Finkelman, Paul. "Slavery in the United States: Persons or Property?" In *The Legal Understanding of Slavery: From the Historical to the Contemporary*, edited by Jean Allain, pp. 109–10. New York: Oxford University Press, 2012.

Finnis, John. "Aquinas' Moral, Political, and Legal Philosophy". *Stanford Encyclopedia of Philosophy*. Last updated March 16, 2021. https://plato.stanford.edu/entries/aquinas-moral-political/.

———. *Natural Law and Natural Rights*. 2nd ed. New York: Oxford University Press, 1980.

———. "The Rights and Wrongs of Abortion". In *The Philosophy of Law*, edited by Ronald Dworkin, pp. 129–52. Oxford: Oxford University Press, 1977.

Fitzgibbons, Richard, Philip M. Sutton, and Dale O'Leary. "The Psychopathology of 'Sex Reassignment' Surgery: Assessing Its Medical, Psychological, and Ethical Appropriateness". *National Catholic Bioethics Quarterly* 9, no. 1 (Spring 2009): 97–125. http://lc.org/PDFs/Attachments2PRsLAs/2018/061118SexReasssignmentSurgery.pdf.

Fitzmyer, Joseph A. "The Letter to the Romans". In *The New Jerome Biblical Commentary*, edited by Raymond E. Brown, Joseph A. Fitzmyer, and Roland E. Murphy, pp. 830–68. Englewood Cliffs, N.J.: Prentice Hall, 1990.

Flood, Michael "Young Men Using Pornography". In *Everyday Pornography*, edited by K. Boyle, pp. 164–78. New York: Routledge, 2010.

Flood, Michael, and Clive Hamilton. "Youth and Pornography in Australia: Evidence on the Extent of Exposure and Likely Effects". Discussion Paper Number 52, Australia Institute, February 2003.

Foley, Kathleen M. "The Relationship of Pain and Symptom Management to Patient Requests for Physician-Assisted Suicide". *Journal of Pain and Symptom Management* 6, no. 5 (1991): 289–97.

Foley, Kathleen, and Herbert Hendin. *The Case against Assisted Suicide: For the Right to End-of-Life Care*. Baltimore: Johns Hopkins University Press, 2002.

Follett, Chelsea. "The Cruel Truth about Population Control". Commentary, CATO Institute, June 13, 2019. https://www.cato.org/publications/commentary/cruel-truth-about-population-control.

Fonseca, Goncalo L. "The School of Salamanca". History of Economic Thought (website). Accessed February 20, 2022. https://www.hetwebsite.net/het/schools/salamanca.htm.

Francis, Pope. Apostolic Exhortation on the Proclamation of the Gospel in Today's World *Evangelii Gaudium* (The Joy of the Gospel). November 24, 2013.

———. Encyclical Letter on Care for Our Common Home *Laudato Si'*. May 24, 2015.

———. Encyclical Letter on Fraternity and Social Friendship *Fratelli Tutti*. October 3, 2020.

———. "Pope Francis: Cheating to Win in Sport Is 'Ugly and Sterile'". Vatican Radio, August 5, 2015. http://en.radiovaticana.va/news/2015/05/08/pope_francis_cheating_to_win_in_sport_is_ugly_and_sterile/1142609.

Francis, Saint. "Peace Prayer of Saint Francis". Loyola Press (website), 2022. https://www.loyolapress.com/catholic-resources/prayer/traditional-catholic-prayers/saints-prayers/peace-prayer-of-saint-francis/.

Freeman, Bill. "Science or Miracle? Holiday Season Survey Reveals Physicians' Views of Faith, Prayer and Miracles". WorldHealth.net, December 22, 2004. https://www.worldhealth.net/news/science_or_miracle_holiday_season_survey/.

Friedman, Milton. "The Social Responsibility of Business Is to Increase Its Profits". *New York Times Magazine*, September 13, 1970.

Fryar, Cheryl D., Rosemarie Hirsch, Kathryn S. Porter, Benny Kottiri, Debra J. Brody, and Tatiana Louis. "Drug Use and Sexual Behaviors Reported by Adults: United States, 1999–2002". *Advance Data from Vital and Health Statistics*, no. 384. Hyattsville, Md.: National Center for Health Statistics, 2007. https://www.cdc.gov/nchs/data/ad/ad384.pdf.

Gallagher, Paul. "The Irish Monastery Movement". *Federalist*, March 1995. http://american_almanac.tripod.com/monks.htm.

Gandhi, Mahatma. *Young India*, January 5, 1922.

Gatehouse, A.M.R., N. Ferry, M.G. Edwards, and H.A. Bell. "Insect-Resistant Biotech Crops and Their Impacts on Beneficial Arthropods". *Philosophical Transactions of the Royal Society B: Biological Sciences* 366, no. 1569 (2011): 1438–52. https://www.ncbi.nlm.nih.gov/pmc/articles/PMC3081576/#.

Gaventa, William C., and David Coulter. *Spirituality and Intellectual Disability: International Perspectives on the Effect of Culture and Religion on Healing Body, Mind, and Soul*. Philadelphia, Pa.: Haworth Pastoral Press, 2001.

Gehring, Darlynne, and Gail Knudson. "Prevalence of Childhood Trauma in a Clinical Population of Transsexual People". *International Journal of Transgenderism* 8, no. 1 (2005): 23–30.

George, Robert. *Conscious and Its Enemies: Confronting the Dogmas of Liberal Secularism*. Wilmington, Del.: ISI Books, 2016.

Gilles, Gary. "How Pornography Distorts Intimate Relationships". MentalHelp.net, 2020. https://www.mentalhelp.net/blogs/how-pornography-distorts-intimate-relationships/.

Gilman, Stephen E., et al. "Risk of Psychiatric Disorders among Individuals Reporting Same-Sex Sexual Partners in a National Comorbidity Survey". *American Journal of Public Health* 9, no. 6 (June 2001): 933–39.

Glassgold, Judith M., Lee Beckstead, Jack Drescher, Beverly Greene, Robin Lin Miller, and Roger L. Worthington. *Report of the American Psychological Association Task Force on Appropriate Therapeutic Responses to Sexual Orientation*. Washington, D.C.: American Psychological Association, 2009. http://www.apa.org/pi/lgbt/resources/therapeutic-response.pdf.

Gold, Rachel Benson. "Guarding against Coercion While Ensuring Access: A Delicate Balance". *Guttmacher Policy Review* 17, no. 3 (2014): 8–14. https://www.guttmacher.org/gpr/2014/09/guarding-against-coercion-while-ensuring-access-delicate-balance#.

Golden, Marilyn, and Tyler Zoanni. "Killing Us Softly: The Dangers of Legalizing Assisted Suicide". *Disability and Health Journal* 3 (2010): 16–30. https://dredf.org/wp-content/uploads/2012/08/PIIS1.pdf.

Grant, Edward. *God and Reason in the Middle Ages*. Cambridge: Cambridge University Press, 2001.

Green, Josie. "100 Top-Grossing Movies of All Time". 24/7 Wall St. (website), September 3, 2021. https://247wallst.com/special-report/2021/09/03/100-top-grossing-movies-of-all-time-4/11/#:~:text=Snow%20White%20and%20the%20Seven%20Dwarfs%20%281937%29%20%3E,%241%20billion%20%3E%20Estimated%20ticket%20sales%3A%20110.6%20million.

Greenfield, P. M. "Inadvertent Exposure to Pornography on the Internet: Implications of Peer-to-Peer File-Sharing Networks for Child Development and Families". *Applied Developmental Psychology* 25, no. 6 (2004): 741–50.

Gregory XVI, Pope. Apostolic Letter Condemning the Slave Trade *In Supremo Apostolatus*. December 3, 1839. PapalEncyclicals.Net. Last updated February 20, 2020. https://www.papalencyclicals.net/greg16/g16sup.htm.

Gsellman, L. "Physical and Psychological Injury in Women Following Abortion: Akron Pregnancy Services Study". *Association for Interdisciplinary Research in Values and Social Change Newsletter* 5, no. 4 (1993): 1–8.

Gutierres, S. E., D. T. Kenrick, and L. Goldberg. "Adverse Effect of Popular Erotica on Judgments of One's Mate". Paper presented at the Annual Meeting of the American Psychological Association. Anaheim, Calif., August 1983.

Guttmacher Institute. "Emotional and Mental Health after Abortion". 2022. https://www.guttmacher.org/perspectives50/emotional-and-mental-health-after-abortion.

Haas, John. "Begotten Not Made: A Catholic View of Reproductive Technology". United States Conference of Catholic Bishops, 1998. https://www.usccb.org/issues-and-action/human-life-and-dignity/reproductive-technology/begotten-not-made-a-catholic-view-of-reproductive-technology.

Hackett, Conrad, and David McClendon. "Christians Remain World's Largest Religious Group". Pew Research Center, 2017. https://www.pewresearch.org/fact-tank/2017/04/05/christians-remain-worlds-largest-religious-group-but-they-are-declining-in-europe/.

Handy, Bridget. "Born-Alive Abortion Survivors Protection Act Fails in US Senate". *Live Action News*, February 4, 2021. https://www.liveaction.org/news/born-alive-abortion-survivors-protection-reintroduced-senate/.

Hansen, Jens Morten. "On the Origin of Natural History: Steno's Modern but Forgotten Philosophy of Science". In *The Revolution in Geology from the Renaissance to the Enlightenment*, by Gary D. Rosenberg, pp. 159–80. Boulder, Colo.: Geological Society of America, 2009.

Hansen, Randall, and D. Kind. *Sterilized by the State: Eugenics, Race, and the Population Scare in Twentieth-Century North America*. Cambridge: Cambridge University Press, 2017, pp. 107–9, https://www.tandfonline.com/doi/abs/10.1080/14743892.2017.1340068?journalCode=rach20.

Hare, John. "Religion and Morality". *Stanford Encyclopedia of Philosophy*. Fall 2019 ed., edited by Edward N. Zalta. https://plato.stanford.edu/archives/fall2019/entries/religion-morality.

Hartoonian, Narineh, Jeanne M. Hoffman, Claire Z. Kalpakjian, Heather B. Taylor, James K. Krause, and Charles H. Bombardier. "Evaluating a Spinal Cord Injury—Specific Model of Depression and Quality of Life". *Archives of Physical Rehabilitation* 95, no. 3 (2014): 455–65. https://www.archives-pmr.org/article/S0003-9993(13)01151-9/pdf.

Hartung, Adam. "Why Cheating In Sports Is Prevalent—And We Can't Stop It". *Forbes*, January 23, 2016. https://www.forbes.com/sites/adamhartung/2016/01/23/why-cheating-is-prevalent-and-we-cant-stop-it/?sh=788ae944a0e7.

Heiler, Friedrich. "The History of Religions as a Preparation for the Cooperation of Religions". In *The History of Religions*, edited by Mircea Eliade and J. Kitagawa, pp. 142–53. Chicago, Ill.: University of Chicago Press, 1959.

Heimlich, Russell. "Mystical Experiences". Pew Research Center, December 29, 2009. https://www.pewresearch.org/fact-tank/2009/12/29/mystical-experiences/.

Hendin, Herbert. "Commentary: The Case against Physician-Assisted Suicide: For the Right to End-of-Life Care". *Psychiatric Times* 21, no. 2 (2004). https://dredf.org/wp-content/uploads/2012/10/hendin-psychiatric-times-2004.pdf.

Hendin, Herbert, and Kathleen Foley. "Physician-Assisted Suicide in Oregon: A Medical Perspective". *Michigan Law Review* 106, no. 8 (2008): 1613–40. https://repository.law.umich.edu/mlr/vol106/iss8/7/.

Henig, Robin Marantz. *The Monk in the Garden: The Lost and Found Genius of Gregor Mendel, the Father of Genetics.* Boston: Houghton Mifflin, 2000.

Herrell, Richard, Jack Goldberg, William R. True, Visvanathan Ramakrishnan, Michael Lyons, Seth Eisen, and Ming T. Tsuang. "Sexual Orientation and Suicidality: A Co-Twin Control Study in Adult Men". *Archives of General Psychiatry* 56, no. 10 (October 1999): 867–74.

Herzog, David B., and John T. Herrin. "Near-Death Experiences in the Very Young". *Critical Care Medicine* 13, no. 12 (December 1985): 1074–75. https://journals.lww.com/ccmjournal/citation/1985/12000 /near_death_experiences_in_the_very_young.21.aspx?__cf _chl_jschl_tk__=8797e12212c5dfb336fc09fa8bf733840b007c05 -1611342662-0-abxwfzl68qczaih1xunhx7_prwfwrhnexcpja6flu- 9it8kknoywurtxf9jgaxrbqby5t4sx2cad4fjmsbih_hncfhckmj-.

Hippocrates, *The Hippocratic Oath.* Translated by W. H. S. Jones. In *Oxford Reference,* 2022. https://www.oxfordreference.com/view /10.1093/acref/9780191826719.001.0001/q-oro-ed4-00007207.

Hitti, Miranda. "Religion, Spirituality May Slow Alzheimer's". WebMD, April 13, 2005. www.webmd.com/alzheimers/news /20070101/religion-spirituality-slow-alzheimers#1.

Holden, Janice. *Handbook of Near-Death Experiences: Thirty Years of Investigation.* Westport, Conn.: Praeger Press, 2009.

Hughes, Donna Rice. "How Pornography Harms Children". Protect Kids.com, 2001. http://www.protectkids.com/effects/harms.htm.

Hughes, Robert Jr. "Does Extramarital Sex Cause Divorce?" *Huff-Post,* August 8, 2012. https://www.huffingtonpost.com/robert -hughes/does-extramarital-sex-cau_b_1567507.html.

Hull, Megan, ed. *Pornography Facts and Statistics.* Umatilla, Fla.: Recovery Village, 2021. https://www.therecoveryvillage.com /process-addiction/porn-addiction/related/pornography-statistics/.

Humphry, Derek. *Let Me Die before I Wake: Hemlock's Book of Self-Deliverance for the Dying.* New York: Grove Press, 1984.

Ignatius of Loyola. *Spiritual Exercises.* From "14 Rules for the Discernment of Spirits". *Scepter* (blog), August 3, 2018. https:// scepterpublishers.org/blogs/scepter-blog-corner/14-rules-for -the-discernment-of-spirits-by-st-ignatius-of-loyola.

———. *The Spiritual Exercises of St. Ignatius.* Translated by Louis J. Puhl, S.J. Chicago: Loyola University Press, 1951.

Institute for Social Ecology. "Peter Singer and Eugenics". 2015. http://
social-ecology.org/wp/2005/01/peter-singer-and-eugenics/.

International Office of Catholic Education. "Global Catholic Education Report 2020". June 2020. http://oiecinternational.com/wp
-content/uploads/2020/06/GCE-Report-2020.pdf.

Irenaeus. *Against Heresies*. Translated by Robert Schihl and Paul Flanagan. From "Post-Apostolic Fathers of the Church". Catholic
Biblical Apologetics (website). Last updated 2004. http://www
.freerepublic.com/focus/religion/2476599/posts?page=1.

Irwin, Terence. *The Development of Ethics: A Historical and Critical
Study*. New York: Oxford University Press, 2008.

Jacobson, Sansea. "Thirteen Reasons to Be Concerned about *13
Reasons Why*". *Brown University Child and Adolescent Behavior Letter*
33, no. 6 (2017): 8. https://onlinelibrary.wiley.com/doi/10.1002
/cbl.30220.

James, William. *The Varieties of Religious Experience: A Study in Human
Nature*. New York: Longmans, Green, 1902.

Jay, Meg. "The Downside of Cohabiting Before Marriage". *New York
Times*, April 14, 2012. https://www.nytimes.com/2012/04/15/
opinion/sunday/the-downside-of-cohabiting-Vbefore-marriage.
html.

Jeremias, Joachim. *The Eucharistic Words of Jesus*. London: SCM Press,
1966.

———. *New Testament Theology*. New York: Charles Scribner's Sons,
1971.

John XXIII, Pope. Encyclical Letter on Christianity and Social Progress *Mater t Magistra*. May 15, 1961.

———. Encyclical Letter on Establishing Universal Peace in Truth,
Justice, Charity, and Liberty *Pacem in Terris* (Peace on Earth). April
11, 1963.

John Paul II, Pope. Address to the Fiftieth General Assembly of the
United Nations. October 5, 1995.

———. Address to the International Committee of the Red Cross.
Geneva, June 15, 1982. In *L'Osservatore Romano*, English edition,
July 26, 1982.

———. Address to the Third General Conference of Latin American
Bishops. Puebla, Mexico, January 28, 1979.

———. Apostolic Exhortation on the Role of the Christian Family
in the Modern World *Familiaris Consortio*. November 22, 1981.

————. *Crossing the Threshold of Hope*. Edited by Vittorio Messori. New York: Knopf, 1994.

————. Encyclical Letter on Human Work *Laborem Exercens*. September 14, 1981.

————. Encyclical Letter on the Hundredth Anniversary of Rerum Novarum *Centesimus Annus* May 1, 1991.

————. Encyclical Letter on the Relationship between Faith and Reason *Fides Et Ratio*. September 14, 1998.

————. Encyclical Letter for the Twentieth Anniversary for Populorum Progressio *Sollicitudo Rei Socialis* (On Social Concern). December 30, 1987.

————. Encyclical Letter on the Value and Inviolability of Human Life *Evangelium Vitae*. March 25, 1995.

————. Encyclical Letter *Veritatis Splendor* (The Splendor of Truth). August 6, 1993.

————. Post-Synodal Apostolic Exhortation on the Encounter with the Living Jesus Christ *Ecclesia in America* (The Church in America). January 22, 1999.

Johnson, Sara, Robert Blum, and Jay Giedd. "Adolescent Maturity and the Brain: The Promise and Pitfalls of Neuroscience Research in Adolescent Health Policy". *Journal of Adolescent Health* 45, no. 3 (2009): 216–21. https://www.ncbi.nlm.nih.gov/pmc/articles/PMC 2892678/.

Johnson, Todd M., Gina A. Zurlo, Albert W. Hickman, and Peter F. Crossing. "Christianity 2017: Five Hundred Years of Protestant Christianity". Center for the Study of Global Christianity, Gordon-Conwell Theological Seminary, 2017. https://www.gor donconwell.edu/wp-content/uploads/sites/13/2019/04/IBMR 2017.pdf.

Josephson Institute. "Josephson Institute's Report Card on American Youth: There's a Hole in Our Moral Ozone and It's Getting Bigger". November 30, 2008. http://questgarden.com/85/27/9 /091104072905/files/press-release.pdf.

Justinian. *Institutes*. Translated by J. B. Moyle. 5th ed. Oxford: New College, 1913; Project Gutenberg, last updated February 6, 2013. https://www.gutenberg.org/files/5983/5983-h/5983-h.htm.

Kafka, Franz. *The Trial*. Gloucestershire, Eng.: Simon and Brown, 2016.

Kant, Immanuel. *Grounding for the Metaphysics of Morals*. 3rd ed. Translated by James W. Ellington. Indianapolis, Ind.: Hackett Publishing, 1993.

———. *Kant's Critique of Practical Reason and Other Works on the Theory of Ethics*. Translated by T. K. Abbott. New York: Barnes and Noble, 2004.

———. *Opus Postumum*. Vol. 21. Berlin Critical Edition. Berlin: Georg Reimer, 1960.

Kass, Leon. "Preventing a Brave New World". *New Republic Online*, June 21, 2001. https://web.stanford.edu/~mvr2j/sfsu09/extra/Kass3.pdf.

Keener, Craig. *Miracles: The Credibility of the New Testament*. Grand Rapids, Mich.: Baker Academic Publishing, 2011.

Kelman, Herbert. "Compliance, Identification, and Internalization: Three Processes of Attitude Change". *Journal of Conflict Resolution* 2, no. 1 (1958): 51–60. doi:10.1177/002200275800200106.

Keown, John. "Further Reflections on Euthanasia in the Netherlands in the Light of the Remmelink Report and the van der Maas Study in Euthanasia". In *Euthanasia, Clinical Practice and the Law*, edited by Luke Gormally, pp. 219–40. Linacre Centre, 1994.

———. "The Law and Practice of Euthanasia in the Netherlands". *Law Quarterly Review* 108 (1992): 51–78.

Kerr, Emily. "The Future of Solar Is Bright". *Science in the News*, March 21, 2019. http://sitn.hms.harvard.edu/flash/2019/future-solar-bright/.

Kim, Scott. "How Dutch Law Got a Little Too Comfortable with Euthanasia". *Atlantic*, June 8, 2019. https://www.theatlantic.com/ideas/archive/2019/06/noa-pothoven-and-dutch-euthanasia-system/591262/.

Kindall, W. Henery, and David Pimentel. "Constraints on the Expansion of the Global Food Supply". *AMBIO* 23, no. 3 (1994): 198–205.

King, Martin Luther, Jr. *Letter from a Birmingham Jail*, April 16, 1963.

King, Michael. "A Systemic Review of Mental Disorder, Suicide, and Deliberate Self Harm in Lesbian, Gay and Homosexual People". *BMC Psychiatry* 8, no. 70 (2008): 1–17.

Kirby, Peter. "Didache". *Early Christian Writings*, 2022. http://www.earlychristianwritings.com/didache.html.

Koenig, Harold. "Religion, Spirituality, and Health: The Research and Clinical Implications". *International Scholarly Research Notices* (2012), https://www.hindawi.com/journals/isrn/2012/278730/

———. "Religion, Spirituality, and Health: A Review and Update". *Advances in Mind-Body Medicine* 29, no. 3 (2015): 19–26. https:// pubmed.ncbi.nlm.nih.gov/26026153/.

———. "Research on Religion, Spirituality, and Mental Health: A Review". *Canadian Journal of Psychiatry* 54, no. 5 (2009): 283–91. https://journals.sagepub.com/doi/pdf/10.1177/070674370905400 502.

Koenig, Harold, H.J. Cohen, L.K. George, J.C. Hays, D.B. Larson, and D.G. Blazer. "Attendance at Religious Services, Interleukin-6, and Other Biological Parameters of Immune Function in Older Adults". *International Journal of Psychiatry in Medicine* 27, no. 3 (1997): 233–50.

Koenig, Harold, J.C. Hays, D.B. Larson, L.K. George, H.J. Cohen, M.E. McCullough, K.G. Meador, and D.G. Blazer. "Does Religious Attendance Prolong Survival? A Six-Year Follow-Up Study of 3,968 Older Adults". *Journal of Gerontology, Medical Sciences* 54A (1999): M370–M377.

Koester, Helmut. "The Great Appeal: What Did Christianity Offer Its Believers That Made It Worth Social Estrangement, Hostility from Neighbors, and Possible Persecution?" Frontline, WGBH Educational Foundation, April 1998. pbs.org/wgbh/pages/front line/shows/religion/why/appeal.html.

Koester, Helmut, and James M. Robinson. *Trajectories through Early Christianity*. Philadelphia: Fortress, 1971. Reprint, Eugene, Ore.: Wipf & Stock, 2006.

Kübler-Ross, Elizabeth, and D. Kessler. *On Grief and Grieving: Finding the Meaning of Grief through the Five Stages of Loss*. New York: Scribner, 2014.

Kurland, Robert. "23 Famous Scientists Who Are Not Atheists". Magis Center, June 5, 2021. https://www.magiscenter.com/23 -famous-scientists-who-are-not-atheists/.

L'Arche USA. "About L' Arche". 2022. https://www.larcheusa.org /who-we-are/charter.

Lake, Rebecca. "Infidelity Statistics: 23 Eye-Opening Truths". May 18, 2016. https://www.creditdonkey.com/infidelity-statistics.html.

Larsen, William J. *Essentials of Human Embryology*. New York: Churchill Livingstone, 1998.

Las Casas, Bartolomé de. *In Defense of the Indians: The Defense of the Most Reverend Lord, Don Fray Bartolomé de las Casas, of the Order of Preachers, Late Bishop of Chiapa, against the Persecutors and Slanderers of the Peoples of the New World Discovered across the Seas.* Translated and edited by Stafford Poole. DeKalb, Ill.: Northern Illinois University Press, 1992.

Lasch, Christopher. *The Culture of Narcissism: American Life in an Age of Diminishing Expectations.* Danvers, Mass.: W. W. Norton, 1991.

Lassi, Stefano, and Daniele Mugnaini. "Role of Religion and Spirituality on Mental Health and Resilience: There Is Enough Evidence". *International Journal of Emergency Mental Health and Human Resilience* 17, no. 3 (2015): 661–63. https://www.omicsonline.org /open-access/role-of-religion-and-spirituality-on-mental-health -and-resilience-there-is-enough-evidence-1522-4821-1000273 .pdf.

Lauby, Sharlyn. "Ethics and Social Media: Where Should You Draw the Line?" Ethics Resource Center, March 12, 2012. https://www .americanexpress.com/us/small-business/openforum/articles /ethics-and-social-media-where-should-you-draw-the-line/.

Laumann, Edward O., Stephen Ellingson, Jenna Mahay, Anthony Paik, and Yoosik Youm, eds. *The Sexual Organization of the City.* Chicago: University of Chicago Press, 2002. https://press.uchicago .edu/Misc/Chicago/470318.html.

Lee, Ryan. "Gay Couples Likely to Try Non-monogamy, Study Shows". *Washington Blade*, August 22, 2003.

Leiby, R. "Whose Death Is It Anyway? The Kevorkian Debate; It's a Matter of Faith, in the End". *Washington Post*, August 11, 1996.

Leo XIII, Pope. Encyclical Letter on Capital and Labor *Rerum Novarum*. May 15, 1891.

Levy, Michael H. "Medical Management of Cancer Pain". In *Principles and Practice of Pain Management*, edited by Carol A. Warfield, pp. 235ff. New York: McGraw Hill, 1993.

Lewin, Roger. "Is Your Brain Really Necessary?" *Science* 210, no. 4475 (1980): 1232–34. https://science.sciencemag.org/content/210 /4475/1232.

Lewis, C. S. *The Abolition of Man.* New York: HarperOne, 2001.

————. *The Four Loves*. London: Geoffrey Bles, 1960; Project Gutenberg, 2014. Chapter 5. https://gutenberg.ca/ebooks/lewiscs-four loves/lewiscs-fourloves-00-h.html#chapter05.

————. *Mere Christianity*. New York: Macmillan, 1952.

————. *Surprised by Joy: The Shape of My Early Life*. New York: Harcourt, Brace & World, 1955.

Lincoln, Abraham. Gettysburg Address. Gettysburg Pa., November 19, 1863. http://www.abrahamlincolnonline.org/lincoln/speeches /gettysburg.htm.

Lipka, Michael. "Millennials Increasingly Are Driving Growth of 'Nones'". Pew Research Center, 2015. https://www.pewresearch .org/fact-tank/2015/05/12/millennials-increasingly-are-driving -growth-of-nones/.

Lipka, Michael, and Tim Townsend. "Papal Saints: Once a Given, Now Extremely Rare". Pew Research Center, April 24, 2014. https:// www.pewresearch.org/fact-tank/2014/04/24/papal-saints-once-a-given-now-extremely-rare/#:~:text=Recent%20popes%20 are%20known%20for,refusing%20to%20convert%20to%20Islam.

Livio, Mauricio. "Comments". *Nature*, November 10, 2011.

Locke, John. *Second Treatise on Government*. Edited by C. B. Macpherson. Indianapolis: Hackett Publishing, 1980.

Lorber, John. "Is Your Brain Really Necessary?" In *Hydrocephalus in fru̇hen Kindesalter: Fortschritte der Grundlagenforschung, Diagnostik und Therapie*, edited by D. Voth, pp. 2–14. Stuttgart, Germany: Enke Verlag, 1983.

Losada, Ángel. "The Controversy between Sepulveda and las Casas in the Junta of Valladolid". In *Bartolomé de Las Casas in History*, edited by Juan Friede and Benjamin Keen, p. 279–309. DeKalb, Ill.: Northern Illinois University, 1971.

Low, Robbie. "The Truth about Men and Church". *Touchstone*, June 2003. https://www.touchstonemag.com/archives/article.php ?id=16-05-024-v.

Lutgendorf, Susan K., Daniel Russell, Philip Ullrich, Tamara B. Harris, and Robert Wallace. "Religious Participation, Interleukin-6, and Mortality in Older Adults". *Health Psychology* 23, no. 5 (2004): 465–75.

Macke, John. "Religious Scientists: Canon Nicolaus Copernicus". *Religious Scientists of the Catholic Church* (blog), 2020. https://

www.vofoundation.org/blog/religious-scientists-canon-nicolaus
-copernicus-1473-1543-heliocentricism/.

Macpherson, Ignacio, Maria Victoria Roque, and Ignacia Segarra.
"Ethical Challenges of Germline Genetic Enhancement". *Frontiers in Genetics*, September 3, 2019. https://www.frontiersin.org
/articles/10.3389/fgene.2019.00767/full.

Malthus, Thomas. *An Essay on the Principle of Population*. London: J.
Johnson in St. Paul's Church-Yard, 1798.

Manning, Wendy D. "Cohabitation and Child Wellbeing". *Future
Child* 25, no. 2 (2015): 51–66. https://www.ncbi.nlm.nih.gov/pmc
/articles/PMC4768758/.

Markets and Markets. "Hydroponics Market by Type (Aggregate Systems, Liquid Systems), Crop Type (Vegetables, Fruits, Flowers),
Equipment (HVAC, Led Grow Light, Irrigation Systems, Material
Handling, Control Systems), Input, and Region—Global Forecast
to 2026". January 2021. https://www.marketsandmarkets.com
/Market-Reports/hydroponic-market-94055021.html.

Marquardt, Elizabeth. *Between Two Worlds: The Inner Lives of Children
of Divorce*. New York: Crown Publishers, 2005.

Marsh, Jason, and Jill Suttie. "5 Ways Giving Is Good for You".
Greater Good Magazine, December 13, 2010. https://greatergood
.berkeley.edu/article/item/5_ways_giving_is_good_for_you.

Martin, Michael M., Daniel J. Capra, and Faust F. Rossi. *New York
Evidence Handbook: Rules, Theory, and Practice*. 2nd ed. New York:
Aspen Publishers, 2003.

Martin, Rachel. "Sorting Through the Numbers on Infidelity".
National Public Radio (website), July 26, 2015. https://www.npr
.org/2015/07/26/426434619/sorting-through-the-numbers-on
-infidelity.

"Martin Niemöller: 'First They Came for the Socialists ...'". *Holocaust Encyclopedia*. United States Holocaust Memorial Museum,
Washington, D.C. (website). Last edited March 30, 2012. https://
encyclopedia.ushmm.org/content/en/article/martin-niemoeller
-first-they-came-for-the-socialists.

Martyr, Justin. *The Second Apology of Justin Martyr*. Chapter 4, "Why
the Christians Do Not Kill Themselves". From *Ante-Nicene Fathers*.
Vol. 1, edited by Alexander Roberts, James Donaldson, and A.
Cleveland Coxe. Buffalo, N.Y.: Christian Literature Publishing,

1885. Revised and edited for New Advent by Kevin Knight. https://www.newadvent.org/fathers/0127.htm.

May, William E. *Catholic Bioethics and Gift of Human Life*. 2nd ed. Our Sunday Visitor Publishing, 2008.

———. *An Introduction to Moral Theology*. 2nd ed. Huntington, Ind.: Our Sunday Visitor Publishing, 2007.

Mayer, Lawrence, and Paul McHugh. "Sexuality and Gender: Findings from the Biological, Psychological, and Social Sciences". Special issue, *New Atlantis* 50 (Fall 2016). https://thenewatlantis.com/wp-content/uploads/legacy-pdfs/20160819_TNA50Sexuality andGender.pdf.

McKenzie, John L. *Dictionary of the Bible*. New York: Macmillan, 1965.

McKinsey Global Institute. "The Demographic Deficit: How Aging Will Reduce Global Wealth". *McKinsey Quarterly*, March 2005. http://www.mickeybutts.com/globalagingQuarterly.pdf.

McNally, Thomas, C.S.C., and William G. Storey, D.M.S., eds. *Day by Day: The Notre Dame Prayer Book for Students*. Notre Dame, Ind.: Ave Maria Press, 2004.

McNaspy, C.J. *Lost Cities of Paraguay: Art and Architecture of the Jesuit Reductions, 1607–1767*. Chicago: Loyola University Press, 1982.

McWhirter, David P., and Andrew M. Mattison. *The Male Couple: How Relationships Develop*. Englewood Cliffs, N.J.: Prentice-Hall, 1984.

Meier, John P. *A Marginal Jew: Rethinking the Historical Jesus*. Vol. 2, *Mentor, Message, and Miracles*. New York: Doubleday, 1994.

Merton, Robert K. "The Self-Fulfilling Prophecy". *Antioch Review* 8, no. 2 (Summer 1948): 193–210.

Miller, Jon. "Hugo Grotius". *Stanford Encyclopedia of Philosophy*. Last updated January 8, 2021. http://plato.stanford.edu/entries/grotius.

Moore, Keith L. *Before We Are Born: Essentials of Embryology*. 7th ed. Philadelphia: Saunders, 2008.

———. *The Developing Human: Clinically Oriented Embryology*. 7th ed. Philadelphia: Saunders, 2003.

Moore, Peter. "1 in 5 Americans Say They've Been Unfaithful". You Gov.com, June 2, 2015. https://today.yougov.com/topics/lifestyle/articles-reports/2015/06/02/men-more-likely-think-cheating.

Munsell, Eylin Palamaro, Ryan P. Kilmer, James R. Cook, and Charlie L. Reeve. "The Effects of Caregiver Social Connections on Caregiver, Child, and Family Well-Being". *American Journal of Orthopsychiatry* 82, no. 1 (2012): 137–45. https://www.ncbi.nlm .nih.gov/pmc/articles/PMC3345204/.

Musk, Elon. "The World's Population Is Accelerating toward Collapse and Nobody Cares". CNBC, July 6, 2017. https://www .cnbc.com/2017/07/06/elon-musk-the-worlds-population-is -accelerating-toward-collapse-and-nobody-cares.html.

Naddaf, Gerard. *The Greek Concept of Nature.* New York: State University of New York Press, 2005.

Nahm, Michael. "Reflections on the Context of Near-Death Experiences". *Journal of Scientific Exploration* 25, no. 3 (2011): 453–78.

———. "Terminal Lucidity in People with Mental Illness and other Mental Disability: An Overview and Implications for Possible Explanatory Models". *Journal of Near-Death Studies* 28, no. 2 (2009): 87–106. www.spiritualscientific.com/yahoo_site_admin /assets/docs/Lucidity_at_Death_Nahm_M.9131800.pdf.

Nahm, Michael, and Bruce Greyson. "The Death of Anna Katharina Ehmer: A Case Study in Terminal Lucidity". *Omega* 68, no. 1 (2014): 77–87. http://journals.sagepub.com/doi/10.2190 /OM.68.1.e.

———. "Terminal Lucidity in Patients with Chronic Schizophrenia and Dementia: A Survey of the Literature". *Journal of Nervous and Mental Disease* 197, no. 12 (2009): 942–44.

Nahm, Michael, Bruce Greyson, Emily Williams Kelly, and Erlendur Haraldsson. "Terminal Lucidity: A Review and a Case Collection". *Archives of Gerontology and Geriatrics* 55, no. 1 (2012): 138–42. http://www.sciencedirect.com/science/article/pii/S016749431 1001865?via%3Dihub.

National Catholic Bioethics Center. *Catholic Guide to Palliative Care and Hospice.* 2019. https://www.ncbcenter.org/store/catholic-guide-to -palliative-care-and-hospiceenglishpdf-download.

National Center for Biotechnology Information (National Institute for Health). "Physicians' Observations and Interpretations of the Influence of Religion and Spirituality on Health". 2010. https:// www.ncbi.nlm.nih.gov/pmc/articles/PMC2867458/.

National Conference of Catholic Bishops. *Economic Justice for All: Pastoral Letter on Catholic Social Teaching and the U.S. Economy.* Washington, D.C.: National Conference of Catholic Bishops, 1986.

National Educational Testing Service. "Academic Cheating Fact
Sheet". 1999. http://www.glass-castle.com/clients/www-noch
eating-org/adcouncil/research/cheatingfactsheet.html.
National Institute on Alcohol Abuse and Alcoholism (NIAAA).
"Alcohol Facts and Statistics". Updated June 2021. https://www
.niaaa.nih.gov/publications/brochures-and-fact-sheets/alcohol-facts
-and-statistics.
National Sexual Violence Resource Center. "Statistics about Sexual
Violence". 2015. https://www.nsvrc.org/sites/default/files/publi
cations_nsvrc_factsheet_media-packet_statistics-about-sexual
-violence_0.pdf.
National WWII Museum. "Research Starters: Worldwide Deaths
in World War II". Accessed February 22, 2022. https://www
.nationalww2museum.org/students-teachers/student-resources
/research-starters/research-starters-worldwide-deaths-world-war.
Neighbors, Clayton, "Are Social Norms the Best Predictor of Outcomes among Heavy-Drinking College Students?" *Journal of Studies on Alcohol and Drugs* 68, no. 4 (2007): 556–65. https://www
.jsad.com/doi/abs/10.15288/jsad.2007.68.556.
Newman, John Henry. *The Idea of a University*. South Bend, Ind.:
Notre Dame Press, 1982.
———. Unpublished manuscript entitled "Proof of Theism". In *The
Argument from Conscience to the Existence of God according to J. H.
Newman*, edited by Adrian Boekraad and Henry Tristram. Lon-
don: Mill Hill, 1961.
Nolan, James L. *Doing the Right Thing at Work: A Catholic's Guide
to Faith, Business and Ethics*. Cincinnati: St. Anthony Messenger
Press, 2005.
Nugent, Colleen N., and Jill Daugherty. "A Demographic, Attitu-
dinal, and Behavioral Profile of Cohabiting Adults in the United
States, 2011–2015". *National Health Statistics Report*, May 31, 2018.
https://www.cdc.gov/nchs/data/nhsr/nhsr111.pdf.
O'Rahilly, Ronan, and Fabiola Miller. *Human Embryology and Teratology*. 3rd ed. New York: Wiley-Liss, 2001.
O'Rourke, Mark A., M. Colleen O'Rourke, and Matthew F. Hudson. "Reasons to Reject Physician Assisted Suicide/Physician Aid
in Dying". *Journal of Oncology Practice* 13, no. 10 (2017): 683–86.
https://ascopubs.org/doi/full/10.1200/JOP.2017.021840.

Otto, Rudolf. *The Idea of the Holy: An Inquiry into the Non-Rational Factor in the Idea of the Divine and Its Relation to the Rational.* Oxford: Oxford University Press, 1923.

Panzer, Joel S. "The Popes and Slavery: Setting the Record Straight". *Catholic Answers*, January/February 1996. From the website of EWTN. https://www.ewtn.com/catholicism/library/popes -and-slavery-setting-the-record-straight-1119.

Parboteeah, K. Praveen, Martin Hoegl, and John B. Cullen. "Ethics and Religion: An Empirical Test of a Multidimensional Model". *Journal of Business Ethics* 80, no. 2 (2008): 387–98.

Parker, Wayne. "Key Statistics about Kids from Divorced Families". July 15, 2020. https://www.thespruce.com/children-of -divorce-in-america-statistics-1270390

Parnia, Sam, Ken Spearpoint, Gabriele de Vos, Peter Fenwick, Diana Goldberg, Jie Yang, Jiawen Zhu, et al. "AWARE—AWAreness during REsuscitation—A Prospective Study". *Resuscitation* 85, no. 12 (2014): 1799–805. http://www.horizonresearch.org/Uploads /Journal_Resuscitation__2_.pdf.

Pascal, Blaise. *Pensées.* New York: E.P. Dutton, 1958; Project Gutenberg, 2006. http://www.gutenberg.org/files/18269/18269 -h/18269-h.htm.

Patients Rights Council. "Facts about Hemlock and Caring Friends". 2013. http://www.patientsrightscouncil.org/site/hemlock-and -caring-friends/.

———. "Ten Years of Assisted Suicide in Oregon." 2013. http:// www.patientsrightscouncil.org/site/oregon-ten-years/.

Patterson, Philip, and Lee Wilkins. *Media Ethics: Issues and Cases.* 8th ed. New York: McGraw-Hill, 2013.

Paul III, Pope. Papal Bull on the Enslavement and Evangelization of Indians *Sublimus Dei.* May 29, 1537. PapalEncyclicals.Net. Last updated February 20, 2020. https://www.papalencyclicals.net /paulo3/p3subli.htm.

Paul VI, Pope. Apostolic exhortation *Evangelii Nuntiandi* (Evangelization in the Modern World). December 8, 1975.

———. Apostolic Letter on a Call to Action on the Eightieth Anniversary of Rerum Novarum *Octogesima Adveniens.* May 14, 1971.

———. Encyclical Letter on the Development of Peoples *Populorum Progressio.* March 26, 1967.

————. Encyclical Letter on the Regulation of Birth *Humane Vitae*. July 25, 1968.

Pearce, Fred. "The World in 2076: The Population Bomb Has Imploded". *New Scientist*, November 16, 2016. https://www.newscientist.com/article/mg23231001-400-the-world-in-2076-the-population-bomb-did-go-off-but-were-ok/.

Pellegrino, Edmund. "Compassion Is Not Enough". In *The Case against Assisted Suicide: For the Right to End-of-Life Care*, edited by Kathleen Foley and Herbert Hendin, pp. 41–51. Baltimore: Johns Hopkins University Press, 2002.

————. "The False Promise of Beneficent Killing". In *Regulating How We Die*, edited by Linda L. Emanuel, pp. 71–91. Cambridge: Harvard University Press, 1998. https://repository.library.george town.edu/handle/10822/712105.

Peplau, Letitia Anne, and Hortensia Amaro. "Understanding Lesbian Relationships". In *Homosexuality: Social, Psychological, and Biological Issues*, by William Paul. Edited by James D. Weinrich, John C. Gonsiorek, and Mary E. Hotvedt, pp. 233–47. Beverly Hills: Sage, 1982.

Perkins, H. Wesley. *The Social Norms Approach to Preventing School and College Age Substance Abuse: A Handbook for Educators, Counselors, and Clinicians*. San Francisco: Jossey-Bass, 2003.

Perry, Samuel, and George H. Hayward. "Seeing Is (Not) Believing: How Viewing Pornography Shapes the Religious Lives of Young Americans". *Social Forces* 95, no. 4 (June 2017): 1757–88. https://academic.oup.com/sf/article-abstract/95/4/1757/2877697?redirect edFrom=fulltext.

Peterson, P. G. *Gray Dawn: How the Coming Age Wave Will Transform America and the World*. New York: Random House, 1999.

Pew Research Center. "Religion and Science in the United States: Scientists and Belief". November 5, 2009. https://www.pew forum.org/2009/11/05/scientists-and-belief/.

Pies, Ronald, and Annette Hanson. "Twelve Myths about Physician Assisted Suicide and Medical Aid in Dying". July 17, 2018. https://www.hcplive.com/view/twelve-myths-concerning-medical-aid-in-dying-or-physicianassisted-suicide.

Pilzer, Paul Zane. *Unlimited Wealth: The Theory and Practice of Economic Alchemy*. New York: Crown Publishers, 1990.

Piquerez, Sophie J. M., Sarah E. Harvey, Jim L. Beynon, and Vardis Ntoukakis. "Improving Crop Disease Resistance: Lessons from Research on Arabidopsis and Tomato". *Frontiers in Plant Science* 5 (2014): 671. https://www.ncbi.nlm.nih.gov/pmc/articles/PMC42 53662/.

Pius XI, Pope. Encyclical Letter on Reconstruction of the Social Order *Quadragesimo Anno* (After Forty Years). May 15, 1931.

Pius XII, Pope. Address to Participants in the VIII Congress of the World Medical Association. September 30, 1954.

Plotner, Tammy. "The Expanding Universe—Credit to Hubble or Lemaitre?" *Universe Today*, November 10, 2011.

Pohle, J. "Eucharist". In *The Catholic Encyclopedia*. Vol. 5. New York: Robert Appleton, 1909. https://www.newadvent.org/cathen/055 72c.htm.

———. "Sacrifice". In *The Catholic Encyclopedia*. Vol. 13. New York: Robert Appleton, 1912. https://www.newadvent.org/cathen/133 09a.htm.

Pollak, Michael. "Male Homosexuality". In *Western Sexuality: Practice and Precept in Past and Present Times*, edited by Philippe Ariès and André Béjin, translated by Anthony Forster, pp. 40–61. New York: B. Blackwell, 1985.

Pontifical Council for Justice and Peace. *Compendium of the Social Doctrine of the Church*. 2004. Reprint, April 2005.

———. *Contribution to World Conference against Racism, Racial Discrimination, Xenophobia and Related Intolerance*. August 31–September 7, 2001.

Popper, Karl, and John Eccles. *The Self and Its Brain: An Argument for Interactionism*. New York: Routledge, 1984.

Pottie, Colin, and John Sumarah. "Friendships between Persons with and without Developmental Disabilities". *Mental Retardation: A Journal of Practices, Policy and Perspectives* 42, no. 1 (2004): 55–66.

Pradhan, Elina. "Female Education and Childbearing: A Closer Look at the Data". *World Bank Blogs*, November 24, 2015. https:// blogs.worldbank.org/health/female-education-and-childbearing -closer-look-data.

Pratt, David. "John Eccles on Mind and Brain". *Sunrise Magazine*, June/July 1995. http://systems.neurosci.info/VisualSub/eccles .htm.

Prentice, David. "Adult Stem Cells: Successful Standard for Regenerative Medicine". *Circulation Research* 124 (March 2019): 837–39. https://www.ahajournals.org/doi/10.1161/CIRCRESAHA.118.313664.

Quadir, Iqbal. "How Mobile Phones Can Fight Poverty". *TED Talk*, 2006. https://www.ted.com/speakers/iqbal_quadir.

Ramsey, Paul. *The Just War: Force and Political Responsibility*. Rowman & Littlefield Publishers, 2002.

Ratzinger, Joseph Cardinal. Mass *Pro Eligendo Romano Pontifice* [for the election of the Roman Pontiff]. Homily of His Eminence Joseph Cardinal Ratzinger, Dean of the College of Cardinals. April 18, 2005.

Reardon, David. "The Abortion and Mental Health Controversy: A Comprehensive Literature Review of Common Ground Agreements, Disagreements, Actionable Recommendations, and Research Opportunities". *SAGE Open Medicine* 6 (October 2018). https://www.ncbi.nlm.nih.gov/pmc/articles/PMC6207970/.

Reardon, Sara. "Massive Study Finds No Single Genetic Cause of Same-Sex Sexual Behavior". *Scientific American*, August 29, 2019. https://www.scientificamerican.com/article/massive-study-finds-no-single-genetic-cause-of-same-sex-sexual-behavior/.

Redman, Melody, Andrew King, Caroline Watson, and David King. "What Is CRISPR/Cas9?" *Archives of Disease in Childhood—Education and Practice Edition* 101 (2016): 213–15. https://www.ncbi.nlm.nih.gov/pmc/articles/PMC4975809/.

Richardson, Bradford. "Insurance Companies Denied Treatment to Patients, Offered to Pay for Assisted Suicide, Doctor Claims". *Washington Times*, May 31, 2017. https://www.washingtontimes.com/news/2017/may/31/insurance-companies-denied-treatment-to-patients-0/.

Riché, Pierre. *Daily Life in the World of Charlemagne*. Philadelphia: University of Pennsylvania Press, 1988.

Ridley, Matt. *The Evolution of Everything: How New Ideas Emerge*. New York: Harper, 2015.

Riley, Naomi Schaefer. "The Young and the Restless: Why Infidelity Is Rising among 20-Somethings". *Wall Street Journal*, November 28, 2008. https://www.wsj.com/articles/SB122782458360062499.

Ring, Kenneth, Sharon Cooper, and Charles Tart. *Mindsight: Near-Death and Out-of-Body Experiences in the Blind*. Palo Alto, Calif.: William James Center for Consciousness Studies at the Institute of Transpersonal Psychology, 1999.

Roberts, Sam. "Lennart Nilsson, Photographer Who Unveiled the Invisible, Dies at 94". *New York Times*, February 1, 2017. https://www.nytimes.com/2017/02/01/world/europe/lennart-nilsson-photographer-embryo-life-magazine-dies.html.

Rommen, Heinrich. "*De Legibus* of Francisco Suarez". *Notre Dame Law Review* 24, no. 1 (1948): 71–81.

Ronenberg, Corina, Edward Alan Miller, Elizabeth Dugan, and Frank Porell. "The Protective Effects of Religiosity on Depression: A 2-Year Prospective Study". *Gerontologist* 56, no. 3 (2016): 421–31. https://academic.oup.com/gerontologist/article/56/3/421/2605601.

Rosenfeld, Michael, and Katharina Roesler. "Cohabitation Experience and Cohabitation's Association with Marital Dissolution". *Journal of Marriage and Family* 81, no. 1 (September 2018): 42–58.

Roser, Max. "Economic Growth". Our World in Data (website), 2013. https://ourworldindata.org/economic-growth.

Ross, Eric B. *The Malthus Factor: Population, Poverty, and Politics in Capitalist Development*. London: Zed Books, 1998.

Rowland, David. "Phases of Human Sexual Response". In *The SAGE Encyclopedia of Abnormal and Clinical Psychology*, pp. 1705–6. Thousand Oaks, Calif.: SAGE Publications, 2017. https://scholar.valpo.edu/cgi/viewcontent.cgi?article=1061&context=psych_fac_pub.

Roy, Abhijit, and Mousumi Roy. "Antecedents and Consequences of Impending Population Implosion in the Developed World: Implications for Business Systems". *International Journal of Sustainable Society* 7, no. 2 (2015): 151. https://www.researchgate.net/publication/281422730_Antecedents_and_consequences_of_impending_population_implosion_in_the_developed_world_Implications_for_business_systems.

Rue, Vincent M., Priscilla K. Coleman, James J. Rue, and David C. Reardon. "Induced Abortion and Traumatic Stress: A Preliminary Comparison of American and Russian Women". *Medical Science Monitor* 10, no. 10 (2004): SR5–SR16. https://www.medscimonit.com/download/index/idArt/11784.

Ruse, Austin. "The Myth of Overpopulation and the Folks Who Brought It to You". United States Conference of Catholic Bishops (website). http://www.usccb.org/about/pro-life-activities/respect -life-program/the-myth-of-overpopulation-and-the-folks-who -brought-it-to-you.cfm.

Russell, Stephen T., and Jessica N. Fish. "Mental Health in Lesbian, Gay, Bisexual, and Transgender (LGBT) Youth". *Annual Review of Clinical Psychology* 12 (2016): 465–87. https://www.ncbi.nlm.nih .gov/pmc/articles/PMC4887282/.

Sacred Congregation for the Doctrine of the Faith. *Declaration on Euthanasia*. May 5, 1980.

Sadler, T. W. *Langman's Medical Embryology*. 10th ed. Philadelphia: Lippincott Williams & Wilkins, 2006.

Saghir, Marcel T., and Eli Robins. *Male and Female Homosexuality*. Baltimore: Williams and Wilkins, 1973.

Sandfort, Theo. G. M., Floor Bakker, Francois G. Schellevis, and Ine Vanwensenbeeck. "Sexual Orientation and Mental and Physical Health Status". *American Journal of Public Health* 96, no. 6 (June 2006): 1119–25.

Sandfort, Theo. G. M., Ron de Graaf, Rob V. Bijl, and Paul Schnabel. "Same-Sex Sexual Behavior and Psychiatric Disorders: Findings from the Netherlands Mental Health Survey and Incidence Study (NEMESIS)". *Archives of General Psychiatry* 58, no. 1 (January 2001): 85–91.

Sanger, Margaret. "The Eugenic Value of Birth Control Propaganda". *Birth Control Review*, October 1921. https://eugenics.us/the-eugenic -value-of-birth-control-propaganda-by-margaret-sanger/128.htm.

Sartre, Jean-Paul. *No Exit*. New York: Samuel French, 1958.

Schall, James. "Captain Francis: The Pope and Sports". *Catholic World Report*, June 30, 2014. http://www.catholicworldreport.com/2014 /06/30/captain-francis-the-pope-and-sports/.

Scheidel, Walter. "Human Mobility in Roman Italy, II: The Slave Population". *Journal of Roman Studies* 95 (2005): 64–79.

Schmitz, Michael. *Made for Love: Same-Sex Attraction and the Catholic Church*. San Francisco: Ignatius Press, 2017.

Schneider, J. P. "Effects of Cybersex Addiction on the Family: Results of a Survey". *Sexual Addiction & Compulsivity* 7, nos. 1–2 (2007): 31–58.

————. "Effects of Cybersex Problems on the Spouse and Family". In *Sex and the Internet: A Guidebook for Clinicians*, edited by A. Cooper, pp. 169–86. New York: Brunner-Routledge, 2002.

Schonfeld, Zach. "Wives Are Cheating 40% More Than They Used To, but Still 70% as Much as Men". *Atlantic*, July 2, 2013. https://www.theatlantic.com/national/archive/2013/07/wives-cheating-vs-men/313704/.

Schumpeter, Joseph. *History of Economic Analysis*. New York: Routledge, 1954.

Schwadel, Philip, and Aleksandra Sandstrom. "Lesbian, Gay and Bisexual Americans Are Less Religious Than Straight Adults by Traditional Measures". Pew Research Center, May 24, 2019. https://www.pewresearch.org/fact-tank/2019/05/24/lesbian-gay-and-bisexual-americans-are-less-religious-than-straight-adults-by-traditional-measures/.

Scroggs, Robin. *The New Testament and Homosexuality*. Philadelphia: Fortress Press, 1983.

Second Vatican Council. Declaration on Religious Freedom *Dignitatis Humanae*. December 7, 1965.

————. Dogmatic Constitution on the Church *Lumen Gentium*. November 21, 1964.

————. Pastoral Constitution on the Church in the Modern World *Gaudium et Spes*. December 7, 1965.

Seeger, Raymond J. "Eddington, Mystic Seeker". *Journal of the American Scientific Affiliation* 36, no. 1 (March 1984): 36.

————. "Heisenberg: Thoughtful Christian". *Journal of the American Scientific Affiliation* 37 (December 1985): 231–32.

————. "Planck, Physicist". *Journal of the American Scientific Affiliation* 37 (December 1985): 232–33.

Seneca. *De Clementia*. In Vol. 1 of *History of European Morals from Augustus to Charlemagne*, by William Edward Hartpole Lecky, pp. 199–200. New York: D. Appleton, 1870.

Shermer, Michael. "Why Malthus Is Still Wrong". *Scientific American*, May 1, 2016. https://www.scientificamerican.com/article/why-malthus-is-still-wrong/.

Shultz, David. "Divorce Rates Double When People Start Watching Porn". *Science*, August 26, 2016. https://www.sciencemag.org/news/2016/08/divorce-rates-double-when-people-start-watching

-porn#:~:text=The%20study%2C%20a%20working%20paper,non
-porn%2Dconsuming%20peers.

Singer, Peter. *Should the Baby Live? The Problem of Handicapped Infants (Studies in Bioethics)*. 1985. Reprint, Oxford: Oxford University Press, 1988.

Sison, Alejo Jose G., Ignacio Ferrero, and Gregorio Guitian, eds. *Business Ethics: A Virtue Ethics and Common Good Approach*. New York: Routledge, 2018.

Skegg, Keren, Shyamala Nada-Raja, Nigel Dickson, Charlotte Paul, and Sheila Williams. "Sexual Orientation and Self-Harm in Men and Women". *American Journal of Psychiatry* 160, no. 3 (March 2003): 541–46.

Skinner, Kevin. "Can Pornography Trigger Depression?" *Psychology Today*, November 3, 2011. https://www.psychologytoday.com/us /blog/inside-porn-addiction/201111/can-pornography-trigger -depression.

Smith, Martin L., James Orlowski, Charles Radey, and Giles Scofield. "A Good Death: Is Euthanasia the Answer?" *Cleveland Clinic Journal of Medicine* 59, no. 1 (1992): 99–109. https://www.ccjm .org/content/ccjom/59/1/99.full.pdf.

Socarides, Charles W. "The Desire for Sexual Transformation: A Psychiatric Evaluation of Transsexualism". *American Journal of Psychiatry* 125, no. 10 (1969): 1419–25.

Solzhenitsyn, Aleksandr. "A World Split Apart". Commencement address at Harvard University, 1978. https://www.americanrhetoric.com/speeches/alexandersolzhenitsynharvard.htm.

Southern Cross Bioethics Institute. "Euthanasia Practices in the Netherlands". Accessed February 15, 2022. http://www.bioethics .org.au/Resources/Online%20Articles/Other%20Articles/Euthana sia%20practices%20in%20the%20Netherlands%20-%20Brian%20 Pollard's%20third%20Document.pdf.

Spektorowski, Alberto, and Liza Ireni-Saban. *Politics of Eugenics: Productionism, Population, and National Welfare*. London: Routledge, 2013.

Spitzer, Robert. *Christ versus Satan in Our Daily Lives: The Cosmic Struggle between Good and Evil*. Vol. 1 of the Trilogy *Called Out of Darkness: Contending with Evil through the Church, Virtue, and Prayer*. San Francisco: Ignatius Press, 2020.

————. *Credible Catholic Big Book*. Vol. 2, *Evidence of Our Trans-physical Soul*. Magis Center, 2017. CredibleCatholic.com. https://www.crediblecatholic.com/pdf/7E-P1/7E-BB2.pdf#P1V2.

————. *Credible Catholic Big Book*. Vol. 13, *Four Levels of Happiness*. Magis Center, 2017. CredibleCatholic.com. https://www.crediblecatholic.com/pdf/7E-P6/7E-BB13.pdf#P1V13.

————. *Escape from Evil's Darkness: The Light of Christ in the Church, Spiritual Conversion, and Moral Conversion*. Vol. 2 of the Trilogy *Called Out of Darkness: Contending with Evil through the Church, Virtue, and Prayer*. San Francisco: Ignatius Press, 2021.

————. *Finding True Happiness: Satisfying Our Restless Hearts*. Vol. 1 of the Quartet *Happiness, Suffering, and Transcendence*. San Francisco: Ignatius Press, 2015.

————. *God So Loved the World: Clues to Our Transcendent Destiny from the Revelation of Jesus*. Vol. 3 of the Quartet *Happiness, Suffering, and Transcendence*. San Francisco: Ignatius Press, 2016.

————. *Healing the Culture: A Common-Sense Philosophy of Happiness, Freedom, and the Life Issues*. San Francisco: Ignatius Press, 2000.

————. *The Light Shines on in the Darkness: Transforming Suffering through Faith*. Vol. 4 of the Quartet *Happiness, Suffering, and Transcendence*. San Francisco: Ignatius Press, 2017.

————. *New Proofs for the Existence of God: Contributions of Cotemporary Physics and Philosophy*. Grand Rapids, Mich.: Eerdmans, 2010.

————. *The Soul's Upward Yearning: Clues to Our Transcendent Nature from Reason and Experience*. Vol. 2 of the Quartet *Happiness, Suffering, and Transcendence*. San Francisco: Ignatius Press, 2016.

————. *Spirit of Leadership: Optimizing Creativity and Change of Organizations*. Seattle: Pacific Institute Press, 2000.

————. *Ten Universal Principles: A Brief Philosophy of the Life Issues*. San Francisco: Ignatius Press, 2011.

Spitzer, Robert, and James Sinclair. "Fine-Tuning and Indications of Transcendent Intelligence". In *Theism and Atheism: Opposing Arguments in Philosophy*, edited by Joseph Koterski and Graham Oppy, pp. 351–58. New York: Macmillan Reference Library, 2016.

Spooner, W. A. "The Golden Rule". In vol. 6 of *Encyclopedia of Religion and Ethics*, edited by James Hastings. New York: Bloomsbury T&T Clark, 2000.

Stagnaro, Angelo. "A List of 244 Priest-Scientists (from Acosta to Zupi)". *National Catholic Register*, November 29, 2016. https://www.ncregister.com/blog/a-list-of-244-priest-scientists-from-acosta-to-zupi.

Stanley, Scott, and Galena Rhoades. "Before 'I Do': What Do Premarital Experiences Have to Do with Marital Quality among Today's Young Adults?" National Marriage Project (University of Virginia), 2014. http://before-i-do.org/.

———. "Premarital Cohabitation Is Still Associated with Greater Odds of Divorce". Institute for Family Studies, October 17, 2018. https://ifstudies.org/blog/premarital-cohabitation-is-still-associated-with-greater-odds-of-divorce.

Steffens, Barbara A., and Robyn L. Rennie. "The Traumatic Nature of Disclosure for Wives of Sexual Addicts". *Sexual Addiction & Compulsivity* 13, nos. 2–3 (2006): 247–67.

Stein, Edith. *On the Problem of Empathy*. Vol. 3 of *The Collected Works of Edith Stein*, translated by Waltraut Stein. Washington, D.C.: Institute of Carmelite Studies Press, 1989.

Steinhoff, Uwe. *On the Ethics of Torture*. Albany, N.Y.: SUNY Press, 2013.

Stem Cell Connect, Charlotte Lozier Institute. "Treatments". 2022. https://www.stemcellresearchfacts.org/.

Stevens, K. R., Jr. "Emotional and Psychological Effects of Physician-Assisted Suicide and Euthanasia on Participating Physicians". *Issues Law and Medicine* 21, no. 3 (2006):187–200.

Stevens, Pippa. "The Battery Decade: How Energy Storage Could Revolutionize Industries in the Next 10 Years". CNBC, December 30, 2019. https://www.cnbc.com/2019/12/30/battery-developments-in-the-last-decade-created-a-seismic-shift-that-will-play-out-in-the-next-10-years.html.

Stills, Joshua. "How Franz Kafka's '*The Trial*' Hides a Religious Narrative". *The Social Matter*, 2017.

Stritof, Sheri. "Essential Cohabitation Facts and Statistics". Spruce.com, August 4, 2017. https://web.archive.org/web/2017072101 1555/https://www.thespruce.com/cohabitation-facts-and-statistics-2302236.

Stuckey, Jon C. "Blessed Assurance: The Role of Religion and Spirituality in Alzheimer's Disease Caregiving and Other Significant Life Events". *Journal of Aging Studies* 15, no. 1 (March 2001): 69–84.

Suarez, Francisco. *On Creation, Conservation, and Concurrence: Disputationes Metaphysicae 20–22.* Translated by A.J. Freddoso. South Bend, Ind.: St. Augustine Press, 2002.

Sullenger, Cheryl. "Planned Parenthood Profited from Selling Aborted Baby Parts, One PP [Planned Parenthood] Location made $25,000 in Three Months". *LifeNews*, April 15, 2020. https://www.lifenews.com/2020/04/15/planned-parenthood-profited-from-selling-aborted-baby-parts-one-clinic-made-25000-in-three-months/.

Swanson, Ana. "144 Years of Marriage and Divorce in the United States, in One Chart". *Washington Post*, June 23, 2015. https://www.washingtonpost.com/news/wonk/wp/2015/06/23/144-years-of-marriage-and-divorce-in-the-united-states-in-one-chart/?utm_term=.54c2dd176ca0.

Tanzi, Rudolph. Cited in "Exploring Frontiers of Biology", by Michael Nahm on his website, 2012. http://www.michaelnahm.com/terminal-lucidity.

Tarne, Eugene C. "Netherlands Forcible Euthanasia Case and the Slippery Slope". Charlotte Lozier Institute Bioethics, July 21, 2017. https://lozierinstitute.org/netherlands-forcible-euthanasia-case-and-the-slippery-slope/.

Taylor, Lauren R. "Has Rape Reporting Increased Over Time?" *National Institute of Justice Journal*, no. 25 (July 2006): 28–30. https://www.nij.gov/journals/254/Pages/rape_reporting.aspx.

Ten Eyck, Katrina F., and Michelle K. Borras. *Called to Love: John Paul II's Theology of Human Love.* New Haven, Conn.: Catholic Information Service, Knights of Columbus, 2014. http://www.kofc.org/en/resources/cis/cis406.pdf.

Theerman, Paul. "James Clerk Maxwell and Religion". *American Journal of Physics* 54, no. 4 (1986). https://aapt.scitation.org/doi/abs/10.1119/1.14636.

Thomas, Clarence. "Abortion and Eugenics". *First Things*, May 28, 2019. https://www.firstthings.com/web-exclusives/2019/05/abortion-and-eugenics.

Thomas, Glen. *Teaching Students with Mental Retardation: A Life Goal Curriculum Planning Approach.* New York: Merrill Publishing, 1996.

Thomson, Judith Jarvis. "A Defense of Abortion". *Philosophy and Public Affairs* 1, no. 1 (Fall 1971): 47–66. Reprinted in *The Philosophy of Law (Oxford Readings in Philosophy)*, edited by Ronald Dworkin, pp. 112–28. Oxford: Oxford University Press, 1977.

Thoreau, Henry David. *On the Duty of Civil Disobedience*. London: Simple Life Press, 1903.

Thornton, Arland, William G. Axinn, and D. Hill. "Reciprocal Effects of Religiosity, Cohabitation, and Marriage". *American Journal of Sociology* 98, no. 3 (1992): 628–51. https://www.journals .uchicago.edu/doi/abs/10.1086/230051?mobileUi=0&.

Tierney, Brian. *The Idea of Natural Rights: Studies on Natural Rights, Natural Law, and Church Law 1150–1625*. Grand Rapids, Mich.: Eerdmans Publishing, 1997.

Tittle, Charles R., and Michael R. Welch. "Religiosity and Deviance: Toward a Contingency Theory of Constraining Effects". *Social Forces* 61, no. 3 (March 1983): 653–82.

Tolkien, J. R. R. *The Letters of J.R.R. Tolkien*. Edited by Christopher Tolkien and Humphrey Carpenter. Boston: Mariner Books, 2000.

Tooley, James. *A Beautiful Tree: A Personal Journey into How the World's Poorest People Are Educating Themselves*. Washington, D.C.: CATO Institute, 2013.

Toynbee, Arnold. "Christianity and Civilization". In *Civilization on Trial*. New York: Oxford University Press, 1948. http://www .myriobiblos.gr/texts/english/toynbee.html.

Turilli, Matteo, and Luciano Floridi. "The Ethics of Information Transparency". *Ethics and Information Technology* 11 (June 2009): 105–12. https://link.springer.com/article/10.1007/s10676 -009-9187-9.

Turner, Jonathan H. *The Institutional Order*. New York: Addison-Wesley Educational Publishers, 1997.

Twenge, Jean M., A. Bell Cooper, Thomas E. Joiner, Mary E. Duffy, and Sarah G. Binau. "Age, Period, and Cohort Trends in Mood Disorder Indicators and Suicide-Related Outcomes in a Nationally Representative Dataset, 2005–2017". *Journal of Abnormal Psychology* 128, no. 3 (2019): 185–99. https://www.apa.org/pubs/journals /releases/abn-abn0000410.pdf.

United Kingdom National Health Service. "Natural Family Planning (Fertility Awareness)". Last reviewed April 13, 2021. https://www .nhs.uk/conditions/contraception/natural-family-planning/.

United Nations. *Millennium Development Goals Report*. New York: United Nations, 2015. http://www.un.org/millenniumgoals/2015 _MDG_Report/pdf/MDG%202015%20rev%20%28July%201%29.pdf.

————. *Universal Declaration of Human Rights*. 1948. https:// www.un.org/en/universal-declaration-human-rights/.

United States Conference of Catholic Bishops. "Catholic Education". 2022. https://www.usccb.org/offices/public-affairs/catholic-education.

————. *Forming Consciences for Faithful Citizenship: A Call to Political Responsibility from the Catholic Bishops of the United States—with New Introductory Letter*. Washington, D.C. United States Conference of Catholic Bishops, 2007.

————. "Torture Is an Intrinsic Evil". 2012. https://www.usccb .org/issues-and-action/human-life-and-dignity/torture/upload /torture-is-an-intrinsic-cvil-study-guide1.pdf.

"United States Population and Number of Crimes 1960–2019". DisasterCenter.com, 1997–2019. http://www.disastercenter.com /crime/uscrime.htm.

Unseld, Matthias, Elisabeth Rotzer, Roman Weigl, Eva K. Masel, and Michael D. Manhart. "Use of Natural Family Planning (NFP) and Its Effect on Couple Relationships and Sexual Satisfaction: A Multi-Country Survey of NFP Users from US and Europe". *Frontiers in Public Health* 5, no. 42 (March 13, 2017). https://www.ncbi .nlm.nih.gov/pmc/articles/PMC5346544/.

U.S. Department of Energy, Alternative Fuels Data Center. "Hydrogen Production and Distribution". Accessed January 11, 2022. https://afdc.energy.gov/fuels/hydrogen_production.html.

Van de Ven, Paul, Pamela Rodden, June Crawford, and Susan Kippax. "A Comparative Demographic and Sexual Profile of Older Homosexually Active Men". *Journal of Sex Research* 34, no. 4 (1997): 349–60. https://www.jstor.org/stable/3813477.

Van Lommel, Pim, Ruud van Wees, Vincent Meyers, and Ingrid Elfferich. "Near-Death Experience in Survivors of Cardiac Arrest: A Prospective Study in the Netherlands". *Lancet* 358, no. 9298 (2001): 2039–45.

Ventura-Junca, Patricio, and Manual J. Santos. "The Beginning of Life of a New Human Being from the Scientific Biological

Perspective and Its Bioethical Implications". *Journal of Biological Research Biological Research* 44, no. 2 (2011): 201–7. https://scielo.conicyt.cl/scielo.php?script=sci_arttext&pid=S0716-9760201100020013#:~:text=The%20zygote%20contains%20a%20new,an%20original%20cell%2C%20the%20zygote.

Vermont Catholic. "Preparing for the Year of Creation". Winter 2016–2017. http://www.onlinedigeditions.com/publication/index.php?i=365491&m=&l=&p=1&pre=&ver=html5#{%22page%22:74,%22issue_id%22:365491}.

Viviano, Benedict. "The Gospel According to Matthew". In *The New Jerome Biblical Commentary*, edited by Raymond E. Brown, Joseph A. Fitzmyer, and Roland E. Murphy, pp. 630–74. Englewood Cliffs, N.J.: Prentice Hall, 1990.

Vollset, Stein Emil, Emily Goren, Chun-Wei Yuan, Jackie Cao, Amanda E. Smith, Thomas Hsiao, Catherine Bisignano, et al. "Fertility, Mortality, Migration, and Population Scenarios for 195 Countries and Territories from 2017 to 2100: A Forecasting Analysis for the Global Burden of Disease Study". *Lancet* 396, no. 10258 (2020): 1285–306. https://www.thelancet.com/journals/lancet/article/PIIS0140-6736(20)30677-2/fulltext.

Vusse, Leona Vande, Lisa Hanson, Richard Fehring, Amy Newman, and Jaime Fox. "Couples' Views of the Effects of Natural Family Planning on Marital Dynamics". *National Library of Medicine National Center for Biotechnology Information* 35, no. 2 (2003):171–76. https://pubmed.ncbi.nlm.nih.gov/12854299/.

Walker, Kris. "The Cost of Biofuel Production". AZO Cleantech, May 13, 2013. https://www.azocleantech.com/article.aspx?ArticleID=337.

Wallace, William. *Galileo and His Sources: Heritage of the Collegio Romano in Galileo's Science.* Princeton, N.J.: Princeton University Press, 2014.

Wan, William. "Teen Suicides Are Increasing at an Alarming Pace, Outstripping All Other Age Groups, a New Report Says". *Washington Post*, October 17, 2019. https://www.washingtonpost.com/health/teen-suicides-increasing-at-alarming-pace-outstripping-all-other-age-groups/2019/10/16/e24194c6-f04a-11e9-8693-f487e46784aa_story.html.

Wang, Hao. *A Logical Journey: From Gödel to Philosophy.* Cambridge: MIT Press, 1996.

Warner, Jennifer. "Premarital Sex the Norm in America: Premarital Sex Research Shows by Age 44, 95% of Americans Have Had Unmarried Sex". WebMD, December 20, 2006. https://www.webmd.com/sex-relationships/news/20061220/premarital-sex-the-norm-in-america.

Watts, Graeme. "Intellectual Disability and Spiritual Development". *Journal of Intellectual and Developmental Disability* 36, no. 4 (December 2011): 234–41. https://www.ncbi.nlm.nih.gov/pubmed/21992689.

Weaver, Gary R., and Bradley R. Agle. "Religiosity and Ethical Behavior in Organizations: A Symbolic Interactionist Perspective". *Academy of Management Review* 27, no. 1 (January 2002): 77–97.

Weigel, George. "Is Europe Dying? Notes on a Crisis of Civilizational Morale". Columbian College, George Washington University. History News Network. Accessed March 8, 2022. http://historynewsnetwork.org/article/12295.

West, Christopher. *Good News about Sex and Marriage: Answers to Your Honest Questions about Catholic Teaching.* Cincinnati: St. Anthony Messenger Press, 2005.

——. *Our Bodies Tell God's Stories: Discovering the Divine Plan for Love, Sex, and Gender.* Grand Rapids, Mich.: Brazos Press, 2020.

——. *Theology of the Body for Beginners: A Basic Introduction to John Paul II's Sexual Revolution.* West Chester, Penn.: Ascension Press, 2004.

Wild, S.J., Robert. "Pastoral Letters." *The New Jerome Biblical Commentary.* Englewood Cliffs, NJ: Prentice Hall, 1990. pp. 891–902.

Wolfinger, Nicholas H. "Counterintuitive Trends in the Link between Premarital Sex and Marital Stability". Institute for Family Studies, June 6, 2016. https://ifstudies.org/blog/counterintuitive-trends-in-the-link-between-premarital-sex-and-marital-stability.

Woods, Thomas. *How The Catholic Church Built Western Civilization.* New York: Regnery History, 2012.

World Health Organization. "Abortion". 2022. https://www.who.int/news-room/fact-sheets/detail/abortion.

Worldometer. Accessed January 10, 2022. https://www.worldometers.info/world-population/.

Wright, Jonathan. *The Jesuits: Missions, Myths and Histories.* New York: Harper Perennial, 2005.

Wright, Laura Jamison. *Chosen to Heal: Gifted Catholics Share Stories of God's Miraculous Healing Power.* Immaculate Heart Press, 2013.

Wright, Paul J. "U.S. Males and Pornography, 1973–2010: Consumption, Predictors, Correlates". *Journal of Sex Research* 50, no.1 (2013): 60–71. https://pubmed.ncbi.nlm.nih.gov/22126160/.

Wykstra, Stephanie. "Microcredit Was a Hugely Hyped Solution to Global Poverty. What Happened?" *Vox*, January 15, 2019. https://www.vox.com/future-perfect/2019/1/15/18182167/microcredit-microfinance-poverty-grameen-bank-yunus.

Xiridou, Maria. "A Study of Young Dutch Homosexual Men". *AIDS*, May 2, 2003, pp. 1029–38.

Ybarra, Michele L., and Kimberly J. Mitchell. "Exposure to Internet Pornography among Children and Adolescents: A National Survey." *CyberPsychology & Behavior* 8 (2005): 473–86.

Zichichi, Antonino. *Galilei, Divine Uomo.* Italy: Casa editrice Il Saggiatore, 2001.

Zillmann, Dolf, and Jennings Bryant. "Pornography's Impact on Sexual Satisfaction". *Journal of Applied Social Psychology* 18, no. 5 (1988): 438–53.

Zucker, Kenneth J., and Susan J. Bradley. *Gender Identity Disorder and Psychosexual Problems in Children and Adolescents.* New York: Guildford Press, 1995.

Zucker, Kenneth J., Susan J. Bradley, Dahlia N. Ben-Dat, Caroline Ho, Laurel Johnson, and Allison Owen. "Psychopathology in the Parents of Boys with Gender Identity Disorder". *Journal of the American Academy of Child and Adolescent Psychiatry* 42, no. 1 (2003): 2–4. https://pubmed.ncbi.nlm.nih.gov/12500069/.

Zusmann, Kate. "How Many People and Animals Died in the Colosseum?" Rome.Us, 2022. https://rome.us/ask-us/how-many-people-and-animals-died-in-the-colosseum.html.

NAMES INDEX

SUBJECT INDEX

The Abolition of Man (Lewis), 42n2, 344
abortion, 198–248
  Catholic Church and, 197–99, 294, 421–22
  conception and, 207–8, 217
  conscience and, 233–34
  dependency of preborn and, 228–30
  dignity of all human persons and, 237, 240, 244
  disabled persons and, 197, 234–51
  divorce and, 168
  Down syndrome and, 225, 234, 241–42
  embryology and, 207–8
  embryonic stem cells and, 259
  emotional health and, 231–34
  ensoulment and, 215–17
  eugenics and, 197, 225, 234–52
  failed abortions, 242–43
  fetal body parts and, 259–60
  fetal defects and, 225
  forced abortions, 165–66, 173, 175, 182, 189
  genetic uniqueness and, 205–8, 220, 236
  incomplete development of preborns and, 222–27
  infanticide and, 225, 240–44
  invitro fertilization and, 252–55
  Jesus' teachings and, 197–98
  legal basis of, 24, 199–201, 208n23, 219–22, 235–36, 242–43, 416–17, 420
  letting die contrasted with, 227–29
  modern culture and, 199
  natural rights and, 416–17, 420–30

  overview of, 22, 197–201
  personhood and, 198–222, 227–30
  post-abortion syndrome and, 231–34
  resources for post-abortion syndrome following, 233
  responses to arguments in favor of, 222–31
  right to life and, 200–201, 204–5, 219–23, 229–30, 235
  slavery and, 219–21, 226–27
  slippery slope and, 240–44
  soul and, 208–18
  studies on negative effects of, 231–34
adultery, 82–87
  artificial birth control and, 165
  Catholic Church and, 45
  conscience and, 25, 87
  conversion and, 83
  definition of, 82–83
  divorce and, 77–78, 83–85
  Evil One and, 85–87
  homosexual lifestyle and, 55
  increases in, 77, 86
  intentions as sufficient for, 84, 88–89, 112
  Jesus' teachings and, 43, 55, 82–87, 112
  justice and, 84
  modern culture and, 45, 73, 86–87
  Old Testament and, 82–83
  overview of, 21, 82–83
  pornography and, 138–40, 144
  punishment for, 83
  sexuality and, 85
  social norming and, 73, 77, 87
  studies on negative effects of, 63, 85

near-death experience evidence
for, 209–10, 216
personhood and, 208–18
philosophy of mind evidence for,
213–18
reevangelizing the culture and,
478–79
terminal lucidity evidence for,
211–12, 237
The Soul's Upward Yearning (Spitzer),
209, 213, 478–79
spiritual well-being. *See also* religion
cohabitation and, 64
components of, 131
disabled persons and, 238–39
divorce and, 63
homosexual lifestyle and, 126–28,
130–35
lessons for strengthening of, 131
marriage and family and, 63–64,
315–16
moral teachings and, 33, 41
NFP and, 168–72
objective moral norms and, 333–35
pornography and, 148–52
sexuality and, 53–55, 57–58, 67–69
stem cells. *See* embryonic stem cells
studies on negative effects
abortion and, 231–34
adultery and, 63, 85
artificial birth control and, 165
cohabitation and, 91–95
divorce and, 63–64, 77–79, 140
gender identity and, 157–62, 189
homosexual lifestyle and, 119–28,
188
moral teachings and, 22–23, 27,
33, 41
objective moral norms and, 334,
346–47, 361
pornography and, 138–52, 188–89
premarital sex and, 63, 90–91,
96–97
Sublimes Dei (Paul III), 380–81
subsidiarity principle, 36, 430–35,
439, 446–47, 468, 471

suicide. *See also* physician-assisted
suicide
Catholic Church and, 289, 295
emotional health and, 289
euthanasia and, 265
homosexual lifestyle and, 121–22
Jesus' teachings and, 289
Summa Theologica (Aquinas), 291, 404

The Tell-Tale Heart (Poe), 349–50
Ten Commandments, 42–43, 308,
326, 344
Theology of the Body (John Paul II),
52–54, 81
13 Reasons Why (television series), 288
torture, 292–95
transphysical consciousness. *See* soul
transsexuals. *See* gender identity and
sex change
The Trial (Kafka), 350
Trilogy (Spitzer)
Volume I of, 19, 26, 31, 51, 126,
357, 485, 503, 506, 508
Volume II of, 26, 28–29, 43–44,
46, 85, 131, 355, 358–59, 486,
492, 495, 498, 502, 504, 508
truth, 304, 513–18

United Nations Fund for Population
Activities (UNFPA), 175
United Nations Millennium
Development Goals (MDGs), 435,
463–64
United Nations Universal Declaration
of Human Rights (1948), 356,
417–18, 423, 470–71
universal destination of goods, 36,
428–32, 434, 462
unjust laws, 402–4, 418, 423, 470
Unlimited Wealth (Pilzer), 177

YMCA, 327n40
youth emotional health, 23, 122–23,
288–89